RICHARD ELLIS

DOLPHINS AND PORPOISES

DOLPHINS AND PORPOISES

RICHARD ELLIS

ALFRED A. KNOPF   NEW YORK   1989

THIS IS A BORZOI BOOK
PUBLISHED BY ALFRED A. KNOPF, INC.
Copyright © 1982, 1989 by Richard Ellis
All rights reserved under International and
Pan-American Copyright Conventions.
Published in the United States by Alfred A. Knopf,
Inc., New York, and simultaneously in Canada by
Random House of Canada Limited, Toronto. Distributed
by Random House, Inc., New York.

Library of Congress Cataloging in Publication Data
Ellis, Richard, [date]
    The book of dolphins and porpoises.
    Bibliography: p.
    Includes index.
    1. Dolphins. 2. Porpoises. I. Title.
QL737.C43E44 1982   599.5'3   82-47823
ISBN 0-679-72286-6

Manufactured in the United States of America
First Paperback Edition

For Elizabeth and Timothy

Book III (*Duodecimo*), Chapter I (*Huzza Porpoise*).
This is the common porpoise found almost
all over the globe. The name is of my own
bestowal; for there are more than one sort
of porpoises, and something must be done to
distinguish them. I call him thus because he
always swims in hilarious shoals, which upon
the broad sea keep tossing themselves to
heaven like caps in a Fourth-of-July crowd.
Their appearance is generally hailed with delight by the mariner. Full of fine spirits, they
invariably come from the breezy billows to
windward. They are the lads that always live
before the wind. They are accounted a lucky
omen. If you yourself can withstand three
cheers at beholding these vivacious fish, then
heaven help ye; the spirit of godly
gamesomeness is not in ye.

HERMAN MELVILLE
Moby-Dick

The nature of the animal might parallel
certain traits in ourselves—the outrageous
boastfulness of porpoises, their love of play,
their joy in speed. We have watched them for
many hours, making designs in the water,
diving and rising and then seeming to turn
over to see if they are watched. In bursts of
speed they hump their backs and their beating
tails take power from the whole body. Then
they slow down and only the muscles near the
tails are strained. They break the surface, and
the blow-holes, like eyes, open and gasp in air
and then close like eyes before they submerge.
Suddenly they seem to grow tired of playing;
the bodies hump up, the incredible tails beat,
and instantly they are gone.

JOHN STEINBECK
The Log from the Sea of Cortez

CONTENTS

Color illustrations follow page **192**

PREFACE

In November 1979, just before I was to leave for Argentina to dive with the right whales, I submitted the manuscript for what was supposed to be a comprehensive book on the cetaceans of the world. I had written hundreds of thousands of words about whales, dolphins, and porpoises; completed hundreds of drawings and dozens of paintings; and made careful, alphabetized lists of bibliographic references. I went to Península Valdés and frolicked with the right whales, the dusky dolphins, and the sea lions, and when I returned home three weeks later I expected to hear that the manuscript was being edited. Instead, I found that my editors had decided that there was too much material for a single book, and they were hoping the material could be efficiently divided into two parts, one of which—*The Book of Whales*—would be published in 1980, and the second some time later.

We struggled with this division. It was easy to identify those cetaceans that were unequivocally whales, such as the rorquals: the blue, fin, sei, Bryde's, and minke whales. Also the right, bowhead, humpback, and gray were surely whales. All the foregoing species are mysticetes; that is, they are whales with baleen plates rather than teeth. (*Mysticete* comes from the Greek and means "mustache whale.") The pygmy right whale, a curious sort of miniature baleen whale, also had to be included. There is no question that the great cachalot is a whale. Ask a child—or an adult, for that matter—to draw a whale, and you are very likely to get a grinning, square-headed creature with a fountain of water spouting from its head. When we included the sperm whale, we also had to include its diminutive relatives, the pygmy and dwarf sperm whales. So far, every animal included in the whale book had the word whale in its vernacular name. Did that mean that everything called a whale was a whale?

It was becoming clear that we would have to divide the books between those animals that were whales and those that were not, but there seemed to be a large number of animals that were called whales, but were not. The beluga and the narwhal, which make up the entire family Monodontidae, were included in the whale book. Out of a total of seventy-six species of cetaceans, we had identified fifteen for inclusion. That left a number of large families, including the beaked whales (Ziphiidae), the freshwater dolphins (Platanistidae), and the dolphins and porpoises (Delphinidae). From a glance at this list, not only was it obvious that the Ziphiids belonged in volume one—they were, after all, known as whales—but the name of the present volume also suggested itself.

Since I had originally written a book that I wanted to call "Cetaceans," there were many cross references from dolphin to whale to porpoise. It now became necessary to eliminate many of these interspecies references, since each book would have to stand on its own. Even though the work was still intended to be an inclusive study of the world's cetacean species, its two-volume, time-separated format obviously meant that it would be possible to own (or read) one half and not the other, and it had to be edited accordingly.

I spent the first six months of 1980 revising the whale sections so they would be independent of any dolphin references. I also continued to add material at a rate that thoroughly distressed and alarmed my editors. New material was constantly appearing, and finally I was chosen to serve as a member of the American delegation to the International Whaling Commission. Among other things, this meant that in July of 1980, as the publisher was uneasily planning to set type, I was in Brighton, England, surrounded by many of the world's leading cetologists. Not only could I ask them questions (during tea breaks and at dinner) about those areas of my soon-to-be-published book that I had been unable to resolve previously, but the actual fate of many of the whales I had written about was being decided at this very meeting. I returned from England with a suitcase full of notes and papers, intending to bring the whale book right up to the minute.

Publication was scheduled for October, and in August I was still calling and writing in with changes, revisions, additions, and corrections. I was finally informed that Knopf was running a publishing house and not a newspaper, and that my almost daily calls to "stop the presses" could no longer be tolerated. Reluctantly, I let it go—it was like sending a child out into the world to earn its own living—and *The Book of Whales* appeared in November of 1980.

In January 1981, I began what I thought were going to be simple revisions of the porpoise and dolphin manuscript chapters. I had, after all, already written the book, and I thought that I would just have to tighten it up, remove the material that had been incorporated into the whale book, delete the cross references, and perhaps make a couple of additional explanatory illustrations. I had not reckoned with the gremlins that had been at work on my manuscript while I was distracted with the production of the whale book. During that time they had somehow removed whole sections, and in their place they had inserted strangely garbled versions of my original text. It was also evident that there was a massive conspiracy of cetologists who had been waiting until I was almost finished with the revisions to publish new and revealing material on almost all the porpoises and dolphins.

I was faced with an enormous amount of fresh information that I had to read, digest, and somehow incorporate into the text. Instead of making a few corrections and drawings, I found that I was beginning again to write the book I thought I had already written. Even as I write this preface (after the chapters on individual species have been completed), I know that the research goes on, and many of the statements made in this book will eventually have to be qualified, amended, or even apologized for. In the first draft, for example, I wrote that so little was known about the Chinese river dolphin (*Lipotes*) that "it is hoped that the status of this animal can somehow be made known to the world." In 1978, however, with the "opening" of the People's Republic of China, various Western scientists, in conjunction with resident Chinese cetologists, investigated the behavior and ecology of the *baiji,* and published the first new material on this heretofore little-known species since 1914.

Throughout the long gestation period of this book, I came to rely on the assistance and advice of many people. It would be impossible to isolate those who helped me only with the porpoises and dolphins, since most of the preparatory work was done for all the cetaceans. I listed many who helped with the whales in volume one, and many of them, along with a number of people who added substantially to my knowledge of the smaller cetaceans, must be recognized for their help in the preparation of this book: Dr. William Aron, Northwest & Alaska Fisheries Center, Seattle; Dr. Peter Beamish, Ocean Contact, Trinity Bay, Newfoundland; Dr. Michael A. Bigg, Pacific Biological Station, Nanaimo, B.C.; Drs. David and Melba Caldwell, University of Florida at St. Augustine; Lieutenant Lewis Consiglieri and Marilyn Dalheim, National Marine Mammal Laboratory, Seattle; Greg Donovan of the International Whaling Commission; Dr. W. E. Evans and Stephen Leatherwood, Hubbs–Sea World Research Institute, San Diego; Al Giddings, Ocean Films, Ltd.; Natalie Goodall, Ushuaia, Argentina; Dr. John D. Hall, Kasilof, Alaska; Jeff Jacobsen, Arcata, California; Charles Jurasz, Auke Bay, Alaska; Dr. Ricardo Mandojana; Dr. Bruce Mate, Oregon State University at Newport; Dr. John E. McCosker, Steinhart Aquarium, San Francisco; Dr. James Mead, U.S. National Museum, Washington, D.C.; Dr. Murray Newman and Ray Lord, Vancouver Aquarium; Dr. Kenneth S. Norris, University of California at Santa Cruz; Dr. William F. Perrin, NMFS, La Jolla; Dr. Giorgio Pilleri, Brain Anatomy Institute, Bern, Switzerland; Dr. John H. Prescott, New England Aquarium, Boston; Karen Pryor; Graham J. B. Ross, Port Elizabeth Museum, South Africa; Dr. Warren E. Stuntz, NMFS, La Jolla; Dr. Leighton R. Taylor, Jr., Waikiki Aquarium, Honolulu; Einar Vangstein, International Whaling Statistics, Sandefjord, Norway; William A. Watkins, Woods Hole Oceanographic Institution; F. G. Wood, Naval Oceans Systems Center, San Diego; and Dr. Bernd Würsig, University of California at Santa Cruz.

When I went to Japan in 1981, a great many people were particularly hospitable, kind, and helpful, but I am especially indebted to Dr. Hideo Omura, Whales Research Institute, Tokyo; Dr. Seiji Ohsumi, Far Seas Research Laboratory, Shimizu; Dr. Nobuyuki Miyazaki, National Science Museum, Tokyo; Dr. Teruo Tobayama, Kamogawa Sea World; and numerous employees of the Japanese Whaling Association, including Motonobu Inagaki, Shigeru Hasui, Chuichi Ohmura, Hisao Mizuno, and my friend and interpreter, Kunio Arai.

It seems that everyone at Knopf helped me put this and the previous volume together, but among those who were the most helpful when it seemed that there were too many changes and not enough time were Ashbel Green, Nancy Clements, Dennis Dwyer, and Albert Chiang. All the color and black-and-white photographs in this book were taken by Bob Mates.

As in the past, I am grateful to my wife, T.A., whose support—often in the face of a consuming obsession—made it possible for me to devote so much time to the porpoises and dolphins, and perhaps reveal some of the reasons for that obsession.

RICHARD ELLIS
New York, New York
January 1982

DOLPHINS AND PORPOISES

Common dolphin *(Delphinus delphis).*

INTRODUCTION

So, in human relations with porpoises, let us first recognize that they are part of enormously complicated systems in the sea, whose intricacy we can scarcely hope to understand fully. Next, let us gain enough wisdom about their basic biology for us to lay guidelines that will let us tamper with them in such a way that their integrity, both as species and as parts of the living web of the sea, remains intact and responsive to the flux and flow of the world. Finally, let us look with wonder at all the capabilities of these superbly adapted marine mammals, for themselves, and not for any relation they may have to human affairs.

K. S. Norris
The Porpoise Watcher (1974)

That there are forty-three species of porpoises and dolphins included in this book will come as a surprise to those who thought there were only a couple of different small cetaceans, a porpoise and a dolphin. In the classification that follows, it will be seen that the great majority of the species—twenty-nine out of the forty-three—are known as dolphins. Five are called porpoises, six are "whales," and the remainder are known by some sort of colloquial rendition of their native names: Franciscana, tucuxi, and vaquita. It is therefore obvious that most small cetaceans are dolphins, but it is equally obvious that some are not. It should be possible, then, to identify those characteristics that define a dolphin (or a whale or a porpoise), and write a selectively definitive statement to the effect that "If the animal has these characteristics it is a dolphin, and if it has those, it is a porpoise." But this is not possible.

The first problem that arises is one of language. Since this book is written in English, I have selected common names that have attained a certain degree of acceptance in the popular and scientific literature. That is not to say that everyone agrees on these names; in many cases the opposite is true. In the species descriptions that follow, I have often made reference to these differences of opinion regarding the popular names of various small cetaceans, quoting the appropriate arguments when necessary. (Similar problems exist in various other languages, but that is beyond the scope of this discussion.) K. S. Norris, perhaps America's foremost cetologist, has long insisted on calling many of the small cetaceans "porpoises," despite the often overwhelming opposition to such a practice. For example, in his 1961 "Observations on Pacific Cetaceans of Californian and Mexican Waters" (written with J. H. Prescott), only the common dolphin (*Delphinus*) bears that appellation; all the others—with the exception of the killer whales, the

pilot whales, and the false killer whales—are called porpoises of one sort or another: Gray's long-snouted porpoise, Pacific bottlenose porpoise, northern right whale porpoise, Pacific striped porpoise. These names have not endured, and only a cetologist would recognize "Gray's long-snouted porpoise" as *Stenella coeruleoalba*, otherwise known as the striped or blue-white dolphin. For all Norris's considerable influence on the study of odontocetes, the animals he wants to call porpoises (with the exception of the true porpoises of the genus *Phocoena*) are now generally referred to as dolphins. In 1964, when R. L. Brownell published a paper concerned with many of the same species that Norris and Prescott had discussed three years earlier, he called them Pacific common *dolphin*, northern right whale *dolphin*, Pacific striped *dolphin*. The problem has been taken to bizarre extremes in the "tuna-porpoise" problem, where the cetaceans caught in the tuna nets are usually referred to as dolphins.

Insofar as the genera *Lagenorhynchus*, *Stenella*, and *Tursiops* are concerned, the problem seems to have no solution. It will continue to be a question of personal preference on the part of the author, and these small cetaceans are as likely to be referred to as porpoises as they are as dolphins. I have chosen to follow D. W. Rice's 1977 *List of the Marine Mammals of the World* for the English common names, a compilation which agrees in the main with other such reputable lists, such as Mitchell (1975), and IWC 1977.* In these works, the only animals referred to as "porpoises" are those belonging to the closely related genera *Phocoena*, *Neophocoena*, and *Phocoenoides*. In other words, the only authentic porpoises to be found in this book are the harbor porpoise (*Phocoena phocoena*), the vaquita (*Phocoena sinus*), the spectacled porpoise (*Phocoena dioptrica*), Burmeister's porpoise (*Phocoena spinipinnis*), the finless porpoise (*Neophocaena phocaenoides*), and the Dall porpoise (*Phocoenoides dalli*). All these animals are characterized by small, chisel-shaped teeth, and no visible beak.

May we therefore say that everything else is a dolphin? Unfortunately not. If we could employ only the scientific nomenclature, the problem would not exist, for every cetologist knows the animal referred to as *Stenella coeruleoalba*. It is only when we encounter such names as Euphrosyne dolphin, Meyen's dolphin, Gray's long-snouted porpoise, blue-white dolphin, striped dolphin, and streaker porpoise (not to mention *suji-iruka*, *polosatyi prodel'fin* or *dauphin bleu et*

---

*Of course there are some differences in these lists, and I have taken some liberties myself. Where Rice refers to the "Ganges susu," I have chosen to call it the Ganges River dolphin, following the precedents established by Pilleri in various detailed discussions of this and related species.

blanc) that it becomes increasingly difficult to identify the animal being discussed. Some of the remaining animals are dolphins, and some of them are known as whales, although they do not even remotely resemble the great filter feeders that we usually associate with that name.

All the animals in this book are odontocetes; that is, they are "toothed whales." In the order Odontoceti, there are five families, only two of which are discussed herein, the Platanistidae and the Delphinidae. (The other odontocetes are the Monodontidae [beluga and narwhal]; the Physeteridae [sperm whale, pygmy and dwarf sperm whale]; and the Ziphiidae [beaked whales]—all of which were included in *The Book of Whales*.) There are only four genera of Platanistids, which are primarily—but not exclusively—restricted to inland rivers and lakes. That leaves thirty-nine members of the family Delphinidae, which includes all the various dolphins, porpoises, and "whales" discussed above.

Most are dolphins, but the inclusion of a number of small "whales" in the Delphinidae (and therefore in this book) is a compelling argument for the abolition of all vernacular names. *Orcinus orca* is a large delphinid which has acquired the name "killer whale"; in order of descending size there are also the pilot whales *(Globicephala)*, the false killer whale *(Pseudorca)*, the melon-headed whale *(Peponocephala)*, and the pygmy killer whale *(Feresa)*. None of these "whales" differs appreciably from the other delphinids; they all share the characteristics that are used to define the family,* and only the killer whale, where the males can

reach a length of 30 feet, could possibly be considered a whale on the basis of size. (The melon-headed whale, which reaches a maximum length of 9 feet, was originally classified with the dolphins of the genus *Lagenorhynchus* until Nishiwaki and Norris [1966] put it into its own genus and gave it its present name.) It has been suggested that dolphins have beaks and porpoises do not, but this does not apply in several cases. While it is true that all the porpoises (genus *Phocoena*) are beakless, the same can be said of Risso's dolphin *(Grampus griseus)* and the Irrawaddy River dolphin *(Orcaella brevirostris)*, as well as all the "whales" included in the Delphinidae.

It is obvious that the semantic problems of porpoise vs. dolphin cannot be simply resolved. Some of the small cetaceans are porpoises, some are dolphins, and some are whales. In the interests of brevity, however, I will use the term "dolphin" throughout this discussion to refer to those species included in Delphinidae and Platanistidae, and "porpoise" for the Phocoenidae.

Although they differ in a number of characteristics, the freshwater dolphins have enough features in common to define the family. They are fairly small animals with a long, slender beak, clearly demarcated from a prominent forehead. The dorsal fin is usually low, and in some species it can hardly be called a fin at all. In *Platanista* and *Inia* it is only a ridge that rises to a point slightly aft of the midpoint of the back. All members of the family have the seven cervical (neck) vertebrae separated, which allows them unusual head mobility. It has been suggested (Layne and Caldwell 1964) that these unfused vertebrae may be an adaptation for slow swimming (or, conversely, that fused cervical vertebrae are beneficial to fast swimmers), and also that increased head movement is connected

---

*In a textbook on mammalogy, Cockrum (1962) defines the family Delphinidae as follows:

The dentition is varied. Teeth are in both jaws and are usually numerous with up to 260 teeth present, but *Grampus* has only four to fourteen teeth confined to the anterior part of the lower jaw. The skull has the lacrimal and molar bones indistinct and articulating posteriorly with the squamosal. The rostrum is as long as, or longer than, the cranial portion. Postcranial features include the two most anterior cervical vertebrae fused. The phalanges are varied, and there are fewer than eight double-headed ribs. External features

include the presence of a dorsal fin and the presence of a tail at the junction of the flukes. The tail is notched posteromedially, and the anterior limbs are sickle-shaped. Size varies from small to medium (4 to 30 feet in length).

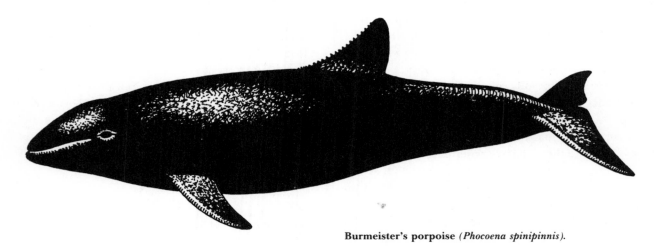

Burmeister's porpoise *(Phocoena spinipinnis).*

with directional hearing, a prerequisite for species living in water where the visibility is often severely limited. The flippers of the platanistids are unusually large, and the flukes are usually wider in proportion to the rest of the body than those of similar-sized oceanic species. All the platanistids have long snouts, and in most there are some bristles on the upper and lower portions of the beak, presumably serving as tactile sensors. Where eyes are present they are small, and the two species of the genus *Platanista* have almost no eyes at all, but only a lensless organ with an optic nerve that is a mere thread. The acoustic abilities of these animals are unusually well developed, as might be expected of animals that live in habitats with hardly any visibility.

The specific order of the classification seems to be another variable, with any number of possibilities in the literature. As in the case of nomenclature, I have chosen to follow Rice (1977), who includes this caveat in his introduction:

The carcasses of marine mammals are large, greasy, bloody, and often putrified before they are brought to the attention of biologists. They are difficult and expensive to collect and to preserve for study. As a result, some kinds are represented in scientific collections by only a few skulls and their external appearance is poorly known. Thus, any list of marine mammals, especially of the smaller cetaceans, can only be regarded as provisional.

Since the earliest seafaring days, dolphins have been intimately involved in the lore and mythology of the sea. In the fourth century B.C., Herodotus wrote of the poet Arion, whose life was saved by dolphins. After winning a poetry contest in Sicily, Arion was traveling home to Corinth, carrying his prizes. The sailors on board coveted his treasures, and threatened to kill him if he did not turn them over. Arion asked to play his cithara one last time, and the sailors agreed. After he had played a high-pitched and spirited song, Arion threw himself off the quarterdeck and into the sea. The sailors claimed his treasure, certain that he

ORDER ODONTOCETI

Family Platanistidae
Genus Inia
Inia geoffrensis (Amazon River dolphin; Boutu)
Genus Lipotes
Lipotes vexillifer (Chinese river dolphin; Baiji)
Genus Pontoporia
Pontoporia blainvillei (Franciscana; La Plata River dolphin)
Genus Platanista
Platanista gangetica (Ganges River dolphin; Ganges susu)
Platanista indi (Indus River dolphin; Indus susu)

Family Delphinidae
Genus Steno
Steno bredanensis (Rough-toothed dolphin)
Genus Sousa
Sousa chinensis (Indo-Pacific humpback dolphin)
Sousa teuszii (Atlantic humpback dolphin)
Genus Sotalia
Sotalia fluviatilis (Tucuxi)
Genus Tursiops
Tursiops truncatus (Bottlenose dolphin)
Genus Stenella
Stenella longirostris (Spinner dolphin)
Stenella attenuata (Pacific spotted dolphin)
Stenella clymene (Clymene dolphin)
Stenella plagiodon (Atlantic spotted dolphin)
Stenella coeruleoalba (Striped dolphin)
Genus Delphinus
Delphinus delphis (Common dolphin)
Genus Lagenodelphis
Lagenodelphis hosei (Fraser's dolphin)
Genus Lagenorhynchus
Lagenorhynchus albirostris (Whitebeak dolphin)
Lagenorhynchus acutus (Atlantic white-sided dolphin)

Lagenorhynchus obliquidens (Pacific white-sided dolphin)
Lagenorhynchus obscurus (Dusky dolphin)
Lagenorhynchus australis (Peale's dolphin)
Lagenorhynchus cruciger (Hourglass dolphin)
Genus Cephalorhynchus
Cephalorhynchus commersonii (Commerson's dolphin)
Cephalorhynchus eutropia (Black dolphin)
Cephalorhynchus heavisidii (Heaviside's dolphin)
Cephalorhynchus hectori (Hector's dolphin)
Genus Lissodelphis
Lissodelphis borealis (Northern right whale dolphin)
Lissodelphis peronii (Southern right whale dolphin)
Genus Grampus
Grampus griseus (Risso's dolphin)
Genus Peponocephala
Peponocephala electra (Melon-headed whale)
Genus Feresa
Feresa attenuata (Pygmy killer whale)
Genus Pseudorca
Pseudorca crassidens (False killer whale)
Genus Globicephala
Globicephala melaena (Longfin pilot whale)
Globicephala macrorhynchus (Shortfin pilot whale)
Genus Orcinus
Orcinus orca (Killer whale)
Genus Orcaella
Orcaella brevirostris (Irrawaddy River dolphin)
Genus Phocoena
Phocoena phocoena (Harbor porpoise)
Phocoena sinus (Vaquita)
Phocoena dioptrica (Spectacled porpoise)
Phocoena spinipinnis (Burmeister's porpoise)
Genus Neophocaena
Neophocaena phocaenoides (Finless porpoise)
Genus Phocoenoides
Phocoenoides dalli (Dall porpoise)

had drowned, but song-loving dolphins had gathered around the ship, attracted by the music, and one of them took the musician on its back and carried him to safety.

Dolphins have been the subject of numerous ancient Greek and Roman legends, mostly concerning dolphins who befriend people or rescue them from the sea.* Dolphins appear on Greek and Roman coins and cups, and they have been immortalized on the famous "Dolphin Frieze" at the Palace of Knossos, on the island of Crete. They have always been regarded as lucky, "an omen of good fortune, fair weather, and steady winds" (Kellogg 1940). These attributes did not stop mariners from occasionally taking a dolphin for food, especially whalers, who were sometimes at sea for three or four years and needed a respite from their diet of salt pork and weevil-infested biscuit. In *The Yankee Whaler* (1942), Clifford Ashley wrote of his experience with dolphins being caught from a whaler:

. . . that night we had the first fresh meat in weeks, and for two days we feasted on porpoise steaks and liver. The steaks are a trifle oily, perhaps, but the liver is as good as any. Sea-pig he is called by the sailors. The cook tried-out the head and jaw oil, the cabin boy saved the teeth, and Mr. Gomes cut the crotch from the flukes for a talisman, and nailed it to the cutting stage—the first catch of the season.

Tales of dolphins leading ships away from danger are difficult to accept, because it is almost impossible to assume that a dolphin, no matter how "intelligent," could understand that a reef is potentially dangerous

*There are any number of popular works devoted to discussions of the dolphins' place in history and literature. Among the most useful of these are Alpers' *Dolphins: The Myth and the Mammal* (1960) and Devine and Clark's *The Dolphin Smile* (1967). Of course, one can also consult the original sources, such as Herodotus, Pliny (Younger and Older), Homer, Aristotle, and Oppian.

for a ship. Of course dolphins can locate and identify submerged features through the use of their echoranging faculties, but it is difficult to imagine that a wild animal would lead a strange object, such as a ship, away from a submerged object that it could easily avoid itself. However, it is just as unlikely that a dolphin would swim head on into an obstacle, so a sailor following the dolphin's normal course would be avoiding obstacles anyway, and could therefore assume that the dolphin was leading him.

The same mythology applies to tales of dolphins and sharks. There seems to be no truth to the story of sharks and dolphins being natural enemies. In one series of experiments (Gilbert et al. 1971), after a captive bottlenose was trained to butt a sandbar shark, a similar-sized bull shark was introduced into the tank. The dolphin avoided the newcomer completely. There are undoubtedly circumstances where dolphins and sharks come into conflict; for example, if a juvenile dolphin required protection from a possible predator, the parent dolphin would probably protect its young. Any number of dolphins have been found with shark-bite scars (Wood et al. 1970), but it is reasonable to assume that the opposite has not occurred. (Dolphins would probably not attack large sharks, since their dentition is designed for the catching and eating of small prey.) Wood (1953) reported that a group of dolphins became noticeably excited when a seven-foot sandbar shark was introduced into their tank at Marineland of Florida, but at Miami's Seaquarium, bottlenoses coexisted for years with a large tiger shark. Leatherwood and colleagues (1973) examined various species of dolphins in the tuna nets, and speculated that "healthy, uninjured adult animals are less likely to fall prey to shark attacks than sick, injured or young animals." Most of their observations involved sharks feeding on dead porpoises, but they

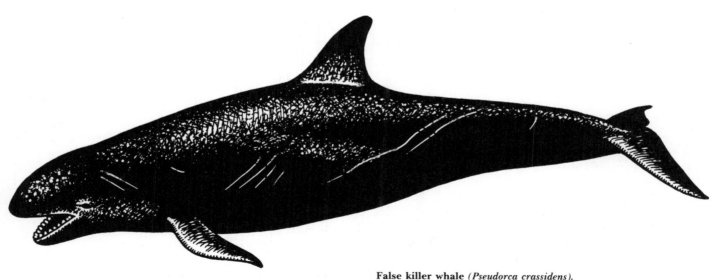

False killer whale (*Pseudorca crassidens*).

6

did see a couple of attacks (by hammerheads) on healthy adult spinners and spotters. We can examine shark-bite scars on captive dolphins or those trapped in the tuna nets, but of course we can never know how many dolphins did *not* survive the predations of sharks. Rather than assume that the presence of dolphins in inshore areas indicates the absence of sharks, it might be more logical—and safer—to assume that the presence of dolphins means that sharks are around as well. They both might be feeding on the same schools of baitfish. (Off the coast of Uruguay, nets set to catch sharks are often hauled in containing Franciscana dolphins [*Pontoporia*] as well as various shark species.)

There are many recorded instances of cetaceans coming to the aid of one of their number when it is in trouble. This has been described as "epimeletic" (care-giving) behavior, and has been summarized in detail by Caldwell and Caldwell (1966), in a comprehensive review of the literature. They have broken down epimeletic behavior into three categories: *standing by* (remaining in the vicinity of an injured or distressed companion without rendering assistance); *excitement* ("swimming violently in circles around the injured animal," biting harpoon lines, or even charging a ship); and *supporting behavior* (actually keeping the injured animal afloat). (The authors also catalog "nurturant behavior," the concern of females for their young, but this is a pattern of most mammals, and not unique to dolphins. Dolphin mothers, however, are usually fiercely protective of their young.) Caldwell and Caldwell review the literature by families, and it would therefore be redundant to repeat their individual observations and references. (Many of these and other observations of epimeletic behavior are incorporated into the species accounts that follow.) They

conclude that "standing by is apparently characteristic of the order Cetacea. . . . Excitement when a congener is wounded is reported sporadically throughout the order." The reports of dolphins saving each other are often exaggerated, as are the stories of dolphins saving swimmers or guiding ships. However, since there is no question that many species of cetaceans manifest a genuine concern for their own kind, it is possible to assign to them some sort of instinctive compassion.

By far the best known of all small cetaceans is the bottlenose dolphin, which happens to be the species that has been studied most extensively in captivity and in the wild. Because of its coastal habitat, it is often visible from strategic vantage points on shore. Occasional fortuitous circumstances have allowed the observation of other species in the wild, so we have more than the ubiquitous bottlenose upon which to base some of our generalizations. For example, the killer whale populations of Puget Sound and Vancouver Island have been monitored for several years (Bigg 1979; Balcomb et al. 1980), and in Plettenberg Bay, South Africa, Saayman and colleagues (1972) were able to observe the behavior of the little-known Indo-Pacific humpback dolphin (*Sousa chinensis*). From the cliffs of the island of Hawaii, Norris and Dohl (1980a) discovered a population of spinner dolphins (*Stenella longirostris*) that could be observed with binoculars, and the long-term behavior of this species, previously known only from a couple of captive animals at Sea Life Park, Hawaii, and its unfortunate involvement in the tuna nets, was partially revealed. Bernd and Melany Würsig, a husband-and-wife team of cetologists, have studied various delphinids in the waters of Península Valdés, Argentina, including bottlenoses, duskies, and even the almost totally unknown Bur-

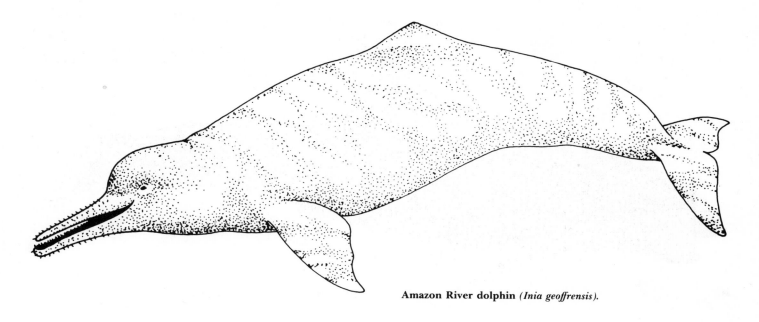

Amazon River dolphin *(Inia geoffrensis).*

meister's porpoise, *Phocoena spinipinnis* (Würsig and Würsig 1979, 1980; Würsig et al. 1977). W. F. Perrin has been following the "tuna-porpoise" problem in the eastern tropical Pacific almost since its inception, and as a result of his studies of the various dolphins that have been trapped in the nets (*Stenella* spp. and *Delphinus,* for the most part), the mysteries of these hitherto unknown dolphins have been greatly resolved. No catalog of intensive studies of small cetaceans would be complete without mentioning the encompassing studies of various species—but especially the platanistids—of Pilleri and colleagues of the Brain Institute of Bern, Switzerland. In addition to these concentrated studies, there have also been innumerable recorded observations of various species in the wild, or stranded, or in captivity, and a compilation of these reports will gradually reveal some of the previously hidden secrets of the dolphins.

From these observations of captive and wild dolphins, a picture is beginning to emerge that is probably best characterized by its diversity. There is so much variation in the delphinids—not to mention the platanistids—that we must not make the mistake of generalizing in anything but the broadest of terms. All delphinids are fusiform (spindle-shaped) animals, with a single blowhole, paired pectoral fins, and of course teeth, but these may number from 8 to 250. The teeth of the killer whale are large and conical, while those of the porpoises (Phocoenidae) are tiny chisel-shaped affairs, and the Dall porpoise's teeth are so small that the gums protrude beyond them, forming a characteristic band of "gum teeth."

The dolphins range in size from the killer whale at a maximum of 30 feet, down through the 5-foot harbor porpoise *(Phocoena phocoena)* and the Franciscana *(Pontoporia blainvillei),* whose 5-foot length includes a 1-foot beak. They range in weight from the 10-ton killer whales to the 65-pound harbor porpoise, and while some species can jump 20 feet out of the water, others barely show their dorsal fin while breathing, and never jump at all. The platanistids obviously never have the opportunity to dive very deeply in their riverine habitat, but some open-ocean species—such as the pilot whales—have been known to descend to depths of 2,000 feet, and in this case, as in so many of the situations involving dolphins in the wild, we are not at all sure what the limits are.

Dolphins are all social animals; that is, they spend their lives in the company of their conspecifics in schools. (The word "pod" is generally used to refer to aggregations of the larger whales.) Norris and Dohl (1980b) broadly define a school* as "any aggregation of aquatic animals that regularly swim together." Cetaceans may school for protection from predators, or the school may function as a more effective food-gathering system. It also serves as an efficient framework for breeding activities: "seemingly the need for mechanisms allowing location of sexually ready animals over long distances is reduced in the close confines of dolphin schools" (Norris and Dohl 1980b).

Observations of small captive groups have shown that there is a definite social structure within these groups, but we cannot extrapolate those limited observations to all species. In the breeding colony of *Tursiops truncatus* at Marine Studios (later Marineland) of Florida, M. C. Tavolga (1966) saw that "There was definite evidence of dominance in the colony in the sense that certain animals were never molested by others, and were more aggressive and less fearful. The adult male was dominant over all other animals in the tank, followed in turn by a group of adult females, a group of juvenile males, and a group of infants." In observations of other captive delphinids a similar hierarchy was observed, even among animals of different species, such as the spinners and spotters at Sea Life Park, Hawaii (Bateson 1974). At Marineland of New

*The word "school" is thought to be derived from *shoal,* one of the meanings of which is "a large number of fish, porpoises, seals, whales, etc., swimming together." The Oxford English Dictionary says that "the early history of the word is uncertain, but its etymology is identical with *scolu,* an Old English word meaning 'troop,' or 'division of army.' " It has nothing whatever to do with a school as an institution of learning.

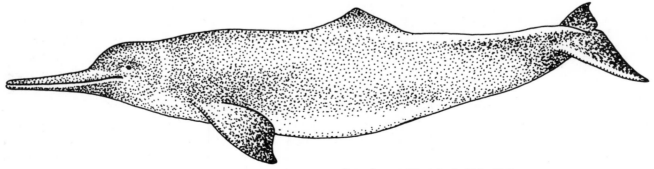

Franciscana *(Pontoporia blainvillei).*

Zealand, Robson (1976) observed that the dominant animal in the captive group of common dolphins was a female named Brenda, but since male odontocetes usually grow larger than females, the males appear to be the dominant animals. This is most evident in observations of killer whales—in captivity and in the wild—where the males grow so much bigger and stronger than the females that there would appear to be no question of dominance and leadership of these powerful animals. The obvious sexual dimorphism between adult male and adult female orcas—males may reach a length of 30 feet and have a 6-foot-high dorsal fin, while the females rarely exceed 20 feet in length, and have a much smaller, more falcate fin—and their inclination to remain close to the surface have made possible what is probably the only detailed survey of social interactions among wild cetaceans, where males and females can be individually identified (Heimlich et al. 1980).

The composition of delphinid schools varies greatly, and is undoubtedly a function of the specific requirements of each species. Some animals, such as harbor porpoises, are most often encountered in small groups of three to five animals, while the average size for a school of bottlenose dolphins is about twenty. Because of their hunting propensities, killer whale groups are often referred to as "packs," and they can range in size from eight to fifty animals. (In the Puget Sound–Vancouver Island area, where these animals have been extensively studied, the groups are referred to as "pods," i.e., A-Pod, J-Pod, etc.) There are occasional sightings of much larger aggregations of killer whales, where groups of several hundred or even thousands are seen together, but the explanation for these groupings is lacking. The spotted dolphins set on by the tuna fishermen in the Pacific are found in schools that range from 50 to 2,500 animals (Stuntz 1980), and estimates of the school size of common dolphins have ranged all the way up into the millions (Cousteau and Diole 1975).

In some way connected with schooling behavior, although not understood at all, is the inclination of some species of small cetaceans—and some of the larger ones as well—to beach themselves en masse. Among the delphinids, the most notorious mass stranders are the false killer whale *(Pseudorca)*—a single stranding of 835 animals has been reported—and the pilot whales, whose strandings have formed the basis for an industry in Scotland, Iceland, and the Faeroe Islands. Almost all cetaceans have been known to beach themselves individually or in groups, and while there have been many hypotheses, no clear explanation has yet emerged for this puzzling phenomenon. It may be navigational breakdown, fear of predators, chasing of prey, tidal cycles, illness, or even a desire to return to the origin of their land-based ancestors. Aristotle wrote, "It is not known for what reason they run themselves aground on dry land; at all events, it is said that they do so at times, and for no obvious reason," and this is as true now as it was in the fourth century B.C.

The possibility of maintaining various delphinid species in captivity has greatly affected our attitudes toward them. This is as much a function of size as anything else, since it was the largest whales that were hunted for meat and oil, and the smaller ones that fit into the aquarium tanks and pools. Much of our information on the baleen whales—and the sperm whale as well—has come directly from the whaling records. It was only the whalers who were willing to venture to the remote, inhospitable regions where their quarry lived, and who could therefore provide the limited amount of information that we have on the lives of these leviathans. (Of course, most of the records that were kept in the early whaling days were intended for future generations of whalers, but some of the information on the size, color, migration patterns and habits leaked out.) Captain William Scoresby (1820) hunted—and wrote about—the great Arctic whale (now known as the bowhead, and considered the most endangered large whale in the world). Drs. Beale and Bennett (1839; 1840) accompanied British sperm whalers, and the accounts of their voyages, aside from providing information on the whales and the whalers, served as some of Melville's most important primary sources in the writing of *Moby-Dick.* Charles Melville Scammon (1874) was another whaling captain who described his adventures and the whales of the northwest coast of North America, and he provided the first warnings about the dwindling population of California gray whales. As whaling became more mechanized, various journals—originally established to document the whaling industry—appeared, such as the *Discovery Reports* (of the British Antarctic Survey), *Norsk Hvalfangst-tidende* (the *Norwegian Whaling Gazette*), the *Reports of the Whales Research Institute* (Tokyo), and the increasingly technical *Annual Reports of the International Whaling Commission.*

It was only in the mid-twentieth century, as it became apparent that the whales were not an inexhaustible resource, that studies—often printed in the journals mentioned above—began to appear on the habits and biology of the whales, apart from information on how to kill and process them, or how many should be killed in any particular season. By then it was too late for many species: the blue, humpback, gray, and right whales were so depleted that their hunting was banned altogether, and the remaining "great" whales—the fin, sei, Bryde's, minke, bowhead, and sperm*—are hunted by the remaining whaling nations in ever-decreasing numbers.

It has always been different with dolphins. They were hunted, to be sure, and there are still nations that use dolphin meat for human consumption, and the oil and bones for various industrial and agricultural purposes. In Japan, for example, there is a long history of dolphin fishing, particularly of the striped dolphin (*Stenella coeruleoalba*), and these animals appear regularly in the fish markets. Numerous other species of small cetaceans are hunted in Japanese waters, and Miyazaki (1980) lists "catch records of 14 species from 7 families [that] are represented from the daily fishing record of the fishermen's cooperative at Taiji." (This fishery should not be confused with the unfortunate slaughter of the dolphins that the Japanese fishermen of Iki-shima believed were stealing their fish.) In Iceland, Scotland, the Azores, and the Faeroe Islands, pilot whales have been hunted for centuries by a drive fishery, where the animals are herded into shallow bays and then killed with spears and knives. We have also learned about the previously unstudied spinner and spotter dolphins (*Stenella* spp.) of the eastern tropical Pacific, where millions of these animals died because the tuna fishermen were unable—or unwilling—to take the necessary measures to ensure that the only animals that died in the nets were the ones they were trying to catch. As a result of this sad spectacle—some 6 million dolphins are thought to have died in this fishery since about 1965—Pryor and Norris (1978) could write, "A massive air-sea survey undertaken in 1977 has given us more simultaneous information about porpoise distribution than we have ever had before for any species."

For the most part, however, our information about dolphins comes as a result of our ability to keep them in captivity and there observe, train, and test them. Defran and Pryor (1980) list 28 species (out of the total of 43) of small cetaceans that have been maintained in captivity, ranging from the popular bottlenose to the little-known finless porpoise. (For species that have never been successfully kept in tanks, the captive observations are enhanced by reports of the behavior of various small cetaceans in the wild, but these are often fleeting views of a small cetacean at a distance, or a brief glimpse of a rare delphinid as it appears off the bow of a ship occupied in activities other than dolphin watching.)

The differences between the reports of whalers and those of dolphin trainers have surely tempered our attitudes toward the various cetaceans. The factor of size must also be considered: even if we were disposed to put a blue or a fin whale in a situation where it could be observed conveniently, the problems of housing and feeding it would be practically insurmountable. Only one baleen whale has been successfully kept in captivity for any length of time; a gray whale named Gigi was maintained for a year at Sea World in San Diego, but when she reached a length of 26 feet and a weight of 7 tons, it became too difficult—and too expensive—to keep her, and she was released.

The history of captive dolphins is a long one, probably beginning in the mid-nineteenth century with harbor porpoises or bottlenose dolphins in Europe. By 1897 belugas were being taken in Canada for (unsuccessful) exhibition in England, and in 1913, a group of bottlenose dolphins was captured at Cape Hatteras, North Carolina, for exhibition at the New York Aquarium. It was not long before the popularity of these animals was recognized, and in 1938, Marine-

*At the 1981 IWC meeting, quotas on all species except minkes were reduced from the previous year's figures. Because of a technicality, the Japanese quota for North Pacific sperm whales for the 1982 season will be deferred until a special meeting to be held in the spring of 1982, and it is possible that the quota will be set at zero, essentially ending sperm whaling.

Striped dolphin *(Stenella coeruleoalba).*

land of Florida at St. Augustine opened its doors, the first such institution in the United States. It was here that the first captive breeding colony of bottlenose dolphins was established, and also where many of the early behavioral studies of this species were conducted. (McBride 1940; McBride and Hebb 1948; Tavolga and Essepian 1957, etc.) Wood (1977) reports that there were twenty-seven calves born between 1939 and 1960, including several that were born to females that had themselves been born at Marineland. (Wood followed Arthur McBride as curator of Marineland, and his observations, published in 1953, were among the earliest on the underwater sound production of bottlenose dolphins.) Since that time, oceanariums and aquariums have proliferated into a multimillion-dollar business, and every one has its contingent of performing cetaceans, almost always bottlenoses, although killer whales, Pacific white-sided dolphins, belugas, pilot whales, and false killer whales are also popular performers.

Most of the information we have on the breeding activities of dolphins has been obtained from observations of captive specimens, and, not surprisingly, the bottlenose dolphin leads all the rest. According to the report of a Dolphin Breeding Workshop held in San Diego in 1975 (Ridgway and Benirschke 1977), over 150 *Tursiops* calves have been born in captivity; no other species even comes close. It goes without saying that we cannot know much about the breeding of wild dolphins, but in some cases, we can apply the knowledge gathered from captive specimens to their wild brethren. We have a considerable amount of information about the breeding habits of bottlenoses, considerably less about the common dolphin and the killer whale, both of which have reproduced in captivity but the young did not survive, and almost no information at all about most of the other delphinids. There is also a small body of data on the hybridization of dolphins in captivity, since there have been a number of incidents where parents belonging to different species, having been kept together for some time, produced hybrid calves. So far, all captive hybrids involve one bottlenose dolphin parent, including a *Tursiops* x *Grampus* cross at Enoshima Aquarium in Japan; a *Tursiops* x *Steno* calf born at Sea Life Park in Hawaii; and a *Pseudorca* x *Tursiops* calf that was born at Kamogawa Sea World in Japan in May 1981.* In the same month, a near-term fetus of a *Globicephala* (pilot whale) x *Tursiops* was stillborn at Sea World, San Diego (Antrim and Cornell 1981).

The dolphins, porpoises, and whales are animals of the interface; they are creatures that live in the water but depend on air. As one might expect of a group so diverse, they vary greatly in their relative proximity to the surface. Some cetaceans live in such shallow waters that they can never be more than 10 meters from their air supply, while others spend their lives in the deep blue pelagic waters where they may never get closer to the bottom than 1,000 meters. Wherever they live, cetaceans have to breathe air regularly, and while some deepwater species dive to great depths in pursuit of their prey, they must always return to the surface to replenish their vital oxygen supply. There are only a few instances where accurate information exists on the depth-of-dive capabilities of small cetaceans (the sperm whale and the bottlenose whales of the genus *Hyperoodon* are believed to be the deep-diving champions of the cetacean world, with dives of a mile or more in depth), but some of the

*These hybrids are discussed in greater detail in the pertinent species accounts, as is the only suspected wild hybridization of delphinid species, Fraser's (1940) discussion of "three anomalous dolphins" that stranded on a remote Irish coast in 1933, discussed in the chapter on the bottlenose.

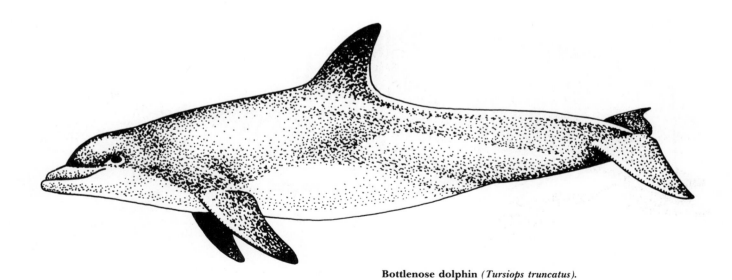

Bottlenose dolphin (*Tursiops truncatus*).

dolphins can also make remarkably deep dives. Captive killer whales and pilot whales were trained to retrieve submerged objects as part of a U.S. Navy program, and they easily reached 875 and 2,000 feet respectively (Bowers and Henderson 1972). A bottlenose dolphin named Tuffy was tested to see how deep he could go, and he managed to get to 1,500 feet (Ridgway 1966). After affixing a radio tag to a wild-caught common dolphin, Evans (1974) discovered that the animal could dive to depths in excess of 800 feet. The killer and pilot whale experiments proved that the animals could reach these depths, but not that they would make such dives in the course of their ordinary existence. (In fact, killer whales are known for their inclination to remain near the surface, and the fact that the trained killer could dive to 875 feet is only an indication of the remarkable adaptability of this animal.)

Speed in the water is another matter: high speed is an indication of the needs of a particular animal's ecological program, either to catch its prey or to avoid being caught itself. Some of the smaller dolphins, such as the spotters and the Pacific white-sided dolphin, have been timed over measured courses and found to be capable of sprint speeds of up to 20 knots. The Dall porpoise has not been timed over such a course—the species does poorly in captivity—but it has always been considered among the speediest of small cetaceans. By inference, the killer whale, which occasionally feeds on these swift little porpoises, must be fast enough to catch them, and must also be listed among the fastest of all cetaceans.*

*It does not necessarily follow that a hunting animal must run down its prey at speed. Killer whales are known to hunt in packs, and they have been seen to herd their prey—either small cetaceans or fish—into a tight group, so that they could dash in and pick off their victims one by one.

One of the fascinating aspects of the behavior of small cetaceans is the inclination of many species to ride the bow waves of moving vessels. The common dolphin can do it for hours at a time. There are even circumstances where cetaceans can be identified at sea by this propensity: of the "blackfish" (pilot whales, false killer whales, melon-headed whales and pygmy killer whales), only the false killer is known to be a bow rider. We have no way of knowing why certain species ride bow waves while others do not, or, for that matter, why some species do it at all, but it may be for the sheer enjoyment of moving so fast without expending very much effort. Among the better-known bow riders are the common dolphin, the bottlenose, some species of lags, particularly the Pacific white-sided dolphin (*Lagenorhynchus obliquidens*), and the spinner dolphin (*Stenella longirostris*). Although Risso's dolphin (*Grampus griseus*) is not well known as a bow rider, one individual named Pelorus Jack was famous for accompanying vessels in New Zealand waters for more than twenty years.

Previously, observers believed that dolphins riding before fast-moving vessels were somehow swimming faster than the vessels, but it was eventually determined that the dolphins were actually utilizing the "pressure wave" of the vessel for a free ride. (Bottlenose dolphins have also been observed "body surfing," and also riding the breaking stern wake of a fast-moving ship.) Norris and Prescott (1961) discussed this "assisted locomotion" in various small cetaceans, and noticed that "none of the animals regularly beat its tail when stationed close to the bow . . . on several occasions the porpoises turned partly or entirely on their sides and it was then obvious that the flukes were held stationary in relation to the body." Hertel (1969) developed various formulas for

Dall porpoise (*Phocoenoides dalli*).

the hydrodynamics of swimming and wave-riding dolphins and concluded,

The dolphin can utilize . . . the bow wave of a rapidly moving ship because it can attain such a high velocity in the open sea that it is able to position itself in the forward slope of a rapidly advancing wave; it is so mobile that without difficulty it can produce, in appropriate orientation to the ship, the equilibrium of forces and momentum; its body is favorably proportioned for high velocities and its skin properties reduce the fluid resistance to minimal levels; its shape is favorable for the utilization of the pressure field, because a sufficient pressure difference between bow and stern is provided because of its length; and it knows how to make use of these many advantages.

For all the detailed analysis of fluid mechanics, however, Hertel is no closer than Norris and Prescott to discovering why the dolphins do it. They wrote, "It seems very unlikely that bow-riding is a pattern that has arisen *de novo,* but is more likely one in which a natural behavior pattern has become adjusted to an unnatural situation, since the advent of sea-going vessels fast enough to provide a satisfactory bow wave. Exactly what the natural behavioral precursor has been is a mystery." It is interesting to note that Payne (1974) gives Norris as the author of the suggestion "that the porpoises' ability to ride a bow wave may be a natural extension of skills developed through riding the bow wave of whales." Payne is discussing the association of dusky dolphins with the right whales of Península Valdés, Argentina, and since right whales are among the slowest swimmers of all the great whales, it seems unlikely that the speedy dolphins would have learned to ride the bow waves of vessels moving at speeds of 25 to 35 knots by practicing on whales that cannot go much faster than 6 to 8 knots.

The exact mechanisms by which small cetaceans find and capture their food—they are all eaters of fish, squid, various crustaceans, or combinations thereof—are, surprisingly, poorly known. Animals in captivity

Rough-toothed dolphin *(Steno bredanensis).*

are seen to snatch at fish or squid and then swallow them, and this does not seem to be particularly mysterious or difficult, but in the open ocean it is considerably more complicated to find and catch a school of moving prey than it is to grab a dead fish as it floats by in a tank.

Although they have not all been tested, most odontocetes are believed to be capable of sending out some sort of signals, which are then used for echolocation. This is a system whereby sounds are emitted—sometimes in a highly directional fashion—and as they bounce off whatever prey object or other obstacle is in their path, the returning echoes are read and analyzed. At this level, the system appears deceptively simple; even the small-brained insectivorous bats can do something very similar when they navigate and chase their prey in the dark by sending out high-frequency squeaks and reacting to the echoes. If bats can do this, there should be no reason why large-brained dolphins should have any trouble with the same system, and they probably don't. However, because dolphins do this—and everything else, for that matter—underwater, we have found it considerably more difficult to determine exactly what is going on, and in fact the large-brainedness of the dolphin raises more questions than it answers. (Human beings also have large brains, as do elephants, but neither species has proven to be a particularly good echolocator. We did invent sonar and radar, however, which serve the same purpose.) The echolocation capabilities of odontocetes have been the focus of some of the most concentrated of all cetacean studies. For sheer volume, no other subject in the cetological literature can approach the acoustics of odontocetes. There have been countless papers written on the capabilities of various dolphins—primarily the easily maintained and easily trained bottlenose—and numerous books as well. To list them all would be unnecessarily burdensome (in the 1979 "Animal Sonar Systems," a compilation of papers on acoustics, there is a forty-page bibliography of publications on echolocation in odontocetes published between 1966 and 1978), but several books can be recommended. There are two collections edited by R.-G. Busnel (1969 and 1979); another two edited by W. N. Tavolga (1964 and 1967); and extensive sections on recording, communication, echolocation, and recognition in Norris (ed.), *Whales, Dolphins and Porpoises* (1966), and pertinent chapters in Herman (ed.), *Cetacean Behavior: Mechanisms and Functions* (1980).

Dolphins are highly dependent on sound in their natural habitat. This is to be expected, given the medium in which they live, where sound can travel for great distances and at great speed, and where light is greatly inhibited and therefore vision must be a limited sense. The earliest acoustic experiments with dolphins, such as those recorded by Wood (1953) and Schevill and Lawrence (1956), indicated that the dolphins were echolocators, and subsequent experiments showed that the acoustic senses of these animals were extraordinarily sophisticated. By 1963, Schevill listed twenty-three species of cetacean "the sound of which have been identifiably recorded." Since that time many more cetacean species have been reliably recorded, and by now it is assumed that all odontocetes are echolocators to a greater or lesser degree, although most of the experimental work has been done with the bottlenose dolphin. As Herman and Tavolga (1980) summarized, "some general adaptations for communication can be seen across species that reflect the common influence of the aquatic habitat, and most cetacean species are highly vocal, although a few, such as the harbor porpoise or other Phocoenidae, seem puzzlingly reserved in vocal output. Possibly, even these animals are highly vocal in ultrasonic portions of the frequency spectrum that are not well sampled by most recording techniques."

In 1964, Schevill identified the sounds of odontocetes as "impulsive, broad-band clicks, narrow-band squeals ('whistles'), which may be made simultaneously, and complex sounds." The "complex sounds" have been variously described as yelps, barks, squeals, and yaps, and detailed analysis indicates that these are composed of click series that are too rapid for the human ear to detect. Cetaceans have no vocal cords, and the manner in which they produce their sounds is not known; and since the animals can produce two types of sounds simultaneously, the problem is even more complex. Investigators have suggested various sources for the production of sounds: "Within the air passages of odontocetes are several structures possibly capable of sound production. These are the larynx and its *additus laryngis* and associated arytenoid cartilages . . . the entrances to the premaxillary nasal sacs, the nasal plugs, the tubular sac slits (Evans and Prescott 1962), the vestibular sac entrances, and the lips of the blowhole, plus the possibility of mechanical sounds being produced by the claps of the jaws" (Norris 1964). In attempts to answer the questions of sound production, researchers have pumped air through the nasal sacs of a dead spotted dolphin *(Stenella attenuata)*, "and a variety of sounds similar to those made by live dolphins resulted" (Hollien et al. 1976). Most evidence seems to favor the nasal area rather than the larynx, especially because sound production is thought to involve the passage of air, and to date no explanation has been provided of how air affecting the larynx could be transmitted back to the lungs. (Only infrequently are bubbles released in conjunction with the production of sound, but in the region of the nasal sacs and plugs it is possible for the air to be recycled.) Dissection of dead animals has produced only inferential information, so various cetologists decided to try to examine living dolphins in the act of transmitting sounds. Norris and colleagues (1971) actually X-rayed a living spinner dolphin *(Stenella longirostris)* as it made squeals, and they noticed "movements of the nasal plugs following inflation of the premaxillary sacs," but they were still puzzled as to how the sounds could be made without the release of air. Hollien and colleagues (1976) X-rayed living bottlenose dolphins, and while they observed no evidence of laryngeal involvement in sound production, they did find that "there is extensive activity occurring in the nasal sac system . . . during phonation." They concluded that "the dolphin larynx does not function in the production of sound—at least not for those animals investigated, and that whistle and pulse type phonations originate from nasal sac constrictions and resonances." They could not discover how "the dolphin is able to mediate the trapped air in order to emit the different types of acoustic signals observed to originate from this region."

Another structure in the head of the dolphin that has long puzzled acousticians is the "melon," the reservoir of oil that is found in the forehead of all odontocetes and reaches its greatest degree of specialization in the spermaceti organ of the sperm whale. Somehow associated with sound transmission—although the mechanism is unclear—the melon is believed by some to be an "acoustic lens," focusing the sounds that emanate from the animal's head (Norris 1964). In their 1972 discussion of the possible function of the spermaceti organ (they suggested that it serves as a "reverberation chamber used in the production of the unique burst-pulse signals of the sperm whale"), Norris and Harvey reported on tests of the melon oil of the bottlenose, in which it was determined that the oil was a good sound transmitter, but not as effective as spermaceti oil. This is not surprising when one considers the great differences in distance that the sound has to travel in the head of the dolphin as compared with that of the sperm whale; the distances in the dolphin's head can be measured in inches, while the spermaceti organ in a full-grown sperm whale might be 20 feet long. In some of his early experiments, Norris also suggested that the bottlenose hears through its melon: ". . . I was quite unprepared for the scientists to report that their porpoises heard almost as well through their *foreheads* as through their throats and jaws! Sounds played there were 5.5 times as effective as those played over the pinhole external ears. How a porpoise might hear with its forehead escapes me to this day. No acoustic nerve penetrates that area, and there seems to be no route for sounds hitting there to get directly to the ear" (Norris 1974).

Animals that are so dependent on sound obviously have to have a well-developed sense of hearing, but like the mechanics of sound production, the mechanics of sound reception in odontocetes are also poorly understood. Although odontocetes have external ears, they are usually no more than a pinhole

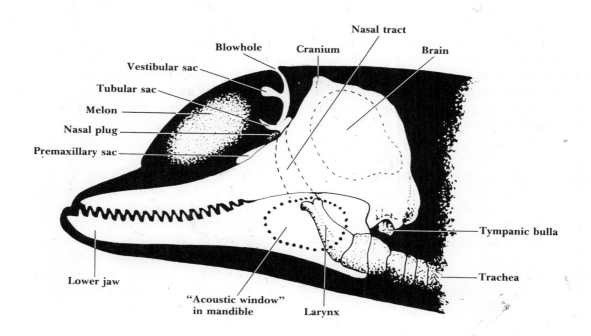

Schematic drawing of the head of a bottlenose dolphin showing those features associated with sending and receiving sounds.

located behind the eye, and "the meatus [auditory canal] and the ear drum of the porpoise no longer function in the hearing process" (McCormick et al. 1979). The porpoise* hears by a method known as bone conduction, which McCormick and colleagues first described in 1970. In *The Porpoise Watcher* (1974), Norris devotes an entire chapter to "The Jaw-Hearing Porpoise" and discusses his finding of a porpoise jaw-bone on a remote beach in Baja California:

What peculiar jaws they were! Most land animals have stout jaws adjusted to the forces of chewing or tearing, or of pulling up grass or the leaves from trees. One can see strong flanges where the jaw muscles attach. Nothing like this seemed to be represented in the porpoise jaw. In fact, it was so thin towards its rear end that I could see sunlight shining through the translucent bone, which at its center was less than a millimeter thick. . . .

Nothing in nature as bizarre as this is created unless the forces of survival hold out value for it. Why, I wondered, did a porpoise find it useful to have a jaw this thin and delicate as the finest porcelain, and a nerve and blood vessel canal that consumed the whole rear end of the jaw?

Norris identified the actual sound receptors as pockets of fat in each side of the mandible, which transmit the incoming sound to the bulla (ear bone), "thence to this tiny bone strut to the inner ear and brain." When Norris wrote that in 1974, he followed it by saying, "All of this is supposition, supported here and there with just enough fact to allow various scientists to explain what they see in different ways." Continuing experimentation over the next five years has proven that Norris's "supposition" was very likely correct, for in 1979 he wrote, "It seems clear now that the environmental sounds enter the odontocete mandible by passing through overlying blubber through what I have termed the 'acoustic window', penetrating the very thin 'pan bone' of the rear mandible, enter the mandibular fat body and are transmitted to the middle ear." Regardless of the mechanism, it appears that dolphins hear very well indeed. Popper (1979) wrote, "It is apparent, in spite of limited data, that several species of odontocetes have exceptionally good hearing, capabilities that are, as far as is now known, rivaled by few other mammals."

*In many of the technical and experimental studies here referred to, the terms "porpoise" and "dolphin" are—once again—used interchangeably. Most of the experimental work has been done with the bottlenose, but some other species of odontocetes have also been used as subjects, particularly the harbor porpoise in the Soviet Union, and common dolphins and Pacific white-sided dolphins in the United States. In 1964, Schevill wrote, "Our knowledge is still depressingly limited, being based on a very few individuals of one species, *Tursiops truncatus*. We extrapolate cheerfully from this short base, with the encouragement that all other known odontocete clicks are very much like those of *Tursiops*."

Lacking any more specific information, we have assumed that dolphins feed by echolocating their prey, then chasing it down and gobbling it up with their tooth-studded jaws. As far as it goes, this is a perfectly reasonable theory, but under close analysis some disturbing questions arise: How do the dolphins catch enough fast-moving fishes on each dive? What if the prey species is not a schooling fish, and it disperses when attacked? How could it be possible for a large, warm-blooded animal to capture enough small organisms so that it could obtain more energy from its food than it had to expend in catching it? (It must be remembered that the air-breathing dolphins have to interrupt their hunt every time they have to surface for a breath, while their piscene prey can remain underwater indefinitely.) There are observations of dolphins herding prey fishes against rock walls (Saayman et al. 1972); against the "wall" of the surface (Würsig and Würsig 1980); "against the wall [of a tank] where they can be more easily caught" (McBride 1940); and even driving them out of the water altogether to catch them in the receding waves (Hoese 1971). But these are isolated cases, and presuppose some sort of barrier against which the fishes can be herded. Even the water's surface, obviously always present, is not useful as a barrier for those animals that feed at depth.

We have formed some fairly good ideas of how dolphins find their prey—echolocation has been successfully demonstrated in captive animals—but we are not at all sure what cetaceans in the wild do about actually catching it. Many of the odontocetes are believed to hunt at depths ranging from a couple of hundred feet to a couple of thousand; the evidence for this comes from the known habitat of fish and squid species that are found in the stomach contents of examined dolphins (Fitch and Brownell 1968). Many of the small fishes and cephalopods are deep-dwelling creatures, and their pelagic habitat does not provide anything even approximating a wall against which they could be herded. How then can the deep-diving dolphins catch enough fish to make each feeding dive productive?

It is possible that the odontocetes are capable of a technique so incredible that it requires a total readjustment of our notions about feeding in the ocean. In 1963, a short article appeared in a Soviet publication entitled "The Whale—an Ultrasonic Projector." The authors Bel'kovich and Yablokov suggested that the sperm whale might be able to use its great nose somehow to project sounds loud enough to stun its prey. Other Russian scientists followed up on this concept, and in 1972 A. A. Berzin wrote (about the feeding habits of the sperm whale): "If the animal dives to the bottom, it swims with wide open mouth. When mobile squid and fish are discovered, the ultrasonic beam narrows and focusses on them, then its frequency sharply increases and the prey is stunned and then seized."*

If one superimposes this theory on many of the previously unexplained aspects of the feeding behavior of sperm whales—and, by extension, of the smaller odontocetes—it begins to make sense, regardless of how preposterous it might appear at first. For example, the teeth of sperm whales do not erupt until they are about ten years old, and yet they feed themselves from when they are weaned until that time, subsisting mostly on squid. Examination of the stomach contents of captured sperm whales has shown that the squid rarely exhibit tooth marks, even when they are found in the stomachs of mature animals, so it is possible to speculate that the teeth are not used in feeding at all. The jaws of the sperm whale are poorly suited for swallowing large numbers of squid at once, but their forcepslike conformation seems to be better designed for plucking individual animals from the sea, or even from the sea floor. (A better design for mass feeding is the great maw of the baleen whale, where thousands of shrimp or other small organisms are engulfed in each mouthful.) If the sperm whale immobilizes its prey, it probably uses the great nose and spermaceti organ as a sound generator, an idea that was suggested by Norris and Harvey in 1972, although they hesitantly described the sound produced as a "tiny 'sonic' boom, somewhat in the manner of production of sound by snapping shrimp."

If we accept the idea that the sperm whale can "ensonify" its prey, a great many of the mysteries of sperm whale behavior are suddenly explained. For example, it has been demonstrated that sperm whales plow along the bottom sediment at great depths, picking up various edible and inedible objects from the sea floor, including stones, sand, shoes, bundles of wire, sponges, etc. (Nemoto and Nasu 1963; Berzin 1972). More significantly, they also become entangled in submarine telegraph cables on the bottom at depths in excess of 3,500 feet (Heezen 1957). It is possible that the sperm whale plows through the sediment in search of food, but it is difficult to imagine a less productive method of food gathering, especially when the animal has to hold its breath to reach these great depths. On the other hand, if the sperm whale uses its spermaceti organ as a generator of sonic booms—of much greater magnitude than was originally suspected—it then becomes possible to postulate an immobilization function for the sounds, and therefore the animal would be probing along the bottom—and occasionally becoming entangled in cables—if it expected the food it had immobilized or killed to be lying on the bottom.

The sperm whale is *sui generis,* and it is not to be considered a large porpoise. The complex arrangement of sacs, tubes, and valves in its titanic nose has no homologues in the delphinids. There are, however, other similarities—in structure as well as behavior—between the great cachalot and the smaller odontocetes. They all have teeth (which is the characteristic that separates the odontocetes from the baleen whales, or mysticetes), and they all have a reservoir of oil in their "foreheads." They are all sound producers and, perhaps most significantly, they all have a pronounced cranial asymmetry. According to Wood and Evans (1980):

The odontocete skull is unique among mammals, including mysticetes, in its asymmetry, the result of enlargement of dorsal elements on the right side. No reversal of this symmetry has been reported. The degree of asymmetry varies, reaching its most extreme form in the sperm whale, *Physeter,* and pygmy sperm whales, *Kogia.* . . . Some years ago it was suggested that the puzzling asymmetry of the odontocete skull was an adaptation related to the development of a sound-producing organ, and represented a modification of the skull having to do with echolocation. . . .

Much research has been conducted on the production, function, and reception of odontocete sounds, and, as usual, the species that has been the primary subject of this research has been the bottlenose. But what applies to the bottlenose does not automatically apply to other dolphins. Just as we cannot easily transfer observations of one delphinid species to another, we cannot apply theories of sperm whale behavior to the smaller cetaceans. And yet the similarities in behavior might be very helpful in explaining the feeding mechanisms of the smaller odontocetes. As of this writing, Norris and Møhl are planning to publish a paper with the working title "Can Odontocete Cetaceans Immobilize Their Prey by Sound?" Norris has described the possibilities:

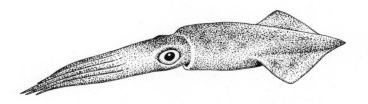

The common Pacific squid, *Loligo opalescens,* one of the predominant food items of California coastal porpoises and dolphins.

---

*I wrote about the feeding habits of the sperm whale in some detail in my 1980 *Book of Whales,* but I did not accept the concept of the whale as ultrasonic projector—although I was not able to explain the feeding of this species by any other techniques—and I wrote that the idea was "incredible." Although *Physeter macrocephalus* is obviously not a porpoise or a dolphin, it is an odontocete, and therefore its feeding habits are appropriate in a discussion of the smaller cetaceans.

The story about toothed whales immobilizing their prey by sound goes like this. We have a small series of field observations of seemingly unharmed prey that have lost escape reactions in the presence of porpoises or some of the larger toothed whales like the false killer whale. These include being able to scoop up fish with a dipnet, or seeing mahi-mahi lying immobile with the whales circling. These things I regard as circumstantial and with other potential explanations.

Then I released a series of fish into a group of three captive spinner porpoises and found them ensonifying the fish. After more than one hour the school broke up, individual fishes lost contact with the school, changed color, one was sucked down the drain, and others were obviously debilitated. Why? Well, it could be sound; it could be lactic acid debt from being chased, it could be oxygen. But it could be sound too.

We ran experiments in Europe and found that both fish and squid can be immobilized by sounds near those most intense for odontocetes. The latest sound intensities for *Tursiops* are very high indeed, and thus there seems to be the power. So, our final conclusion is that we suspect the mechanism, but we feel it needs definitive proof. . . .*

At the Fourth Biennial Conference on the Biology of Marine Mammals, held in San Francisco in December 1981, Norris presented this theory for the first time, and in the abstract, he wrote, "Much additional information, none of it conclusive, will be presented" (Norris and Møhl 1981).

Whether or not odontocetes use their sounds to stun or kill their prey is still an unknown. There is no question, however, that they are capable of generating very loud noises indeed. While diving with an agitated bottlenose at San Francisco's Marine World, D. C. Reed (1981) reported that the dolphin "did something peculiar, a move I had never seen before. A kind of somersaulting forward roll underwater, gray head down and torso following, a front flip that turned into a half twist as her tail moved across and around and up—the movement seemed almost slow in its grace.

*Letter to author, February 1981.

. . . An impact like a car crash lifted me half my body's length in the air. . . . I heard a whistling SEESEESEESEE in my left ear. . . . Pain, as if somebody had shoved a sharpened pencil into my ear." The dolphin had broken his eardrum with a sound.

The question of dolphin intelligence is an extraordinarily complicated one, since very few people are altogether sure what intelligence is (in humans or dolphins), or how to measure it. Dictionary definitions for human intelligence include "the capacity to apply knowledge," and "a faculty of thought and reason," but there are rarely quantitative elements included in this sort of definition, so even if we decide we know what it is, we still don't know if one species—or one individual, for that matter—has more of it than another. One of the simplest ways to decide how intelligent dolphins are is to compare them to humans. In 1978, after nearly two decades of dolphin research, John Lilly wrote, "We deduce that the human-sized brain in Cetacea correspond to human computational power and that the larger cetacean brains are capable of extensions of computations into the past and into the future beyond the range of the human." (In the same discussion, he also wrote, "If the whales and dolphins begin to injure and kill humans in the water, I am sure that the Cetacea realize that our navies would wipe them out totally, at a faster rate than the whaling industry is doing at the present time.")

Since the publication of his first book (*Man and Dolphin*, 1961), Lilly has been preoccupied with the concept of interspecies communication, particularly with bottlenose dolphins, presumably as a manifestation of the intelligence of the dolphin. In his early work he wrote,

Scientifically, it is very appropriate to identify with their position by increasing our knowledge of what that position is, and how it differs from ours. At the same time, we must tentatively remove them from the category of the chimpanzee, the cat, the dog, and the rat in our thinking about them. It is probable that their intelligence is comparable to ours,

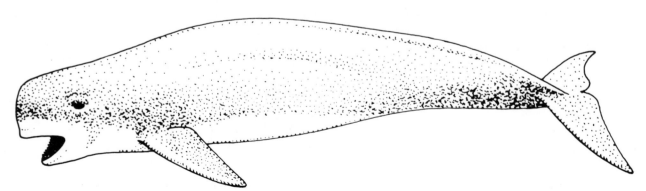

Finless porpoise *(Neophocaena phocaenoides).*

though in a very strange fashion. To accomplish anything of importance with them, we must overcome our self-immolation, xenophobia, and various taboos which we carry to our work with these animals.

This sort of thinking, expressed in Lilly's numerous books and publications, has probably given more people the wrong ideas about dolphins and their intellectual abilities (not to mention the intellectual abilities of certain researchers) than any other body of work in the cetological—or pseudocetological—literature. The idea of talking to dolphins—and expecting them to answer—is anthropocentrically arrogant, and has virtually no scientific validity, unless we assume that English-speaking people represent the highest form of intellectual achievement in the world. In his discussion of the misinterpretations of dolphin research, J. H. Prescott (1981) wrote:

J. C. Lilly reported on the intelligence of dolphins and speculated upon their use of language. Dr. Lilly reported that dolphins were capable of learning and repeating words, and speculated that the combination of words was contactual expression, defending this supposition on the basis that dolphins had a larger brain size than any other mammal, including man. Brain size was equated with intelligence, and intelligence extrapolated to language. Review and analysis of the results indicate that Dr. Lilly's initial results were no more than mimicry. Other investigators were unable to reproduce the results of his experiments, while the popular press shaped public impression regarding brain size, intelligence, and communication.

It is highly likely that dolphins can communicate with one another, since they have had to develop some sort of communication system in the low-visibility medium in which they live. This does not necessarily suggest a higher level of intelligence, as almost all social animals, from bees to wolves, must be able to convey some sort of information to members of the group. It may be in the form of wing movement, whinnies, chest beating or howling, but whatever the device, it is likely to have evolved in the context in which the animal lives. For instance, if wolves have to communicate over long distances, it is altogether reasonable to expect some sort of loud, carrying sound to have been developed. Living in a world of sound, however, the dolphin had to find some nonvisual way of communicating with its fellows. The dolphin "language," while not clearly understood by human listeners, probably serves them very well in their environment. In other words, dolphins developed a system of clicks, whistles, barks, and yelps because it was the best-designed system for the circumstances in which they live. We must examine the dolphin's capabilities in the light of its own ethology, and not attempt to

force it into an ill-fitting mold of dolphin-as-apprentice-person. When we try to teach dolphins to talk, play ball, or retrieve objects, we are demonstrating not so much the animal's intelligence as its responsiveness to operant conditioning, which Pryor (1973) has defined thus:

A stimulus is paired with food as reinforcement, and used to mark desirable actions. The sound of a whistle is often used; it can be emitted rapidly by a human and is perceived above and below the water by a porpoise. Leaps and other freely occurring behavior can be conditioned and brought under stimulus control in a matter of days. Artificial or "shaped" behaviors such as ball-playing, retrieving objects, or locating targets by echolocation while blind-folded are trained by the psychology laboratory technique known as successive approximation, in which the trainer selectively rewards behavior while gradually raising and modifying his criteria until the desired response is obtained.

Later (1981) she wrote, "There is little coercion, however, in the porpoise-trainer interaction (even food deprivation is hazardous, and seldom used) and this has an effect on both trainer and animal. The animal is, as it were, training the trainer to give fish, and thus is shaped to find new ways to elicit fish. . . ." (Commenting on Lilly's theories about "communication," Pryor wrote that "anyone can communicate just fine with a whistle and a bucket of fish.")

Another approach to the investigation of dolphin intelligence has been what L. M. Herman (1980) referred to as their "cognitive characteristics," defined as "the intellectual specializations, capabilities and limitations of a species, as traced and measured through behavioral experiments and observations." In his experiments, Herman tested the memories of bottlenose dolphins for sounds and visual stimuli, and discovered (not surprisingly) that "the visual memory . . . was remarkably limited as compared with the auditory memory abilities," another instance where the auditory dominance of cetaceans is clearly demonstrated. The dolphins were also shown to be excellent mimics—of sounds and motor behaviors—and Herman concluded that "their joint emergence in one species may be limited to cetaceans among infrahumans . . . because no mammalian species other than *Homo* has been shown capable of vocal mimicry."

Unlike Lilly's attempts to converse with dolphins, Herman began a series of experiments designed to test the dolphin's ability to respond to auditory commands. (No attempt was made to have the dolphins respond. "Two way communication requires some means for the dolphin to reply in the auditory language, but this is technically very difficult. . . .") In summarizing his work, Herman wrote:

The capacities for vocal mimicry, the conditionability of vocalizations, the advanced rule learning capabilities, and other demonstrated intellectual traits suggest that dolphins, like some of the greater apes, may be capable of learning an imposed language in the laboratory setting. The demonstration of such capability in a delphinid species would press us toward the reconsideration of the foundations for the evolution of language in humans, and further underscore the convergence in cognitive characteristics of primate and dolphin. Recent work at our laboratory demonstrated that the dolphin was capable of comprehending simple auditory or gestural language elements and their combination into two-word and three-word sentences. Further work on such comprehension is currently underway.

Even though the definition of intelligence is a variable, it is usually assumed that brain size is a factor in the equation. (Whatever intelligence is, an animal with a tiny brain is not going to have very much of it.) The sperm whale, therefore, with the largest brain ever known to exist on earth, should be the smartest animal that ever lived, followed by the larger baleen whales (the largest animals ever known), the elephants, large delphinids (killer and pilot whales), bottlenose dolphins, and then *Homo sapiens.* Obviously, this linear progression does not work*; there must be some sort of a correction for body size in proportion to brain size. In an essay presented at the 1980 IWC Conference on Cetacean Behavior, Intelligence, and the Ethics of Killing Cetaceans, H. J. Jerison (1980) wrote:

The measure is structural encephalization, as estimated from brain/body relations. . . . Encephalization is measured by the ratio of the volume of the brain to the surface area of the body; it's not the brain/body weight ratio.

This measure is relevant for an interesting reason. The volume of the brain (or its weight) reflects the amount of information the brain can handle. This is due to several features of the brain's geometry that are not always fully appreciated. First, the brain consists of nerve cells and other cells that are, on the average, surprisingly similar to one another in different species. Second, the number of these cells that are packed into a brain is directly related to the size of the brain. And, third, the number of connections that nerve cells make with one another also seems to be related to the size of the brain. So brain size is a measure of total information-processing capacity as this would be described in information-theory. The body's surface gets into the picture, because it is related to the expected information-processing capacity for an average animal. By taking the ratio of brain size to body surface we estimate total processing capacity, adjusted for the amount required to handle ordinary body functions for average animals. That is a useful definition of intelligence from a neurobiological perspective.

We therefore have a means by which "neurobiological intelligence" can be calculated, and Jerison concludes,

We know too little about the nature of the adaptations among whales that require encephalization, but this is certainly due primarily to the technical difficulties in working with completely aquatic animals and to the weaknesses of our scientific institutions when faced with what must be exotic adaptations. The brain is too demanding an organ in the

*Melville seems to have believed it would. Of the sperm whale he wrote, "Genius in the Sperm Whale? Has the Sperm Whale ever written a book, spoken a speech? No, his great genius is declared in his doing nothing to prove it. . . . If hereafter any highly cultured poetical nation shall lure back to their birthright, the merry May-day gods of old; and livingly enthrone them again in the now egotistical sky; in the now unhaunted hill; then be sure, exalted to Jove's high seat, the great Sperm Whale shall lord it."

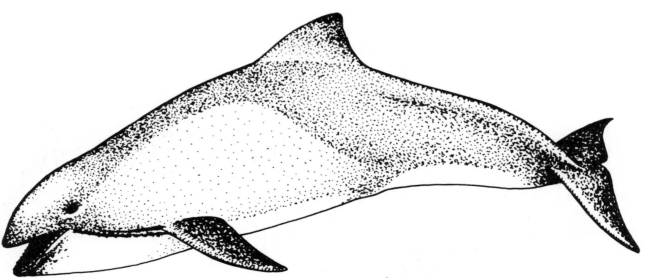

Harbor porpoise *(Phocoena phocoena).*

economy of the body for us to assume that such considerable expansion would occur without large amounts of tissue. . . . We can assume that unusual mental processes occur in whales and we should also assume that these will be quite different from those that we know in ourselves.

Gihr and Pilleri (1979) calculated the cephalization ratio on the basis of a "body length–body weight to body weight–brain weight relationship," and in a highly technical study (well suited for the workers of the Brain Anatomy Institute of the University of Bern), they concluded that the species with the highest level of cephalization were "the smaller marine Odontoceti, *Phocoena phocoena, Tursiops truncatus, Grampus griseus, Orcinus orca,* as well as *Inia,* the Amazon dolphin, a member of the Platanistoidea."

Even when we recognize the magnitude of cetacean intelligence—as a function of the relative magnitude of the cetacean brain—we are still a long way from understanding how it is applied to the everyday business of living underwater. We know that a large proportion of the brain is devoted to the analysis and processing of auditory information:

Basic to the echolocation capability of odontocetes is their neuroprocessing of such sounds—the integration, analysis, and interpretation of acoustic information contained in the echoes. . . . Although there is much variation in the size of odontocete brains, both absolutely and by whatever index of cephalization one chooses to use, in general the brains of these animals are characterized, in gross morphology, by large size, with greater width and height than length; great development of the cerebral hemispheres; and intricate convolutions of the cortex. [Wood and Evans 1980]

There have been other suggestions advanced for the development of the large brain in cetaceans.

Among the more unusual is that of Fichtelius and Sjölander (1972), who wrote that "the brain of modern man is not as remarkable as we like to believe. As a result of cultural evolution, and particularly as a result of the invention of writing, the greatest part of its capacity lies outside the individual." Because the dolphin has not developed writing—and therefore "culture"—its communications capabilities have had to develop in a compensatory fashion. Whereas humans can store their collective information in books and computers, dolphins, lacking the hands to build these artifacts, have had to develop the massive brains to store all the knowledge in dolphin history. In his discussion of the anatomical basis of intelligence, Morgane (1974) wrote, "It does seem that the quantity and quality of gray matter (the neocortex) in brains can be taken as a definite index of relative efficiency of those brains in the regulation of behavior."

We have not yet developed a reliable system for measuring the intelligence of cetaceans. There is no question that they are extremely capable animals, with a highly sophisticated auditory sensitivity, but all of the criteria suggested as gauges of their intelligence fail because of our fundamental inability to bridge the gap between those sound-oriented water-dwellers and our own land-based, vision-oriented sensibilities. By some still unrevealed evolutionary path, the dolphins developed their capabilities for a completely aquatic existence, just as bats developed theirs for a life that is lived in the dark, upside-down, and in the air. We know that dolphins are proper mammals—they breathe air, are warm-blooded, give birth to live young which they nurse—but we are still uncomfortable with their fishlike shape and habits. (The only other mammals that spend their entire lives in the water are the sirenians—the manatees and dugongs.

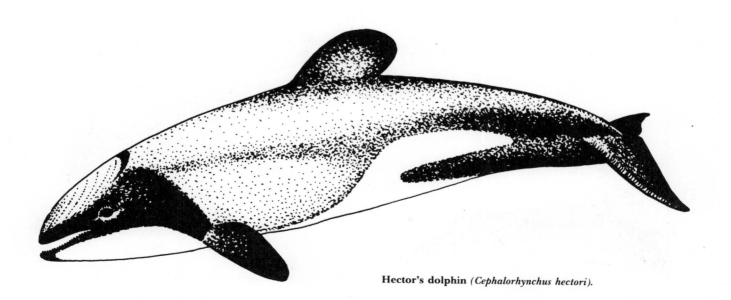

Hector's dolphin (*Cephalorhynchus hectori*).

All other aquatic mammals—seals, sea lions, walruses, otters—come ashore for some of their activities.)

It is here that the major problem arises. Life in the water is totally different from life on the land or in the air. Water does not transmit light very well, but it is a superb conductor of sound. (Sound travels approximately five times faster in water than it does in air.) Therefore, animals that live in the water must perforce depend on their auditory senses more than their eyesight. No matter how well an animal sees (and some dolphins see quite well, even in the air; remember how a bottlenose can leap 20 feet out of the water to grab a fish with its teeth), the very medium in which it lives—no matter how clear—does not permit an emphasis on vision except in short-range situations. It is this situation, not some supernaturally sensitive sensory apparatus, that has been responsible for the cetaceans' dependence on hearing. It is the best thing to use under the circumstances. (The same is true for bats with their ability to echolocate insects in the dark. They use high-frequency sounds to find their prey because neither they nor any other creature can see in total darkness. Some see better in reduced light than others, but an animal that had to depend exclusively on its vision to find its prey in the dark would soon starve.) As an indication of this lack of dependence on vision, it has recently been suggested that some species of dolphins may do their hunting at night when the prey is more accessible, and when vision would be totally inoperative (Norris and Dohl 1980a).

Although we do not understand the language of the dolphins, it now seems clear that it is a well-developed communications system, originated by large-brained creatures whose capabilities—I eschew the word *intelligence,* which seems to have no true meaning in the interspecies context—are among the most remarkable on earth. The dolphins exist in a world where they are almost totally integrated in the medium in which they live. As human divers know, in the enveloping, primeval world of water, which itself constitutes such a large proportion of the animal's corporeal being, gravity as we know it vanishes, and it is replaced by the sublime feeling of weightlessness. In the water, the dolphin is one with its environment, in a way that we landlocked humans can only dream about.

The dolphins could very easily represent a parallel evolutionary path where the large, convoluted brain and the effective transmission and reception of information have developed for completely different purposes, and which may cause us to question our view of our own purpose. "Be fruitful and multiply," it says in Genesis, "and replenish the earth, and subdue it; and have dominion over the fish of the sea and the fowl of the air, and of every living thing that moveth upon the earth." Examining this concept of having dominion over "every living thing that moveth upon the earth," the scientist and poet Loren Eiseley wrote:

If man had sacrificed his hands for flukes, the moral might run, he would still be a philosopher, but there would have been taken from him the devastating power to wreak his thought upon the body of the world. Instead he would have lived and wandered, like the porpoise, homeless across currents and winds and oceans, intelligent, but forever the lonely and curious observer of unknown wreckage falling through the blue light of eternity. This role would now be a deserved penitence for man. Perhaps such a transformation would bring him once more into that mood of childhood innocence in which he talked successfully to all things living but had no power and no urge to harm. It is worth at least a wistful thought that someday the porpoise may talk to us and we to him. It would break, perhaps, the long loneliness that has made man a frequent terror and abomination even to himself.

Commerson's dolphin (*Cephalorhynchus commersonii*).

BOUTU
(AMAZON RIVER DOLPHIN)

Inia geoffrensis de Blainville 1817

The boutu, also called boto and bufeo, is a thickset, long-snouted dolphin with a pronounced forehead and a small eye located above the corner of the mouth. It has a ridge on its back instead of a dorsal fin, and dorsal and ventral keels on the tail stock. The flippers and flukes are disproportionately large, perhaps as an adaptation to its slow swimming habits, "since in a slow moving dolphin larger control surfaces are probably necessary to maintain maneuverability and stability" (Layne and Caldwell 1964). As a converse to this, it might be noted that some of the fastest of the oceanic dolphins, such as the right whale dolphin (*Lissodelphis*) and the Dall porpoise (*Phocoenoides*), have disproportionately *small* flippers and flukes. One unusual characteristic of this species is the presence of a sixth "finger" in the bones of the forelimb. This is unknown in other cetacean species, and since it occurs in "almost all the specimens of *Inia* so far examined" (Pilleri and Gihr 1976), it is to be considered "characteristic and physiologically normal in the hand of the Amazon dolphin." The boutu has small but functional eyes, and it has been known to raise its head out of the water to observe activity on the surface (Layne 1958). The ear opening is conspicuous, and although dolphins do not rely on this aperture for hearing, it is known that the boutu has a well-developed sense of hearing. Both the upper and lower portions of the beak are sparsely covered with stiff hairs which point toward the rear.

The boutu is not a lovely animal. Caldwell and Caldwell (1969a) described it thus:

It is a beady-eyed, humpbacked, long-snouted, loose-skinned holdover from the past. The grapefruit-sized lump perched atop of the head adds nothing to its ridiculous appearance. Nor does it entrance by its behavior, for it is so lethargic that it frequently causes concerned persons to report that "one of your dolphins is dead." We have been fooled ourselves even though familiar with this tendency of the beast to curl up on the bottom of the tank and apparently go to sleep—sometimes on its back. To research scientists, however, the ugly dolphin is a thing of beauty. It represents a valuable opportunity to study a once widespread group of marine dolphins, most of whose members have long since been relegated to fossil beds.

There are a number of conflicting reports on the maximum size of this animal, ranging from 4 feet (1.2 meters) to 9.8 feet (3 meters), with the true figure probably lying somewhere in between. Six adult specimens captured in Bolivia in 1968 and 1976 ranged in length between 1.45 meters and 2.16 meters (Pilleri and Gihr 1977). There are 33 or 34 teeth on each side of the lower and upper jaws—although there are some geographical variations—and the "two halves of the lower jaw are fused together for a considerable portion of their entire length" (Norman and Fraser 1938), making this jaw essentially a tooth-studded rod, rather like an attenuated Y. (The lower jaws of most other odontocetes are roughly V-shaped, the two mandibles coming together at the forward end.)

The range of color variation in this species is extensive, and early observers were puzzled by the apparent differences. In 1900, Beddard wrote: "Its color variations are rather extraordinary unless they can be set down to sex, which has been denied. Some individuals are wholly pink, others are black above and pink below." Subsequent observations have indicated that these variations are in fact a function of age: the younger animals are dark gray, lightening with age, until they achieve the "strikingly flesh-colored or pinkish" coloration of the adult (Layne 1958). The Portuguese name for this species in Brazil is *boutu vermelho*—"red dolphin."

In the South American jungle rivers which it inhabits, the boutu is often seen in the company of another "Amazon dolphin," *Sotalia fluviatilis.* The two are quite dissimilar in appearance, and can easily be told apart. *Sotalia* is a smaller animal, grayish in color, with a proper dorsal fin and a much shorter beak. The two species do not seem to interact, however, and in 1958 Layne wrote that "no interplay of any sort was ever observed between them."

In the wild, boutus are not gregarious; they are sometimes seen in pairs or in groups of three and four animals, but more frequently, solitary individuals are sighted. (In 1958 Layne reported that 58 percent of his sightings of boutus in the upper Amazon were single animals.) They are slow swimmers, and seem to prefer the quieter portions of the rivers. Pilleri and Gihr (1977) wrote that "they prefer to stay near the shady banks where the river is deeper and the water calm." When surfacing to breathe, the animal is almost horizontal, and usually only the melon and blowhole appear; the beak and eyes are seldom seen. When making deeper dives, the boutu shows a steep arch of its back, creating a humped "triangle" before it descends. The boutu often swims in shallow water, and it has been observed rolling on its own long axis, perhaps in an attempt to clean or scratch itself (Pilleri 1969).*

As with all platanistids, the seven cervical vertebrae of the boutu are not fused, and this arrangement permits the animal a most uncetacean flexibility of the head and neck. It is capable of a 90-degree lateral

---

*Ivan Sanderson (1956) wrote that the boutu uses its flippers "to cross mudbanks, like a sea lion galumphing over a beach, raising its forequarters off the ground when completely out of the water." Recent studies of captive specimens have not substantiated this charming image.

flexion of the head, and in captivity a specimen was seen to reach down "back beneath" itself to pick up an object from the bottom of its tank (Layne and Caldwell 1964). From the examination of the stomach contents of captured boutus, it has been seen that the animal normally feeds on fish and crabs, and its teeth are modified for the two separate functions of grasping and chewing. The front teeth are sharp and conical, and they are used to grasp the prey and hold it in the forcepslike jaws. The boutu then works the fish toward the rear of the mouth, where it is "vigorously chewed" (Layne and Caldwell 1964), then swallowed head foremost. The rear teeth are ridged and equipped with a supplementary lobe, the better to chew with. Pilleri (1969) observed "well advanced dental caries" in the teeth of this species, but was unable to explain this peculiar phenomenon.

Even though the boutu has functional eyes, hearing is believed to be its dominant sense. This is true of most of the freshwater dolphins, and although sound rather than light is the primary vehicle for cetacean communication, hearing is even more dominant in species that live in cloudy or turbid waters. In tests conducted on three males exhibited in the Duisberg Zoo (West Germany), the sonar field of the boutu was identified as being "directed forward in a cone around the beak" (Pilleri 1979). These three males—all from the Beni River in Bolivia, and now believed to represent a distinct species, *Inia boliviensis*—were fed live trout, which they appeared to echolocate effectively. "Every time the fish changed direction, the dolphin followed it with its head." When nets were set for the capture of these animals in the Río Negro in Brazil, the animals so effectively avoided the nets (presumably by

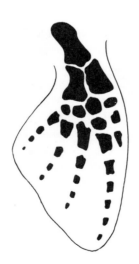 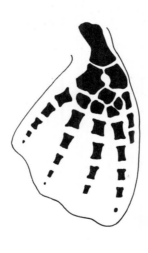 

Comparison of the right forelimb (manus) of three species of freshwater dolphins. Left to right: *Pontoporia blainvillei,* *Platanista gangetica, Inia geoffrensis.* **Only** *Inia* **has six "fingers" on each forelimb. (After Pilleri et. al. [1976])**

the use of their echolocating clicks) that they had to be herded into the nets by local people standing in the water (Waterman 1967). The sounds made by the boutus have been described as "more or less constant pulsed sonar activity," and "when a young animal was seen in a school, yelps or barks were sometimes heard" (Norris et al. 1972).

A completely freshwater species, the boutu is found in various rivers in northern South America, including the Amazon and its tributaries, and the Orinoco River system in Venezuela. It has also been reported from northern Peru, Ecuador, and Colombia. Collecting and observing expeditions have concentrated on the area of Leticia, Colombia (Allen and Neill 1957); the Río Negro in Brazil (Waterman 1967); the Beni in Bolivia (Pilleri 1969); and the Apure in Venezuela (Pilleri 1979). Mitchell (1975b) has written: "While only one species is currently recognized in this genus, there are several well-separated populations. The Orinoco and Amazon populations could be considered separate subspecies, while the population from Bolivia may prove to be a separate species." In 1977, Pilleri and Gihr published a paper in which they differentiated the boutu from the Bolivian lowlands from that of the Amazon and Orinoco basins.* They

have designated the Bolivian species *Inia boliviensis* d'Orbigny 1834 (noting that it was first described by the French naturalist Alcide d'Orbigny after the 1817 description was published of *Inia geoffrensis* by de Blainville). The physical differences between the two species can be found in the smaller brain and larger number of teeth of *boliviensis*, but the main specific determinant is a geographical one, since they are separated by "a 400 km stretch of rapids in the River Madeira" (Pilleri and Gihr 1977), and unable to cross this barrier they are therefore unable to interbreed. Also on geographical grounds, Pilleri identifies a subspecies of *geoffrensis* which he calls *Inia geoffrensis humboldtiana*, found in the rivers of Colombia and Venezuela and eastward to the Guianas. This subspecies has fewer teeth per jaw than the others (25 on each side of each jaw whereas *boliviensis* has an average of 33), and is uniformly darker in color than the other species. In Venezuela the animal is known as *tonina*, and is "a deep grey in colour, quite different from the pale grey or pale pink of the Bolivian species" (Pilleri 1979). In a 1980 discussion of the taxonomy of the genus, Pilleri and Gihr differentiated *geoffrensis* and *boliviensis* on the basis of color as well as other considerations. "While the dolphins from the Orinoco [*I. geoffrensis*] are rather dark in colour, the Beni dolphins [*I. boliviensis*] which we observed at different ages and at different times of the year were all pale pink to greyish pink."

*It is likely that these are indeed valid species, but I have chosen to include them in a single account. The variations in morphology are small, and the major distinctions drawn by the authors are geographical.

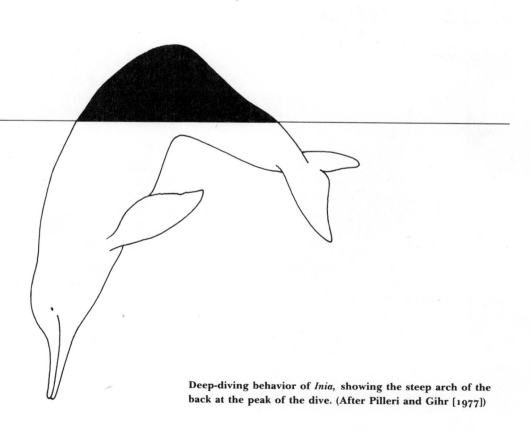

Deep-diving behavior of *Inia*, showing the steep arch of the back at the peak of the dive. (After Pilleri and Gihr [1977])

Until about 1974, there was a fishery by professionals for *bufeos,* where special nets were used. The skin was used for leather and the blubber as fat for cooking (Pilleri and Gihr 1977). Even more than in the local economy, however, this animal figures prominently in the folklore. In the Amazon there is a wide and varied body of mythology and fable associated with the boutu, including the purported aphrodisiac properties of its eye (presumably eaten), and the ability of its teeth to cure toothache. There are stories to the effect that it could sprout legs and walk away if penned up (Allen and Neill 1957), or it could take advantage of hapless young girls during celebrations, bearing the blame for siring children whose male parent was otherwise unidentified. Beddard reports that the boutu could be versatile in its victim and its transmutation; it could also assume the form of a long-haired woman and entice young men into the water, where they would drown. There are reports of boutus saving the lives of people whose canoes had overturned, and even some stories (e.g., Beddard 1900) of their attacking people in the water. In some areas the natives will not use the oil for illumination because they believe that blindness will result (Norman and Fraser 1938).

The boutu is not a shy animal, and it will often come close to boats and canoes in the water, often taking canoe paddles in its mouth or peering out of the water to observe passing boats. In one extraordinary account, F. B. Lamb (1954) reported that a fisherman on the Tapajós River in Brazil could call "his" boutu by tapping on the side of his canoe with the paddle, and "whistling a peculiar call." The dolphin would then chase fish from the deeper waters of the river to the shallows, where the fisherman would spear them. When the canoe (with Lamb in it as an observer) moved across the river, the dolphin would be there waiting for them. Lamb wrote: "this differed from the random feeding habits I have seen porpoises engage in on other occasions," since the dolphin stayed with them for over an hour. Busnel (1973) cites this as one of the few documented instances of symbiotic interaction between man and dolphin.

Since the 1956 expedition to Leticia, Colombia, to collect freshwater dolphins for exhibition, there has been a small industry in the acquiring of these animals for aquariums around the world. Herald (1967) reported that seventy living boutus had been brought into the United States since 1956, but the survival rate has been unfortunately low. In 1966 a group of seven animals was collected in the Amazon and brought to Marineland of Florida. They were extensively studied (see Caldwell and Caldwell 1969 a and b) and, as of 1981, at least two were still alive in the United States; one (Chico), at the Shedd Aquarium in Chicago, and another at the aquarium at Niagara Falls, New York. In 1968, after a conception in captivity—the male and female had been in the Fort Worth (Texas) Zoo for six years—the first boutu was born in the United States. It was delivered tail first, and appeared to have trouble staying afloat. Its mother tried to push it to the surface, but it died without ever successfully breathing. Postmortem examination showed that it weighed 15 pounds and was 32 inches long (Huffman 1970). In the absence of any other data from the field, it is assumed that this is about the average size for a newborn boutu.

In the wild as well as in captivity, the boutu is a fairly placid animal, whose unusual appearance and low-key behavior—in contrast, say, to the highly physical and "intelligent" behavior of the bottlenose dolphin—intrigues the observer. The boutu often swims upside down; it "rows through the water with its wide flippers"; or it just sits "with its flippers and tail flukes on the bottom of the tank, moving its head in all directions as if it were watching the outside with its very small eyes" (Nishiwaki 1972). In 1969 Herald wrote: "as soon as food is placed in the tank [in the Steinhart Aquarium in San Francisco] the dolphins turn on their backs and begin a search pattern which apparently allows them to use their sonar more effectively." (Later experiments at the Duisberg Zoo indicated that they did this only in the case of food that was not moving, and they fed on live fish in the "normal" position, that is, with the dorsal surface uppermost.) Defran and Pryor (1980) reported a specimen of *Inia,* "well-trained to perform a discrimination task, which gave a series of over fifty wrong responses in a row, thus calling attention to the fact that the fish being delivered to her by a feeding machine were dried out and inedible; when the fish were replaced, the animal returned immediately to 100% correct responses." A specimen (illustrated in Huffman [1970]) was trained to jump partly out of the water for a fish, and Pilleri (1969) recorded a boutu that could retrieve a weighted ring thrown into the water.

Further observations (e.g., Pilleri et al. 1980) have shown the boutu to be a playful animal, prompting the observers to remark that they "were struck by the dolphins' highly developed sense of curiosity. They were spontaneously interested in any new object placed in the tank and at once began investigating it." Captive animals at the Duisberg Zoo in Germany were observed to play with all sorts of floating objects such as buckets and brushes, but they were particularly interested in deck-tennis rings, which they would play with for hours, carrying one on the upper or lower jaw, or passing the rings to each other. It is also interesting to note that the play repertoire of the animals increased as they matured; that is, as they became more

adept at the manipulation of the objects, the play became "more varied and sophisticated."

In their study of the characteristics of cetaceans in captivity, Defran and Pryor (1980) characterized the boutu as follows:

Some of the more conspicuous behavior previously reported for the bottlenose dolphin has also been reported for the bouto, including play, orientation to humans, sexual activity (mostly masturbation) and various solitary swimming and surface activities. While quantitative comparisons are not possible, it appears that both the frequency and range of activities displayed by bouto are attenuated with respect to those seen in the bottlenosed dolphin. An exceptional lack of timidity was observed by M. Caldwell (1966). In none of the 10 bouto they tested was there a fright or flight reaction to the introduction of sound measurement apparatus into their enclosures. The authors noted that this pattern was in sharp contrast to the initial fright reactions of most bottlenosed dolphins they had tested with the same apparatus.

They further comment: "*Inia geoffrensis* is rated as markedly superior to *T. truncatus* in its ability to be controlled by auditory signals. *Inia geoffrensis'* natural habitats in turbid river waters favor the use of hearing."

It had been assumed that the platanistids, the most "primitive" of all the odontocetes, were also the least intelligent. Of the four genera in the family, *Platanista, Pontoporia, Lipotes,* and *Inia,* three of them rank at the bottom of the cephalization-ratio list of Gihr and Pilleri (1979), but surprisingly, *Inia* is near the top of the list, along with such clever animals as the bottlenose dolphin and the killer whale. (In another list, compiled by Wood and Evans [1980], *Inia* is not ranked quite so high, but the authors say that the species "trains well, and is an excellent experimental animal.") A high encephalization ratio does not necessarily indicate intelligence, but it certainly places *Inia* in some particularly "intelligent" company.

FRANCISCANA (LA PLATA DOLPHIN)

Pontoporia blainvillei Gervais 1844

One of the smallest of all cetaceans, the Franciscana reaches a total length of perhaps 6 feet (1.75 meters) and a maximum known weight of 133 pounds (50 kg). It is grayish brown above with lighter underparts. The flippers are wide but not large, and the flukes are relatively small as well. It is the only one of the platanistids with a real dorsal fin. The Franciscana has the longest beak, relative to body size, of any dolphin, and it used to be known as *Stenodelphis,* which can be translated as "narrow dolphin." Since the animal itself is usually plump, one assumes that *steno* refers to the beak. In this beak (or in the jaw itself) there are 50 to 60 small, sharp teeth in each half of each jaw, bringing the total to over 200 in some cases.

The name "Franciscana" is of unknown origin, but one suggestion connects it to the monks of the Franciscan order, the "gray friars" who were involved in the earliest European settlement of Uruguay (Van Erp 1969): the grayish color may be responsible for its curious name. Although it looks considerably more "dolphinlike" than other freshwater species—in fact, it is not really a freshwater inhabitant at all—the cervical vertebrae are unfused, a characteristic of the family Platanistidae.

The Franciscana feeds on small fishes, cephalopods, and crustaceans found in the shallow waters of the La Plata estuary between Uruguay and Argentina. A recent analysis of the feeding habits of this species (Brownell and Praderi 1976) has shown that croakers (*Cynocion*) make up over 60 percent of its diet, which also includes toadfishes, anchovies, and squid.

The eyes of the Franciscana, like those of all the platanistids, are small and weak, but because this species lives in shallow oceanic habitats where "light conditions are good . . . and the water shows very little cloudiness" (Pilleri 1971a), it probably has the best eyesight of all the platanistids. In a study of the brain of this species, Pilleri (1971a) noted that it has the thickest optic nerve of all the freshwater dolphins. Even with fairly well-developed eyesight, the Franciscana probably locates its prey by echolocation. The teeth have been described as "quite long, slender as toothpicks, [and] marvellously adapted for catching and holding soft-bodied prey" (Kellogg 1940).

This species is unusual in that the females are generally somewhat larger than the males. Juveniles are very small, measuring 27 inches (70 cm) at birth, with a weight of only 22 pounds (10 kg). The calves are born after a gestation period of ten and a half months, and are weaned at less than one year of age (Kasuya and Brownell 1979). The young animal has a short snout; as it matures the beak becomes more elongated. The species is not known to school; it has been observed in pairs, in groups of three to five animals, and alone (Pilleri 1971a).

It is found from Península Valdés, Chubut, Argentina, north to Río Grande do Sul, Brazil. By far the greatest concentration is at the wide mouth of the La Plata River in Uruguay, whence comes one of its common names. Unlike the other freshwater species, the Franciscana does not inhabit the river itself, but is restricted to the coastal waters of Uruguay, Argentina, and Brazil.

If it were not for a shark fishery begun in 1941 in Uruguayan waters, this little dolphin would be even less known than it is. (In 1969 Ingeborg Van Erp discovered that very few Uruguayans had ever heard of "their" dolphin—or the shark fishery for that matter —since the country's attention is focused inland, and

fishing is not a major industry.) In 1942, because supplies of cod-liver oil were drastically reduced by the effects of German U-boat attacks on Allied shipping, alternate sources of vitamin A were sought. Shark liver was discovered to be a rich source of this vitamin, and soon a small-scale shark fishery had developed off the Uruguayan coast, especially in the province of Rocha, off Punta del Diablo. The sharks taken in the nets were the sevengill, various species of hammerheads, the sand tiger, and the particular shark toward which the fishery was directed, the soupfin. These sharks are not known to prey on free-ranging dolphins (Brownell 1975), but they have attacked dolphins when both are trapped in the nets, or when the dolphins are entangled and unable to escape.* There is one recorded instance of epimeletic ("care-giving") behavior for this species where a female tried to pull her calf free from the net in which it was entangled (Pilleri 1971a).

In the early days of the fishery, the dead dolphins were just dumped overboard, but eventually the fishermen discovered that the oil was useful for waterproofing the hulls of their boats and for lubricating pulleys and capstans (Brownell and Praderi 1976). Vitamin A has now been synthesized, and there is no longer a need to catch sharks for this purpose. The shark fishery continues, however, with the current "in-

*With their ability to echolocate, it is curious that the Franciscanas cannot avoid the nets. Similar species, such as the boutu, proved themselves so adroit at avoiding nets that this approach had to be abandoned and the animals harpooned (Layne 1958). In a discussion of the brain development of various cetaceans, Gihr and colleagues (1979) have suggested that the low degree of cephalization of this species might be responsible for its inability to avoid the nets. In the same waters, the highly cephalized *Tursiops truncatus* is never caught in the nets. Put simply, the La Plata dolphin might not be intelligent enough to learn from experience.

Adult female and calf Franciscana dolphin (*Pontoporia blainvillei*), showing the long beak of the mature animal and the shorter one of the juvenile.

cidental" catch of dolphins, for now the shark meat is dried, salted, and sold as *bacalao,* the dried fish eaten by inhabitants of various South and Central American countries. Some 100 tons of *bacalao* are processed every year in the province of Rocha, and as long as the shark nets are set, the Franciscanas will be caught in them. There is no estimate of the total population, but between 600 and 1,500 dolphins are killed annually (Brownell and Praderi 1970).

CHINESE RIVER DOLPHIN (BAIJI)

Lipotes vexillifer Miller 1918

On February 18, 1914,* Charles M. Hoy, the son of an American missionary in Hunan Province, was duck hunting in Tung Ting Lake. When a school of dolphins passed within range, Hoy shot one in the back. He later reported that when he neared the wounded animal it "gave out a subdued bellow somewhat after the nature of a noise made by a buffalo calf" (Hoy 1923). He described the animal as weighing 297 pounds, with jaws that showed a distinct upward curve. He gave the color as pale blue-gray, but from a distance it looked white. From its stomach he removed "about two quarts of a single species of eel-like catfish that inhabits the mud at the bottom of the lake." Hoy retained the skull and the cervical vertebrae, which he delivered to the U.S. National Museum (Smithsonian Institution) upon his return to America. (In his 1923 paper he had written, "I noted that these bones serve as a means of identification in the porpoise and dolphins group of Cetacea or whales.") The material was examined and described by G. S. Miller, who realized that it represented a new species and

named it *Lipotes vexillifer.* The name *Lipotes* comes from the Greek *lipos* meaning "fat," and *vexillifer* is Latin for "flagbearer."

In 1921 another specimen was described (Pope 1932), and another was collected by G. F. C. Corfield in 1922 (Brownell and Herald 1972). Events in China from 1922 to the present have included a major revolution and a world war, and among the many things that were slighted during this period was cetological research. It was known that a river dolphin lived in Tung Ting Lake, and that it was related to the other platanistids. The cervical vertebrae that Hoy had saved were unfused, which is one of the diagnostic characteristics of this family. It also had a long snout, degenerate eyes, and broad flippers. Other than its basic physical appearance and restricted habitat, however, hardly anything was known about it.

In a brief description in their 1938 book *Giant Fishes, Whales and Dolphins,* Norman and Fraser wrote, "The Chinese River Dolphin is never seen except in Tung Ting Lake and around its mouth," and they then quote at some length from Miller's 1918 paper. In Kellogg's 1940 *National Geographic* article on whales and dolphins we read that "the Chinese White Flag Dolphin today is restricted to the fresh-water Tung Ting Lake in Hunan Province, China, some 600 miles up the Yangtze River." Kellogg further commented that the fishermen are reluctant to capture this dolphin because they believe it to be descended from a princess who flung herself into the lake. In subsequent mentions of this little-known animal, the story of the princess was usually repeated, its restricted habitat was always included, and even some elaboration on its habits began to appear in the popular literature, presumably as a result of an author's having to describe an animal about which hardly anything was known. For example, in Sanderson's *Living Mammals of the World* (Hanover House, n.d.), there appears this quote: "Although the lake is connected to the main river, these animals never go downstream; on the

---

*This is the date given in Hoy's 1923 paper, but Brownell and Herald (1972) report a "hand-written letter . . . from Hoy to Miller" that gives February 18, 1916, as the date.

other hand, at certain seasons they leave the lake and go up small tributary streams and even into ditches, so that it is hard to see how they ever turn round and get back again." In *Mammalian Species,* a series of short, definitive monographs published by the American Society of Mammalogists, Number 10 is on *Lipotes vexillifer* (Brownell and Herald 1972). Even after collecting all of what was known about this species to date, the authors were not able to improve much on Hoy and Miller. They described the animal's size, its habitat, its tooth count (about 33 on each side of the upper and lower jaw), and wrote that its blowhole was "somewhat rectangular." In the same report, the authors wrote, "nothing is known about the genetics or the physiology of *Lipotes.*"

Dr. Georg Pilleri, of the Institute of Brain Anatomy in Bern, Switzerland, has been collecting and publishing information on the various species of freshwater dolphins, traveling to India for the Ganges and Indus River dolphins, to the South American jungles for the two species of *Inia,* and to Uruguay for the Franciscana, or La Plata River, dolphin. Pilleri's *Investigations on Cetacea* includes papers on other species of cetaceans, but there is a pervasive emphasis on the platanistids. In Volume 7 (1976) he presented a discussion, "The Current Status of Research on the Chinese River Dolphin," which includes this somewhat plaintive note: ". . . we also know nothing about the behaviour and the bioacoustics . . . we should be extremely grateful if the Chinese authorities would make it possible to carry out comprehensive research on *Lipotes vexillifer,* either in their own institutes or in cooperation with other experts."

The literature on *Lipotes* seemed to consist of Hoy's discussion, upon which most other accounts were based, and on Miller's 1918 description. When China was finally opened to Westerners, Georg Pilleri's wish was answered, and in 1979, two *Lipotes* expeditions were mounted, one consisting of members of the Hydrobiology Academia Sinica at Wuhan, and the other from the Department of Biology, Nanjing Normal School. Pilleri was on both expeditions. On April 14–19 and then April 27–30, a voyage was made on the research vessel *Ke-Hu* to the lower reaches of the Chang Jiang River (formerly known as the Yangtze). From May 10 to 15 members of the Wuhan group made a survey of the middle reaches of the Chang Jiang River, and then made an additional survey on their return voyage (Chen et al. 1979).*

If there was any one thing that could be gleaned from the earlier literature on the baiji it was that the animal inhabited Tungting Lake, yet the expeditions

*All the 1979 observations in this part of the account are taken from Chen et al. (1979) and Zhou et al. (1979).

explored the river and did not once visit the lake (now known as Dungtinghu). There seems to be no question that Hoy's specimen came from the lake, but according to the Chinese scientists, the species can no longer be found there. The lake, which used to be China's largest, has been reduced in size by "discharge of floods into the lake, reclamation and cultivation of lakeside land, repair of dikes and the extension of embankments along the lake shores. . . ." It is now smaller than Poyanghu, and has lost its title as China's largest freshwater body. In addition, increased sedimentation has resulted from these actions, and it is believed that *Lipotes* has completely abandoned the lake in favor of the river.

From discussions with Chinese scientists, Pilleri learned that the Chinese river dolphin—correctly known now as baiji, or bai-ji—has been known for well over 2,000 years, and the earliest known description was published in the *Er-ya,* a book dating from about 200 B.C. Part of this description follows:

Ji is a dolphin. Its body shape is similar to that of Qin. The tail is like Ju. Large belly. Beak small and long. Many sharp teeth which interlock when biting. Nose sited in middle of forehead. Can produce sound. Flesh scarce but much fat. Viviparous. Feeds vigorously on small fish. The length of the large individuals may reach ten feet.

(*Qin* is the sturgeon [*Acipenser*], and *Ju* is the finless porpoise [*Neophocaena*], both of which are found in the river.) Pilleri (1979) also quotes several legends of the baiji in oral Chinese literature, two of which involve *Lipotes* and the other porpoise of inland China waters, *Neophocaena.* In both stories it is a woman who is transformed into the baiji, while the man becomes the *ju,* the finless porpoise. Pilleri further reports that he "was told another legend by the fishermen of Wu-Hu which confirmed the identification of the two species as man and woman."

In the past, the baiji acquired a number of vernacular names, including "whiteflag dolphin" and "whitefin dolphin." These appear to have resulted from erroneous translations, or attempts to render the name *vexillifer* into English.* *Ji* means "dolphin" in Chinese, and baiji means simply "grayish-white dolphin." In the first report published in English by Chinese scientists on this species, Chen (1981) wrote, "In China, as a matter of fact, *Lipotes* has always been called 'Baiji-tun.' "

The dolphin population of the river is sparse, and

*In a note in his *List of the Marine Mammals of the World* (1977), Rice gives *pei c'hi* and whitefin dolphin as the vernacular names, and quotes a personal communication from M. Nishiwaki to the effect that "the English name whiteflag dolphin is based on an erroneous interpretation of the Chinese."

during the two expeditions, the scientists saw fewer than 30 animals. They were usually seen in groups of "several—sometimes even more than ten—individuals." "*Lipotes* has a habit of grouping," wrote Chen, and "when the ship went near, the group broke up into small groups of about two individuals each, and these smaller groups either followed one after another or kept within a distance of 1–2 km. When the ship left, the smaller groups gathered into a large group again." They were also seen in groups of two, four, or six individuals. They tend to remain in deeper waters "near the mainstream," but Chen observes that "sometimes they go to the shallow waters near shore or near sandbanks or may even enter river branches for food. Sometimes they are found to be stranded in such places."

At the surface, the baiji is particularly difficult to see, because it raises just the melon, the blowhole, and part of the back out of the water when it breathes. The "interval between two surfacings varies from 5 to 135 sec, usually about 20 sec" (Chen 1981). The beak and tail are rarely seen, but infrequently an animal will lift the front half of its body out of the water so that the snout and flippers can clearly be seen. The Chinese river dolphin is often seen in mixed schools with the finless porpoise, but their behavior is totally different. The finless porpoise is much more abundant in the river, and considerably less shy; it even approaches boats occasionally. *Lipotes* is shy of boats and people, and dives whenever ships come near. "If the baiji is approached by motor boat, it would often make a long dive, change direction under water, swim right underneath the boat and surface behind it" (Zhou et al. 1979). Fishermen often find specimens that have been killed or badly wounded by boat propellers. Chen reported that "the greatest threat . . . is the hook fishery which is the most common practice in the river. We have investigated the causes of the death of nearly one

hundred individuals between 1950 and 1980, and found that nearly 50 percent were killed by the hooks. It seems very likely that *Lipotes* was caught while ingesting fish that had already been hooked up."

The eyes of the Chinese river dolphin, like those of all the other platanistids, are degenerate, but they are less regressive than those of the Indus and Ganges River dolphins, which are totally blind. Zhou and colleagues (1979) have arranged the platanistids in descending order of visual acuity, from the Franciscana, which can see quite well in the relatively clear coastal waters of the La Plata River delta, to the animals of the Indian subcontinent, which live in waters "which are almost totally dark a short distance below the surface." The Amazon River dolphin (*Inia*) and the Chinese river dolphin fall between these two extremes. The latter has small but functional eyes, located higher up on the head than those of any freshwater dolphin. Its eyes are also oriented forward, which would enable the animal to see better when it was swimming closer to the surface of the river. Like all the platanistids, *Lipotes* has a well-developed capability for echolocation. According to Yeh and Pilleri (1980), "the sonar used by dolphins is more efficient than manmade sonar systems," and because of the increasingly turbid nature of its habitat, this species has had to rely more and more on its sonar. ("The deforestation of the river banks once thickly wooded with deciduous trees has led to the land being eroded and washed down into the river with the result that the water has become increasingly turbid" [Yeh and Pilleri 1980].) These authors suggest that this species—and probably others—can alter the shape of the melon to vary the sonar beam pattern, but this has not been observed in living specimens of *Lipotes*. Calves are born in March and April, and are about 3.28 feet (1 m) in length. There was one sighting of a newborn calf on the lower reaches of the river.

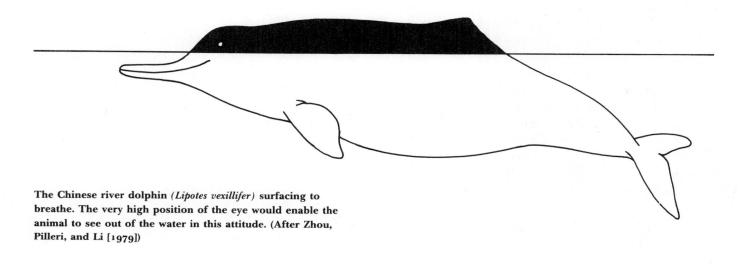

The Chinese river dolphin (*Lipotes vexillifer*) **surfacing to breathe. The very high position of the eye would enable the animal to see out of the water in this attitude. (After Zhou, Pilleri, and Li [1979])**

As an indication of the advances being made in the research on this species, there is even a report of one in captivity in China. Because it is the first record of a captive baiji, it is here reproduced in full from Chen's 1981 report:

On January 11, 1980, fishermen of Jiayu County, Hubei Province, caught a live *Lipotes* that had entered a pool of shallow water near a sandbank. We transported it back to the institute successfully by using the "dry" method. This male *Lipotes* with the pet name Qiqi, weighed 36.5 kg. and was 1.47 m in length. It has been kept provisionally in a 17.8 × 8 m cement pond. At first Qiqi was very shy and moved away rapidly whenever anyone tried to go near him. But now, after five months of careful rearing, it has become accustomed to the new environment, and comes eagerly to the feeder for fresh fish. Even the sound of our footsteps will attract his attention and he would come near the edge of the pond and play around. Some preliminary studies have been made, including the recording of his echo-signals, the observations on his physiology and behavior, and the technique of rearing in captivity.

Qiqi was injured by hooks during capturing. Soon after he reached our institute, the infection got so serious that he had to be kept out of water for emergency treatment for over sixty hours. Now that the wounds have mostly healed, Qiqi is eating more and becoming more active.

Mitchell (1975a) wrote that "the status of the population is unknown." In 1976 the *Red Data Book* assigned the Chinese river dolphin "indeterminate status," indicating that its numbers were unknown and that until more information could be collected, no hunting should take place. It now appears that the Chinese have long been aware of the declining population of their only endemic freshwater dolphin—the finless porpoise is also found in Indian waters and the Inland Sea of Japan—and they have assigned it "first grade protection, which is the same accorded to the Giant Panda." Pilleri (1979), discussing the possibility of saving this species, wrote, "Clearly the task will not be an easy one. The Chinese have, however, achieved success in far more difficult enterprises. Moreover, they have an enormous experience in breeding both land and water animals, having developed skills which are seldom to be found in other countries. If they succeed in saving *Lipotes vexillifer* in this way, it will certainly be a splendidly original achievement."

The problem, however, may not be with the hunters or fishermen, but with the dolphins themselves. In an examination of the comparative cephalization ratios (body length and body weight to brain weight), Gihr and Pilleri (1979) found the baiji to be one of the lowest species on the list.* Although we cannot as-

cribe human "intelligence" values to Pilleri's cephalization ratios, we can make the simple observation that those animals with the highest ratios (such as the bottlenose dolphin) are able to behave in a self-protective manner, while those on the lower end of the scale seem not to be able to defend themselves from new or unique dangers. A case in point is the baiji's inability to avoid boats. Its low brain-to-body ratio may be interpreted as an indication of relatively low cetacean intelligence. All odontocetes have the ability to echolocate (and therefore "see" objects that they might encounter underwater), but some animals may not be able effectively to process the information they receive. Gihr and colleagues (1979) have written, "*Lipotes* is less capable of *Neophocaena* of defending itself against the increasing anthropogenic impact on the Yangtze River. It is probable that a less efficient sonar apparatus and indeed a less highly developed brain is the main cause of the vulnerability of the Chinese river dolphin." It is difficult to imagine what can be done, short of banning all motorboat traffic on the river, to protect the baiji. We can, if we choose, protect dolphins from our own predations, but we cannot protect the dolphins from themselves.

GANGES RIVER DOLPHIN (SUSU)

Platanista gangetica Roxburgh 1801

The Ganges River dolphin, found only in the river system of the Indian subcontinent, is also known as the susu. This word is derived from the Hindi words *sus, sous, susu, susa,* and *sunsar,* all onomatopoetic transliterations of the sound the animal makes when it surfaces to breathe. It is also known as *susuk, sishuk, shushuk* and *sishumachh.* In Sanskrit it is called *savsar,* "which means 'sea' or 'ocean,' presumably meaning an animal of the sea which shows that the ancients knew the marine origin of the animal" (Jones 1976a).

The Ganges River dolphin was first described by William Roxburgh in 1801, and therefore his name and the date have become part of the animal's full scientific name.* In 1878 the animal was described in great detail by John Anderson, M.D., superintendent

---

*They analyzed data on several species of cetaceans, and found the highest were the bottlenose dolphin, the harbor porpoise, the

boutu, Risso's dolphin, and the killer whale. The sperm whale, the fin whale, the humpback, and the gray whale were in the middle range, and at the low end of the scale were the right whale, the blue whale, and the platanistids (excluding the boutu).

*It has sometimes been written with the name LeBeck (or LeBeck) and the same date, but Pilleri (1978) has shown that Roxburgh, a Scottish botanist who became superintendent of the Botanical Gardens in Calcutta in 1793, was the original author, and while LeBeck did publish a paper describing the animal in 1801, it now seems likely that he referred to Roxburgh's account.

of the Indian Museum in Calcutta and a professor of comparative anatomy. Anderson's monograph is a model of detailed observation, and includes virtually every aspect of the animal's morphology and known behavior—including its feeding habits; he managed to keep one alive for ten days in a pool in Calcutta. Until quite recently, most of our information on the Ganges River dolphin was based on Anderson's account. As a study of the interior and exterior aspects of the animal Anderson's discussion is meritorious, but since it normally lives in waters so murky that it cannot be seen except when it surfaces, his account is limited to those observations he could make of captive or dead specimens, and therefore much of the work that followed his was based on speculation. Anderson wrote that he examined the stomach contents of one specimen, and found "paddy, seeds of the Kudoo grass, remains of beetles . . . and a solitary undigested bee." This led subsequent authors to assume, for the better part of the next hundred years, that the animal got its food from the bottom. For example, in Norman and Fraser's 1938 discussion of the species, we read that "the animal procures its food by probing in the mud of the rivers in which it lives," and shortly thereafter, Kellogg (1940) wrote that "it must be guided to its food by the sense of touch in its long snout." Slijper (1962) wrote that the "Gangetic Dolphin which feeds mainly at the bottom of turbid rivers probably used its long jaws for stirring up the mud." It appeared that this image—which is false—of the animal grubbing in the mud survived even the discovery of the remarkable sonar capabilities of dolphins.* It did seem logical, after all, that this animal had to catch its food some-

how, and its long snout and sharp teeth—not to mention its virtual absence of eyes—made it appear ideally suited for "probing in the mud."

Early accounts, and unfortunately some more recent ones, pictured the Ganges River dolphin as a primitive, degenerate creature, whose eyes had atrophied as a result of millennia of occupying the murky waters, and therefore had to rely on mud-grubbing for its sustenance, which was likely to be of a somewhat lesser quality than the food of the swift, seagoing dolphins. Seeds, beetles, and bees are not really the food of "lively ocean rangers."

In November 1968, a group of four scientists (a veterinarian, a photographer, a cetologist, and an ichthyologist) traveled to West Pakistan for the purpose of collecting specimens of the Ganges River dolphin, which they planned to bring back to the Steinhart Aquarium in San Francisco. Under the leadership of E. S. Herald, the director of the aquarium, they caught only three young females, but since these animals represented the first captive susus since Anderson's 1878 study, the information the group gathered was highly significant. In his 1969 report,* Herald wrote that Anderson's studies were "so comprehensive that this may have served to stifle the interests that zoologists of the region might have otherwise had in this interesting creature."

The dolphins were transported from Karachi to Tokyo to San Francisco, a distance of some 11,000 miles ("the flight travel record for cetaceans"), in four days and thirteen hours. The three animals lived for less than two months and did not feed voluntarily, so they had to be force-fed, but during that time a number of revealing observations were made. The side-

---

*Arthur McBride is usually credited with the discovery that dolphins in Florida waters could avoid his nets by some "specialized mechanism" associated with sound. His startlingly accurate prediction was published in 1948, and subsequent investigators (such as Schevill and Lawrence) confirmed his hypothesis. A more detailed account of this discovery can be found in the discussion of the bottlenose dolphin, the animal that was the subject of the original studies.

*Herald's comprehensive account of the expedition appeared in the same year as the article in *Science* by Herald et al., but it is much more complete, incorporating all the laboratory reports from the various consulting scientists, while the *Science* article is a summary, emphasizing the side-swimming of the observed animals. Quotes in this section are from Herald's report, unless otherwise noted.

swimming of the species was noted for the first time, and it was pointed out that Anderson had kept his specimen in a "filled bathtub," which was presumably "too narrow for the animal to show its normal swimming pattern." The echolocating capabilities of these animals with eyes that can barely differentiate between light and dark were recorded, their respiration rates and swimming behavior were noted, and when they died (two of pneumonia and the third of complications following a jaw injury that occurred during capture), the autopsies revealed many unsuspected anatomical characteristics. The eye structure was closely examined, as were the skin, skeleton, and internal organs. The blubber layer was discovered to be much thicker than had been suspected (almost 2 inches in some areas), and the various medications that had been injected into the animals had not penetrated the fat, and were therefore ineffective.

In 1966 Dr. George Pilleri examined the head of a Ganges River dolphin. His interest in the species was piqued, and he organized an expedition to East Bengal and Northern India to collect specimens, but "due to unfavorable conditions it yielded few results" (Pilleri 1970a). Another expedition left Switzerland for the Indus and Brahmaputra Rivers in 1969, and was "crowned with success." Two live specimens were transported from the Indus River* to the Institute of Brain Anatomy at Bern, and Pilleri and his colleagues began what has now become one of the most extensive studies in the history of cetology. Beginning with the description of the first expedition to India in 1967, the Institute of Brain Anatomy has assembled a virtual textbook on the biology, habits, history, and taxonomy of the platanistids, and concurrently has produced the most comprehensive discussion of the other freshwater dolphins of South America and China. There have been other studies of the Amazon River dolphin, the La Plata River dolphin, and even the rare and little-known Chinese river dolphin, but *Investigations on Cetacea,* the journal of the Institute of Brain Anatomy, under the editorial and scientific direction of Pilleri, has concentrated heavily on the family Platanistidae. There is no other journal in cetology—and perhaps in all biology—where such emphasis is placed on a single family.

The Ganges River dolphin is usually a soft, brownish-gray color, which darkens as the animal matures. (Norman and Fraser [1938] described the animal as "lead black," but Kasuya [1972] gives "pale brown with a tinge of gray" as the color of a 113-centimeter (44-inch) male. The first female collected by Herald (1969)—which he described as "extremely fat and chunky"—was "suffuse pinkish red on the underside grading to dark gray above." The earlier literature gives 8 feet as the maximum length for this species, and although Pilleri measured one at 240 centimeters (7.8 feet), they are usually smaller. (The three females collected by Herald ranged from 107 to 121 centimeters [41 to 46 inches] in length, and the largest weighed 59 pounds.) The species is characterized by a long narrow snout, "squared-off" flippers, and only the merest hint of a dorsal fin, a slight triangular peak behind the midpoint of the back. The blowhole is slitlike in form, running parallel to the animal's long axis, and set slightly to the left of center. The susu has an impressive array of sharp teeth—about 29 or 30 on each side of each jaw. The lower teeth are longer than the uppers, and they are visible when the animal's mouth is closed.* A certain degree of sexual dimorphism is evident in this species: the snout of the female is proportionally longer than that of the male, so if there are a male and a female of the same weight, the female will be longer. The species has visible ear openings, and an eye that is a small, lensless dot in a slight depression above the angle of the mouth.

The Ganges susu is almost totally blind. Its eyes, usually described as "regressive" or "degenerate," have become almost useless. The waters of the Ganges River system are murky in the extreme, with a visibility that often does not exceed 2 to 4 centimeters (.78–1.56 inches). Pilleri and colleagues (1976) examined numerous specimens, and wrote that the eye "has no lens, the ciliary body is atrophic, the optic nerve is very thin and the eye muscle nerves are lacking entirely. . . . Although a retina is present, it is virtually impossible for such an eye to perceive images. It can at the most determine the direction of the light and distinguish between light and dark."

If the animal is almost completely blind and does not root around in the mud to find its food, how then does it manage to feed itself?† It turns out that this "primitive" dolphin has certain behavioral and

---

*Although the Indus River dolphin was identified as a new species by Blyth in 1859, in his 1878 monograph Anderson maintained that it was not distinct from the Ganges species. Until the publication of Pilleri's 1971 paper, Anderson's determination was accepted. Therefore, the two animals collected in the Indus were technically *Platanista gangetica,* because the species *P. indi* was not resurrected until 1971.

*The presence of these sharp teeth, even in juveniles, raised the question, according to Herald (1969), "as to the method by which a young dolphin with such frightful dentition could obtain milk from the mother without leaving the parent a mutilated shred. F. G. Wood came up with a good suggestion—i.e., that the area at the base of the jaw where the teeth were not erupted had to be the area used to obtain milk. By pressing that part of the mouth against the mammary slits, the susu could undoubtedly obtain its necessary nourishment."

†Although *P. gangetica* and *P. indi* are distinct species, their habits and biology are so similar that I have combined them in this account. The differences, discussed in the following section, are anatomical, osteological, and, of course, geographical.

anatomical adaptations that enable it to function quite efficiently in its nonvisual habitat: it has a remarkably well developed sonar capability. By sending out a series of rapid clicks and then reacting to the returning echoes as the sound bounced off objects in the water, the Ganges dolphin exhibits an extraordinary ability to echolocate. A lead shot 4 millimeters (just over 1/8″) in diameter was "immediately located, inspected, and collision with it avoided" (Pilleri et al. 1976). Dolphins in captivity could also easily locate transparent plastic balls filled with water, and they could also distinguish different species of fish, dead and alive. The sending of signals obviously requires the reception of the echoes, and therefore it is not surprising to discover that the susu has a particularly well-developed sense of hearing. Purves and Pilleri (1973) wrote that the "sense of hearing . . . in *Platanista* in particular is extremely delicate and capable of analyzing minute quanta of sound energy."

The mystery of the feeding methods of *Platanista*, long a matter of speculation, has now been resolved. Instead of probing in the mud, the Ganges dolphin is an effective predator on living fishes, locating them by its efficient sonar apparatus and snapping them up in its pincerlike jaws. Animals observed in captivity fed at night for the most part, and were extremely adept at catching live fishes in their tanks. They would snare the fish at right angles to the snout, surface, inhale, then dive again to swallow the fish. (*Platanista* exhales just before reaching the surface, and it echolocates the surface of the water just as it does everything else in its environment.)

The skull of the platanistids is unique. On either side of the head, a crest of bone projects from the facial portion of the skull. These crests are believed to perform an important function in the sonar orientation of the animal. Purves and Pilleri (1973) have postulated a sound-gathering function for these crests, as contrasted with those species, such as the bottlenose, in which the primary hearing function has been assigned to the lower jaw (Norris 1964). "The general shape and orientation of the crests suggests the act of cupping the hands in front of the mouth or the use of a megaphone to give directional reinforcement to the

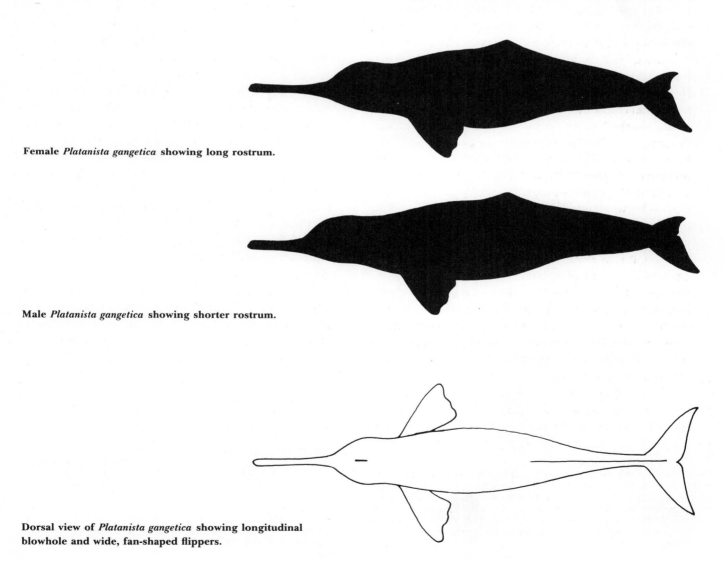

Female *Platanista gangetica* **showing long rostrum.**

Male *Platanista gangetica* **showing shorter rostrum.**

Dorsal view of *Platanista gangetica* **showing longitudinal blowhole and wide, fan-shaped flippers.**

DOLPHINS AND PORPOISES 35

voice, and there seems to be little doubt that this principle is involved in the maxillary crests of *Platanista.*" The crests, therefore, would seem to serve dual purposes with regard to sound: they help with both reception and transmission.

The structure of the throat in *Platanista* is different from that of any other dolphin, and here again a sonar function has been postulated. All the platanistids are characterized by unfused vertebrae in the neck region, which gives them unusual mobility of the head. Pilleri (1979) identified the larynx as the sound-production organ of this species, and wrote "that there is a great deal of evidence to show that the clicks in all toothed whales are produced exclusively in the larynx." Pilleri and colleagues (1976) have written, "It has still not been firmly established whether the sound is produced in the upper nares as Norris et al. [1971] suggest, or by the larynx, but all the anatomical and experimental evidence so far accumulated from the study of *Platanista indi* strongly suggests the latter method. . . ."*

Since *Platanista* swims on its side, it therefore orients its throat toward the object it would inspect, rather than facing the object head on, as do most other odontocetes that have been observed. Pilleri and colleagues (1976) have identified three distinct modes of echolocation behavior: (1) *explore,* to "obtain a general acoustic image of the surroundings during normal swimming; (2) *locate,* to "detect the position of an object by sonar"; and (3) *inspect,* to "examine an already located object." When strange objects were introduced into the tank of a captive animal at Bern, "the dolphin usually remains motionless with the object opposite its throat at an angle of approx. 30° to the angle of the rostrum."

Observing captives in Bangladesh, Aminul Haque and colleagues (1977) reported that "the dolphin swam on one side nodding the head continuously in 'yes' motion." This constant "nodding" was also observed at Bern, where the scientists had identified two distinct sonar fields—both produced by the larynx—one from the "forehead" and one from the throat. They suggested that the head movement might be necessary to eliminate the "blind spot" in the sonar field, where the two beams of sound do not overlap.

During the 1969 expedition to Assam, Pilleri (1970a) observed: "At night: swimming on the side (particularly the right side) is clearly visible. This mode of swimming can always be observed in shallow water. The animal will venture into zones where the depth of the water is no more than 20 cm" (7.8 inches). It was not until specimens were observed in captivity, however, that the unique nature of this behavior was revealed. In 1969 the first platanistids were observed in captivity (excluding Anderson's in 1878). Two dolphins from the Indus River were transported to Switzerland and placed in tanks at the Brain Anatomy Institute at Bern. Pilleri and colleagues (1970) reported, "Although the dolphin can swim on either side . . . it nearly always swims on its right side." Subsequent observations (at Bern and at the Steinhart Aquarium in San Francisco) led to more detailed descriptions of this "method of progression previously unknown in cetaceans" (Herald et al. 1969). Side-swimming is considered to be useful for moving in shallow water, because an up-and-down tail motion would be impossible where the tail would have to come out of the water on the upstroke or hit the bottom on the downstroke. An additional puzzle concerning the swimming habits of these dolphins involves rolling. When other cetaceans—such as the common dolphin—rotate on the long axis, the flippers are rotated in the same direction simultaneously, but in *Platanista,* "the flippers and the tail flukes do not appear to be involved in the process. The whole animal revolves effortlessly as if controlled by some internal alteration in the centre of buoyancy. It can even perform this maneuvre when stationary" (Pilleri et al. 1976).

During side-swimming, the Ganges dolphin often drags the lower flipper along the bottom, an activity that observers have associated with a sense of touch. (Since the animals usually swim on their right sides, it is the right flipper that is usually in contact with the bottom.) Pilleri and Gihr (1976), in "The Function and Osteology of the Manus of *Platanista gangetica* and *Platanista indi,*" have this to say about the flippers:

*There is still considerable controversy concerning the actual source of cetacean sounds. Norris (1964) wrote that "evidence is already relatively secure for production of echolocation sound trains in the nasal sac of the forehead." He was discussing the sound production of the bottlenose dolphin, and it now seems likely that the great differences in the structure of the head—bones, sacs, blubber, and musculature—between the bottlenose and the platanistids would account for quite different methods of sound production. The fact that both produce trains of high-frequency clicks might be an example of the principle of convergence, where two separate evolutionary paths produce the same results, even though the development of the mechanism has been independently reached.

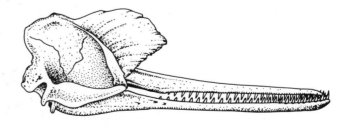

The skull of *Platanista gangetica,* showing maxillary crests.

"Whereas the main function of the flipper of other dolphins is to act as a stabilizer during swimming, in the two *Platanista* species . . . it also fulfils an important function of touch. These virtually blind dolphins that are side-swimmers grope along the muddy floor of their biotope. . . . In *Platanista* the two sensory functions, sense of touch and sonar location, are both vital for its orientation." Another function of side-swimming might be the orientation of the eye toward the light source. Since the eye of this species can only distinguish light from dark, an effective way of maintaining the most efficient swimming position might be the positioning of one eye toward the incident light source. Even with its greatly reduced visual apparatus, the Ganges River dolphin would therefore be making the best use of all of its sensory faculties.

According to Pilleri and colleagues (1971), the animals never stop swimming. They are also constantly sending out sonar signals, except for the moments when they come to the surface to breathe. Since they are continuously swimming and echolocating—only 3- to 5-second interruptions have been recorded in the signals—the animals appear to sleep very little, and they manifest "probably the shortest period of sleep established so far in a mammal" (Pilleri et al. 1976). The waters in which these animals live are marked by strong currents, especially during the monsoon season, and the water is so murky that constant sonar orientation is necessary, as is constant movement. "Under these conditions," wrote Pilleri and colleagues in 1976, "long periods of sleep involving a complete standstill of the swimming movements and orientation apparatus would be lethal."

Platanista is generally a slow swimmer, with recorded speeds in captivity of 1.9 meters (6.2 feet) per second, as compared to an average of 7.8 meters (26.5 feet) per second for the common dolphin, an oceangoing species. *Platanista* is capable of short bursts of speed, and can also leap completely out of the water, especially in panic situations. A. K. M. Aminul Haque and colleagues (1977) reported that a specimen of the Ganges susu was seen "chasing a big fish at tremendous speed." (In the same paper, the authors reported an attack on a goose, "while the latter was, in its characteristic manner, probing the pond-bottom for food.") The Ganges River dolphin usually breathes almost invisibly with only the blowhole appearing above the surface, but there are some instances in which the long pointed snout appears, and most infrequently, when the animal puts its entire head out of the water (Pilleri 1970a).

An analysis of the brain–body weight ratio of the Ganges River dolphin (and its close relative, the Indus River dolphin) has revealed "the lowest relative brain weight of all species [of odontocetes] examined to date" (Pilleri and Gihr 1970). It is difficult to interpret these findings without resorting to some degree of anthropomorphism, but it is possible to assume that this is among the least "intelligent" of the dolphins. With its relatively small brain it is obviously capable of processing the acoustic information it receives, but it may not be able to deal with the additional threat imposed upon it by the existence of hunters or barricades in the rivers.

Perhaps one of the most startling suggestions made by Pilleri and his colleagues at Bern is that the susu swims in circles "and that it is structurally incapable of doing otherwise" (Pilleri et al. 1976). Even

The separate dorsal and ventral sonar beams of Platanista. (After Pilleri [1979])

when an animal was towed behind a boat, the rope "had to be mounted on a metal swivel" to keep the rope from knotting, because the animal was inclined to swim in a circle. After a meticulous examination of the musculature, the scientists at Bern concluded that the animal cannot swim in a straight line, and therefore it "must be constrained to swim all its life in circles, however large or small they may be."

Copulatory behavior has been observed once: two animals "emerged vertically above the water and came together in a vertical contact with their flippers enlaced. A good half of the body of the animal was visible above the water and the tail was agitated furiously to keep the body vertical" (Pilleri 1971). What happens after copulation, however, has been a subject of much speculation. In 1878 Anderson wrote, "some of my informants record that the period of gestation is 8 or 9 months" and, for lack of any better information, this figure has been regularly repeated in accounts of the species. (In 1967, Rice wrote that "such a short gestation period is highly questionable".) Given the size of the animal at maturity, the 8- or 9-month figure is very low, and after examining 22 specimens in Bangladesh, Kasuya (1972) remarked "the gestation period may probably be about one year." The newborn susu is about 50 centimeters (20 inches in length), and has been described as dark grey or pinkish red in color (Pilleri 1972a). According to Pilleri and Bhatti (1978), calves leap almost completely out of the water when surfacing to breathe. Females reach sexual maturity at about 6 feet (185 centimeters), and males at 5 1/2 feet (Kasuya 1972). The susu is not gregarious, and under natural conditions—that is, when it is not being chased by hunters—it is rare to see two or more animals together (Jones 1976a).

Since almost everything about this species is unusual, it may not be altogether surprising to discover that it has bad breath: "Like those observed in the Indus, the Brahmaputra dolphins exhale a peculiar unpleasant odour, vaguely reminiscent of excrement. This odour could be smelt quite distinctly when the animals swam near the bank" (Pilleri 1970a). In 1976 Pilleri and colleagues wrote, "We can offer no explanation as to the cause of the strong odour described."

The Ganges susu is found throughout the rivers of northern India, especially the Ganges-Brahmaputra-Meghna system, and also in Nepal and Assam in the foothills of the Himalayas. W. F. J. Mörzer Bruyns (1971) reports it "on the Hoogly River to Calcutta, where during the summer it comes downstream to just below Budgebudge." Before the construction of the dam at Kaputi on the Karnaphuli River (1954–55), the species was plentiful in the river. Some six or seven

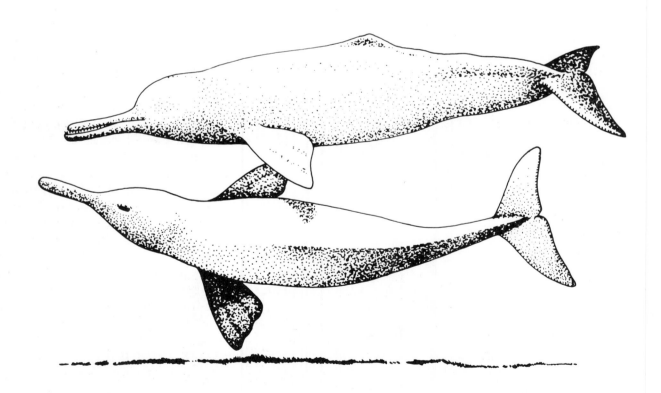

Ganges River susu, *Platanista gangetica*, showing "side-swimming" and the longitudinal blowhole.

years after the construction of the dam, the population has apparently been eliminated upstream. (See the account of the Indus River dolphin for further discussion of the effects of these dams on the populations of the Ganges dolphin.)

There is no fishery for this species in Pakistan, and its mortality is almost entirely a function of habitat destruction. (According to Pilleri [1970a], the fishermen have never reported stranded animals.) Jones (1976a) estimates a total Ganges dolphin population of "between 4,000 and 5,000, a very satisfactory population when compared to the few hundred of *Platanista indi* surviving in the Indus River." As of this writing, the situation with the Ganges susu appears to be fairly stable, but, as Jones wrote in a 1976 report to the Food and Agricultural Organization (FAO) of the United Nations,

The Ganga-Brahmaputra system drains about 2,000,000 sq km of land in which live about 300 million people, nearly a tenth of the world's population. . . . It is not necessary that we should wait till a critical situation, as has happened to the Indus susu, before we contemplate taking steps for its conservation and protection. Its habitat . . . comes within one of the most densely populated and food deficit areas of the world.

INDUS RIVER DOLPHIN

Platanista indi Blyth 1859

The Indus River dolphin is very similar to the species that lives in the Ganges River. They can be differentiated only by certain characteristics of the skull, and by other minor—but consistent—anatomical differences. Both varieties are blind, long-snouted, side-swimming dolphins, with wide flippers and flukes, and a low peak where the dorsal fin would normally be.

Although this species was originally described by Blyth in 1859, later authors, unwilling or unable to differentiate the animal from its Ganges River counterpart, lumped the two together. In his 1878 monograph on the Platanistidae, Anderson did not differentiate between the two, and they were therefore treated as a single species until 1971, when Pilleri and Gihr published "Differences Observed in the Skulls of *Platanista gangetica* (Roxburgh 1801) and *indi* (Blyth 1859)." In this paper, significant differences were identified in the two species, which "permits even the uninitiated to distinguish between the two species from an examination of macerated skulls." In 1972 Kasuya wrote that there were indeed differences between the two forms—he added differences in the proportions of the tail region to Pilleri's skull variations —but he felt that the evidence was "still insufficient" to consider them as separate species, and he preferred a subspecies distinction, *Platanista gangetica gangetica*, and *Platanista gangetica indi*. Further examinations have confirmed Pilleri's original conclusions, and they are now considered totally separate. (In the 1968 *List of the Marine Mammals of the World*, Rice and Scheffer included only the Ganges dolphin, but in the 1977 version of the work, both species are included.)

In 1853 Sir Robert Owen described a particularly small specimen, and believing it to be a new species, he named it *Platanista minor*. The skull was less than 12 inches long, as compared with the skull of a mature adult animal, which might be twice that length. Owen had obviously examined a juvenile and assumed it to be an adult. Although Rice (1977) maintains that "Owen's name has priority," Pilleri and Gihr, in a 1977 discussion of the nomenclature, hold that Owen's *minor* is invalid: "the proposal to name the Indus dolphin *Platanista minor* runs counter to the stability of the zoological system and we would reject it for this and other reasons." Such an argument is convincing from Pilleri, the acknowledged expert on the Platanistidae.

Since the two species were considered synonymous for almost a century, it is not surprising to find a substantial overlap in the literature concerning them. We read in Norman and Fraser (1938) that the susu "is confined to the River Ganges and the River Indus, in each ranging from the sea as far upstream as depth and the absence of rocky barriers will permit." While there are clear osteological and geographical reasons to differentiate the Ganges dolphin from the Indus, the basic biology of the two species is so similar that my discussion of their habits and habitat are combined in the previous account.

The differences identified by Pilleri and Gihr in their 1971 publication concern the nasal crests, formed by the frontal bones of the skull, and visible behind the great maxillary crests that characterize the genus. In the susu, the nasal crest is well defined and as much as 10 millimeters in height, while in *indi* the crest is poorly defined, and it only projects 1 to 4 millimeters.* When Kasuya (1972) plotted the various measurements given by Pilleri, he discovered a difference in the "length of tail" (measured from the notch in the flukes to the anal slit); in the Ganges specimens this measurement was 6.7 centimeters shorter than in the Indus dolphins. "This difference is too large to consider as individual variation or personal deviation from the measurement." Kasuya then discusses the Pleistocene division of the Ganges and Indus Rivers, and attributes the morphological differences (even though he does not grant them full-species status) to "separate evolution," after the two rivers had become separated. Both rivers begin in the Himalayas. The Indus runs through Pakistan, and the Ganges through eastern India and Bangladesh. The middle reaches of both rivers, where the dolphins live, are separated by almost fifteen hundred miles of the Indian highlands. The former range of the animal was the Indus River from the Himalayan foothills to the sea, and included the main Indus tributaries, the Jhelum, Chenab, Sutlej, and Ravi Rivers. Currently, the species is restricted to the Indus between the Sukkur and Taunsa barrages, and to a small stretch of the Chenab River below the Panjnad barrage.

Now that the two species have been clearly differentiated, some observations that previously would have been ascribed to either species can be applied to one. (That is not to say that both species would not—or could not—behave in the same manner, but where the origin of the particular animals is known, the behavior is assigned to one species.) A case in point is the "play behavior" observed and recorded by Pilleri and colleagues (1980) of four Indus dolphins in captivity in Europe. The animals were observed over a period of several years, from 1972 to 1978, and in their 1980 discussion, the authors presented the first detailed observations of play in these dolphins.*

The dolphins were immediately interested in any new object placed in their tanks, and investigated it immediately by means of their sonar signals. They were especially interested in the hydrophones hanging in the tank, and would play with them for protracted periods of time, mouthing them and twisting the cords together. They also played with tennis balls floating on the surface—pulling them below and then allowing the balls to bob up again—and a small turtle: a female dolphin would "send it staggering sideways with a smart blow of the beak, exactly like a golfer propelling the ball with a powerful sideways swing of his club." Playful swimming behavior consisted of loops, dives, headstands, and figure-eight patterns.

Play behavior increases with age in these dolphins (as it does with the Amazon River dolphin). In their summary of the play behavior of the freshwater dolphins *Platanista* and *Inia,* the authors wrote, "The Cetacea so far studied . . . show far more parallels in terms of play behavior with primates than with carnivores. . . . Play behavior ensures the acquisition of experience in the broadest sense and presupposes learning ability. Only superior animals with a highly developed capacity for learning can really play at all."

After Pilleri led his 1969 expedition to the Indus region, he published the first descriptions (in the cetological literature) of the barrages or headworks that have been built at strategic points along the river to control the water of the irrigation canals. "The total length of the canal system is 10,000 miles and 33 million acres of land are irrigated annually. It is essentially the largest essentially continuous block of irrigation development in the world" (Taylor 1965). As of 1974 there were six barrages in the Indus, and additional ones in the above-mentioned tributaries. These barrages are impassable to the dolphins, and they not only prevent the normal seasonal migrations, but they effectively isolate individual populations, which makes them particularly vulnerable to hunting. Kasuya and Nishiwaki (1975) assign an even more ominous function to the barrages: the irrigation efforts actually drain the water from the river, and the water level is so lowered that the animals cannot survive. ". . . if the utilization of water for irrigation increases in future, the survival of this dolphin population will be impossible."

---

*This is unfortunately rather technical, but it is just the sort of information that taxonomists rely on to differentiate one allied species from another. When there is a consistent, recognizable difference—even one that is visible only to anatomists—there can be a differentiation of species.

*For purposes of their discussion, Pilleri and colleagues referred to play as "one of the least understood categories of behavior," but characterized it as activity that "lacks any specific earnest context . . . appears meaningless in so far as they [the animals] do not fulfil their normal biological functions at the time . . . ," and "the goal of play lies in itself."

In November 1969 Pilleri and his colleagues visited the Indus between the Sukkur and Taunsa barrages and observed the dolphins in the wild but made no population counts (Pilleri 1970a). Two years later he returned to Pakistan and made "the first count of *Platanista indi . . .* in any river." There were an estimated 40 animals between Sukkur and Chak, and the total number for this portion of the river was between 65 and 70 animals (Pilleri 1972a). It was apparent even then that the species was in serious trouble. Another population census was conducted in 1974, and yielded a count of no more than 150 animals between the Guddu and Sukkur barrages, a distance on the river of some 170 kilometers (105.4 miles). In December 1974 the Ocean Research Institute of Tokyo conducted a survey in Pakistan to "know the present range of distribution of the dolphin and to estimate the population" (Kasuya and Nishiwaki 1975). Using personal observations, designated observers, and reports from fishermen, Kasuya and Nishiwaki estimated the total population at 450 to 600 animals, "the lowest estimation [that] has ever been made on this population."

The barrages make the animals easier prey for the *bhulangshikari,* the dolphin hunters. (One of the names for the river dolphin in Pakistan is *bhulaan.*) In this area, unlike the Ganges region, the dolphins are hunted. The meat is eaten by some castes, and the blubber oil is used for medicinal and veterinary purposes. The dolphins are caught from boats with specially constructed nets, but often the nets can be thrown from platforms erected in the river, and, to demonstrate the vulnerability of this species to hunting, the nets are sometimes thrown directly from shore. Pilleri and Zbinden (1973) wrote that "this stock is being progressively and rapidly reduced owing chiefly to the persistent dolphin-catching activities of local fishermen."

The study of the Indus dolphin is unique in cetological literature because almost the entire population can be observed during a visit to its home range. It was for this reason, as well as its apparently imminent demise, that cetologists kept returning to the Indus region to study the dolphin. In 1978 another survey was conducted by Pilleri and Bhatti, and they encouragingly reported an increase in the number of dolphins seen. They attributed this to "protective measures instituted by the Pakistani Authorities (decree of the Sind Government of 27 Dec 1974) and the creation of a nature reserve on the lower Indus river" (Pilleri and Bhatti 1978). Because of the great length of the Indus —over 1,800 miles—Pilleri and his associates assumed that there would be more dolphins upstream of the Guddu barrage, but unfortunately there were not. In their 1979 report, Pilleri and Pilleri discovered that "dolphins were far less common in the Punjab region," and in two excursions, only nine dolphins could be seen. It appears that the dolphin catchers of the Punjab are moving southward, and killing the animals as they go.

If the foregoing account of year-by-year expeditions to the Indus valley appears excessively detailed, this can be attributed to the precarious situation of the Indus dolphin and the desire of certain cetologists to study it in its native waters before it is too late. Furthermore, this is the only dolphin—in fact, the only cetacean—where almost every known individual can be counted. This is a far cry from the sophisticated mathematical models used in population estimates of the pelagic species; in this case, one simply has to stand on the banks of a river and count the dolphins as they surface. Of course, if they can be so easily counted, they can be just as easily hunted, especially since they are restricted to enclosed stretches of the river. The dolphin hunters have been catching the animals for centuries, but it is only within the past sixty years or so that the barrages have made their task so much easier.

Known to science since 1859, "rehabilitated" in 1971, the Indus susu may not survive the combined threats of human industry and human insensitivity. Of all the cetaceans it is the most seriously threatened. It seems possible, then, that the first cetacean to become extinct in the foreseeable future will not be one of the "great" whales that were hunted so mercilessly by the whalers in the nineteenth and twentieth centuries and defended so fiercely by the "save-the-whales" forces, but instead a blind side-swimmer caught with hand-thrown nets by people who believe its oil can cure rheumatism.

ROUGH-TOOTHED DOLPHIN

Steno bredanensis Lesson 1828

Before 1964, virtually nothing was known about this species in life, and cetacean literature was replete with admissions of this ignorance. Since its original description by Lesson in 1828, this animal has been an enigma to cetologists. It was originally named *Delphinus rostratus* (from the Latin *rostrum* meaning "beak"), and like so many of the Delphinidae, it has gone through a host of nomenclatural changes. Its present name, according to Hershkovitz (1966), was assigned by Lesson "based on a drawing by Van Breda [hence *bredanensis*], of a stranded dolphin, the skull of which had first been matched with a skin of *Inia geoffrensis* Blainville, and named *Delphinus frontalis* Cuvier." In 1835, Hamilton described the original specimen as follows:

Cuvier received from M. Van Breda, professor of natural history at Gand, a drawing which, with an examination of certain crania, led him to recognise the existence of a new and authentic species of the order (*Oss. Foss.* v. 400). The specimen of which our plate is a representation was stranded at Brest and there faithfully delineated. The animal examined by M. Van Breda was eight feet long; its dorsal fin was elevated and near the middle of the body; its pectorals were scythe-shaped; its tail was crescent-shaped and curved in the middle. But what especially characterises it is the profile of the head, which insensibly loses itself in that of the snout, contrary to what is remarked in the Dolphin genus. All the upper parts of this species are of a sooty-black, and the lower of a rich rosy hue. These portions are not separated by a distinct and uniform line; on the contrary, their junction is quite irregular, and many small black patches are figured on the fairer colour. The total number of teeth are from eighty-four to ninety-two. It would appear to inhabit the Atlantic. This appears to be all the information which has been produced regarding this animal.

Because this description was based on an actual specimen, it remained the best available for more than a century, since most subsequent records were concerned with stranded remains—often only skeletons or skulls. The known distribution of the species, therefore, is based almost entirely on these remains, because there have been very few documented observations of the rough-toothed dolphin in the wild.* It would appear to be rare throughout the world.

The original specimen was discovered at Brest, on the Brittany coast, establishing the North Atlantic as one area in which the species can be found. Later discoveries of skulls in various other locations have expanded the range to the point where Mitchell (1975a) could write, "Distribution in tropical and subtropical waters, occasionally a few animals have

stranded in colder water areas outside their normal range. Seems to occur in the Mediterranean in small numbers." Skulls were found on the beach in Marin County, California, in 1946, and in the Galápagos in 1964 (Orr 1951, 1965), which added the eastern North Pacific and the equatorial Pacific to the animal's range. (Of the California specimen, Leatherwood and colleagues [1972] wrote: ". . . it was presumably a straggler or dead animal which washed in from a considerable distance away. The normal range is probably futher to the south and west.") A group of sixteen animals (of which only twelve were examined), was found stranded on the Gulf Coast of Florida in 1961, which represented the first recorded observation of the animals in the flesh in Florida waters. (Miller and Kellogg [1955] had previously reported the species from the Tampa area, but only from skeletal material.) From the collected material—often a single report from one area or another—it appears that the rough-toothed dolphin is a panoceanic, warm-water species, but nowhere common. A 1.9-meter female was found washed ashore at Moclips, Washington, in August 1980, "a very rare occurrence for this species which has heretofore not been reported north of Stinson Beach, California" (Balcomb 1980). Ellerman and Morrison-Scott (1951) list its distribution as follows: "recorded from France, Portugal, Holland; Japan, according to Kuroda; Aden District; Bay of Bengal (near Nicobar Islands, Blanford); Java; Zambesi, South-East Africa; Florida." Caldwell and colleagues (1971) have reported the species from the Caribbean, from a single skull obtained in 1969.

The infrequency of sightings at sea is probably related to the overall rarity of the species, but it may also be a function of the animal's inclination to remain underwater. Norris and colleagues (1965) wrote, ". . . we were suspicious that *Steno bredanensis* is primarily a diving species. When seen at sea, schools are extremely difficult to follow. They travel submerged most of the time and when approached will dive for

*Some authors, such as Fraser (1938, 1966), refer to this animal as the "rough-toothed dolphin," while others, such as Norris (1965, 1969, 1974), call it the "rough-toothed propoise." In the list I have chosen to follow in this book, Rice (1977) uses "rough-toothed dolphin."

long periods. Our collectors report that they have timed such dives at 15 min duration." The species does not seem to be a bow-rider, although there is a photograph (in Leatherwood et al. 1972), of a "small group of rough-toothed dolphins [riding] the stern wake of a vessel near Hawaii. . . ."

While it is not possible to say that this species is abundant anywhere, it does seem to favor some areas more than others. Mörzer Bruyns (1971) wrote that "the great number of very old skulls in Dutch museums indicate that in the last century mass strandings must have occurred in Indonesia," and Nishiwaki (1967) wrote, ". . . sometimes they are caught in the waters adjacent to Japan. . . . Occasionally they are found in the fish market at Shiogama (near Sendai City). . . . A school of this species were caught on the Izu Peninsula in September 1965, and kept in oceanaria about half a year."

In 1964 the first rough-toothed dolphins were captured in Hawaiian waters, where they seem to be not uncommon. Tomich (1969) reports that "sightings have been frequent in deeper water some five miles off the Waianae coast in the past five years," and once "an estimated 300 were seen at one time." K. S. Norris, who was eventually to use the species in a series of open-ocean deep-diving experiments, was informed of the capture of the first specimen by Karen Pryor, then the dolphin trainer at Sea Life Park. According to Norris's 1974 account, Pryor described the animal to him as "the most grotesque-looking porpoise she had ever seen . . . great goggle eyes, his body randomly covered with round pinkish spots about the diameter of a silver dollar. Furthermore, he had a ski snoot that would do credit to Bob Hope." When Norris went to Hawaii to see this exciting new acquisition, he realized that it was a rough-toothed:

I have yet to see an uglier porpoise. The homeliness of older animals is even greater, since they tend to become obese and heavily scarred. The lips and foreheads, especially of old animals, are often white with crisscrossed scars, which I now believe to come from encounters with squid, a major part of their diet. . . . At the first glance and ever afterward I have been struck by the resemblance of these *Stenos* to extinct ichthyosaurs, seagoing reptiles from the age of dinosaurs. Its long snout lined with stout, pointed teeth, the big brown protruding eyes, and the reptilian head contours are part of this impression, as are the barrel-chested, chunky body and the large paddle-shaped fins and flippers.

The rough-toothed dolphin gets its common name from the presence of small vertical ridges on the teeth, which number 20 to 27 pairs in each jaw. Another osteological peculiarity is the elongation of the symphasis of the mandible, the point at which the two halves of the V-shaped lower jaw come together, ac-

counting for almost one fourth of the length of the lower jaw (True 1889). The most noticeable characteristic of the living animal, however, is the sloping forehead, which Mörzer Bruyns described as "like that of a pike." The long snout blends smoothly into the forehead, with none of the visible demarcation that is found in the other long-snouted dolphins. The dorsal coloration has been described as slate-black or purplish black, and the undersides are lighter, often suffused with a pinkish hue. The lips and the snout are often white, and the animals are usually marked extensively with scratches and a profusion of lighter colored spots, about one to two inches in diameter.* (If we accept the description of the animal as "purplish black" and of the spots as "pinkish," we have what is surely the most unusually colored of all cetaceans: a dolphin that is purple with pink polka dots.) The dorsal fin is high and triangular, and the flippers are proportionally large. Maximum size for the rough-toothed dolphin is about 8 feet (2.4 meters), and it may weigh as much as 350 pounds.

*Norris (1974) wrote that he believed that these spots were the healed scars of wounds made by the "cookie cutter" shark, *Isistius brasiliensis:* "The polka dots also proved to be scars and are much more common in older animals. Each is a sharply raised mound of pinkish white scar tissue, surrounded by the normal gray-colored skin." Jones (1971) identified this 18-inch (45.72 cm) shark as the culprit in many of these "attacks" on various cetaceans, and Norris also wrote, "Most Hawaiian porpoises and whales are dotted with scars from this source, especially those that live far offshore and those that feed deep below the surface."

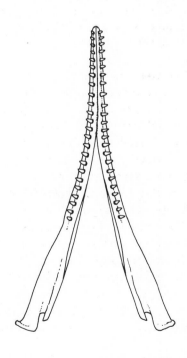

The characteristic mandible (lower jaw) of the rough-toothed dolphin, *Steno bredanensis.* The two halves are fused for about one-fourth of their length.

There are very few records of strandings for this species; in addition to the Florida mass stranding in 1961, seventeen animals swam onto the beach at Kihei, Maui, in 1976. They came in over a reef, and some of them were badly scarred and scraped in the process. Wood (1979) reports that "they were remarkably free of parasites," and that "only one animal had what appeared to be a severe pathological condition in the form of constricted arteries." Of those animals taken "several miles out, at least one returned, but apparently the others swam away." One of the survivors was taken to Sea Life Park, where it "accepted food within a few hours of being placed in the tank," and was alive and well at least until the original submission date of Wood's report, April 1978. The stomachs of the mass-stranded animals in the 1961 Florida incident contained some remains of octopus, but otherwise there is little information on the diet of this species in the wild. Defran and Pryor (1980) have speculated that the species "might have unusual feeding habits, perhaps feeding on large prey," and they cite an observation where "groups of these animals have recently been observed in Hawaii feeding on and sharing 9-kg mahi-mahi."

The rough-toothed dolphin is unusual among small cetaceans because there is so little information available on its natural history. In this respect, not much has changed since the earlier remarks about our ignorance of the habits of this animal in the wild, but with the capture and subsequent training of various specimens at Sea Life Park in Hawaii, a picture has begun to emerge that is most unusual. Of his early observations of this species, Norris (1974) wrote:

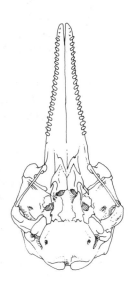

Ventral view of the skull of *Steno bredanensis*, showing the elongated narrow rostrum. (After Hall and Kelson [1959])

We soon came to know this animal as one full of surprises, not once docile to every human order, as our old friend the bottlenose porpoise is apt to be, but insisting upon a degree of dignity and equality with humans. It proved to have extraordinary manipulative capacities, being able to do such things as open gates with its mouth, or pulling the hypodermic needle from one of its schoolmates who was being given penicillin. If handled carefully, it became the tamest of any trained porpoise. *Stenos* just simply impress one as intelligent, however you define it.

In a series of tests designed to measure the diving capabilities of dolphins, Norris and colleagues (1965) trained a female rough-toothed dolphin named Pono to dive to where a buzzer had been lowered, push the buzzer to indicate that she had reached that depth, and then return to the surface. Since this work was to be conducted in the open ocean, Pono was first trained to come to a "recall signal" which would bring her back to the boat on command (Norris 1965). In the tests it was seen that Pono could easily dive to 30.5 meters (100 feet), and the experimenters felt that "she was not being pressed to maximum performance." She made 51 dives during the 1 3/4 hours of testing, which "is impressive, not only for the number, but for the effortless way in which the dives were performed." Pono dived easily, straight down, and when she returned to the surface, she did not even seem to be breathing hard. When the buzzer was at 30.5 meters, Pono refused to dive any more, "and began rapidly circling ahead of the boat, slapping the water with both her flippers and her flukes, signs of agitation well-known to porpoise trainers" (Norris et al. 1965). Pono became more and more agitated, and "finally, she turned directly out to sea and was gone." The observers saw several small sharks in the vicinity of the buzzer, and one shark that was over 12 feet long "coming directly towards the place where the *Imua* [the research vessel] had been drifting." As Norris (1974) wrote in his popular account of the event,* "Later I learned the probable answer to why the sharks had congregated around the instrument cable. Some remarkable experiments in Florida had shown that sharks are strongly attracted to pulsing low-frequency sounds. The buzzer we had required Pono to press made just such a noise. Thus each time she signalled a successful dive to us she also gathered sharks from the surrounding sea and insured the fate of our tests!"

Pono apparently approached a fishing boat the

---

*Both Norris and Pryor have discussed Pono's diving and subsequent departure in the scientific literature and in their respective popular books. While the details agree, there is a tendency toward more colorful description in the nontechnical publications, especially since Pono's trainer, Dottie Samson, was especially fond of the dolphin, and her loss was a "wrenching separation from a dear friend" (Norris 1974).

day after her precipitous departure, and Norris believes he spotted her a month later, swimming with a wild school. "Though we had tried hard to find and recapture Pono, in retrospect our work with her was the best kind of experimental interlude. We had caught her, brought her into our world, and learned much from her. And then, before these relationships could settle into a humdrum and tedious affair, she took her leave and returned to the school where all her old ties existed."

In another series of deep-diving tests, a male named Kai was trained to swim through a hoop that was equipped with an electric eye, a beam of light that would be broken when he passed before it. No more buzzers to attract sharks. Kai "reliably reached depths of 150 feet," and after five days during which he made over 300 dives, he also chose not to return to the "humdrum and tedious affair" of living in a tank: "He was circling and breathing off the *Imua's* port side, as usual, when he suddenly changed his pattern and circled the whole ship. He looked at the hoop, at the cage, and at us; and then he took off, headed for the horizon, leaping and chasing a flying fish ahead of him as he went, a wild animal who had suddenly chosen to be free" (Pryor 1975).

At Sea Life Park, the animals were trained to perform in the daily "porpoise shows," and because they were unique, their behavior as captive animals was closely monitored. In 1973 Pryor wrote, "The Rough-toothed Porpoise is even bolder and more investigative than the Bottlenosed Porpoise, has a long attention span, 'loves a puzzle,' and is the trainer's choice for complex and prolonged tasks. However, they are potentially dangerous swimming companions as they are hot-tempered. Rough-toothed porpoises might be said to be unforgiving: trainer error such as confusion or contradiction in the presentation of reinforcement may produce a strong emotional response." As an example of "just as much aggression as will serve its purpose and no more," Pryor (1973) recounts the story of a female who was kept in a tank with her calf and frequently solicited stroking from her trainer. "The calf occasionally situated itself between mother and trainer while the mother was being stroked. When the calf was approximately a month old, the trainer in this situation stroked the calf. The mother swung her tail from the water, reached up and out, and struck the trainer a sharp but not dangerous blow across the shoulders, and then with no further apparent fear or anger continued to solicit stroking for herself."

This was no ordinary calf that the female was keeping from being stroked: it was the first hybrid ever born in captivity to cetaceans of two different species. The female had been captured off Hawaii in 1969, and had been kept with two male bottlenoses until the

birth of the calf on October 4, 1971. The calf was therefore a *Tursiops* x *Steno* hybrid, the first such animal ever born. The actual birth was not observed, but it seems to have taken only "a few minutes." (The report describing the hybrid calf and the care given it by its rough-toothed mother is by Dohl, Norris, and Kang 1974.) The calf looked like neither parent, but in its early days it seemed to resemble the bottlenose more than the rough-toothed. It had a suggestion of a "forehead" (more than its mother's but less than its father's) and a dorsal fin that "was intermediate in shape between the large barely falcate *Steno* fin and the much more deeply falcate fin of *Tursiops*." During the first few weeks, the calf positioned itself close to its mother, and "echelon swimming" was observed, where the calf swims in a position just below the dorsal fin of the female and moves through the water with no apparent motion of its own flukes. In this situation, however, the observers noted that "the calf's right pectoral was pressed against the mother's side [which] goes far toward explaining how this locomotive pattern works and may have well taken place during other observations of newborn behavior where observation was more distant and hence more difficult."*

The calf grew to full size, and eventually acquired more *Steno*-like features, including a lengthened snout and more protruding eyes. Since there are those (e.g., Fraser 1966) who consider *Steno* to belong to a separate family, the Stenidae, this would represent one of the few known interfamilial hybrids for any vertebrate species, but more recent classifications, such as Rice's 1977 *List of the Marine Mammals of the World,* place the species in the Delphinidae. If this is accepted, then the cross breeding, while interesting, is not quite so significant. Dohl and colleagues concluded their discussion of the hybrid with this statement: "In our opinion this viable hybrid raises a question with regard to the distinctness of the families Delphinidae and Stenidae."

In a further series of experiments with the rough-toothed dolphin, Norris and Evans (1967) identified the remarkable directionality of the echolocating clicks of this species—and, by inference, those of other odontocetes. At Sea Life Park an animal was trained to position itself at one end of a tank as a fish was dropped into the water at the other end. "As the fish hit the water on the opposite side of the tank the porpoise turned, gave a burst of echolocation clicks at

---

*Norris and Prescott (1961), in their discussion of "assisted locomotion," attributed this phenomenon to an applicable hydrodynamic theory, but they also noted that the juvenile's pectoral fin (of the Pacific white-sided dolphin) was "nearly or actually touching the adult's side just below the dorsal fin." Since Norris participated in both studies, it would appear that the contact between mother and calf had, in fact, been noted. Perhaps the distinction here is between "pressing" and "touching."

the fish and swam directly towards it, emitting further bursts of signals as it went." From their analysis of the recordings of the sounds made by this animal, the authors concluded, "The sound field emitted by the rough-toothed porpoise was found to be very narrow and to be directed forward of the emitting animal. Further, it was highly structured with regard to frequency, the highest frequency components only occurred in front of the animal, and dropped off very rapidly on either side of this highest frequency component." Immediately on the midline (the o degree test sector), clicks of 208 kHz were recorded, representing some of the highest-frequency sounds ever recorded from odontocetes. In a comparison of the characteristics of the sounds emitted by various odontocetes, Popper (1980) recorded only the boutu to have click sounds of comparable frequency, and this species is an inhabitant of muddy waters, where it has to depend much more strongly on its echolocating faculties. (In a comment to Norris and Evans' discussion, W. E. Schevill is quoted as saying, "This work of Norris and Evans on a pelagic animal is particularly interesting to me in showing great precision in echolocation even in high seas species.") The species has also been recorded to whistle (Norris 1969), and the whistles were believed to travel a distance of 1,800 yards (1,640 meters) underwater. It was also noted that animals at sea made quite different sounds from those in captivity, probably because of the reflective nature of the walls of the tanks.

Rough-toothed dolphins have proven to be among the most amenable of all small cetaceans to training. For the porpoise shows at Sea Life Park they were trained to perform the regular leaps, rolls, and tail slaps, but there came a time when the trainers decided that "the show was getting a little too good, a little too slick, a little too polished" (Pryor 1975), and they decided to try something different: they would show the audience the actual mechanics of porpoise training. Working with a female named Malia, Karen Pryor and Ingrid Kang let her into the tank:

Malia swam around for a while, waiting to be given a cue. After two or three minutes, she slapped her tail impatiently, and Ingrid reinforced that. Then Malia swam around again; nothing happened, she slapped her tail in annoyance, and Ingrid reinforced it again. That of course was enough for Malia; she got the message and slapped, ate her fish, slapped, ate, slapped repeatedly. In less than three minutes she was motorboating around the tank pounding her tail on the water, and the audience burst into uproarious applause (Pryor 1975).*

*Karen Pryor was the head trainer at Sea Life Park when Malia was being trained, and has documented the events in both the scientific and the popular literature. The abbreviated accounts here

For the next few days the trainers reinforced her natural behaviors, such as head slaps, upside-down swimming, rising out of the water and porpoising, but they soon realized that they were running out of new material.

Malia solved the problem. On the last show of the third day, we let her out of her holding tank, and she swam around waiting for a cue. When she got no cues, instead of launching herself into a series of repetitions of old behavior, she suddenly got up a good head of steam, rolled over on her back, stuck her tail in the air, and coasted about 15 feet with her tail out: "Look, Ma, no hands!" It was a ridiculous sight. Ingrid, I, the training assistant, and six hundred people from Indiana roared with laughter. Ingrid reinforced the behavior, and Malia repeated it a dozen times, each time coasting farther and looking funnier.

She then went on to invent new behaviors on a regular basis: "She spun in the air like a spinner. She swam upside down, drawing lines in the film of silt on the tank floor with her dorsal fin. She revolved on her long axis underwater like a corkscrew. She thought of things to do spontaneously that we could never have imagined, and that we would have found very difficult to arrive at by shaping." It was becoming apparent to the trainers that the dolphin understood the criterion "only those actions will be reinforced which have not been reinforced before," and to certain observers, such as the behaviorist Gregory Bateson, this "was an example of higher order learning, a combining of facts to learn a principle; he called it deutero-learning" (Pryor 1975).

To determine whether this unusual learning ability was characteristic of the genus or Malia was particularly receptive to this sort of thing, it was decided to repeat the experiment with another animal.* A female named Hou was chosen, "a very different individual than Malia. She was much more easily discouraged, and in the first sessions, she developed a pattern of circling, porpoising, circling, over and over again, offering no new behaviors, hung up in a superstitious pattern that could go on for many long minutes." For fourteen sessions, Hou followed the same pattern, much to the discouragement of her trainers. In session

are taken from her book *Lads Before the Wind* (1975) and various discussions in behavioral and other scientific publications (Pryor 1973; Pryor et al. 1969).

*It may be necessary to indicate a difference in individuals insofar as training is concerned. There are many discussions of different populations behaving differently (see the bottlenose and common dolphin accounts for examples), but there is also the distinct possibility—often overlooked in the anthropocentricity of the investigators—that individual animals differ widely in their capabilities. We are more than willing to grant this individuality to humans, but we often tend to believe that when you've seen one bottlenose, you've seen them all. There is no reason to assume that all dolphins have the same mental capabilities, any more than there is to assume the same for humans, dogs, or chimpanzees.

15, however, she appeared "unusually active in the holding tank," and thereafter "the topography of Hou's aerial behaviors became so complex that while undoubtedly novel, the behaviors exceeded the powers of the observers to discriminate and describe them" (Pryor et al. 1969). By session 16 Hou had once again demonstrated that a rough-toothed dolphin could learn the principle, "Only new kinds of behavior will be reinforced." Pryor (1975) describes the behavior of Hou:

From then on, Hou was a changed animal. She showed us a lot of anger signals. She seldom went back to her stereotyped pattern of porpoising and circling. She came up with novelty after novelty, sinking head downwards, spitting water at the trainer, jumping upside down. We went back to the old stuff for some filming sessions, but that didn't confuse her. By the thirtieth session she had offered a new behavior in six out of seven sessions consecutively, had calmed down to the point of giving us the reinforced response and *only* the reinforced response, once she heard the whistle, and had started two sessions with a novel response and no errors at all.

Pryor points out (in both the popular and the technical accounts) that this sort of behavior is not necessarily indicative of any degree of cleverness peculiar to the porpoise—and she indicates that she could have conditioned the same response in pigeons —but she also writes that the trainers "had provoked originality," which is, if not particular to porpoises in general, perhaps unique to the rough-toothed dolphin.

As an epilogue to her chapter on "the creative porpoise," Pryor tells the story of the time the trainers got Hou and Malia mixed up, and as part of the regular porpoise show, they inadvertently put each one through the other's routine:

Hou had done Malia's part of the show, getting the cues confused but offering the behaviors so well that we didn't realize that she didn't "know" them, and even managing the hoop jump, which normally takes weeks to train. Malia had done all Hou's blindfold stunts correctly, on the first try, nervously, but again well enough so that we thought it was Hou. I stopped the departing audience and told them what they had just seen. I'm not sure how many understood or believed it. I still hardly believe it myself.

INDO-PACIFIC HUMPBACK DOLPHIN

Sousa chinensis Osbeck 1765

In 1889, when F. W. True compiled his revision of the Delphinidae, he had to rely to a great extent upon the published works of others, as well as on his own examination of skeletal materials. Many of the areas from which the dolphins came were then only recently—if at all—opened to science, and information on many of the nominal species was quite sparse. If there were only a couple of descriptions of a particular species, and if these descriptions did not seem to duplicate other descriptions, then it appeared that the specimen was a representative of a "valid" species and should be included. The specimens True examined for the genus *Sotalia* (which he differentiated from all other small cetaceans) seemed to represent a fairly homogeneous group, although there were very few specimens to work from. "It will be necessary," wrote True, "for me to treat of the species with much reserve, since I did not have the opportunity of examining carefully all the types and must therefore base my opinions partly upon the descriptions and drawings which have hitherto been published."

Under the heading *Sotalia,* True named and described the following species: *Sotalia gadamu, S. lentiginosa, S. guianensis, S. brasiliensis, S. pallida, S. tucuxi, S. fluviatilis, S. plumbea,* and *S. sinensis.* From the information available to him, True believed that these all represented valid species, although he was certainly willing to admit that there would be changes in the future, as additional information became available: "A naturalist can, however, scarcely be regarded as deserving censure for having described the skeleton of a species the external appearance of which is unknown to him. If the description is full and accurate it must be accepted, and cetologists must be content to wait patiently until the acquisitions of new specimens make a complete description possible."

Subsequent authors have generally followed True's example (with minor digressions), but until recently the diversity of this genus was recognized by almost all authors, and most of the species listed by True were included in their works.* Even the *List of the Marine Mammals of the World* (Scheffer and Rice 1963; Rice and Scheffer 1968) demonstrated this diversity. The 1963 edition listed three South American species, one West African, and four Indo-Pacific varieties, and by 1968 there were only two South American species (they alone retained the name *Sotalia;* the others had become *Sousa*), one African, and four Indo-Pacific. It was around 1974, however, that the great taxonomic revolution for humpback dolphins took place. In Montreal, April 1–11, 1974, a meeting sponsored by the International Whaling Commission was held, the objectives of which were to review the relevant published literature, catch statistics, and other data in order to compile for each species of dolphin, porpoise, and small whale the relevant data on status and possible geographic subdivisions of species, the initial size of each stock, recent catches, and information on the present status of populations" (Mitchell 1975b). As part of the report of this meeting (published by the Fisheries Research Board of Canada), there appeared a "list of the smaller cetaceans recognized," and only *Sotalia fluviatilis* (tucuxi), *Sousa chinensis* (Indo-Pacific humpback dolphin), and *Sousa teuszii* (Atlantic humpback dolphin) were included. In a note referring to *Sousa chinensis*, Mitchell wrote:

Two species are recognized: *S. teuszii* from west Africa and *S. chinensis* from South Africa, Indian Ocean south to Australia, and in the western Pacific from Australia north to southern China. Other nominal species, the identity of which need study, are *S. lentiginosa, S. plumbea,* and *S. borneensis* (synonyms of *S. chinensis*).

The die was cast. Subsequent lists (Rice 1977; IWC 1977) adhered to this revision and, at least as far as the

list makers were concerned, *lentiginosa, plumbea,* and *borneensis* had vanished. (Not everyone agreed with the list makers, and because observations of what looked very much like the earlier descriptions of *lentiginosa* or *borneensis* continued to be published, these species have not entirely disappeared. In fact, there are numerous cetologists, such as Pilleri, who believe that *lentiginosa* and *plumbea* are valid species.)

It is clear, however, that descriptions published prior to 1975 (and some published after that date) refer to a multitude of species as if they were distinct, but because I have chosen to follow Rice's 1977 list for the taxonomic structure of this book, all these diversified accounts are lumped under the general heading of the Indo-Pacific humpback dolphin.

All humpback dolphins share certain characteristics: Adults range in length from 7 to 9 feet, and they may weigh as much as 330 pounds (150 kilograms), although these figures will vary from population to population. All varieties have a sloping "forehead," a relatively long, narrow beak, and teeth that number between 23 and 37 pairs in each side of each jaw (again varying with the particular population). Responsible for the species' common name is the double-step dorsal fin (sometimes described as a dorsal ridge upon which the dorsal fin is situated), which is present to a greater or lesser extent in all humpback dolphins, although it may be more exaggerated in adult males. This fin is diagnostic even when the actual species or type designation is not possible. In 1966 Fraser wrote, "It is not clear that the females . . . develop similar prominences in old age."* In fact they do, and in the South African study made by Saayman and Tayler (1979), the authors were almost totally incapable of differentiating males from females. In some specimens, there are also pronounced dorsal and ventral keels, which may be an example of sexual dimorphism, since these are more prominent in adult males.

In the coastal waters of the Far East, a type of white dolphin has long been known, as first described by the Swedish missionary and naturalist Peter Osbeck. According to Flower (1870), Osbeck wrote that while lying at anchor in the Canton River, "snow white dolphins tumbled about the ship but at a distance they seemed to be nothing different from the common species, except the white color." Flower eventually obtained a "fine skeleton" from "our zealous member Mr. Robert Swinhoe, H.B.M. Consul at Amoy." According to Flower's report to the Zoological Society of

---

*Obviously, one cannot list all the works in which such lists appeared, but most of the responsible publications prior to 1972 listed these various species of *Sotalia* (or *Sousa,* as it came to be called). These include Norman and Fraser (1938); Hershkovitz (1966); Mörzer Bruyns (1971); and Nishiwaki (1972). In addition to these semitechnical works, almost all the popular "encyclopedias" of recent years (e.g., Coffey 1977) list every species, probably to make sure that they haven't left anything out.

*In this discussion, Fraser describes (from photographs) two male specimens from East Africa (Berbera, Somaliland, and Zanzibar), the first ever recorded from East Africa. Although Fraser does not specifically identify the Berbera and Zanzibar specimens as *S. lentiginosa/plumbea,* other authors (Pilleri and Gihr 1972) have done so, and thus added this previously unsuspected area to the species' range.

London, Swinhoe described the animal as "milky white with pinkish fins and black eyes," but in 1889 True wrote that "a good figure of the exterior and measurements are still desiderata." In his discussion of this species (known as *Sotalia borneensis*) in Borneo, Banks (1931) described it as "some seven feet long with pure white skin marbled with grey spots on the back, a pattern which may have given rise to the illusion of the spotted dolphin in Bornean waters." There has been substantial cross-reference of *chinensis* and *borneensis* since both of them have been described as white dolphins of Far Eastern coastal waters. Norman and Fraser (1938) differentiate them on the basis of the dorsal fin—"low and not concave behind" in *borneensis*—and of course the distribution: *chinensis* is ostensibly found farther east than *borneensis*. (Hershkovitz [1966] gives "China Seas, from Sarawak north along the Chinese coast and into the Canton and Fuchow Rivers, and 750 miles up the Yangtze at least as far as Hankow" as the distribution for *chinensis,* and "South China Sea from Sarawak to Gulf of Thailand"

for *borneensis*. Without the conclusive evidence of any morphological differentiation between the two species of white dolphins, and the apparent overlap of their ranges in Sarawak, a strong argument could be made for conspecificity.) C. A. Gibson Hill (1949) described the white dolphin thus from Malayan waters: "It is a beautiful glossy white, dappled with grey on the upper parts. Little is known of this species, but it would seem to occur mostly in estuaries, and to be rather ponderous and leisurely in its movements." Harrison (1960) described it as "large, slow and tame—white and pink as a baby's bottom—it literally shines out of the South China Sea as much as half a mile away. It is easy to watch, occurring in large, slow-moving schools. We have seen many hundreds, usually close in to shore and sometimes well inside the Sarawak River estuary."

There are very few records of the white dolphin from the coasts of Australia, but in 1972, Gaskin described a "white dolphin, *Sousa* sp. in captivity in Queensland. This may be a species or subspecies new to science, for which the name *Sousa queenslandenesis*

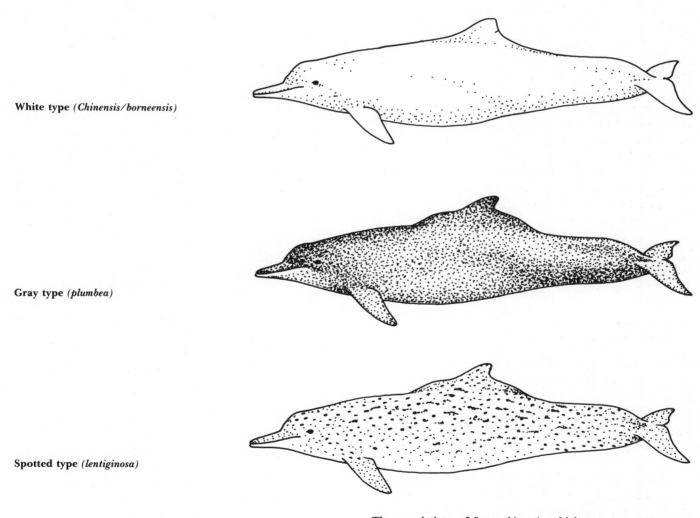

White type *(Chinensis/borneensis)*

Gray type *(plumbea)*

Spotted type *(lentiginosa)*

Three variations of *Sousa chinensis*, which may represent distinct subspecies, or even species: Note the absence of the dorsal ridge in the white type.

might be considered. However, a thorough and systematic comparison between this population and Asian *Sousa* has so far been precluded by lack of specimens." Gaskin's description is, in fact, a caption for a photograph of the animal in Queensland, and in his 1975 review of the systematics of this species, Mitchell also reproduces a photograph of a light-colored dolphin (possibly the same specimen), with the entire picture caption reading as follows:

The Indo-Pacific hump-backed dolphin *Sousa* cf. *S. borneensis* (= *Sousa chinensis* of this report), was originally described from Sarawak. The species is relatively common along northeastern Australia where it occurs close to the coast and penetrates estuarine areas. There are reports of these animals heaving themselves over banks when water is very shallow at low tide. They are kept in captivity in two Queensland oceanaria at present.

White dolphins appear to be restricted to the waters of Southeast Asia, China, and Australia, and of all the species of *Sousa* (if indeed there are different species), they appear to be entitled to the name *chinensis*, especially since Osbeck first described the animal from Chinese waters, and the skeleton, collected by Swinhoe and described by Flower in 1870, also came from China. In a review of the various types of *Sousa*, Pilleri and Gihr (1972) separated *borneensis* and *chinensis* geographically and anatomically, and suggested that while the former "is a well-defined species characterized by distinctive external features (low dorsal fin with no concave caudal edge)," it is not so easy to distinguish *S. chinensis* from *S. plumbea*: "Osteological differences are very slight and apart from them there is only the difference in the color of the body. Due to the lack of adequate investigation material and documentary photographs of *chinensis*, it is impossible to decide whether these porpoises should be classified as a local race of a separate species. In spite of the striking osteological resemblance, they may well represent two different species distinguished exclusively by external characteristics."*

Farther to the west in the Indo-Pacific region, the situation becomes considerably more confusing. Here the humpbacks are not white, so they are much more likely to be identified as other species—such as bottlenose dolphins—and of course, there is no agreement on which species of *Sousa* occurs where.

It is this inability to isolate particular types in particular areas that was responsible for the lumping together of all Indo-Pacific humpbacks under the name *chinensis*. If any population could have been shown—on the basis of osteological, exterior, or any other criteria—to be distinct from any or all of the others, it would surely have been designated as a full species. Since this did not occur to the satisfaction of the list makers, all varieties, from the white dolphins of Borneo to the spotted dolphins of South Africa and the solid gray dolphins of the Persian Gulf, have been lumped together as a single species. However, as Rice (1977) points out, "The taxonomy of the humpbacked dolphins is greatly in need of revision. Several nominal species have been described, but individual, sexual, age, and geographic variations have not been adequately studied."

True (1889) recognized *S. gadamu*, *S. lentiginosa*, and *S. plumbea*,* based again upon the scanty descriptive materials available to him. For *lentiginosa*, for example, True had only the "type skull with its mandible and a second broken mandible, all of which are in the British Museum." The species had originally been described and illustrated by Owen (1866), who described a 7-foot, 10-inch specimen (captured by fishermen of Vizapatagam, India) as "pretty uniformly bluish cinereous, or slaty, freckled with irregular small spots or streaks of brown or plumbeous pigment, the streaks longitudinal and flecked with white. The undersurface is a shade lighter than the rest of the body." Other observers, particularly Lydekker (1904, 1908), examined and illustrated specimens of humpback dolphins from the waters of India. At first Lydekker differentiated *lentiginosa* from a "new species" that he named *Sotalia fergusoni* after Harold Ferguson, the director of the Travancore Museum, but then he realized that the animals were probably the same, "the absence of spotting [in *fergusoni*], being a feature of immaturity" (Lydekker 1908). Norman and Fraser identify *Sotalia lentiginosa* as "another Indian species known to the Vizapatagam fishermen as the Bolla Gadimi," and then repeat Owen's description of the animals' freckled appearance.

Often encountered in the same areas as the spotted dolphin is an animal usually referred to as the plumbeous dolphin. True quotes Cuvier's description of this species, as follows: "Uniform lead gray, except for the tip and the underside of the lower jaw, which are whitish." Norman and Fraser further describe the plumbeous dolphin as "a marine species from the Malabar coast of India. The snout is very long; from its tip to the eye is one-sixth the body length. The

---

*One is reminded of Fraser's 1966 discussion of the differences between various species of *Lagenorhynchus*. Lacking sufficient skeletal material to differentiate *L. obscurus*, *L. cruciger*, and *L. australis*, Fraser separated them on the basis of pigmentation patterns. He wrote, "On body coloring *L. cruciger* and *L. australis* may be distinguished specifically, but on the cranial proportions so far used the indications are that they are very much alike."

*The name *"gadamu"* comes from the Indian name for the animal, while *lentiginosa* and *plumbea* are from the Latin. *Lentigo* is Latin for "freckle" and refers to the spotted nature of these animals, and *plumbea* means "lead," obviously a reference to the gray color.

dorsal fin is long, but a little elevated, and the posterior border is only feebly indented. . . . Teeth number 34–37 in each row, and the length of the animal is about 8 feet."

In 1963, Tietz described a "speckled dolphin" from South Africa, which he believed was undoubtedly *Sotalia lentiginosa*—even though it had no spots, but was leaden gray in color. (Three animals were captured in Algoa Bay and transported to the Port Elizabeth Aquarium, thus becoming the first recorded specimens of *S. lentiginosa* [or *plumbea*], to be maintained in captivity. They prospered for about two months, then suddenly died of unknown causes.) In the Shatt-al-Arab (the confluence of the Tigris and Euphrates rivers forming a channel to the Persian Gulf in Iraq), Mörzer Bruyns (1960) observed humpback dolphins, which he called *Sotalia plumbea*, and which he designated the "ridge-backed dolphin of the Indian Ocean." They were 8 to 9 feet in length, and gray in color, "but covered with numerous little white spots like spatters of white paint." In his illustration of this animal, he shows the trailing edges of the flukes as white. Nishiwaki (1972) lists and describes *S. plumbea*, *S. chinensis*, *S. borneensis*, and *S. lentiginosa*, and in that same year Pilleri and Gihr of the Brain Anatomy Institute of Bern, Switzerland, published their observations of various cetaceans of Pakistan, including one they referred to as *Sousa plumbea*.

In the region of the Indus delta they found that the animal (which the local people refer to as *malar*) was "uniform bluish grey; it had no spots and the lower part and tip of the lower jaw are white." The authors also observed the living animals in the mangrove zones, and were able to identify certain behavior characteristics for the species, including the way it raises its long snout out of the water when it breathes, and how it sometimes raises its flukes when it dives. Other observers (e.g., Gibson Hill 1949) described the animal as "placid and slow-moving," but Pilleri and Gihr noticed some young animals "leaping energetically into the air." In the muddy waters of the Indus delta, Zbinden and colleagues (1977) observed the plumbeous dolphin,* and described them as swimming in a "leisurely fashion." They saw the animals in pairs or small groups—never more than 12—and they also observed animals of different sizes swimming together. When a single animal of undetermined gender swam on its side with one flipper out of the water and "beat it 5 or 6 times rhythmically on the surface of the water," they suggested that this might be some sort of mating display. When the dolphins were found in areas known to be inhabited by a species of fish known

*In this paper, the authors carefully identify "five Afro-Asian species of *Sousa*," as follows: *Sousa teuszii*, *S. lentiginosa*, *S. plumbea*, *S. chinensis*, and *S. borneensis*.

as the *boro* their sounds were recorded. They were heard to emit whistles, clicks, and creaks, as well as transitional vocalizations between these types of sounds. Zbinden and colleagues published a detailed analysis, the first discussion of the sounds produced by this species.

While the Swiss scientists were cruising around the Indus delta looking for cetaceans, some South Africans had found them almost in their own front yard. At Plettenberg Bay, humpback dolphins could be observed from the cliffs surrounding the bay, and they were seen to be an inshore species, even more so than the bottlenose dolphins, which also inhabited the same bay. Unlike the bottlenoses, the humpbacks were seen in small groups, usually no more than 10 or 12 animals, but more often as pairs or singles. Saayman and colleagues (1972) described the color of the animals as ranging from "off white in young calves to grey, through grey-brown to bronze, often with a deep purplish tinge on the dorsal surface." They were not altogether certain of the name of the animal they were observing, and they wrote, "It is described as *Sotalia lentiginosa* by Tietz (1963) and *Sousa plumbea/lentiginosa* by P. J. H. Van Bree (pers. comm.), but its taxonomic status is by no means settled." (Pilleri and Gihr [1972], in their distribution map of the various species of *Sousa*, indicated that *Sousa plumbea/lentiginosa* had been found in South Africa, in the Persian Gulf, and also at the tip of the Indian subcontinent. In 1973, Saayman and Tayler wrote that the species "was now called *Sousa plumbea* or *lentiginosa*.")

In 1973 Pilleri and Gihr mounted another expedition, this time to "Southwest and Monsoon Asia (Persian Gulf, Indus Delta, Malabar, Andaman Sea and Gulf of Siam)." They found both species of *Sousa*, which they differentiated by the presence of spots in *lentiginosa*, their absence in *plumbea*. Despite Lydekker's 1908 assertion that the absence of spotting was "a feature of immaturity," Pilleri and Gihr (1973) saw fully mature animals with and without spots. Off Qishm Island in the Straits of Hormuz they reported "a large animal, more than 2 m long and light grey in colour. The whole body was covered with small elongated spots that were clearly visible. . . . In spite of the short observation time, it was easily identified as *lentiginosa*. This removes all doubt as to the existence of this species." In addition to making these field observations, they captured three adults: "Their back was steel grey in colour, and they had elongated spots . . . to indicate that the animals belonged to the species *Sousa lentiginosa*." They also encountered animals they identified as plumbeous dolphins, which they described as "light grey," and of this species, they wrote, "The plumbeous dolphin is a neritic species that occurs both in the mangrove zone (Indus delta) and in the open sea in the vicinity of coasts and islands." When followed, the small schools split up into pairs or groups of three, unlike the bottlenoses, in which the "constant compactness of the school, even in flight, is very characteristic." They also observed "vertical surfacing," which they described as follows:

Two animals would thrust their whole head vertically out of the water, rapidly and simultaneously, and appear belly to belly. It is difficult to say whether this was a mating behaviour pattern or whether the animals were copulating. Vertical surfacing was only observed in larger communities of more than 10 animals. While the adult animals exhibited this behaviour, the younger ones were always seen making full or half leaps in the same area. Adult animals of the same community swam energetically in circles.

Interestingly, both species were seen in the Hormuz Straits, "in the area known as the best fishing grounds for shrimp," but hardly anything is known of the feeding habits of these animals. When observers from Bern visited the Indus delta in 1978–79, they were able to write (of the plumbeous), "we still know very little about behaviour; feeding habits at different times of year; or seasonal migrations and breeding seasons. . . ." According to Pilleri and Pilleri (1979), there is no fishing for this or any other species of cetacean in the region of the Indus River delta, but "unselective industrialization of the Delta area presents a serious threat to an ecosystem on which very little information is available to date."

Saayman and Tayler (1979) conducted a three-year study of the humpback dolphins that live off Robbe Berg, Plettenberg Bay, South Africa. Theirs is one of the few detailed investigations involving wild, free-swimming dolphins, and was possible only because of the fortuitous configuration of the land—Robbe Berg is a steep-cliffed peninsula that forms the southern boundary of Plettenberg Bay—and the inshore habits of the dolphins themselves. Unlike many other long-term observations of dolphins where the animals were kept in captivity, these were totally free, undisturbed and undetected by the observers who were on the cliffs, equipped with binoculars, cameras, clipboards, tape recorders and other implements of the dolphin watcher's trade.

One cannot apply all the observations made of this population to humpback dolphins in general, since it is not known if this is the same species found in such locations as Shatt-al-Arab, Sarawak, or China, but we can probably assume that some of these details apply to other members of the genus.

The humpbacks of South Africa are an inshore species, even more so than the better-known bottlenose dolphin. It is their affinity for shore that made

this study possible, since the dolphins were visible, in water of great clarity, all the year round.* Five distinct age classes were recognized: Calf I, Calf II, Juvenile, Grayback, and Whitefin. As the off-white newborn dolphins matured, they became darker in color, and finally, at what is assumed to be physical maturity, the adult animals were "characterized by a remarkable girth and the whitening of the dorsal fin and adjacent areas. In some animals this whitening extended to the tip of the rostrum and flukes, and appeared to be an index of advancing age."

Contrary to earlier reports—especially of the humpbacks in Southeast Asian waters—the dolphins of Plettenberg Bay were extremely active animals, given to fast swimming, leaps, inverted swimming, and front and back aerial somersaults. "A spectacular form of display occurred when individuals performed inverted backward somersaults: the dolphin swam inverted, reared its tail out of the water and, becoming completely airborne, performed a full backward somersault and reentered the sea flukes first, belly down, and facing the direction from which the approach was made." When two groups of humpback dolphins met in the bay, there was much flipper contact, fast swimming, and "the tendency of participating animals to form a compact group which circled slowly in a clockwise direction." Because the observers were so far from the animals, feeding could be observed only from a distance. The actual prey species are not known (although one stranded specimen had been feeding on mullet), but the feeding behavior "was characterized by long-jumping and high-speed chasing, the dolphins swimming inverted, belly uppermost. Large schools of fish were seen to run ahead of the dolphins, which pursued them in open water . . . and seized their prey behind the neck with a sideways movement of the head and then manipulated the fish with the tongue so as to swallow them head first." Much of the perimeter of Plettenberg Bay is composed of reefs, and it is assumed that reef fishes make up the majority of the humpback's diet, rather than such pelagic species as yellowtail or leerfish, both of which are plentiful in the bay. In captivity in Port Elizabeth, humpback dolphins "spent much time poised vertically, head downwards, above the reefs in the tank and investigated crevices and crannies with their long rostrums, snapping with a sideways motion of the head at any rock-dwelling fish which emerged. This behaviour possibly gave some

*All information in this account of feeding, behavior, etc., is taken directly from Saayman and Tayler's 1979 study, "The Socioecology of Humpback Dolphins." Where quotations appear in the account, they have been taken verbatim from the study. Otherwise, the material has been paraphrased by the author in the interest of brevity.

indication as to their mode of hunting at depth under normal conditions."

Plettenberg Bay is also the sometime habitat of other cetaceans, including southern right whales, common dolphins, and killer whales, which were not seen to chase or harass the resident population of humpback dolphins. (It was also the scene of an inshore appearance of a very rare pygmy right whale [Ross et al. 1975], which was filmed there in one of the only instances in which this species was observed alive and positively identified.) Bottlenose dolphins appeared frequently in the bay, and the two species appeared to swim and perhaps even "play" together.* There appear to be some humpback dolphins that are permanent residents of the bay—at least they were recognized by the observers over the three-year observation period—but the complete social organization of these animals is not completely understood. The structure of the groups, which may number as many as 25 animals but are usually smaller, seems to be somewhat flexible, with some animals associating with others on a temporary or fluctuating basis.

The Indo-Pacific humpback dolphin, under numerous aliases, inhabits the coastal waters of the entire Indo-Pacific region, from the Cape of Good Hope up the east coast of Africa to the Red Sea; to the entire coast of India and Sri Lanka, and Indonesian waters up the coast of Vietnam, north to the South China Sea from Amoy to the Canton River. They are also found throughout the Moluccas, off New Guinea and northeastern Australia. There are gray humpbacks in South Africa, speckled ones in India, and white ones in Borneo. Although they inhabit the waters of some of the most densely populated countries in the world, the humpbacks remain some of the world's least-known

animals. (There are other species that live in the high Antarctic or far offshore in the deep tropical Pacific, but most of the humpbacks live within sight of land.) There is probably enough variety to suggest that there are valid subspecies—if not valid species—but the necessary taxonomic work has not been done, and therefore by default the various forms are lumped together here under this species. It appears that only the list makers favor this designation, for the students of the various populations have persisted in using the different names, and we are faced with a situation where no one seems really certain which species is being discussed. There are many recent references to *lentiginosa/plumbea*, and Saayman and Tayler (1979) managed to write an entire account of the behavior of the humpback dolphins of South Africa without ever referring to the species by name: throughout the study, they referred to them as *Sousa* sp.

ATLANTIC HUMPBACK DOLPHIN

Sousa teuszii Kükenthal 1892

The Atlantic humpback dolphin is similar in general characteristics and appearance to the preceding species, but it is regarded as distinct because of its isolated West African habitat and certain minor morphological differences. Discussing the differences in humpback dolphins, Pilleri and Gihr (1972) wrote, "To sum up it may be said that *S. teuszii* is a clearly defined tropical species from West African waters distinguished from *S. plumbea* and *lentiginosa* by certain characters the most important of which are craniological." There does not seem to be the variability of color that is evident in other members of the genus; most of the specimens described have been "slaty grey on the sides . . . and imperceptibly paler grey in the ventral regions" (Cadenat 1956). This species reaches a

---

*Although it is describing the behavior of dolphins in human terms, it is hard to resist the temptation to describe the exuberant behavior of some dolphins as play (see especially the bottlenose dolphin). We really do not know what the animals are doing, but much of this behavior does not appear to have any useful function, and it certainly looks like fun.

length of about 8 feet (2.5 meters), and a large male was weighed at 365 pounds (166 kilograms). The Atlantic humpback has a smoothly curved forehead and a long, narrow beak. The teeth number 30 or fewer in each row, another feature which differentiates the species from the Indo-Pacific varieties, which may have as many as 37. The distinctive dorsal fin is particularly evident in adult males, but since only a small number of specimens have been collected, it is not known if females develop in the same way. Females have prominent dorsal and ventral keels, "but not obviously in the form of a hump" (Fraser 1966). The first specimen was collected in the harbor of Douala in the Cameroons, by Edouard Teusz. He brought it to Professor Willy Kükenthal, who described it and named it after Teusz in 1892.

In Kükenthal's description there are a number of curious references that have been regularly repeated in the literature, and have led to a curious picture indeed. Kükenthal mentions the animal having leaves, mangrove fruits and grass (*"Blätter und Mangrovefrüchte, weniger Gras"*) in the stomach, which was interpreted as indicating a vegetarian dolphin, the only one known.* Since the 1892 animal was unique for many years, Kükenthal's description remained the only available information. In 1938, F. C. Fraser, writing in *Giant Fishes, Whales and Dolphins,* said that the species was "noteworthy as being the one cetacean believed to feed exclusively on vegetable matter." Kükenthal also wrote that the skin was about as thick as that of a manatee and, most surprising of all, that its blowhole protruded in pipelike extensions, "like the erect ears of a hippopotamus." The thickness of the skin and the strange shape of the blowhole have been interpreted recently thus: "The blubber is very thick. The blowhole sticks out in a tube-like form, making a small hump" (Nishiwaki 1972). None of this makes much sense, especially since the Indo-Pacific humpbacks and the closely related tucuxi, have diets that consist of fish; they have thin skin and a normal blowhole. How could these strange misconceptions have developed?

The problem was addressed by Jean Cadenat, a biologist with the Institut Français Afrique Noir, at Dakar, Senegal. Cadenat examined a female specimen in 1955, the first animal examined in the sixty-three years since Kükenthal's description of the type specimen. (F. C. Fraser had described the second specimen in 1949, but it was from a skull, and he therefore had no opportunity to comment on the leaves, grass, or hippo ears.) In his examination of the 1955 specimen —and in subsequent animals as well—Cadenat could find no evidence of a vegetarian diet. In one, he discovered the remains of a grunt and other fishes (Cadenat and Paraiso 1957), and the blowhole looked like that of any other dolphin. In one attempt to explain the vegetable matter in the stomach of Kükenthal's specimen, Walker (1964) suggested that the material was originally eaten by fish which were then eaten by the dolphin. Walker did not deal with the thickness of

*The full title of Kükenthal's paper is "Sotalia teuszii n. sp., ein pflanzenfressender (?) Delphin aus Kamerun." *Pflanzenfressender* means "plant-eater."

Male (top) and female Atlantic humpback dolphin *(Sousa teuszii),* **showing marked sexual dimorphism. (After Cadenat)**

the skin or the peculiar blowhole, and Cadenat suggests that the problem may have occurred as a result of confusion with the animals examined. Cadenat reports that the Senegalese manatee is found in the same waters as the dolphin, and that they have been observed together. In fact, Cadenat examined a specimen of the humpback dolphin from Joal, Senegal, which had been captured in a shark net with a manatee. There is, therefore, a strong possibility that either Teusz or Kükenthal was describing aspects of two totally different animals. Manatees do have very thick skin, and they eat only vegetable matter, but the strange matter of the protruding blowhole will probably remain a mystery.

Since the initial discovery of this species in the Cameroons in 1892, almost every new occurrence has extended the range. The 1949 skull described by Fraser came from Senegal, "two thousand miles west of the Cameroons"; Cadenat's specimens were taken in Senegal; and in 1970, the species was observed in Mauritania, "more than 700 miles north of the previously known limit" (Fraser 1973). From the limited records—Pilleri and Gihr (1972) list all fourteen of the known specimens—it is possible to postulate a discontinuous range from the Cameroons around the hump of West Africa through the Gulf of Guinea; from Senegal to Mauritania.

In 1970, R.-G. Busnel, a French acoustical biologist, was in Mauritania on the northwest coast of Africa, where he observed what he described as "a symbiotic relationship between man and dolphins" (Busnel 1973). The Imraugens, a coastal fishing tribe at Cape Timris (19°23′N, 16°32′W), had long been in the habit of working with dolphins. As Busnel describes the activity, "the fishermen sit on the shore, and some of them stare fixedly at the sea. They look for a slight color change of the seawater, produced by a school of mullet." When the school is sighted, one of the fishermen wades into the sea and begins to beat the water violently with a stick. The dolphins are attracted ("this signal is, in fact, an imitation of the noise of the mullet, which, after jumping, splashes into the water"), and the fish are driven toward the men who have entered the water with their nets. "The dolphins swim vigorously around the fishermen, and sometimes between their nets and their legs close to the beach." After about half an hour of frenzied feeding on the part of the dolphins, and a huge catch (sometimes up to four tons of fish) on the part of the fishermen, the dolphins depart. Both predators—men and dolphins—are capable of catching mullet on their own, "but apparently they take the opportunity to hunt together, a true example of symbiosis.*

*There are other examples of men and dolphins working together. At Twofold Bay, Australia, killer whales were seen to "herd"

Photographs of this performance show the high, curved dorsal fin of the bottlenose dolphin, but one can also see the unmistakable silhouette of the Atlantic humpback dolphin. If Cadenat's reports on the stomach contents were not enough to discredit the story of a vegetarian dolphin, surely this account of the dolphin seen feeding on mullet should put that story to rest forever.

TUCUXI

Sotalia fluviatilis Gervais 1853

In their introduction to a discussion of this species, Norris and colleagues (1972) wrote:

The tucuxi *(Sotalia fluviatilis),* a small stenid porpoise living throughout the Amazon Basin, including brackish and probably saline waters adjacent to the distributary mouths of the main river, is very poorly known. It is not at all secure whether one or as many as five species of this genus occupy South America, and rather little is known of its ecology and nothing of its sounds.

The possible variations are based on size, geography, and color, but even those who would "split" the genus usually offer some sort of disclaimer, *viz.,* "some scientists include this species [*S. tucuxi*], as well as *S. pallida,* with *S. fluviatilis,* and attribute the differences in body color to age variation" (Nishiwaki 1972). Those animals that might be considered separate species are as follows: the buffeo blanco, a light-colored animal reported from upstream in the Amazon; the tucuxi, a brownish-gray variety; the Brazilian dolphin, common in the bay of Rio de Janeiro; and the Guiana dolphin, dark in color and reported from Lake Maracaibo, Venezuela, and the offshore waters and rivers of Guiana. Walker (1964) has given a detailed catalog of the various color forms in his discussion of the genus *Sotalia:*

S. brasiliensis ranges from pale bluish gray to blackish above, and white below. The color of the back extends to a circle around the eye, onto the pectoral fins, in an oblique band on the flanks, and to the sides of the tail. The dorsal fin is the same color as the back except for an area of bright yellow on each side near the top; the sides of the dolphin are a yellowish orange. *S. guianensis* ranges from blackish, dull

humpback whales toward the whalers, who would harpoon them, permitting the killers to "take the lips and tongue without interference" (Gaskin 1972). Anderson's 1878 report of fishermen in Burma, where "each fishing village had its guardian dolphin [*Orcaella brevirostris*] that drew the fish into their nets" is another example, and there is the account of an Amazon River dolphin that scared fish from deep to shallow water in the Tapajós River where they could be more easily speared by fishermen (Lamb 1954).

lead gray, or brown above, and from pinkish, violet gray to white along the lateral margins and on the ventral side. The pectoral fins are the same color as the back. Fresh water *Sotalia* are bluish or pearl gray above; the color is darker on the anterior part of the body. The pectoral fins, both below and above, are the same color as the back. The under parts are pinkish white to white. A prominent band of the ventral coloration extends upwards on the sides of the body to slightly above the level of the eye; the dorsal color, however, extends down to a distinct line from the corner of the mouth to the base of the pectoral fin and includes the eye. The tip of the beak and the apex of the dorsal fin are conspicuously white. The large dolphins are noticeably paler above.

Assuming all these descriptions are accurate—although it must be said that the report of bright yellow spots on each side of the dorsal fin is a bit unexpected—it will still be seen that there is a great variety in the appearance of these animals in South American waters, and that the confusion as far as the number of distinct species is concerned is understandable. Like their close relatives in the genus *Sousa* these animals need much more study before accurate species and subspecies classifications can be determined.* To further confuse matters, wherever these Amazon dolphins occur there is usually one or more species of a totally different kind of dolphin, with which it might be confused by the uninformed. In offshore waters there is the bottlenose dolphin, which, like some species of tucuxi, is grayish above and lighter below, but the bottlenose has a shorter, stubbier beak and a much higher and more curved dorsal fin, and is a larger animal besides. In its riverine habitat, another dolphin is often seen with the tucuxi. It is the Amazon River dolphin, or boutu, a much larger animal with a long narrow snout, and a low triangular ridge instead of a dorsal fin.

*Until at least 1963, all these dolphins, including the ones we now refer to as *Sousa*, were classified in one genus, *Sotalia*. In Scheffer and Rice's *List of the Marine Mammals of the World*, the genus *Sotalia* includes *S. pallida, guianensis, chinensis, borneensis, lentiginosa, plumbea,* and *teuszi.*

The tucuxi—whose name was given to it by Amazon Indians, and is sometimes spelled "tookashee"—is one of the smallest cetaceans, reaching a maximum known length of about 5 1/2 feet (1.7 meters) and a weight of 100 pounds (45 kilograms). The beak is relatively long, and the forehead gently sloping. There are about 30 pairs of teeth in both the upper and lower jaws. (One reference describes the lower jaw as having "thirty-one rather snaggled teeth in a disordered row on the lower jaw" [Nishiwaki 1972], but the correct description should be 31 teeth, snaggled or not, *on each side* of the lower jaw.) There are very few pictures of this species, but when it is illustrated (e.g., True 1889; Walker 1964; Leatherwood et al. 1976), it can be seen that the animal has a low, broad-based dorsal fin, with no suggestion of the "hump" that characterizes many of the types included in the genus *Sousa*. The trivial name *fluviatilis* comes from the Latin *fluvius,* meaning "stream," and refers to the riverine, or fluviatile, habitat.

They are usually seen in groups of eight to twenty, and they are relatively slow swimmers. They are, however, more active than the boutu, another factor that serves to differentiate them in the wild. They rarely jump clear of the water, but they are said to "swim and roll in tight formation and in nearly perfect synchrony almost touching sides when they appear above the water" (Walker 1964). They are sometimes found in very shallow water, and in one report it is stated, without elaboration or explanation, that "crocodiles submerge when they appear" (Kellogg 1940). Norman and Fraser (1938) called it "Buffeo negro" and wrote, "This species is seen in troops of twenty or thirty and is said to attack the Bouto. . . ." Until someone decides to concentrate on this species (singular or plural), we will have no more precise information than these descriptions of yellow-spotted dorsal fins and attack troops of tucuxis, and there will be no coherent resolution of the taxonomy of the genus.

In 1967, Norris and his colleagues traveled to Amazonas Province in Brazil, to record the behavior and sounds of the two species of Amazon dolphins, the tucuxi and the boutu. They reported that the tucuxi is "very vociferous" and produces a series of short clicks of very high intensity and high repetition rate, as well a single whistle of pure tone and rising frequency. The tucuxi also produces what the authors refer to as a "characteristic intense brief double click" (Norris et al. 1972).

Although the various color forms are not fully accounted for, it can still be said that the tucuxi—in all its forms and all its habitats—is found throughout the rivers and lakes of northern South America, primarily the Amazon and its tributaries, as far west as the Peruvian Andes. It also inhabits the coastal waters of Venezuela, Guiana, and Surinam, and perhaps the Atlantic coast of Central America as well, from Panama to Venezuela (Bössenecker 1978).

This dolphin is held in high esteem by the natives, and is not hunted for food or oil. Earl Herald (1967) referred to it as the "sacred dolphin," and Bössenecker (1978) wrote that while the Indians had often seen them "in an area 100 to 2,000 m from the river mouth [the Magdalena in Colombia] . . . 5 or 6 were regularly seen up to 600 m up the river. Local fishermen recalled that this behavior had never changed within their memory and stated that they had never attempted to catch any dolphins, for superstitious reasons. In fact, it was difficult to persuade local people to help in catching for this reason." (During the California Academy of Sciences Expedition to the Amazon in 1965, when one of the animals drowned in the capture net, the expedition party cut it up, broiled it, and ate it. According to Waterman [1967], "The fishermen were aghast at this apparently barbarous cuisine.")

Some specimens have been collected for exhibition and study in aquariums, but they are delicate little animals, and special care must be taken with regard to their capture and transportation. The California Academy Expedition captured five animals and got them as far as Florida, but when they had to be transported by truck for some of the journey, four of them died. Herald, who led the expedition, wrote in 1967, "The sacred dolphin, or tookashee, has a very fast respiration rate—once every 30 seconds. If one of these animals became entangled in the net it had to be removed quickly or it would drown. Tookashee are also very susceptible to shock, and so had to be handled with great care." The remaining animal survived the trip, and lived at the aquarium at Niagara Falls for approximately four years.

In 1977 another expedition went to Colombia to collect tucuxi for exhibition in Europe. In all, 80 dolphins were rounded up, of which 24 were selected for transportation to Europe. Of this number, "three died within three weeks of arrival with lung problems, and one died after two months with severe hepatic degeneration of unknown cause. The remaining animals are healthy and well acclimatized" (Bössenecker 1978). Some of these animals were trained, but they were not particularly responsive: " 'Sinbad' was trained quite easily to retrieve a plastic ball and return it to the trainer, although he could become confused if the trainer did not stand at the same place." Although Bössenecker claims that the tucuxi he collected were the first maintained in captivity, this distinction has to fall to the single survivor of the 1965 expedition. Nevertheless, the collection, transport, and exhibition of 24 of these little-known cetaceans has added substantially to our knowledge. In his conclusion, Bössenecker wrote:

We have established that the range extends far to the west of Lake Maracaibo and northwards up the Caribbean coast to Panama. We have established a range size of from 60 to 188 cm, and have suggested that maturity may occur around 160 to 170 cm. Certainly females of 167 cm can be in lactation. . . . We have seen that this species is very easy to handle, and that, although nervous in the water, can adapt well to captivity given time, making it very suitable for display.

BOTTLENOSE DOLPHIN

Tursiops truncatus Montagu 1821

The bottlenose dolphin is the most familiar of all the smaller cetaceans because of its appearance in porpoise shows,* children's books, movies, and television programs. It is a sturdy animal that can reach a length of 13 feet (3.9 meters) and a weight of 1,430 pounds (650 kilograms). Most specimens are smaller, however, averaging about 9 feet in length and weighing perhaps 500 pounds. Adult males are somewhat larger than females, and at maturity both sexes achieve a heavy-bodied appearance.

The bottlenose has generally a silvery gray color, but descriptions of its appearance have ranged from black to lead-colored to purplish gray. Most animals are darker above and lighter below, sometimes showing a distinct "cape" pattern, and there is often a clear demarcation between the dorsal and the ventral areas. Some mature animals are covered with a profusion of small spots (Caldwell and Caldwell 1972b), and there

---

*As a demonstration of the confusion surrounding the common name of this animal, the reader is advised to review the list of references for this species. Some authors prefer "porpoise" and others use "dolphin," while some even use the names interchangeably. In addition, the animal is also called "bottle-nose," "bottlenose," and "bottlenosed" dolphin. (Or porpoise.)

are records of all-white animals as well. (A full albino named Carolina Snowball was captured off the coast of South Carolina in 1962, and lived for three and a half years at the Miami Seaquarium.) The overall coloration of the animal is subdued, but there are variations nonetheless: some individuals have a pronounced eye-to-flipper stripe; others have a visible eye ring; while on others there is a visible pattern of lines running from the blowhole forward to the junction of the melon and the rostrum.

The dorsal fin is high and gracefully falcate, and the lower jaw projects beyond the upper, giving the animal its familiar pugnacious look. The beak itself, obviously responsible for the name "bottlenose," is short and stubby, and the mouth is drawn into a "permanent grin—a feature which makes this naturally friendly animal even more likable" (Baker 1972). There are 23 to 25 pairs of sharp, sturdy teeth in each jaw—conical in younger animals, but usually worn down in mature animals. The bottlenose is a graceful and surprisingly flexible animal, with great mobility in the region of the neck, since five of its seven neck vertebrae are unfused, unlike those of many of the other oceanic dolphins, where the seven cervical vertebrae are fused. The bottlenose can bend its neck so that its head is at right angles to its body. During normal swimming, the bottlenose breathes by exposing just its blowhole, and in some areas where it coexists with other similar species, such as the tucuxi, this behavior is diagnostic: the tucuxi characteristically pokes its rostrum out of the water as it surfaces to breathe (Saayman et al. 1972).

In Russian, the bottlenose is known as *bolshoi delfin;* the French call it *grand souffleur;* in German it is *grosser Tummler;* in Swedish it is *oresvin,* the Portuguese know it as *peixe-boto;* and the Japanese name is *hando* (or *bando*) *iruka.* In the scientific literature, the animal was originally known as *Delphinus tursio,* from a 1780 description of a specimen from Greenland by Otho Fabricius. Of this description, Flower (1883) wrote:

The type of this group is *Delphinus tursio* of Bonnaterre and Cuvier, so named because it was supposed to be the *D. tursio* of Fabricius, a very doubtful identification, especially since, as I am informed on the high authority of the late Professor Reinhardt, no specimens of this species have even been seen from Greenland, its range in the northerly direction not extending so far.

It would appear that Fabricius was describing some other species, but we will probably never know what it was. Hershkovitz (1966) simply dismisses it as "(= *Delphinus tursio* of Bonnaterre and authors, and not of Fabricius, which is unidentifiable)."

With its distinctive grin, short snout, and high, curved dorsal fin, the bottlenose is easily recognized at sea. In certain areas of its wide range, however, it might be confused with other dolphins. For example, the young of the Atlantic spotted dolphin are unspotted, and the similarity between the two has led to a number of erroneous reports of the two species swimming together. On the northern coast of South America, the Guiana dolphin resembles the bottlenose but it is a much smaller species, rarely reaching a length of 5 1/2 feet (1.7 meters).

The major problem with identification, however, concerns the bottlenose itself, rather than similar species. With regard to various subspecies, races, variations, and discrete geographical populations, there exists a taxonomic tangle of enormous complexity. In his 1889 *Review of the Delphinidae,* F. W. True listed no fewer than four "valid" species (*Tursiops tursio, T. catalania, T. abusalam,* and *T. gillii*), and then suggested that *T. aduncas* "may or may not prove to be distinct, but as we have not had access to the original description of this species, we venture no opinion regarding it." The literature on the bottlenose is crammed with new species and revisions (True confirmed the existence of *T. catalania* from two South African skulls in 1914), and the identification of a new type seems to be a pet project of cetologists. From the examination of a skull of an animal that had been caught in an Uruguayan shark net, Pilleri and Gihr (1972b) resurrected the name *T. gephyreus*, originally proposed by Lahille in 1908, since the skull they examined "differed clearly" from *T. truncatus* and *T. aduncus*. (In another discussion also published in 1972, the same authors wrote, "In no other cetacean genus are the systematics as contested as in *Tursiops*," and they then proceed to separate the genus into three distinct species, *truncatus, aduncus,* and *gilli*.) In some recent works, the names *Tursiops aduncus, T. gillii* (or *gilli*), *T. nuuanu,* and, of course, *T. truncatus* are recommended for specific status, while other authors (e.g., Rice 1977) hold that there is only one worldwide species with geographical races varying in color, tooth count, and body size. Although there has not been a clarification of the convoluted taxonomy of this species, conservative taxonomists recognize a single species *Tursiops truncatus truncatus* with the following subspecies, differentiated by geography and morphology: *T.t. gilli*, tropical Pacific from California to Japan; *T.t. aduncus* from the Red Sea and the east coast of Africa; and *T.t. nuuanu* from the eastern tropical Pacific.* On the basis of detailed examinations of some fifty-eight specimens from South African waters, Ross (1977) concluded that *T. truncatus* and *T. aduncus* are "sufficiently different to warrant full specific status for each group." He also writes, however, that the results "should be viewed as preliminary, pending a global review of the taxonomy of *Tursiops*."

The bottlenose dolphin is an inshore species, rarely spotted more than five hundred miles out, and most frequently observed in groups of about a dozen, often in association with other species. Scammon referred to it as "a 'mongrel breed' of doubtful character, being frequently seen in company with Blackfish, sometimes with porpoises, and occasionally with Humpbacks." Their behavior at sea is characteristic: groups of bottlenoses are often seen leaping out of the water as they swim along, a behavior that has come to be known as porpoising. Tomilin (1957) wrote that they are exuberant and playful, and that they are often seen jumping for no apparent reason. He reports that

they can turn somersaults, and mentions one animal that "broke the surface tail first."

Where observations have been made over time (e.g., Würsig 1978, Würsig and Würsig 1979, Saayman and Tayler 1973), it is becoming apparent that certain populations of bottlenose dolphins have a home range and restrict themselves to that range rather than migrating from one place to another at random. Caldwell (1955) reported observations of a single large animal with a distinctively damaged dorsal fin (a "natural tag") for several years in the Florida Keys, and the Würsigs' studies of the species in the South Atlantic were predicated on the assumption that certain identifiable individuals could be seen from year to year in the same location. (One of the Würsigs' early papers, in fact, described the process of identifying individual animals from the shape of the dorsal fins. Published in *Science* in 1977, it was entitled, "The Photographic Determination of Group Size, Composition, and Stability of Coastal Porpoises [*Tursiops truncatus*].") Shane's 1980 study of the bottlenose dolphins of Aransas, Texas, was based on a year's observations of a local population whose numbers fluctuated from 48 to 164 animals, but the same individuals (given names like Thick Fin, Lumpy, V-tip and Bent Fin to facilitate the recording of individual appearance and behavior) were seen regularly throughout the year. Caldwell and Caldwell (1972b) have speculated that the dolphins may have "a very restricted home range of only some 10 miles or so, a traveling range to another spot, and then another restricted home range on the other end, somewhat like a dumbbell in overall shape." Within these "home-ranging" populations, there seem to be great variations in the group structure, with animals appearing at one time in the company of certain others, but at other times with a totally different group. As described by the Würsigs (1977), "the fluidity with which additional animals appeared and disappeared (presumably to join other groups), far surpasses the individual interchanges between known 'open' groups of most terrestrial mammals."

*To further confuse matters, the name *nuuanu,* which is a Hawaiian word, does not refer to the species found in the Hawaiian area; that is *T.t. gilli.* The name was introduced by Roy Chapman Andrews in honor of the ship that J. T. Nichols was on (the *Nuuanu*) when he described this "apparently new porpoise" (Andrews 1911).

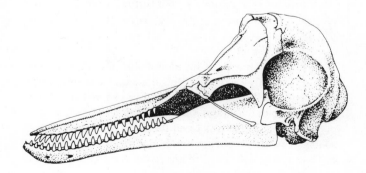

The skull of *Tursiops truncatus.*

One of the most extensive case studies of a wild bottlenose dolphin population was carried out by Wells, Irvine, and Scott (1980), in the waters of the Gulf Coast of Florida near Sarasota, during 1970 and 1971, and then again from 1975 through 1978. The study area encompassed some 85 square kilometers (53 square miles) and contained what was probably a single resident "herd" of perhaps 100 animals. For over 3,000 individual sightings (some of the animals were tagged and released; others were identifiable by natural tags), the average group "consisted of 4 or 5 dolphins, but ranged up to approximately 40 individuals." The "home ranges" of the various groups (defined as "the area over which an animal normally travels during its routine activities") differed from group to group, with the females with calves having the largest ranges, the females without calves being the next largest, and then the subadult females and the adult males, both apparently restricted to the northern portion of the study area, in the vicinity of Sarasota Pass and Palma Sola Bay. Most of the subadult males did not often enter into the areas frequented by the adult males. Even though this herd was observed and photographed for a protracted period of time, the nature of the animals continues to make comprehensive hypotheses difficult. The authors wrote, "Unfortunately the volume of data available on inshore odontocete social ecology does not begin to approach that collected for terrestrial mammals." The difficulty of observing the activities of wild dolphins combined with the often easy availability of captive specimens means that observations of captive animals are probably going to be the most comprehensive available, but investigators must always be mindful that captivity itself may inflict some "unnatural" behavior patterns on the dolphins.

In various areas off the South African coasts, Saayman, Tayler, and Bower (1973) studied the behavior of free-ranging bottlenose dolphins (identified as *Tursiops aduncus*), and their observations have contributed materially to the still-limited knowledge of the behavior of this animal in the wild. They saw "large schools, estimated most frequently to number about 500 individuals," but these schools were frequently deployed in subgroups of 25 to 50 animals.

Feeding behaviour was readily identifiable. Herding of food-fish was generally carried out by all groups and subgroups combined. The dolphins swam at high speed, many of them long-jumping in the chase. Single individuals leaped several times in succession and slapped the water with their flanks, making an audible report. A number of variations in herding and feeding procedures were observed. For example, in the late afternoon, approximately 200 dolphins entered Plettenberg Bay deployed in two lines, forming a spearhead. The dolphins swam at high speed, with many leaping individuals,

and, now strung out into a single line-abreast formation, were apparently driving fish ahead of them. A small group on the periphery speeded ahead and then turned back towards the sweeping line of dolphins. As the two groups converged, with the food-fish apparently trapped between them, the orderly line disintegrated and, for several minutes, dolphins criss-crossed over the area and fed in a disorganised mass.

Also at Plettenberg Bay, Tayler and Saayman (1973) reported the peculiarly aggressive (or perhaps maliciously playful) behavior of a group of approximately 20 "fully adult" dolphins. They were herding and harassing a group of fur seals for no apparent reason. The dolphins circled the seals,

diving under and around them; the flurries of white water and the close proximity of individual dolphins and seals indicated that some form of physical contact was taking place. At this point, the seals appeared to become agitated, some of them leaping at speed repeatedly clear of the water ("porpoising"). Some dolphins on the periphery of the group then commenced to leap repeatedly and slap down heavily on their sides, a form of behaviour generally associated with fish herding procedures. Two dolphins in the rear of the group constantly circled around those seals lagging behind and appeared to be preventing their escape from the encircling cetaceans.

The authors wrote that the "significance of this encounter was not at all obvious. . . ."

In the wild, bottlenoses eat a variety of food organisms, which they usually swallow whole. There is, however, evidence that some individuals behead larger fishes before swallowing them (Norris and Prescott 1961), and Caldwell and Caldwell (1972a) describe a situation where a freshly captured 6-foot (and therefore juvenile) animal could not be made to eat unless the trainer manually broke the heads off the fish that were being offered to the dolphin; the animal refused to eat fish where the heads had been *cut* off. Often the teeth of mature specimens are worn down (Fraser 1934), and Tomilin comments on the "remarkably worn state of the teeth," indicating that this species bites the fish in two before swallowing it. He further cites the instance where a dolphin was taken with a fresh—but headless—scorpion fish in its stomach. The stomachs of a number of animals from the Gulf of Mexico were examined, and the prey species were recorded: the prevalent food item was mullet, then came gizzard shad and various other fish in lesser quantities. The bottlenose dolphin also eats squid, eels, sharks (although not always successfully—one choked and died on a leopard shark), and almost anything else it can catch. They also seem to feed at almost any depth; Tomilin recorded an instance of a bottlenose being caught and drowned in a flounder net set at 90 meters (298 feet), and at the opposite end of the scale, these versatile animals have been observed feeding completely out of the water: Hoese (1971) described the situation where pairs of dolphins in a Georgia salt marsh were feeding on fish by working inshore waves until the fish became stranded on the shore, at which time the dolphins came all the way out of the water to get the fish, and then returned to the water on the next receding wave.

In Golfo San José in Argentina, Würsig (1978) observed that the group's structure—with the exception of the predictable mother-calf bonds—seemed to depend on feeding situations as much as on any other observable determinants. Dolphins in the Black Sea were observed by Bel'kovich and his colleagues, and in a report written in 1978, these observations were summarized as follows: The Crimean dolphins assembled in small subgroups that were part of a larger, relatively stable population that could be seen throughout the year. The herd was apparently "led" by a large male, who would "determine the degree of hazard or investigate anything new." There were also "scouts," groups of two to four animals that searched for food, perhaps corresponding to the "senior male squads" of the Pacific spotted dolphins (*Stenella attenuata*) described by Pryor and Kang (1980). Actual hunting for fish was described as a cooperative effort, with the scouts detecting the fish and the rest of the school assembling to feed. The dolphin herd was seen to surround the schooling fish and then feed on them, often while maintaining a constant circling motion (the "carrousel" technique). Taylor and Saayman (1972) described similar hunting techniques for the Indian Ocean bottlenose. In addition to this "surround" method, the Crimean dolphins also drive the fish toward shore, toward the surface (a photograph in Caldwell and Caldwell [1972b] shows "wild dolphins feeding on leaping mullet," which would indicate that the mullet had been herded against the "wall" of the water's surface), and even in the direction of fishermen's nets. Similar behavior was observed by Busnel (1973) in the waters of Mauritania. Bottlenose dolphins, working with humpback dolphins, would appear when fishermen of the Imraugen tribe beat the water with sticks, and the dolphins would drive mullet into the nets of the waiting fishermen. Since the fishermen provided the "wall" and the dolphins were also seen feeding on the fish, Busnel described this as a "symbiotic association . . . man and dolphin take common advantage of a common prey, the mullet."

There are numerous reports of bottlenose dolphins adapting their feeding strategies to changing artificial (nonnatural) conditions. In Texas waters where shrimp boats operate, the dolphins often follow the shrimpers to pick up the trash fish that are dis-

carded as the nets are hauled in (Gruber 1979). Norris and Dohl (1980) discuss other examples of this "learned behavior" for bottlenoses, which "seems to translate into a heightened importance of learning in the social patterns of odontocetes." Norris and Prescott (1961) mentioned two additional examples of the "remarkable degree of flexibility in the feeding of the species." In one instance, a school of Pacific bottlenoses in San Diego Bay regularly traveled some eighteen miles to Imperial Beach, "to feed around the Navy garbage buoy, where the fleet anchored in the harbor dumped its daily load of refuse." They also recorded a situation where dolphins would dash toward shrimp boats that were hauling in their nets, often from as far as two miles away. "One cannot help but conclude," they wrote, "that these animals hear and recognize the specific sounds produced by the boat winching in its net, and from very considerable distances."

Observations of groups in captivity have revealed a definite social structure, particularly apparent in the spring mating season, but present all year round. Tavolga (1966) viewed a "stable, self-perpetuating group [at Marine Studios in Florida], to which the only additions were by birth," from 1951 to 1955, and could therefore compile data on the long-term relationships among the animals. There were twelve bottlenose dolphins, five males and seven females, in the tank. (A female Atlantic spotted dolphin died during the study.) "In the colony of animals under observation there was definite evidence of dominance or a 'peck order,' though this dominance was not as strict as that seen in some other animals."

The adult male, the largest animal in the colony, was dominant over all others. Throughout most of the year he swam alone, or with one of the adult females for short periods. During the spring months he swam habitually with one or another of the females for periods of several weeks, when conception presumably took place (Tavolga and Essapian 1957). On these occasions the female involved was submissive to him, swam constantly with him, and left only to feed for periods of a minute or two, returning to his side when he yelped. When he initiated courtship activities, she cooperated. She returned to her normal activities with the other females only when the courtship period was terminated at the option of the male.

The remaining animals could be divided into three groups: the adult females, the younger males, and the juveniles, all of which were born in 1953. (Tavolga suggested that "evidence of acclimatization is indicated by the fact that the animals were actively reproducing while under observation.") The mature females were nonaggressive, but they were more curious and often initiated new activities in the tank. The young males spent most of their time together, they were more mischievous than any of the others, and their activities "were often destructive to the peace and quiet of the community of animals, but they might have served to use up excessive amounts of energy that would have been used otherwise in the wild state." The youngest animals were all dependent on their mothers, and were "the most submissive animals in the tank." It is not possible to apply directly the observations of captive animals to their wild counterparts, but there is no reason to assume that the social organization of free-swimming bottlenoses differs substantially from that observed in the tank at Marineland. In a tank, however, long-range movements are not possible, so some behavioral changes could possibly take place. The presence of a dominant male in a wild herd, for example, would put the younger males at a disadvantage, and they might leave the group. Sergeant and colleagues (1973), observing the social structure of wild bottlenoses in northeast Florida waters, wrote that there is the possibility "that herds of subordinate males will be found." It is believed that bottlenose dolphins reach maturity at about 12–13 years of age, and that they have a life span of approximately 25 years.

From numerous observations of these animals in captivity, it has been noted that they are almost obsessively sexual. Males only a few months old initiate sexual behavior with other dolphins—male and female—and often with turtles and even inanimate objects, and they continue to behave in an often embarrassingly overt sexual manner in captivity. Bottlenose dolphins are by far the most commonly bred cetaceans in captivity, and in North America alone as of 1977, there had been 107 recorded births (Cornell and Asper 1978). In Marineland of Florida, no fewer than 25 Atlantic bottlenose dolphins were born between 1939 and 1963, of which 6 had been conceived in the wild and 19 in captivity (Wood 1977). Three generations were raised in the institution, and provided an unparalleled view of the behavior of breeding dolphins.*

For some unknown reason—perhaps related to this obsessive sexuality and perhaps not—all known (and one suspected) instances of cetacean crossbreeding have involved the bottlenose. In June 1933 three dolphins were found stranded together at Blacksod Bay, Ireland. When he examined the carcasses, F. C. Fraser, the British Museum's expert on small ceta-

ceans, was unable to identify them. They were dark above and light below; two of them had short beaks, and the third was beakless. To Fraser, the one with the longest beak looked like a bottlenose, but, as he wrote in 1940, "the other two were not within the range of variation of any known form of dolphin." Fraser performed a complete examination of the three, which had beached together—itself an unusual occurrence, which "suggested the possibility of the three specimens being inter-related"—and concluded that they bore a resemblance to both Risso's dolphin and the bottlenose. At Enoshima Aquarium in Japan, three different female bottlenose dolphins gave birth to calves that were probably sired by a male Risso's which had been kept in the same tank. The first calf, a female, was born on September 29, 1978, and was alive and well as of March 1981.* The other two, another female and a male, lived for less than a year each (Hirosaki et al. 1981). In a Hawaiian oceanarium in 1971, a calf was born to a female rough-toothed dolphin that had been kept in a tank with three male bottlenoses, and the calf grew to full maturity, manifesting the sloping profile of its mother and the gray coloration of its sire (Dohl et al. 1974). On May 3, 1981, at Kamogawa Sea World in Japan, a female bottlenose gave birth to a calf that was sired by a false killer whale which had lived in the same tank for nine years. (In previous years, the female had miscarried twice.) The calf—a female like all the other captive-born hybrid bottlenose calves—was almost black in color like its father, but it showed the light-colored "fetal folds" that are often present in newborn delphinids, and it had a short, whitish beak.†

After a gestation period of about 12 months, a calf about 3 1/2 feet long (1.1 meters) is born, tail first. As the fetus is expelled, the female comes about rapidly, presumably in an attempt to break the umbilical cord. Contrary to most popular accounts, the mother does not assist its newborn offspring to the surface for its first breath (McBride and Kritzler 1951), but she will help the infant if it appears to be having difficulty. In most observations of births in captivity, another female (sometimes referred to as an "auntie") accompa-

---

*Because of the comparative ease with which the bottlenose reproduces in captivity, the species has been the subject of numerous studies, which, by extension, have greatly enriched our knowledge of all odontocetes. A Dolphin Breeding Workshop was held at the San Diego Zoo in December 1975, and the results published in 1977 as *Breeding Dolphins: Present Status, Suggestions for the Future.*

*It is hard to imagine anything more disconcerting to a student of cetaceans than to encounter a species he cannot recognize. A color photograph of the *Tursiops* x *Grampus* hybrid was used in 1979 as the Christmas card for the Whales Research Institute in Tokyo. Of course it was identified inside the card (as *Tursiogrampus grisecatus*), but when I opened the envelope and saw a shiny gray, short-beaked dolphin, I was struck dumb: I had been studying pictures of these animals for years, and before me was an animal I couldn't even begin to identify.

†I saw this animal some three weeks after it was born, and made the description and the accompanying drawing from life. According to a letter I received from Teruo Tobayama, the Director of Kamogawa Sea World, the hybrid calf lived for 276 days, and then died of unknown causes in February 1982.

nies the mother during and after delivery. "Immediately after birth, the female turns on her side to allow the infant to suckle, resuming her normal upright position only after the newborn dolphin has become proficient in this procedure" (Tavolga 1966). In nursing, the baby presses the mother's belly in the region of her nipples and forms a tube with the palate of its upper jaw and its tongue, through which the milk passes from the mother to her baby. Young dolphins have been observed to try solid food as early as 6 months after birth, but they are not fully weaned until they are about 18 months old, and some individuals have been observed suckling at the advanced age of 29 months (Ross 1977). The mothers are extremely protective of their calves: "They keep the calves close to their sides, sweep or push them away from new or unusual objects, remove them from the vicinity of other animals falling into the water after a jump or in the midst of a fight, and in general, watch them constantly. They do not allow the young animals to stray, and retrieve them at once if they do so" (Tavolga 1966).

The young dolphin is in vocal communication with its mother almost from the moment of birth, using weak whistling signals that can be heard with hydrophones and that can often be seen as a stream of bubbles emanating from the baby's blowhole. The first sounds made by a newborn dolphin are "tremulous and quavery," indicating that the infant will eventually learn to control its communications. Since it has now been demonstrated that every individual dolphin has its own "signature whistle" (Caldwell et al. 1971), it is believed that the mother dolphin is able to recog-

nize her own baby by the tone and quality of its whistle (Hickman and Grigsby 1978). (As early as 1953, Wood had written that "whistling may constitute a form of communication between a mother porpoise and her infant, enabling one to find the other. . . .") Caldwell and Caldwell (1972a) reported that juveniles separated from their mothers "often whistle constantly for hours, even days, a behavior which suggests emotional unrest." The same authors also discuss the forming of attachments between adults, where an adult female had spent her entire captive life (ten years) with the same male. When the two were separated, the female "refused to perform and for two days and three nights remained in the center of the small tank bobbing up and down and vocalizing constantly. She refused to eat and paid no attention to her usual training props . . . except to violently flip them out of the tank if they happened to come near her snout." When the two tankmates were reunited, the female resumed her normal behavior, and "there were no further manifestations of the unusual behavior observed when she was in isolation."

If a bottlenose dolphin is injured, other individuals will often assist it. (Adult females appear more likely to do this than adult males, however.) When an animal was stunned by a dynamite blast, two others came up beneath its flippers and supported it until it could breathe normally (Siebenaler and Caldwell 1956). Norris and Prescott (1961) report a case of a bottlenose dolphin that assisted a "stricken" adult Pacific white-sided dolphin at Marineland of the Pacific. There are other reports (Hubbs 1953; Moore 1955) of female bottlenoses supporting the remains of juve-

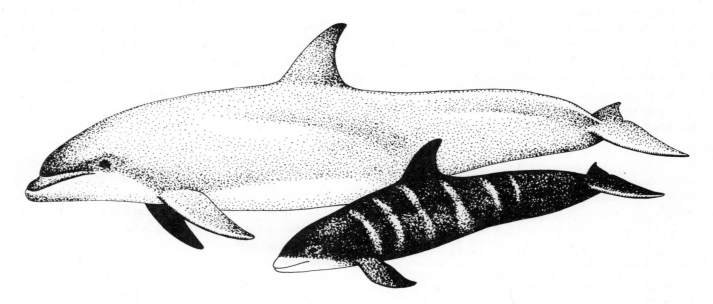

The result of a *Pseudorca* (false killer whale) x *Tursiops* cross. The hybrid calf, shown with its *Tursiops* mother, was born on May 3, 1981, at Kamogawa Sea World, Japan (drawn from life).

niles that had apparently been killed by sharks.* There is no evidence, however, to support the popular concept that dolphins will drive sharks away from swimmers. Since sharks and porpoises often feed on the same organisms, the presence of porpoises might indicate the presence of sharks, instead of indicating that the waters are safe for human swimmers. Sharks and dolphins have even been kept in the same oceanarium tanks, and they do not seem to be "natural enemies." When a sandbar shark was introduced into the tank at Marineland of Florida, "the greatest volume of whistling ever heard by the writer" (Wood 1953) occurred. "For some minutes the porpoises, obviously excited, bunched together and stayed well away from the shark. Then some of them began to make sudden passes across the shark's bow, causing it to swerve sharply to one side." When a 6-foot tiger shark was introduced into the tank (several months after the sandbar shark had died), the porpoises again exhibited signs of excitement, "bunching together, staying in that part of the tank farthest from the shark, and speeding up their already accelerated swimming whenever they came closest to the shark. . . . However, within 20 minutes they had apparently become accustomed to its presence and accorded it little more attention."

In the wild, sharks are probably aware of small cetaceans as potential food sources, and some cetaceans may regard sharks as a threat, particularly when there are females accompanied by calves. Since one of these situations calls for an active response, while the other is passive, or at best defensive, it is not surprising to discover that dolphins are often found with shark-bite scars. Wood and colleagues (1970) reported that "at least half of the 75 or so animals [bottlenose dolphins] that we have either captured or have found washed up on the beach . . . have had some degree of shark scarring." An attempt to train a captive bottlenose dolphin to repel sharks was conducted at the Mote Marine Laboratory in Sarasota, Florida. The dolphin was conditioned to butt a sandbar shark, but when a bull shark was introduced into the tank, the

dolphin "refused to approach and harass it" (Gilbert et al. 1971).

Also in the realm of fantasy is the oft-repeated story of the dolphin saving the swimmer in trouble. It would take deductive reasoning abilities far beyond those of even the smartest dolphin to be able to identify a swimmer in trouble—to a dolphin, all human swimmers probably look like they're in trouble—and then decide which way to push it for the swimmer's survival. The dolphin's natural reaction, assuming it had any motivation at all to "save" a swimmer, would probably be to seek deeper rather than shallower water. As F. G. Wood (1973) remarked, "We are not likely to hear reports of assistance from people who are pushed out to sea."

Even though they are social animals, bottlenose dolphins are not often found stranded in numbers. They do, however, strand individually: in the extensive studies of cetaceans stranded on British coasts from 1913 to 1977, some 217 bottlenose beachings were recorded, ranking it second for this period, behind the harbor porpoise, which has a total of 779 (Sheldrick 1979). On the east coast of the United States, however, the bottlenose has the dubious distinction of being the most frequent strander of all cetaceans. Commenting on this phenomenon, Mead (1979) wrote that the two commonest stranders (the other again is the harbor porpoise) "are the commonest elements of the coastal fauna. Other distribution records indicate that both of these species normally occur near shore in relatively large numbers and are certainly the dominant cetacean elements in these areas." While this does not explain the stranding phenomenon, it does point out the obvious: the commonest species will be the most frequent stranders. Of the 58 animals examined in Ross's 1977 study, 26 of them had stranded on South African beaches. The bottlenose dolphins may avoid the multiple strandings common to other species because of their familiarity with shoal waters, and "because they are familiar with the peculiarities of these surroundings" (Dudok van Heel 1966).

The compilation of statistics brings us no closer to a solution of the mystery of cetacean strandings, but one case in which a "reason"—albeit anthropomorphic—can be suggested is described by Tomilin: a live female was found beached at Novorossisk, "with an already dead suckling 122 cm at its side. The tails of both animals were in the water." Wood (1979) distinguishes live strandings, in which the animal comes ashore apparently of its own volition, from beaching, where it has been dead or injured and washed ashore accidentally. According to his research, there have been very few live strandings of bottlenoses: ". . . two involved captive animals kept in fenced enclosures. A

*To demonstrate that this sort of behavior may not be indicative of "intention," Evans and Bastian (1969) cite the obviously counterindicative evidence of a dolphin supporting the carcass of a leopard shark that the dolphin herself had killed. (The incident was originally described by Norris and Prescott in 1961.) In reporting the incident, Evans and Bastian wrote, "In this case we would be obliged to conclude that the attribution of intention to these actions was groundless." To describe an action as indicative of a resemblance to human situations simply because we can explain it in no other way—or perhaps because the observers are biased to find "humanlike" behavior where it does not exist—is poor reasoning and faulty science as well. Evans and Bastian caution against the assumption that the animals possessed "understanding" simply because they exhibit the behavior that might be used to demonstrate this understanding, and call this "the most vicious sort of circular reasoning."

Tursiops stranded alive on the Irish coast with a full-grown spotted dogfish 'firmly wedged head-first in its oesophagus'; one stranded on a North Carolina beach and refused to swim away when pushed off; and two animals, a 280 cm female and a 302 cm male, stranded together at, appropriately, Strand-on-the-Green in Middlesex, England, 'many miles' from the mouth of the Thames."

The bottlenose is a fast, powerful swimmer, capable of tremendous leaps out of the water. Scientists have long wondered how fast a bottlenose could swim, and then, how it could swim so fast. (In 1936 Sir John Gray published a paper in which he demonstrated that porpoises should not be able to swim as fast as they do, a situation that subsequently became known as Gray's Paradox.) Although there have been reports of dolphins swimming 20, 30, or even 50 mph, speed trials conducted by the U.S. Navy in Hawaiian waters showed that the maximum speed attained by a free-swimming bottlenose was 14 knots (Lang and Norris 1966).* The bottlenose is by no means the fastest of the dolphins: in subsequent trials a Pacific spotter was clocked at 23 knots (Lang and Pryor 1966), and while it has not been tested under controlled conditions, the Dall porpoise is believed to be even faster for short sprints.

Those instances where the speed of a bow-riding dolphin has been estimated in excess of 35 mph are not necessarily exaggerations. Recent studies (e.g., Fejer and Backus 1960, Hertel 1969), have shown that this can be accomplished with the assistance of the pressure wave created by the forward movement of a ship under way. In many instances, the dolphins have been observed to make no swimming motions at all (some early observers attributed the dolphin's speed under these circumstances to oscillations of the tail too rapid to see), and they have even been observed to drop their flukes to take full advantage of the pressure wave. They can turn on their sides as they are pushed along at speeds far greater than they could achieve under their own power. The same principle is applied to surfing: bottlenose dolphins have been seen surfing in the wake of a fast-moving vessel (Norris and Prescott 1961) and even "bodysurfing" in waves close to shore, where they ride the curl of a wave until it begins to break, "pulling out" just before the wave collapses in shallow water (Caldwell and Fields 1959). Like bow riding, this behavior probably does not serve any practical purpose for the dolphin, and therefore, it is possible to interpret it as play.

Most actions of wild animals can be said to have some survival value. For most terrestrial mammals, daily actions are devoted to the everyday necessities of eating, reproducing, and resting. Except in juveniles, "play" is a concept that is uncommon in all but a few land mammals, and of these, many are partially aquatic. Perhaps there is something in the world of water that encourages playfulness: otters and sea lions come to mind as animals that play regularly in and around the water. Primates—including ourselves—have intricate patterns of play, often involving water. For the fully aquatic dolphin, however, play appears to represent a very significant portion of its behavioral repertoire. In a 1974 essay, Bunnell wrote, "Extreme playfulness and humor are conspicuous in dolphins and may be found in whales also, although they are harder to observe. Despite its low status in puritanical value systems, play is a hallmark of intelligence and is indispensable for creativity and flexibility. Its marked development in Cetaceans makes it likely that they will frolic with their minds as well as their bodies." In captivity the animals invent games, and will play with almost anything in their tanks, from feathers and bits of shell to fish, turtles, pelicans, inner tubes, and beach chairs. In one instance, two captive dolphins were teasing a moray eel, and when they could not get it out of a rock crevice, one of the dolphins swam away, captured a spiny scorpion fish, and shoved the fish into the crevice, driving the eel into the open so that the dolphins could continue to play with it (Brown and Norris 1956). They are also known to invent games that involve human participation, ranging from teasing divers in their tanks to throwing things out of the tank for a person to throw back. Unfortunately, playing with small thrown objects often ends badly for the dolphin, since they are apt to swallow things such as coins, often for no other reason than to keep the object from another dolphin (Caldwell and Caldwell 1972a). Bottlenose dolphins even play with their own noises. The Caldwells wrote: "In our communication studies, we have been made to feel extremely foolish on more than one occasion by getting excited over wildly different sounds coming through our earphones until we were able to correlate the sounds with a young *Tursiops* resting in the tank, blowing bubbles, and obviously just playing with the many different sounds that his noisemakers could produce."

Tayler and Saayman (1972) have described one of the few observations of "play in the wild," where they saw "two to four immature animals disporting together, leaping over non-participating adult dolphins, chasing each other . . . single animals played, tossing scraps of fish skin or seaweed . . . frequently chased

*During these tests the dolphin, whose name was Kieki, was swimming in the open ocean, free to leave at any time if he was so inclined. (He wasn't.) Also during these tests, it was considered an unnecessary shark attractant to have the divers carrying pieces of fish with which to reward Kieki. The "Porpoise National Bank" was established, where instead of a piece of fish as a reward, the dolphin was given a plastic disk, which, according to Norris (1974), "he could trade for a fish until the bank was empty."

butterflies as they flew out of the water." The extent of play in captive animals is probably largely a function of their not having much to do, and certainly, if they are not involved in some sort of experiment or exhibition, they don't have to work very hard for their food. The bottlenose dolphin is a naturally energetic animal, and in a tank, with nothing to do but swim in circles and wait for feeding time, it is very likely to become bored.

When they are young, bottlenose dolphins sleep, watched carefully by their mothers, but as they mature, they only seem to doze, resting near the surface between breaths. Since breathing in a dolphin is a voluntary rather than a reflex action, the animal cannot fall into the state of semiunconsciousness that characterizes the sleep of many terrestrial animals. "Porpoises do not breathe as land mammals do," wrote Wood in 1973; "instead of inhaling and exhaling continuously, they take a breath and hold it." Careful planning has to accompany this exercise, since the animal has to arrange to be in exactly the right place when the inhalation takes place. The animal doesn't have to be there for very long, however, since Lawrence and Schevill (1956) have shown that the bottlenose can exhale and inhale in 0.3 second. According to Ridgway (1966) "Most marine mammals breathe less frequently than their terrestrial counterparts. In order to compensate, they take 'deeper' breaths and take more oxygen from the air than they breathe." Ridgway also noted that bottlenose dolphins breathe about once or twice per minute on average, but when stressed or excited, they will breathe more frequently. Although it may seem longer, a bottlenose dolphin usually does not hold its breath for more than 7 minutes, and this duration usually accompanies a particularly deep dive. When Tuffy, the deep-diving bottlenose of the Naval Bioscience Facility at Point Mugu, California, dived to 300 meters (984 feet), he was down for 7 minutes and 15 seconds (Ridgway 1966). One aspect of these deep-diving experiments was the investigation of physiological changes that took place at depth. Tuffy was trained to push a plunger and take a photograph of himself when he reached maximum depth, and in the pictures that were produced, it was seen that his thoracic (chest) region was remarkably collapsed. In addition to this thoracic collapse, Ridgway lists the following "adjustments" that deep-diving cetaceans can make to the increasing ambient pressure: large, distensible veins that can engorge with blood and fill space as air is compressed; lungs that contain large amounts of elastic tissue; and resilient trachea that allows the respiratory passages to collapse beyond the limits of the sea-level dead-space volume.

Taking into account the various nominal subspecies, the bottlenose dolphin is found in practically all the coastal waters of the world, including enclosed bays, lagoons, and even shallow streams that feed into the ocean. Although it is sometimes found in fairly high latitudes, it is not an inhabitant of polar waters. The bottlenose is commonly encountered in the western North Atlantic from New Brunswick to the Caribbean and Mexico, and in the eastern Atlantic from Norway to the Mediterranean and the Black Sea (the Russians call the Black Sea dolphin *Tursiops truncatus ponticus*), and to the northwest coast of Africa. In the Southern Hemisphere, the bottlenose is found on both sides of South America, off South Africa, Australia, and New Zealand, and in the Indian Ocean. The various other subspecies inhabit waters other than those mentioned above, and it is those, particularly the Indo-Pacific forms, that are so confusing to taxonomists.

Because of its coastal habitat and fearless nature, the bottlenose has probably been known to people ever since the first seaman noticed the exuberant behavior of this sleek animal. Pliny mentions the "tursio," which he says "bears a strong resemblance to the dolphin; it differs from it, however, in a certain air of sadness" (Sanderson 1956). The first direct contact was probably a predatory one on the part of *Homo sapiens,* since the dolphins would regularly ride the bow waves of ships and could be easily harpooned. Whalemen often supplemented their meager diet with meat from various small cetaceans, and Melville wrote, "Porpoise meat is very good, you know."

The early records are sparse, but we know there was a fishery for bottlenose dolphins on the east coast of the United States early in the nineteenth century, and by 1884, there were at least two full-scale net fisheries for this species, one at Cape May, New Jersey, and another at Cape Hatteras, North Carolina. (In discussing his visit to the Hatteras fishery, F. W. True [1885] wrote that porpoise fishing had been carried out there for at least a hundred years.) In both areas, the method was pretty much the same: boats would find and encircle schools of dolphins in inshore waters, then nets would be thrown around the school to entangle and drown them. Those that were not drowned were stabbed with knives. True (1885) wrote that "very few individuals escape, and those mostly by leaping over the nets, breaking the meshes, or running out near the beach." For the season of 1884–85 (November to May), True (1890) reported that the Hatteras fishery took a total of 1,268 bottlenose porpoises.* The flippers and the dorsal fin were cut off

*In the *Fisheries and Fishery Industry Report* for 1887, Clark wrote that "an average catch in former years was from four to five hundred porpoise to the season, requiring from five to six for a barrel of oil." But these figures—presumably contemporaneous with the fishery—

and thrown away; then the skin and blubber were stripped off and boiled down in the try kettles. The mandible (lower jaw) was removed, and its oil extracted separately. This was the *sine qua non* of the porpoise fishery, the so-called porpoise-jaw oil. According to Clark (1887) "Watchmakers were then using olive oil as the only fitting oil for watches; but by experimenting with porpoise-jaw oil they found it superior to the olive or any other oil, consequently the sailors and fishermen found a ready market for any they were able to obtain." Total catch records for the Hatteras fishery are unclear, probably because accurate records were not maintained, but Mitchell (1975b) estimates a cumulative catch of some 17,000 bottlenose dolphins, the only species caught in this fishery, by the time the fishery closed down in 1893.* As far as can be ascertained, the Cape May fishery operated for only two years, from 1884 to 1886, and seems to have taken approximately 200 porpoises per year (Mead 1975). The "fishery" for this species in U.S. waters is now restricted by the Marine Mammal Protection Act of 1972, and consists only of federally permitted live captures for exhibition and research purposes. In other areas, however, there have been directed fisheries for bottlenose dolphins, and some of these are still being carried on. The Soviets and the Turks fish for this species in the Black and Azov Seas (although again the figures are difficult to obtain); off the coast of India various small cetaceans have been hunted for centuries; and in the Caribbean and off the west coast of South America fishermen continue to take almost all species of inshore porpoises and dolphins, including the bottlenose.

In February 1978, one of the most gruesome episodes in the history of humans and dolphins occurred. Over 1,000 bottlenose dolphins and false killer whales were herded into a shallow bay at Iki Island, Japan, where they were clubbed, shot, and stabbed to death. The Japanese fishermen killed the dolphins because they claimed that these "gangsters of the sea" were eating the fish that the fishermen thought belonged to them. In other words, the dolphins were slaughtered for pursuing their normal prey. A worldwide public outcry followed, but again in 1980 the Japanese fishermen of Iki-shima killed the dolphins that they thought were depriving them of their livelihood. Under the eyes of American filmmakers (who had gone to Iki to "inhibit the slaughter"), the fishermen herded 800 dolphins into a bay at Tatsunoshima, and butchered them as the filmmakers stood helplessly by. In an apparent attempt to overcome the objections that they were just leaving the dolphin corpses on the beach to rot, the Iki fishermen fed the corpses into a huge grinder that reduced the carcasses to fertilizer. (It was during this episode that Dexter Cate, an American schoolteacher from Hawaii, cut the fishermen's nets and freed another 200 dolphins that were being held until they could be shredded. Cate was arrested for "interfering with business," kept in jail for three months, then released and deported because his visa had expired while he was in jail.)

In 1913 five bottlenose dolphins were caught in the Hatteras area and shipped to the New York Aquarium. They had been netted in the regular fashion, and then five of them "were dragged away from the net with a rope tied around the tail" (Townsend 1914). (This manner of handling apparently injured one of the animals, "which soon became deformed and cannot participate in the rough gambols indulged in by the others. . . .") They were transported from Hatteras to New York (a two-day journey by boat), in "long narrow boxes large enough to accommodate them without rubbing . . . and kept supplied with sufficient cold water to support and cover them. . . ."* C. H. Townsend was the director of the New York Aquarium at that time, and in 1914 he published his firsthand observations of the "world's best single exhibit of captive wild animals:"

The captive porpoises are very lively and keep swimming day and night, rising to blow usually with each circuit of the pool. Being kept in shallow water [the circular pool was 37 feet in diameter and 7 feet deep] they probably breathe oftener than they would in deep water. They often swim under the water, belly up, like seals, but never lie on the bottom or bask at the surface as the latter do. Visitors ask whether they ever rest—a question not easy to answer. If they do, it is apparently without cessation of forward motion. Nevertheless they are quieter at night when most of the lights are cut off, and do not indulge in boisterous play. For a time two of them habitually moved from left to right, while three took the opposite course, but this practice soon became less regular and is apparently breaking up. Sometimes the speed is slow, but more often it is quite rapid. Occasionally they indulge in a bit of racing that makes high waves, the water surging up to the coping of the pool. A porpoise *speeding* around the pool can make a right-angled turn as quickly as a frightened fish, without lessening speed.

---

are quite low. In a more recent analysis of the data, Mead (1975) reports that the Hatteras fishery probably took some 2000 animals per year.

  *Mead (1975) gives this date as "the close of the fishery," but in his 1914 discussion of the Hatteras dolphins that were brought to the New York Aquarium, Townsend gives catch figures for the fishery from 1907 to 1914, including such numbers as 1,550 porpoises in 1909, 1,278 in 1910, and 1,073 in 1914.

  *Two previous attempts to ship dolphins from Hatteras to New York ended in failure: "all the animals, eight in number, died en route because they were unfortunately carried without water in the shipping tanks, and could not survive the journey without the cooling and supporting medium of water."

There is no evidence that the porpoise can see out of water. In throwing a fish the head is often thrust well above the surface, but the animal seems always intent on its plaything, entirely disregarding the visitors leaning over the rail five or six feet away. While a fish thrown into the water is promptly seized, the porpoise pays no attention to a fish suspended by a thread two inches above the surface. If the eyes of porpoises and other whales were fitted for observation above the surface of the water, as are the eyes of seals, they might long ago have learned to use them in the same way.

In fact, bottlenose dolphins see quite well in air as well as in water. In one study (Pepper et al. 1972) their visual acuity in air was favorably compared to that of antelope or red deer, animals noted for the high level of their aerial vision. Why would a dolphin need to see well in air? There are records of bottlenoses feeding on flying fish (Ljungblad et al. 1977), and there are other instances where the dolphins were seen feeding on fish that were jumping out of the water (Caldwell and Caldwell 1972b); being driven up onto the beach (Hoese 1971); or herded up against a steep back whence they began jumping and were caught in midflight (McBride and Kritzler 1951). In captivity the aerial vision of dolphins is important for various games, such as the throwing and catching of objects, and leaping high out of the water to take a fish from a trainer, but these are manifestations of existing capabilities, not visual adaptations. (In these activities, the dolphins also have to be able to compensate for the refraction of the water and calculate the actual position of a trainer or a hoop as opposed to the perceived image of the object from under the water.) On one occasion ("more out of playful curiosity than anything else" on the part of the trainers), a dolphin was allowed to watch television. When the researchers noticed that the dolphin was "swimming rapidly around in the tank, vocalizing loudly, and violently tossing his ball high in the air again and again," they feared that "something terrible might be wrong," and rushed to the side of the tank. They found that the dolphin had been watching a televised baseball game (Caldwell and Caldwell 1972b).

Even after bottlenose dolphins had been maintained in captivity, they were still generally regarded as peculiar, fishlike mammals; a source of oil along with their larger relatives. Some early descriptions of the bottlenose are interesting for their ignorance of the animal's capabilities. For example, in Kellogg's (1940) article on whales and dolphins in the *National Geographic,* a photograph of a bottlenose dolphin bears this caption:

Like a dog taught to stand up and beg, a dolphin rises for a fish. With its tail lashing beneath the surface, this tame

Bottlenose Dolphin in a large tank at Marineland, near St. Augustine, Florida, stands half out of the water to take mullet from an attendant's hand. A bell is rung to call the dolphins to "meals."

Not everyone thought of dolphins as seagoing dogs, of course, and some scientists made some remarkably good guesses about the senses of the cetaceans. In 1930, the anatomist A. B. Howell discussed the acoustic senses of marine mammals, and wrote this about hearing:

But there must be a gradual accommodation to this change —a gradual increase in ability to receive water borne vibrations and a gradual decrease in the power to receive those transmitted by air. And there must be some change in the quality of the reception also, for it is unthinkable that during the thousands of years since the abandonment of atmospheric hearing in the Cetacea they receive sounds under water only after the same fashion as we do when the head is submerged. . . .

There is abundant evidence that whales are sensitive to certain water borne vibrations which cannot possibly be transmitted through their auditory or Eustachian tubes. Hence these waves must be transmitted through some solid part of the head, but we have no means of ascertaining which part is most resonant. . . .

It has been reported that porpoises are peculiarly sensitive to the waves that are transmitted by the sonic depth finder and will disappear in great haste and apparent discomfort when one of these contrivances is put in operation. This fact suggests that the Cetacea may be sensitive to water borne sound waves of a character and after a fashion that we do not yet understand. The transmission of the sounds that reach them and the ears themselves are so different from anything connected with our own acoustic apparatus that my personal opinion is to the effect that we know nothing whatever about the matter.

The dolphins at the New York Aquarium apparently did not live beyond 1916 (Devine and Clark 1967), and therefore it was not until the late 1930s that the real potential of the bottlenose was suspected. The species had been observed playing and jumping for fish in the newly built Marine Studios (later Marineland) in Florida, which opened in 1938, but then had to close until 1946 because of the war. In his 1973 discussion of the history of Marineland, F. G. Wood wrote:

In 1946 the oceanarium reopened. The colony of porpoises was reestablished and in February of the following year one of its members gave birth to a healthy female calf named Spray. The first of a number of bottlenose dolphins born at the Florida Marineland, Spray was to live for 22 years and herself give birth to five calves. . . . The opportunity to observe these exotic animals at close hand dispelled some erroneous beliefs . . . and provided a host of new information. It was apparent that the porpoises had good vision in air as well as water; that they made a variety of sounds, especially when excited; they slept in brief naps at intervals during the day and night; and if there was a current in the tank they continued to swim while sleeping; they exhibited a wide and imaginative variety of sexual behaviors.

When Arthur McBride, the curator of Marine Studios, tried to capture some dolphins for the reopened oceanarium, he observed that the porpoises could somehow avoid the nets he had set for them, and with remarkable foresight, he wrote, "May we not suspect that the above described behavior is associated with some highly specialized mechanism enabling the porpoise to learn a great deal about his environment through sound?" (McBride 1956). Even earlier, however, when McBride wrote one of the first popular articles on the dolphin—it was called "Meet Mr. Porpoise," and appeared in *Natural History* magazine in 1940—he discussed the animals' ability to locate fish thrown in the water, and wrote, "The possibility is offered, therefore, that the porpoise, by their sense of hearing, locate the schools of mullet." McBride's successor as curator of Marineland was F. G. Wood, and when he arrived he discovered that captive bottlenose dolphins made a variety of sounds, including jaw claps, whistles, rasping and grating sounds, combined mewing and rasping sounds, barks, and yelps. He noticed that the rasping sounds (which he described in 1953 as ranging from "a brief toneless grating noise to a high pitched, rather musical meandering lasting two or three seconds") could be induced by "introducing almost any strange (to the porpoises) object into the tank—for example, a white enameled pail, a dumbbell-shaped sound projector, a length of pipe, etc."

The general pattern of behavior under these circumstances is always the same; the porpoises bunch together and swim at a faster rate around the tank. They accelerate while passing the object, but crane their necks to look at it as they go by. Rasping sounds, usually brief, are heard at this time. Generally within only a few minutes (the Marineland porpoises have been subjected to many unfamiliar objects) their swimming slows and the younger animals (those which were born in the tank) approach the object more closely, and even pause and appear to examine it. If it is the hydrophone they are examining, the "rusty hinge" noise and related rasping or grating sounds are, of course, quite pronounced when heard through the listening equipment.

To Wood it was apparent that these "rusty hinge" sounds "possess the characteristics necessary for a pulse-modulated type of echo-ranging, and the behavior of *Tursiops* at the time it emits these sounds certainly suggests that they might be used for echo-

location or even what might be termed 'echo-investigation' " (Wood 1953). Other investigators, including Schevill and Lawrence (1956) and Kellogg (1958), were also working on the "echolocation" capabilities of the bottlenose, but the extent of this capability would not be known—if indeed it is known even now—for many more years. In 1961, Norris and colleagues successfully demonstrated that the bottlenose dolphin could navigate and locate objects in the water without the use of vision; they covered the eyes of a captive female named Kathy with latex suction cups, and observed that the animal at first "navigated beautifully, totally without sight. . . . Kathy could easily locate a target as small as an inch in diameter, apparently from across the entire thirty-five foot tank, without sight" (Norris 1974).* When attempting to capture bottlenose dolphins for Marineland of the Pacific in 1958, Norris and Prescott (1961) made some observations that were also particularly important in identifying the bottlenose dolphin's ability to echolocate and echonavigate in situations where its vision was useless: "By their occasional surfacing and their tail beats we could see the animals head into the trap, turn away from the net ahead when they were an estimated 100 feet from it, orient to the 20-foot opening that we were straining to close, race directly for it and through it without any searching behavior whatsoever. Quite obviously these animals were able to sense this opening a long way from it in very murky water in which visibility was only a few feet at best."

In further experiments with Kathy, Norris and his coworkers dropped fish into the tank with the blindfolded dolphin:

As Kathy zeroed in on a reward fish dropped near a hydrophone, she made her clicks in a rather regular fashion. At the first splash of the fish, she wheeled around in the water and headed directly for the splash, giving out trains of clicks at the same time. We felt that this initial location of the target was accomplished by the use of two capabilities. First, Kathy seemed to possess a remarkable ability to localize the position of the splash, simply by using her extremely acute directional hearing. Then, when she was headed in approximately the right direction, she began to pick up the echoes of her clicks as they bounced off the sinking fish. These brief, but intense, clicks began to come faster as she swam toward her target. By the time she picked up the tidbit, we could detect as many as 416 clicks per second. There was another interesting thing we noticed; Kathy waggled her head up and down and around in circles just before she snapped up a sinking fish. If she temporarily lost the fish, or if we

*Norris's original experiments with Kathy took place in 1959, and were officially described in the *Biological Bulletin* (Norris et al. 1961). A more anecdotal account of the events appears in his 1974 book, *The Porpoise Watcher,* and whenever possible I have chosen the more popular terminology. Both sources are listed in the references for this section.

dropped it an inch or two from the hydrophone, these head waggles became extreme. At the same time the hydrophone picked up a tremendous concentration of clicks. It seemed obvious to us that she was trying to find her fish with these clicks and to discriminate it from the nearby hydrophone. She looked for all the world like a miner peering into the crevices of a mine shaft with his head lamp.

The manner (although not the method) by which Kathy was locating objects dropped into her tank was revealed when the investigators noticed that she could track pieces of fish above and to the side of her head while blindfolded, but she seemed to lose them when they dropped below the level of her snout. Norris (1974) wrote:

Sure enough, she always failed to find those fragments that drifted below the level of her upper jaws, even though they might be only an inch away. However, any fish that drifted above her jaws she snapped up at once. All the while we could hear her making her rusty hinge noises. Porpoises have no sense of smell, and Kathy could not see, so we were forced to conclude that her actions were the result of her echolocation ability. If so, she seemed either to be putting out a beam of sound from her fatty forehead (called the "melon" by whalers), or was receiving echoes there, or perhaps both.

The investigators also noticed "sound scanning," that is, side-to-side head movements, which indicated to Norris and colleagues (1961) "that the animal probably sends, and may also receive, sound in a directional fashion during echolocation." Of this capability, Kellogg (1961) wrote:

Auditory scanning may be thought of as more complex than visual scanning, for it represents a combination of two already complex processes. Auditory scanning consists of (a) the emission of a continuous series of sound signals for the purpose of echolocation and (b) binaural localization. It might be characterized as "binaural-echolocalization."

Above and beyond this activity is the perceptual process itself. The stream of information produced by auditory scanning must be instantly analyzed by the amazing brain of the animal. The mechanical counterpart of such a receptor system would be a sonar apparatus with one transmitter and two independent receivers, plus an electronic computer capable of decoding and processing the data—all within a single compact unit.

At approximately the same time that the early dolphin research was taking place, other researchers were investigating the echolocating capabilities of bats. (D. R. Griffin, the person known as the "father" of animal sonar research, published his first paper on the subject in 1938, but his major work, *Listening in the Dark,* did not appear until 1958.) Prior to Griffin's pioneering work, people simply had no idea how bats managed to navigate and catch their insect prey in total darkness.* Echolocation in bats and dolphins is now the accepted explanation for their behavior, but not long ago the concept—in fact the very word echolocation—was unknown to science. In a 1979 summary of the early history of echolocation research, Griffin had this to say about the nature of his revelations:

This is now so rudimentary that it is difficult to realize how unexpected was the discovery that bats actually orient their flight by hearing echoes of sounds generated for this purpose. For example, the distinguished physiologist Selig Hecht was so incredulous when he heard our reports of these experiments at a meeting of the American Zoological Society around Christmas, 1940 that he seized Galambos by the shoulders and shook him while complaining that we could not possibly mean such an outrageous suggestion. Radar and sonar were still highly classified developments in military technology, and the notion that bats might do anything even remotely analogous to the latest triumphs of electronic engineering struck most people as not only implausible but emotionally repugnant. It was partly to overcome this sort of resistance that I suggested the general term echolocation to cover the wide variety of orientation mechanisms, natural and artificial, based on the emission of probing signals and the location of distant objects by means of echoes.

It soon became apparent that dolphins shared these remarkable capabilities with bats, but Norris realized that it still was not known if the dolphin could *not* navigate with its hearing faculties blocked: "we had not performed the complementary experiment—the one akin to Spallanzani's plugging his bat's ears with wax." An experiment was therefore devised wherein those organs thought to be the dolphin's hearing apparatus—not the ear openings, which are only tiny holes, but the melon and the upper jaw—were to be masked. If the dolphin could not navigate with its "ears" blocked, it would indicate that hearing was necessary for this navigation. When Norris and his colleagues tried to put a rubber mask over Kathy's upper jaw and melon, the dolphin adamantly refused to wear it and shook it off every time, "perhaps all we could expect from an intelligent animal faced with the loss of sight and hearing."

*The Italian Lazzaro Spallanzani (1729–99) was probably the first investigator of this subject; when he blinded bats he found that they flew perfectly well, but when he plugged their ears, he discovered that "they collided blindly and at random with whatever obstacles were set in their path" (Griffin 1959). Known as "Spallanzani's bat problem," the mystery of bats' navigation and feeding remained unsolved for nearly two centuries. In a 1939 book entitled *Bats,* the mammalogist G. M. Allen wrote that the bats heard the humming of their insect prey, and "no doubt it is the echo of vibrations set in motion by air currents that they really perceive."

The mechanisms of sound production and reception have remained among the dolphin's most closely guarded secrets: "Despite years of discussions, special seminars, experiments, morphological descriptions and several studies of functional anatomy, uncertainty still exists, and the details of production of the vast variety of sounds found in the repertoire of cetaceans is still an unsolved mystery" (Green et al. 1979).

From the earliest identification of the sounds made by the bottlenose dolphin, an enormous amount of attention has been directed toward the classification and analysis of the sounds themselves, and also their function in the life of the dolphin. Using fairly simple equipment (a single sending and receiving hydrophone), Wood (1953) was able to identify whistles, rasping and grating sounds, combined mewing and rasping sounds, barks, and yelps. He wrote that "there may be some significance in the fact that the 'rusty hinge' sound is clearly associated with investigative behavior or manifestations of curiosity on the part of *Tursiops*," and "there appears to be good evidence that whistling may constitute a form of communication between a mother porpoise and her infant, enabling one to find the other in the event of separation. . . ." Wood was correct on both counts, but in 1953 no one was aware of the sophisticated nature of the acoustic system of the bottlenose dolphin: it serves two purposes, communication and echolocation, and the animals are capable of utilizing both aspects simultaneously.

The sounds known as whistles are pure tones, while the rasping, creaking, mewing, and barking noises are actually composed of rapid bursts of clicks. According to Caldwell and Caldwell (1972b), "The pulsed sounds are in turn broken down into those regular series of clicks which are used for environmental exploration or echolocation, and those bursts of clicks which we often term 'burst pulse sounds' and which we believe are communicative since they vary with the type of behavior the dolphin is manifesting when they are emitted." Numerous studies of the different sounds made by dolphins have been conducted by various researchers, some of them highly specialized. For example, Drs. David and Melba Caldwell of the University of Florida have extensively studied the whistle sounds of the bottlenose, and they have published records of the sounds made by infants and adults; they have identified individual "signature whistles," and they have recorded the ability of the dolphins to mimic mechanical as well as natural sounds. Each dolphin has its own individual whistle, slightly different from that of any other dolphin, and it may serve to identify one individual to its fellows. Hickman and Grigsby (1978) wrote, "An individualized signature whistle has been shown (Caldwell, Hall and Caldwell 1971) to have meaning to a dolphin who hears it.

One meaning is to identify the vocalizer." The Caldwells (1979a) discovered, "Dolphins learn to recognize each other's whistle so well that with a little practice they can correctly identify another animal's whistle within only 1/2 second of listening time." Dolphins are also excellent auditory mimics, and they have been known to replicate an electronically produced signal by using their own whistle (Caldwell and Caldwell 1972c).

The ability of bottlenose dolphins to repeat sounds that they have heard has led some researchers down some curious paths. The most controversial of these has been John Lilly, a neurophysicist who began his dolphin research in 1955 when he and a number of other doctors attempted to map the cerebral cortex of a dolphin in captivity at Marineland of Florida. Because of the almost total lack of knowledge at that time of the biology of dolphins, the animal was improperly anesthetized, and it died on the operating table. Eventually, Lilly constructed a full-scale research facility on the island of St. Thomas in the American Virgin Islands, and there continued his research, most of which was directed toward "interspecies communication"—talking to dolphins and trying to get them to talk to him. He wrote:

The great difficulty in developing a type of vocal communication between man and these water-borne mammals that are used to living and communicating under water is obvious. We speak in air, we hear best in air. Speaking under water is a difficult feat for us. The dolphins seem to be a bit ahead of us: they can also vocalize in air. Their natural air-borne sounds are not very loud, not as loud as ours, except with training. Apparently they hear poorly in air, but nobody has yet measured how badly their hearing suffers in air as opposed to their hearing in water, which is excellent. Therefore, in order to meet these animals more than halfway, we must devise a technique of speaking under water and a technique so that when we are in air and they are in water we can hear them "speaking" under water and they can hear us speaking in air. [Lilly 1961]

Attempts to get dolphins to imitate human speech were important aspects of Lilly's program, and in one instance a female researcher lived with a male dolphin for 63 days, talked to him, played with him, and addressed the problem of his "sexual needs." Lilly's books have been widely publicized, and he has probably been the individual most responsible for the popular conceptions—and misconceptions—about dolphins. For example, Robert Merle wrote *Day of the Dolphin* (1969), based largely on Lilly's work. In this book, dolphins actually do learn human speech. Commenting on it, F. G. Wood (1973) wrote, "Many readers, previously conditioned by accounts of the intelligence and linguistic ability of the porpoise, apparently found the work cogent and even profound." Of John Lilly, Robert Stenuit (1968) wrote; "a member of an impressive number of scientific societies, committees, councils and associations, inventor of various instruments and author of countless publications. He has become famous in the United States (and too much so for a scientist, insinuate certain colleagues who do not share the limelight), and journalists have labelled him, quite against his will, 'the man who makes fish talk.' " (Later in *The Dolphin, Cousin to Man,* Stenuit wrote, "The first thing I shall ask a dolphin, once I can speak to him, is to lead me to the wreck of some galleon loaded to the gunwales with gold and jewellery. . . .") Lilly has been called "the father of modern dolphin research" (Brown 1979) and "scientifically unsound and naive" (Tavolga and Tavolga 1962). It is probably safe to say that he is not the father of modern dolphin research, but we must hold him accountable for some of the popular attitudes about the possible uses of dolphins for military purposes. In *Man and Dolphin* (1961) he wrote: "If they are military types they could be very useful as antipersonnel self-directing weapons. They could do nocturnal harbor work, capture spies let out of submarines or dropped from airplanes, attacking silently and efficiently and bringing back information from such contacts. They could deliver atomic nuclear warheads and attach them to submarines or surface vessels and to torpedoes and missiles." In 1970, Caldwell and Caldwell wrote the following on the subject of the language of dolphins:

Dolphins do not talk. They are fascinating animals but they do not talk. . . . The popular press of recent years has given a good deal of play to the speculation that dolphins do have a whistle language, or as one author terms it *delphinese.* Some advocates of this or closely related theories have fine academic backgrounds (albeit not in animal communication) and their words and work have been accepted by a majority of the public including some scientists. This has been most natural for there exists in all of us a deep rooted need for certain myths and fantasies. In new or little known areas of research one or two individuals of good professional background can exert great influence on public thinking, particularly if their approach is such that it does satisfy our communal need for fantasy.

From 1955 to 1968 Lilly was involved in various dolphin projects, and then he left the field of "delphinology" to pursue the more personal goals of mind expansion and self-awareness. He has now returned to his dolphin studies, and has written another book, *Communication Between Man and Dolphin* (1978), in which he elaborates again on the theme of talking to dolphins.

Other sounds made by bottlenose dolphins are far more complex than their whistles, and enable the animals to perform feats of echolocation that are truly extraordinary.

Clicked signals are composed of discrete clicks of sound, usually very broad-band in character, which may be heard as individual bursts of sound, or as trains of clicks, or when the repetition rate is very high, may be heard as a single signal whose frequency reflects the rate (Watkins 1967). Such high repetition rate sounds have been given a variety of names such as squawks, barks, chirps, etc. Many of these appear to be social signals even though their production often appears to be generically related to echolocation click production. The slower repetition rate clicks have been implicated in echolocation behavior (Schevill and Lawrence 1956), since they have always been associated with discriminative behavior in situations where the animal could not see, and often when it could (Norris and Evans 1967). [Norris 1969]

Experiments with blindfolded dolphins (to ensure that they are not using vision) have shown that the animals can, by the almost instantaneous processing of returning echoes, perform a variety of discrimination determinations. In a 1979 paper on the echolocation of the bottlenose, W. W. L. Au lists the following accomplishments:

Results of discrimination experiments have shown that Tursiops can detect a 10% difference in the diameter of metallic spheres (Norris, Evans and Turner 1967), material composition and thickness differences as small as 0.1 cm in metallic discs (Evans and Powell 1967), differences between plates shaped as circles, triangles and squares independent of their cross sectional areas, as well as a 6% change in the diameter of the circles (Barta and Evans 1970; Fish, Johnson and Ljungblad 1976), and an 0.8 dB difference in the target strength of corprene cylinders (Evans 1973) . . . Nachtigall, Murchison and Au (1978) reported on the ease with which a *Tursiops* could discriminate between foam cubes and cylinders of different sizes. Hammer and Au (1978) found that an animal could recognize differences in the wall thickness of aluminum cylinders that were as small as 0.16 cm. They also found that the animal could detect differences between free-flooded aluminum, bronze and steel cylinders of equal dimensions.

The means by which the dolphins achieve this sophisticated sonar are not clearly understood, but Kellogg (1961) was able to put the problem of "acoustic analyzing" in a clearer perspective when he wrote,

The process by which such distinction is accomplished can be understood by comparing it to vision or to optics. Daylight or white light contains all the wave lengths of the visible spectrum. Yet, when white light is used to illuminate a red surface, red light is all that is reflected back. The same white signal reflects only green from a green surface, blue from a blue surface, and so on. The remaining wave lengths from the original light source are absorbed by their respective targets. The "coefficients of reflection" of the different surfaces are not the same.

By comparing the acoustic abilities of the porpoise to our own, we can begin to get an idea of the way the system works. In the same way that brass and aluminum look different to us, they "sound" different to a porpoise.

In 1971, Diercks and colleagues described a series of 1969 experiments with a dolphin named Scylla that demonstrated still another capability of the bottlenose dolphin, passive sonar. Scylla was blindfolded and a series of transducers were affixed to her head to monitor any noises she might make. A live fish was dropped into the training tank, and "the porpoise, without emitting any detectable echolocation signals, positioned herself adjacent to the fish as it swam around the perimeter of the pool. *No* echolocation signals were detected by any of the ten hydrophones during this circuit" (Evans 1980). Until this time, it was assumed that the sonar of dolphins was an active sense, that is, the dolphins would send out click trains and respond to the returning echoes. When Scylla could track (and eventually catch) a fish without emitting a sound, it showed that the dolphins also react to the sounds of other animals, and their echolocating capabilities are even more complex than they were originally thought to be. Evans (1980) wrote, ". . . as we can see from the experiment just described, echolocation must not be viewed as distinct from another acoustic capability—receiving and interpreting other sounds in nature."

There was a time when the ocean was thought to be a "silent world" (Cousteau 1953), but it has since been discovered to be incredibly noisy, especially to those creatures with a well-developed sense of hearing. In 1980 L. H. Herman wrote,

The underwater world of the dolphin is filled with sound of both physical and biological origin. In its journey through this world, the dolphin hears almost the full range of acoustic energy present, save perhaps for the exceptionally low subsonic noise. The sound of shoaling water, the noisy chorus from the deep-scattering layer, the croaks of fishes, the whine of an engine or the low rumble from a large ship, the "screams" of a killer whale, and the whistles, buzzes, and other sounds from its own or allied species may all have significance for the individual's biological and social well-being. . . .

The vision of odontocetes seems to be a well-developed sense, and they probably use this faculty as well as any other creature of the sea. Those species, such as bottlenose dolphins and killer whales, that spend so much time near the surface, where the light level is higher, must depend even more strongly on their eyes. Cetaceans do not have distinct eyelids, but they can close their eyes by utilizing the musculature of horizontal skin folds, one above and one below each eye. Listing the areas where vision might "help promote key functions in their life," Madsen and Herman (1980) include "(a) orientation and navigation in space and time and the coordination of group movements; (b) prey detection and capture; (c) predator defense; (d) identification of conspecifics, of age and sex classes, and of individuals; and (e) communication of behavioral states."

With the passage of time, we learn more and more about the capabilities of dolphins, particularly the bottlenose,* but there are still many unanswered questions about the sonar capabilities of this and other odontocetes. We do not know, for example, why animals with such advanced acoustic sensitivities blunder into fishermen's nets and purse seines, which should have ample "acoustic reflectivity" to warn the dolphins of their presence. Evans (1980) suggests that it might be the "porpoise's inattention or its concentration on pursuing prey."

Early experimenters were inclined to assign an extraordinarily high intelligence to dolphins, based mostly on the size and convolutions of its brain and its unusual trainability. Lawrence and Schevill (1954) said that bottlenose dolphins are "truly remarkable animals, not only in their aquatic adaptations, but also in their intelligence," and in 1956, Brown and Norris wrote of the bottlenose, "still we say that it is intelligent because its behavioral range seems to far exceed that necessary for survival, learning is rapid and requires very little repetition, a degree of reasoning ability seems present, and the species indulges in pure play, not for the sake of reward." Currently, scientists are trying to avoid making the dolphin into "a little man in a wet suit" (Caldwell and Caldwell 1968), and there are numerous authors who do not believe that dolphins are anything special at all. In *Sociobiology* (1975), E. O. Wilson has written, ". . . it is important to emphasize that there is no evidence whatever that dolphins and other delphinids are more advanced in intelligence and social behavior than other animals. In

*Many researchers have suggested that the extraordinary echolocating capabilities of the bottlenose dolphin are related to the limited visibility in the waters in which it usually lives, and are not necessarily a demonstration of the animal's inherent superiority. Certain other fresh water dolphins, some of which are totally sightless, also have excellent echolocating capabilities, and conversely, some of the open ocean species that live in relatively clear water probably do not rely as heavily on echolocation. Norris (1969) reported that "even though *D. delphis* [the common dolphin] emits typical click trains at sea, it may become disoriented when introduced into a tank filled with dirty water and may hit the walls frantically, force its head out of the water, and sometimes may drown in its frenzy. In another instance a trained Pacific white-sided dolphin, *Lagenorhynchus obliquidens,* was blindfolded and promptly ran into the tank wall, and only after a period of days did it learn to navigate blindfolded."

intelligence the bottlenosed dolphin probably lies somewhere between the dog and the rhesus monkey." Still, there are those who believe that dolphins are special, and books will continue to be written and meetings convened on the subject of cetacean intelligence.

In April 1980, a symposium was convened in Washington, D.C., under the auspices of the International Whaling Commission to discuss cetacean behavior, intelligence, and the ethics of killing cetaceans. The part of the meeting that was not concerned with humane methods of killing whales was devoted to discussions of the intelligence of cetaceans, and it was soon apparent that the participants not only could not agree on what intelligence was, they could also not determine how to find out. Wood and Evans (1979) wrote: "It is a common tendency to think of large brains as indicating 'intelligence,' although there is no universally agreed upon definition of the term. Jerison (1973) avoids the usual difficulties by suggesting that "biological intelligence may be nothing more (or less) than a capacity to construct a perceptual world.' " Whatever the criterion of intelligence—human or cetacean—if it has anything at all to do with brain size, the bottlenose will be found near the top of the scale. Of all known mammals, only the larger baleen whales, the sperm whale, the elephant, and the killer whale have brains that are actually larger than that of an adult bottlenose dolphin, and when various ratios are applied that refer to brain weight to body weight, the bottlenose comes out at the top. In a paper given at the IWC conference, Ridgway (1980) said, "The surface area-to-volume ratio is about one-third larger for those odontocetes than for man (i.e., the cetacean brain is more convoluted)." He concluded his remarks by saying, "The IWC should encourage scientists and governments in obtaining measures on cetaceans so that we can start to understand why cetacean brains are so large." As Hockett (1978) has written, "Brains are metabolically expensive, and don't get bigger (phylogenetically) unless in some fashion they are more than paying for their upkeep." We still don't know why the bottlenose dolphins have such large brains, but we are doing everything we can—short of asking the dolphins themselves—to find out.

We cannot ask the dolphins questions and expect them to answer in English (or Russian, Japanese, or Danish, for that matter), but we can make rational attempts to identify their intellectual capacities. In 1980, L. M. Herman wrote:

Descriptions of the brain of the bottlenosed dolphin (*Tursiops truncatus*) and of some other Delphinidae uniformly remark on its large size, quality, and complexity. . . . These descriptions hint at the intellectual potential of the species, which ultimately depends on brain structure and organization. . . . However, it is behavior, not structure that measures the intellectual dimensions and range of the species or what may be called its cognitive characteristics. By "cognitive characteristics" I refer to the intellectual specializations, capabilities, and limitations of a species as traced and measured through behavioral experiments and observations.

Herman has extensively studied these "cognitive characteristics" in bottlenose dolphins, and he thus defines his experimental goal: "to describe through experiments how and how well an organism selects, encodes, stores, retrieves, analyzes, and manipulates information to achieve successful performance. In this manner the capabilities and limitations of the animal as an information processing system are revealed."*

Because of the environment in which the bottlenose dolphin lives, it is to be expected that its auditory capabilities would far surpass its visual senses:

. . . the auditory system of the bottlenosed dolphin, and other cetaceans, is richly elaborated. Auditory centers occupy a large portion of the huge cerebral cortex, though the location of these centers is still under study. The amount of cortex devoted to audition or sound production seems to greatly exceed that necessary for effective echolocation, judging by the excellent capabilities of the very small-brained echo-locating bats. Based on this "surplus" cortex, it may be expected that the auditory information-processing capabilities are sophisticated, efficient and complex.

Herman meticulously reviewed the literature on memory processes in various animals and carefully documented his findings before beginning his own experiments with captive bottlenose dolphins. He was particularly concerned with concepts of memory (auditory, visual, and spatial), conceptual processes, and language learning. When dolphins were asked to remember individual sounds and sound sequences they performed well over time, but their "visual centers are not nearly as elaborate as auditory centers, and it might be expected that complex visual information-processing capabilities are correspondingly limited, as compared with auditory capabilities." (When the visual information was supplemented with associated sounds, that is, when the visual materials were "named," the experimental success rate rose dramatically.) Spatial working memory (the ability to remember locations or the physical relationship between objects) was not demonstrated to be particularly impressive in the dolphins tested.

In experiments to test for the conceptual process

*The most recent summary of this work is contained in *Cetacean Behavior: Mechanisms and Functions* (1980), edited by Herman, in the section entitled "Cognitive Characteristics of Dolphins." Most of the quotations, unless otherwise identified, are from Herman's book.

("the manipulation of information," or the use of stimuli received by the various auditory or visual centers), Herman and his colleagues required captive dolphins to discriminate between two signals. They had to identify the "correct" sound, no matter when it came in the sequence, and it seemed that "an almost endless variety of sound pairs could be discriminated on their first appearance and responded to reliably thereafter." As usual, the dolphins scored higher on tests that required the use of their acoustic abilities.*

As noted earlier, one of the most interesting characteristics of the bottlenose dolphin is its talent for mimicry, vocal as well as motor. Herman defines "true" mimicry as that "in which the animal initiates new behaviors not in its species' typical repertoire. . . ." He writes that some birds are able to copy human speech, but they are "poor at motor mimicry, and non-human primates have little facility at vocal imitation. . . . It will be seen that dolphins have capabilities for both true motor and vocal mimicry, though the evidence is largely informal and incomplete."

Herman lists a number of examples of motor mimicry, including the bottlenose (originally described by Brown et al. 1966) that successfully imitated the spinning leap of a Pacific spinner dolphin immediately after seeing the spinner perform once. (Spinning leaps are not part of the normal repertoire of the bottlenose.) Tayler and Saayman (1973) described the extraordinary mimicry of two female Indian Ocean bottlenoses as seen in the Port Elizabeth Oceanarium in South Africa. One of the dolphins began to imitate the behavior of a young male Cape fur seal that occupied the same tank, and included in her repertoire such undolphinlike (and yet very seal-like) movements as swimming on her side with one flipper extended out of the water; scratching herself ("comfort movements") with her flippers in the same way the seal groomed himself; and mimicking the seal's sleeping posture, where she swam on her back with her flippers pressed flat against her belly. The two dolphins also imitated other occupants of their tank, including skates, fish, turtles, and penguins, and would also attempt to copy the movements of the tank cleaners, which resulted in the primitive use of tools by the dolphins: they would use a piece of broken tile to scrape algae off the glass. In discussing the un-

precedented use of tools, the authors wrote: "It is therefore remarkable that the virtually limbless dolphin, specialised for high-speed locomotion in a three dimensional aquatic environment, all but barren of inanimate objects, can readily demonstrate in captivity unconditioned and spontaneous behavioural sequences, including the elementary use of tools, on a level comparable to that displayed by nonhuman primates when similarly placed in captive surroundings." Perhaps the most unusual imitative behavior of all the Port Elizabeth dolphins was performed by Dolly, a six-month-old calf that had been born to one of the females:

At the end of an observation session, a cloud of cigarette smoke was once deliberately released against the glass as Dolly was looking in through the viewing port. The observer was astonished when the animal immediately swam off to its mother, returned and released a mouthful of milk which engulfed her head, giving much the same effect as had the cigarette smoke. Dolly subsequently used this behaviour as a regular device to attract attention.

In their discussion of the imitative behavior of these dolphins, Tayler and Saayman (1973) wrote, "The refined reproduction of these motor performances necessitated a highly developed ability to perceive detail, to retain the perception for long periods of time in the absence of the stimulus originally provoking the act, and to practice and ultimately to elaborate the behavior imitated as to culminate in new modes of behavioural integration."

Vocal mimicry has been discussed earlier, and there is no question that bottlenose dolphins can imitate various sounds that they hear above and below the surface of the water. In his discussion of Lilly's claim to have heard "words," Herman wrote, "Unfortunately, Lilly's observations were not well-documented, nor, in some cases, substantiated by other on-the-scene observers."

The major aspect of Herman's studies, however, has been what he refers to as "language learning," in which he attempted to condition dolphins to respond to simple auditory commands, one-way communication (man-to-dolphin). The animal would respond to a series of arbitrary sounds representing various objects in their tank (a ball, a pipe, or a hoop), which it was directed to touch, fetch, or "mouth" (to place in the mouth). The dolphin (a female named Kea) was then required to perform the directed action only relative to the named object, so that the instructions became two-word strings, such as "touch ball," "fetch hoop," or "mouth pipe." "In this final syntactical arrangement, Kea performed almost flawlessly with all nine two-word combinations of three objects and three actions." She was then to be trained to bring the

*In one series of experiments Herman and Arbeit (1973) replicated tests that had earlier been performed with a Pacific bottlenose, *Tursiops gilli*. They reported that "the differences in the rate of learning and in the final level of performance reached were enormous." This is at least one way of differentiating the species, and some investigators (e.g., Nishiwaki 1972; Pryor 1975) believe that *T. truncatus* is more readily "trainable." (It must be noted however, that in a comprehensive study of various species of cetaceans in captivity—where the two species of *Tursiops* were ranked separately —Defran and Pryor [1980] found very little difference in the "trainability ratings" of the two species.)

designated object to a named trainer, and she "quickly learned to bring the object only to the named male trainer," which was therefore a three-word string of commands that she had to understand.

The succeeding steps, of differentiating between the two named trainers and constructing various three-word instructions comprised of object, action, and agent, were never carried out. It was at this point in May, 1977 that Kea, along with our second dolphin Puka, the subject of our visual learning and memory studies, was abducted, late at night, by two recently discharged tank cleaners. The dolphins were taken from their tanks, motored some forty miles in a small van, and abandoned in the ocean in remote waters known to have a large shark population. Each dolphin had been nurtured in tanks or enclosed lagoons for eight to twelve years, had been hand-fed throughout, and was highly socialized toward humans. They were never recovered, and almost certainly died not long after their abandonment. Irvine (1972) has documented the strong attachment of captive dolphins to their home pens and the extreme stress when suddenly placed in unfamiliar environments, projecting a tragic picture of the emotional stress of Kea and Puka at their end.

Kea was seen again after her release, badly injured: "Ugly blistering cuts on her left flank suggested that she had been thrown up against a coral reef, and her eye had been bruised so badly that it was swollen shut" (Lubow 1977). Attempts to recapture her failed, and she was never seen again. The two men who had "freed" the dolphins were tried and found guilty of theft, but the issue they hoped to raise, whether people could "own" dolphins, was not admitted at their trial. Two other dolphins, named Phoenix and Akeakamai, have been trained to pick up where the work of Kea and Puka was so abruptly and disastrously terminated, but they are still a long way from reaching the levels attained by Kea in the language experiments. In summarizing his work on the study of cognition in dolphins, Herman (1980) wrote:

The dolphin is capable of forming and generalizing response rules, as evidenced by its efficiency in solving new instances of old auditory problems governed by a common rule, or in improvising motor behaviors governed by a requirement for novelty. The dolphin may be able to represent its world through arbitrary auditory symbols, as inferred from the encouraging results in the studies of auditory language comprehension. The conditional memory tests, in which one sound in memory was represented by another, or a visual signal by an auditory one, additionally suggest competency in manipulating auditory symbols.

The dolphin seems highly proficient at some imitative behaviors, including sharing a capability with the human for *both* vocal and motor mimicry. The imitative talent has value for socially cooperative or socially convergent species like dolphins and supports an apparent ability to learn motor tasks easily by observation.

It would require a separate book to relate the accomplishments of all the scientists and all the dolphins that have been involved in the numerous and varied research projects over the last thirty years. Fortunately, there are a number of excellent works available, to which the reader is hereby directed.*

Bottlenose dolphins have been trained to jump 20 feet out of the water and to dive to depths of 1,000 feet. They have been trained to play basketball, retrieve lost objects, climb out of the water, swim upside down, jump through flaming hoops, do the hula and the twist, walk on their tails, "sing" on command, and accept "money" instead of fish as a reward for a performance. (In training, only positive reinforcement has been used, never punishment.) In their study of eleven species of cetaceans in captivity, Defran and Pryor (1980) described the bottlenose as

playful and gregarious, these animals may engage in a wide variety of daily activities. Individuals may spend a significant amount of time manipulating objects in their tank or carrying about some toy, leaf or other chance debris on their rostrum. Spontaneous diversions such as balancing a ball between the pectoral fins may arise suddenly and disappear just as quickly. Play with other cetaceans is common, including chases or even "keep-away" games. Bottlenosed dolphins housed with other aquatic animals such as sea lions, turtles, eels, and fish are frequently reported to manipulate, or even harass these other species by pushing, towing, threatening, or biting them. Aerial displays including breaching and porpoising and aquatic behaviors such as fast swimming in circular or irregular patterns are often seen.

The bottlenose is by far the most popular of all captive cetaceans. Of the 359 in captivity in North America as of August 1976, 286 were bottlenoses. Cornell and Asper (1977) and, at the same time, Defran and Pryor (1980) wrote that the worldwide population of captive bottlenoses was probably in the area of 450.

*The most comprehensive of these is *The World of the Bottlenosed Dolphin,* by David and Melba Caldwell (1972), a thorough, easily readable and nonscientific compilation of most of the current information on the animals. Antony Alpers' *Dolphins: The Myth and the Mammal* (1960) is, obviously, less up to date, but it contains some solid scientific material, as well as thorough coverage of the interactions of dolphins and man, especially the story of Opo. Dr. K. S. Norris, a charter member of the advance guard of dolphin researchers, has written an anecdotal and enjoyable account of his experiences, called *The Porpoise Watcher* (1974). W. N. Kellogg, another scientist who participated in many of the early acoustic experiments with porpoises, has summarized his and other studies in *Porpoises and Sonar* (1961). Highly recommended—but very hard to find—is F. G. Wood's *Marine Mammals and Man* (1973), in which he summarizes much of the history and natural history of human relationships with marine mammals, mostly bottlenose dolphins, but also killer whales, pilot whales, and sea lions.

Despite its permanent grin and engaging personality, the bottlenose is not always easily manipulated. There are numerous accounts in the literature of experiments during which the animal refused to come out of its enclosure or sulked in the far end of its tank, regardless of what the trainers had in mind. In this regard, Caldwell and Caldwell (1972b) have written, "It is difficult, if not impossible to induce a large male dolphin to do anything at any time that he is not inclined to do." Although most dolphins in captivity are docile, there are instances (e.g., Shurepova 1973) where a male repeatedly attacked his trainer, and the trainer, fearful for his safety, had to leave the water. At the Port Elizabeth Oceanarium, a male bottlenose named Daan copied the window-cleaning activities of a diver in his tank, using "a seagull feather while emitting sounds almost identical to that of the diver's air-demand valve and releasing a stream of bubbles from the blowhole in a manner similar to that of exhaust air escaping from the diving apparatus." During a fifty-four-day period, while he repeatedly "cleaned" the window with food fish, seaslugs, stones, and paper, Daan "actively prevented divers from approaching the window by open-mouthed threats, jaw clapping and by forcibly pushing them away" (Tayler and Saayman 1973). When Tuf Guy was acquired by the U.S. Navy for the research program at Point Mugu, California, he was almost totally intractable, butting and biting everyone. A trainer, Deborah Duffield, spent time with him, and eventually, his name shortened to Tuffy, he became one of the Navy's prize pupils, working freely in the open ocean, and diving to depths of 1,000 feet. Dr. S. H. Ridgway, then the veterinarian at the Point Mugu project, paid Tuffy the ultimate compliment: he dedicated his book *Mammals of the Sea: Biology and Medicine* to him.*

There are well-documented cases of wild dolphins that have permitted people to play and swim with them. Off the coast of Wales, a particularly large animal regularly allowed divers to swim with him in the open ocean (Dobbs 1977, 1978). When Dr. Horace Dobbs described Donald, the animal was curious and mischievous, given not only to initiating encounters with human divers but also to disrupting diving classes, fishing operations, and attempts to film him. He would lift the anchor of a moored boat and then tow the boat away, the anchor chain in his mouth. (One of the boats was the "7-tonne yacht, *Aquarius of Arne*.") The same animal, now known as Beaky, appears again in the literature of British delphinology, and in various locations including the Cornwall coast

*L. M. Herman also dedicated his book *Cetacean Behavior: Mechanisms and Functions* (1980) to the two bottlenose dolphins Kea and Puka, who had been stolen from his research facility in Hawaii and released in the open sea, probably to die.

and the waters of the Isle of Man. Beaky/Donald was a large male, estimated to be 11 1/2 feet long and to weigh 800 pounds, and by 1977, he was not only towing boats, but also behaving in a sexually aggressive way toward women divers, and, "on two occasions . . . attempting to carry women away with him . . . one woman enthroned on his nose like a ballerina" (Lawrence et al. 1979). Christina Lockyer (1978), one of Britain's foremost cetologists, has studied Beaky, and she is of the opinion that he was "solitary and probably an outcast." Since this obviously gregarious animal was never seen in the company of other dolphins, his behavior has been interpreted as highly abnormal for a wild bottlenose.

In 1955, at Opononi Beach on the North Island of New Zealand, a wild dolphin came into shoal water and allowed bathers to handle her, play ball with her, and even hold her head out of the water. She never behaved in an aggressive fashion like Donald/Beaky, and the interpretation of her actions, while no less curious, was much more relaxed and pleasant. She was named Opo, after the town, and she became such a celebrity that thousands of people would crowd the beach every weekend to see her:

It was noticed that the dolphin seemed both to hear and enjoy the laughter of the crowd, and the people were sure she liked an audience. When one of her tricks had produced a cry of approval, she would make an exultant leap, high out of the water, showing all her gleaming lines in the sunlight. But she never did this when bathers or children were near. [Alpers 1960]

Opo died in March 1956, apparently stranded in a tide pool, and the town of Opononi deeply mourned her loss, as did other New Zealanders who had heard of this unique animal. Saayman and Tayler (1973) described another incident where wild bottlenoses allowed humans to handle and even ride them: in Fish Hoek Bay, off South Africa, two females came into the area where people were swimming, and remained with the bathers as long as no person brought a strange object into the water; as soon as that happened, the dolphins swam away.

It is altogether too easy to identify with these winsome creatures, and to ascribe to them human qualities that they simply do not possess. They are undoubtedly "intelligent" in ways we may never be able to measure or understand; theirs is truly another world, lived for the most part in another medium. For a proper understanding of the bottlenose, we must see the animal as a dolphin, not as a semihuman that just happens to live in the water, waiting for us to strike up a conversation. M. C. Tavolga, summarizing a 1966 discussion of the behavior of the bottlenose, warned:

One of the most deceptive, and therefore one of the most dangerous, pitfalls awaiting the observer of dolphins is reliance on anthropomorphism. The bottlenose dolphin in particular, and many other dolphins in general, have built-in smiles, and exhibit types of behavior which endear them to the observer. Thus the observer is led to describe the behavior of the animal in human terms, and to ascribe to the animal motives that he cannot be sure are actually there, as he is incapable of seeing inside the mind of the animal to determine its purposes. Some descriptions of dolphin behavior abound in statements of purpose that can properly be ascribed only to humans. It is sincerely to be hoped that such accounts, most of which are misleading and probably inaccurate, will not gain credence in the literature to the extent that they are believed implicitly by other workers in the field.

SPINNER DOLPHIN

Stenella longirostris Gray 1828

If there is any good at all to be derived from the slaughter of hundreds of thousands of dolphins, it might be the exposure of the animals to scientific scrutiny. The spinner dolphin was almost totally unknown, even in those inshore waters where it is now known to be common: in his survey of Hawaiian mammals, for example, Tomich (1969) wrote that the spinner is "apparently widespread in tropical and temperate open seas; said to be common in Hawaiian waters."

Before 1963, when spinners were first captured and exhibited at Sea Life Park in Hawaii, almost nothing was known about this species, and although it appeared in various early works on cetology (under numerous different names), its appearance was almost invariably accompanied by categorical admissions of ignorance. In 1889, for example, F. W. True made the following assessment of the genus (at that time known as *Prodelphinus*):

The genus comprises a large number of nominal species, for the most part founded upon single skulls. Nearly every large collection contains a considerable number of skulls which may be assigned to this genus. It is found, however, in many cases that when a large number of these skulls is brought together they tend to form a continuous series. The differences between the extremes of these series are often striking and perfectly definable, but in the middle they melt away and elude definition. From this fact and from the absence of material the task of revising the species of this genus is a very difficult and disheartening one.

In 1938 Fraser wrote, "A host of species has been described, about none of which is there very much information concerning habits. Many of the forms are known only from skulls, but here we shall confine description to the more noteworthy species of which there is at least some account of external appearance." In his 1940 discussion of the cetaceans of the world, Kellogg resolved the problem by ignoring it completely, and does not mention the species at all. In a paper that was published in 1966, Fraser wrote (of the genus now known as *Stenella*):

It seems likely that most of these dolphins are gregarious. It would be helpful to know about the composition of the schools of these and other species. . . . Systematic collecting might provide some of the answers; at least it would assuredly produce more positive information than the sporadic trickle of specimens on which cetologists, for the past 200 years, have had to base their results.

The situation has changed so drastically in the past fifteen years or so that the problem is no longer one of too few specimens, but too many. Hundreds of thousands of dolphins of the genus *Stenella* have been killed "incidentally" in the eastern tropical Pacific tuna fishery, and the literature on these species has increased accordingly. By 1978—just twelve years after Fraser complained about the "sporadic trickle of specimens"—Pryor and Norris could write: "Thousands of porpoise specimens have been measured, dissected, computerized, and compared, so that we now probably know more about *Stenella* biology, physiology, and systematics than about any other small cetacean." These thousands of specimens had been killed in the tuna fishery, but even before this problem arose, the spinner dolphin was being exhibited at Sea Life Park in Hawaii, and it was becoming something less than a complete mystery.

When the oceanarium opened in 1963, there were four spinners exhibited there; animals which had been caught offshore in the waters of the Hawaiian Islands. Since they were so rare, they quickly became the focus of some rather intensive studies, and cetologists from all over the world came to look at the first captive spinners. (The name *longirostris* simply means "long beak.") Masaharu Nishiwaki, one of Japan's foremost cetologists, saw the animals in Hawaii and wrote, "Sea Life Park . . . has a beautiful ocean dolphin whose snout is longer than that of *S. longirostris*. It may be a new species." (Nishiwaki 1967) The animals seen in Hawaii were fairly small, slender dolphins with a long narrow snout. The maximum length for this species is about 7 feet (2.1 meters) and adults weigh between 120 and 135 pounds. The general coloration is muted, and consists of a dark dorsal field or "cape," a lighter band below, and lighter underparts. There is an eye-to-flipper stripe, and the upper part of the beak is usually darker than the lower part. They are timid, gentle animals, and it was discovered that they would perform their unique aerial maneuvers in captivity; the dolphins would leap into the air and rotate several times on their long axis before splashing down.

While those spinners were entertaining the visitors at Sea Life Park, however, other spinners were drowning in the tuna nets and being unceremoniously kicked overboard. The tuna fishermen were "setting on porpoise," which meant that they would use the highly visible schools of dolphins (mostly spinners and the spotted dolphin, *Stenella attenuata*) to indicate the presence of yellowfin tuna. The association between the dolphins and the tuna is still poorly understood, but as soon as it was discovered that the presence of dolphins meant the presence of tuna, the fishermen changed their tactics from a hook-and-line to a purse seine operation. As the nets were drawn around the tuna, the dolphins would become entangled in the mesh and drown, or be hauled aboard the boats alive, then thrown overboard. Initially, the fishermen did not know how to get rid of the porpoises once they had them in the net, "so they hauled the entire contents of the net on board, sorted out the fish, and then threw the porpoise overboard, often injuring or killing many of them" (Perrin 1968).

In 1972, the first year that an attempt was made to keep some sort of record of the number of porpoises killed, the total was well over 300,000. (This is an estimate based on the extrapolation of data from a limited number of tuna boats with observers aboard. Additional information was gathered from foreign boats which did not have observers, but reported their catch figures to investigators.) Between 1960—about the time the tuna fishery converted from pole-and-line fishing to setting on porpoise—and 1975, the number of porpoises killed has been estimated at between three and five million.*

With the passage of the Marine Mammal Protection Act of 1972, it became illegal for Americans to harm cetaceans or other marine mammals. Initially, the tunamen were exempted from the provisions of the act, and were only required to abide by quotas that were to be set in 1974. In the two years that the fishermen had to research and resolve their problem and bring their porpoise kills to a "near-zero level," they did absolutely nothing but fish in the same manner. The total number of spotters and spinners killed in 1972 was estimated at 334,800, and in 1973 the number was 175,300 (Perrin et al. 1975). (The authors pointed out that "these estimates must be considered minimal," because only dead animals were counted. "No attempt was made to take into account the injured animals some of which can be presumed to have died after release from the net.") After the two-year "grace period" had expired, conservation groups brought suit against the National Marine Fisheries Service for failing to comply with the Marine Mammal Protection Act and allowing the fishermen to operate in direct contravention of that act. After a nineteen-month court battle (during which the fishing went on as usual), U.S. District Court judge Charles Richey handed down a decision in favor of the porpoises. Part of that decision reads as follows:

The court realizes that the per-ton cost of catching tuna in some ocean areas may rise if purse-seiners are prevented from fishing "on porpoise" until the requirements of the MMPA are satisfied. But steps which ensure the protection and conservation of our natural environment must, almost inevitably, impose temporary hardships on those commercial interests which have long benefited by exploiting that environment. The people of this country, speaking through

---

*By far the most common species caught in the nets has been the Pacific spotter, followed by the spinner. Also involved—but to a lesser degree—were the common dolphin, the bottlenose dolphin, and the very rare Fraser's dolphin. It was not only the United States fishing boats that ensnared and killed the dolphins, but also the fleets of Canada, the Congo, Costa Rica, Ecuador, South Korea, Mexico, Netherlands Antilles, New Zealand, Nicaragua, Panama, Senegal, Spain, and Venezuela (Allen and Goldsmith 1979).

their Congress, declared that porpoise and other marine mammals must be protected from the harmful and possibly irreversible effects of man's activities.

An appeal by the tuna fishermen allowed them to continue unrestricted fishing until the end of 1975, by which time another 100,000 porpoises had been killed.

By then, however, the fishermen knew how to release porpoises from their nets: they would throw the engines into reverse when approximately half the net had been hauled in, a process known as "backing down." This sinks the corkline at the far end of the net, allowing the porpoises to escape over the line, which is now below the surface. (The tuna remain lower in the nets, and do not swim out over the top.) The addition of the "Medina panel" and the "super apron," both fine-meshed net sections that prevent porpoises from becoming entangled, also helped to lower the porpoise kill figures.

It was a period of chaos. The government did not know how many porpoises there were, and therefore it could not predict whether these huge kills would endanger the species. The fishermen were trying to lower the porpoise mortality rate without sacrificing their all-important profits.* The scientists were attempting to discover the answers to all sorts of critical questions: What kinds of porpoises are these? How many are there? What do they eat? Why do the porpoises and the tuna stay together? How do we get the porpoises out of the nets?—or, put another way, how do we keep them from coming in in the first place? As the behaviorists and zoologists wrestled with these and other problems, the fishermen continued setting on porpoise. Although the government has now assigned maximum kill figures to the fishermen, the compromise is satisfactory neither to the fishermen nor to those who would protect the porpoises. For 1977, the limit was 62,429; for 1978 it was 51,945; for 1979 it was 41,610; and for 1980 it was 31,150. (While these figures may still seem high for "incidental" kills, it is important to remember that the number of porpoises killed in 1972 was more than ten times the quota for 1980.)

The quota for 1981 (and for each of the following four years) is 20,500 porpoises, but another problem has cropped up which may render the previous controversy moot. Aerial surveys of the eastern Pacific

fishing area indicated that the earlier population estimates—upon which the kill quotas were based—were too high, and there may be fewer dolphins than was originally suspected. If this is the case, the government may be forced to declare the species endangered, which would mean no more setting on porpoises at all. If this were to happen, the fishermen have threatened to sell their ships and their services under foreign flags, where there are no restrictions on the number of porpoises that can be killed. If the government rules against the fishermen, they will fish under foreign flags, and if it rules that they may continue to set on porpoises, another 20,500 porpoises will be killed every year. This would mean that despite its Marine Mammal Protection Act of 1972, the United States continues to be the country that condones the slaughter of more cetaceans than any other nation in the world.

W. F. Perrin (1972, 1975a, 1975b), studying the spinners caught in the tuna fishery, has identified four races or subspecies, but he has not assigned names to them because "the taxonomy is unsettled, and the nomenclature used here [1975b] is provisional." The physical characteristics of animals taken from different areas are distinctive enough to warrant their nomination as subspecies:

One that occurs near the coast of Central America is relatively long, slender, and gray. A second race, called "eastern spinner" occurs along the coast of Mexico and seaward about 800 km and is relatively short, slender, and gray. A third, called "whitebelly spinner," occurs in far offshore waters west to about 145 W long., and is relatively short, robust, and white below. A fourth form occurs in Hawaiian waters and possibly to the south and west and is relatively long, robust, and white below.*

The dorsal fins of the various races also differ. The easternmost races ("Costa Rican" and "eastern" spinner) have the most pronounced reversal at the tip; in these animals the fin looks very much as if it had been put on backward. The unusual characteristic is not apparent in the Hawaiian or "whitebelly" races. Mature males, again in the easternmost varieties, also show the development of a peculiar "ventral keel," the function of which is unknown. (Perrin [1972] suggested that it might serve as a secondary sex characteristic, to enable estrous females to identify males of the same species in mixed aggregations.) This keel is a

---

*These fishermen should not be viewed as a group of rugged individualists struggling against a capricious government ruling that threatened their livelihood for the sake of a couple of dolphins. The American Tunaboat Association is a well-organized group backed by the enormous power and resources of some giant multinational food corporations, including Ralston-Purina (Chicken of the Sea), H. J. Heinz (Star-Kist), and Castle & Cook (Bumble Bee). These corporations own a substantial proportion of the tuna fleet.

*In 1979, Perrin, Sloan, and Henderson published a paper in which a stock of spinners from south of the Equator in the eastern Pacific was identified as "modally different from dolphins of the same species just to the north in coloration, size, shape and skeleton." These animals most resemble the Hawaiian spinners, but they are substantially different from the "eastern whitebelly" spinners found just to the north, off Costa Rica.

regular feature, composed of ordinary connective tissue, and not a tumor or other abnormal growth. Spinners have more teeth than any other dolphin—except perhaps the subspecies of the common dolphin *Delphinus delphis tropicalis*—with 46 to 65 per side in each jaw, or well over 200 in many individuals.

Although the study of this species has been concentrated on the Pacific populations, spinners are also inhabitants of the tropical Atlantic. They have been reported from the Caribbean (Caldwell et al. 1971), as well as the waters of Senegal and Venezuela. In most instances, species identification was confirmed by observations of the animals actually spinning, but there have been some records based on the examination of skulls and on infrequent stranding records. Because of its pelagic habits, the spinner is not often found

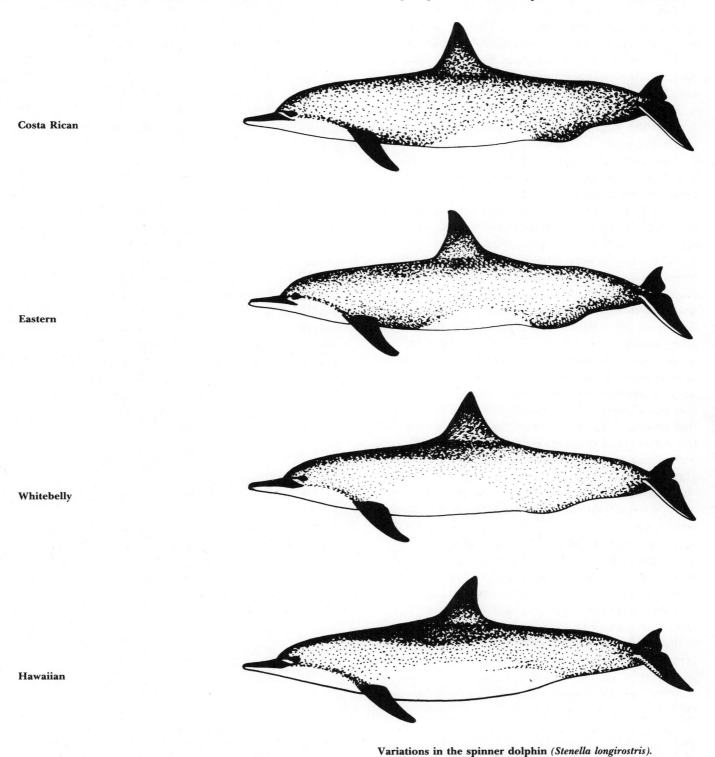

Costa Rican

Eastern

Whitebelly

Hawaiian

Variations in the spinner dolphin *(Stenella longirostris).* **Note particularly the shape of the dorsal fin and the ventral keels. (After Perrin [1975b])**

stranded, but there are a few records of single strandings (Schmidly and Shane 1978; Shane 1977) and two instances of mass stranding, both in Florida. Layne (1965) reported 36 animals that stranded on Dog Island on the Gulf Coast in 1961, and Mead and colleagues (1980) described 28 that came ashore in the area of Casey Key, near Sarasota, in July 1976. The total number of dolphins in the school was estimated at between 50 and 150 animals, and despite efforts to save them (some were taken to the Mote Marine Laboratory in Sarasota, others to Sea World at Orlando), all those that came ashore died. Necropsies did not reveal anything unusual that might explain the stranding, but as Mead and colleagues (1980) point out, "The causes of mass strandings are still very little understood." Apparently, the dolphins made a considerable amount of noise as they came ashore, and the authors reported "much squealing and crying" which probably represented the distress calls of the animals, unimpeded by water.

Perrin (1975b) quotes Pernetty's 1769 observation of animals that "leaped at least three or four feet high and turned round not less than three times in the air, as if they had been on a spit," and there have been other early references to the unusual actions of this species. In 1963, Hester and colleagues published a description of the spinning behavior of animals that they referred to as *Stenella microps* in the tropical Pacific, but which are now known to have been *S. longirostris.* They wrote that the animals could spin clockwise or counterclockwise, and that the same animal "could reverse direction in subsequent leaps." They were unable to assign any function to the spinning; it was not to dislodge parasites (some had none); nor was it a courtship display (both sexes and all ages indulge); and they concluded "that some other explanation must be sought for this behavior." (Whittow [1977] speculated that the animals keep warm by producing additional metabolic heat through spinning.)

Some insights into the behavior of spinners were gained at Sea Life Park (Pryor 1973, 1975) and even in the tuna nets (Norris et al. 1978; Pryor and Kang 1980), but only observation in the wild, unimpeded by tanks or nets, could provide information about the natural history of the spinner dolphin. This sort of thing is not easy to accomplish for animals that are primarily residents of the open ocean and highly mobile besides, but an opportunity presented itself at Kealakekua Bay off the island of Hawaii, where the animals appeared regularly:

These Kealakekua porpoises represented one of those rare opportunities a naturalist occasionally encounters. Sometimes a rare or difficult-to-observe species presents, at some special place or time, an unparalleled chance to look into its life patterns. The trouble with watching porpoises is that they are shy and fast-moving. One may spend the greatest part of his time just trying to find the animals, as we had done off Oahu. These Kealakekua Bay porpoises came in virtually every day to rest, and equally important, they did so in a limpid bay that is usually flat calm. [Norris 1974]

From 1970 to 1973, Norris and Dohl (and numerous assistants) watched the spinners of Kealakekua Bay. Norris published some of his observations in the *The Porpoise Watcher* (1974), but it was not until 1980 that the full report came out.

It was seen that the Hawaiian spinners are nocturnal feeders, moving inshore in the morning after eating and resting for the better part of the day.* The nocturnal feeding behavior could not be observed, but during the day the spinners could be seen as they approached the bay. In the periods that Norris and Dohl characterized as "subsidence into rest," the dolphins gradually slowed down, and the schools became more tightly compressed. After a period of "subsidence" that might take as long as two hours, the dolphins achieved what the researchers called "rest," which was defined by the lack of aerial behavior and an increase in synchronous swimming and diving. The interdependence of these animals—a factor that made them particularly difficult to train individually in captivity—prompted Norris (1974) to write, "They ceased to act like porpoises and began to act like herrings." (At no time in this discussion do Norris and Dohl suggest that the animals are actually asleep, although they did write, "Once quiescent, resting schools are difficult to disrupt." They must always be alert for possible predators—especially sharks—and this has been suggested as a reason for their moving into shallow waters.)

By midafternoon the dolphins begin to move around more actively for a short period that Norris and Dohl called "arousal." During this time, they exhibited "sudden aerial behavior—a complete spin or headslap for instance," which was interpreted as a signal to other resting dolphins that feeding time was approaching. The highest levels of aerial activity were seen during arousal, and later during feeding. Norris and Dohl catalog the aerial behavior of these energetic little dolphins and also give a plausible suggestion for the function of this unique behavior.

The activity that gives this animal its common name is accomplished in the following manner:

---

*These observations, of course, can apply only to those spinners that have an inshore area to move into. The offshore varieties may also rest during the day, but since they live hundreds of miles from the nearest land, they cannot do it in protected bays and lagoons.

The spinner dolphin rushes to the surface as if about to make an arcing leap, and the last instant, when most of the body is out of the water, tips its flukes slightly and flexes its tail stock, causing the airborne animal to spin about its longitudinal axis. As many as four revolutions may be made in the course of such a leap (Hester et al. 1963). The dolphin may literally appear to flicker as flippers, flukes, and the dorsal fin flash by. The animal falls back into the water, usually partly on its side, and its rapidly rotating body scoops out a hollow of water around the sinking animal. The hollow then collapses producing a welter of spray and a discernible clap of sound. [Norris and Dohl 1980]

The aerial repertoire for the spinner also includes the "tail over head leap," which the authors describe as "the most active and perhaps physically demanding behavior pattern. . . . The animal bursts from the water at a rather high angle, slings its tail over its head in a wide arc, usually trailing a spiral of spray, and enters tail first, often slapping its tail flukes against the water with a loud 'thwack' in the process." Spinners also indulge in backslaps, headslaps, and tailslaps, all of which make noise. It is, in fact, the noisemaking aspect of these actions that the authors feel is their most important property: they serve as communication signals over distance or when vision would not be useful. (Captive spinners at Sea Life Park were recorded to display their aerial behavior most energetically at night.) These dolphins, like most other odontocetes, are believed to be echolocators, with clicks and whistles that can be directly aimed, but the sounds gener-

The spinner dolphin, *Stenella longirostris*, is able to make as many as four rotations on the long axis while in the air.

ated by splashes and slaps are omnidirectional, and probably serve a social rather than a food-finding function.*

The activity cycle of spinners, feeding at night and resting during the day, can serve—at least in theory—to explain the association of spinners and spotters in the open waters of the Pacific:

Spinner dolphins may seek the schools of spotted dolphins for refuge during rest in the open sea. We believe this may be true because spotted dolphins feed during the day, while spinners are nocturnal feeders, and spinner dolphins have been observed to join spotted dolphin schools in the morning. . . . If such rest association occurs, the spinner dolphins are associating with alert animals in this oceanic area. Related to this the yellowfin tuna seine fishermen chase and encircle dolphins to catch tuna, most fish apparently follow the spotted dolphins. Since the association between tuna and dolphin is probably food based, the tuna may be following the dolphin species that are actively searching for food. That is, like the tuna, the spinner dolphin may follow active dolphin schools.

Because there are no bays and lagoons in the open Pacific, the spinners substitute schools of spotters as their "places of refuge."

In captivity (they have only been exhibited at Sea Life Park in Hawaii) the spinner has been described as "timid, easily frightened, fearful of objects, highly dependent on the presence of other dolphins . . . and not easily induced to allow itself to be touched, to manipulate objects, or to wear equipment or props of any kind" (Defran and Pryor 1980). Describing the development of the first porpoise show in Hawaii, Pryor (1975) wrote, "It was easy to decide that spinners would go in Whaler's Cove. They were bona fide, authentic Hawaiian porpoises . . . [and] the spectacular spin would look best out under the sky. . . ." The spinners performed their spectacular in-unison spins from 1963 onward, but they have proven to be too much trouble to train, and as of 1981, they are no longer used in the shows (Pryor, personal communication).

In the tuna nets, these high-strung animals behave in the expected fashion. (One of the earliest suggestions for resolving the problem of porpoises in the nets was to train a captive to lead the wild ones out of the nets, but given the nature of the spinner's personality, it was hardly the ideal animal to haul out to

sea in a tuna boat and then dump into the sea to perform intricate—and individual—maneuvers.) Perrin and Hunter (1972) experimented with five spinners, three trained and two "naive" (freshly captured) animals, trying to determine how to get the animals out of the nets once they were trapped. The animals in the experiments frequently failed to escape through the openings provided for this purpose, and the authors concluded, "It is to be expected that great difficulty will be encountered in inducing wild porpoise to pass through an opening in the perimeter of a purse-seine enclosure."

As part of the continuing program to resolve the problems of dolphins in the nets, various behaviorists actually entered the nets during the fishing procedure to observe the dolphins. These studies (Norris et al. 1978; Pryor and Kang 1980) supported the earlier descriptions of the nature of the spinners. They remained subordinate to the spotters, and they also whistled more and blew more bubbles than the spotters, both of which actions have been interpreted as distress signals (Pryor and Kang 1980). Because of their constant movement, trapped spinners were more likely to come in contact with the mesh of the nets, and therefore more likely to become entangled. It was further reported that there was a suppression of aerial behavior in the trapped spinners, "another indication of the level of fear in these animals" (Norris et al. 1978).

In the early history of the tuna fishery, there were no records kept of the numbers of dolphins of various species that were killed. They were considered a nuisance to the fishermen, since a lot of time—and therefore a lot of money—had to be spent in getting them out of the nets. They were also an important element in the fishing industry, however, since the fishermen would have a difficult time locating the tuna without sighting the dolphins first. In a 1969 discussion of the problem, Perrin asked, "Will the fishery remain viable if pressure on the porpoise populations is sufficient to depress them?" and "What is the nature of the relationship between the porpoise and the tuna?" The fishermen did not address these problems immediately; they simply continued to set on porpoise. According to the data collected by the Porpoise Stocks Workshop convened in 1979, the following are the numbers of spinners killed from three of the four stocks, the eastern, northern whitebelly and southern whitebelly; the Hawaiian spinners are not involved in the fishery.

1973: 64,877
1974: 61,753
1975: 69,722
1976: 38,608
1977: 5,031
1978: 4,351

*A similar hypothesis has been advanced for the "noisy" aerial behavior of the dusky dolphins in Patagonia (Würsig and Würsig 1980). These dolphins feed during the day, so their activities can be more easily observed. Their "noisiest" leaps, when the dolphins land on their backs or sides, are presumed to communicate their location to other distant dolphins, or perhaps even to herd the anchovies on which they feed into tighter schools to facilitate feeding.

During the 1979 season, 1,410 spinners were killed (Allen and Goldsmith 1980). The spinners are killed in considerably lower numbers than the spotters. For both species, however, the numbers killed in the early years of the fishery seem to have significantly depleted the populations. According to William Aron (quoted in Cahn 1980), "We have so much more data today than we had in 1976 that the new population assessment is probably more accurate than the old one. The tuna fleet over the past three years has done a remarkable job in reducing mortalities. But it appears that serious damage to the stocks was done in the early years of purse seining in the eastern Pacific."

CLYMENE DOLPHIN

Stenella clymene Gray 1850

From a skull in the British Museum collection, J. E. Gray (1850) described what he regarded as a new species, *Stenella clymene*. With the passage of time, the species was incorporated into other descriptions—in 1889 True regarded it as synonymous with *Prodelphinus froenatus*—and by the middle of the twentieth century, it had virtually ceased to exist in the cetological literature. Since dolphins do not read this literature, however, the species did not disappear but continued to swim—unrecorded, to be sure—in its usual haunts.

In 1965, two female dolphins—believed to be mother and calf—were collected at Bunces Pass, near St. Petersburg, Florida, and while they were colored much like the spinner dolphin, their snouts were shorter. The animals were brought to Marineland at St. Petersburg, where they "lived for a short time" (Caldwell and Caldwell 1975). Photographs of the dolphins appeared in the Caldwells' paper, and also in Leatherwood, Caldwell, and Winn's 1976 *Whales, Dolphins and Porpoises of the Western North Atlantic*, where the authors wrote that these "small, short-snouted dol-

phins . . . are spinners, although their classification is uncertain. There may be several species or geographical races of spinners in the Atlantic." In their 1975 description, Caldwell and Caldwell wrote, "This dolphin appears to belong to the same species or form as that described by Cadenat and Doutre [1958]," and also referred to several conversations with W. F. Perrin, in which the "short-snouted spinner dolphin" was discussed.

At the Marine Mammal Meetings in San Diego in 1977, Perrin, Mitchell, van Bree, and Caldwell presented the first paper in which the short-snouted spinner was nominated as a new species: "*S. clymene* closely resembles *S. longirostris* in color pattern and tooth shape and is obviously closely related to it, but it has a short, broad rostrum, is more robust in build, and has fewer teeth." One of the problems with this species is that its skull, because of the shorter rostrum, closely resembles that of *Stenella coeruleoalba*. Therefore, when skulls were found that could not be referred to *longirostris* because of the obviously short snout, they were assumed to be *coeruleoalba*. As Perrin and colleagues wrote in the description of *S. clymene*, "This discordant resemblance of the skull of *clymene* to that of one species and the external appearance to that of another perhaps accounts for the longstanding uncertainty concerning the existence of the species."

Perrin and colleagues (1981) examined many of the records and the specimens that had been used in the various descriptions—including the British Museum specimen that Gray had described in 1850—and concluded that the species was indeed a valid one. Therefore, their full description of the clymene dolphin is entitled "A Rediscovered Tropical Dolphin of the Atlantic," and it is not a new description that is being published, but a "redescription." In this paper they suggest that the animal should be known as the "clymene dolphin," from the name originally used by Gray. (In Greek mythology, Clymene was the daughter of Oceanus by Tethys, the wife of Iapetus, and the mother of Atlas, Prometheus, and Epimetheus.)

In general appearance, the clymene dolphin resembles the spinner, with a dark "cape," a lateral band of a lighter grayish or brownish color, and white underparts. It is more robust than the spinner, and of course its snout is shorter. It therefore has fewer teeth, averaging about 38 to 49 per row, while the spinner has 47 to 64. The tip of the beak is black, and there is a light stripe that runs from the junction of the beak and the melon to the blowhole. Very little is known of the behavior of these animals in the wild, although Perrin and colleagues (1981) have reported that they have been seen to spin, but "the spinning leaps observed . . . were not as high or complex as those exhibited by the closely related spinner dolphin." A photograph reproduced in *Whales, Dolphins and Porpoises of the Western North Atlantic* shows these animals riding the bow wave, so this behavior can be added to our limited knowledge of their repertoire. Perrin and colleagues report that this dolphin has been observed at sea only in deep water—250 to 5,000 meters or deeper—and that they probably feed on small fishes and squid, like their better-known relatives.

The range of the clymene dolphin is still uncertain, but a review of the literature reveals reports of this animal from Florida (Caldwell and Caldwell 1975), the Gulf Coast of Texas (Schmidly et al. 1972; Schmidly and Shane 1978),* the Caribbean (Caldwell et al. 1971), the mid-Atlantic, the deeper offshore waters of West Africa (Cadenat and Doutre 1958), and New Jersey (Ulmer 1980). From these records, it can be seen that the species is known only from the temperate and tropical waters of the Atlantic.

In a discussion of the "historical zoogeography of tropical pelagic dolphins," Perrin, Mitchell, and van Bree (1978) have written, "At least five species [*S. attenuata/frontalis, S. plagiodon, S. longirostris, S. clymene, S. coeruleoalba*] of the delphinid species *Stenella* exist in the tropical Atlantic, whereas only three of these species [*S. attenuata, S. longirostris, S. coeruleoalba*] occur in the other tropical waters of the world." The authors suggest that, "during Pleistocene glacial periods, the Cape of Good Hope (southern tip of Africa) was a barrier isolating the tropical Atlantic from the Indopacific," and during interglacial periods, the Cape and its attendant currents (the Agulhas and Benguela) might have "acted as a one-way filter admitting tropical, Indopacific pelagic forms to the tropical Atlantic." It is interesting to note that the clymene dolphin and its close relative, the spinner, share the same range,

---

*Since many of these records were obtained before the "rediscription," they naturally refer to different species which have since been shown to be the clymene. For example, the three specimens described by Schmidly et al. (1972) were called *Stenella frontalis*, but when the photographs were examined, it was seen that they were clymene dolphins.

The short-snouted spinner dolphin, *Stenella clymene* (top) compared with the long-snouted spinner, *Stenella longirostris*.

both species having been recorded from Florida, Texas, the Caribbean and the coast of Africa.

When a clymene dolphin stranded at Ocean City, New Jersey, in June 1976, F. A. Ulmer (1980) wrote that it was "one of the most exciting cetological events in New Jersey in recent years." A 6 1/2-foot (1.86-meter) male had been found alive on the beach by a policeman, and despite efforts to send the animal back to sea, it reappeared on the beach several hours later, "dead this time." It was an exciting event because of the rarity of the species, but also because most other records were from tropical or subtropical waters, so this animal was probably a stray or, as the scientists say, "extralimital."

SPOTTED DOLPHIN

Stenella attenuata Gray 1846

Throughout the tropical oceans of the world, there can be found a group of slender spotted dolphins that have been a source of confusion to cetologists for centuries. Because they are creatures of the open ocean—and also because they are to be found far from the normal shipping lanes as well as far from land—they are not often seen. Early studies of small cetaceans (characterized by the usual nomenclatural changes) gave these animals short shrift. True (1889) examined only skeletal material and other scientist's descriptions, and combined three species: *Prodelphinus malayanus, P. attenuatus* and *P. froenatus.* He wrote, "The relationships of these three species (if such they be) are so close that I have thought best to consider them conjointly." In 1938 Fraser was still referring to the species as *Prodelphinus,* and aside from identifying the characteristic that separates this genus from the otherwise similar *Delphinus* (the palate of the common dolphin is deeply grooved, while that of *Prodelphinus*

(= *Stenella*) shows no such grooving), he supplies very little information. He names six species *(attenuatus, plagiodon, froenatus, malayanus, coeruleoalbus,* and *euphrosyne),* but then wrote, ". . . in none of these species is coloration sufficiently distinctive to make identification an easy matter." Of the six species discussed, none was identified as occurring in the Pacific Ocean, an obvious indication of the lack of observers, not the lack of dolphins.

Kellogg (1940) wrote that "great schools of . . . *Stenella graffmani* are frequently seen in the Pacific Ocean in coastal waters northward at least to Acapulco, Guerrero, Mexico, and southward to Gorgona Island off Colombia." In 1966, Hershkovitz repeated Kellogg's distribution for the species, but it was obvious that the great pelagic herds of Pacific spotted dolphins were still to be discovered. In a 1966 discussion of the genus *Stenella,* F. C. Fraser wrote that cetologists needed more than the "sporadic trickle" of specimens that they had had to work with over the past two hundred years.

Unbeknownst to Fraser, at the very time his remarks were published, the tuna fishermen of the eastern tropical Pacific had discovered the spotters, and they had been killing hundreds of thousands of them every year since 1959.

In the mid-1960s, a young graduate student in zoology named William F. Perrin, working on his Ph.D. dissertation on *Stenella* at UCLA, heard that some of the animals were somehow involved in the tuna fishery. (In the past, tuna had been caught by chumming them up with bait until the fish were feeding in such a frenzy that they would bite anything, even unbaited hooks, and they were hauled out of the water as fast as the men on the rods could yank them up.) By about 1960 setting on porpoise had largely replaced the hook-and-line techniques, and by 1966—the same year that Fraser's plaint was published—62 percent of the tuna caught in the Pacific were caught in association with dolphins (Perrin 1969c). The species of dolphins most involved in this fishery are the spinner and the spotter. Fraser's "sporadic trickle" of specimens had become a roaring waterfall.

The fishermen initially look for a commotion on the horizon which would indicate the presence of feeding seabirds or leaping dolphins (or both), which might indicate the presence of tuna. For reasons that are still unknown, schools of tuna congregate beneath the herds of dolphins, so the fishermen look for the dolphins' usual commotion (these dolphins are renowned for their leaping and splashing, and they congregate in herds that sometimes number in the thousands, so they are not particularly difficult to see). When the tuna boat is within range, speedboats known as pongas are lowered, and these small boats with high-powered outboard motors herd the dolphins into a tightly milling herd. When the dolphins have been compactly herded, the seiner lowers its net and surrounds the herd, attempting to trap the dolphins and the tuna, which are still congregating beneath them.

At first the mile-long purse seine is open, making a "wall" around the dolphins and the tuna that is open at the bottom, but for some reason—perhaps having to do with the much colder water at the 200-meter depth of the bottom of the net—the animals being herded rarely escape beneath it. During this circling operation, the pongas continue to roar around the perimeter of the school, creating an additional barrier to the dolphins by their noise and wake. When the dolphin school is completely encircled by the net, it is "pursed": the fishermen close it at the bottom by a cable that passes through a series of rings, and everything in it is trapped. The net is then drawn in through a power block, one of the inventions that made this sort of operation possible, and it is stacked methodically on deck as the enclosure gets smaller. In the early history of this fishery, everything in the net was hauled aboard; the valuable tuna were kept and the dolphins and trash fish were dumped overboard.

Although the tuna fishermen had no reason to publicize the massive slaughter of dolphins, the information managed to leak out, and it soon became apparent that the dolphins were dying in numbers almost impossible to imagine. Extrapolating from the early—and irregular—data accumulated by the fishermen, scientists have postulated that as many as 100,-000 dolphins were killed in 1959, even before the entire fleet had converted to the purse-seining techniques (Smith 1979). By 1960, when more boats had been converted, an estimated half million dolphins died in the nets.* The figures were not easy to obtain,

*Before scientists began their examination of the dolphins caught in this fishery, there were no records kept of the different

but eventually the U.S. Government—under tremendous pressure from various humane and conservation groups—began to monitor the tuna fishery. In a report published in 1979 by the National Marine Fisheries Service's Southwest Fisheries Center at La Jolla, California, the total number of dolphins killed between 1959 and 1972 was estimated at 3,796,658. Even these figures are considered low, because they included only dead animals: "No attempt was made to take into account the injured animals some of which can be presumed to have died after release from the net" (Perrin et al. 1975).

It was the dolphins from this fishery that the scientists began to study, and from a little-known animal, the spotter (and the spinner as well) soon became some of the most intensively studied of all small cetaceans. In a few short years, the various types of *Stenella* were being examined from every conceivable viewpoint: they were measured, weighed, photographed, and counted; they were observed at sea and in the nets; parasites were identified, and predators (other than the fishermen) were observed as well. Catalogs of behavior—known as ethograms—were compiled; different populations were identified; and steps were finally being taken toward the identification of the individual species.

In 1968, Perrin was referring to the Pacific spotted dolphin as *Stenella graffmani*, but by 1975 he recognized it as *S. attenuata* with three subspecies, only one of which was named. (It was *S. attenuata graffmani;* the other two are identified as *Stenella attenuata* subspecies A and B.) In 1975b Perrin (whose dissertation was entitled *Variation of Spotted and Spinner Porpoise (Genus Stenella) in the Eastern Tropical Pacific and Hawaii,* and who is considered the expert on this taxonomically troublesome genus) concluded that there was only one species, and wrote, ". . . I therefore provisionally apply the name *Stenella attenuata* to the eastern Pacific and Hawaiian spotted porpoise, implying that a single species exists from the west coast of the Americas to at least the southern Atlantic and that True was correct in referring Gray's (1846) type to this species."*

According to his careful examination of the specimens collected in the tuna fishery and elsewhere, Perrin has identified two races from the eastern tropical Pacific, one from Hawaii, and a fourth from south of the Galápagos Islands (Perrin et al. 1979). In the tropical Pacific the coastal form is relatively large, robust,

species. Later studies revealed that the commonest species used for setting on porpoise was the spotter, followed by the spinner, the common dolphin, and some other species, but in much lesser numbers.

*In a more recent paper, however, Perrin, Mitchell, and van Bree (1978), have revived the possibility of more than one species, and they refer to the spotted dolphins of the Atlantic, Pacific, and Indian Oceans as *Stenella attenuata/frontalis?*.

and heavily spotted; the offshore race is smaller and more slender, spotted to a varying degree; and the Hawaiian form is smaller yet, and less spotted than the other two forms. The "southern" ones (from south of the Galápagos) are less heavily spotted and smaller than their northern counterparts. All four forms are differentiated by variations in cranial dimensions in addition to size and coloration, and they have not been observed or captured together.

However many varieties there are—and whatever their names—all the spotted dolphins share certain characteristics.* They are small, slender animals, reaching a maximum length of about 8 feet (2.44 meters) and a weight of 250 pounds (112.5 kilograms). The spotting pattern varies from population to population, but it generally consists of a lightly spotted dark dorsal area, and a lighter ventral area which is covered with dark spots. In mature animals there is a "cape" and an eye stripe, as well as variations in the coloration of the mouth. One of the identifying characteristics of this species (singular or plural) is the white-tipped beak of adults. (This appears in adolescent animals at about the age of four [Kasuya et al. 1974], but does not seem to be quite as prevalent in the eastern Pacific races.) After a gestation period of about eleven and a half months, a calf is born that is a uniform dark gray or purplish gray in color, with white ventral surfaces and no spots. As the animals mature, they pass through various stages, including a "two-tone" phase, and as they approach sexual maturity, more and more spots appear. Fully matured individuals are often seen in what has been referred to as a "fused stage," in which the spots have converged and overlapped to the extent that the animal appears to be an almost solid gray (Perrin 1969a).

The eastern spotted dolphin is an offshore species that Rice (1977) records from "the tropical Atlantic, Indian and Pacific Oceans." It has been observed from strandings and sightings in the South Atlantic; at the Cape of Good Hope and Cape Horn (Hershkovitz 1966); at Durban, South Africa (Best 1969); and the Solomon Islands (Dawbin 1966). Although the range occupied by these animals is vast, there appear to be some areas where they do not occur. Daugherty (1972) records only one stranding record from the coasts of California, and Perrin (1975a) could find "no recorded sightings of the spotted porpoise" in the

*Mitchell (1975) lists four possible names for the unresolved "spotted dolphins," but writes:

The species S. coeruleoalba and S. longirostris are well defined and accepted by most experts. In addition to these two species, there are probably two more species, both spotted. One occurs in all tropical seas, the other may be restricted to the Atlantic. There is no agreement on what these should be called. The following names each may belong to either of these two species: S. dubia (G. Cuvier, 1812), S. frontalis, (G. Cuvier, 1829), S. attenuata (Gray, 1846), S. plagiodon (Cope, 1866).

700-mile-wide band between the westernmost limits of the recorded range (at about 145°W) and Hawaiian waters. It has also been reported from the Seychelles and Sri Lanka in the Indian Ocean. Nishiwaki (1966) discussed two herds of dolphins that he identified as *Stenella attenuata,* which had been driven ashore in Japan by the *oikomi,* or drive-fishery, method. He asserts that this species is "very rare; this report is the first one from Japanese waters." Other Japanese observers, however, have not found the spotter so rare; Ohsumi (1972) lists the spotter as "common" around the middle of the islands of Japan, from Chiba Prefecture south to Miyazaki Prefecture, and also off the southern coast of Japan in the East China Sea. Miyazaki and colleagues (1974) list spotted dolphins as "fairly common, and [along with *Stenella coeruleoalba*] have been the object of commercial hunting at several places on the Pacific coast of Japan." For their detailed study, "Growth and Reproduction of *Stenella attenuata* in the Pacific coast of Japan" (1974), Kasuya, Miyazaki, and Dawbin examined 750 specimens from a total of 2,239 that were "caught by the driving method at Kawana or Futo on the east coast of Izu Peninsula, or at Taiji on the coast of Kii Peninsula." Approximately 20,000 dolphins of various species—mostly spotters and striped dolphins—are killed annually in Japan for human consumption. The animals are also used for food in Taiwan, where they are killed with hand harpoons. A drive fishery also exists in the Solomon Islands, but there the animals are destroyed for their teeth. As of 1966, when Dawbin studied this phenomenon, porpoise teeth were still a valid currency, and approximately 1,000 teeth were required to make a necklace that was worth A$50. Each spotter has about 150 usable teeth, so six or seven animals had to be killed to make one necklace. The dolphins would be driven into shallow water by the clanging together of stones. ("Noise is intensely disturbing to most of the local species of porpoise . . . some schools will not cross between two noise-making canoes spaced a half mile apart.") As the noise intensifies and the canoes close in, the dolphins "mill about frantically until some of those in the shallows of three or four feet of water suddenly plunge vertically and bury part of their heads in the softish sandy mud bottom. Here they remain with tails oscillating above the surface," until the people in the canoes and those on the beach rush in and drag them ashore. The heads are cut off and cooked to loosen the teeth, and some of the meat is eaten, "but there is far more meat than can be used and the wastage is great" (Dawbin 1966).

In the waters off Hawaii, spotters were collected and exhibited regularly at Sea Life Park. They were colloquially known as *kikos,* from the Hawaiian word for "spots." Under the direction of Karen Pryor, they were trained to perform various tricks, including jumping over bars, swimming through hoops, and playing water polo. The spotter is the fastest-swimming dolphin that has been accurately timed. Tests using two Hawaiian animals resulted in a maximum speed of 21.5 knots (almost 25 mph) for short sprints (Lang and Pryor 1966). This is considerably faster than the top speed of the bottlenose dolphin, usually considered to be a cetacean speedster, which was only 15 knots (Lang and Norris 1966). Two animals were used, according to the trainer, "because kikos hate solitude" (Pryor 1975).

The species has also been identified in the southwest Pacific between Japan and New Guinea (Miyazaki and Wada 1978), but the greatest concentration of these animals so far reported has been in the eastern tropical Pacific, where millions of them have been caught in the tuna nets since 1959. Most of this activity has taken place in the region west of Mexico and Central America, from Cabo San Lucas (the southern tip of Baja California) south to Lima, Peru, and as far offshore as the Revillagigedo and Clipperton Islands. This area encompasses millions of square miles of open ocean, and it appears to be the primary habitat of the spotter dolphin.* In an area of this size, it is obviously impossible to count the dolphins, but there have been various attempts at estimating the total population, primarily to determine the number that could be removed from it by the tuna fishermen. (Prior to the interest shown by conservationists in preserving the dolphins, the population estimates were, at best, academic exercises.)

One of the by-products of the tuna-porpoise controversy was the initiation of the Dedicated Vessel Program, wherein a tuna boat would perform its regular functions with a team of biologists aboard, not only to monitor the porpoise kills but also to study the behavior and biology of the porpoises in the nets. Observers had been aboard the *Elizabeth C.J.* in 1977, and their report was published in 1978 (Norris, Stuntz, and Rogers). On this cruise, porpoise behavior was observed from a helicopter, from the ship, and underwater by observers in the nets. In 1978, another team of researchers went aboard the *Queen Mary,* another tuna seiner out of San Diego, and observed the social behavior and school structure in pelagic spotters and spinners (Pryor and Kang 1980). These studies—and others—contributed substantially to the information on these heretofore little-known animals, and enabled us to see the dolphins as something more

than unknown creatures that seemed to share the same habitat as the yellowfin and skipjack tuna.

From the air, for example, it was seen that the "undisturbed" dolphins—that is, those that were not being herded or chased—swam slowly, spread out, and with 20 to 30 body lengths separating the individuals. When chased by speedboats, however, the porpoises crowded together, with only 2 to 3 lengths between them. In this "running mode" they also began moving much more rapidly—as might be expected—making long, low leaps out of the water.*

Once surrounded by the nets, the behavior of the dolphins changes radically. Norris and colleagues (1978) described a variety of behaviors, including "milling," where "a large percentage of the school remains essentially in one area while swimming and diving." They also saw some leaping activity, but this appeared to take place early in the set, and soon subsided. In the nets, they saw dolphins at the surface with their heads out of the water (they called this "head-up" behavior), and also with their tails out of the water ("tail up"). A group hanging vertically in the water in the head-up mode was described as "rafting." In the nets, the animals also aligned themselves in discrete "layers," and after coming to the surface to breathe, they would return to their original positions: "Layers are defined as discrete bands of animals more or less horizontally oriented relative to the water surface. The exception to a horizontal orientation were rafting individuals which tended more toward a vertical orientation relative to the surface. As many as four individual layers, at depths estimated to be 5 m, 9 m, 12 m, and 15 m, could be detected at any one time in a set" (Norris et al. 1978). In most cases, spinners and spotters remained segregated from each other, forming small groups of 4 or 5 animals, and with certain exceptions, the behavior of the two species was similar. (For example, spinners tended to move around more in the nets, and remained more on the periphery of a mixed assemblage.) The observers commented that the "passive behavior" of the animals in the nets, where the dolphins sank slowly to the bottom of the net, was probably a reaction to a situation of great stress, induced by the boats, nets, noise, wake, etc., and may be comparable to the behavior of the spotters in the Solomon Islands, where the animals buried their heads in the sand to escape the loud clattering noises made by the rock-clanging hunters. Norris and colleagues comment:

---

*Smith (1979) has estimated that the ranges for the three major stocks of spotters are as follows: coastal, 199, 817 square miles; northern offshore, 3,605,244 square miles; southern offshore, 924,-416 square miles, for a total range of 4,727,477 square miles, a larger area than that of all fifty American states.

*In a study published in 1980, Au and Weihs demonstrated mathematically that in the "running mode," these long leaps are the fastest and most efficient mode of swimming. Even though more energy is required for jumping, the time spent out of the water, and therefore with no water resistance, compensates for the additional expenditure of energy.

These responses are not hard to understand when one considers that the animals may come from open waters where no barriers are present at all, and no confinement. Thus, confinement in a tuna set is utterly foreign to these animals, as are corklines (they know nothing about barriers unless it is learned in a tuna net), purse rings, motor noise and the other features of a set.

In a survey of various species of dolphins in captivity, Defran and Pryor (1980) found that spinners and spotters are "timid, easily frightened, fearful of objects, highly dependent on the presence of other dolphins, and . . . reacting adversely to novelty." Thus the very characteristics so undesirable for animals on exhibition might be exactly the protective mechanisms required for survival in the wild—except when hunted by tuna seiners, when these characteristics prove fatal. In the conclusion of their 1978 report, Norris and colleagues pose a series of questions that they feel must be answered if the tuna fishery and the porpoises* are to be preserved:

We still need to know precisely why, and under what circumstances, porpoises die. We need to know if knowledge of capture and confinement is the information of a few porpoises, or of every animal. How often are they caught? How far do they roam? Do schools intermingle? Are young animals selectively hurt by seining? Do spinners sleep with spotters? Who finds the food? Do tuna benefit?

In the summer of 1978, another team of investigative biologists was aboard a tuna seiner, but this time the investigators were concentrating primarily on the behavior of the animals in the nets. The goals of their study were as follows:

1. To determine and describe porpoise behavior patterns that indicate such characteristics as fatigue, fear, aggression, courtship, and panic, so the patterns can be recognized by others in the future.
2. To investigate the composition and behavior of subgroups within captive schools.
3. To determine the importance of conditioned behavioral patterns in the responses of the porpoise to the fishing operation.
4. To observe the social behavior of captured porpoises over a longer term by holding the purse seine open at the prebackdown stage for several hours on two or three sets.
5. To observe the porpoise as they leave the backdown channel and to follow and observe the school for as long as possible after release. [Pryor and Kang 1980]

The investigators were in the water with the dolphins and carefully recorded their underwater observations, often writing underwater on specially prepared slates. On this cruise, seventeen "sets" were made, nine on spotters and eight on combined spinner and spotter schools. Since most previous descriptions of the behavior of small cetaceans have been the result of observations of captive animals or of animals viewed from a distance,* this exercise represented a new and unique opportunity in cetology.

In the nets, the dolphins exhibited many of the actions that are believed to be characteristic of their behavior in the wild, with the obvious exception of those actions directly associated with the seines themselves, for example, "rafting," which they described as "probably a behavior seldom engaged in by free animals," but one that "reduces the likelihood of getting into trouble." The various escape techniques, usually associated with certain actions on the part of the captain when hauling in the nets, are also unrelated to the normal behavior of free-swimming dolphins. Both Pryor and Kang had experience as trainers of spinners and spotters at Sea Life Park in Hawaii, so they were relatively familiar with the behavior of these animals in captive situations, and they were able to prepare a "dictionary" of actions in advance, which allowed them "to identify actions which might be indecipherable to a novice observer, such as gaping (a threat display often anthropomorphically misinterpreted as 'smiling' by laymen) and to notice small movements, such as scanning, which might be overlooked were they not already known to have significance." Within the schools, various subgroups were recognized, some of which are probably typical for all cetaceans—and probably all mammals—such as the mother-baby pair and mother-young groups, but they observed that male spotters form "senior male squads," a grouping that appears to be unique. These are compact groups of from 3 to 8 animals, and these squads were seen in every one of the seventeen sets:

The typical behavior pattern of dominant male subgroups was coordinated cruising (very close to touching) in formation with no animal in advance of another, surfacing, breathing, diving and cruising again, at a constant but slow speed. Members of dominant spotter male subgroups bore conspicuous white rostrum tips, visible at the extreme range of visibility, before the animals' shapes could be seen, described as "shining," "like stars," and "flashing."

---

*Throughout this report they refer to the animals as "porpoises." In the abstract, however, this sentence appears: "The porpoise species involved were the spotted dolphin, *Stenella attenuata,* and the spinner dolphin, *Stenella longirostris.*" So much for the "porpoise-dolphin" controversy.

*Würsig and Würsig (1977, 1979) reported on bottlenose dolphins observed from the cliffs of Golfo Nuevo, Argentina; Saayman and Tayler (1973) did the same in South Africa; and Norris and Dohl (1980) watched Hawaiian spinners at Kealakekua Bay, but all these observations were restricted to surface observations. Pryor and Kang were in the water with temporarily captive wild dolphins.

Courting behavior, threats, fights, and other actions were also observed, as well as echolocating (identifiable by short, sideways movements of the head, and clicks audible to the divers). In what has been called the "affiliative mode," male and female pairs were seen swimming together with their pectoral fins overlapping, an action that the investigators described as "holding hands." Pryor and Kang formulated a "tribe hypothesis" in which they suggest that the various subgroups "do not operate independently of each other, but are linked into larger groupings which are socially affiliated and probably to some degree genetically related groupings which we call tribes. . . . Animals in the nets which swim in the same subgroups may be assumed to be well acquainted with each other." They further suggest that these "tribes" are organized around the dominant male subgroups, where "the whole school or tribe . . . benefits from the acquired experience of the oldest males."

Among the "behavioral events" recorded by the observers in the nets were "female and young interactions, courtship, aggressive interchanges, bubble displays, neonate transport, and subgroup composition and relationships. Data suggest much learned behavior and surprisingly low stress levels." Although the dolphins were obviously in an anomalous situation, it was assumed that much of their behavior was "normal," and could therefore be applied to an ethogram of the species in the wild.

Special care was taken on these dedicated vessel cruises, and very few dolphins died. Norris (1977) reports that during twenty sets made when he was aboard the *Elizabeth C.J.,* a total of 11 porpoises were killed. On the seventeen sets of the *Queen Mary,* Pryor and Kang recorded the deaths of 3 animals.

Many of the dolphins observed during the *Queen Mary*'s sets seemed to have had some experience with the nets, that is, they appeared to know when they were going to end up in the net, and they stopped swimming. They also appeared to know how to escape over the corkline during the "backdown" maneuver, which indicated that at least some of the animals had been entrapped before, and did not panic when they were in the nets.

On a few occasions, whitetip sharks were seen in or around the nets, but during the *Queen Mary* sets, no contact between sharks and dolphins was observed. In another study, however, "several attacks on living animals were seen" (Leatherwood et al. 1973). A new threat now seems to have been added, since there is a report of false killer whales, and perhaps pygmy killer whales, also attacking dolphins as they are being herded by the speedboats. Perryman and Foster (1980) write that "these whales may attack free-swimming dolphins and also occasionally feed on dolphins that are released from the purse seine." They collected a total of 49 "separate aggressive interactions," and most of these involved the false killer whale. Other larger cetaceans involved in these "interactions" were killer whales, which were long believed to

"Senior male squad" of Pacific spotters, *Stenella attenuata.*

92

be the only species of cetacean that preyed on others. The authors suggest that this is not normal predatory behavior, but it is possible that these are "unique situations created by the purse seine fishery . . . the concentrated and excited animals leaving the net at backdown are probably more vulnerable than a free-swimming school."

What was originally called "passive behavior" on the part of spotters trapped in the nets, in which the animals were "frustrated" and would eventually "scull awkwardly off the net and rise to the surface" (Norris 1977), has since been provisionally described as an example of "capture myopathy," where "capture stress was probably causing some mortality in porpoises involved in the eastern tropical Pacific tuna fishery" (Stuntz 1980a). In other words, the stress of the chase and the capture, rather than being something that the dolphins can become accustomed to, may be stressful enough to kill some of them.

When they are not being trapped in tuna nets or eaten by sharks or false killer whales, is there any information on the *natural* causes of death in dolphins? Perrin and Powers (1980) have identified the nematode parasite *Crassicauda* sp. as a possible cause of natural mortality in spotters, and from the examination of some 700 skulls, they suggest that parisitism may be responsible for as much as 11 to 14 percent of the natural deaths of spotters in the Pacific. (All the dolphins they examined had been killed in the tuna nets, but they were able to classify the extent of the parasite-related damage to the skulls, and thereby predict the natural mortality that would have occurred if the animals had not been trapped.)

In the early history of the purse-seine fishery, techniques were developed to protect the porpoises, if not for humane reasons, then certainly to reduce the labor required to get the dead dolphins out of the nets, and, probably even more important, to preserve at least some of the dolphins for the future of the tuna fishery. After all, if there were no more dolphins to set on, they would have to go back to the old hook-and-line style of fishing, and these multimillion-dollar purse seiners, now capable of bringing in a million dollars' worth of tuna on a single voyage, were not going to have a horde of fishermen hanging over the rails with bamboo poles in their hands.

Techniques were developed to release the dolphins from the nets. At first, the release operation consisted of "backing down": when about half of the net had been hauled in, the vessel was put into reverse, "and as the vessel begins to move backward, the net is drawn out into a long, finger-shaped configuration. At the far end of the finger, water pressure against the webbing causes the net to sink. The porpoises literally have the net pulled out from under

them" (Norris et al. 1978). This worked moderately well, but still thousands of dolphins drowned every year. The backdown technique was mentioned by Perrin as early as 1969, but in that year, a total of 518,407 porpoises of all species were killed, and in 1970, the number was 502,815 (Smith 1979). Obviously, some captains were less interested in getting the porpoises out of their nets than they were in keeping the tuna in (sometimes the tuna escaped during backdown), and with half a million porpoises dying annually, it would be difficult to say that the system to protect them was working very well. The American public and its congressional representatives were becoming aware of this egregious slaughter of the dolphins, and under great pressure, the Marine Mammal Protection Act of 1972 was passed. Upon its passage, the tuna industry was given a two-year "grace period" to reduce its dolphin kills, but from the numbers of dolphins reported killed during that period, it was apparent that the fishermen were doing little to reduce dolphin mortality. In most cases, the records of dolphins killed was extrapolated from sample tuna boats, since it was obviously impossible to have an observer aboard each vessel, counting the dolphins that died in the nets. Nevertheless, there have been estimates prepared of the dolphin kill for all the years when any sort of records were kept, and they were summarized in a 1979 report of a Status of Porpoise Stocks Workshop that was held in La Jolla in August 1979. The number of spotters from all three populations (coastal, northern offshore, and southern offshore) killed are as follows:

1973: 114,087
1974: 74,590
1975: 83,859
1976: 57,185
1977: 12,149
1978: 12,805

Backdown procedures and the addition of fine-meshed panels (the "Medina panel" and the "super-apron") to prevent the dolphins from getting snared in the nets contributed to the reduction in kills, but the most important factor was pressure—congressional, judicial, and public—on the fishermen.* With the dramatic reduction in kills, it seemed that the problem was almost solved, even though there were those who believed that *any* porpoise deaths were too many. As of October 1980, a quota of 20,500 porpoises (all

*From 1972 onward, the American public was becoming more and more sensitive to the problems of cetaceans, from the IWC to tuna fishery. It was painfully apparent, therefore, that the United States, a leader in whale conservation, was paradoxically responsible for more cetacean deaths than any other nation, even the modern pelagic whalers.

species) was set by the U.S. Government, and since the previous years' kills did not even reach the permitted quota, it appeared that the problem had subsided.

At the Porpoise Stocks Workshop at La Jolla, however, some of the earlier data were analyzed, and some disturbing results emerged. A more careful analysis of the population data indicated that the earlier estimates—upon which the quotas were based—were seriously flawed, and the actual number of spotters in the eastern tropical Pacific was much lower than had been previously assumed. Earlier estimates had been based on observer and crew-member estimates of school size from tuna vessels, while the 1979 figures were based on aerial observations (Smith 1979). The figures and formulas are (as usual) particularly convoluted, but as an example, the 1979 report states that the population of offshore spotted dolphins is at 34 to 55 percent of its 1959 level, which is below the OSP (optimal sustainable population)* range, while the same population analyzed in 1973 (for the 1976 report) was at "92 to 95 percent of the 1959 level, which would imply that it is in the OSP range" (Smith 1979). In real numbers, the estimated population of spotters in the eastern tropical Pacific was not the 4 million dolphins that had been estimated to make up the population in 1959, but a figure that was probably closer to 3 million. This sounds like a lot of dolphins, until it is placed alongside the number that are believed to have been killed throughout the fishery: from 1959 to 1978, a total of 4,180,613 spotted dolphins were killed. The "recruitment rate," or the reproductive abilities, of the dolphins make up for the apparent discrepancy, but if more than 4 million spotters were killed in twenty years, it can be seen that the actual numbers—as well as the OSP—are critical.

This is an enormously complex issue, and it is still continuing as of this writing. The lines are not particularly clearly drawn: conservationists sometimes find themselves on the side of the tuna fishermen, who say that if they are prohibited from setting on porpoise by U.S. regulations, they will sell their ships to foreign countries, and fish under flags which have no such restrictions. If that were to happen, the dolphins would have no protection at all. The tuna fishermen, on the other hand, feel that they have been cooperating with the environmentalists by significantly reducing their kills, and now they find themselves threatened with a total shutdown if the government declares the spotters "depleted."*

As long as spotters and spinners associate with tuna, and as long as people eat tuna—at least until there is some resolution of the mystery of the association of the dolphins and the fish which might enable us to separate them before the dolphins enter the nets —some dolphins will die in the tuna fishery. The saddest reflection of all is that millions had to die—perhaps to the detriment of entire species—while humans argued over the arcane questions of OSP, fishermen's rights, and backdown techniques.

ATLANTIC SPOTTED DOLPHIN

Stenella plagiodon Cope 1866

Also known as the Gulfstream spotted dolphin or the longsnouted dolphin, this is a medium-sized spotted dolphin that appears to be restricted to the Atlantic Ocean. Like all other members of the genus, the spotted dolphin has experienced a number of name changes, and even now its taxonomy remains unsettled. The confusion exists because this species closely resembles the Pacific spotted dolphin, which might be easily distinguished from the Atlantic form were it not for the occasional appearance of the Pacific species— under various names—in Atlantic waters (Perrin et al. 1978). Although the distinctions between the two are still not clarified, the Atlantic spotter is usually a more robust animal, and more heavily spotted.

Kellogg (1940) described the "long-snouted dolphin" thus: "From a distance these dolphins appear very dark, almost black, above, and paler beneath. At closer range the white spots on the purplish-gray upper parts are conspicuous, and as the dolphin rolls at the surface the lighter flanks speckled with white or gray spots may be clearly seen." Since the spots are not visible at a distance, it might be possible to confuse this animal with the bottlenose dolphin, but the latter is a larger animal with a stockier build and a proportionally shorter snout.

The Atlantic spotter begins life as an unspotted animal, but it soon acquires the pattern of overall marks. Caldwell and Caldwell (1966) point out that this is one of the few cetaceans where the pattern of the juveniles differs from that of the adults: "Similar

---

*This is the definition given of OSP in the 1979 "Report of the Status of Porpoise Stocks Workshop": "Optimum sustainable population is a population size which falls within a range from the population level of a given species or stock which is the largest supportable within the ecosystem to the population level that results in maximum net productivity. Maximum net productivity is the greatest net annual increment in population numbers of biomass resulting from additions to the population due to reproduction and/or growth less losses due to natural mortality."

*According to the Marine Mammal Protection Act of 1972, a species may be considered depleted if the population "(A) has declined to a significant degree over a period of years; (B) has otherwise declined and that if such decline continues, or is likely to resume, such species would be subject to the provisions of the Endangered Species Conservation Act of 1969; or (C) is below the optimum carrying capacity for the species or stock within its environment." If a species is declared depleted, there may be no taking of it at all.

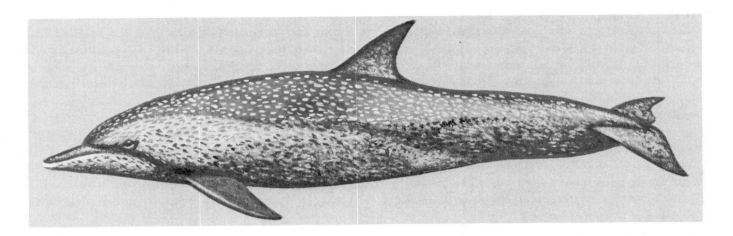

variation, in which the young is plain and the adult spotted, has been reported for the narwhal . . . and for *Stenella graffmani* in the eastern North Pacific. . . . Species of cetaceans with adults and young of different colors or shades of the same color, but with the same color pattern, are not as unusual. The unspotted character of the juveniles is clearly demonstrated in Caldwell and Caldwell (1966), where several excellent photographs of a mother and calf are reproduced. They describe the color of the calf as shading "from dark purplish-gray on the dorsal side to white on the ventral," and the trailing edges of the flukes are described as "notably darker than the rest of the fluke." In their description of the coloration of adults, Caldwell and Caldwell differ from Kellogg's description when they maintain that "in *plagiodon* the spots are apparently always dark on a light ground," and suggest this as a characteristic that may be used to differentiate the species from other spotted dolphins. In the case of adults, moreover, the spots get larger, resembling "blotches," but there is no record of their fusing together to form a solid color, as has been suggested. An area that is prominently spotted in mature adults is the underside of the lower jaw, and there is often some white on the lips, but not the prominent white tip to the rostrum. The spots probably serve partially as an intraspecies recognition device, but it is "more likely that they are a camouflage to help protect the animals from possible predators such as killer whales, in the sparkling and often white-capped waves which are common in their normal open-sea environment" (Caldwell and Caldwell 1966). Atlantic spotters can reach a maximum length of 8 feet (2.4 meters), and they have 30 to 36 teeth in each lower jaw row and 28 to 35 in each upper row, fewer than any other member of the genus. *Plagiodon* can be translated as "sloping teeth," from the Greek *plagios* ("sloping") and *odon* ("tooth").

Spotted dolphins congregate in large schools of 100 or more animals, but smaller groups of less than 50 (usually 6 to 10) are more common. "The small gray calf swims alongside its mother, invariably between the fore flipper and the caudal flukes, both rising and sinking in unison. A sucking fish, the remora, adhering to the fore flipper or to the side of the tail of one of the dolphins, at times has been mistaken for the calf" (Kellogg 1940). A far more frequent mistake is the misidentification of the solid-colored juveniles for bottlenose dolphins, leading to erroneous reports of mixed schools of the two species. For the most part, spotted dolphins are found further offshore than bottlenoses, but Caldwell and Caldwell (1966) report that during the spring off Florida, "spotted dolphins appear so regularly each year so close to shore that they are collected for display by the same means that are used for capturing *Tursiops;* namely, by seines worked in very shallow water (usually wading depth) immediately adjacent to or within less than a mile of the beach."*

When the first oceanariums were opening up in Florida, this species was often captured for display, along with the more popular bottlenose dolphin. The dolphin collector for the Miami Seaquarium was Captain W. B. Gray, and he describes the capture of the "spotted porpoise," which he refers to as *Stenella graffmani:* "This is the type usually noticed cavorting ahead and about ocean steamers well away from any point of land. They are very playful by nature and when attracted by the commotion of a moving ship will race to it from miles away. It seems they are curious and often play along with the vessel for several miles as a form of amusement. They seem to delight in sporting along in this manner and have no difficulty in keeping pace with a boat traveling thirty miles an hour or more." Spotters were captured as they rode the bow

---

*Caldwell and Caldwell's discussion—and the following descriptions—of the methods used for capturing dolphins were written before the passage of the Marine Mammal Protection Act of 1972, and in U.S. waters dolphins may now be collected only by permit and by certain approved techniques.

wave of the collecting vessel by means of a "tail grabber," a device like a giant ice tongs attached to the end
of a long pole. After the dolphin had been "tail-
grabbed," it was played for a time on the end of the
rope, and eventually brought aboard for transport to
Miami. "When the spotted porpoises are brought to
the Seaquarium, they must be placed in a separate
tank because this variety is more nervous and timid
than any other. The bottlenoses are very domineering
and seem to resent any other porpoises in their domain. They do not take to coexistence. If they were so
inclined, you would see them practicing it in their
natural element. In other words, they do not mix"
(Gray 1964).

At Marineland of Florida, some of the earliest
observations of these animals in captivity were recorded by F. G. Wood (1953). In a tank with ten bottlenoses, there were two male spotted dolphins. (Wood
repeats that the spotted dolphins were "apparently
dominated by the bottle-nosed porpoises.") The spotters were heard to whistle frequently, and also to produce a sound described as "yapping," particularly
when being chased by a bottlenose or when passing in
front of or behind a tiger shark that had been introduced into the tank: "Each yap was accompanied by a
stream of bubbles from the porpoise's blowhole, so
there was no question as to who was making the noise.
At another time the bull *Tursiops* in the tank was observed chasing a male *Stenella,* whether in play or in
anger was not clear, and the spotted dolphin was emitting the same kind of sounds" (Wood 1973). In a later
series of experiments conducted at various facilities in
Florida, Caldwell and Caldwell (1971) recorded click
trains emitted by spotted dolphins which they identified as "environmental exploration or echolocation." It is not surprising to learn that this species is
an echolocator, but it is useful to have had this ability
experimentally demonstrated. The animals were also
heard to emit "squawks," "squeals," and "barks," and
the authors suggest that this species—like the bottlenose—is capable of producing an individual signature
whistle. In a series of underwater observations made
off the east coast of the United States from North
Carolina to Florida, the Atlantic spotter was recorded
in the wild, swimming in small schools, and often
swimming upside down underwater. In this same series of televised observations, the dolphins were also
seen to have barnacles attached to the trailing edges
of their flukes (Sutherland and May 1977).

Because this species is uncommon in inshore waters—except perhaps in Florida waters at certain times
of the year—its range is poorly known. It is believed
to be restricted to the western North Atlantic from
Cape May, New Jersey, south to Panama. Hall and
Kelson (1959) have listed it from "Cape Hatteras and

Texas; channel in front of Port Aransas, thence southward to South American waters," but Caldwell and
Caldwell, in their 1966 detailed study of the range of
this species, "find no published records or specimens
in collections to form the basis for the note that this
species occurs in South America. . . ." Schmidly and
Shane (1978) have written, "Based on the number of
observations and recorded strandings, the spotted
dolphin is the second most common cetacean in Texas
waters." (The most common is the bottlenose.) Wood
(1979) reports two strandings of spotters in Florida,
one of which involved two males that were found alive
in a man-made saltwater lake on Marathon, one of the
Florida Keys: "The only access from the Gulf of Mexico was by two culverts, each 91 cm in diameter and
12 m long. The approach from the Gulf was a small
cove, rocky and shallow. This event was all the more
remarkable because, as trainers at oceanariums know,
delphinids generally exhibit great reluctance to pass
through constricted openings and must be patiently
trained to do so." In the West Indies, Taruski and
Winn (1976) reported "short beaked dolphins that
have numerous spots" at several locations. They rode
the bow wave, and were "generally on the banks,"
indicating a preference for shallow water. Taruski and
Winn recognize a distribution pattern drawn by Caldwell and colleagues (1971), where they identify the
spotted dolphins around the Antilles as *Stenella frontalis* (= *attenuata*), and those "near the continents" as
S. plagiodon. They go on to comment, "Obviously without an adequate collection of animals this decision
must remain tentative." Caldwell and Caldwell discuss
the possibility of this species occurring in the eastern
Atlantic, and cite several references to indicate that it
may have been sighted off the Ivory Coast. One specimen is currently residing at the Brighton Aquarium in
England, where it performs along with three bottlenose dolphins.

A particularly friendly male nicknamed Sandy was
consorting with divers in the warm waters off the
Bahamian island of San Salvador (Murphy 1979; Linehan 1979; etc.). Sport divers shot hundreds of rolls of
film and waxed rhapsodic over their contact with a
wild dolphin, but it should be emphasized that this is
highly unusual behavior for an animal that is normally
timid, and almost always seen in large groups. Sandy
visited and posed for divers for about a year (1977–78)
and then disappeared, "probably frightened off by
hordes of, no doubt, well intentioned divers" (Sheffe
1980).

An even more unusual situation involving this
species has been occurring regularly off the Bahamas
in recent years. A group of filmmakers and musicians
discovered an extraordinarily friendly and cooperative
school of spotters in the clear, warm waters of Little

Bahama Bank, just off the east coast of Florida. The spotters were found to be willing to swim with divers who attracted them by playing music on underwater speakers: "Fear was nowhere in evidence. The dolphins played tirelessly around the boat as long as we stayed down, intensely curious about our actions. Occasionally they would stray out of sight, but always return for more. . . . We dived, twisted, rolled; they emulated our movements, maintaining a constant, high-pitched chatter that resembled the sound of air escaping from the pinched neck of a child's balloon, undulating in and out of the high frequency limits of our hearing range" (Sheffe 1980). As with so many species of small cetaceans, mere observation of the animals in their natural habitat is greatly increasing our knowledge. Fortunately, this is one species of *Stenella* that did not have to be slaughtered in vast numbers before we could begin to learn something of its habits.

STRIPED DOLPHIN

Stenella coeruleoalba Meyen 1833

Although it is best known from Japanese waters, the striped or blue-white dolphin (*coeruleoalba* means "blue-white") can be found widely distributed throughout the temperate and tropical waters of the world. It has been reported along the entire west coast of North America, from the Bering Sea and British Columbia through Washington, Oregon, and Southern California as far south as Cabo San Lucas, the southern tip of Baja California (Hubbs et al. 1973). Most of these records refer to the stranding of a single animal or the sighting of a school at sea, and in 1978, writing of the occurrence of this species in the eastern North Pacific, Leatherwood and Reeves wrote, "these records represent either extralimital straying or suggest an offshore distribution." It is also rare in the eastern North Atlantic, with a total of four known

strandings on British coasts from 1913 to 1977 (Sheldrick 1979), but Duguy (1977) says it is "the commonest species in the Mediterranean and Gibraltar." It is also known to strand off the east coast of North America, having been recorded from Halifax to the Gulf of Mexico. Reporting on a specimen that stranded at Cape Henlopen, Delaware, in 1978, Ulmer (1980) wrote, "Striped dolphins seem to prefer the warmer waters of the Gulf Stream at our latitude and so are rarely seen close to shore in New Jersey." (In 1962, however, Schevill and Watkins reported a group of about 200 in deep water over the lower Hudson Canyon some 140 miles southeast of New York City.)

In the late 1870s, a single skull placed this species in the New Zealand cetacean fauna, but over 100 years passed before another specimen turned up. On November 15, 1971, a dolphin stranded at Mission Bay, Auckland, obviously of this species (Baker and Stephenson 1972). Also in 1972, in *New Zealand Whales and Dolphins*, Baker wrote that the "striped dolphin probably comes close to the New Zealand coast only in the summer months. . . ."* There are scattered reports of the blue-white dolphin from South Africa, the Caribbean, Hawaii, and the eastern and western tropical Pacific. The single known specimen from Hawaii was captured in the Ala Wai Canal, "a brackish canal running through Honolulu behind Waikiki Beach on March 2, 1958" (Hubbs et al. 1973), and Miyazaki and Wada (1978) report sightings of schools of striped dolphins from Japan south all the way to the Solomon Islands. Their observations indicate an offshore habitat for the species, as do Perrin's data (1975a) on the eastern tropical Pacific tuna fishery, where occasional schools of these animals are set on by the purse seiners. (Of the 1,874 sets recorded by Perrin from 1971 to 1975, only 4 were on this species,

*The species is not mentioned at all in two other books about the cetaceans of New Zealand; Gaskin's 1972 *Whales, Dolphins & Seals, With Special Reference to the New Zealand Region*, and Robson's 1976 *Thinking Dolphins, Talking Whales*.

known as the streaker dolphin to the tuna fishermen.) Perrin wrote: "In addition to the published locality records (Hubbs et al. 1973) we now have 36 more records, including three for which specimens were collected. The known range has been extended south to below the equator and east to the Panama Bight."

It is curious that an animal that was apparently well known as early as 2000 B.C. should still remain such an enigma. (In 1977 Fraser wrote that the dolphins pictured in the frescoes in the Queen's Palace at Knossos were "recognizable as *Stenella coeruleoalba*, a species known to occur in the Mediterranean.") Part of the mystery may be attributed to the inability of taxonomists and other observers to identify the animals as the same species throughout their extended range. Since 1833, when Meyen described the first specimen (which had been collected in the vicinity of the La Plata River in South America, and where no subsequent specimens have been recorded), the species has undergone some forty-five name changes, including such unfamiliar appelations as *Orca tethyos, Tursio dorcides* and *Clymeria burmeisteri* (Hershkovitz 1966). Until fairly recently it was known as *Prodelphinus*

euphrosyne, and Norman and Fraser (1938) further divided it into two distinct subspecies, *P. euphrosyne* and *P. coeruleo-albus*, the first of which had a dark snout, and the second a white snout. (It was the same Fraser who, with Noble in 1970, combined all striped dolphins into a single species, *Stenella coeruleoalba*.) Even today there are digressions, because there are two versions of the eye-to-flipper stripe, a single and a double variety. Some taxonomists (e.g., Nishiwaki 1972) continue to separate the striped dolphins into two species, *S. coeruleoalba* and *S. styx*, but in the most recent classifications—such as Rice's 1977 *List of the Marine Mammals of the World*—there is only one recognized species.

In addition to the confusion over its scientific nomenclature and classification, this species has been blessed with a bewildering variety of common names, including blue-white dolphin, Euphrosyne dolphin, Meyen's dolphin, striped dolphin, long-snouted dolphin, streaker dolphin and streaker porpoise. In Japanese it is known as *suji-iruka* ("striped dolphin"), except where it is referred to as *ma-iruka*, which means "common dolphin," but does not mean the animal we call the common dolphin (*Delphinus delphis*), simply

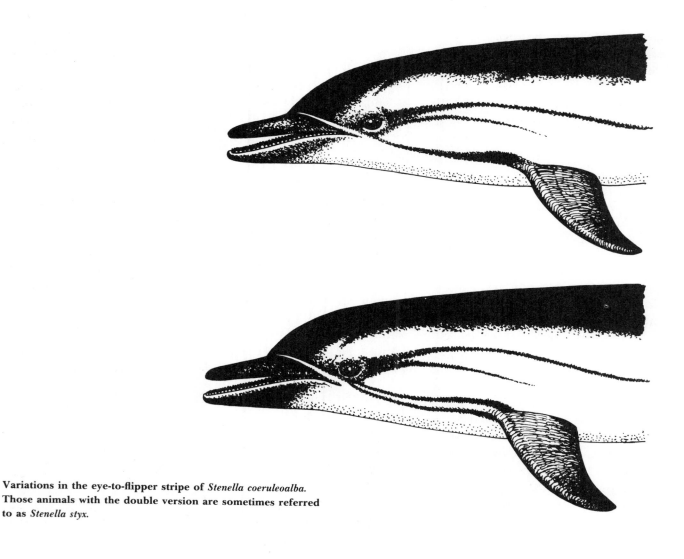

Variations in the eye-to-flipper stripe of *Stenella coeruleoalba.* **Those animals with the double version are sometimes referred to as** *Stenella styx.*

98

that the animal is plentiful in a given area (Ohsumi 1972).

Its resemblance to the common dolphin has also contributed to its obscurity. A close examination of specimens reveals numerous differences between the two species, but at sea the two strongly marked animals can easily be confused. Even though the common dolphin is smaller and has a shorter snout and a different pigmentation pattern, misidentifications frequently occur. For example, Norris and Prescott (1961) examined a stranded specimen from the waters of Playa del Rey (Los Angeles County, California), and observed, "After examining this very distinctive animal it became apparent to us that we had, in all probability, been seeing *Stenella euphrosyne* with fair regularity in the San Pedro Channel area. We had dubbed them 'bull *Delphinus*' because of their large size and resemblance to the common dolphin. . . . The dorsal pattern and form is sufficiently similar to *Delphinus bairdi* that they apparently went unidentified as a form new to us." The species is usually described as "dark blue" or "steel-blue," but Norris and Prescott wrote (of the Playa del Rey specimen) that "the initial report . . . was of a brown animal. . . . No mention was made of any bluish coloration. It was the brownish coloration that made the freshly dead animal resemble *Delphinus bairdi* sufficiently so that we feel we could have confused them in the field."

Throughout its broad distribution the blue-white dolphin strands fairly frequently, although it most often shows up as a singleton stranding and not in groups. Mead (1979) reports that it is often found alive on the beach of the eastern United States; only the shortfin pilot whale, with a 50 percent record of live strandings exceeds the 36 percent live-stranding record of the striped dolphin. Mead further points out that the blue-white dolphin is often confused with the common dolphin, "and since *S. coeruleoalba* is the lesser known of the two, the identification is more likely to be given to *D. delphis.*"

Most descriptions (including Meyen's, which is given below in a translation from the 1833 German by Fraser and Noble in 1970),* emphasize the blue color-

ation and the stripes. The back is dark blue, the undersides white, and the dark stripes trailing back from the eyes and on the flanks are diagnostic. Fraser and Noble (1970) referred to the stripe running from the eye along the flank to the anal region as the "main plimsoll line." They analyzed various illustrations of "Meyen's dolphin," and were unable to find a single picture of this species with a white beak, including Meyen's original illustration, in which he described the beak as "dazzlingly white." In most instances, the beak is darker on the upper part and lighter—but not white—on the lower jaw.

This species can reach a maximum length of 10 feet (3.28 meters), as compared to 8 feet (2.4 meters) for the common dolphin. Like other members of the genus *Stenella,* it has an ungrooved palate. (The grooves in the palate of *Delphinus* differentiate that genus from *Stenella.*) The striped dolphin has approximately 45 teeth in each tooth row, for an average total of 180.

After a twelve-month gestation period, a calf about 3 feet long (100 centimeters) is born. It will begin to feed on solid food at about three months, but lactation in the nursing female lasts about a year and a half, indicating a fairly long mother-calf relationship (Miyazaki 1977). Because specimens are often found with the scars of squid suckers around their mouths, it was previously assumed that this species was predominantly a squid eater (Nishiwaki 1972). Further studies have shown that their diet is more varied: they eat fish, particularly lanternfish (myctophids), squid, and shrimp. The lanternfish and squid have luminous organs, so it might be inferred from this diet that this species of dolphin feeds in relatively deep water (Miyazaki et al. 1973).

In the eastern North Pacific, the North Atlantic, and the various other locations where this species is encountered so infrequently, very little is known about it. (In his handbook of the *Marine Mammals of California,* Orr [1972] wrote, "little is known regarding its habits.") Since there is now considered to be a single, worldwide species, we can rely upon the Japanese studies of the western North Pacific population to provide more detailed information on the natural history of the striped dolphin. According to Nishiwaki (1967), "This species is very common in Japan, forming about half of the harvest of the dolphin fishery."* For hundreds of years striped dolphins were hunted

---

Delphinus coeruleo-albus w. sp. Tab. XLIII, fig. 2.1/11 natural size, female 5 1/2 feet. The head round and very domed, on the other hand the snout is very flat and with a somewhat protruding lower jaw. On each side of the jaws 48 to 50 teeth which are very conical and very sharp-pointed and curved somewhat inwardly. It resembles *Delphinus delphis* whose beak-like snout is much shorter and particularly ventrally is more compressed. The flippers and dorsal fin in our species are more pointed and not so pronouncedly falcate. The colour distinguishes our species very conspicuously; the entire back with the brow as far as the beak is a dark steel blue. From the dorsal fin a narrow, very dark blue-coloured stripe runs anteriorly and suddenly peters out. From the eye there runs a very narrow blue stripe along the flank towards the tail where, in the region of the anus, it terminates widely. The flipper is blue grey and is connected to the coloured eye-circle by a stripe. The belly, the beak and the remainder of the body are dazzlingly white.

This beautifully marked dolphin inhabits the waters off the east coast of South America; we harpooned it in the region of the River Plate. The entire skeleton is in the Royal Anatomical Museum, Berlin.

*The remaining half is made up of various other species, none of which are caught as often as the striped dolphin. Nishiwaki (1975) lists the following species as "still used for human consumption in Japan": Dall porpoise, bottlenose dolphin, Pacific spotted dolphin, Risso's dolphin, false killer whale, and Pacific white-sided dolphin.

by hand harpoon or harpoon gun, but since 1973 the driving method (*oikomi*) has been used (Miyazaki 1980). This method, as described by Ohsumi (1972), consists of driving the dolphins into a bay, where they are captured: "This method was also called "net method," because nets are used after a school of dolphins are driven into a bay. This method depends on the behavior of dolphins that they are very sensitive to underwater sounds and are gregarious. A school of dolphins are driven into a bay by noise under-released from many fishing boats. As soon as the school is driven into a bay, fishermen set a net at the mouth of the bay. Some of them are taken up by net and some driven ashore." In 1972, Nishiwaki described the susceptibility of the species to this type of fishery:

These animals are very cowardly, and large herds can be chased into a bay for harvesting. Several to more than ten boats participate in the drive in which the dolphins are scared in the proper direction by slapping the water surface, by throwing stones, or by beating a trumpet-shaped device designed to produce underwater noise.

In a later paper, Nishiwaki (1975) wrote, "Drive fisheries often kill whole schools of dolphins. Requests to fishermen to release young animals have almost always been ignored. The fishermen argue that if they released an infant, it would soon die, and also, that the meat of infants is more tender, and therefore brings a higher price than does adult meat."

Because of the concentrated hunting of this species, it is not surprising that Japanese scientists have accumulated a considerable body of information on the striped dolphin. Various Japanese cetologists (but especially Noboyuki Miyazaki, who is considered an expert on this species) have extensively studied the migration routes, school structure, growth and reproduction, and population estimates.*

The striped dolphin, which is generally considered an offshore species throughout the rest of its range (Nishiwaki 1967), passes close to the Pacific coast of the Japanese islands during two peak seasons: from October through March the schools are heading south, and from May through July they are on their northward migration (Miyazaki 1980). They are caught at various locations, including Arari, Futo, Kanawa, and Taiji, but dolphin fishing is not practiced throughout Japan. As Nishiwaki (1975) pointed out:

*In addition, the examination of large numbers of specimens also produces all sorts of anomalies, including hermaphroditic dolphins (Nishiwaki 1953); protruded hind limbs (Ohsumi 1965); a two-headed "monster" fetus (Kawamura and Kashita 1971); and a Siamese-twin fetus (Miyazaki 1980).

In Japan, dolphin fishing is carried out exclusively in areas where local people, or people in nearby districts, like to eat dolphin meat. There is a cultural stigma attached to those who eat dolphin, for it is not considered a luxurious food. Therefore, dolphin consumption is restricted to people in local communities, primarily those in coastal and mountainous districts where the climate is very cold.

At the southern tip of the Kii Peninsula lies the village of Taiji, where whaling of all kinds has been carried out for over eight hundred years (Nicol 1979). Miyazaki (1980) has analyzed the catch records of Kii from 1963 to 1979, and has found a yearly average of 916 striped dolphins, with the annual kills ranging from 331 animals to 2,397. In a study of the composition of the schools, Miyazaki and Nishiwaki (1978) studied a total of 5,958 dolphins taken from 45 schools caught at the Izu Peninsula (southwest of Tokyo) from 1963 to 1973. They classified the schools into three types: juvenile, adult, and mixed, and then found that the adult schools could be further subdivided into two categories, mating and nonmating:

In the years when the Kuroshio currents came closely to the fishing area in the coast of Izu, number of adult schools is superior, but in other years, the number of juvenile schools is dominant. Calves remain in the adult schools for about one to two years after weaning and then move into the juvenile school. Young females which once left the adult school and got into the juvenile school, rejoin the adult school. Major numbers of those females choose the non-mating school to go in, and only remainders join the mating school, while nearly equal number of males seem to go into the mating and non-mating schools after they reach sexual maturity. The males which chose the non-mating school change to the mating school when they attain sexual maturity. In the adult school, fully matured females seem to gather together and are joined by the socially mature males, then they form a unit of the mating school. One mating school holds several such units. After most of the females are fertilized, socially mature males seem to leave the mating school. The mating school naturally turns into the non-mating school.

Further examination provided Miyazaki (1977) with substantial information on the growth and reproduction of this species. Born at a length of approximately 3 feet (1 meter), the striped dolphin reaches 1.66 meters at one year of age, and 1.8 meters at the age of two. Nursing lasts about 18 months, and the males attain sexual maturity at about 6.7 years of age and females at about 8.7 years. Tomilin (1957), who based his information on Japanese data, wrote that the maximum age for this species is about 18 years, but Kasuya and Miyazaki (1975) calculated (from the examination of dentinal tooth layers) that "the maximum age of a female striped dolphin is about 50

years" and wrote, "This observation may suggest that the length of lifetime of dolphins is longer than expected from tooth layers."

There is no way of precisely determining the number of striped dolphins in the western North Pacific, but because of this species importance to the Japanese dolphin fishery, there have been many attempts at stock estimates, so as to arrive at some sort of figures on which to base the continuing exploitation. In 1967, Nishiwaki wrote that "about 20,000 of this species are killed annually, so the population of at least 250,000 animals must inhabit the far offshore waters." In 1972, the same author wrote that "this is the most abundant species in Japanese waters, and despite annual harvests of from 10,000 to 20,000 individuals, there is no indication that the population is declining." In Ohsumi's 1972 "Catch of Marine Mammals, Mainly of Small Cetaceans, by Local Fisheries Along the Coast of Japan," he did not break down the totals caught (except to divide them into seals, whales, and dolphins), but from 1957 to 1970 he reports a total of 299,575 dolphins killed. By 1975, Nishiwaki had raised his estimate of the total Japanese population of striped dolphins to "400,000 to 600,000," but in the same year Kasuya and Miyazaki calculated that over 100,000 animals had been removed from the population between 1942 and 1953, with an annual catch of "at least 10,000 dolphins," and concluded that the total population of the striped dolphins from the late 1950s to the early 1960s ranged between 218,-000 and 255,000 animals. The conclusion of their 1975 study reads as follows:

The population of *S. coeruleoalba* off the Pacific coast of Japan was initially more than 320 thousand. It had been decreased by exploitation to the level of about 220 to 250 thousand by the late 1950's to the early 1960's. The present status is estimated to be 130 to 180 thousand, which is close to the level producing the maximum sustainable yield of 4,000 to 6,000 dolphins per annum. Possibly this population is a small coastal population migrating seasonally along the Pacific coast of Japan Islands. A driving fishery started for this population in 1973 at Taiji on the coast of Kii Peninsula (Miyazaki et al. 1974) has increased the total catch of the dolphin in recent years. This tendency will continue, and has an effect, if any adequate regulation is not introduced, to decrease the population rapidly.

COMMON DOLPHIN

Delphinus delphis Linnaeus 1758

Perhaps no other small cetacean has been the subject of so much misinformation and misidentification as the common dolphin. Even its name, which comes from the Greek *delphys* meaning "womb," has been applied to the entire class of animals that share some of its characteristics. Its own attributes have been ascribed to other species, while the characteristics of numerous other species have been assigned to it. It is supposed to be the quintessential dolphin of the ancient world, represented in story and in fable, appearing on cups, coins, and friezes,* and yet there is enough uncertainty about its identification—even in modern times—that it has only recently emerged from the all-purpose "dolphin" classification, and become recognized for its own, very special characteristics.

Obviously, the problem begins with the name. The Greeks knew the various small cetaceans as "dolphins" and differentiated them from fishes, but unfortunately they did not distinguish among the species. (The problem has been further compounded by the existence of a fish, *Coryphaena hippurus*, which is also known as "dolphin.") It is here that the "porpoise-dolphin controversy" can no longer be considered a

---

*It was long considered the subject of the famous "dolphin friezes" at Knossos on the island of Crete (Sanderson 1956), but in 1977 no less an authority than F. C. Fraser decided that the animals shown in these friezes are really blue-white dolphins, *Stenella coe-ruleoalba*.

mere semantic or linguistic problem, since it appears that incorrect nomenclature has contributed substantially to thousands of years of confusion. If the common dolphin had exclusively retained the name "dolphin," we might have avoided all the misinformation. The literature, both ancient and modern, is replete with stories of dolphins saving swimmers, swimming with boys, guiding ships, and performing all sorts of noble and notable deeds that have assured the animal a permanent place in the history of human-and-animal relationships. These stories have been told extensively elsewhere, and it is unlikely that they apply to the species here under discussion. There are numerous instances, of course, where the stories could refer to *Delphinus genus,* with its speed in the sea, its highly distinctive coloration, or its bow riding, but most of the tales are more likely to involve the bottlenose dolphin. Of course we cannot prove that the animal that saved Arion when he was thrown overboard was not *Delphinus,* but we can document many recent instances where small cetaceans approached swimmers and even allowed themselves to be handled, and they have almost all been the bottlenose.*

In W. N. Kellogg's *Porpoises and Sonar* (1961), we read, "The particular animal which was admired in these distant times was undoubtedly the common dolphin of the Mediterranean, *Delphinus delphis.* Yet similarity between the Mediterranean species and its relative, the bottlenose porpoise, is close enough to make the early descriptions applicable to either organism." There follows a catalog of the accomplishments of dolphins in ancient times, including Pliny's tales of "the friendship and love existing between young boys and porpoises." We cannot determine if the tales are true, let alone what the species of cetacean was, but the distinctions become blurred by time and the individuality of each species gets less clear and we are once again reading about "dolphins." This in fact is the name of Cousteau and Diolé's 1975 book, where the problem is taken to its most unfortunate extremes. The book is ostensibly about *Delphinus* in the Mediterranean, and it contains probably the best collection of color photographs of these animals ever published. However, when it is convenient to make a particular point the authors often use pictures of other species, without bothering to identify them. Photographs of bottlenoses, duskies, white-sided dolphins —and in one instance a killer whale—are merely identified as "dolphins," and by the time one reaches the

Appendix and the "clarifications," the book and the reader are hopelessly confused. (On a page with four cetaceans illustrated, there are only three names, one of which is *Phocoena cephalorhynchus,* a nonexistent combination of two generic names.)

It is indeed unfortunate that the common dolphin has been overshadowed by its more visible and better-documented relatives, because this species is enormously interesting, even without having to resort to fables of saving swimmers or feeding on bread. (It is also important to note that the common dolphin is not an inshore species, rarely being found close to the shore, while the bottlenose is frequently encountered in sight of land.) It is one of the most spectacularly patterned of all cetaceans, among the fastest, and certainly ranks among the highest jumpers. In the wild it has been seen to aggregate in schools that may number in the millions, and it can dive to over 800 feet (243 meters). It is a slender creature, reaching a length of 8.5 feet (2.55 meters), and a weight of some 200 pounds. At the same age, males are slightly larger than females, and the tail stock is narrow, without the dorsal or ventral keels often seen in other species of delphinid.

If it were not enough to confuse this species with other small cetaceans, especially the bottlenose, there are also problems within the world's populations of the common dolphin, since there seem to be distinctions that can be drawn at least on the subspecies level; some authors believe that there are several different species, not just the worldwide common dolphin. Most of the taxonomic arguments involve the physical structure of the animals—particularly the length of the snout and the number of teeth—but there are also behavioral differences between the various populations, and what is applicable to New Zealand dolphins may not apply to those found in California waters.

The species is found throughout the subtropical and temperate waters of the world, and with the exception of the killer whale, which is also found in the ice packs of both poles, the common dolphin is probably the most widely distributed cetacean in the world.

*The only other species that has approached swimmers in recent years has been the Atlantic spotted dolphin. In several instances (discussed in the section on this species), Atlantic spotters have been involved with humans in the wild, once where a single dolphin regularly approached divers in the waters off San Salvador, and another in which divers in the Bahamas were able to swim with an apparently cooperative school of these animals.

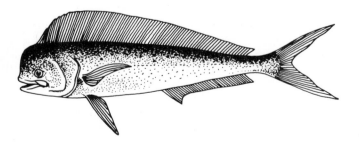

The dolphin fish, *Coryphaena hippurus,* also known as the dorado or *mahi-mahi.*

Allowing for the possibilities of subspecies in some of these areas, it is known from both coasts of North America as far north as British Columbia on the west; in Europe from the coasts, the Mediterranean, Black, and Azov Seas; the coasts of Africa and Southeast Asia; both coasts of South America; the Indian Ocean; Australia and New Zealand; and the coastal waters of Japan. In their study of the zoogeography of Cetacea, Marcuzzi and Pilleri (1971) indicate that the range of the animal is primarily coastal (except in the Indian Ocean), but there is evidence that the species occurs in substantial numbers thousands of miles from land. It has been frequently implicated in the eastern tropical Pacific yellowfin tuna fishery (Perrin 1975), and it is also known from various island groups in the Pacific, including Hawaii (Tomich 1969). Although none were reported from the 1976 Japanese whale-marking cruise in the western tropical Pacific, the authors (Miyazaki and Wada 1978) did report that the common dolphin had been seen in the Ogasawara and Marianas Islands in 1972. The species seems to be primarily a warm- and temperate-water inhabitant, although there are occasional reports of common dolphins in the waters of Nova Scotia, Iceland, and Greenland. In her report on the various species of cetaceans stranded at Tierra del Fuego, Goodall (1977) lists the common dolphin and writes that it is a species "that was not even supposed to be in the area."

It is a fairly common strander in areas where it might be expected to turn up—although it usually strands singly despite its great abundance—and also in some rather unusual places. On British coasts it is second only to the harbor porpoise in stranding frequency (Sheldrick 1979). In 1937, an "invasion" of the squid *Todarodes sagittatus* in British waters seems to have been responsible for numerous strandings of common dolphins, some of them multiples, with as many as six animals stranded together (Fraser 1946). On the east coast of the United States, where a systematic recording of strandings has recently been initiated, Mead (1979) has collected records of some 44 stranded common dolphins. There are documented accounts of the species stranding on Long Island and New Jersey coasts (Ulmer 1980), and a photographic record of two common dolphins that ascended the Hudson River in New York: one was found 73 miles upriver, and the other apparently swam 145 miles up, to Van Wies Point, approximately four miles south of Albany (Stoner 1938). Wood (1979) includes a record of a female common dolphin that was first seen three quarters of a mile up Bushman's Creek, Eastern Cape, South Africa, where she "charged the sandbank" and was dead by the time the observers reached her.

In the past, when the graceful little dolphin with the intricate coloration was not being confused with the bottlenose, it was occasionally accurately described. In 1834, Dewhurst (who refers to the species as *Delphinus didelphis*) wrote, "They are gregarious, and, like the porpoises, frequently sport about on the surface, leaping out of the water so as to be entirely visible . . . they are said to change their color before death; but this is probably an error, arising from a different reflection of the rays of light, when the body is in motion or at rest."

Soon the question of different species had arisen, and it is still far from resolution. Captain Scammon collected two females off Point Arguello, California, which were described by W. H. Dall in 1873, and on the basis of the "great length of the beak as compared with the braincase, and the remarkably deep channels in the maxillary bones on each side of the palatal ridge," he erected a new species, *Delphinus bairdii.* * (The differentiating factor between *Delphinus* and all other similar long-snouted, small delphinids is the presence of the grooves on the palate. True [1889] wrote, "The most salient characteristic by which this genus, in its present restricted limits, is distinguished is the presence of the lateral grooves in the palate.") In 1889, True listed numerous other species of *Delphinus*, including *D. major, D. fulvofasciatus, D. fosteri, D. janina, D. pomeegra, D. bairdii, D. moorei, D. algeriensis* and *D. albimanus*, and after examining the specimens and the various descriptions, he concluded that there were four valid species: *D. delphis, D. longirostris, D. capensis*, and *D. roseiventris*.

In the cetacean section of *Giant Fishes, Whales and Dolphins* (1938) F. C. Fraser wrote, "There have been described, as distinct from *Delphinus delphis*, a host of forms which, almost without exception, may be regarded as synonymous with the common species, but mention should be made of the Red-bellied Dolphin (*D. roseiventris*), which has the under part of the body pale rose colour. It is small in size, 3 feet 10 inches, stout in form and frequents the Molucca Sea and Torres Strait." Many of the forms, however, have persisted in the literature (*D. roseiventris* not among the survivors, at least with that name), and Hershkovitz (1966) recognized *D. delphis, D. ponticus*, and *D. bairdi* only as subspecies, while Nishiwaki (1972) lists *D. delphis, D. capensis*, and *D. bairdi* as distinct species, differentiating them on the basis of rostrum length, color pattern, and distribution. Mitchell (1975a) has summed up the state of the taxonomy of the common dolphin as follows:

---

*Like Baird's beaked whale, *Berardius bairdii*, the new species was named for Spencer F. Baird of the Smithsonian Institution, "to whose never tiring courtesy and unfailing liberality nearly every American naturalist is more or less indebted" (Dall 1874).

At least three morphologically distinct populations exist in the northeastern Pacific (Banks and Brownell 1969; W. E. Evans unpublished data). These include northern coastal and offshore stocks, ranging primarily from central California to inside the Gulf of California. In the southern part of this range, from southern California to the eastern coast of Baja California, a more neritic form occurs, the long-snouted form called *D. bairdii* by Banks and Brownell (1969). A third form occurs in the warmer waters off Central America. Southern and seaward limits of distribution of this form are not known. Other recognized local forms exist in the Black Sea (Tomilin 1957), in the Mediterranean (Gihr and Pilleri 1969), along the Atlantic coasts of Europe and Africa (van Bree and Purves 1972), in the Indian Ocean (van Bree 1971), Japan (Nishiwaki 1965), and elsewhere. Seasonal changes in the latitudinal distribution of long- and short-snouted forms in the eastern Pacific, western Pacific, and eastern Atlantic may be related to sea-surface temperature. The number of recognized populations can be expected to increase greatly with research.

In 1977, Rice listed only *D. delphis,* but added, "the extremely long-snouted Arabian form, *D. d. tropicalis* van Bree 1971, may be a distinct species (van Bree 1972)."

There is no question that there are differences in the various populations that can warrant at least sub-specific status. Evans's work on the species in the eastern North Pacific has fulfilled Mitchell's prediction that "the number of recognized populations can be expected to increase greatly with research," and in 1978, van Bree and Gallagher wrote, "The occurrence of *D. delphis* in the same area as *D. tropicalis* makes it plausible that *D. tropicalis* is a distinct species and not a sub-species of *D. delphis.*" Even though there appear to be valid and often consistent anatomical distinctions within the genus *Delphinus,* the variations are here incorporated into a single account, with applicable disclaimers, especially for those geographically distinct populations where behavior seems to be appreciably different. It is possible that further research will identify greater differences in the populations, and it is to be hoped that a comprehensive review of the taxonomy will result.

The common dolphin is a graceful, streamlined, and beautifully marked animal, and it is easy to see how it became the subject of veneration in ancient times. There is no doubt that it follows ships, and it rides gracefully before them so it has been often observed at sea. Tomilin (1957) describes the animals as follows: "Very slender, perfectly streamlined pelagic cetaceans of small size (up to 2.5 m) with a clearly defined long and narrow beak, a tall, posteriorly falcate dorsal fin, and pointed, narrow flippers with a falcate upper margin." The long beak is separated from the forehead by a V-shaped groove, another diagnostic feature of the species, but difficult to observe at sea. The coloration varies from population to population, but it can be generally described as consisting of a dark dorsal "cape" which begins at the forehead and continues back to the flukes, which are dark on the dorsal as well as the ventral surface. In various publi-

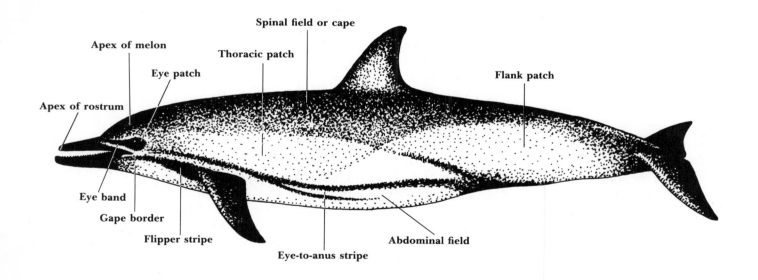

The "most complex pigmentation pattern" of all cetaceans: the crisscross pattern of *Delphinus delphis,* with the components identified according to the terminology of Mitchell (1970).

cations, the back of this species has been described as black, but Gaskin (1972) writes, "The dorsal surface . . . is actually a rich purplish-brown in life, fading to grayish black after death." As Mitchell (1970) points out, few authors have indicated the elapsed time between the death of the animal and the moment at which the photograph was taken. Timing becomes critical within hours—even minutes—after death: contrast between lightly and darkly pigmented areas is quickly lost in the overall darkening process which accompanies postmortem change.* The rest of the coloration—which Mitchell (1970) describes as "probably the most complicated within the Cetacea"—consists of a "bridle" around the eyes, an eye-to-flipper stripe, a lip patch, an eye-to-anus stripe (sometimes doubled), and the "thoracic patch and flank patch [which] form a figure eight as they are juxtaposed on the animal" (Mitchell 1970). "The thoracic patch," continues Mitchell in his discussion of the pigmentation patterns of cetaceans, "is worthy of special note, since it is one of the few brightly colored markings found on any species of delphinid." (Only the Atlantic white-sided dolphin shows a similar color in adult animals; juvenile killer whales are sometimes yellowish on those areas that are white on adults.) The dorsal fin of the common dolphin is often grayish with darker borders, and the underparts are white, which accounts for the name "white-bellied porpoise" among tuna fishermen. (Perrin [1972] also recognizes an offshore race of the spinner dolphin, which he calls the "white-belly spinner.")

In addition to the diagnostic grooves on the palate of this species, the common dolphin also has a great many small, sharp teeth, which "interlock perfectly, and, being sharply pointed and curved backward, are very effective for catching and holding slippery fish" (Kellogg 1940). The animals described as common dolphins from the Mediterranean and *D. bairdii* from California have approximately 50 teeth in each side of each jaw, for a total in the area of 200. The specimens referred to *D. tropicalis* (van Bree 1971; van Bree and Gallagher 1978), have a longer rostrum and a correspondingly higher number of teeth. Totals of

*Interestingly, one similarity between the dolphin fish and the dolphin mammal is the fading of the colors after death. In life, the fish is a veritable rainbow of green, blue, and gold, with a pattern of blue spots, and the color fades dramatically in death. In *Childe Harold's Pilgrimage*, Byron wrote (with reference to the fish, certainly):

> Parting day
> Dies like the dolphin, whom each pang
>   imbues
> With a new color as it gasps away,
> The last still loveliest, till—'tis gone,
>   and all is gray.
>   Canto IV, Stanza 29

59 to 60 teeth were counted in the tooth rows of those Indian Ocean specimens known as *tropicalis,* giving this variety of *Delphinus* the distinction of having as many as 250 teeth, more than any other mammal.

Common dolphins are ichthyophagous, known to feed on anchovies and other small fishes, and they eat a lot of them. Harmer (1927) quotes a report of 7,596 otoliths (ear bones) of small fishes taken from a single specimen, and Tomilin (1957) cites two studies where over 15,000 otoliths were counted in individual specimens. The actual manner in which the dolphins catch these fishes is not known, but both the dolphins and the fishes aggregate in huge numbers. Tomilin writes that schools of 200,000 to 300,000 dolphins are known to aggregate over schools of anchovy and sprat in the Black Sea.

There are other reports of huge schools of common dolphins, including Robson's (1976) description of a herd that was 51 kilometers (32 miles) in length by half a mile in width: "As the boat steamed across the path of the herd we tried to estimate the number of dolphins in all. We marked off by eye an area of about forty-two metres square (fifty yards square) and tried to count the dolphins in that area. It averaged out at about twenty-three or twenty-five each count and we concluded that a quarter of a million dolphins was a very conservative estimate." Cousteau and Diolé (1975) quote the acoustician R.-G. Busnel as having seen "dolphins assembled in schools that stretched to a length of thirty-five or forty miles," and "Once en route to Dakar, his ship was completely surrounded by dolphins with the animals spaced out so that there was only one dolphin to every twenty square yards of surface. He estimates that some of these schools com-

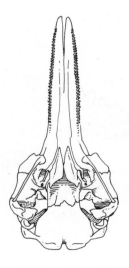

Ventral view of the skull of *Delphinus delphis.* Note the long narrow rostrum, the numerous small teeth, and the characteristic grooves on the palate. (After Hall and Kelson [1959])

prised several million dolphins." It is hard to imagine anyone counting "several million dolphins," but there seems to be no question that the animals gather in huge herds. In his study of the common dolphin off southern California, Evans (1975, 1976) reports sightings of groups that ranged in size from 10 to 30 animals to 3,000 or 4,000. Norris and Prescott (1961) reported seeing common dolphins forming "a single broad rank, two to five animals deep and many animals in width." In the Mediterranean, Pilleri and Knuckey (1969) observed the dolphins "on parade," which they described as "the whole school swimming in a line with groups of 2–3 animals following one another. . . ."

Of all the bow-riding cetaceans, the common dolphin seems to be the most accomplished. While most bow riders make short sorties, this species has refined the skill to such an extent that it can do it for hours at a time. Gaskin (1972) records one instance where four dolphins rode the bow wave of a vessel in New Zealand waters for "a distance of 60 or 70 miles." With the help of a moving vessel, the common dolphin is able to achieve what appears to be extraordinary speed (Tomilin says that it is "justly considered the fastest cetacean species"), estimated at up to 60 knots (Pilleri and Knuckey 1969). These authors were describing the bow riding of the animal: "They climb the bow wave and then leap out of the crest of the wave at top speed to fall into the water with an enormous splash." Tomilin (1957) quotes a report where a destroyer traveling at 30 mph was unable to overtake a school of dolphins. More conservative observers are willing to grant the species great speed, but not in the 50 mph range described by Cousteau and Diolé. (Gunter [1942] called such speeds "preposterous.") Even at top speed, the common dolphin probably cannot go much faster than 25 knots.*

In *Moby-Dick* Melville described the "huzza porpoise" thus:

This is the common porpoise found almost all over the globe. The name is of my own bestowal; for there are more than one sort of porpoises, and something must be done to distinguish them. I call him thus, because he always swims in hilarious shoals, which upon the broad sea keep tossing themselves to heaven like caps in a Fourth-of-July crowd. Their appearance is generally hailed with delight by the mariner. Full of fine spirits, they invariably come from the breezy billows to windward. They are the lads that always

live before the wind. They are accounted a lucky omen. If you yourself can withstand three cheers at beholding these vivacious fish, then heaven help ye; the spirit of godly gamesomeness is not in ye.

Common dolphins at sea are often seen leaping from the water as they traverse their broad range, and in this activity, as with all the others that involve relative power, they seem particularly competent. They can be seen associating with other species, such as the striped dolphin in the Mediterranean and the Pacific white-sided dolphin in the North Pacific. All of these animals are famous jumpers, and from a distance the massed schools have been likened to a squall on the horizon. (Robson [1976] called the effect "a scud of wind breaking the water.") The common dolphin jumps frequently and in all configurations, from headfirst entries to bellyflops; Pilleri and Knuckey (1969) observed one animal that leaped from the water making a 360-degree roll before reentry. In the wild, Tomilin (1957) recorded an animal that could leap out of the water to a height that "seemed to exceed the body length of the animal two or three-fold," and Robson (1976) claimed that a trained dolphin "broke the dolphin world high jump record with a jump of 6.6 metres (21 feet 6 inches)."

It would appear that an animal capable of these prodigious leaps and great speeds would have few enemies in the wild, but there are records of common dolphins with shark-bite scars (Wood et al. 1970; Leatherwood et al. 1973), and there are two remarkably similar accounts of the techniques used by killer whales to hunt these swift little dolphins. Brown and Norris (1956) observed a school of killers circling a school, crowding them tighter and tighter. "Finally, one of the killers veered off, rushing the school, while the others continued circling. In this fashion the killers ripped at the school one at a time, killing many of the dolphins. The water was red with blood." It has been shown that hunting killer whales "scream" (Schevill and Watkins 1966), and Robson (1976) observed a herd of dolphins in New Zealand waters "dashing around in a panic, rushing first one way then the other. But, whichever way they went, they seemed to run up against a wall of sound, growing louder and louder, frightening them more and more, until, not knowing which way to turn, they began to swim frantically around in a circle; a circle of terror hemmed in even closer by a terrifying wall of sound."*

Despite its clearly evident appearances, sometimes in huge schools, throughout the world's oceans,

---

*To the best of my knowledge, the common dolphin has not been timed over a measured course; most of the estimates of its great speed are exactly that: estimates. Species that have been clocked, such as the Pacific spotter, Pacific white-sided, and bottlenose dolphins (the spotter was the fastest), do not seem to be able to exceed 21 or 22 knots. It seems unlikely that the common dolphin could surpass these other species by a factor of three.

*Ordinarily, the underwater sounds of cetaceans cannot be easily heard above the surface. Robson says he was 500 meters from this incident when he observed it, but he describes the sound he heard as "an incessant bleep bleep bleep, a terrifying sound."

very little was known about the common dolphin until W. E. Evans began a detailed study of their behavior. (He wrote his 1975 Ph.D. dissertation, "The Biology of the Common Dolphin," at the University of California.) His extensive studies of the distribution, migration, feeding, diving behavior, and other aspects of the biology of this animal have brought it from the vague status of an animal known mostly from probably erroneous identifications in the past and fables in mythology, to one of the most extensively studied of all small cetaceans: Leatherwood and Reeves (1978) wrote that Evans' studies "have revealed more about *Delphinus* than any other wild dolphin in the eastern North Pacific."* In 1961 Norris and Prescott wrote that the common dolphin was "one of the most abundant species in southern California waters," but when Evans began concentrating his efforts on this species, he found out just how abundant it really was. He wrote that it is "indeed the most 'common' dolphin in southern California waters, representing 53% of all the odontocete cetaceans encountered in 654 observations" made over ten years from aerial surveys, naval observations and tuna fishing vessels. (The second most abundant cetacean in these waters is the Pacific white-sided dolphin, accounting for 14 percent of the total sightings.) The movements of the common dolphins in the study area were not random, as had been previously assumed: they were related to the movements of food sources, with the dolphins "locating highly productive areas, exploiting them and then moving on in search of new feeding grounds." Evans discovered that the dolphins were "catholic" feeders, preying on those species which are the most abundant or catchable—mostly anchovies in the fall and winter, and deep-sea smelt and various lantern fishes during the spring and summer.

Evans was also involved in some of the earliest attempts at radiotelemetric studies of wild dolphins, where a radio beacon was affixed to a newly captured animal, which was then released into the open sea, where it could rejoin its school and its movements could be tracked. This technique has greatly expanded the ability of scientists to learn about the movements of wild dolphins, since only surface observations could be made in the past, and for animals that aggregate in such enormous numbers and travel over such great areas, these observations were somewhat less than totally revealing. As Evans wrote in 1971, "Several years of trying to unravel the mysteries of herd movement and distribution by conventional methods of observation and tagging have resulted in little knowledge for

the time invested." The radiotelemetry techniques could not resolve questions of population size or home range, but they turned out to be extremely useful in identifying diurnal/nocturnal behavior, diving behavior (some of the radio packs were equipped with pressure transducers to record depth of dive), and individual movement over time and distance. It was discovered, for example, that a herd of dolphins might travel as much as 120 kilometers (75 miles) in a twenty-four-hour period, and there were other observations that herds of 200 to 300 animals might travel 270 miles (kilometers) over a ten-day period.

In all, eight dolphins were outfitted with radio packs, and in conjunction with aerial observations, it was learned that their movements were closely correlated with the sea-bottom topography in the area Evans refers to as the "Southern California Continental Borderland," with herds of dolphins orienting particularly to sea mounts, canyons, and escarpments, areas considered considered to be productive of the small planktonic animals fed upon by the small fishes, which in turn make up the bulk of the diet of the dolphins. Diving behavior was also correlated with the vertical migrations of the deep scattering layer (DSL),* with the deepest dives recorded after sunset and before dawn, the period when the DSL rises into the diving range of the dolphin. During their nocturnal deep diving, common dolphins usually go down to about 200 feet, but Evans recorded one dive of 846 feet. The longest dive was recorded at about four minutes, but most of the dives lasted less than a minute (Evans 1976). They did not seem to dive to the bottom in areas where the depth of the ocean varied from 400 to 1,000 meters, but they seem to confine their activities to the upper 150 feet of the water column. (Using echo-sounding equipment in the waters of the Hudson Canyon off New York, Edwards and Livingstone [1960] recorded feeding common dolphins that did approach the bottom, where the depth was about 200 feet. The different behavior may be related to the different bottom topography, or to the different habits of the Atlantic prey species.) In discussing Evans's work, Norris and Dohl (1980) wrote:

Delphinus schools off southern California and Baja California were found to congregate with considerable predictability over escarpments and seamounts which might be as much as

---

*Evans' studies have not, however, done much for the problem of the vernacular name of the dolphin. In a number of instances, he refers to the animal as "the common dolphin or the saddle-back porpoise."

*The deep scattering layers were long a mystery to oceanographers. Sonar equipment showed the existence of echoes where there was no bottom, and charts were marked with shoals rising from the deep and marked "ED"—existence doubtful (Dietz 1962). It was discovered that the cause of these echoes was a layer of living organisms, ranging from copepods to squid, that rises at night to feed on plankton. In the darkest hours of the night, the DSL is closest to the surface; it is deepest at the height of the day. The DSL is believed to be composed mostly of lantern fish, crustaceans, and colonial jellyfish.

2000 m below the surface. It is surmised that the dolphins may be able to "hear" such topography by passive listening, even though it is too deep to reach by diving, since there is an increase in ambient sea noise in such areas. Increased density of scattering—layer organisms exist over such sea-bottom topography as compared to sea bottom with less relief, and the stomach contents of dolphins feeding over areas of high relief contain fishes and squids of the vertical migrant layers, as well as surface anchovies.

Norris and Prescott (1961) recorded common dolphins feeding at the surface, and on one occasion, above the surface: "Several times the dolphins were seen catching sauries in mid-air as they both leapt above the surface. In one instance a fish was caught in mid-leap, an estimated 1.5 feet above the surface. One dolphin was observed to jump out of the water upside down and catch a leaping saury while in this position."

One of the products of Evans's extensive research was the identification of no fewer than four populations of common dolphins in the waters of southern California and Baja California, differentiated by the length of the snout and by geographical distribution. He identified the following stocks: (1) short-snouted Pacific, (2) short-snouted Baja California, (3) short-snouted tropical eastern Pacific, and (4) long-snouted neritic [inshore]. The short-snouted varieties are found all along the coast of western North America, all the way to northern South America, but the long-snouts seem to be restricted to the waters off Baja California. In a 1976 summary of this work, Evans wrote: "At present, because of intrapopulation variability demonstrated, it would be premature to suggest any change in the current taxonomic status of *D. delphis* in the northeastern Pacific. More detailed study of the extensive material available from the four groups perviously mentioned, which is now underway, may change this, especially in the case of the neritic long-snouted population, which may warrant at least sub-specific status."

The common dolphin is a known echolocator, producing click sounds that enable it to locate and identify objects and obstacles in its environment. Dreher and Evans (1964) recorded a school of about 180 dolphins feeding on sauries, where many examples of "chorusing" (more than one animal taking up and continuing a contour started by another) were heard, as well as various "trills." Evans (1971) reported that "an echolocation capability comparable to that of *Tursiops* has been reported." Like many other odontocetes, the common dolphin is capable of producing whistles and clicks simultaneously (Busnel and Dziedzic 1966), but with this species as well as the others that share these capabilities, we do not know how this is accomplished. These animals also have some means of navigating by sight or by "passive sonar," where they navigate by listening to the natural echoes produced in the sea, making no sounds of their own. Busnel and Dziedzic called this "silent navigating," and wrote that it always occurred "with good weather, a glassy sea, clear water, and a visibility approximately 70 to 80 m in depth." In this context they also mention that the schools they observed were "swimming very fast in a straight line, 2 to 3 m apart, in the direction of the sun. . . ." Other observers have correlated the movements of dolphin herds with the sun's transit; Pilleri and Knuckey (1969) wrote that "schools of dolphins always swim in the same direction when navigating: Depending on the time of day, they either swim from east to west or west to east—never N-S or S-N." Evans (1971) also noticed this solar orientation, but he warned that this observation should be "treated with caution," since there could be other factors—such as the movement of prey species—that more directly affect the dolphin's movement.

The whistle of delphinid species is both a communication device and a stress signal, depending upon the circumstances under which it is emitted and received. When Busnel and Dziedzic (1966) recorded dolphins at night in the Mediterranean—presumably in the process of feeding—they heard echo-ranging, [clicks], "a sort of squealing, and a few whistles." A variety of other signals was recorded, resulting in the classification of five different types of whistles, clicks, or combinations. Dreher (1966) recorded the "whistle contours" of captive bottlenoses, pilot whales, and common dolphins, and discovered that the common dolphins had the widest range of all the species tested: they utilized 19 different whistle sounds, while the bottlenose was recorded to make 17 different whistles. These various sounds were loosely correlated to the observed behavior of the animals, but it was not possible to identify the sounds as "language." When the conspecific tankmate of a male common dolphin died in Marineland of the Pacific, the male "circled her body, whistling constantly" (Brown and Norris 1956).

The mating behavior of these animals has been observed (Essapian 1962), and there is at least one record of a baby common dolphin born in captivity. In recording the birth, Robson (1976) wrote that a large friendly male was caught at the same time as the female, but since the animals were captured in March 1968 and the birth was observed in July, there is no reason at all to assume that this male was the father. (The gestation period for this species is approximately 11 months.) The baby was born tail first, and "the whole parturition, from the first labours until the calf started to breathe, took fourteen minutes." The calf lived for sixteen weeks at Marineland of New Zealand, being escorted around the tank by its mother and an "auntie," before succumbing to a staphylococcus infection. (Apparently this species does not do well in captive births: Cornell and Asper [1977] recorded no survivors among those born in North American aquariums and oceanariums.)

The behavior of captive individuals from different geographical locations often differs enough to suggest support for the idea of distinct subspecies. For North American specimens, Defran and Pryor (1980) gave this profile of the species in captivity: "Most descriptions of common dolphins in captivity suggest a shy, easily frightened animal that adapts poorly to the confinement of captivity and, once there, has little inclination to play and is reluctant to socialize with other tankmates." In his discussion of the various small cetaceans involved in the California "live-capture fishery," Walker (1975) described the common dolphin as "the most delicate . . . and the most difficult to keep in captivity." When brought to the oceanariums, these animals are usually in an advanced state of shock: "Upon introduction into the pool, a single, naive animal, left alone, quite often swims in an erratic fashion with low amplitude tail beats, occasionally bumping into the walls." Of the 22 common dolphins captured for display between 1966 and 1972, Walker reports that they had all died by 1975. Most died within the first 60 days, and only 15 percent survived more than a year. Cousteau's attempts to handle the common dolphins from the Mediterranean were inconclusive—especially since the animals shown in the illustrations are often other species—and they attempted only to handle animals in a floating pen before returning them to the ocean. In studies of dolphins in the Soviet Union—presumably individuals from the Black Sea—Yablokov and colleagues (1972) observed that a male common dolphin played with a live piked dogfish (a small shark), dragging it around the tank and throwing it up in the air. When observed in competitive situations, the Black Sea dolphins appeared "afraid of the bottlenose dolphin" that shared their tank, supporting Defran and Pryor's assessment.

In New Zealand, however, a totally different situation obtains. Gaskin (1972) wrote that this species "has proven amenable to training," and Frank Robson, the trainer at Marineland at Napier, was intimately involved with the species, since it was the first animal exhibited at the oceanarium.* He found that

the common dolphin was "most uncommonly clever and cooperative and could be trained to be first-class performers." A female named Dipper "broke the dolphin world high jump record with a jump of 6.6 metres (21 feet 6 inches) and repeated this day after day in her performance. We felt that she was entitled to smile as broadly as any bottlenose dolphin." For the shows, the common dolphins of New Zealand's Marineland were trained to race one another, play baseball, and tow boats with small children in them. These dolphins also demonstrated a clear dominance hierarchy, and it was an adult female named Brenda "who took over the whole pool as soon as she got into it and within days had asserted her authority over all the others. If anything did not please Brenda, then every other dolphin got the sharp end of her beak. Whatever job she wanted in a ball game or trick she had to have."

With regard to the behavior of one individual common dolphin toward another, there also appears to be an intrapopulational difference, but it may also be that there is not enough information to produce an accurate sample. For the California animals, Brown and Norris (1956) described an instance where a female named Pauline was captured and brought to Marineland of the Pacific. She seemed to be so stressed that she could not keep herself afloat, and the trainers had to use a set of "dolphin water wings" consisting of four glass jars to keep her from sinking. When a newly caught healthy male was introduced into the tank, he "sometimes swam under her and nudged her to the surface. Before long Pauline was swimming fairly normally and the two animals became inseparable until the day of Pauline's death two months later." After Pauline died, the male circled the tank whistling constantly, refused food, and he died three days later. In the Mediterranean, Pilleri and Knuckey (1969) recorded the care-giving behavior of the common dolphin for members of its own species when several animals immediately came to the assistance of a dolphin that had been harpooned:

They supported the wounded animal with their flippers and bodies and carried it to the surface. It blew 2–3 times and then dived. The whole incident lasted about 30 seconds and was repeated twice when the animal appeared unable to surface alone. All the animals including the wounded dolphin then dived and swam quickly out of sight. During the

*Robson's experiences are documented in his *Thinking Dolphins, Talking Whales* (1976), but only a limited number of his observations can be included here. Except where otherwise noted, references to the training of common dolphins are from Robson's book. Interpretation of these observations, however, must be tempered with the realization that Robson's training methods were something less than orthodox. He talked to the animals ("Look after the baby while Bess feeds"), and he believed that he had psychic powers which enabled him to communicate with dolphins by thought. Of his training methods, he wrote: "He will fix his eyes on the dolphin's eyes and concentrate as hard as he can on an appeal to the dolphin

to respond to and obey his wishes. . . . A very experienced trainer can make the dolphin increase her speed at this point by giving her strong thoughts of praise and encouragement while at the same time keeping up the thought that she must swim to the given spot."

chase only a few leaps were seen and the animals stayed around the yacht instead of fleeing, as they had done until this time.*

In his observations of the New Zealand common dolphin, Robson carefully pointed out that "when compassion was distributed, some of the common dolphins were left out," and he mentions a case where a female, upon the death of her calf, "refused to be left out and insisted on performing with the others." This appears to be a situation where too many human qualities are assigned to the dolphins; Robson expected the dolphin to feel "grief" at the death of her offspring, and he also felt that her insistence on performing so soon after this tragic experience showed a lack of "compassion." There are, on the other hand, numerous recorded instances (cited in Tomilin 1957) of "strongly developed maternal and filial instincts in this species." It should be borne in mind that the normally protective obligations of motherhood in mammals and the need for a juvenile to remain close to its mother for protection and sustenance do not necessarily indicate consciously protective behavior.

As might be expected with an animal so widely distributed and so abundant, the species has been hunted for centuries. In his 1975 survey of the dolphin fisheries of the world, Mitchell indicates that it has been hunted for food and oil in Israel, Japan, and Venezuela, and the species is "incidentally" taken in purse seines and shark nets off South Africa and the Ivory Coast. In the U.S. tuna fishery in the eastern tropical Pacific, this species has been the third most numerous—after the spinner and the spotter—taken in the tuna nets, accounting for about 10 percent of the total number of dolphins killed for the years 1971–74 (Perrin 1975). Conservative estimates indicate that about a million dolphins died in the nets during that period, so approximately 100,000 common dolphins perished at the hands of the tuna fishermen. The animal is still being hunted in the Azores by sperm whalers, although Clarke (1980) reports that they are only taken after a day's sperm whaling, and not sought intentionally. They are "harpooned when

*This sort of behavior is often cited as evidence of a higher intelligence in cetaceans, since they appear to show a genuine concern for their own kind, a characteristic that seems to be lacking in those creatures of lower intelligence. In E. O. Wilson's *Sociobiology* (1975) the care-giving incident of the common dolphin is accompanied by this disclaimer:

By itself the behavior is not as complicated as, say, nest building by weaver-birds or the waggle dance of honeybees. It could well represent an innate, stereotyped response to the distress of companions. Drowning that results from an incapacitating injury must be one of the chief causes of mortality among cetaceans. The automatic response of offspring and other relatives contributes greatly to inclusive fitness and is likely to have been fixed in the innate behavioral repertory of the species.

they conveniently come to the bow." In his 1971 discussion of Azorean whaling, Housby wrote that the harpooner learns his skill by "throwing at dolphins," and the catch is "sold by the kilo. In flavor dolphin meat resembles steak, and is very popular with the islanders."

It is in the Black Sea that the common dolphin has been most heavily exploited. Russia and Turkey, the countries that comprise most of the borders of this inland sea (Bulgaria and Romania have some shoreline on the west) have intensively fished for dolphins for many years. Tomilin (1957) reports that the animals, mostly common dolphins but also bottlenoses and harbor porpoises, were hunted at first by shooting but then by purse seining. This method, using nets that may be as much as a mile wide, is very similar to that employed by the American tuna fishermen, but in the Black Sea it is the dolphins that are the object of the fishery. While herding the dolphins, fishermen clang cobblestones together (Tomilin refers to this as the "telephone") to panic and drive the dolphins into the nets. "The method of Soviet dolphin catchers has been successfully adopted in Bulgaria, which had no dolphin fisheries of her own before the war," according to a report quoted by Tomilin. Even though Soviet catch figures for the Black Sea fishery include all three of the aforementioned species, "it is known that the common dolphin *Delphinus delphis* has historically been the predominant animal in the catch" (Smith 1976). In the twentieth century (with time out for World War II), the number of dolphins caught in the Black Sea is staggering. Mitchell (1975) summarizes the catch statistics at approximately 110,000 to 130,000 animals per year from 1931 to 1941, and for later years he quotes that catch as: "USSR 75,000, Turkey 40,000, Romania 5,000, Bulgaria 2,000–3,000. About 200,000 porpoises are caught annually, which is about 20 per cent of the population." (Different sources are quoted for these figures, and Mitchell writes, "catch statistics . . . do not appear to be readily available in the published literature.") In a 1976 study of the status of the small cetacean populations in the Black Sea, Smith estimates that the fishery peaked in 1938 with a catch of 135,000 to 140,000 animals, and has been in decline since then. "It is apparent that a fishery directly on these animals has reduced their abundance to marginal levels" (Smith 1976).

Apparently the Soviet dolphin fishery ceased in 1966, but the Turks continue to slaughter the animals in vast numbers. Between 1951 and 1957, something on the order of 175,000 dolphins were killed annually. Berkes (1977) wrote that "Turkey is the only country in the world reporting a major catch of *Delphinus* according to FAO statistics." He gives the figures for the

Turkish dolphin fishery in metric tons, and these figures can be converted to numbers of animals as follows:

1965: 52,000
1966: 236,000
1967: 8,000
1968: 88,000
1969: 332,000
1970: 136,000
1971: 176,000
1972: 176,000
1973: 176,000

According to the IWC report in which these figures are included, "No explanation is given of the wide year-to-year variation in the catch." Berkes has noted that the Turks hunt the dolphins for their oil, the rest of the carcass going for fish meal. The Turkish fishermen shoot the animals, and they are given free bullets by the government, and they are sold guns at government-subsidized prices.

FRASER'S DOLPHIN

Lagenodelphis hosei Fraser 1956

During a reorganization of the cetacean collection at the British Museum of Natural History in the 1950s, a skeleton was discovered that bore only this identification: "White Porpoise (?). *Lagenorhynchus* species, purchased from Dr. C. Hose, Lutong River, Baram, Borneo." The registration number on the skeleton indicated that it had been acquired by the museum sometime before 1895. When F. C. Fraser examined the specimen, he realized that it was different from any other known species. He published his description of this new species in the *Sarawak Museum Journal* in 1956, and noted that while the specimen resembled two known genera, it obviously belonged to neither. He

concluded that "it is a new form of dolphin having affinities with both *Lagenorhynchus* and *Delphinus*, but generically different from either. It is proposed that Hose's Sarawak Dolphin may be named *Lagenodelphis hosei.*"

After the publication of Fraser's 1956 description, Ernest Hose, the brother of Dr. Charles Hose, wrote to Tom Harrison, the director of the Sarawak Museum, and told him that it was he who had collected the specimen, and that "it was not possible to recognise the color of the skin, it was so very decomposed." When Charles Hose sent the skeletal material to Dr. Sidney Harmer at the British Museum, "he must have been drawing on his imagination" to have described the specimen as white. This correspondence was published in 1957, so now there was a new species of dolphin, but even the faintest clues as to its actual appearance had been proven erroneous.

On January 21, 1971, the tuna seiner *Larry Roe* was working some 500 miles (800 kilometers) west of Costa Rica, near Cocos Island. As they pulled in their nets, the fishermen discovered approximately 25 dolphins of an unknown type. Before they were discarded, a large male and a small calf were photographed by an observer aboard the vessel. On February 17, 1971, a pregnant female of the same species was collected south of Durban, South Africa, and two days later, an adult male was taken in the same area. An adult male washed ashore at Coff's Harbor, New South Wales, on March 1, 1971, and in February 1972, another female was collected at Durban. Later that year, three specimens, all females, were collected in a set on yellowfin tuna 1,587 miles (2,560 kilometers) west of the Cocos Island location of the first tuna set, this time near Clipperton Island (Perrin et al. 1973). In 1973, two more records were published in the *Reports* of the Whales Research Institute of Tokyo (Tobayama et al. 1973): one was a single animal that stranded on May 25, 1972 on a beach at Kamogawa, Japan, and another that had been found at Kao-hsiung, Taiwan. (The Kao-hsiung specimen had actually been found in 1969, but it was not identified until Hung Chia Yang came to the Ocean Research Institute in Tokyo and conferred with cetologists there.) Two more animals were collected during a Japanese whale-marking cruise in the western tropical Pacific in 1976 (Miyazaki and Wada 1978a).

While hardly an overwhelming number of specimens (Miyazaki and Wada list all twelve known specimens), it is fascinating to realize that prior to its description by Fraser in 1956, there were no records whatsoever of this species, either from beached specimens or from those taken at sea.

In 1976, Leatherwood and colleagues wrote of this species in the western North Atlantic: "Although Fraser's dolphins have yet to be described for the western North Atlantic Ocean, they are included here as 'possibles' because of the recent discovery that their range is far more extensive than previously known." The prediction has indeed proven correct, and the species has now been definitely recorded for the tropical Atlantic: in 1976, two females were taken at sepa-

rate times at the fishing village of Barrouallie on the island of St. Vincent in the Lesser Antilles, and Caldwell and colleagues (1976) also recorded the skull of a male that had been collected at the same village prior to 1972.

Fraser's dolphin (sometimes called the "short-snouted whitebelly dolphin" or the "Sarawak dolphin") is dark grayish above and lighter below, with a series of lateral stripes. The coloration has been variously described as "grayish yellow" (Miyazaki and Wada 1978a) or "dark greyish blue with a brownish hue" (Perrin et al. 1973), and there are a "bridle," "eye stripe," and "lip patch," using the terminology of Mitchell (1970). The species can be distinguished by the small size of the dorsal fin and flippers, both of which features are dark in color. Fraser's dolphin has a short but distinct beak, more clearly defined than that of the various species of *Lagenorhynchus,* but considerably shorter than that of *Stenella* or *Delphinus.* At sea, this rare animal might be confused with the striped dolphin, but the smaller size, smaller appendages, and different pigmentation pattern should en-

Lagenorhynchus

Lagenodelphis

Delphinus

Comparison of body shapes.

able the observer to differentiate the animals. From the limited number of specimens examined, it has been estimated that the species averages a body length of about 7 1/2 feet (2.26 meters). There are approximately 40 teeth in each side of the upper and lower jaws.

Almost nothing is known of the natural history of Fraser's dolphin. It has been taken in the tuna fishery in the eastern tropical Pacific (Perrin 1975), but in such small numbers as to make this a statistically insignificant sample. Tobayama and colleagues (1973) reported "only squid beaks and otoliths of fish" in the stomach of the Kamogawa specimen, and suggested that "they eat food without diving to depth." One of the specimens examined in Barrouallie was found to have consumed "a large, very red shrimp, fish otoliths, cephalopod beaks, and two isopods" (Caldwell et al. 1976).

Several observations of Fraser's dolphin at sea suggest that the species aggregates in fairly large schools. Berzin (1978) described three schools near the Equator, "one group very large, probably 800 animals," and a Japanese vessel, operating north of New Guinea, reported three separate schools, one of 200 to 300 animals, a second of 40 to 50, and a third of 400 to 500 Fraser's dolphins. The last school was seen together with a school of melon-headed whales, which shows that "Fraser's dolphins may rarely mix with other species" (Miyazaki and Wada 1978b). In only one instance did any of the animals approach the research vessel, supporting Mitchell's (1975) suggestion that the species is particularly shy of boats, "possibly accounting for its obscurity."

The scattered records for this species suggest a much wider range than was previously assumed. The type specimen is from Sarawak, Borneo, and the spe-

cies has been collected from the eastern tropical Pacific; South Africa; eastern Australia; Japanese waters; Taiwan; the western tropical Atlantic; and the western Pacific, north of New Guinea. It is therefore possible to assign this species a distribution that includes the entire tropical Pacific and Indian Oceans, as well as the tropical Atlantic, but there are no estimates of total numbers, so the sightings and collecting records might represent only isolated populations.

WHITE-BEAKED DOLPHIN

Lagenorhynchus albirostris Gray 1846

There is no accepted vernacular name for the animals of the genus *Lagenorhynchus*—which can be translated as "flask-beaked"—although they are sometimes referred to as "plowshare-headed dolphins" (Mitchell 1975b), an awkward appellation that does little justice to these exuberant and beautifully marked creatures. "Lags," a contraction of the scientific name, is often used, but it is more a slang expression than an accepted common name. Each species, of course, has one or more common names, usually descriptive of its color pattern, but as a group the genus is nameless.

Despite its common and scientific names (*albirostris* is literally translated as "white beak"), the beak of this species is not always white. In the western North Atlantic, the short but distinct beak is sometimes gray, or even speckled. In many instances, however, the beak is white, and Harmer (1927) wrote, "The white-beaked dolphin is readily recognized by several characters, among which the white beak to which it owes its popular name is the most obvious. I have seen no specimen in good condition in which this feature was not sharply marked. . . ." Bierman and Slijper (1948) have written that the beak "may show a mottled gray or even a dark gray color," and Jonsgard (1962) includes photographs of a specimen with the comment, "notice the darkish snout." Since the beak on this animal is only about 2 inches long, it may not always be visible, no matter what color it is.

The primary field mark for this species, therefore, is the light area on the back, behind the dorsal fin. The dark-gray back is also marked with a diffuse pattern of chevrons, stripes, and blazes, more prominent in some geographical areas than in others, and the throat and belly are white. The white-beaked dolphin reaches a maximum length of about 10 feet (3.1 meters), and it is usually encountered in schools of 10 to 20 animals, although it sometimes aggregates in enormous schools, numbering in the thousands.

In the North Atlantic, the only other short-beaked, black-and-white dolphin is the white-sided dolphin. The two can be distinguished by the white area on the back of the white-beaked variety; a profile that is shorter and somewhat stubbier than that of the Atlantic white-sided dolphin; and the dorsal fin of the white-beaked dolphin that is higher, more gracefully falcate, and placed farther back than that of the white-sided dolphin. As its name implies, the white-sided dolphin has a white blaze on its side, aft of the dorsal fin, but it has no white on its back. The caudal keels of the white-beaked dolphin are not as pronounced as those of the white-sided, and the former has fewer teeth in each jaw, with 22 to 25 sharply pointed teeth on each side of each jaw, as compared to 30 to 40 teeth in the jaws of the latter.

Because of its cold-water habitat, this species has been said to have an especially thick layer of blubber (Kellogg 1940). The white-beaked dolphin feeds on squid (therefore one of its common names in Newfoundland, "squidhound"), octopus, cod, herring, and crustaceans. Like many other small odontocetes, it appears to be an opportunistic feeder, and will eat whatever food is available. Kellogg also reported that "stomachs of these animals have been found packed with the undigested bones of whiting, claws of hermit crabs, and horny parts of the common whelk, a mollusk used in dyeing purple." Although not well known as bow riders, white-beaked dolphins are sometimes attracted to boats, and Jonsgard (1962) reported that the animals "swam close to the boat on several occasions." In Newfoundland the species is also known as "spinner," because of its occasional habit of emerging from the water and rotating a couple of times on its long axis (Peter Beamish, personal communication). Fraser (1946) records a school of about 20 or 30 animals, "some of them very small, and they leaped out of the water occasionally sometimes going into it again

sideways instead of in the normal manner. It was noted too that the animals sometimes swam on their side when under water." Records of juvenile specimens stranded on British coasts indicate that the size of a newborn white-beaked dolphin is about 4 feet (1.2 meters); at sizes just a little larger than that, the teeth have not erupted, and there was milk in their stomachs (Harmer 1927).

This dolphin is the most northerly of the North Atlantic lags, found from Cape Cod and Newfoundland north to western Greenland and the Davis Straits. It is more numerous even farther north, in the Barents Sea and off the coast of Norway, and it shows a "striking preference for the North Sea, and may occur at any time of year" (Harmer 1927). It is the predominant small cetacean in the waters of northern Norway, especially in the Norwegian Sea.

There are some reports of this species being taken in various small whale fisheries in Norway, Iceland, Scotland, and Ireland (Mitchell 1975b), but they are usually "incidental" to the species being hunted, either minke whales or pilot whales. Sanderson (1956) wrote that the Greenlanders hunted this species regularly, because "the animal just happened to be very common in their sea-country, while they needed it for food." According to records kept on both sides of the Atlantic, there has been a marked increase in strandings of this species in recent years. Sergeant (1979) attributes this to an overall cooling trend in the North Atlantic, since "*L. albirostris,* a cool-water species rather typical of the North Sea and northward, has increased in British waters and has tended to displace *T. truncatus* [in total strandings] in the southern North Sea (Netherlands)." In the British Museum's reports on strandings on the shores of the British Isles (Fraser 1974), this species has moved up from seventh place in total strandings to fourth, and in the North Sea, it has moved up to become the third most frequent strander, after the harbor porpoise and the bottlenose dolphin (Sergeant 1979).

ATLANTIC WHITE-SIDED DOLPHIN

Lagenorhynchus acutus Gray 1828

This is a gregarious, lively species—its common name in Newfoundland waters is "jumper"—often seen in large aggregations, sometimes numbering 1,000 animals or more. Harmer (1927) wrote of a group in the Shetlands where "there were thousands around the boat. The water seemed alive with them."

The white-sided dolphin of the North Atlantic reaches a maximum length of about 9 feet (2.75 me-

ters) and has 30 to 40 teeth in each side of the upper and lower jaws. The upper part of the short, ill-defined beak is always dark, but the lower jaw is sometimes lighter. The entire back of the animal, including the sharply curved dorsal fin, is black. There are a pair of distinctive, light-colored blazes on the flanks, below and behind the dorsal fin. These two blazes are juxtaposed, and may give the impression of being a single, light area. The rearmost of these is tan or yellowish in color, and the lower, forward, one is white. This "flash," often seen as the animal leaps from the water, is considered the most distinctive field mark, for no other dolphin in the North Atlantic is similarly adorned. Gavin Maxwell (1952), writing of a specimen that had been harpooned in the Hebrides, wrote, "the dolphin . . . was a male, a little over seven feet long, graceful and streamlined as a swallow, the flared markings on his side looking as though they had been drawn in conscious design to enhance an image of speed and beauty." The tail stock is distinctive in this species: the dorsal and ventral keels are sharply pronounced, narrowing abruptly just before the flukes. There is a prominent eye-to-flipper stripe, a dark area around the vent, and the flippers and flukes are dark. Schevill (1956) reported a very light-colored specimen off Cape Cod, "almost white all over its back and sides."

Because the yellowish flash is so unusual in cetaceans, it has been a subject for speculation and discussion. Why should this animal alone display this color? (The common dolphin has a tan thoracic patch, and the "white" areas of young killer whales are often yellowish, but these are the only other instances in which colors other than black, dark blue, white or gray are seen in pelagic dolphins.) Mitchell (1970), emphasizing that "there is almost no evidence bearing directly on delphinid pigmentation patterns," writes:

Lagenorhynchus acutus seems to be the only living species of *Lagenorhynchus* to have evolved distinct white and brownish-yellow patches on the side, in addition to a distinct, dark spinal field and a white abdominal field. . . . *L. acutus* is analogous to *D. delphis* among the *Stenella-Delphinus* group in combination of black and brown pigments and in the distinctiveness with which each area is demarcated. It may be that all of these species are endemic to continental shelf regions, if they are not strictly coastal in habitat.

In a discussion of the coloration of this species, Waller and Tyler (1979) wrote that the "buff-colored streak would remain visible only at shallow depths [while] the lower white stripe would remain visible at greater depths . . . and might therefore function as a recognition marker during schooling or feeding. . . ." It is possible that the yellowish flank blaze could serve as a "recognition marking" as the animal leaps from the water, since this color, so quickly rendered invisible in water is particularly visible in air, and this flash may enable the species to readily identify its conspecifics at considerable distances as they jump.*

The white-sided dolphin is often confused with the white-beaked dolphin, the only other lag from the North Atlantic. The dark back from dorsal fin to flukes is diagnostic of the white-sided, as are the white and tan blazes and the exaggerated caudal keels. This species is somewhat the smaller of the two Atlantic varieties, but this information is only useful where some sort of comparison is possible.

Even though this is an abundant animal in the offshore North Atlantic, very little is known of its life

*Würsig (1978, 1980) has suggested that the closely related dusky dolphin communicates its feeding activities over distance by various types of leaps and the subsequent reentry noises. There is no other lag in the waters inhabited by the dusky, but the white-sided dolphin, whose range often overlaps that of the white-beaked dolphin, might use this marking as a visual signal to others of its own species.

history. Males seem to grow somewhat larger than females, but from the examination of the teeth of stranded specimens, it was suggested that females live longer, averaging 27 years maximum, compared to 22 years for males (Sergeant et al. 1980). Calves are born in midsummer after an 11- or 12-month gestation period, and they are about 3 1/2 feet (1 meter) long at birth (Fraser 1934). From numerous records of this species stranding on various European coasts, we have obtained an idea of their diet. They seem to be primarily fish eaters, consuming mackerel, herring, and various other species. They have also been found with squid and some crustaceans and mollusks in their stomachs, which suggests some bottom feeding as well as midwater and surface feeding.

Two recent multiple strandings in New England have provided a substantial amount of new information on the biology of this species, since previous assumptions were based on the examination of small numbers of specimens—usually singletons or double strandings, such as those recorded by Gresson in Ireland in 1968 and 1969—and therefore, no group comparisons were possible, an obvious requirement for generalizations about a species. On May 15, 1973, about 20 animals stranded at Wellfleet, Massachusetts, and of these, 13 were examined in detail. Then on September 6, 1974, "a large herd stranded alive at Lingle Cove, Cobscook Bay, Maine . . . of which many died and 59 complete specimens were trucked to the New England Aquarium, frozen and examined in detail" (Sergeant et al. 1980). In both strandings, females outnumbered males, and there was an absence of immature animals between 2 1/2 and 6 years of age. "But these," wrote the authors, "predominate in single strandings and occasionally form loose groups." Sergeant and colleagues, who examined the specimens in detail (and from whose account these quotes have been taken), found 15 animals of lengths less than 150 centimeters, which they assumed were suckling calves. The absence of "older immatures" (180–200 centimeters) in the sampled herds suggests that these animals do not remain with a reproductive herd. "One may conclude that immature *L. acutus* of both sexes, on reaching the age of weaning, tend to leave or be driven away from the reproductive herds, and either lead solitary lives, form themselves into loose groupings, or attach themselves to groups of other species of delphinids." (There are numerous instances of this species having been spotted with schools of pilot whales, and an instance where a single animal was seen "swimming with two killer whales.")

The two *Lagenorhynchus* species of the North Atlantic. The white-sided dolphin (top) can be identified by the black upper jaw, the yellowish "flash patch," and the exaggerated keels on the tail stock. The white-beak dolphin (below) has a light-colored (but not always white) upper jaw, and a light area on the back just behind the dorsal fin.

The Atlantic white-sided dolphin is found off-shore from the Gulf Stream and the Laborador Current, from the Hudson Canyon off New York City, and there is one record of a specimen stranded in Virginia, "which extends the southern distribution approximately 700 km southwest of Schevill's (1956) sighting [off Cape Cod]" (Testaverde and Mead 1980). In the eastern North Atlantic, they are fairly common off the Shetland and Orkney Islands, and in the North Sea off southern Norway. In the table of stranding frequencies for the British coasts from 1913 to 1966, Fraser (1974) records this species as ranking eleventh in total strandings. (The white-beaked dolphin is fifth overall, and a glance at the map showing the actual locations of the strandings clearly indicates the overlap of the range of the two North Atlantic lags in the British Isles. Both species have stranded from the Shetlands in the north to Cornwall in the south, and there does not appear to be any geographical pattern that would correspond to a northerly or southerly preference for either species in the North Sea.) The white-sided dolphin is particularly plentiful in southern Norwegian waters, and Jonsgard (1962) has written that "there does not seem to be any reliable evidence for including the waters of northern Norway in the range of this species," further supporting the idea that the white-sided dolphin is the more southerly of these two species.

These animals are sometimes taken in substantial numbers in a drive fishery in the Norwegian fjords, where the fishermen trap the dolphins as they enter the bays in pursuit of herring. Sometimes, after the animals have entered the fjord, a net is run across the opening, and then the dolphins are taken with hand harpoons (Jonsgard and Long 1959). At other times, "the animals are maneuvered into a confining situation where they are either entrapped or immediately driven ashore and killed" (Mitchell 1975b). They have occasionally been driven ashore in Newfoundland as well, where Sergeant and Fisher (1957) have reported catches of up to 250 animals, but they write that "these figures may be exaggerated." When 52 animals were harpooned one after another in Norwegian waters, they did not panic, nor did they demonstrate any of the supportive behavior sometimes exhibited by other members of the genus (Jonsgard and Nordli 1952).

Even though the two North Atlantic representatives of the genus are relatively common in the off-shore waters of some of the most densely populated areas in the Western Hemisphere, there have been virtually no efforts made to capture or exhibit either species. They do occasionally approach boats, but they do not seem to come close enough to have made capture feasible. Townsend (1914) reports that one of the genus (species unidentified) was exhibited in the New York Aquarium after having been cast ashore, but it was "too badly injured to live more than a few weeks."

PACIFIC WHITE-SIDED DOLPHIN

Lagenorhynchus obliquidens Gill 1865

We have observed that this species has a wider range, congregates in larger numbers, and exhibits more activity, than any other of the Dolphin family. They are seen in numbers varying from a dozen to many hundreds, tumbling over the surface of the sea, or making arching leaps, plunging again on the same curve, or darting high and falling diagonally sideways upon the water, with a spiteful splash, accompanied by a report that may be heard at some distance. [Scammon 1874]

This common resident of the coastal waters of Pacific North America and Japan reaches a length of about 7 feet (2.13 meters) and a weight of perhaps 300 pounds (131 kilograms). The white stripes on the flanks, the hooked, bicolored dorsal fin, and the short, dark beak are good field marks. The curvature of the dorsal fin becomes more pronounced in older animals, and is therefore an indication of maturity (Brown and Norris 1956). It is a high-spirited animal, a strong swimmer, and a frequent jumper. (One overenthusiastic individual jumped 10 feet onto the deck of a research vessel, but observers quickly returned it to its proper element [Dearborn 1968].) It is almost obsessively active as it jumps, dives, frolics, rides bow waves, and somersaults, apparently for the sheer joy of it. These lags are often seen in huge schools numbering in the thousands, and also in mixed aggregations with common dolphins and northern right whale dolphins. In 1874, describing the activities of this species, Scammon wrote:

At first we could hear a harsh rustling sound, as if a heavy squall of wind, accompanied with hail, was sweeping over the otherwise tranquil sea; and, as the moon burst through the clouded sky, we could see a sheet of foam and spray surging towards us. In a few moments the vessel was surrounded by myriads of these Common Porpoises, which, in their playful movements, and for the space of one hour, whitened the sea all around us for as far as the eye could discern, when they almost instantly disappeared.*

*Scammon called this animal the "striped or Common Porpoise," but he illustrated the animal we now know as the Pacific white-sided dolphin, and he further identified it as *Lagenorhynchus obliquidens*. The common name of this species seems always to be changing; Norris and Prescott (1961) called it the "striped porpoise"; Brownell (1964) referred to it as the "Pacific striped dolphin"; and Hall (1970) knew it as the "Pacific white-striped dolphin."

Obliquidens means "slanting teeth," but the teeth of this species—about 30 in each side of the upper and lower jaws—do not appear to be noticeably different from those of the other lags.

In the wild, the mixed schools present the appearance of a frothing, leaping multitude of small cetaceans, and a certain proximity is required to differentiate the species that may occur together. The common dolphin has the characteristic crisscross or "saddle" pattern, a yellowish thoracic patch, and a long slender beak, while the white-sided dolphin has a short, dark beak, a hooked dorsal fin, and light-colored longitudinal stripes that have been referred to as "suspenders." Even in mixed groups, it would be difficult to confuse the right whale dolphin with the white-sided, since the right whale dolphin has no dorsal fin at all. Another small cetacean of the North Pacific is the Dall porpoise, but this is a strongly marked, stout-bodied black-and-white animal that does not jump, but rather speeds up to the bows of moving vessels, creating a characteristic "rooster tail" of spray. There have been occasional observations of oddly colored examples of this species, including Brown and Norris's 1956 mention of an animal that was snowy white except for a "mottled gray area running dorsally from the snout to the tail stock." In another case, an animal was seen in the company of normally pigmented dolphins, but it had a totally uncharacteristic color pattern, including a large white patch over the eye, and stripes where white-sided dolphins do not normally have stripes (Brownell 1965a). These irregularly colored animals are rare and unusual, but they can confuse the untrained observer.

According to Nishiwaki (1967), this species is "the most widespread in the North Pacific." In the west, it is found from Kamchatka and the Kurile Islands south to the Philippines. Its range extends to the

Bering Sea (but not into it), and to the Aleutian chain, across the Pacific to the coastal waters of North America, from Alaska to Baja California, and occasionally as far south as Panama. It is particularly abundant in Japanese waters, where Nishiwaki (1972) has estimated a total population of between 30,000 and 50,000 animals, and off the coasts of North America, where Brown and Norris (1956) have called it "probably the most common cetacean in southern California waters." It is found primarily close to large land masses, and not as much in deep, offshore waters. Nishiwaki (1967) indicates that it ranges over the entire North Pacific, but Tomich (1969) reports "no specific records from Hawaii."

In both the eastern and the western portions of its range, the white-sided dolphin is often encountered in large schools, upwards of 1,000 strong. One observation recorded a school that was one and a half miles across, and "thirty minutes were required for it to pass at a rate of two or three knots.faster than the speed of the ship" (Wilke et al. 1953). These animals are extraordinarily energetic, perhaps even more so than any of the other lags, and much given to mass breachings, somersaults, and lusty splashing. This energy has been exploited in porpoise shows, where they have been trained to leap out of the water in jumps that Daugherty (1972) calls "particularly breathtaking." At sea they ride bow waves and follow ships, often "body surfing" the wake of a fast-moving vessel. A captive female named Notty was the subject of a number of hydrodynamic experiments to determine the actual swimming speed of dolphins, and her maximum speed was recorded at 15 knots, or a little over 17 mph (Lang and Daybell 1963). The researchers had expected this species to demonstrate greater speeds, but it has been pointed out that the tests—conducted in a tank at General Dynamics, San Diego—might have been "adversely affected by one or more environmental factors." White-sided dolphins, therefore, might be faster than the tests on Notty indicated.

In 1957, K. S. Norris had an ideal opportunity to observe the bow-riding technique of this species:

Two adults of *Lagenorhynchus obliquidens* took up station at the bow of the Marineland collecting vessel *Geronimo* and stayed there for 20 minutes. The vessel was traveling at 8 1/2 knots, as judged from engine revolutions that had previously been checked against speed. Every movement of the animals could be seen clearly and we were even able to determine that both were females when they rolled onto their backs. Both animals stayed at the bow, with only an occasional beat of their flukes, during the entire period. Some of the periods during which no tail beats at all occurred were timed at 7, 7, 15, 30, 34, and 47 seconds, respectively.

The animals guided themselves by bending their heads and bodies slightly, and by tiny movements of their pectoral flippers. These positioning movements allowed the porpoises to slip onto their sides or even to spin completely over without losing station. [Norris and Prescott 1961]

These lags are sometimes seen in the company of larger whales, in situations that are comparable to the behavior of the dusky dolphin with the right whales of Patagonia. In one instance, after following a sei whale, the whalers noted that a group of white-sided dolphins stayed with a sei, and in another case, these dolphins were seen "jumping in the vicinity of three juvenile humpback whales" (Brownell 1964). On other occasions, white-sided dolphins have been seen in the company of Risso's dolphins, and blue-white dolphins "feeding from horizon to horizon" (Wahl 1977).

In California waters, the main food item of this species is the northern anchovy, although it has also been reported to feed on other small fishes and squid. The dolphins follow the seasonal movements of the prey species: when the anchovies move closer to shore in the summer and fall, the dolphins follow; and in the winter and spring, both dolphins and anchovies are found farther from land (Norris and Prescott 1961). (Würsig and Würsig [1980], in discussing the movements of the dusky dolphin in Patagonian waters, note that the same dependence on prey species is apparent, only there it is the southern anchovy.) When actually feeding, these dolphins seem to separate into smaller groups of 10 to 20 animals, but in their seasonal movements they move in huge schools.

There are no recorded mass strandings for this species, and it appears to strand singly and relatively infrequently. In his extensive study of the literature on the stranding phenomenon, F. G. Wood (1979) cites only one reference to a stranded Pacific white-sided dolphin, and that was a captive animal that beached itself while being trained by the Navy at Point Mugu, California. Apparently, something panicked Pat while she was being worked, and she streaked for shore, only to be picked up "thrashing in the shallows" by her trainers and returned to her pen. Cowan and colleagues (1981) reported 10 animals that stranded on southern California beaches between 1970 and 1973, and a literature survey by Leatherwood and colleagues (1981) revealed records of 166 strandings of Pacific white-sided dolphins in the northeastern Pacific from 1855 to 1977.

There are a number of instances recorded of white-sided dolphins remaining in the vicinity of injured or captured conspecifics (Caldwell and Caldwell 1966), and one particularly moving account of an adult female that "stayed between a harpooned individual and the ship, frequently forcing its way between the dying beast and the ship, and pushing it away" (Hubbs 1953). At Marineland of the Pacific, Norris and Prescott observed two captive white-sided dolphins that assisted a newly captured Dall porpoise that had apparently been injured in the capture process: ". . . two adult females of the species *Lagnorhynchus obliquidens* swam to it and placed their snouts upon its flanks at the posterior insertion of its pectoral flippers. With their bodies extending obliquely outward from its body at about 20°, they forced the stricken animal back to the surface" (Norris and Prescott 1961).

Another interesting behavior was observed for this species by the same authors. Also at Marineland of the Pacific, they recorded "echelon swimming," which they described as follows:

A half grown female individual of *Lagenorhynchus obliquidens* was seen positioning itself alongside an adult and coasting this way for as many as three complete circuits of the 80-foot tank. The distance of these glides was often so great that it was soon obvious that the animal was somehow obtaining a "free ride." Repeated observations revealed that the smaller animal positioned itself alongside the adult above the latter's mid-line with its pectoral flipper nearly or actually touching the adult's side just below the dorsal fin.*

Captive animals have been observed and tested in various California facilities, and among other things,

---

*The authors mention a number of other species, including pilot whales, common dolphins, bottlenose dolphins and killer whales, where "baby porpoises . . . are always seen swimming in close company with an adult animal." They cite a hydrodynamic study (Kelly 1959), in which "it has been shown that the idea of a porpoise getting a free ride is not at all unreasonable from the standpoint of hydrodynamic theory," and discuss in some technical detail the mechanics and forces necessary to achieve this phenomenon: "The attractive force can be thought of as due to Bernoulli's Law, which relates the increase in speed of a fluid passing through a restriction to a decrease in pressure. The forward thrust is a component of the vector sum of the pressure forces, and is due to the staggered position of the two bodies."

their visual acuity has been shown to be excellent (Spong and White 1971); but of course vision cannot be very important underwater, since light does not travel very far in water, and therefore, no matter how well an animal sees, it must rely on other senses for long-range discrimination. Caldwell and Caldwell (1971) wrote that this species is "one of the odontocete cetaceans which emits whistles," and in experiments with three animals captured off Los Angeles, they were able to identify "individual signature whistles," specific sounds made only by an individual dolphin and thought to serve as a means of identification. Defran and Pryor (1980) have written that this species "may solicit stroking . . . and for such a small animal it is unusually aggressive to other species of cetaceans, more so even than *T. truncatus* and *O. orca,* and in fact, is reported to be 'quite a pest,' especially for slow-moving animals such as pilot whales.* It is much less restricted to group activity than *Stenella* and *Delphinus,* and is much more interested in strange objects and quite likely to play with toys." Unfortunately, this species has "a usual captive life span of only one or two years," but Caldwell and Caldwell (1972) comment that they are "beautiful animals and warrant simple training procedures." One curious aspect of the behavior of captive white-sided dolphins is their willingness to associate with killer whales. In many places where killer whales are exhibited, their tankmates are likely to be Pacific white-sided dolphins. The little lags appear quite unafraid of the orcas often ten times their

*There is at least one recorded instance where the "slow-moving" pilot whale became so annoyed at the "pestering" antics of a white-sided dolphin that it chased the dolphin around the tank at speeds far in excess of those previously thought possible for pilot whales (Norris and Prescott 1961).

size and play and jump with their larger cousins, apparently unaware of the killer whales' reputation for gobbling up small cetaceans. (At the Vancouver Aquarium in 1980, I saw Whitewing, the companion of Hyak, a 20-foot killer whale, steal half a fish right from the mouth of the feeding killer.)

In Japan, these animals (known as *kama-iruka,* or "sickle dolphins," because of the shape of the dorsal fin) are sometimes hunted for food, but they are generally considered more difficult to catch than other species. "They are not hard to kill," wrote Wilke and colleagues in 1953, "but they are hard to hit. They emerge and dive so quickly that success often depends as much on skill in anticipation as skill in shooting." In May and June of 1949, a single company in Japanese waters took 697, and one vessel is reputed to have killed 200 in a single day (Wilke et al. 1953). Tomilin (1957) wrote that the Soviets have no active fishery for this species off their coasts, but he points out that "their blubber has a rather high content of fat, and their meat is of excellent quality; tender, tasty, somewhat resembling beef."

DUSKY DOLPHIN

Lagenorhynchus obscurus Gray 1838

Although the trivial portion of its scientific name suggests obscurity, the word *obscurus* in this case probably means "indistinct," and refers to the blending of the light and dark areas of the dolphin's coloration. There is nothing indistinct about its overall appearance, since this is another one of the strikingly colored lags, with a black-tipped rostrum and lower jaw, a dark dor-

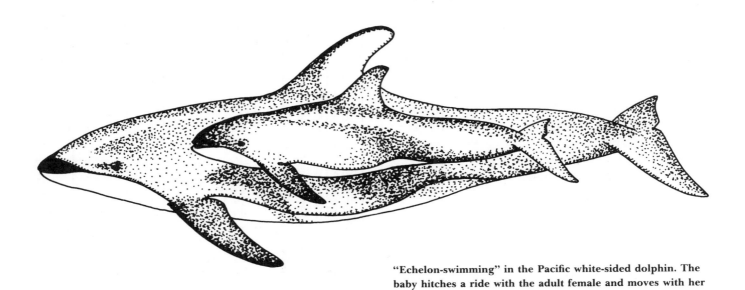

"Echelon-swimming" in the Pacific white-sided dolphin. The baby hitches a ride with the adult female and moves with her without expending any effort.

sal surface with trailing dark blazes, and a swooping white stripe that originates forward of the dorsal fin and widens as it joins the light-colored flank patch behind the dorsal fin. The dorsal fin itself is bicolored like that of the Pacific white-sided dolphin, but it is not as sharply hooked. In this species, as in all lags, the flippers and the flukes are dark, and there is an eye-to-flipper stripe which separates the white throat from the grayish upper body. Adults of this species reach a maximum length of about 7 feet (2.13 meters), and they have 30 pairs of teeth in each jaw.

This dolphin has a circumpolar distribution in warm temperate and cold temperate waters of the Southern Ocean off South America, South Africa, Kerguelen Island, southern Australia, and New Zealand, "where it is one of the most common cetaceans" (Gaskin 1972).

It would be difficult to confuse this species with the other two Southern Ocean species of *Lagenorhynchus,* the hourglass dolphin or Peale's dolphin, since they are markedly different in pattern of pigmentation and, to a lesser extent, in general proportions. Nothing in the taxonomy of the lags is simple, however, and there is another name for this species which regularly appears in the literature: *Lagenorhynchus fitzroyi.** Nishiwaki (1972) identifies (and illustrates) it as a separate species, and it appears in Coffey's 1977 "encyclopedia" as a distinct species, along with *L. superciliosus, L. thicolea,* and *L. wilsoni*—all of which were synonymized by Fraser in 1966.† In Fraser's own book (*Giant Fishes, Whales and Dolphins* [1938], written with J. R.

Norman), however, there appears an illustration of *L. fitzroyi* (called "Fitzroy's Dolphin") and also another animal identified as the "Dusky Dolphin (*Lagenorhynchus obscurus*)." This could easily be passed off as just another case of necessary taxonomic revision, except that the illustration for this latter animal shows a long-snouted creature with a wide dorsal fin that looks like some sort of *Stenella-Delphinus* hybrid. It is now accepted that *fitzroyi = obscurus,* but the identity of the long-nosed "dusky dolphin" in *Giant Fishes, Whales and Dolphins* is a mystery.

The dusky dolphin is one of the three southern species about which very little was known until recently. (In 1974, Brownell wrote of this species, "Nothing is known about the food habits or other aspects of its life history.") When Roger Payne went to Península Valdés in southern Argentina to study the right whales there, he and his colleagues discovered the added cetological bonus of a large population of dusky dolphins swimming in the same inshore waters as the great whales. There are numerous reports of the dolphins and the whales "playing" together, where the duskies would ride just ahead of the slower-moving whales, perhaps taking advantage of the pressure wave created by the swimming whale, or sometimes just circling the whale as it swam (Payne 1974). Bernd Würsig, then a graduate student, accompanied Payne to Golfo San José from 1973 to 1975, specifically to study the dolphins. He studied the habits and behavior of these previously little-known animals, and even affixed radio tags to some of them to better track their movements (Würsig 1976). He observed that they travel in groups of from 6 to 15, although they band together in aggregations as large as 300 animals

*Named for Captain Robert Fitzroy, master of the *Beagle,* aboard which Charles Darwin made his 1831–36 voyage around the world. Fitzroy illustrated the first known specimen of the dusky dolphin, whatever its scientific name.

†One of the species often mentioned as part of the genus is *Lagenorhynchus electra.* In a 1947 discussion of the genus, Bierman and Slijper suggested that many of the synonyms could be combined, and also pointed out that one of the nominal species, *L.*

electra, was "certainly a different species." It turned out to be not only a different species of *Lagenorhynchus,* but a completely new genus as well: *Peponocephala electra,* the melon-headed whale.

when feeding. Their main food item (in Patagonian waters) is the southern anchovy, which they eat by herding the schools of fish into a tight mass against the surface, feeding on them from below as the gulls, terns, albatrosses, petrels, and cormorants take advantage of the situation from above.*

At one time it was assumed that the Pacific white-sided dolphin was the only one to somersault in the wild (Leatherwood et al. 1976), but observations of the duskies in Golfo San José have shown that they too perform spectacular acrobatics, and the full somersault is included in their repertoire. "A single dolphin may excite the whole school," wrote Bartlett in 1976. ". . . if one begins to breach others will follow suit, executing a series of graceful leaps and somersaults as beautiful as we have ever seen among whales and dolphins." Würsig identified at least three different types of leaping behavior, and suggested that each leap served a specific function within the communication lexicon of the species. First there is the "head-first reentry leap," in which the dolphin makes a simple leap out of the water and returns without much of a

splash. Würsig believes that this may be a means of looking for feeding birds at the surface, which would indicate the presence of schools of anchovies. If and when the anchovies have been located, the dolphins make "noisy" leaps, which involve a much greater degree of splashing during reentry, and where the dolphin may land on its back or side, apparently to create as much noise as possible. This type of leap may communicate the location of prey fishes to other dolphins, or it may frighten the anchovies into a tighter school. After feeding, the dolphins display their most spectacular leaps: they somersault, backflip, and even spin on the long axis in midair, an action so unusual that it has given the (unrelated) spinner dolphin its common name. For these exuberant displays, Würsig suggests that "the dolphins seem to be performing, and it is difficult to imagine that they do so for any reason other than 'pure joy.' " The high activity level after feeding may serve a "social function . . . as individuals reaffirm and strengthen social and possibly sexual bonds. . . . We suggest that individual animals have taken care of the basic requirement of feeding and are now prepared to spend time socializing and 'playing' " (Würsig and Würsig 1980).

Bottlenose dolphins are also found in the protected waters of these Patagonian gulfs, but the two

*Bernd and Melany Würsig have published extensively on their observations of the dusky dolphins of Patagonia, and, except where otherwise noted, these observations of feeding, jumping, and communicating are taken from their various published works.

The Pacific white-sided dolphin (above) is found only in the North Pacific, from Japan to southern California. The dusky dolphin (below) does not have as sharply hooked a dorsal fin as the white-sided and is found in the waters of southern South America, Australia, New Zealand, and South Africa.

species do not appear to interact: "they did not appear to take notice of each other, although both species independently sought contact with southern right whales, sea lions, and the boat" (Würsig and Würsig 1980). Dusky dolphins are active bow-wave riders, and will often approach from a distance at the sound of an engine to ride along with a power boat (Ellis 1981).

In 1972, Gaskin wrote that this species was "amenable to training," but did not elaborate. It turned out to be one of the most "amenable" and trainable of all dolphin species, according to Frank Robson, who was in charge of the capture and training of dolphins at Marineland of New Zealand. A number of dusky dolphins were exhibited there, and Robson was obviously favorably impressed with this species:

Dusky dolphins go a lot further than Common dolphins to justify the generalisations made about the species. They really are loveable and quiet and full of compassion for man and dolphin. They are less mischievous, more serious and more docile than Common dolphins. They are very intelligent with a large brain comparable in size and weight to that of a human. They will perform tricks in shallow water that a Common dolphin would not attempt and they can manoeuvre better at speed (Robson 1976).

They were trained to jump in unison, jump over poles, jump through hoops (sometimes aflame), and "tail-walk," or raise themselves out of the water, and, by rapid sculling beats of their flukes, move backward.

Since he was also in charge of the capture operations for this oceanarium, Robson had many opportunities to observe dusky dolphins in New Zealand waters. He observed their feeding behavior: "They feed only on the surface when in shallow water, and an examination of the contents of their stomachs shows that they feed much nearer the bottom than the Common dolphins. They frequent the reefs more and their larger gullets allow them to swallow large fish such as blue cod." He also observed mating behavior, but aside from the observation that "each time it was in very clear water at a depth of about nine metres," he gives no details. On newborn dusky dolphins:

Dusky dolphin calves are born in an area near the shore and in close proximity to reefs, probably because of the absence of sharks in this area during winter. They are the most adorable creatures imaginable, about 0.6 metres (twenty-four inches) in length and weighing about 4.5 kg (ten pounds). They are black on the topside and a beautiful shiny white underneath. They take up a position on the mother's port side, above the eye level, in line with the blowhole. They give the impression of being fastened there for the first few weeks. They only leave this position to go under the mother for a feed.

Robson also wrote that they "have great compassion for one another," and describes a situation where a baby dusky was trapped in a set line and drowned. The mother tried to come up on the beach after her calf but did not strand herself because, "the calf being dead, she received no answer to her communication signals." She swam in circles for a week in the area where her calf had died, and finally "it was obvious from her swimming behaviour—close to the surface, stopping and starting, rapid breathing—that the end was near and she actually died before our eyes . . . from grief, for I can see no other explanation."

Although Robson has extensively studied strandings in New Zealand—a notorious "problem" area for cetaceans of all species—he reports no instances of stranded duskies, either singly or in groups. Brownell (1965b) reported a 6-foot (1.83-meter) specimen "washed ashore" in New Zealand, one of the few recorded strandings for this species.

PEALE'S DOLPHIN

Lagenorhynchus australis Peale 1848

In this species, sometimes known as the "blackchin dolphin," the dark back meets the dark coloration of the forehead and chin, and these features, combined with a dark eye stripe, give Peale's dolphin a dark face, unique among the lags. It has a white flank patch similar to that of the hourglass dolphin, but it lacks the corresponding light zone in the region of the flippers. Peale's dolphin reaches a length of about 7 feet (2.1 meters), and has 30 teeth on each side of each jaw, for a total of about 120.

This is one of the species that Bierman and Slijper (1947) suggested ought to be incorporated into *L. cruciger*, and although the species is now considered valid by most taxonomists, there are still disputes. It is so little known that it is often included in other species, not because of characteristics that would classify it differently, but because there is so little information that conservative taxonomists are inclined to wait until more specimens are collected and examined. In 1966, F. C. Fraser wrote (of *L. cruciger* and *L. australis*), "The situation is like that of the lion and the tiger, whose external appearance leaves little doubt that they are two very different kinds of cat, but whose skulls are so alike that a slight convexity at the lower border of the mandible and a slight projection at the tip of the nasal in one and not in the other are the distinguishing criteria." Although the cranial proportions are much alike in the two species, the strong and consistent differences in pigmentation patterns are sufficient to accord each one specific status. (In her

discussion of skulls collected at Tierra del Fuego, Goodall [1978] wrote, "Since there are very few differences between the skulls of *Lagenorhynchus australis* and *L. cruciger,* all will provisionally be included in *Lagenorhynchus australis* until further comparisons can be made.") As far as the external appearance is concerned, Fraser's 1966 discussion of the comparative patterns of the three southern varieties, and Mitchell's subsequent essay on cetacean coloration (1970), seem to have resolved the problem conclusively.

From observations made off the Chilean coast (Aguayo 1975), it would appear that this species does not form large groups. In sixteen separate sightings, no more than eight animals were seen on any occasion, and more often, the reports were of "one animal," or "two animals." Goodall (1978) reported that this species "is regularly seen by fishermen, and often rides the bow waves of boats." As far as diet is concerned, we can probably assume that it eats fish and squid, and there is one record of a specimen being found with the remains of a small octopus in its stomach. Schevill and Watkins (1971) observed Peale's dolphins on a research voyage off the coast of Chile, and found this species to be the most abundant small cetacean in those waters. They also recorded the pulsed sounds of the animals, which consisted of low-frequency clicks and rapidly pulsed sounds. No "squeals" were heard, which they found surprising, "since we have heard squeals from *L. albirostris, L. acutus, L. obliquidens,* and the *obscurus* of New Zealand."

The species is known only from southern South America and the Falkland Islands. (*Australis* comes from the Latin for "southern.") On the west coast of South America, it has been recorded as far north as Río Inio, Chile (43°20′ S), and on the east from Comodoro Rivadavia, Argentina (45°50′ S) (Brownell 1974). Seventeen specimens (not all of them complete; some consisted of just skulls or vertebrae) were collected by Goodall (1978) on the protected beach of San Sebastián Bay, Tierra del Fuego. She wrote, "My experience is that Peale's dolphin is very common throughout the channels and bays of Tierra del Fuego, but more numerous in the southern part, such as the Beagle Channel. . . ." She also wrote that "Peale's dolphin, since it is common in the channels and inclined to play around boats, is one of the species harpooned for *centolla* [southern king crab] bait," or caught in the nets of fishermen in the Beagle Channel or the Straits of Magellan.

Unlike the North Atlantic lags, which strand frequently, this species, like the Pacific white-sided dolphin, does not appear to do so. The scarcity of stranding records is primarily attributable to the lack of observers in this mostly uninhabited part of the world, but even in areas where there are both people and records of stranded cetaceans, the species does not seem to figure prominently in the records. Goodall (1978) wrote, "In spite of this being one of the most common species in Fuegian waters, there have been very few strandings. Perhaps the preference of Peale's dolphin for fiords and deep water bays means that sick or dead animals would be broken up on the rocky beaches of southern Fuegia."* Goodall did record several stranded specimens, however, which would suggest that this dolphin does strand, albeit infrequently.

The animal is named for Titian Ramsay Peale, the son of Charles Willson Peale, the famous colonial American portraitist and naturalist. From 1838 to 1842, the U.S. Exploring Expedition, under the command of Charles Wilkes, USN, roamed the world in

---

*In other cetaceans, a preference for deep water does not necessarily mitigate the stranding impulse. Species that are deepwater inhabitants, such as sperm whales and beaked whales, are known stranders, and the two North Atlantic lags, regular inhabitants of the fjords and bays of Norway, strand quite often.

search of new and exotic animals, with Titian Peale aboard as artist-naturalist. In 1858 the folio "Mammalogy and Ornithology" was published in Philadelphia, and this species is described and illustrated as "*Delphinus obscurus*," captured off Patagonia. In the same publication, another animal was described and named *Sagmatias amblodon*, captured off Tierra del Fuego in 1839. In 1923 a specimen that matched the description of *Sagmatias* was found beached at Chiloé Island, Chile, and a subsequent investigation (Kellogg 1941) showed that it was none other than Peale's dolphin. In the typical taxonomic scramble that accompanies this genus, various scientific names for the species have been replaced by various others—Hershkovitz (1966) maintains that it should be known as *Lagenorhynchus cruciger*—but the animal still bears Peale's name, if not the name he gave it.

HOURGLASS DOLPHIN

Lagenorhynchus cruciger Quoy and Gaimard 1824

The prominent hourglass markings give this species its common name, and also make it easy to identify. But it is extremely rare, and as of 1974, it was known from a total of five museum specimens (Brownell 1974). A specimen was harpooned from a research vessel rounding Cape Horn, and the very fact of its capture was noteworthy (Nichols 1908). Beamish (in Brownell 1974) has photographed these elusive animals in action, and with their spectacular coloration, they are a dramatic sight as they leap and plunge in the waves alongside the vessel. In addition to the two white areas that define the "hourglass," this species can also be identified by its low, broad-based dorsal fin, and the pectoral fins which are longer and more curved than those of the other lags. A captured male was measured at a length of 5.3 feet (1.63 meters), and

a female was recorded at 6 feet (1.83 meters), so it is assumed that the species is relatively small at maturity.

In the Antarctic, the only other small odontocetes are Commerson's dolphin, which is smaller and more robust, with a totally different black-and-white pattern; and the spectacled porpoise, a small animal that is white below and black above, more or less laterally divided down the middle, and with white flippers. The dusky dolphin is not found as far south as the hourglass, and Peale's dolphin may overlap in some portions of the range, but the striking color pattern of the hourglass is diagnostic. The name is derived from the "hourglass" pattern of white on the black flanks of the animal.

The hourglass dolphin is the only lag known from deep in the Antarctic. Almost all records are from offshore locations at latitudes higher than 55°S. There are some sightings from the Falkland Islands, South Georgia, Bouvet Island, and Cape Horn.

Almost nothing is known about this animal in its natural habitat. In Edward Wilson's (1967) 1901–04 journals of Robert F. Scott's *Discovery* expedition, he makes occasional references to black-and-white dolphins, "very boldly marked," and "a great many handsome black and white dolphins," but the species is unnamed until a plate, in which he illustrates animals that are obviously of the hourglass variety. In his notes for the plate, he wrote, "A school of these porpoises played around our bows for a long time today. . . . The one with a scimitar shaped dorsal fin was the biggest of the whole school. So far as I could see, no other individual has this long curved dorsal fin. . . ." In his book *Whaler's Eye* (1962), which concerns the Antarctic, Christopher Ash describes

The most beautiful creature to be laid upon our deck . . . a dolphin shot with a rifle by Gunner Hem. This species is so rarely seen that it has no common name, so it must be called

Lagenorhynchus cruciger. When the frozen dolphin was delivered to the British Museum (Natural History), we found that it was the first to come to Britain. [This is the very specimen pictured in the photographs accompanying Fraser's 1966 discussion of *Lagenorhynchus.*] Color photographs were taken of the whole body, and especially of the head to show the kohl-rimmed eyes, and the way in which the coloring looked as though it had been laid on with an overcharged brush that had run dry at the end of the stroke. . . . It had needle sharp interlocking teeth; and as we had guessed, it had been feeding on small squid.

Fraser (1964) reported about forty of these animals swimming with fin whales, and Matthews (1948) observed seven dolphins, "almost certainly of the species *L. cruciger,* that played round the bows of the whaler *Don Ernesto,* making 9 or 10 knots." While aboard the Japanese research vessel *Chiyoda Maru No. 5,* Gaskin (1972) observed animals of this species "riding the bow wave of vessels . . . [and they] consistently showed spinning behavior." These observations, although sparse, indicate an energetic and playful nature for these little-known dolphins of the Antarctic.

The name *cruciger* is derived from the Latin *crux,* meaning "cross," and *gerere,* "to bear." In the original description of the species (Quoy and Gaimard 1824), there is an illustration showing an animal with a wide

black stripe running the length of the back, and a narrow band intersecting it at right angles just behind the flippers, giving the impression of a cross. The actual specimen was not examined, but "seen at sea, and drawn from a distance." In his 1966 discussion of the genus, Fraser points out "the inadequacy of sight records and . . . the difficulties facing the cetologist because of the lack of adequate information." In reality, there is nothing at all resembling a cross on the animal, but according to the rules of zoological nomenclature, *cruciger* was the name first applied to the species, and it must be retained.

COMMERSON'S DOLPHIN

Cephalorhynchus commersonii Lacépède 1804

There are four nominal species in the genus *Cephalorhynchus,* which means "head-beak" (*kephalos* = "head"; *rhynchus* = "beak" or "snout"), and refers to the sloping forehead which merges directly into the snout with no appreciable beak. All four are restricted to the high southern latitudes, and each has its own range: *C. hectori,* New Zealand; *C. eutropia,* Chile; *C. heavisidii,* South Africa; and *C. commersonii,* southeastern South America. They are strongly marked in

The two *Lagenorhynchus* species of the Southern Ocean. The hourglass dolphin (above) has a peculiarly shaped dorsal fin and long, sickle-shaped flippers, while Peale's dolphin (below) has an all-black face.

shades of black and white, or black, white, and gray, leading one author (Grzimek 1975) to suggest the name "skunk dolphins" for the genus. Other than this, there is no accepted generic name, although "short-nosed dolphins" and "southern dolphins" have been used. The ventral surfaces of the four species are strongly marked, with a characteristic black patch in the genital area, but this feature is not visible except in beached specimens.

All species are small, not exceeding 6 feet (1.83 meters) in length, and most specimens have been measured at less than that. They have between 25 and 32 pairs of small teeth in each jaw and may be recognized at sea around Cape Horn, the Cape of Good Hope, or the waters of New Zealand, by their uniquely rounded dorsal fin.

A strikingly marked species, Commerson's dolphin is also known as the piebald dolphin or the Jacobite (*jacobita* in Spanish), "the latter being Commerson's own name for it"* (Norman and Fraser 1938). Except for the conspicuous pigmentation, this species is typical of the genus, with a rounded dorsal fin, and a maximum size of about 5 feet (1.5 meters). There are 30 pairs of teeth in each jaw.

The only other black-and-white small cetacean with which this one could be confused in southern South American waters is the spectacled porpoise. Commerson's dolphin is black at either end and white in the middle, while the spectacled porpoise is black on top and white on the bottom. (The southern right whale dolphin can also be found in sub-Antarctic waters, but this slender animal with no dorsal fin would

*Jacobites in British history were the supporters of the exiled Stuart king James II after the revolution of 1688. As far as I can ascertain, they did not wear black-and-white costumes, nor did they have much to do with dolphins. *Jacobins*, however, in addition to their place in the French Revolution, were monks known for their distinctive hood or cowl. There are also domestic pigeons called Jacobins, which have reversed feathers on the nape. Perhaps the coloring of this dolphin suggested the monk's cowl to Commerson. (Philibert Commerson sailed as naturalist on Bougainville's 1766–69 voyage around the world.)

be difficult to confuse with any other dolphin.) According to Mitchell (1970), the Dall porpoise of the North Pacific has developed a "strikingly similar" color pattern. This may be an example of adaptive convergence, where unrelated animals develop similar characteristics, presumably for the same purpose. Although we can only speculate as to this purpose, it might be for camouflage, for this disruptive pattern could help the animal avoid the killer whale, the predator that Harmer (1922) says is the "principal enemy" of Commerson's dolphin.

Very little is known of the biology of this species. It is usually seen in groups of no more than 3 animals and in shallow waters. It is said to be shy of boats (Brownell 1974), but there are several published photographs of the animals leaping from the water (e.g., Cadot in Brownell 1974; Erize in Stephen 1973), and I have seen a film of 15 or so Commerson's dolphins pacing a U.S. Coast Guard icebreaker in the Antarctic. It might therefore be said that, while these animals do not ride bow waves (none of the cephalorhynchids do), they will occasionally pace a vessel from alongside.

This dolphin is the southernmost representative of the genus, found in the waters of Cape Horn and Tierra del Fuego. (The other South American species, the black dolphin, is found farther north, along the coast of Chile.) Mermoz (1980) refers to the species as "very common in the southeastern Atlantic south of 42°S." Commerson's dolphin is occasionally seen in the waters of Península Valdés, and all the way south to Tierra del Fuego along the Argentine coast, but its primary habitat seems to be Tierra del Fuego and the Straits of Magellan. It has also been reported from South Georgia and Kerguelen Island (Angot 1954). On the beach at San Sebastián Bay in Tierra del Fuego, Goodall (1978) recorded 33 "nearly complete skeletons from 1975 to 1978," and skeletal or cranial material from another 58 animals for the same period. There is no directed fishery for this species in Argentine waters, but Goodall and Cameron (1980) report that they are sometimes trapped and drowned in fishing nets around Tierra del Fuego, and some specimens are also taken to be used as bait for the king crab fishery.

It is fortunate indeed that Natalie Goodall has become interested in the cetaceans of Tierra del Fuego (see "Housewife at the End of the World," *National Geographic*, January 1971), for she now maintains an observation post in one of the most remote but cetologically productive locations on the face of the earth. Starting with the collection of bones on the beaches, she has progressed to the presentation of reports on the appearance and natural history of the cetaceans of her distant outpost. Few people have observed Commerson's dolphins in any significant numbers, but Goodall and Cameron (1979) have provided some unique and fascinating data. From beached specimens they recorded the sexual dimorphism of the genital patches—another similarity to the Dall porpoise, the animal that probably represents the Northern Hemisphere analogue of Commerson's dolphin. The coloration of fetal and juvenile specimens—heretofore unreported—is black and gray, the gray turning to white as the animal matures. (Mermoz [1980] described newborn calves as "completely brown.") The rounded flippers of the adults were observed to be serrated along the leading edge, a peculiarity that has not been seen in any other cetacean. (Two species of porpoises, Burmeister's and the harbor porpoise, have tubercles on the dorsal fin—in fact, that is the derivation of the scientific name of one of them: *spinipinnis* means "spiny fin," but these are present in juveniles as well as adults, while the serrations on the flippers of Commerson's dolphins were found only on adult animals.) The small serrations were on the left flipper, never on the right, and there is no apparent explanation for this curious phenomenon.

Other observers have since gone to the Southern Ocean to investigate this and other species. Watkins and Schevill (1980) recorded the underwater sounds of Commerson's dolphins in the Straits of Magellan, but "only a few sounds were heard . . . and they were not repeated enough by nearby animals for certain attribution." The acousticians later recorded captive specimens at Mystic Marinelife Aquarium in Connecticut, and they described the sounds as "low level, 1 to 3 sec or longer sequences of 2 to 100 or more clicks per sec, 0.2 to 0.5 sec click bursts at 50 to 80 per sec, and 0.5 to 2 sec pulsed 'cry' sounds—all often characterized by variable lower frequency emphases (1 to 6 kHz). . . ."

Mermoz (1980) reported on the behavior of Commerson's dolphins in Patagonian waters, primarily in the harbor of Comodoro Rivadavia. Here they are known as *tonina overa: tonina* is a common name for all small dolphins, and *overa* ("egg-colored") refers to the animal's white flanks. He said that the animals spent a great deal of time in the kelp beds, and although actual feeding was not observed, the possible prey species in the area are silversides, sardines, and anchovies. "When some Commerson's dolphins were caught for a German zoo [see Gewalt below], we could see that the other dolphins began to swim slowly near the captive ones. Acoustic distress signals from those entrapped in the net may have attracted the others. We saw this every time we succeeded in trapping a dolphin (Mermoz 1980).

In November 1978, an expedition from the Duisberg Zoo in Germany traveled to southern Argentina to collect Commerson's dolphins, since "this species has never before been exhibited in zoological gardens or oceanaria" (Gewalt 1979). Before they captured some of the animals in Bahía San Jorge, the collectors described the free-swimming animals as "very swift and flexible swimmers and though they swam very near our boat, it was quite impossible to catch them with a sling, a net or by hand." Finally, the animals were trapped in a larger net, and two males and four females were transported to Germany. Four of the animals died within a couple of weeks (post mortem revealed "infections, lung worms and pneumonia"), and the fifth was "killed by an accident." As of February 1980, the sole survivor was in excellent condition: "With its skin smooth like lacquer, this charming animal looks like a small *Orca*. The Jacobita has made good contact with our three white whales (*Delphinapterus leucas*) and goes through a splendid training programme together with these big white cetaceans" (Gewalt 1979).

Gewalt correctly described the dolphins at the Duisberg Zoo as the first of the species to be held in captivity, but his November 1978 expedition only preceded the arrival of Commerson's dolphins into the United States by one month. In December of that year, four dolphins had been collected in Argentine waters, and en route to their ultimate destination, which was Japan, they landed at John F. Kennedy International Airport in New York. National Marine Fisheries Service agents at JFK confiscated the shipment because it was without proper documentation. The shipping and "packing" arrangements had been barbarous: the animals had been crammed for more than two days into small wooden boxes with a little water sloshing around the bottom. Of the four, one was dead, another moribund, and of the remaining two, a male and a female, one died within two weeks. That left only a small female, badly deformed, "probably as a result of not being able to move in the ship-

ping box'' (Kezer 1979). The dolphin—named ''Carmelita''—lived for over two and a half years at the Mystic Marinelife Aquarium, gamely trying to swim in a normal fashion, but since her tail stock was so deformed, her flukes were almost totally useless, and she had to paddle with her flippers.* In July 1981, Carmelita, the only Commerson's dolphin in North America, died of multiple complications.

BLACK DOLPHIN

Cephalorhynchus eutropia Gray 1849

Since it was first described by J. E. Gray in 1849 from a specimen collected by R. Dickie, RN, this species has remained almost a complete mystery, even to this date. True (1889) examined two skulls in the British Museum (one of which was the type specimen), and later purchased another skull, ''also said to have been received from the coast of Chili.'' He believed that the species was distinct from the South African form (*Cephalorhynchus heavisidii*), but he wrote, ''We know nothing of the skeleton or the external form of this species.''

In 1893, Dr. R. A. Philippi published a description and an illustration of a small dolphin from Chilean waters, based on material provided by Dr. C. Perez Canto, which he named *Phocoena (Hyperoodon?) albiventris* Perez. In 1896, Perez Canto published his own description, translating Philippi's Spanish into French along the way. When True (1903) reviewed the descriptions and designations chosen by Philippi, he questioned the choice of name (''why the name *Hyperoodon* should be applied is not at all clear, as nothing about it suggests the genus in any way''), and wrote:

Philippi's figures of the skull show that it is a *Cephalorhynchus*, and his measurements agree with the type-skull and other specimens of *C. eutropia*, except that the beak appears to be a little longer. Dr. Perez Canto's description and figure of the exterior show that the color-pattern resembles that of other species of *Cephalorhynchus* except that the posterior lateral white mark is not divided by an interiorly divided arm of black, to form a trident. . . . As the exterior of *C. eutropia* has remained unknown hitherto, this identification, if correct, is of much interest.

The dolphin was described as very dark greenish black on the back, head, flanks, and fins, with a white throat and belly, and a white spot behind the flipper. There was a dark line on the sides which runs from front to back but does not show in the illustration of Philippi.

Since this turn-of-the century flurry of interest in the black dolphin, almost nothing new has been added to the literature. In 1938 Norman and Fraser were still calling the species *Cephalorhynchus albiventris* (even though Flower had determined that it should be *C. eutropia* in 1883), and they described it as ''a rare South American species.'' In 1972, Nishiwaki published this description of the black dolphin, which he refers to as the ''white-bellied dolphin'': ''The adult body length is about 1.4 m. The dorsal fin is rounded and the flippers are small. There is a marked curvature in the posterior edge of the tail flukes. The body is generally gray with white spots at the throat, behind the flippers, and on the abdomen.'' Nishiwaki provides no accompanying illustration, but from the published illustrations—all of which are drawings, such as those appearing in Beddard (1900) and Mörzer Bruyns (1971)—it can be seen that the descriptions of Philippi and Perez Canto were used for reference, and that the

---

*This unfortunate incident probably represents a unique situation, since it may be the first record of a cetacean swimming without the use of its flukes. In a 1961 discussion of whales without flukes,

Gilmore wrote, ''no one, so far as I know, has seen a whale propelling itself even slowly with its flippers alone, much less at a rapid rate—nor even a porpoise in an oceanarium.''

general appearance of this animal is very much like that of Heaviside's dolphin.

Marcuzzi and Pilleri (1971) have indicated that this species shares the same range as Commerson's dolphin on the eastern coast of South America, but Brownell (1974) points out that this is erroneous, since all the known records for the black dolphin are from the Chilean coast. According to Aguayo (1975), it inhabits the coastal waters between Concepción Island (37°S) and the fjord region (55°S) near Isla Navarino. Goodall (1979) lists this species (which she calls *Delfin chileno o negro*) as belonging to the cetacean fauna of Tierra del Fuego, but she does not provide an illustration.

Nothing at all is known of the natural history of this animal, but it can be assumed that it resembles the better-known members of the genus in such respects as diet (small fish, squid, and shrimp) and a wariness of ships, which may account for its obscurity. Norris (quoted in Aguayo 1975) reported that this species was "very shy and refused to allow close approach." While on a cetacean observation cruise in Chilean waters in 1964, Clarke, Aguayo, and del Campo (1978) saw several small porpoises that "could have been, with regard to size and colour pattern, the white-bellied dolphin *C. eutropia* as described by Perez Canto," but the observers were never close enough to make an accurate identification. At Navarino Island, Watkins, Schevill, and Best (1977) "encountered eight or nine *C. eutropia*," and recorded their sounds as "cries at a very low level in the ambient noise." The sounds made by this species were very similar to those recorded by the same authors for the three other species of *Cephalorhynchus*, and the authors suggest that their similarities to the various species of *Phocoena* "appear to be a response to the equivalent ecological niches that they occupy in similar hemispheres."

Along the Chilean coast, the black dolphin has been seen in groups of up to 14 animals, and Aguayo (himself a Chilean) suggests that the name "Chilean dolphin" be used to denote this species in the future.

HEAVISIDE'S DOLPHIN

Cephalorhynchus heavisidii Gray 1828

A little-known, strongly marked species, Heaviside's dolphin* was described as follows by Gray in his original discussion of the new species (quoted by Flower 1883):

Type is *heavisidii,* described by Gray from a stuffed specimen in the British Museum. 4 feet long from Cape of Good Hope, "with rather a peculiar distribution of colours with the greater part of the surface being black, but with very distinct white markings beneath consisting of a transverse band in front of, and a triangular spot behind each of, the pectoral fins; and of a longitudinal line on the belly, which separates just beneath the dorsal fin into three equal forks, the central one of which is continued in its direct course, while the lateral ones extend obliquely up the sides."

Flower further characterizes the species as having "an obtusely triangular (not falcate) or rounded dorsal fin, ovate or oblong pectoral fins, and rather short rounded snout without groove separating distinct beak."

Very little is known about the life cycle of this species, but studies are currently being conducted by P. B. Best of Cape Town (personal communication). According to Best (quoted in Mitchell 1975a), the species is known only from western South African waters, from Cape Cross to Cape Town, and they are sometimes taken inadvertently in fishing nets. Fewer than 100 animals per year are killed in this manner.

In 1975, four animals were captured in Pater-

---

*There is a note in Mitchell (1975a) that reads "as long as the International Commission on Zoological Nomenclature has not taken a decision to the contrary, species names originally written with 'ii' must be used." This means that the trivial (species) name of this animal is *"heavisidii,"* not *"heavisidei,"* as it often appears. The man for whom it was named was a certain Haviside, the captain of an East Indiaman, whose name was mispelled (Fraser 1966). In Beddard's *Book of Whales* (1900), the name is spelled "Heavyside."

noster Bay, South Africa, and held for a week in a cemented-in rock pool. During that time their sounds were recorded and found to consist "entirely of clicks and pulse-series or relatively restricted bandwidths. No squeals (whistle-like sounds) were heard at any time" (Watkins et al. 1977). The only behavioral observations made during this period were the following: "Most of the time the animals were either swimming in a circle around the tank or stationing themselves vertically, head down, and well below the surface for up to 1 min at a time. The latter was a conspicuous behavioral feature but it did not correlate with any particular sounds."

Although the killer whale and Heaviside's dolphin are in no way similar in temperament, habits, or size, a number of authors (Norman and Fraser 1938; Mitchell 1970; etc.) have remarked on the similarity of the pigmentation patterns of the two. Mitchell wrote:

Mimicry of *Orcinus orca* by *Cephalorhynchus heavisidii* does not necessarily connote similarity of predators, or even functional similarities in the hunting and capture of prey species, but a third possibility is that *C. heavisidii* itself is a potential prey species of *O. orca*, and by attempting to mimic the young of the latter, it is in the situation where the predator precipitates the need for mimicry on the part of the prey.

HECTOR'S DOLPHIN

Cephalorhynchus hectori Van Beneden 1881

Unlike its close relatives in the waters of Chile, South Africa, or southeastern South America, this species is fairly common and often observed.* It is found only in New Zealand waters, and never more than five miles from shore. Oliver (1922a) referred to it as "the common white-nosed porpoise, never seen far from the coast." One report (Harrison 1960) of this species from the South China Sea has caused certain authors (Hershkovitz 1966; Marcuzzi and Pilleri 1971, etc.) to posit an extended range throughout Indonesian waters and north to Borneo, but Harrison's sighting ("a low rounded dorsal fin which slopes back and a length of 6–7[?] feet") is almost certainly a case of mistaken identity (van Bree 1972).

Barely reaching a length of 5 feet (1.5 meters),

*On the other hand, Frank Robson, an inveterate New Zealand cetacean watcher and professional collector wrote, "The only Hector's dolphin I have seen in Hawke's Bay waters was dead—caught in a net set. It was one of a herd of eleven. I knew that fishermen in the Bay had been seeing black and white dolphins for five weeks but as luck would have it my first sight of the beautiful creatures was in death."

Cephalorhynchus heavisidii (top) **and** *Orcinus orca,* **showing similarity of pigmentation patterns (not drawn to scale).**

this animal can be easily recognized by its dark-colored, rounded dorsal fin, which Flower (1883) described as "being rounded in outline unlike that of any other cetacean but rather resembling the adipose fin of a Salmon on a large scale." There are black markings on the head and tail, and the body is a silvery gray color. A feature unique to this species is the "forehead" coloration, which consists of a dark, curved line forming a crescent which defines a light-colored area, finely streaked with black, which sweeps down toward the poorly developed beak. The ventral pattern is also unique, but of course it cannot be seen except in beached animals. Like the other members of the genus, Hector's dolphin has 27 to 32 pairs of small sharp teeth in each jaw. According to Baker (1978), this dolphin is a fish eater, and it may be a sometime bottom feeder in the shallow inshore waters in which it lives. There appears to be no evidence to support Gaskin's (1972) reference to shellfish, crustaceans, and squid in the stomachs of these animals.

Hector's dolphin—also referred to as the "little pied dolphin"—is often found in "green" or muddy waters at the mouths of rivers where the water has been roiled by land runoff after the rains. Baker (1978) wrote that even though it swims close to shore, its "small size, and fast, low and silent method of surfacing makes it very difficult to see in other than calm conditions." It is often observed in small groups of 2 to 4 animals, although larger aggregations have been reported. (Baker's 1978 discussion mentions "one exceptional school of 200–300 individuals. . . .") Unlike other members of the genus, it is not a particularly shy animal, and will approach boats entering New Zealand harbors or follow fishing trawlers. It is also known to enter the estuaries of the Clarence, Wanganui, Wairau and Grey Rivers (Gaskin 1972). One interesting observation records an individual that stayed in a net when another dolphin (its mate?) was trapped, and left only when the trapped animal was released (Mörzer Bruyns and Baker 1973). Speed at sea has been es-

timated at 4 to 6 knots, with bursts up to 10 knots. On an expedition to capture some of these animals for Marineland of New Zealand at Napier, the hunters sighted numerous dolphins of this species and commented that "they moved a lot faster around the boat than the dusky dolphins, and would not stay at the bow" (Abel et al. 1971). When an animal was captured (and for some reason named Narwhal), "at least a dozen others surrounded the boat, just lying on the surface. . . ." Now that the animal could be maintained in captivity, it could be closely observed and photographed, and the problems of its color variations and subspecies could be better resolved.

In F. W. True's 1889 discussion of the family Delphinidae, he included a description and illustration of "*Cephalorhynchus albifrons,* the white-headed dolphin." Norman and Fraser (1938) also listed it as a valid species, stating, "The whiteness of the head distinguishes this species from those nearly allied to it." At that time, it appeared as if there were two distinct species of *Cephalorhynchus* in New Zealand waters: a dark-colored animal and a light one with a white head.

In 1873, Sir James Hector had described a new species of dolphin from New Zealand, which he called *Electra clancula,* and the illustration shows an animal with a white head. The Belgian cetologist P. J. Van Beneden (1881) later described a dark-headed small dolphin from the same region, which he named *Electra hectori.* By 1885, Hector, "on the advice of Professor William Flower . . , referred his specimens to *Cephalorhynchus* Gray, and adopted Van Beneden's specific name *hectori,* stating that the main differences in colour (of the nose and forehead) between Van Beneden's and his own material were of small importance" (Mörzer Bruyns and Baker 1973). In 1946, W. R. B. Oliver "became acquainted with some very light coloured specimens *C. hectori,* living in the neighborhood of Pelorus Sound and Wairau Beach. He obtained photographs of the animals . . . and, without having had a specimen in his hands, created in 1946 a new subspecies, *Cephalorhynchus hectori bicolor*. A rather inappropriate act; the more so as he did not compare his subspecies with the nominate form (i.e., the original descriptions)" (van Bree 1972).

It was not until 1972 that van Bree published his analysis of this convoluted situation* and stated, "there is no subspecific difference between *bicolor* and the nominate form and . . . the pattern and colours in *Cephalorhynchus hectori* may vary considerably." The following year, Mörzer Bruyns and Baker concluded that there was only one form, namely, "the pied form of Hector's dolphin such as described by Hector (1872) and Oliver (1946), most other descriptions being based on cast specimens which had largely lost their original colour pattern through deterioration of one kind or another." Baker (1978) concluded that Hector's 1873 description "contains a mixed description of *L. obscurus* and *C. hectori*, under the name *Lagenorhynchus clanculus* or *Electra clancula*." Baker was extremely lucky to be able to find the actual specimens described by Hector and his successors (since this is a

*It did not come in time for Nishiwaki. In his 1972 detailed catalog of the world's cetaceans, he lists both *hectori* and *albifrons* from New Zealand, and illustrates both: the drawing intended to show *hectori* looks nothing at all like the actual animal, and for *albifrons* the artist has shown a strange, small-finned creature with a color pattern unlike that of any known cetacean.

New Zealand species, most of the skeletal material, casts, and mounts could still be found in New Zealand collections), and he was able to compare the mounted specimens with recently stranded ones or even living animals at Marineland. Most cetologists are not so fortunate; often the type specimens are thousands of miles away, or lost altogether.

NORTHERN RIGHT WHALE DOLPHIN
Lissodelphis borealis Peale 1848

The common name "right whale dolphin" is supposedly derived from the mutual lack of dorsal fin in this genus and in the right whale, but it would be hard to imagine two more dissimilar animals. The right whale is a huge, slow-swimming, ponderous creature, while the right whale dolphin is perhaps the slenderest of all cetaceans. It has been described as "eellike," (Leatherwood and Reeves 1978), and Mörzer Bruyns (1971) wrote that it is "A slim and beautifully shaped dolphin, like a drop of liquid."

These swift, slim animals reach a maximum length of about 10 feet (3.28 meters) and, at this length, a mature male—somewhat larger than the female—would weigh only 180 pounds (81 kilograms).

Ventral views of *C. commersonii* **(top) and** *Cephalorhynchus hectori*

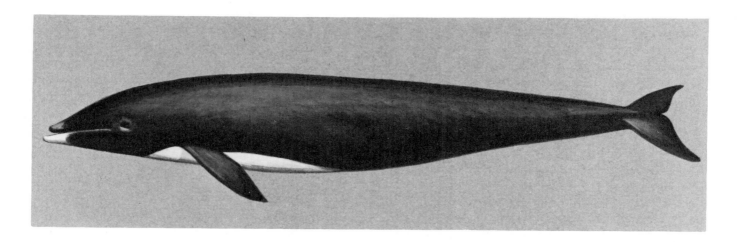

The tail stock is particularly narrow, and the flukes "are no wider than the widest part of the body" (Norris and Prescott 1961). The right whale dolphin is dramatically marked, with jet-black dorsal surfaces and a unique white ventral pattern, the two colors sharply demarcated. There appears to be a difference in the white ventral coloration for males and females: the area around the genital slit in females is wider than the corresponding area in males. The flippers are black, top and bottom, but the flukes are black on the dorsal surface and white beneath, with a trailing border of gray. The tip of the slightly protruding lower jaw is black, and there are about 43 pairs of teeth in each jaw. A distinguishing characteristic of the northern right whale dolphin is its narrow, pincerlike jaws.

Like most cetaceans, this species has undergone a succession of name changes—Scammon knew it as *Leucoramphus borealis* and True (1889) called it *Tursio borealis*—but its present name is a wonderfully appropriate appellation which can be translated as "smooth dolphin of the north wind."

It is a blue-water, offshore species, known from both sides of the North Pacific. Ohsumi (1972) lists it as "very common" in Japanese waters, and in the eastern North Pacific it can be found from the Gulf of Alaska south as far as San Diego. Although the type specimen was collected in 1848 by Titian Peale several hundred miles off the coast of Oregon, the species seems to be most abundant in the offshore waters of southern California. Compared to some of the other delphinids of this region, such as the white-sided dolphin and the common dolphin, whose schools can number in the tens of thousands, the right whale dolphin does not seem to be particularly abundant. Nishiwaki (1972) estimated the total population for the North Pacific at "more than 10,000," but since Leatherwood and Walker (1979) obtained an estimate of some 17,800 animals for their southern California study area, they wrote that Nishiwaki's figure "appears overly conservative."

Because of its relative rarity and offshore habitat, the northern right whale dolphin was very poorly known until recently. In 1940, Remington Kellogg wrote, "Our knowledge of this dolphin's actions when swimming rests solely on the observations of Titian R. Peale. . . . He reported them to be remarkably quick and active, and said that they frequently leap out of the water." In recent times, a number of open-ocean sightings have confirmed Peale's observations, and while our knowledge of the species is somewhat more advanced than it was in Peale's time, Leatherwood and Walker could still write (in 1979) that it is "one of the least-known delphinids of the eastern Pacific." In their study, Leatherwood and Walker summarized sightings from various sources (Smithsonian Institution, National Marine Fisheries Service, University of California, Naval Undersea Center), but they still wrote that the "ranges, seasonal movements and numbers are still rather poorly known." From the collected reports it was apparent that the northern right whale dolphin is a seasonal visitor to southern California waters, arriving in the fall and reaching its peak numbers in midwinter. There are no sightings at all from June to September, and it is not known where the animals go when they are not in California waters. The same seasonality seems to apply to this species off Japan; Kasuya (1971) notes that it is "sighted only in the season from September to June." It is possible that both the eastern and western populations migrate northward in the warmer summer months, since this species is known to prefer colder waters. It is not known from the mid-Pacific, including Hawaii (Nishiwaki 1967).

The northern right whale dolphin is often seen in the company of other cetaceans, particularly the Pacific white-sided dolphin, but it has also been seen in mixed aggregations with pilot whales, Dall porpoises, and common dolphins. Leatherwood (1974) recorded this species riding the pressure wave of gray whales, but it is not an enthusiastic bow rider. When seen together with white-sided dolphins, the species has been known to ride the bow waves of ships; otherwise it moves away from or avoids ships. As Peale noted, it is an extremely active swimmer, and it has been clocked at speeds of "about 20 miles per hour, almost constantly under the water surface" (Nishiwaki 1967). Leatherwood and Walker report an instance where a naval vessel traveling at a known speed of 18 knots was unable to overtake a school of fleeing right whale dolphins. The observations of Norris and Dohl (1980) differ from most other descriptions of the locomotion of this species; in their discussion of "the mode of travel of various species during food-searching," they wrote, "The right whale dolphin (*Lissodelphis* sp.) may at times move very rapidly and spend much time in the air. . . . Its extremely attenuate body may allow it to take three or four rapid propulsive strokes of its flukes while its anterior body is in the air, thus reducing drag. At any rate this species may be seen leaping in dense ranks, traveling considerable distances over the surface with each leap." Other observers describe this leaping as occurring only when the animals are being chased; otherwise, they have been described as "slow-moving herds, usually exposing just the head and blow-hole to breathe, creating only slight surface disturbances that are difficult to detect, even under ideal sea conditions" (Leatherwood and Walker 1979). When pursued, however, "they begin to jump out of the water with regular low-angle leaps" (Norris and Prescott (1961), and they have been observed to jump in unison (Brownell 1964). Herd sizes for this species have been reported to range from single animals to groups of 3,000, but most of the sightings recorded by Leatherwood and Walker (1979) and Kasuya (1971) were of groups that numbered less than 50 individuals.

Very little is known of the biology of these animals, but Norris and Prescott (1961) observed calves that were 24 to 28 inches in length, and they wrote that "color and pattern seemed to be identical with that of the adults." More recent, concentrated study (e.g., Leatherwood and Reeves 1978) reveal that the calf is "cream-colored to grayish with only a muted color pattern . . . it acquires a tuxedoed look early in its first year." Because these animals are difficult to approach, there are very few observations of their behavior in the wild. According to Tomilin (1957), when one is harpooned, the others "do not abandon their congeners, but they stay near the ship. . . ." Attempts to capture these animals have been generally unsuccessful, and Wood (1973) wrote, "The right whale dolphins . . . were caught on only one occasion. They survived the journey to the facility, but died the next day." Walker (1975) described the behavior of netted animals as "unique compared to that of other species. In each instance, the animal became completely immobile on the surface the instant the net-snare was pursued around the head and flippers." If the animals survived the capture procedure, they fared poorly in captivity. At Marineland of the Pacific, one died of "stress" within three days of its capture, and another—the only recorded "successful" capture of this species—lived for 15 months before it died of undetermined causes.

Like many pelagic delphinids, the northern right whale dolphin occasionally beaches itself. All the recorded strandings, however, are of single animals. The examination of the stomach contents of some of these specimens has provided some of the scant information we have on the diet of these animals.* Squid beaks have been identified from some specimens (Scheffer and Slipp 1948; Norris and Prescott 1961), and the examination of other stranded animals as well as those collected at sea indicate that the northern right whale dolphin also feeds on DSL organisms, par-

*Leatherwood and Walker warn against the interpretation of the stomach contents of stranded animals as being indicative of the feeding habits of animals in the wild: "Fish remains identified from the stomachs of some stranded specimens include a pronounced combination of near-shore and offshore fishes. Many of the near-shore fish species are not representative of the normal known distribution of *L. borealis* and were probably ingested just prior to stranding."

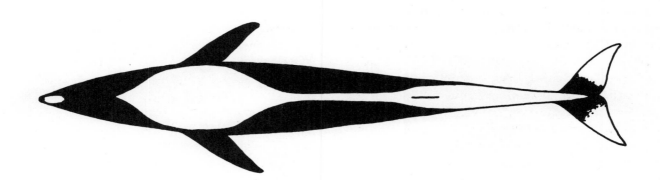

Ventral view of northern right whale dolphin (*Lissodelphis borealis*), **showing pattern.**

ticularly the lantern fishes, but they might not dive too deeply to get them. If, as Leatherwood and Reeves suggest, they are "late evening, nighttime, or early morning feeders," they might dive only to the requisite depth—perhaps as little as 50 meters—to meet the DSL on its nightly upward migration. The inshore/offshore movements have also been correlated with the movements of the Pacific squid, an extremely abundant species in California waters, and one known to represent a significant percentage of the diet of some California porpoises and dolphins.

The sounds of this species have been recorded (Fish and Turl 1977), and it is assumed that, like most of the other deep water odontocetes, it is an echolocator. No whistles were recorded, but the "moans" and "whelps" which sounded like whistles "turned out on later analysis at slower speeds to be a series of high-repetition-rate click trains from a number of animals." Leatherwood and Walker further described the sound production of this species as being "not essentially different from ocean/pelagic delphinids of the *Delphinus/Stenella* types, although whistles were far less common in the *L. borealis*."

No other small cetacean in the Northern Hemisphere resembles this species, but because the dorsal fin is so characteristic of porpoises and dolphins, its absence makes it possible—but not likely—to confuse the animals as they swim with a school of fish or a herd of sea lions. (In his original description, Peale wrote that it is "sometimes mistaken for a Seal.") The southern right whale dolphin is very similar to its northern relative, the primary difference being a variation in coloration. In the North Pacific a number of anomalously colored specimens have been collected with a pigmentation pattern that matches neither the southern nor the northern varieties. Tobayama and colleagues (1969) illustrated one such specimen, and Leatherwood and Walker (1979) included photographs of another. On the basis of such specimens, Nishiwaki (1972) identified a white-bellied subspecies of *L. borealis*, which he named *L. borealis albiventris*. The

specimen described by Tobayama and colleagues was said to have been taken from a mixed school of *L. borealis*, *L. peronii* and *Lagenorhynchus obliquidens* swimming together off Ibaragi, Japan, but *L. peronii* is believed to be restricted only to the Southern Hemisphere, so it is possible to assume that the observers mistakenly identified these unusually colored individuals as *L. peronii*. It now appears that the white-bellied form of the northern right whale dolphin is just an aberrant color form, and Leatherwood and Walker "consider the evidence insufficient to differentiate *Lissodelphis borealis* on a subspecies level."

Despite our still limited knowledge of these animals, the Japanese have been fishing them for years. Since the species is plentiful off the coasts of Japan, there have been various attempts at its commercial exploitation. One company landed 465 right whale dolphins in two months in 1949 (Wilke et al. 1953), and its presence in the dolphin-fishing areas of Japan (Ohsumi 1972) makes it very likely indeed that it will continue to be taken for human consumption.

SOUTHERN RIGHT WHALE DOLPHIN

Lissodelphis peronii Lacépède 1804

The southern right whale dolphin is not quite as slender as its northern relative, but it is the only other blue-water dolphin without a dorsal fin. From the few published photographs of this species (Fraser 1955; Brownell 1974; Aguayo 1975), it would appear that it does not have the narrow, pointed jaws of the northern variety, and its whole head—perhaps because it is white where *borealis* is black—looks heavier and more substantial.

The color pattern of this dolphin is unique: shiny black dorsal field, snowy white underparts (with the white coming much higher up on the flanks than it does in its northern counterpart, where it is restricted

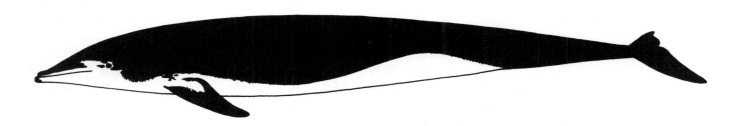

Anomalous color pattern of a northern right whale dolphin taken off Japan. Similarly colored specimens have been seen in California waters, but they are believed to be only color variations, and not subspecies. (After Tobayama et al. [1968])

to a ventral streak), and a white face. The black coloration on the forehead meets in a "widow's peak" just
forward of the blowhole, and the flippers are white on
the dorsal and ventral surfaces. True (1889) describes
the species as having "a broad black spot on the posterior margin of the pectoral fins . . . sometimes absent,"
and although this feature is not mentioned in most
other descriptions, it is shown quite clearly in the photograph of a living specimen in Brownell's 1974
"Small Odontocetes of the Antarctic." In describing
this species, cetologists have noticed some rather
unusual proportions: in the thoracic (chest) region,
the body is somewhat flattened, wider than it is high.
This is clearly evident in the first published photographs of the species, where three animals stranded
alive on a beach in New Zealand, and were then "returned to the sea, apparently none the worse for their
temporary sojourn on dry land" (Fraser 1955). Fraser
observed that this unusual configuration "may be because they are not waterborne, or it may be a stabiliz-
ing factor in an ocean-going dolphin that lacks a dorsal fin." (The northern right whale dolphin, another
pelagic dolphin with no dorsal fin, shows no such thoracic compression.) The southern species is somewhat
smaller than its northern relative, reaching a maximum known length of 7 feet (2.1 meters), although
most individuals are even smaller. (Norman and
Fraser say that the length is "stated to be nearly six
feet," and Gaskin [1972] illustrates the species as measuring 5 feet in length.) The dental arrangement is the
same as in the northern, with about 43 pairs of small,
sharp teeth in each jaw.

In the Southern Hemisphere there are two other
strikingly marked black-and-white small cetaceans,
Commerson's dolphin and the spectacled porpoise.
Neither of these animals moves as fast as the right
whale dolphins, and they have prominant dorsal fins,
while the right whale dolphin has no dorsal fin at all.
One observer wrote that this dolphin, "when swimming, resembles a giant penguin" (Baker 1972). In his

diary of the 1910–12 *Terra Nova* expedition to the
Antarctic, Wilson wrote, "We saw two distinct species
of dolphin today, a very handsome pair, jet black and
pure white, a species I cannot find described anywhere, and the ordinary southern Dusky Dolphin in
large numbers." Because Lillie (1915) recorded the
same event (on October 20, 1910), we are able to
correlate the two accounts, and positively identify the
animals that Wilson could not recognize: "They
seemed to roll over more than the other dolphins we
saw. On October 20th the *L. peronii* came with a herd
of Dusky Dolphins, but they kept separate." It is interesting to note that in their respective hemispheres, the
northern and southern right whale dolphins associate
with the species of *Lagenorhynchus* that occur there: the
Pacific white-sided dolphin in the North Pacific, and
the dusky in the Southern Ocean.

Very little is known of the biology of this offshore
species. Despite its striking coloration, it is rarely seen
—undoubtedly because of the remoteness of its habitat. Like its Northern Hemisphere relative, it is most
often observed in small groups of 50 or fewer, but
there are reports of schools of as many as 600 off the
coast of Chile (Aguayo 1975), and a "huge aggregation of scores of schools totalling over 1,000 animals"
was observed off the Marlborough coast of South Island, New Zealand (Gaskin 1972). Because of its
similarity to the northern variety, it may be assumed
that it feeds on squid and small fishes.

The type specimen (named for François Peron, a
French naturalist who described it to Lacépède in
1802) was collected off the coast of Tasmania. It is a
creature of the high southern latitudes, but is a "marginal Antarctic species" (Brownell 1974). It has been
recorded from both coasts of South America, from
Cape Horn, the Straits of Magellan, the Falkland Islands, and Tierra del Fuego, where Goodall (1978)
discovered "four nearly complete skeletons, 17 cranial
specimens and eight groups of isolated vertebrae."
She wrote that the "eleven cranial specimens from

the Río San Martín area, all beach worn, may represent a mass stranding." She also said that these strandings "indicate that it may occasionally inhabit shallow waters."*

Although Melville does not concern himself very much with the smaller cetaceans in *Moby-Dick*, he offers an accurate portrait of the southern right whale dolphin in the section entitled "Cetology." Since we know that he was aboard the whaler *Acushnet* in the South Seas and elsewhere, we can probably assume that his description is based on firsthand observation:

Chapter III. *(Mealy-mouthed Porpoise).*—The largest kind of Porpoise; and only found in the Pacific, so far as it is known. The only English name, by which he has hitherto been designated, is that of the fishers—Right-Whale Porpoise, from the circumstance that he is chiefly found in the vicinity of that Folio. In shape, he differs in some degree from the Huzza Porpoise, being of a less rotund and jolly girth; indeed, he is quite a neat and gentlemanlike figure. He has no fins on his back (most other porpoises have), he has a lovely tail, and sentimental Indian eyes of a hazel hue. But his mealy-mouth spoils all. Though his entire back down to his side fins is of a deep sable, yet a boundary line, distinct as the mark on a ship's hull, called the "bright waist," that line streaks him from stem to stern, with two separate colours, black above, and white below. The white comprises part of his head, and the whole of his mouth, which makes him look as if he had just escaped from a felonious visit to a meal-bag. A most mean and mealy aspect! His oil is much like that of the common porpoise.

In this section, Melville distinguishes the whales by comparison with the different sizes of books; thus the

*The appearance of animals on the beach does not necessarily indicate that this is their normal habitat. Many deepwater species, such as sperm whales, beach themselves, but this does not mean that they are amphibious. Other factors, still not understood, compel various cetaceans to strand, and they may come from considerable distances to do so,

larger whales are the "Folio" whales, the smaller ones, such as the pilot whale and killer are "Octavoes," and the porpoises are "Duodecimoes." The "Huzza Porpoise" is probably a common dolphin, but he gives no clues as to the particulars of its appearance. From his final comment on the oil, it appears that this "mealy-mouthed porpoise" was brought aboard and rendered down.

RISSO'S DOLPHIN

Grampus griseus Cuvier 1812

Risso's dolphin, sometimes known as the gray grampus or even simply as grampus, is cosmopolitan in distribution but not well known anywhere. Mature adults reach a length of 12 to 13 feet (3.6 to 4 meters), and can be identified by the beakless, rounded profile; high, falcate dorsal fin; and omnipresent scratch marks. The overall color is grayish, lighter in larger (and therefore older) specimens. Scammon (1874) called this species the "whiteheaded or mottled grampus," and wrote that "the prevailing color is very dark, approaching to black, the head and anterior portion of the body—as far as the pectorals in some specimens—are white, in others it is only partially so; and frequently they are seen more or less mottled with light gray to the region of the dorsal fin." There seems to be an almost limitless variation in the coloring of adults, ranging from almost white to almost black. Schevill (quoted in Fraser [1974]) has commented, "I have seen them so pale as to look nearly as white as *Delphinapterus leucas* (the White Whale) except for the dark flukes and fins. I have seen them so dark and unscratched as to approach *Pseudorca* (the False Killer). There seems to be no geographic connection. Both the palest and the darkest I have seen were in the

North Bahamas, but nearly as wide a range has turned up in the New York Bight." In the case of the five animals which stranded on the shores of the Gulf of California, all of the dolphins, which were of similar size, "varied considerably in coloration. One was nearly white all over, the others ranged from dark gray to light gray . . . with white areas of varying size on the belly" (Leatherwood et al. 1979). This pattern on the belly can also vary, as demonstrated by Fraser (1974) in his discussion of a specimen that was caught in the line of a lobster pot at Ballydonegan, County Cork, and killed by the fishermen. After remarking that "there are usually no well-marked boundaries between the darker and lighter areas," Fraser writes that the Ballydonegan specimen had "a light area behind the chin followed posteriorly by a dark transverse band having a lighter patch on the mid-line, and, on its posterior margin, a small mid-ventral, posteriorly projecting promontory—reminiscent of that found in the Pilot Whale."

The melon (forehead) is characterized by a vertical crease, unique to this species. Risso's dolphin also has an easily recognizable dental arrangement, with 2 to 7 pairs of teeth in the lower jaw only. Rarely a specimen is discovered with one or two teeth in the upper jaw, but the lower teeth are usually the only ones visible, and they are not always evenly distributed in the jaw. Fraser (1953) commented on the condition of these teeth, since they are greatly worn down without contact with upper teeth: "Other dolphins having a full complement of teeth in the upper jaw which normally interdigitate with those in the lower jaw occasionally have the lower jaw displaced so that the upper and lower teeth are opposed to one another, and excessive and sometimes damaging wear results. It is difficult to understand how in Risso's dolphin the same condition can be produced in the absence of upper-jaw teeth."

In some respects, Risso's dolphin resembles the pilot whale, but the overall proportions are different, especially as regards the dorsal fin, which is located much closer to the head in the pilot whale, and is much lower and less sharply curved than that of Risso's. In addition, the pilot whale is usually blackish, while Risso's dolphin comes in various shades of gray and is usually lighter in color forward of the dorsal. From a distance, a herd of Risso's dolphins might be mistaken for bottlenoses, because both are energetic swimmers with a high, falcate dorsal fin, but the bottlenose is somewhat smaller and has a distinct beak. Another area of possible confusion lies in the name *Grampus*. This is also one of the vernacular names of the killer whale, but, aside from this, there is no reason to confuse the two species, since killer whales are jet-black with sharply defined white markings.* Certain authors (e.g., Iredale and Troughton 1933; Nishiwaki 1963) have chosen to place this species in an altogether different genus, *Grampidelphis*, and assign the name *Grampus* to the killer whale, but as of this writing, *Grampus griseus* is the accepted name for Risso's dolphin. *Grampus* is thought to be derived from the Latin for "large fish" (*gran* "large"; *piscis* "fish"), and *griseus* is Latin for "gray."

The species has been known as Risso's dolphin—or, more accurately, *dauphin de Risso*, since it was described first in French—ever since the early nineteenth century. The naturalist Giovanni Antonio Risso (whom Cuvier refers to as a *pharmacien à Nice, observateur zélé*) "sent an account of it from Nice with a drawing in 1811 to Paris, when Cuvier, satisfied it was distinct, affixed to it the name of this modest and devoted naturalist" (Hamilton 1835). Cuvier believed it was a different species from the already described *Delphinus griseus*, but it was not, and after a succession of

*Most people, however, are not that familiar with any cetaceans, and if it has a dorsal fin and a spout, it is likely to be taken for a killer whale. When a fisherman off San Mateo County, California, saw several small cetaceans swimming about his boat, he "feared they were killer whales" and shot them. They were Risso's dolphins (Orr 1966).

Ventral view of Risso's dolphin *(Grampus griseus),* **showing two white areas, sickle-shaped flippers, and broad, notched flukes.**

concurrent name changes (for what was believed to be two different species), the correct name was determined to be *Grampus griseus*. Among its other names, this species has been known as *Globicephalus rissii, Delphinus Rissoi, Grampus rissoanus,* and *Delphinus aries* (Hershkovitz 1966).

The "gray grampus" is distributed throughout the tropical and temperate waters of the world, and does not seem to occur in high polar latitudes. A report of the species in the Bering Sea is considered "of doubtful accuracy" (Leatherwood et al. 1980). It has been recorded from Newfoundland south to Cape Horn in the western Atlantic, and from the Hebrides and Shetland Islands to the Cape of Good Hope in the east. The species is known from the Mediterranean, the Red Sea, and the Indian Ocean, and in the western Pacific from the Commander Islands south to New Zealand. Leatherwood and colleagues (1980) reviewed the distribution and movements of Risso's dolphin, with particular emphasis on the eastern North Pacific, since they had access to various fisheries' information that had not previously been examined for specific cetacean sightings. They added a number of sightings and strandings to the records for this species, and reported groups that ranged from 1 to 220 animals, "about a geometric mean of 10.65. About 75% of the groups contained fewer than 20 animals."

This species has been described as "frolicsome," and it is seen leaping clear of the water. (Mercer [1973], however, observed six specimens passing "sluggishly, breaking the surface slightly. . . .") They are often observed in small groups, although Leatherwood and Reeves (1978) make reference to "Risso's dolphins . . . loafing at the surface, arranged in a manner reminiscent of stacked cordwood," which would probably imply a large aggregation. During an aerial

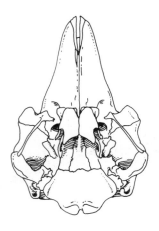

Ventral view of the skull of *Grampus griseus.* **In this view of the underside of the upper jaw the absence of teeth can be seen. (After Hall and Kelson [1959])**

survey of the Gulf of California, Leatherwood and colleagues (1979) reported one school of "50 ± individuals," and Schevill (1954) reported a school of more than 60 animals, swimming in groups of four to six.

Risso's dolphin is primarily a squid eater, and many cetologists believe that the scratches on the bodies of the animals are caused by these cephalopods: "The whitish streaks and blotches often seen on the bodies of these dolphins probably are scars made by the circular suckers, armed with claws, on the arms of the giant squid" (Kellogg 1940). It is not very likely that these 12-foot dolphins feed on the giant squid, which sometimes can reach a length of 50 feet, but Orr (1966) records one specimen found in California that had three pairs of jaws of the squid *Dodisicus gigas,* which is known to reach a length of 12 feet (Clarke 1966). An alternative explanation for the scratches is that "they are the healed scars of wounds caused by the teeth of individuals of the same species" (Norman and Fraser 1938). Given the limited dentition of this species, this suggestion seems considerably less plausible than the first. McCann (1974) includes Risso's dolphin in his list of the Delphinidae that are given to "body-scarring," and writes that the "movement of the jaw is somewhat like that of a pig when attacking an opponent." Baker (1972) described the teeth of adult Risso's dolphins as "rounded like .44 bullets," which would make the suggestion of tooth-inflicted wounds even more questionable, and it is possible that there are other, still unsuspected factors responsible for the extensive scarring of this species.

From the examination of females with almost full-term fetuses, it has been estimated that Risso's dolphin is about 6 feet long at birth. Fraser (1934) records a 10-foot 6-inch female from which a 5-foot 5 1/2-inch fetus was taken, and notes that this fetus was more than half the length of the parent. In 1974, Fraser reported a 13-foot 5-inch female ("which approaches the upper limit of length for the species") with a fetus that was "about 4 ft. 6 in. (1371 mm) long." The smallest specimens of Risso's dolphin that were reported stranded on British coasts between 1913 and 1966 were just under 6 feet in length. (This species is not particularly abundant, but on the shores of the British Isles there have been 66 recorded strandings in that 53-year period.) Maxwell (1952) described an 8 1/2-foot specimen which had stranded in the Hebrides as "a dark buffish color which looked pearly grey in certain lights," but we do not know how long the animal had been out of the water, and the skin color of cetaceans is extremely susceptible to the effects of sunlight. In the examination of a 6-foot 7-inch female captured on the British coast, Murie

(1871) noted that "it was not crisscrossed with scratches, but had instead seven narrow white but grey-edged lines . . . somewhat vertically placed along the sides from the shoulder to about opposite the vent; the front and hinder pairs being cross-barred longitudinally. . . ." This description corresponds closely to the 1872 discussion by Flower of a 6-foot 1-inch animal, and another by Fraser in 1946. All these juveniles had these vertical stripes, which are probably fetal folds, formed as the animal lies curled up in the uterus of its mother. In these young animals the dorsal surface is usually described as quite dark, and the lower surface is white, with the two areas clearly delimited (Flower 1872).

During his three years as a basking shark fisherman in the Hebrides, Gavin Maxwell had ample opportunity to observe Risso's dolphins: ". . . I do not think I am exaggerating if I say that there were very few weeks in which we did not see several schools of them. The schools would range from about a dozen to forty individuals, the average school being about twenty-five, and were always composed of adults and young, the latter swimming close alongside their parents." Because he spent so much time at sea, Maxwell was in an ideal position to record the behavior of these animals, and his book *Harpoon Venture* (1952), while concerned primarily with the shark fishery, gives as much firsthand information on Risso's dolphins as can be found in any scientific publication.

Sometimes we would find a bay full of them; scattered, and each one going in a different direction, swimming more slowly, at seven knots or less. These were probably in the middle of a shoal of fish, and feeding, and it was easier to approach them closely. When they were travelling they seemed very conscious of the vibration of the boat's engines

and kept an average distance of forty yards to port or to starboard when blowing, although we could see them under water at closer quarters.

When travelling, they hold a speed of ten or twelve knots and blow about every thirty yards. The sound of the blow is not as harsh or prolonged as that of a killer, but it is audible at a considerable distance—up to perhaps a quarter of a mile in still weather.

When travelling, Risso's grampus does not show the tail flukes as he sounds except when he is alarmed, and we learned that a flourish of the tail, often ending with a possibly accidental but audible slap upon the water's surface, was always followed by the complete disappearance of the school. I did not time their periods below the surface, but I should say that ten minutes to a quarter of an hour was the maximum, after which they would reappear in the far distance.

When Risso's grampuses are feeding or at play practically no attitude or antic is improbable. The very first one of which I had a clear view was stationary—treading water as it were, and staring at me with his head vertical and three feet clear of the water. The face looked to me like that of a huge lizard, and, as I was seeing mainly the underside of it, it appeared pure white. . . . When playing, Risso's grampuses breach like other whales, shooting high out of the water; they make short rushes along the surface; flourish their tails in the air; remain absolutely stationary at the surface for several seconds at a time; seem, in fact, to get their bodies into every possible and impossible attitude. More than once I saw a dorsal fin remain stationary and high out of the water while the tail lashed violently up and down, showing itself just above the surface at each upward movement.

A unique opportunity to observe a stranding in progress occurred when a family named Fisher, camping along the Baja coast of the Gulf of California, saw five dolphins (identified later from photographs as

A juvenile *Grampus*, showing the characteristic vertical stripes and the marked delineation of the dark dorsal coloration and the white ventral surface. (After Murie [1871])

Risso's dolphin) "seemingly chasing a large school of fish, thought to be mullet, and apparently taking some at the surface, in the presence of numerous gulls."* At about 5:30 P.M. on June 18, 1973, the dolphins ceased their apparent feeding, and one of them headed for the beach and "continued alone up the gradually sloping beach, at first separately, until it was in no more than one foot of water (not enough to cover it). Here for ten minutes it began rooting in the sand." The other four dolphins remained nearby, "even when members of the observing party entered the rapidly shoaling water and touched them." The single animal eventually stranded, and was left on the sand by the receding tide. It died during the night, and the remaining dolphins "were still in attendance, remaining within about 100 feet (30 m) swimming back and forth along the beach." At about six the next morning, the remaining four dolphins had stranded some 300 feet to the south, and within two hours they too had perished. The authors comment, "In a rather major aspect, however, this *Grampus* mass stranding seems to differ in that just before starting to strand, the 5 individuals appeared to be feeding actively, whereas it has generally been thought that stranded cetaceans have little or no recently ingested food in their stomachs."† The five carcasses were towed out to sea, so there was no possibility of a postmortem examination. The "rooting in the sand" behavior of the first strander is reminiscent of the actions of spotted dolphins hunted in the Solomon Islands: when the hunters clang stones together underwater, the resulting noise is thought to cause the dolphins to "suddenly plunge vertically and bury part of their heads in the soft sandy mud bottom" (Dawbin 1966). If the dolphins in the Solomons were driven to bury their heads in the sand by an intense auditory stimulation, it is possible that the behavior of the Risso's dolphin was also related to some painful internal difficulty with the ear, perhaps related to a parasitic infection. (Dawbin also records a school of 30 Risso's dolphins herded ashore in the Solomons, but he makes no mention of their burying their heads in the sand.)

Most of our knowledge of this species has been obtained from the examination of stranded specimens, some observations in the wild, and the occa-

sional exhibition of a captive specimen in an oceanarium or an aquarium. Several animals are on exhibit at Enoshima Aquarium in Japan, and there have been specimens briefly exhibited in Florida and California. In August 1980, a 10 1/2-foot female was captured after stranding in the Fore River near Quincy, Massachusetts. Workers from the New England Aquarium brought the animal to Boston, and after several months of adjusting to captivity, she is being trained to perform along with the bottlenose dolphins.

A pair of "inseparable" males were kept at Marineland of Florida for over a year, and they interacted vigorously with other species, according to Caldwell and Caldwell (1972): "One was moved, and the larger, who occasionally became aggressive toward the large male bottlenosed dolphins, particularly during feeding, gave an indication of actively warding off the large males when his newly acquired companions [female bottlenose dolphins] were trying to feed. On the other hand, this same animal attacked the largest female *Tursiops* on occasion."

According to Evans (1967), this species is a known echolocator, sending out clicks as well as harmonic whistles. (Watkins [1980] includes it in his list of odontocetes that have been recorded making click sounds at sea, but he does not elaborate on the nature of the sounds.) "Given equal body weight," wrote Pilleri and Gihr (1969), "the brain weight of *Grampus* corresponds to that of *Tursiops truncatus*." In their 1979 analysis of the cephalization ratio of various cetaceans, the same authors placed Risso's dolphin at the highest level of cephalization, along with *Phocoena*, *Tursiops*, and *Orca*.

There have been cetaceans sighted at sea which resembled Risso's dolphin, but the particulars do not exactly agree, leading to an observation that "these whales sighted off Chile in 1964 may be a new species, possibly of the genus *Pseudorca* or *Grampus*." These animals, as described by Clarke and colleagues in 1978, were beakless, with a whitish head, but the dorsal fins were much higher and more vertical than those usually seen in Risso's dolphin, and they were much larger—estimated at 20 feet—than any known specimens of Risso's dolphin. The animals were photographed (see Clarke et al. 1978, Pl. III), but there is no way of determining the size of the animals from the picture.

The possibility of distinct species interbreeding in the wild is quite remote, but the only instance in which this must be considered a possibility probably involves *Grampus*. Three "anomalous" dolphins washed ashore at Blacksod Bay, Ireland, in 1933, and were examined by F. C. Fraser, one of the world's foremost authorities on the systematics and anatomy

---

*The actual stranding was witnessed by the Fisher family and subsequently related to S. Leatherwood and C. L. Hubbs, who wrote up the account, sharing authorship with Matilda Fisher. Descriptions of the events surrounding the stranding are from their paper, published in 1979.

†It also appears to be unusual in that the remaining animals, which were presumably healthy, stranded even though the injured animal had died. In numerous other instances of mass strandings, when an injured animal dies, the remaining cetaceans move off. This seems to be a case of apparently healthy animals beaching themselves *because* one of their number has died.

of small cetaceans. He examined the three animals, two females and a male, all between 7 feet 6 inches and 8 feet 10 inches in length, and wrote that one of the three looked like a bottlenose dolphin, but "the other two were not within the range of any known form of dolphin." After a careful examination of the exterior and interior anatomy, Fraser (1940) wrote: "The circumstances of the stranding suggests the possibility of the three specimens having been inter-related; and the position of the three as connecting links, between two genera hitherto acknowledged as being quite distinct, is of very great interest. . . . A successful crossing between *Tursiops* and *Grampus* may be considered." Such a crossing has in fact taken place, but it involved captive animals. At the Enoshima Aquarium in Japan, no fewer than three *Tursiops* × *Grampus* hybrid offspring have been born to a male *Grampus* and a female *Tursiops*. The hybrid has been named *Tursiogrampus grisecatus*, and the first calf, born in 1978, is healthy as of February 1981, but the other two, born later, died in 1980 (Hideo Omura, personal communication).

Although there are occasional strandings of Risso's dolphins, some taken incidentally in net fisheries at various locations (Mitchell 1975b) and some observed in oceanariums, by far the best known and most celebrated Risso's dolphin was Pelorus Jack, who accompanied steamers in the Cook Strait, between North and South Islands, New Zealand. The first time Pelorus Jack was seen is not recorded, but he was known as early as 1888. (There is no evidence, by the way, that Jack was a male, but he was always referred to that way.) "He most often came in sight slightly south of the Chetwode Islands and above a twisted lump of land, poking seaward, called Alligator Head. His entrance was spectacular—a foamy dash, highlighted with a series of leaps which often took him clear of the water. After his display of exuberance and good will, the dolphin would head for the bow of the vessel and continue at that position for several miles" (Cress 1955).*

Although he appeared regularly, Jack seemed to prefer the faster steamers to the slower ones, and would leave a slow vessel if a faster one appeared. The captains of these steamers would often blow their whistles when they saw the dolphin approaching, and then tell the passengers that they had called him. Antony Alpers has written a meticulously researched essay on Pelorus Jack (1960), including an eyewitness description: ". . . we all thronged to the bow of the

---

*Sergeant (1978) has suggested that this highly unusual behavior—remaining in the same bay and alone, as far as could be determined, for more than twenty years—might be explained as the behavior of a "lost" animal which had become separated from its own kind and sought "some form of security" in its restricted habitat and its association with ships.

ship to see a large, silvery-white fish plunging through the waves towards us. As it reached the vessel it turned with it, scraping its body first on one side and then on the other, playfully plunging and springing from the waves. . . ." The animal soon became an attraction of major importance, and tourists would ride the steamers between Wellington and Nelson just to see Pelorus Jack. Mark Twain is reported to have made the crossing during the time of the dolphin's popularity, and even Kipling wrote of having seen him.

Because someone had taken a potshot at the dolphin, an Act of Parliament was passed in 1904 that contained the wording:

During the period of five years from the date of the gazetting of these regulations, it shall not be lawful for any person to take the fish or mammal of the species commonly known as Risso's dolphin (*Grampus griseus*) in the waters of Cook Strait, or of the bays, sounds, and estuaries adjacent thereto.

This is generally thought to be the first time that a law was passed to protect an individual wild animal, as opposed to a species or a particular population. Even though the proclamation was written to protect the "fish or mammal commonly known as Risso's dolphin," everyone knew that there was only one animal to be protected, Pelorus Jack. In 1911, the carcass of a dolphin washed ashore on D'Urville Island, close to Jack's regular route, and virtually the entire New Zealand populace mourned his passing. A week later, however, Jack reappeared at the bow of a steamer, and the nation rejoiced. He continued his activities for another year, but by April 1912 he was gone for good. There was a flurry of talk and recriminations regarding the way he died, including some wild accusations of Norwegian whalers who happened to be in the vicinity, but no evidence was ever presented.

During his lifetime—he rode the bow waves of ships for at least twenty-four years—this animal was thought to be a fish, a goose-beaked whale, or even a beluga. (The beluga is strictly an Arctic creature, occasionally straying as far south as England or New Jersey.) More than half a century after his disappearance, the controversy still continues as to exactly what sort of animal Pelorus Jack was. In 1972, Gaskin wrote that "the famous New Zealand dolphin 'Pelorus Jack' called a Risso's dolphin in many publications, was almost certainly a specimen of *T. truncatus* [the bottlenose dolphin]." (Mörzer Bruyns, in his 1971 discussion of this species, categorically states, "It has never been recorded in New Zealand.") In 1976, V. B. Scheffer, not even bothering with the possibility of confusion, refers to "Pelorus Jack, the famous bottlenose porpoise." As evidence, Gaskin points out that Risso's dolphin is very rare in New Zealand waters, known only from "a single jawbone in the Dominion Museum," and the behavior of the animal, riding bow waves and accompanying ships, "would be quite in keeping with the behaviour that could be expected of a *Tursiops. . . .*"

In a paper published in 1974, A. N. Baker reproduced a photograph of Pelorus Jack taken from the bow of a steamer in 1907, and that seems to have resolved the controversy, since there is no question that it is a picture of a Risso's dolphin. By coincidence, a picture taken by W. E. Evans of a Risso's dolphin at Enoshima Aquarium almost exactly matches the 1907 photo, and both pictures, reproduced side by side in Baker's paper, show the characteristic light head, dark flippers, and falcate dorsal fin. In May 1972, two more specimens stranded in New Zealand, demonstrating at least that they are more common there than Gaskin thought they were. Pelorus Jack entertained people—and quite possibly himself—for many years in New Zealand waters, but it is indicative of the mysterious nature of this species that even the existence of an animal that thousands of

people saw had to be verified by the stranding and death of two others.

MELON-HEADED WHALE

Peponocephala electra Gray 1846

The melon-headed whale is a slim, black, beakless species, reaching a length of 9 feet (2.7 meters). It has an overhanging upper jaw, sometimes described as a "parrot beak," and unpigmented areas around the lips. In the dorsal or ventral view, it can be seen that the head is pointed, more so than in similar species. There are 21 to 25 teeth in each side of each jaw. The dorsal fin is sharply pointed, as are the flippers. *Peponocephala* has a grayish patch on the chest between the flippers, and the genital area is often lighter in color than the rest of the animal.

At sea, the melon-headed whale is almost impossible to differentiate from the pygmy killer whale, although the latter may have visible areas of white extending up the flanks from the belly and a darker "cape." Both species have been seen in Hawaiian and Japanese waters, and both are between 7 and 9 feet in

Risso's dolphin, *Grampus griseus.* Notice the whitish head, with its vertical "crease," and the high falcate dorsal fin, as well as the profusion of scars.

144

length. (The only other species with which these two "blackfish"* might be confused is the false killer whale, which shares the same coloration, but gets to be approximately twice as long as the others, reaching a maximum length of almost 20 feet.) Of the three species of "blackfish," the melon-headed whale has the most teeth: it can have 25 teeth per row, while the pygmy killer has between 11 and 13, and the false killer has between 8 and 11. Animals with larger teeth are predators on larger prey, so it might be surmised that of the three species, the melon-headed whale feeds on the smallest prey, probably squid and small fishes.

From the infrequent records, this species is believed to be gregarious. Peale (1848) records "sixty of these animals [then known as *Phocoena pectoralis*] driven ashore by natives at Hilo, Hawaii. They were considered a dainty food and yielded a valuable stock of oil." In 1965, a group of about 500 animals of this species came into Suruga Bay, Japan (Nishiwaki and Norris 1966). Its swimming habits have been described as follows: "One school of 15 specimens was roaming around just under the surface, dorsal fins exposed and occasionally bobbed up and down, showing the head and upper body clearly with each blast, diving again with a strong arching of the tailstock which has a sharp ridge" (Mörzer Bruyns 1971). A male calf, 43 1/2 inches (112 centimeters) long and weighing 94 pounds (43 kilograms) was caught in a tuna net off Guatemala (Perrin 1976), but its age at that size could not be determined.

*Even though the common name of the pilot whale (*Globicephala* spp.) is blackfish, there are three other black, beakless cetaceans that are also referred to in this way by fishermen in various parts of the world. These are *Pseudorca*, *Feresa*, and *Peponocephala*, and since these species are unrelated, there is no name that could be used for all three in a discussion of their differences or similarities, and I have therefore chosen to call them blackfish.

With these scanty exceptions, "extremely little is known of the ecology and ethology of *Peponocephala*" (Pilleri and Gihr 1973).

The melon-headed whale is known from limited but widely scattered records from temperate and tropical seas. It has been recorded from Japan: the first live specimen was found in the shallows of Hiratsuka Beach, Sagami Bay, in 1963 (Nakajima and Nishiwaki 1965); from Crowdy Heads, New South Wales in 1958 (Dawbin et al. 1970); and from Hawaii, where a newborn specimen was found at Kahuku Beach, Oahu, in 1964 (Nishiwaki and Norris 1966). Specimens were also found on the east coast of Australia in 1969 and 1973 (Bryden et al. 1977), leading the authors to suggest that the range "probably extends throughout the northern half of the east coast of Australia." Human habitation in this area is sparse, however, so "the chances of observation of stranded or live animals along most of the coast is remote." It has also been reported from Thailand, Pakistan, India, Senegal, Guinea, and Indonesia, and the juvenile caught in the tuna seine off Guatemala "extends the known range of the species some 3,000 miles into the eastern tropical Pacific off Central America" (Perrin 1976). There is one apparently accurate record of a single specimen taken in 1912 by Robert Cushman Murphy northwest of St. Paul's Rocks in the Atlantic off Brazil (Goodwin 1945). Until recently, this remained the only record for this species in the Atlantic, but in March and April of 1976, four melon-headed whales were landed in the small whale fishery on the island of St. Vincent (Caldwell et al. 1976), thereby confirming its occurrence in the Atlantic and extending its range to another warm-water area.

Although there have been records of this species —under many different names—since its original description by Gray in 1846, it was not until 1963 that a living specimen was observed. (Aboard the U.S. Exploring Expedition in the years 1838 to 1842, T. R. Peale illustrated an animal referred to as *Lagenorhynchus electra*, which was obviously this species, but he worked from a dead specimen.) The 1963 Sagami Bay specimen was not one of the other "blackfish," that is, it was not a false killer whale or a pygmy killer whale, and it was probably not even a member of the genus *Lagenorhynchus*. (Gray had named the species from an examination of the skull, which does bear great similarities to the skulls of other *Lagenorhynchus* species, but the animal's external appearance—not available to Gray—would obviously place it in another group. This species has a rounded profile and no beak, while the other lags have a sharp snout, and sometimes even a poorly defined beak; and where the melon-head is all black, the other lags are among the most strongly patterned of all small cetaceans.) There were a number of osteological differences as well, including the presence of one more phalange in each digit than *Lagenorhynchus* (Nishiwaki and Norris 1966).

Nakajima and Nishiwaki (1965) described the Sagami Bay specimen as *Electra electra*. On March 23, 1965, the year their paper was published, some 500 animals of this species came into Suruga Bay, Honshu, and almost half of them were caught. Most were used for human consumption, but 15 were brought to the Whales Research Institute in Tokyo. There

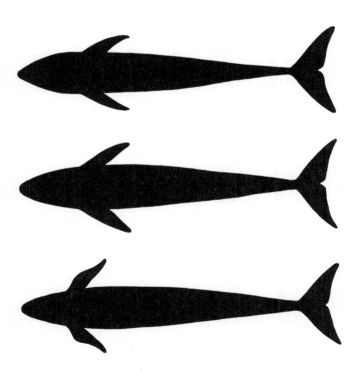

Dorsal view of the three "blackfish": *Feresa* (top); *Peponocephala* (middle); *Pseudorca* (bottom) (not drawn to scale). *Feresa* has a pointed snout, and *Pseudorca* has "humped" pectoral fins.

they were examined by Nishiwaki and Norris, who published their findings in 1966. They discovered that the generic name *Electra* was preoccupied (already in use) by a genus of bryozoans, and they proposed a "new generic name, *Peponocephala*, for the form, which is a delphinid odontocete cetacean most closely allied to the genera *Pseudorca*, *Feresa*, and *Lagenorhynchus*." The name *Peponocephala* was suggested to the authors by F. C. Fraser of the British Museum, and means simply "melon-head." There have been many vernacular names for this species, including "broad-beaked dolphin," "Hawaiian blackfish," "many-toothed blackfish," and "electra dolphin," but since the species was actually named "melon-head," this is the common name that should be employed.

PYGMY KILLER WHALE

Feresa attenuata Gray 1875

Discussing the state of knowledge of this species in 1960, F. C. Fraser wrote:

Perhaps the most remarkable feature about *Feresa* is that this Dolphin, recognized from a skull described by Gray in 1827 and again by another skull described by him in 1875, should not have been encountered for another eighty years, when Yamada at last provided a well-defined locality for the occurrence of the species, and gave the first account of its external form. The specimen secured by Cadenat while increasing the known number of specimens to four, widens the potential distribution of the Dolphin nearly to the possible oceanic limit. Both Mr. Cadenat and Dr. Yamada are to be congratulated on the contribution they have made to the knowledge of what still must be regarded as one of the world's largest rare mammals.

Since 1960, there have been several observations of wild and captive specimens, but it still can be fairly stated that the species is hardly known at all. The reports of its behavior are often contradictory, and there is not enough of a sample to decide which—if any—of the observations represent the typical behavior of the pygmy killer whale.

True (1889) described the species from the two skulls in the British Museum (one of which was identified only as coming from "South Seas") and wrote, "The future development of our knowledge of this genus will be watched with much interest by cetologists. At present there is nothing to add to Gray's original description, and no additional specimens have been discovered." The specimen described in 1954 by Yamada was the first one seen in the flesh by a cetologist. (Obviously, untrained observers had seen others at sea but they did not know what

they were seeing.) The animal had been harpooned off Taiji, Japan, by a dolphin-fishing boat, and although Yamada arrived on the scene after the animal was flensed, he carefully "re-assembled" it for purposes of identification and photography, and subsequently prepared the first skeleton known from this species.

In 1958, a specimen washed ashore at Senegal (Cadenat 1958), and in 1963, a school of 14 animals was discovered near the entrance of Sagami Bay, near Tokyo, and driven to Futo, where they were captured and taken to the Ito Aquarium: "During the driving they seemed obedient and sounded shallowly only three times, each of which was for about three minutes" (Nishiwaki et al. 1965). Characteristically, they raised their heads out of the water at the aquarium, and "they observed the men on the shore with both eyes when they were perpendicular." Except for one male that lived for 22 days, all the other specimens died within the first week of captivity. There were seven males and seven females, ranging in length from 208 to 244 centimeters (6.8 to 8 feet), and on average, the males were larger than the females.

Although there have now been a number of observations of this animal at sea, very little is known of its life history or biology in the wild. A juvenile specimen was collected in the eastern tropical Pacific in 1967, but scientists could only get its basic measurements, since it had been frozen in the hold of a tuna boat before they saw it, and no information was available on its behavior (Perrin and Hubbs 1969). The authors wrote, "It is almost certain that this juvenile porpoise was accompanied by its mother, which apparently escaped during the purse-seining operation." The species appears to congregate in small groups of 10 to 50 animals, but the individual harpooned off Japan was "solitary at sea" (Yamada 1954).

Although most descriptions of the pygmy killer whale indicate that it is black in color, it is really gray, with a "dark spinal field" or a black "cape." (The part that is usually seen as the animal swims, therefore, is black.) This characteristic has been described by Nishiwaki (1966) as "pale wavy stripes along the sides," but there is only one stripe, the line where the cape meets the lighter coloration of the sides. At the junction of these two colors in the region of the eye, a sort of "eyebrow" is formed, which is often clearly visible. (See illustrations in Nishiwaki 1967, 1972.) There is a white patch in the genital region, and the lips are often white as well. Some individuals have a white chin, described by Leatherwood and colleagues (1976) as a "goatee," and illustrated clearly in Caldwell and Caldwell's (1975a) discussion of the pygmy killer whale in Florida.

Of the three unrelated "blackfish" (*Feresa, Peponocephala,* and *Pseudorca*), the pygmy killer most closely resembles the melon-headed whale. The melon-head has a more pointed snout (viewed from above), but "otherwise the two species are virtually indistinguishable in encounters at sea." (Leatherwood et al. 1976). Both are dark-colored, beakless cetaceans, about 9 feet long. (The false killer whale reaches twice this length and has uniquely shaped pectoral fins.) The pygmy killer—a name suggested by Yamada in 1954—does not look much its larger namesake, the "true" killer whale either, but it does have similar dentition, with 11 to 13 pairs of large, conical teeth in each jaw.

This species has narrow flippers that are rounded at the tips, and they may be different in male and females. Pryor and colleagues (1965) have suggested that there may be some evidence of sexual dimorphism: "The flippers of our specimen [in Hawaii] were considerably more rounded and paddle-shaped than those figured by Yamada.. . . . Since our specimen was a young, sexually mature male . . . while Yamada's was an adult female, the difference may be sexual." A prominent feature of this animal seen at sea is the high, erect dorsal fin, as noted by Pryor and colleagues: "The large triangular dorsal fin of the adults distinguished them from any other small whales known to the collecting crew."

In 1963, a single male specimen was captured off the Kona coast of the island of Hawaii and brought to Sea Life Park, where it lived for twenty days before succumbing to a respiratory infection. Observations of the school of about 50 animals from which it was collected indicated that the propensity for these animals to raise their heads out of the water—as noted by Nishiwaki and colleagues of the animals at Ito Aquarium—was also prevalent in the Hawaiian pygmy killers; "they appeared to watch the approaching boat briefly before slipping back into the water" (Pryor et al. 1965). Even during transport to the oceanarium, the pygmy killer showed itself to be something less than completely tractable:

The unusually aggressive nature of the captive was apparent as it was being introduced into the Sea Life Park training tank. During the trip to the oceanarium its handler reported that it snapped at him every time the truck hit a bump. As it was lowered into the tank it again opened its mouth. At first the animal floundered, so the handler held the animal by the dorsal fin at the edge of the tank. During this time the "blatting" sound was repeated.

As the animal was escorted along the edge of the pool it suddenly struggled free. In the next few seconds the animal dashed forward halfway around the tank, dived to the bottom, traversed the tank upside down, and leaped two-thirds free of the water at the point of introduction. Without slackening speed the whale swam in a tight figure eight at the water inlet and then shot partly out of the water and snapped twice at one of us (KP). There was only time to yell a warning when the animal leaped again and snapped at another person 10 ft away. As the personnel backed nervously away from the tank edge, the animal took up station in mid-tank, apparently watching its captors.

It showed absolutely no signs of timidity and "made no attempt to avoid an observer but instead acted as if it expected the observer to move." Discussing this animal in *Lads Before the Wind* (1975), Karen Pryor wrote that it raised its head out of the water, "teeth clashing like a seagoing wolf." After ten days the animal was moved to a tank containing two pilot whales, and it began to circle them aggressively. Although the act was not observed, it was assumed that the pygmy

killer whale killed the smaller of the pilot whales, since it was found dead one morning, and when the animal was necropsied, it was found to have been "killed by a single powerful blow to the temporal region of the cranium" (Pryor et al. 1965). In South Africa, after a pygmy killer was put in its tank, a dusky dolphin was found dead, "bearing long raking tooth marks on both sides of the body, on the caudal peduncle, and at the base of the flipper" (Best 1970). Best points out that this behavior is most unusual in captive cetaceans, for even the killer whale, which preys on smaller cetaceans in the wild, "to date, has displayed little or no aggression to dolphins housed with it." Certainly these two cases are insufficient to establish a general pattern of behavior—no such aggression was observed in the Japanese capture of 14 animals—but it is possible to attribute a nasty disposition to this species in some instances. After her experience with the "seagoing wolf" in Hawaii, Karen Pryor (1975) wrote, "During my years at Sea Life Park, we deliberately never collected another."

In the tuna fishery of the eastern tropical Pacific, however, Perryman and Foster (1980) have collected evidence that this species preys on dolphins. In examining the records of cetacean attacks on the spinners and spotters in the nets, the authors found that the predominant predator was the false killer whale, but they also discovered some reports of attacks on the dolphins by a smaller whale: "The most likely suspect is the pygmy killer whale. The teeth of the externally very similar melon-headed whale . . . are small and appear unsuitable for handling such large prey." One report in which the predators were tentatively identified as pygmy killers was quoted as follows: "The pygmy killer whales surrounded the boat and the net. As they swam through the water they lifted their heads out of the water slightly then slapped [them] down. The porpoise went wild when they knew they were outside the net. They attacked the porpoise by biting them near the blowhole!"

The range of the pygmy killer whale is poorly known. It appears to be a warmwater species, and records include Japan, Hawaii, the eastern tropical Pacific, and Senegal. The first record for the Southern Hemisphere was obtained in 1968, when five animals stranded at Lüderitz, South-West Africa, and another from the Natal coast was collected in the same year, the first record from the Indian Ocean (Best 1970). In May 1971, "five individuals of this species, each estimated to measure about six feet (ca. 1.8 m) in length, were seen circling in shallow water just off the beach at Singer Island, near the pumping station at Palm Beach Shores," Florida (Caldwell and Caldwell 1975a). Sightings have occurred off Texas and the Atlantic coast of Florida, and specimens are infrequently taken in the small whale fishery on the island of St. Vincent in the Lesser Antilles. (Caldwell and Caldwell 1975b). The species has been seen "several times in the lee of Oahu Island; they seem to be regular residents of the Hawaiian area" (Pryor et al. 1965).

In March 1981, a group of underwater photographers in the waters of Kailua-Kona (the same region where the single whale had been captured for Sea Life Park in 1963) encountered a school of 12 to 14 pygmy killers and obtained probably the first underwater pictures of this species in the wild. They also provided some unique and fascinating field observations, which are reproduced here for the first time. (The comments are taken from a letter to me from Al Giddings dated April 10, 1981.)

On March 25, approximately two miles off the town of Kailua-Kona, in blue water, 2000 to 3000 feet deep, Rich Mula, Dan McSweeney and I came upon a group of 12 to 14 of what I believe to be pygmy killer whales. The animals were not moving, the water was flat calm, visibility 100 feet plus. With snorkel gear I quietly slipped into the water; the animals were approximately 30 yards away, slowly milling about, spy-hopping from time to time. Once in the water, but still at the surface, I was approached by a large adult, perhaps 6 feet in length. I then moved away from the Zodiac and we swam together some 5 or 6 feet apart for 20 to 30 seconds. The balance of the animals were visible in the background. The animal swimming next to me then broke away and leisurely returned to the group. . . . The animals seemed to be resting. As I closed the distance to perhaps 15 yards, the large group broke up into smaller groups (2 to 4) and moved off 100 yards of so, and stopped once again. . . . This went on for about five hours. . . . Most of the animals frequently vented a white milky material into the water. On one occasion two animals were swimming belly to belly and vented simultaneously. There were two calves in the group, one quite small, 30 inches or so, the other half grown. From time to time the calves would insert their rostrum into the ventral slit of the attendant animal while swimming, the young animal being on its back and underneath the adult. . . . At one point during our encounter Dan McSweeney actually touched one of the largest adults who was swimming alone at 100 feet or so from the group. This touch instigated a quick vertical dive to about 70 feet; the animal then stopped and shook itself as a golden retriever might upon exiting the water. It then returned to the surface quite rapidly to resume swimming on the surface in front of Dan as before. . . . The tolerant nature of these otherwise wary critters I found very curious. . . . It was our impression that this group might have tolerated us for the following reasons: (1) They had just finished some heavy feeding, thus the extensive venting. (2) They had calves with them, one extremely young. (3) The water was extremely calm, enabling them to drift effortlessly, their blowholes clearing the placid surface water. In short, this family group was fat, full, and resting with accompanying juvenile or newborn animals.

FALSE KILLER WHALE

Pseudorca crassidens Owen 1846

In 1846, Sir Richard Owen described a new species of cetacean from a subfossil skull found buried in the Lincolnshire Fens of England in 1843. He named the species *Phocoena crassidens* ("thick-toothed porpoise"), and although he considered it to be extinct, he qualified this opinion with the disclaimer, "until it should be proved that it still exists in our seas." (In the same year, J. E. Gray described the same specimen as *Orca crassidens* and suggested the popular name "Lincolnshire killer.") For the next sixteen years, this new species of fossil whale was known only from the single skull, but on November 24, 1861, a school of large black dolphins appeared in the Bay of Kiel in the Baltic, southeast of the Danish peninsula. When one of these animals was examined by the Danish zoologist J. Reinhardt (1866), he realized that it was identical to the specimen described by Owen, and he named the new genus *Pseudorca*, or "false orca."

The false killer whale does not resemble the killer whale in its external particulars: it is all black where the orca is strongly patterned with white; it has a comparatively small, sharply curved dorsal fin unlike the tall, vertical fin of the male killer; and where adult male killers have broad, paddle-like flippers, false killers have sickle-shaped pectorals, with a pronounced hump on the leading edge. The skulls of the two species are quite similar, however, and both have about 10 pairs of teeth in each jaw. As befits predators of large prey, both have large, strong teeth, but where the teeth of the killer whale are oval in cross section, those of the false killer are round. When H. F. Ferguson (1903) found a large, black cetacean stranded at Travancore, India, he was not sure of its identity, and he wrote, "From the size of the teeth it is evident that the animal is a 'Killer' or 'Grampus' . . . it approaches more the genus *Pseudorca*, a meagre description of which is given by Beddard in his *Book of Whales*."* (In a note to Ferguson's paper, Lydekker [1903] conclusively identified the animal as a false killer whale.) The French call this species *faux-orque*, and the Spanish *falsa orca*, but the Japanese name is *oki-gondo*, which means "offshore pilot whale." (Gaskin [1972] wrote that " 'false pilot whale' would be a better name, as the two species are frequently confused in stranding records when trained biologists or experienced whalers are not able to go to the scene.")

---

*Beddard's (1900) description was not only meager, it was downright derogatory: "The whale is scarce, and there is not very much to be said about it. It is not precisely evident why systematists have thought to remove it from the genus *Orca*, to which it is clearly very closely allied."

The maximum size usually given for males of this species—females are smaller in this as in most species of odontocetes—is 18 feet (5.5 meters), but it is likely that full-grown males get even larger. Fraser (1946) records several specimens over 18 feet—one was 19 feet, 4 inches—and Tomilin (1957) gives 6 meters (19.68 feet) as the maximum. Purves and Pilleri (1978) have written that the false killer may be "almost exactly comparable to the pilot whale, *Globicephala*, in maximum size, the largest males of each apparently reaching a length of 20 feet and the largest females about 16 feet." Calves are born between 5 and 6 feet long after a gestation period that has been calculated (on the basis of the examination of embryos and near-term fetuses) to be 14 months (Purves and Pilleri 1978).

Off the coast of southern California, Norris and Prescott (1961) observed "a school of what were very likely false killer whales, estimated to number three hundred animals . . . 3 miles west of Santa Catalina Island, California. The elongate school was adjudged to be two miles in length and about half a mile wide. . . . The animals in the school were estimated to range in size from 5 feet to a little more than 10 feet in length. Many of the animals, estimated at 9 feet in length, were accompanied very closely by young." This report had been frequently cited (e.g., Daugherty 1972; Gaskin 1972) as establishing the presence of the species in California waters—several skulls had been found on California beaches (Mitchell 1965), but no live animals had been recorded—and, more significantly, as indicating a smaller adult size for these animals than had previously been suspected. In discussing the size of the false killer whale, Gaskin (1972) wrote, "Specimens sometimes reach 18 feet (Norman and Fraser 1937), but in the North Pacific 7 to 10 feet is more usual (Norris and Prescott 1961)." This is indeed an unusual size range—Norris and Prescott's adults seem to be less than half the size of others—and Purves and Pilleri wrote that Norris and Prescott's

description "would seem to be a case either of mistaken identity or of an underestimation of length. . . . On the basis of the present investigation, the majority of this school, if indeed they had been *Pseudorca crassidens*, would have been suckling juveniles and the largest would have been recently weaned."

The false killer whale feeds on fish and squid, including large prey items such as snappers, amberjacks, bonito, and tuna. It has also been reported that the species "characteristically shakes and dismembers its prey, a habit indicating that it feeds on large organisms" (Scheffer 1978). There is one report of a female false killer catching a mahi-mahi (dolphin fish) in Hawaiian waters and holding it so that a juvenile accompanying her could feed on it (Brown et al. 1966). This propensity for feeding on large fish, especially tuna, has established the false killer as the scourge of the Japanese longline fishery. Nishiwaki (1967) wrote, "They do great damage to the tuna fishery. They do not swim solitary or by small schools, but usually tens of hundreds, even thousands of whales swim gregariously in the water . . . an incident was told that a group had been following a tuna boat for more than 1,000 miles." (Tomilin [1957] quotes a report of a school of false killers that followed a ship [presumably not a tuna boat] from Brazil to the English Channel.)

Perhaps because of this inclination to follow tuna fishermen, false killer whales in the eastern tropical Pacific have become involved in the "tuna-porpoise" problem in a most unexpected way: they have begun to attack the dolphins. In the first report of such behavior, Perryman and Foster (1980) have observed or recorded 49 such attacks. In one instance, the false killers were "herding the porpoise much like the speedboats do, finally cutting out a small section which they attacked." There was another observation of a false killer whale coming "clear out of the water with a full-grown porpoise crossways in its mouth, still struggling." Until this discovery, it was believed that the "true" killer whale was the only cetacean to prey

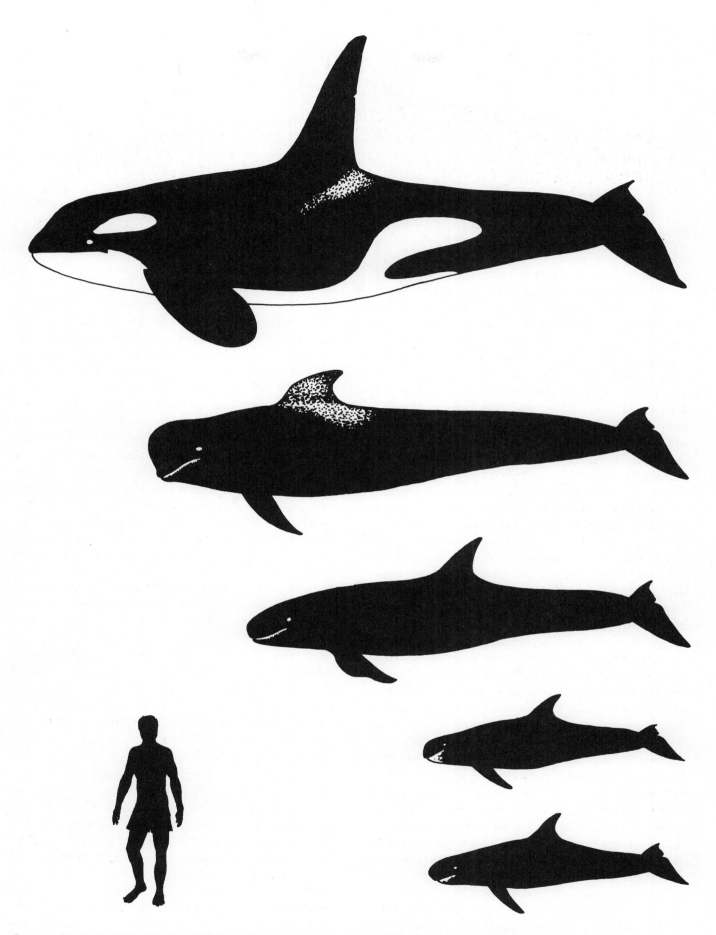

Comparative sizes of killer whale, pilot whale, false killer whale, pygmy killer whale, melon-headed whale, and a man.

upon other mammals. Although other "blackfish," including pilot whales and pygmy killer whales, were tentatively implicated in these attacks, "the false killer whale was the cetacean most often seen chasing or attacking dolphins during fishing operations. Of the 22 interactions in which the whales were identified, 19 were identified or adequately described as false killer whales." Perryman and Foster conclude their report with the following observations:

Since attacks on dolphins by small whales are not reported elsewhere, it is possible that the unique situations created by the purse seine fishery make these animals vulnerable to an otherwise very rare form of predation. A long chase could result in weak or young animals falling behind the school and attracting the interest of predators. The concentrated and excited animals leaving the net at backdown are probably more vulnerable than a free-swimming school.

(It is interesting to note that the killer whale, a known predator on dolphins, has very rarely been seen in the vicinity of the tuna fishing operations [Leatherwood et al. 1980]. This may have more to do with the distribution of the two species than it does with their feeding habits, since killer whales are inclined to be inshore animals, while false killers are more of an open-water species.)

From stranding records and at-sea observations, the worldwide range of the false killer whale has been provisionally determined. It is known—albeit poorly —from virtually all the world's temperate and tropical waters, but it does not inhabit or visit polar oceans. Bullis and Moore (1956) came to the conclusion that to state "all seas" or "cosmopolitan" for this distribution is not accurate enough, and Mörzer Bruyns (1969) wrote that "there are indications that this species invades the temperate coastal zones from a more oceanic habitat in tropical and sub-tropical waters." (Nishiwaki [1967] wrote that "they migrate comparatively far, and the route is not regular and probably capricious.") Mörzer Bruyns concluded, "The habitat is definitely 'deep water,' although a school of 40 false killer whales in the Persian Gulf seemed to be quite happy in 47 m of water."

At sea, the false killer is usually seen in schools of 10 to 40 animals, which appear to be composed of smaller "family" groups of 4 to 6 animals. Norris and Prescott's 1961 report—if the species identification is correct—is an unusually large aggregation for this species at sea,* but, as we shall see, even larger groups

*If they were not false killer whales, the only other species that could have appeared off the California coast was pygmy killer whales or melon-headed whales. The authors admit that the whales they saw might have been pygmy killers, but they felt that they were almost certainly false killers.

sometimes appear on beaches throughout the world. Miyazaki and Wada (1978) recorded schools of 10 to 20 and 10 to 30 animals north of New Guinea in the western tropical Pacific during a whale-marking cruise. In the Spanish Mediterranean between Gibraltar and Marbella, Pilleri (1967) observed a school of about 15 false killers, consisting of adults and calves that were between 2 and 2.5 meters (6 1/2 to 8 feet) in length: "As soon as the yacht came close they divided up into small groups of 4–5 animals . . . only the calves made small leaps out of the water." They also observed a sort of protective behavior, where "each time the yacht or dinghy approached a calf, it was immediately flanked on both sides by two of the smaller adult whales, probably females."

They are fast swimmers, capable of speeds up to 14 knots (Scheffer 1978), and of all the "blackfish" they are the only known bow riders. "When approaching the bow," wrote Mörzer Bruyns in 1969, "they jump out of the water in a low flat arc, just clearing the surface, and usually arrive at the bow wave half a mile astern, playing and jumping for several minutes." In a later discussion, Mörzer Bruyns (1971) wrote, "They ride the bow wave of small boats, but are probably not fast enough to keep up with a big ship."

As far as can be determined, the first specimen in captivity was caught off the California coast in 1963 and exhibited at Marineland of the Pacific. This animal, an 11-foot female named Swifty, adapted unusually rapidly to captivity: by the second day she was feeding, and by the third day she was taking fish from the hands of a trainer (Brown et al. 1966). Eventually, Swifty demonstrated an extraordinary "adeptness at observational learning" (Defran and Pryor 1980) when she was able to mimic the behavior of another dolphin:

After more than three years in captivity, Swifty demonstrated that she knew the game better than anticipated. On the first occasion of this demonstration of observational learning, a single Pacific whitesided dolphin (*Lagenorhynchus obliquidens*) was being taught to backflip. The trainer had spent several days attempting to initiate the behavior and coordinate it with a signal. In this particular instance, the dolphin frequently backflipped spontaneously in the early morning and the trainer was present to capture the activity by using a bridging stimulus to reinforce the activity. During one of these sessions, Swifty departed from her staging position, swam off, and backflipped, not only surprising the trainer but others present. Seeing a 12-foot whale backflip was more than anticipated. A remarkable learning experience. [Prescott 1981]

On another occasion, the same animal "participated in probably one of the most unusual occurrences of spontaneous learning":

During the regular performance of shows at Marineland, "Bubbles," a pilot whale (*Globicephala scammoni*), was the star performer. During one performance, however, Bubbles performed her opening act and then refused to participate further in the show. Swifty swam over, took Bubbles' position, and upon the trainer's command, Swifty accepted all the cues for Bubbles' performance and completed the entire show. More than half of the behaviors had never been performed by nor asked of Swifty.

Defran and Pryor (1980) list "Florida, Hawaii, Japan, West Coast USA" as the locations at which this species is or has been maintained in captivity. Pryor (1973) described the animal in captivity as "fast, agile, volatile, emotional. It learns rapidly, forms intense attachments to other cetaceans and to people, and is excitable and sometimes aggressive. A common threat display consists of swimming full speed as if to ram the offending object or person and then halting abruptly a few feet from contact." It is extremely adaptable to captivity and training, and at two Japanese aquariums —Enoshima and Kamogawa Sea World—false killer whales share top billing with the bottlenose dolphins and killer whales. They perform regular jumps, spins, and head-outs, and at Kamogawa, one of them has been trained to leap out of the water spinning like a giant black spinner dolphin. (At this aquarium in May 1981, a hybrid calf was born to a common dolphin female and a false killer male that had been kept together for over nine years. The calf was black with a short, whitish beak and the humped pectoral fins of its father.)

Although it is considered a rare species in most parts of the world because of its open-ocean habitat, the false killer whale is occasionally hunted in Japanese waters. Ohsumi (1972) lists the species as "common" and writes that while "whales are not caught actively by local fisheries . . . pilot whales and false killer whales are one of the objects of the drive fisheries in Shizuoka, Wakayama, Nagasaki and Yamaguchi Prefectures." In contrast to this, however, Miyazaki (1980) wrote, "As the species has not so much commercial value, the catch of the animal is very few." At Iki Island in February 1978, when Japanese fishermen herded over 1,000 dolphins into a bay and slaughtered them for interfering with their fishery, it could be seen that many of these "dolphins" were false killer whales (Anonymous 1978; Jones 1980).*

*It is not only the Japanese who kill cetaceans for no good reason. In 1937, when a rare false killer whale was sighted in Puget Sound, a group of local sportsmen took after it with guns and harpoons: "After a chase of two hours in which they had great difficulty in approaching the animal, it stranded on a mud bank and they were able to shoot it through the brain. Officers of the state police had been shooting at it with revolvers from shore to no avail" (Scheffer and Slipp 1948).

The false killer whale is a particularly noisy species, and under the right conditions it can be heard vocalizing at distances over 100 yards away. Norris and Prescott (1961) reported that "one of the most striking things about the encounter with these cetaceans [assuming they were *Pseudorca*] was their constant squeaking. The squeaks were loud enough to be heard when the animals were 50 feet or more away. Only a single type of call was noted, which consisted of a rather drawn out high squeak of a constant pitch." Brown and colleagues (1966) described the sounds of the animals at sea as "piercing, harsh, and quite consistent," and stranded specimens have been reported to make "chirps, squeaks, squawks and squeals [that] could be heard distinctly forty or fifty feet from the beach" (Porter 1977).

This species, rarely seen in its natural habitat, is a more than occasional visitor to the shallows and beaches of the world. Its range has been postulated from single and multiple strandings, primarily throughout the temperate zones but by no means restricted to them. It appears to be equally abundant in both hemispheres, and although Slijper (1939) suggested a northern and a southern race, Purves and Pilleri (1978) have concluded "that this distribution is not justified." There have been 18 strandings on British coasts since 1913, including multiples, which are listed as a single occurrence (Sheldrick 1979). Bullis and Moore (1956) listed the species as having stranded all along both coasts of North America, from Puget Sound south to Acapulco on the west coast, and from Cape Hatteras, North Carolina, to Florida, Cuba, and Venezuela in the Atlantic. On the east coast of the United States, a total of 15 strandings have been reported by Mead (1979), including three instances where many animals came ashore at once. The false killer has also been reported to have stranded (usually as a singleton) on the beaches of Spain, France, Italy, Egypt, Brazil, India, New Zealand, Tasmania, and Australia. There is no explanation for the propensity of this—or any other— cetacean to beach itself, but the deepwater habitat of the false killer has suggested to some cetologists that it may become disoriented in shoal waters: "It has been generally stated that the apparent rarity of *Pseudorca* could probably be accounted for by its predominantly pelagic habits, a factor which has also been connected with its tendency to become stranded when in unfamiliar waters" (Purves and Pilleri 1978).

In 1940, Remington Kellogg wrote, "The sporadic appearance in inshore waters during the past 30 years of large schools of False Killer Whales, a species that hitherto has been regarded as rare, is perhaps the most extraordinary happening in the entire history of cetology." These comparatively rare cetaceans are no-torious for appearing *en masse* in shoal waters, and then swimming up onto the beach to die. This has happened all over the world, even in areas where the existence of the species had been unknown or unsuspected. (The first specimens were taken from a school of about 100 animals that appeared in the Bay of Kiel, where they had never been seen before.) As F. C. Fraser wrote in 1936, "The recent reappearance of *Pseudorca crassidens* in different parts of the world has focussed attention on a cetacean which, since its discovery, has been characterised by a tendency to become stranded at irregular intervals and in widely separated regions." He continued, "It is difficult to give any satisfactory explanation for the departure of false killers from their oceanic environment to frequent inshore regions. The times of occurrence are not regular, and the places of the strandings are widely separated, so the probability is remote that the migration is associated with any particular phase of the reproductive life of the animals. It may, however, be associated with feeding." Tomilin (1957) believed that the strandings were certainly associated with feeding: "Like the pilot whale, the False Killer stays in schools, usually far from the coast. Its inshore migrations are associated with those of cuttlefishes. . . . These simul-taneous strandings must have been caused by the in-shore migration of some food species that the two cetaceans have in common, but whether this was herring . . . or some cephalopods, remains unclear." Others have been less inclined to assign the stranding phenomenon to the migration of a food source, and other possible explanations include faulty navigation, parasitic infections that interfere with the animals' echolocation mechanisms, and a desire to return to land in times of stress, as a sort of racial recollection of the cetaceans' origins on land. Dudok van Heel (1962) wrote,

The supposed theory of suicide seems too anthropomorphic to be taken seriously, and a disease causing madness in the animals seems highly improbable because the whales in question look quite healthy. In his book *So Few are Free*, Green (1945) refers to the mass stranding of false killers . . . near Mamre, South Africa, and he even ventures to suppose that these animals tried to find a prehistoric strait to the Indian Ocean, which they might remember because whales grow so old.

Whatever the explanation, the false killer is, along with the pilot whale, the cetacean most inclined to mass strandings. The following list includes many of the most dramatic occurrences: .

WORLDWIDE MAJOR STRANDING RECORDS OF THE FALSE KILLER WHALE

Number of Animals	Location	Date	Reference
835	Mar del Plata, Argentina	1946	Caillet-Bois (1948)
200–300	Mamre, South Africa	1935	Wood (1979)*
150–175	Fort Pierce, Florida	1970	Caldwell et al. (1970)
167	Velanai Island, Ceylon	1929	Pearson (1931)
150+	Dornoch Firth, Scotland	1927	Hinton (1928)
100+	"Near Cape Town," South Africa	1928	Fraser (1936)
97	Muthur Estuary, Ceylon	1934	Deraniyagala (1945)
58	Berg River mouth, South Africa	1936	Smithers (1938)
41	Firth of Tay, Scotland	1935	Fraser (1946)
30	Florida	1976	Porter (1977, etc.)†
21+	Coast of Wales	1934	Fraser (1946)
11	Donna Nook, England	1935	Fraser (1936)

*The reference for this stranding is listed in Wood (1979) as "Green, L. 1945 (?) *So Few Are Free*. Howard B. Timmins, Cape Town. (Not seen.)" In this reference, the stranding is described as follows: "They came in suddenly through the breakers, leaping over the rocks, a farmer told me. It was a determined dash, and those that survived the battering threw themselves on and on until they reached the sand . . . they made tremendous efforts to jump over all obstacles. . . ."

†Because of its recent occurrence—and the present interest in cetaceans—this stranding has been extensively covered in the popular as well as the scientific press. In addition to Porter's 1977 account in the popular magazine *Oceans,* Odell et al. (1979) described the stranding(s) in detail.

Certainly the most spectacular of these records is the simultaneous stranding of 835 false killer whales on the resort beach at Mar del Plata, Argentina. The event took place on October 10, 1946, and "thousands of persons witnessed this frightening harakiri" (Caillet-Bois 1948). If Caillet-Bois's number is not incredible enough, Langguth (1977) quotes a local newspaper as giving a total of 1,200 animals. In a detailed review of the strandings at the various beaches at Mar del Plata—obviously the animals could not all have come ashore at the same place—Marelli (1953) is able to account for only 123 animals. Probably because of the potential exaggerations involved with this event, it is not listed in many of the synopses of false killer mass strandings, such as Dudok van Heel's extensive 1962 list. Tomilin (1957) includes it in the discussion of false killer biology and includes a partial translation of Caillet-Bois's description:

On 10 October, 1946, at 5:00 P.M., 835 false killers ran aground at full speed on the sandy beach of Mar del Plata (Buenos Aires Province). About a hundred of these were stranded along a 200 m stretch of the coastline. Many animals perished very soon, some had a long death flurry, and only a few lived to the end of the following day. . . . Since there was no equipment for trying out cetacean blubber in Mar del Plata (although this town is a fishing center), local authorities, as a sanitation measure, towed the carcasses out to sea.

Caillet-Bois illustrated his article with numerous photographs, and one can clearly see that the beaches are littered with the carcasses of false killers. The only thing in doubt is the total, and it is likely that we will never know how many stranded there, just as we will never know why this group stranded, even if we are able to tell—in the future—why other groups strand.

British cetologists have long been particularly interested in strandings; in the fourteenth century all stranded cetaceans were designated "Royal Fishes" (or "Fishes Royal") and belonged to the crown (Fraser 1977). Since 1913, the British Museum has maintained records of nearly every cetacean stranded on British coasts, so the arrival of hundreds of false killer whales on various shores is of special interest. After the discovery of the species "under the turf" at the Lincolnshire Fens in 1843, the British Isles were not visited by a single false killer whale until 1927, when a large school—perhaps 150 animals—ran ashore at Dornoch Firth, Scotland. M. A. C. Hinton of the British Museum rushed to the scene, expecting to find pilot whales: "A glance showed they were not caa'ing whales as had been anticipated; their peculiar heads, very large teeth, remarkable flippers and black colour at once attracted our attention, and in a few minutes I satisfied myself that I had to deal with a school of

false killers (*Pseudorca crassidens* Owen), hitherto regarded as one of the rarest cetaceans." Hinton (1928) also expected to find the whales neatly collected in one place, but instead, "The whales were scattered up and down the Firth from Tarbet Ness to a point on the Kyle of Sutherland, six miles above Bonar Bridge; that is to say, the chain of whales was thirty miles long." In all, 126 specimens were collected, "the largest series of cetacean skeletons ever brought together."*

The mid-1930s saw a veritable invasion of false killer whales on British coasts; in May 1934, 21 animals stranded on the Welsh coast at Llanmadoc, and another three animals stranded nearby, "undoubtedly associated with the main stranding at Llanmadoc Bay" (Fraser 1946). In November 1935, false killers began to come ashore on the North Sea coasts of England. Fraser (1936) recorded 41 whales from Scotland, and numerous others from various locations on the east coast, including 11 from Donna Nook, Lincolnshire (Fraser 1946).

False killers are usually discovered after they have beached themselves. This was the case in Florida in 1970, where between 150 and 175 whales stranded along the southeast coast. Caldwell and colleagues (1970) wrote, "The whales were alive when stranded, and some were still alive after 24 hours. Efforts by a number of people to drag some of the more active animals back into the water met with typical discouraging results, that is, the whales returned to the beach to strand again, with the possible exception of one or two incompletely documented cases." In the press the whales were first referred to as pilot whales, and then as pygmy sperm whales, but there is no question that they were false killers.†

On July 26, 1976, at least 29 false killers entered shallow water at Captiva Island, on the southwest coast of Florida. One died, four were taken into captivity and later died, and 24 returned to sea (Odell et al. 1979). Three days later, a herd of 30 stranded at Loggerhead Key in the Dry Tortugas, about 200 miles

---

*The study of this enormous quantity of material was not completed until 1978, when Purves and Pilleri published their exhaustive "Functional Anatomy and General Biology of *Pseudorca crassidens* (Owen) with a Review of the Hydrodynamics and Acoustics in Cetacea," which begins with this introduction: "This paper consists mainly of the augmentation, analysis and application to functional morphology of anatomical data obtained from a school of 127 whales . . . which was stranded in the Dornoch Firth in 1927 . . . and in representing an almost complete sample of a single whale population, the collection is unique."

†Because people are so unfamiliar with false killers, many of the strandings of these animals were probably described as those of pilot whales. Mead (1979) wrote, "Many early records of *Globicephala macrorhynchus* probably represent strandings of *Pseudorca crassidens*. The differences between the two are evident enough to anyone familiar with cetaceans, but the literature formerly available to the general biological community was nearly unusable for many species, resulting in most strandings of large, black cetaceans being referred to *G. macrorhynchus*."

(325 kilometers) southwest of the first site. At Logger-head Key, J. W. Porter (1977) documented and photo-graphed the appearance, behavior and eventual return to the sea of 29 of the whales. He also entered the water with the animals, and photographed them underwater. He wrote, "With some trepidation, but no common sense, I entered the water to snorkel close to the group of pseudorcas. The outermost individual broke from the group and headed directly for me. Without any motion that could be unequivocally construed as an attack, other than moving in my direction, the whale lowered its head and slid underneath me. Its body rose slowly, lifting me almost completely out of the water and carrying me toward the beach; it then slowly submerged.") The group was composed of 17 males and 13 females: "Although many of the whales bore minor scars and a few had small open lesions, only one, the large male which eventually died, showed evidence of serious wounds. He lay on his side with his blowhole occasionally submerged, bleeding slowly from his right ear." When the large male died, the remaining 29 whales "loosened the formation around him" and eventually moved off, heading in a northeasterly direction.

Porter concluded his account with the remarks that "the incident is significant because only one individual died, not the entire herd as is so tragically the case in other beachings. This suggests that if clearly sick or injured animals are identified and removed, the others might stand a chance of survival if properly treated during slack tide." Unfortunately, the story did not end on that optimistic note. On August 2, three false killer whales were found dead at Cape Sable, Everglades National Park, and by the end of the month, 20 more skeletons were recovered in the same area. "These animals were probably the same animals that were forced off Loggerhead Key" (Odell et al. 1979). It appears that the false killers were determined to beach themselves, despite the efforts of the Good Samaritans, and in their summary of the "information derived from the recurrent mass strandings of a herd of false killer whales," Odell and colleagues wrote: "It seems reasonably safe to conclude, again, that forcing stranded animals back to sea is a futile effort. If they don't strand again, they may well die at sea and sink. In order to maximize data collection, it may be better to place many of these stranded animals in captivity where they can be observed, treated, and since they will probably die, thoroughly necropsied."*

*There is at least one instance where a stranded whale was "rescued" from its own stranding. In April 1981, a 25-foot male sperm whale beached itself at Coney Island, New York, and after nine days of rest, medication, and (futile) feeding efforts, it was returned to the sea. There is no way of knowing if the animal died at sea, but it did not reappear and strand again on any of the local beaches. The differences between this incident and the various mass

LONG-FINNED PILOT WHALE

Globicephala melaena Traill 1809

The pilot whale is one of the largest dolphins; among the Delphinidae, only the killer whale is larger. There have been reports of this species reaching a length of 28 feet (Harmer 1927), but Sergeant (1962a), in his study of the biology of the pilot whale, contends that the maximum known length is about 21 feet (6.4 meters). There is a pronounced sexual dimorphism in this species: the males are considerably larger and more robust than the females, reaching 20+ feet while the females do not exceed 16 feet, and even this is exceptionally large. A full-grown male can weigh as much as 3 tons (2900 kilograms). Mature males have an exaggerated protuberance on the forehead, or melon, which has been likened to a pot overturned on the whale's head, and accounts for one of its common names, "pothead." According to Norris and Prescott (1961), this protuberance may extend 4 inches or more beyond the tip of the upper jaw. Also in males, the dorsal fin is higher and thicker than in females, the flippers are longer and more curved, and the dorsal crest on the tail stock is more pronounced.

Both males and females appear black (although the color is actually a dark blackish brown), and they have a patch on the chest between the flippers that has been described as "anchor-shaped" and "fountain-jet shaped" (Andrews 1916). From this patch there emerges a thin light line (the "mid-ventral streak" of Mitchell's 1970 terminology) which connects the patch to the teardrop-shaped, light-colored region of the belly and genital areas. (These ventral markings are visible only when the animal is beached, or, in the case of the throat patch, when the animal "eyes out," maintaining a vertical attitude, facing the observer with its head out of the water.) The species is entirely black on the dorsal surface, unlike the short-finned variety, which often has a characteristic "saddle" of a lighter color behind the dorsal fin.* There are some areas where both the long-finned and short-finned varieties occur simultaneously, and there must be a way of differentiating them. Writing of pilot whales in the North Atlantic, Brown (1961) wrote:

strandings discussed above is in the number of whales involved, and also in the fact that the sperm whale could possibly recuperate in a boat basin, whereas the other animals had to remain on the beach. (Ellis 1981)

*Rayner (1939) regarded this saddle as distinctive enough to erect a new species, *G. leucosagamorpha* ("white saddle"), but this species has now been synonymized with *G. macrorhynchus*. Some populations of *macrorhynchus* also have a "post-ocular spot" above and behind the eye, but this too is a variable, and not considered diagnostic (Davies 1960).

156

Two species of *Globicephala* occur in the North Atlantic Ocean, *Globicephala melaena* Traill in the northern waters and *Globicephala macrorhyncha* Gray in the more southerly waters. Externally the two are distinguishable in that the former is black over most of its body except the ventral surface which has a white area below the chin and extending posteriorly as a light-colored stripe along the mid-ventral line of the thorax and abdomen. *G. macrorhyncha* is also black but with an ill-defined grayish area anterior to the dorsal fin, the ventral markings are darker and less clearly distinguished, and it has shorter pectoral limbs than *G. melaena.*

With sophisticated acoustic equipment, we might also identify the species by the nature of their underwater sounds.

It is most likely [wrote Schevill (1964)] that cetaceans, like other animals, use their calls to identify their kind, and we are learning to do the same. We are not yet very good at it, but we can do a little. For example, the North Atlantic species of *Globicephala* . . . are hard to distinguish by eye at sea, but seemed to have a marked frequency difference. The squeals of *G. melaena,* the northern one, range from about 0.5 to 5 kcps, while those of *G. macrorhyncha,* the low latitude form, are between 2 to 12 kcps.

The dorsal fin, which is wide-based, is located considerably forward of the midpoint of the back in adults, but this is a characteristic associated with maturity; in juveniles the fin is located much nearer the middle of the back. The flippers, which in this species are approximately one fifth of the animal's total body length, are located forward of the dorsal fin, and are narrow and sickle-shaped. The name *Globicephala melaena* is literally "globe-headed black," from the Latin *globus* "globe" and the Greek *kephale* "head." *Melas* is Greek for "black."

The unique proportions of this animal, with its squarish head, wide-based dorsal fin, and sickle-shaped flippers, make it possible to differentiate it from other "blackfish"—the false killer whale, pygmy killer whale, and melon-headed whale—all of which have a rounded, sloping snout, and a higher, more falcate dorsal fin. (Of the three, only the false killer whale approaches the pilot whale in size; the other two reach a maximum size of about 9 feet. If the pilot whales are the "southern forms," as described by Davies [1960], where a "whitish mark behind the eye was visible," the inexperienced observer might not be so sure.) There are even reports of white pilot whales, and Hain and Leatherwood (1982) have reported the sighting of a white animal (possibly the same one) off Nova Scotia in 1976 and again in 1980.

There are at least two species of pilot whales, the long-fin from temperate regions and the short-fin from more tropical waters. These two species have been differentiated primarily on the basis of the relative length of their pectoral fins, the presence or absence of a "saddle," and various other anatomical variations. In the 1977 *List of the Marine Mammals of the World,* D. W. Rice wrote, "There appear to be two well-defined species, the ranges of which overlap off the middle Atlantic coast of the United States, off southern Europe, off South Africa, and perhaps elsewhere (van Bree 1971)." In the same year that Rice's comments were published, A. W. F. Banfield wrote (in *The Mammals of Canada* [1977]): "At present the Pacific pilot whale is considered a distinct species, but in future studies it may prove to be a subspecies of the Atlantic pilot whale."

Because of this confusion, the literature on pilot whales contains numerous references to various races and subspecies, many of which enjoy different names. Most authors agree on *melaena* and *macrorhynchus* (although this is often—and, according to Rice, incorrectly—employed as *macrorhyncha*), but in many works *G. scammoni* (or *scammonii*) is recognized, and one may also encounter such names as *G. seiboldi* and *G. leucosagomorpha*. In his discussion of the systematics of the pilot whales, Mitchell (1975a) included this note: "A definite problem exists in the North Pacific, where there appear to be two different kinds of *G. macrorhynchus,* one of which is similar to the Atlantic *G. macrorhynchus* in total length and head shape, and another (the nominal species *G. scammonii*), which is larger and has a different head shape in mature males." As taxonomists change the names of the various species, it becomes increasingly difficult to determine which animal is being referred to, especially in those areas where the species' ranges overlap. With the obvious exception of the discussion of the differences between the species, information on the natural history of pilot whales around the world is quite consistent. Therefore, most of the general observations on group behavior, size, and diet are applicable to both (or all) species.

The length of the fins can be used to distinguish the two species, but one is not always in a position to measure the flipper relative to the body length. As shown by Fraser (1950), the basic cranial difference lies in the arrangement of the maxillaries and the premaxillaries: in the short-fin the premaxillaries (upper bones of the rostrum) completely cover the maxillaries (lower bones of the rostrum), whereas in the long-fin the premaxillaries are narrower. (Of course, only a trained cetologist can make this determination, so it remains extremely difficult to differentiate the two species when they are seen at sea, and only the sometime presence of the "saddle" is a reliable field mark.)*

The long-finned pilot whale is a fairly well-known species; it has been studied extensively in the Newfoundland area, where some 47,000 animals were killed between 1951 and 1961 (Mitchell 1975b). Many of these whales were examined by D. E. Sergeant, and his findings were published in a definitive study of the pilot whale (1962b) that forms the cornerstone of much of our knowledge of the biology of the species. The food of the pilot whale in Newfoundland waters (and elsewhere in its range) is almost exclusively squid. The short-finned squid is the prevalent species in Newfoundland, and similar species of squid are eaten in other areas. Observations from 1951 to 1956

*One way of dealing with this thorny problem is to ignore it completely. Even though there would seem to be no argument regarding the existence of at least two species, some authors choose to lump them together for convenience. For example, in their 1978 discussion of the worldwide distribution of pilot whales, Leatherwood and Dahlheim mention the species differentiation only in reference to "the more temperate species, *Globicephala melaena . . . ,*" and "the tropical species *(G. macrorhynchus).*" Throughout the discussion, however, no distinction is drawn between one species and another, and in reading this paper one has the impression that all pilot whales are the same and can be found throughout the world's tropical and temperate waters.

Adult male (top) and female pilot whales. The males are larger; they have a more hooked dorsal fin, longer, narrower flippers, and more pronounced keels on the tail stock.

indicated that no food items other than this squid had been eaten by the whales taken at the various Newfoundland whaling stations. In 1958 the squid "rather rapidly disappeared from inshore waters, presumably as a result of some unfavorable hydrographic or planktonic conditions which remain unknown" (Sergeant 1962b). Most of the whales "disappeared" as well, but those that remained fed on cod. Sergeant estimated the food intake of an adult pilot whale at about 30 pounds (14 kilograms) of squid per meal, and they appeared to feed three times a day.

The teeth of pilot whales are conical in shape, and there are 9 to 12 pairs in each jaw. Tomilin (1957) described their feeding equipment thus: "The wide rostrum with strong teeth shifted forward allows these teutho-ichthyophagi [squid and fish eaters] to catch both fish and large slippery invertebrates." He also reported dives "to the bottom of the sea; their stomachs may contain solid particles, stones and sand."

These are almost compulsively gregarious animals, always seen in aggregations numbering 15 to 200, and sometimes in even larger, loosely cohesive groups of up to 1,000. They travel in tight ranks when migrating or in danger, but during feeding activities they tend to disperse into smaller, scattered groupings of perhaps 10 to 20 animals. Banfield (1977) has written, "Pilot whales seem to rely a great deal on each other's company. They sleep on the surface in compact groups, often with their flippers touching, with the result that, if one is aroused, all are alerted simultaneously."

Females reach sexual maturity at 6 or 7 years of age and 12 feet in length; males at about 12 years and 16 feet. As a result of this uneven maturation, there is an excess of mature females, and therefore "the species is undoubtedly polygamous" (Sergeant 1962a). Mature males are known to form "bachelor herds," which remain segregated from the females except during the breeding season; this reaches its peak in Newfoundland in April and May. The gestation period is between 15 and 16 months, and calves are usually born from July to October. At birth, pilot whale calves are about 6 feet (1.8 meters) in length, and, as is the case with adults, male calves are larger than females. They are not black at birth, but a brownish gray or tan color, which darkens as they mature. Newborn calves are toothless, but their teeth erupt between the ages of 6 and 9 months, enabling them to catch and eat squid at this time. They are not fully weaned until the age of 2. One report, in which the species identification was speculative, described a newborn calf as being "ashy gray with thin black lines showing in various places on its body. No light ventral markings were seen" (Starrett and Starrett 1955). At Dennis, Massachusetts, when the unborn calves of captured pilot whales were examined, they were "bluish instead of black in color on the back, and grayish white beneath. In every instance they were marked by a spiral line of lighter color, which wound around the body five or six times, and which were supposed to have been caused by the pressure of the placental envelope" (Clark 1887). These lines on the unborn calves—whether dark or light in color—were later identified as "fetal

Differences in flipper length and ventral pattern of long-finned pilot whale (Globicephala melaena) **and short-finned pilot whale** (Globicephala macrorhynchus).

folds formed when they had lain curled up in their mothers' bellies" (Norris 1974).

Pilot whales do not jump in the wild, although they have been trained to do so in captivity, and they have not been recorded as bow-wave riders. They seem to be relatively indifferent to vessels, and Brown (1961) records some instances where they approached vessels, and others where they passed right by ships without paying any attention to them. He also documented a type of behavior in the North Atlantic where

some of the animals took up a vertical position in the water with the head and neck entirely above the surface, sometimes as far back as the flippers. After maintaining this position for up to about half a minute, they sank vertically back into the water. Occasionally this behaviour was varied by slapping the surface with their flippers and there is one record of the whales rising vertically and then rolling over on one side and slapping their tails and flippers on the surface.

Pilot whales display an inclination to follow a "leader," a tendency that renders them particularly susceptible to drive fisheries, and may, incidentally, explain their common name. Even when the leader is injured or dying and has thrown himself (the leaders are usually large males) into shoal water or onto the beach, the rest of the pod will follow. This behavior has been the basis for the fishery in Newfoundland, New England, the Faeroes, the Shetland and Orkney Islands, Iceland, Norway, and all other areas where the long-finned pilot whale has been hunted. In 1820, Captain William Scoresby described the hunting of these whales in the "Feroes":

Being of gregarious disposition, the main body of the drove follows the leading whales, as the flock of sheep follows the wedders. This disposition is well-known by the natives of Shetland and Orkney, and improved to their advantage; for, whenever they are enabled to guide the leaders into the bay, they seldom fail likewise to capture a considerable number of the followers.

According to Mitchell (1975b) the pilot whale fishery of the eastern United States "depended on both stranded whales and schools actively driven ashore." He reports that the "largest single catch on Cape Cod was on 17 November 1884 when 1,500 were killed; 500 more were taken about one month later." In the U.S. Government report on *The Fisheries and Fishery Industries of the United States* (1887), Clark provides the following account of the pilot whale fishery "from the pen of a veteran fisherman of Provincetown":

They make their appearance about the shores of Cape Cod and Barnstable Bay from early in the summer until early in the winter, and when it becomes known that a school of blackfish is in the bay the boats are manned and proceed at once to get in their rear, and as the fish are on the surface of the water the most of the time, it is easy to tell how to manage to keep them between the boats and the shore. And while in this position the men in the boats will make all the noise with their oars they can, and that will cause them to go in the opposite direction from the boats and toward the shore; and when the fish find out that they are in shoal water, by seeing the sandy bottom, they become alarmed and go with all their might till they run fast aground on the sand. The boats then row in their midst, the men, with lance in hand, jump out their boats in the water and butcher them as a butcher would a hog, and it becomes one of the most exciting occasions it is possible to imagine, for the water flies in every direction and the blood flows freely until death puts an end to the great tragedy.

They were hunted for meat, bone, and fertilizer, but the primary product of the pilot whale fishery was the oil, which was known commercially as "blackfish-melon oil," and was used as a lubricant for fine watches and other delicate machinery. When there was not an active fishery, people simply waited for the blackfish to come ashore, as indicated by this tale from Clark (1887):

On one occasion [in a fishing town on Cape Cod] when services were being held in the village church here, the minister being engaged in his sermon, some one in the street cried out "Blackfish!" Many in the congregation heard it, and a rush made for the door, when the minister cried out "Stop!" Some turned about, expecting to be reproved, but the minister in his excitement only said "Now all take a fair start," and joined the crowd himself; and when pursuing the fish shouted out "Hallelujah, hallelujah!" He got his share, which amounted to $25.

Pilot whales run aground singly or in groups, and they have been recorded as doing so throughout their range. The species has always been noteworthy for its propensity for mass stranding; in Scoresby's 1820 discussion of "The Ca'ing or Leading Whale," he lists numerous records of the whales being driven ashore or stranding themselves: "In 1799, about 200 of the deductor species, 8 to 20 feet in length, ran themselves aground at Taesta Sound, Fetlar, one of the Shetland Islands; February 25, 1805, 190 of the same kind, 6 to 20 feet long were driven on shore at the Uyea Sound, Unst, Shetland; and, on the 19th of March, in the same year, 120 more at the same spot. In December 1806, 92 of this species were stranded in Scapa Bay, Orkney, measuring from 15 to 21 feet in length."

In the extensive records of stranded cetaceans kept at the British Museum of Natural History, pilot whales appear with great regularity, and from 1913 to

1966 there were 75 recorded strandings—singletons and multiples. An interesting occurrence is included in Fraser's 1934 report, where a large number of pilot whales did *not* strand: "On Sunday, 10th February 1929 . . . a big school of Pilot Whales (*Globicephala melaena*) entered the harbour at Lerwick, Shetland, and remained all day. The school, estimated to number 500 whales, came close inshore, and, after swimming along both sides of the harbour, assembled in deep water in the centre. . . . The whales were so densely packed that they collided with each other when diving. . . . They were still in the harbour at nightfall, but had disappeared on Monday."

In the 1974 British Museum report Fraser listed 47 pilot whale strandings for the years 1948–66, including multiple strandings of 63 animals in the Orkney Islands in 1955, 36 at County Kerry, Ireland, in 1957, and 148 in East Lothian in 1950. Budker (1968) reported a school of "about fifty pilot whales" that stranded on the coast of Normandy in 1967, but only 16 (10 females and 6 males) "remained high and dry for good." The others were "able to put back safely to sea," which probably means that they were able to refloat on the next high tide.

More mass strandings of this species take place on the coasts of Newfoundland than anywhere else. It might be that these are related to the hunting of squid in shallow waters, but in at least one instance, where more than 200 whales stranded at Bonavista Bay, the stomachs of 12 animals were examined, and only one had squid beaks in its stomach (Geraci 1978). Other records for Newfoundland include a 1979 mass stranding where 170 animals beached themselves and died at Point au Gaul; and in October 1980, some 70 pilot whales expired on the shores of Point Leamington.

The reasons for these strandings are unknown, but some contributory factors may be stress or panic (Nishiwaki [1972] wrote, "Harassment by killer whales is believed to have caused these as well as other species of pilot whales to beach themselves"), navigational difficulties, parasites, or disease. Since pilot whales display a strong tendency to follow a leader, a possible cause for mass strandings might be an injured male beaching himself (again, for reasons unknown), and the rest of the pod—and perhaps even other pods—following him, perhaps to become trapped by falling tides. A cause of death—although in no way an explanation for the stranding—is often sand in the whale's blowhole when it gets itself turned on one side in its thrashing about and suffocates when its breathing apparatus becomes clogged.*

*In an analysis of North Atlantic strandings, Sergeant (1979) hypothesized that the increase in strandings on Canadian and British coasts indicated an increase in pilot whales. This, he felt, repre-

In their study of care-giving behavior of cetaceans, Caldwell and Caldwell (1966) recorded numerous instances of pilot whales "standing by" injured members of the school, and other situations where pilot whales supported dead or dying individuals in the water. The species' gregariousness is certainly a factor; pilot whales appear willing to remain together until death.

It is fairly certain that pilot whales, using the fatty melon in the head as an instrument for the directional broadcast of clicks, are among those odontocetes that are echolocators. They emit clicks and other sounds and react to the returning echoes for navigation, hunting, and communication purposes (Evans et al. 1964). Busnel and Dziedzic (1966) report "whistles, echoranging clicks, creaks, blasts, squeaks," and a combination of a long whistle and a "creaking of more or less strong intensity" among the vocal repertoire of pilot whales, and Brown (1962) heard a "creaking hinge sound" made while a captive male was rubbing against a female. Watkins (1980) identified the longfin as one of the species with "highly directional character of echolocation clicks," and further noted that at sea, this species "produced clicks that often had more low frequency energy and less obvious high frequency emphasis. . . ." In a further breakdown of one of the pilot whale's phonations, Taruski (1979) identified seven different whistle categories, including several that might be interpreted as "signature whistles," that is, a particular sound made only by an individual whale as a means of establishing its identity or signaling its location.

In the eastern North Atlantic, the long-fin is found from Greenland, Iceland, and the Barents Sea, south to the Faeroe, Shetland, and Orkney Islands, Scotland, Ireland, and England. In the western Atlantic, it is found from Davis Strait to the Maritime Provinces of Canada, and south as far as New Jersey (Ulmer 1961) and North Carolina. Brown (1961) analyzed reports from French, British, and Canadian weather ships and merchant vessels, and summarized the North Atlantic distribution of pilot whales as follows:

On the western side of the North Atlantic *G. melaena* has been recorded from as far south as Virginia (Paradiso, 1958), while *G. macrorhyncha* is recorded as far north as southern New Jersey. Sergeant and Fisher (1957) suggest that the zone of interchange between the two species may lie off New York. Paradiso's definite record of *G. melaena* from Virginia suggests that the zone between 38°N and 40°N may be correct.

sented a gradual cooling trend, since the pilot whale, a cool-water species, stranded more frequently during the past twenty-five years than the bottlenose dolphin (a warmer water inhabitant), which had been more abundant—as indicated by stranding records—over the same period of time.

On the eastern side of the North Atlantic *G. melaena* has been recorded southwards to the Mediterranean Sea, and *G. macrorhyncha* from as far north as Madeira. Since the strait of Gibraltar is situated in latitude 35°55′N, the Mediterranean records for *G. melaena* indicate that this species may range further south on the eastern side of the North Atlantic than on the western side.

In the North Pacific, this species was found off the coast of Japan until at least the tenth century (Kasuya 1975), but now only the short-finned species inhabits the western North Pacific. The southern population (sometimes known as *G. melaena edwardi* but physically indistinguishable from its northern counterpart) has been recorded from the Cape of Good Hope (van Bree et al. 1976), New Zealand (Brownell 1974), and Tasmania (Davies 1960). On a 1964 whale-observation voyage off the coast of Chile, Clarke and colleagues (1978) sighted some 200 pilot whales, all of them with the ventral white pigmentation (and some with the white streak behind the eye), so "it appears reasonable to identify the blackfish of the Southeast Pacific as *G. melaena edwardi.*" On the maps accompanying Brownell's 1974 discussion of the small odontocetes of the Antarctic, there are no records of pilot whales close to the pack ice, but there are numerous observations at sea within the Antarctic Convergence (approximately 40°S), and at such islands as Kerguelen, Scott, the Falklands, and New Zealand.

Our knowledge of the taxonomy of these animals is further complicated by their migratory habits. In the waters off Newfoundland, the long-finned pilot whale comes inshore to feed in late June, stays until late autumn (Mercer [1975] reported the latest sighting in Trinity Bay on November 10), and then moves offshore in winter, to the Grand Banks and beyond. Norman and Fraser (1938) record a concentration of pilot whales in the Faeroes in the summer, with lower numbers from September to May. The movements of the whales probably coincide with the movements of the squid, but the behavior of squid is poorly known. Sergeant, in a concurrently published discussion of Dudok van Heel's (1966) account of navigation in cetaceans, said:

In Newfoundland, where the pilot whales approach a deep-water coast, the squid, which form their prey, come in very close indeed, and at times the whales may be seen or heard close to shore. These squid form aggregations in very shallow water, the famous squid-jigging grounds, and we have been unable to explain what the significance of these is, other than that the squid may be taking refuge from the whales.

When a group of pilot whales stranded on the Normandy coast, Budker (1968) wrote that "the local fishermen said that they had never heard of any strandings of whales in this place. However, some days before, they had observed an exceptional quantity of cuttlefish which appeared in the vicinity of St. Vaast."

As of this writing, pilot whales are not considered endangered, although the numbers caught through the years are substantial enough to have seriously depleted even the most abundant species. Harmer (1927) quotes 117,456 as the number of pilot whales killed in the Faeroes from 1584 to 1883; and Sergeant (1962a) reported that over 10,000 whales were killed in the Newfoundland fishery in 1956 alone. The killing of this species is much reduced—the Newfoundland fishery is now closed down, since there is no more commercial whaling in Canada—and pilot whales are often seen today in oceanariums as star performers. (Most of these are probably short-fins, so the behavior of captive animals is discussed in the species account that follows.)

They are still hunted in the Faeroes, but it appears that the populations are in equilibrium with their exploiters (Mitchell 1975b). The Newfoundland fishery inflicted massive depredations on the population of pilot whales there (Mitchell estimates that some 50,000 were killed from 1951 to 1961), and the stock—and therefore the fishery—collapsed, but this may have been the result of the movement of the whales away from the whaling areas for unknown reasons other than whaling. Sergeant's (1979) study of strandings would point toward an increase in the pilot whale populations of the North Atlantic, but stranding records can only present a small part of the total picture.

One of the more peculiar common names for this species is "caa'ing whale" (sometimes spelled "ca'ing"). In explanation, Scoresby (1820) says, "From the property of following a leader, this animal is called, in Shetland, the Ca'ing Whale." Since this does not seem to be a particularly clear explanation, others have suggested alternative derivations: ". . . the breathing of the Blackfish is said to make a bellowing noise, and this seems to be the basis for the name 'Ca'ing,' or Calling Whale" (Kellogg 1940). In 1938 Fraser wrote, "It may be stated that the Scottish name caa'ing whale is connected with the practice of driving or herding the animals and has nothing to do with calling or vocalization of any sort" (Norman and Fraser 1938). The Oxford English Dictionary supports Scoresby and Fraser, but does not offer much in the way of explanation: "[Ca'ing (calling: see CALL) = driving like a herd or flock]." Scoresby also refers to the species as *Delphinus deductor,* from the Latin for "to lead or draw off." When Melville discusses this species, he writes, "Where any name happens to be vague or inexpressive, I shall say so, and suggest another. I

do so now, touching the Black Fish, so called, because blackness is the rule among almost all whales. So call him the Hyena Whale, if you please. His voracity is well known, and from the circumstances that the inner angles of his lips are curved upwards, he carries an everlasting Mephistophelean grin on his face." It sounds very much as if Melville never saw a "Black Fish"; of all the terms that one might apply to the pilot whale, "voracity" is probably low on the list.

SHORT-FINNED PILOT WHALE

Globicephala macrorhynchus Gray 1846

In external appearance, this species is very similar to its long-finned counterpart, with the exception of the relative length of the pectoral fins and the ventral markings. Van Bree (1971) differentiates them as follows:

Globicephala melaena: Long pectoral fins (18–27% of the total length of the animal). Ventrally with a clear white blaze.

Globicephala macrorhynchus: Short pectoral fins (14–19% of the total length of the dolphin). Ventral blaze either absent or rather indistinct.

(Andrews [1916] noted that the Pacific blackfish "has no white on its underparts" and includes a photograph in which this is shown quite clearly.) As noted in the discussion of the long-fin, there are also significant differences in the skull (van Bree 1971):

Globicephala melaena: A more elongated rostrum with rather narrow premaxillae leaving uncovered a one centimetre lateral margin of the maxillae. Normally 9–12 teeth in each toothrow.

Globicephala macrorhynchus: A rather short and broad rostrum with broad premaxillae completely covering the maxillae anteriorly or leaving uncovered a very small margin of the maxillae on one or both sides. Normally 7–9 teeth in each toothrow.

Other authors have reported the presence of a "saddle" in the short-fin,* so there may be a possibility of differentiating the two species at sea, even in those problem areas where the ranges are known to overlap, such as the middle Atlantic coast of the United States, off southern Europe, off South Africa, and perhaps elsewhere. Leatherwood and Dahlheim (1978) described the long-fin as "the more temperate species" and the short-fin as "the more tropical species," so armed with these geographical distinctions and the aforementioned physical differences, it ought to be possible to distinguish the two species.

There are some who believe that there is yet another pilot whale species; they recognize *Globicephala scammoni* (sometimes spelled *scammonii*). Nishiwaki (1972) gives complete descriptions of all three, and says that *scammoni*, which generally lacks the ventral patch, "is found only in the North Pacific. Near Japan, there are records of their being captured south of the Izu Peninsula. Considerable numbers are taken annually off Sanriku, and some specimens are caught near Hokkaidō, but few have been reported in the Okhotsk Sea."† In the literature, the names are constantly being interchanged, and an animal described as "*scammoni*" (as in Norris and Prescott [1961]) is here included in the account of the short-finned pilot whale.

*The killer whale is another large, black cetacean with a "saddle," but the killer's fin is higher and placed farther back. Off Santa Catalina Island, California, in 1977, I saw a small group of pilot whales—obviously short-fins—with saddles, and the entire dorsal fins of the adult animals were of a much lighter color.

†Van Bree, who believes there are only two species, wrote that Nishiwaki's (1967) discussion of distribution in the North Pacific "cannot be based on the results of detailed studies and probably the names of the two species [*scammoni* and *melaena*] should be interchanged on the map."

There is no question that there is still a problem with the proper classification of *scammoni*, but it will not be easily or quickly resolved. I have chosen to combine the accounts, leaving open the possibility that at some future date the problem will be resolved one way or another.

The similarities, of course, are much more noticeable than the differences. They are essentially large, black animals; the males, which are consistently larger than the females, have a broader, thicker dorsal fin, a more bulbous forehead, and a more pronounced ridge on the tail stock. However many species there are, they are all gregarious, they are predominantly eaters of squid, and they all strand more frequently than any other odontocetes.

Because of the history of intensive fishing for the long-finned variety in such places as Norway, Newfoundland, the Faeroes, and the Shetland and Orkney Islands, more is known about the natural history of this species in the wild: Brown's 1961 collection of North Atlantic sighting records added substantially to our knowledge of the behavior of the animal at sea, and Sergeant's 1962 studies of the specimens taken in the Newfoundland fishery represent the most comprehensive work done on this species to date. On the other hand, the short-finned pilot whale is known best from observations made of captive animals—feeding, playing, sleeping.

The species was first exhibited at Marineland of Florida in 1948. From the first captive specimen, a juvenile female that had stranded on the beach at St. Augustine, Florida, observers discovered that this species (or at least this specimen) was nocturnal, inoffensive, and "relatively inflexible [which] seemed to limit the whale to the pursuit of food organisms which are not capable of intricate maneuvers" (Kritzler 1952).

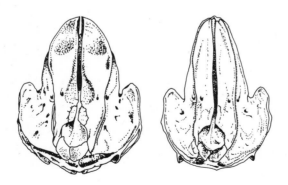

Comparison of the skulls of pilot whales. In *G. macrorhynchus* (left) the premaxillary bones cover the maxillaries, but in *G. melaena* the maxillaries can be seen under the premaxillaries. (After van Bree [1971])

The animal ignored fish that were offered to it, leading to the conclusion (eventually proven correct), that pilot whales are squid eaters by preference. (They have occasionally been observed feeding in the wild on other organisms; Caldwell and Erdman [1963] recorded an observation of the species feeding on tuna.) The first specimen intentionally collected for display was netted in the Pacific off California and brought to the newly built Marineland of the Pacific at Palos Verdes. Named Bubbles, this 12-foot (3.66-meter), 1,500-pound female quickly adapted to captivity. Although she was fed up to 60 pounds of squid per day, she also gobbled up almost an entire school of Pacific barracuda, and once swallowed a small inner tube, which was later recovered, still inflated. Contrary to all expectations about the docility of pilot whales, Bubbles became quite aggressive, and soon reached a stage where divers could not enter her tank for fear of being butted or even bitten. When she was placed in a tank with other animals, including another pilot whale, she became much more tractable (Brown 1960). Whenever pilot whales have been observed in the wild, they have been swimming fairly slowly, usually not exceeding 4 or 5 knots. It was therefore quite a surprise when Bubbles was seen chasing a Pacific white-sided dolphin around their 80-foot-diameter circular tank, and clocked at speeds in excess of 25 mph, or 22.5 knots (Norris and Prescott 1961). Since these early experiments, other pilot whales (all of them probably short-fins) have been exhibited in various oceanariums, and they have proven to be "among the most affable and intelligent of cetaceans" (Reilly 1978). As of 1977, Cornell and Asper recorded a total of seven individuals in captivity in various institutions in North America, and their behavior has been described in this way: "Spyhopping and tail-slapping are frequent *Globicephala* behaviors. *Globicephala* occasionally plays chasing games, and is capable of aggression towards objects, other mammals, and people" (Defran and Pryor 1980). With the exception of the killer whale, whose reputation depends as much on its supposed ferocity as on its size, pilot whales are probably the most dramatic marine mammals that it is possible to see in captivity: They are big, black, and boisterous, and, after all, they are *whales*. *

From studies conducted on trained animals in the open sea, it was discovered that pilot whales are capa-

---

*Brown and Norris (1956) tried once again to eliminate the nomenclatural imbroglio that usually accompanies the dolphin vs. porpoise controversy: "We follow Norman and Fraser (1940) in their definitions of the term *porpoise* and *dolphin; porpoise* refers to the members of the Delphinidae which are small, beakless and with triangular dorsal fins and triangular teeth. *Dolphin* is used for the remainder of the family except for those larger forms distinguished by the name *whale*." This did not really solve the problem, for it was Norris, years later, who described a new species of cetacean, *Peponocephala electra*, the melon-headed *whale*, all of 9 feet long.

ble of enormously deep dives. Kooyman and Andersen (1969) give the maximum known depth for a dive by this species at 366 meters (1,200 feet), but a captive whale named Morgan dived considerably deeper. In a 1970 series of U.S. Navy experiments known as Deep Ops, Morgan was trained to descend with a mouthpiece and clamp, and affix it to a deactivated torpedo on the bottom. Once the whale attached the "grabber," compressed-air balloons would inflate and raise the object to the surface. Morgan easily performed his task at 1,000 feet, and was accurately recorded at 1,654 feet (504 meters). It was thought that he was able to dive to even greater depths—perhaps 2,000 feet (609 meters)—but "his depth of dive transmitter was not working properly, so the depth could not be verified, but he was below the surface for more than 13 minutes. It seems probable that he had gone all the way to the bottom" (Wood 1973). The investigators of the Deep Ops project (Bowers and Henderson 1972) believed that the "trained" depth limit for pilot whales is somewhere between 1,600 and 2,000 feet, "representing a level to which, under training pressure, the animal will 'bounce dive' (that is, dive and make a quick return to the surface)."

Pilot whales in the wild may dive even deeper than Morgan did. In a 1965 report, Norris and colleagues wrote:

Observations by one of us [Norris] suggest regular descents by the eastern Pacific pilot whale (*Globicephala scammoni*) as deep as 366 m during feeding. These large delphinids move into the nearshore waters of Santa Catalina Island, California during the spawning season of the squid, *Loligo opalescens*. The squids aggregate on the bottom in great numbers, spawn and die during the winter and early springtime. Pilot whales can be found diving and feeding upon these squid from close inshore out into relatively deep water. Such whales have been seen rising to the surface after a dive, with squids still in their mouths. Feeding pilot whales typically remain in one general area, diving and returning to the surface for prolonged series of respirations. It is then that they can be caught as they refuse to submerge until several breaths have been taken. On three occasions, while on board oceanarium collecting-boats, pilot whales have been found in such groups in approximately 366 m of water, as determined by fixes on a navigational chart.

When a wild pilot whale was captured in the offshore waters of Southern California, outfitted with a radio beacon and then released, Evans (1974) discovered that the animal made frequent shallow dives during its midafternoon activities (10 dives of not more than 50 feet in a 30-minute period) and less frequent, somewhat deeper dives at sunset. He coordinated the diving behavior of the whale to the movements of the

same species of squid, "known to represent a high percentage of this species' diet."

Pilot whales are known echolocators, and their sounds have been recorded in the wild and in captivity. Norris and Prescott (1961) described the most common sound they heard from these animals as "a distinct staccato popping, which sounded much like the noise created by rubbing a finger over the surface of a balloon." Other sounds recorded for this species include a birdlike chirp, high-pitched whistles, and what Kritzler (1952) described as sounding "like the peevish whining of a young child." In 1964, Schevill reported this: "Once, in the Bahamas, as we were boating a dead *Globicephala macrorhyncha*,* we heard and recorded loud squeals from another that loitered near the boat until the victim was on board, whereupon the survivor stopped calling and rejoined the now distant herd."

In their discussion of "cooperative behavior" among cetaceans, Norris and Prescott (1961) recount this extraordinary story of *Globicephala scammoni* (= *macrorhynchus*):

In one subgroup of three adults, one animal was shot and apparently killed instantly. The animal became rigid upon being hit and its momentum caused it to slide toward the vessel. When it came within about 8 feet of the ship's rail, 2 or 3 feet beneath the surface, the other two animals swam rapidly to it and placed their snouts on top of its head, one on each side of the stricken animal. Their snouts were estimated to be 6 inches apart and even with the tip of the dead animal's rostrum. In this position they forced the dead animal rapidly downward into the water and literally took it away from the ship. The group of animals was not seen again.

Norris and Prescott describe numerous other instances of pilot whales in the Pacific supporting injured animals in the water, standing by animals that were being captured, and one occasion where a small animal was netted and a large female, presumably its mother, "attempted to force the smaller animal away from the boat by draping itself over the restraining line and by actively swimming against the side of the smaller animal. As the little creature was being placed into a stretcher, the adult came up underneath it and bumped it rather violently with its dorsal fin. . . . While the animal was on board the adult circled the vessel, from 20 to 50 feet away from the railing." After the baby was examined and measured, it was decided to return it to the water and its agitated

*According to the rules of the International Commission on Zoological Nomenclature, *macrorhynchus* should be used instead of *macrorhyncha*. "It is a noun in apposition," wrote Rice (1977), "not an adjective, so must retain its original gender." Wherever I have quoted an author who has used *macrorhyncha*, I have retained it rather than changing someone else's spelling.

mother, and the baby "raced off, trailing a stream of bubbles from her blowhole, rejoined the larger animal and disappeared."

Mating behavior has also been identified for pilot whales off Santa Catalina Island, where they were seen lying "venter to venter," and they "thrashed about in the water and waved their pectoral flippers above the surface from time to time" (Norris and Prescott 1961). Captive whales at Marineland of the Pacific were seen to swim rapidly toward each other, and then crash into each other with their heads: "The impact was so great that shock waves could be seen traveling down the bodies of both animals, and the smaller female was forced backward a few feet in mid-water." Norris and Prescott suggested that "the large fatty melon of adult pilot whales may have a function in courtship," since this head-butting was often accompanied by attempts at mating.

The question of cetaceans sleeping has always been a knotty one. There is simply not enough information to determine if some species actually sleep, but as far back as 1874, Scammon reported what seemed to be Pacific pilot whales sleeping: "In low latitudes, during perfectly calm weather, it is not infrequent to find a herd of them lying quite still, huddled together promiscuously, making no spout and seemingly taking a rest. Sometimes they assume a perpendicular attitude, with a portion of the head out of the water, as does the Sperm Whale." Confirmation of this species' propensity for "taking a rest" was obtained from Norris and Prescott's observations of captive specimens: "We have repeatedly observed the captive pilot whales sleeping with eyes tightly closed during the day and at night. . . . During sleep the animals hang almost immobile in the water, with their tails downward at about a 30° angle."

Pilot whales, both long- and short-finned, are among the most notorious of all stranders. In his review of the stranding phenomenon, Wood (1978) says that "*Globicephala* spp. are usually considered to be pelagic species and seem to be more subject to mass strandings than any other cetaceans." The literature is filled with reports like "Pilot Whales Mass Stranded at Nevis, West Indies" (Caldwell et al. 1970), but while such reports contain the date, the location, and the number of stranded whales, they usually contribute very little to our understanding. Like their temperate-water relatives, short-fins come ashore in large numbers and often die on the beach despite all attempts to refloat them. In 1971, 44 of them beached themselves at various locations on the west coast of Florida, and no matter how many times individuals were towed away from the beach, "they continued slowly and deliberately toward the beach in a tight pod" (Fehring and Wells 1976). The whales were finally towed and driven out to sea, but five days later, 13 of the same animals (some of them identifiable by rope burns on the tail stock) came ashore again, this time some 160 miles from the original stranding site.

The behavior of these whales effectively demolishes many of the hypotheses propounded to explain the stranding phenomenon: certainly they were not being chased by predators; they were probably not fatally infested with parasites (if they were, how could they navigate from one beach to another 160 miles away?); and their navigational faculties were probably functional even in what Fehring and Wells referred to as "gently sloping sand beaches." Wood (1979) has hypothesized that stranding cetaceans are seeking refuge on land from some form of stress, as a demonstration of their land-based origins. As Wood points out, however, "the hypothesis is not readily susceptible to experimental confirmation or refutation, nor does it seem likely that further observations could bring about any significant revision of this explanation for strandings." It is likely that we will continue to be confounded by the appearance of pilot whales and other cetaceans on our shores, and despite our learned papers and theories, this remains one of the great mysteries of nature.* In other words, we have not made much progress in resolving this problem since Aristotle wrote, "It is not known why they sometimes run aground on the seashore; for it is asserted that this happens rather frequently when the fancy takes them and without any apparent reason."

The short-finned pilot whale is found in the western North Atlantic from Virginia south to Florida and the Caribbean, Cuba, and the West Indies. In the eastern Atlantic it inhabits an area from Madeira to the northwestern coast of Africa. "It probably occurs in all warm waters of the Indian Ocean and along the coast of northern Australia, but not New Zealand" (Mitchell 1975a). In the Pacific, it ranges from the coast of southern California to Mexico, and in the west from Suruga Bay, Japan, south to the Philippines. It has been reported from Okinawa and from New Guinea waters (Miyazaki and Wada 1978), and although comprehensive records are incomplete, the species can

---

*In *The Book of Whales,* I suggested a "simple recovery function" as the explanation for some strandings. Whales have to breathe air to live, and if they are sick or otherwise stressed and in danger of sinking, those that are near enough to the shore might try to get into shallow enough water so they will not sink and drown. It is possible, therefore, that some cetaceans come ashore on gradually shelving beaches, not, as Dudok van Heel (1966) has suggested, because their echolocating system cannot function in those conditions where there is nothing to reflect the echoes back, but rather because there are no rocks, cliffs, or other impediments to their movement out of the water. That is to say, whales come ashore where they *can* come ashore, and do not come ashore where they cannot. This does not, of course, explain the "why" of strandings, but it might be helpful in understanding the "where."

probably be found in most of the tropical and warmer temperate waters of the world.

In the early days of offshore whaling, pilot whales were not hunted extensively (although the meat and oil were probably utilized when the animals stranded), but occasional whalers sought them out. Scammon describes the nature of the fishery:

Although the Blackfish is taken for its oil, it is not an object of pursuit by the whaler, like the balaenas and the Cachalot. Sperm whalers do not lower their boats for Blackfish, when on the Sperm Whale ground, unless the day is far spent or there is little prospect of "seeing whales." The northern or polar whale-ships pay but little attention to them, except, perhaps, when passing the time "between seasons," cruising within or about the tropics. Occasionally a small vessel is fitted out for hunting Blackfish and Sperm Whale, carrying proportionately limited crew, thereby making the capture of this species of the smaller Cetaceans profitable.

Although the colder-water species has been heavily fished in Newfoundland, Norway, and the various island groups of the North Atlantic, the short-fin has not been so heavily exploited in modern times. There was a fishery in Japan on the Izu Peninsula, where, Mitchell (1975b) reports, 1606 animals were taken between 1957 and 1962. (However, Ohsumi [1975] writes, "After the war, the fishery for these whales flourished until 1949, when 890 whales were caught. . . . Catches are all *G. macrorhynchus,* but the possibility of occurrences of *G. melaena* in northern Japan needs study.") Mitchell also reports a drive-fishery in Okinawa. Clarke and colleagues (1978) have written, "Blackfish meat is edible: in Japan and the Faeroe Islands it is used for human consumption, and in Norway and Newfoundland it is used for animal food, including food for fox and mink farms." (Scammon wrote, "The flesh of the Blackfish is like coarse beef, and after being exposed to the air for a few days, then properly cooked, is by no means unsavory food, and is often used by whalemen as a substitute for the fresh meat of land animals.")

The short-finned pilot whale was the object of a fishery operated out of the island of St. Vincent in the Lesser Antilles. (The other principal target of this fishery was the humpback whale, but numerous other species of cetaceans were also taken opportunistically, including various dolphins, killer whales, and even sperm whales [Caldwell and Caldwell 1975].) Until the passage of the Marine Mammal Protection Act of 1972, the fishery's major product was the melon oil of the pilot whale, which was exported to the United States to be used as a lubricant for fine instruments. The act prohibited the import of this or any other whale product into the United States, and therefore the market for the oil was eliminated. In combination with the reduced number of fishermen, the expense of running the boats—until 1968, very few of the Vincentian boats were powered, but shortly thereafter, they all were motorized—and the elimination of the market caused the eventual downfall of the St. Vincent fishery. Caldwell and Caldwell reported a total of 2,912 pilot whales landed at the port of Barrouallie, St. Vincent, between 1962 and 1974. Another fishery, on the nearby island of St. Lucia, also went after blackfish, "but results so far published . . . deal with chlorinated hydrocarbon residues and heavy metals in tissues from *Globicephala macrorhynchus*" (Gaskin et al. 1974). It now appears that even if we leave the whales alone directly, we can indirectly affect them with our pollutants, presumably by polluting the entire food chain, from the microorganisms that serve as food for the fish and squid all the way up to the whales that consume the squid.

KILLER WHALE

Orcinus orca Linnaeus 1758

The Grampus has the character of being exceedingly voracious and warlike. It devours an immense number of fishes of all sizes, and especially large ones, including cod, halibut, skate, and turbot. When pressed with hunger, it is said to throw itself on every thing it meets with, not sparing the smaller porpoises and dolphins. . . . They are often seen in small herds of six or eight individuals, apparently chasing and amusing themselves; and when thus in company, it is alleged that they frequently attack the true whale—not the young and smaller only, but even the greatest giants of the deep. [Hamilton 1835]

The killer whale is a sort of supercetacean: it can do almost everything better and faster than other whales and dolphins, and it has a reputation of almost mythic proportions. While the bottlenose dolphin is admired for its engaging grin and public performances, and the sperm whale for its place in history and its prodigious feats of eating and diving, the killer whale is renowned for its position as the sea's supreme predator. In 1974, Paul Spong, a student of the species, wrote, "*Orcinus orca* is an incredibly powerful and capable creature, exquisitely self-controlled and aware of the world around it, a being possessed of a zest for life and a healthy sense of humor, and moreover, a remarkable fondness for and interest in humans."

The species has no enemies—except these humans—and its social organization is efficient, complex, and unique. Its role as ocean predator seems to be advertised by its striking markings. Mature males have a taller dorsal fin than any other cetacean: a 6-foot triangular topsail that Gavin Maxwell (1952) de-

scribed as a "blazon of ferocity." The killer whale's reputation probably surpasses its capabilities, but they are prodigious indeed. It is fast—probably the fastest of all cetaceans, and certainly one of the swiftest of all the creatures in the sea; it is immensely strong (a killer whale has been observed to leap so that the tip of its snout was 40 feet above the surface); it is graceful, and, if this were not enough, it is beautiful as well. (It was not always considered beautiful; in the past, the killer whale has been described as "ugly" and "terrifying," but these appellations have in most cases been replaced by terms of admiration.) Randall Eaton (1979a) wrote, "Like man, orca rules its domain, or did, until recently challenged by man. Man and the killer whale are the two most formidable, successful and intelligent social predators ever to live on earth. . . ."

The origins of the name *Orcinus* are obscure, but it might have been derived from the Roman Orcus, another name for Pluto, the god of the netherworld. *Orca* is Latin for "cask" or "barrel," and probably refers to the robust form of the species. There is now a tendency to call the animal by the common name "orca" rather than "killer whale," since it has been shown to be no more than a large, efficient predator, and not a seagoing homicidal maniac. The name "killer whale," or even simply "killer," will probably remain in general use, because its habits in the wild still include large-scale predations on warm-blooded prey, and no amount of oceanarium press-agentry can alter its observed attacks on whales, seals, penguins, and other creatures that people are so fond of. In Spanish, the animal is known as *ballena asesina*, or "as-

sassin whale," but in German its name is merely the descriptive *Schwertwal*, which can be translated as "shoulder whale" and obviously refers to the prominent dorsal fin. The Japanese call it *sakamata*, which can be translated as "a halberd reversed," and refers also to the shape of the dorsal fin (Hawley 1961). Another common name for this species in Japan is *shachi*, a word derived from *shachihoko*, a descriptive term for the upturned decorative elements on castle roofs.

The largest of the Delphinidae, killer whales have been known to reach a length of 31 feet (9.5 meters) and a weight of 9 tons (8,100 kilograms). Males are larger than females, as is the case with all toothed whales, but they are not twice as large, as was earlier believed. Jonsgard and Lyshoel (1970) reported a female that was 27 feet (8.2 meters) in length, and another female, stranded in Newfoundland, was measured at 24 feet 7 inches (Dearden 1958). Males are characterized by the greatly exaggerated dorsal fin, which may be 6 feet (1.8 meters) high, and also by the greatly enlarged flippers, which become paddle-shaped in mature bulls. One 30-foot male, stranded on a beach in Scotland in 1916, had flippers that were 6 feet 8 inches in length and 3 feet 7 inches wide (Harmer 1917). On an animal of this size, the flukes can be 9 feet from tip to tip.

It is a strongly marked animal, with distinctive areas of white on a coal-black ground. Mitchell (1970) refers to the components of the pattern as the "post ocular spot," the "flank patch," and the "post-dorsal saddle," and Evans and Yablokov (1978) have elaborated on this scheme, identifying some 14 separate elements in the piebald pattern. In younger animals, the white areas are often a tawny or yellowish color. The "saddle" is neither white nor tawny but a grayish or brownish color (Scammon [1874] called it "maroon"), and it is extremely variable in shape. In the waters of Vancouver Island and Puget Sound, a photographic record of the populations of killer whales has been maintained for several years, and the primary identifying characteristics of individuals are the size of the animal, the size and shape of the dorsal fin, and the shape of the saddle (Bigg et al. 1976; Balcomb 1978, etc.). In full-grown bulls, the fin is straighter and more erect than in females, and it can even cant forward or flop over to one side or the other. The dorsal fin of a female is much shorter and more falcate.*

The entire pigmentation pattern is variable, with some animals showing much more white than others, and there are even reports of killer whales with no white at all (Scammon; Scheffer and Slipp 1948). Sanderson (1956) mentions a Pacific race that "lacks the white spot on the side of the head," but in Evans' extensive catalog of the variations in pattern, this possibility is not listed. Until recently, it was believed that all killer whales were similarly colored, with minor individual variations. When Evans and Yablokov (1980)† analyzed the pattern on killer whales from various locations, they concluded that the patterns are consistently different in different geographical areas, and therefore, they "suggested that *Orcinus* occur as distinct regional populations." Although the killer whale is worldwide in distribution, the areas from which these distinct populations have been recorded are northwestern Atlantic (Iceland), northeastern Pacific (Puget Sound and Vancouver Island), southwest Atlantic (Argentina), tropical eastern Pacific (Baja California and Mexico), and Antarctic (Ross Sea and McMurdo Sound). The differences in these populations can be seen in the consistent variations in the size and shape of the pigmentation components, the angle of the postocular spot, and, in the Antarctic, the existence of a dorsal "cape," a darker area on the back that does not appear in any other population.

A unique situation was observed in the resident killer whale population of Prince William Sound, Alaska, by Hall (1981), where at least five males were seen to have the same distinctively curved dorsal fin. Hall suggests that "it is possible that the peculiar dorsal fin curve observed in large male killer whales in Prince William Sound represents a sex-linked genetic trait, raising the possibility of a seasonally resident and genetically distinct population of killer whales in the Sound."*

It is easier to see killer whales than it is to record their sounds, but there is evidence that discrete pods also have different "dialects," which are "important in maintaining the cohesion and identity of killer whale social units" (Ford 1980). If pods of British Columbia killer whales can be shown to have different dialects from one another, it is more than likely that populations of the species around the world will be shown to make distinct sounds. Researchers in the Antarctic have recorded the sounds of killers there as being higher-pitched than those of their Northern Hemisphere counterparts (Awbrey et al. 1980). A study of the chromosome structure of the cells of various killer whale populations further supports the theory that the world's killer whales are distinct; in 1979 Duffield and Cornell wrote, "Interpretation of these data strongly support the existence of discrete family units or groups of family units in which inbreeding coefficients are high and exchange between populations limited."

There have been frequent reports of albino killer whales: Carl (1960) collected no fewer than 74 records of all-white or mostly white animals sighted between 1923 and 1959, and in 1970, an all-white calf was captured and released off British Columbia. Chimo, a semialbino with normal markings faintly visible, was exhibited at Sealand, in Victoria, British Columbia (Thornton and Hoey 1979). In Cousteau's 1972 book *The Whale*, there are photographs of an albino "of the Juan de Fuca Strait," but the circumstances under which the animal was photographed are not clearly explained.

---

*This facility for differentiating males from females only applies to mature animals. Until the males begin to surpass the females in size and develop the characteristically tall dorsal fin, it is difficult —if not impossible—to distinguish the sexes. When two killer whales arrived from Iceland at the Vancouver Aquarium in December 1980, they were both believed to be females, and much publicity accompanied their future role as "companions" for the aquarium's male, Hyak. Even though the two newcomers had been examined by qualified veterinarians in Iceland and again in Canada, and certified as females, it was almost three weeks after their arrival that an aquarium visitor reported that one of the "females" was—quite obviously—a male.

†This paper and many of the others dated 1980 were presented at a symposium held at the University of Washington in October 1980 entitled "The Biology and Behavior of the Killer Whale, *Orcinus orca.*" In the bibliography for this chapter, many of the references are to abstracts, the précis of what the paper was about. I attended this symposium, and in addition to the published abstracts, I also worked from my own notes.

*If the males in a given population can manifest a similarly distinct dorsal fin shape, it might explain the discrepancies in the story of Old Tom, a male that is said to have appeared for over 80 years at Twofold Bay, Australia (see p.178). Tom was easily recognized by his distinctively curved and notched dorsal fin, but his longevity is questionable. If a number of individual males—perhaps direct descendants of the original Tom—had similarly shaped fins, then they might be identified as a single animal over such a long period of time.

A sometime characteristic of Antarctic killer whales is the yellowish coloration where other populations are white. From Scott's ill-fated 1911 journey to the Antarctic, there is a reference to the "ugly black and yellow heads of Killer whales" (Huxley 1978); Ponting, the expedition's photographer, referred to the "huge black and tawny head," and other references have confirmed the occurrence of yellow-marked killer whales in the high southern latitudes. In Sapin-Jaloustre's 1953 discussion of the whales of the Antarctic, this description of the *Orque* appears: "*La couleur générale est gris-noir, avec des taches blanches ou jaunes caractéristiques,*" and Liouville's 1913 plates show animals that are black and yellow-ochre (*jaune d'ocre*). The 60 killer whales that Taylor (1957) recorded as trapped in the Antarctic ice were seen to have a "copper coloured sheen," and he attributed this to a film of microscopic animals called diatoms, which may be responsible for the yellowish color in the other records.

Because of the disparity in size and dorsal fins in males and females, early observers believed that the "long-finned" and the "short-finned" killer whales were different species. Scammon wrote: "Both the high and low finned Orcas are found in the same school, yet we have occasionally seen those with the longest and most falcated fins exclusively by themselves." This dimorphism and the wide range of the animal led to the establishment of numerous species, usually based on geography. "It is well known," wrote Scammon, "that there are several species of Orcas, incident to their wide geographical distribution, which includes every zone and hemisphere. . . ." In the past, various names were employed, including *Orca gladiator* (derivation obvious), *O. rectipinna* ("straight fin"), *O. pacifica, O. africana, O. magellanicus,* and so on. At this time, only one worldwide species is recognized, but with consistent variations noted throughout the world.*

As the study of killer whales becomes more directed toward the observation of the animals in the wild—as opposed to the study of captives, where behavior is at least irregular, and possibly totally anomalous—more and more revelations about the unique nature of this animal emerge. In a 1976 study of the killer whales of Vancouver Island waters, Bigg and colleagues identified no fewer than 19 separate pods, with a total of 210 whales. (They defined a pod as "a permanent family unit containing up to 20 individuals," but later investigations have shown that pods are sometimes larger.) They identified two different types of pod, "resident" and "transient": the former permanently inhabits a given area, and the latter, with no permanent home territory, passes irregularly through the territory of the residents. There is no apparent conflict in this behavior; in fact, the residents and transients sometimes join together to form much larger aggregations for varying periods of time. (In this

*After the examination of 323 specimens (205 males and 118 females), Soviet scientists once again raised the possibility of a subspecies: Mikhalev and colleagues (1980) provisionally identified a smaller variety, which they called *Orcinus orca minor.* They differentiated it from the "common" killer whale by its smaller size at maturity and the different rate of accumulation of yellow traces in the ovaries of females, indicating more frequent pregnancies.

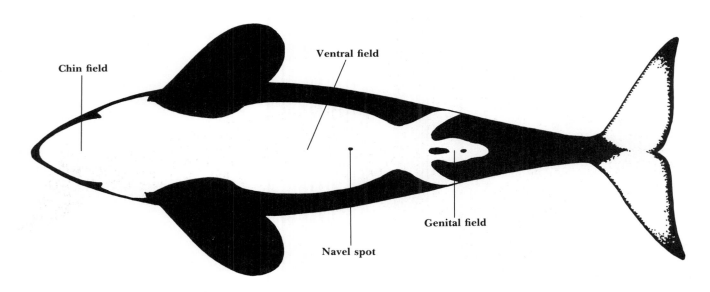

The underside of a killer whale. Notice that the flippers are black on their undersides, while the ventral surface of the tail flukes is white.

study, conducted from 1972 to 1976, individual whales and separate pods were photographically identified. An accurate census could therefore be conducted by recording the appearance of individual whales, identifiable to the researchers as belonging to a given pod, and then adding together the known numbers of the whales in each pod.)

Subsequent research—by Bigg and others*—has revealed an extraordinarily complex social structure which is, as far as we know, unique in the animal kingdom. The pods are indeed family groups, with a remarkable degree of cohesion over time and distance. In the resident pods of the waters of Puget Sound, known as J-Pod, K-Pod, and L-Pod, every whale was identified and assigned a number (J-1, K-4, L-12, etc.) to facilitate description and discussion. Within each pod, the "family" structure was noted, and the

*Orca Survey, under the direction of K. C. Balcomb, was established in Friday Harbor, in the San Juan Islands of Puget Sound, specifically to track and observe the local killer whales. Funded by the U.S. National Marine Fisheries Service (NMFS), the survey has produced information on nearly every whale and pod that frequents the area of Puget Sound and the Strait of Juan de Fuca. This was the most detailed study ever conducted of the behavior of wild cetaceans. Group studies have been conducted of the right whales in the waters of Península Valdés, Argentina, the gray whales of Baja California, and the humpbacks of Hawaii, but only in rare instances have those whales been individually identified. In the Orca Survey territory, not only individuals but males and females are easily distinguished, so behavioral interactions can also be filmed and recorded.

breeding bulls, nursing cows, and juveniles identified, and their behavior recorded. As calves were born, they were photographed and their growth and behavior extensively documented. Continuous monitoring of this population (from 1976 to the present) has produced a wealth of data that are still being analyzed.

There is the expected association of calves with their mothers, but even when the calf is weaned, it may continue to swim with its mother, at least until another calf is born, but perhaps for as long as ten years (Bigg 1980). Heimlich and colleagues observed the surface associations of the Puget Sound killer whales and noted that certain whales associated with certain others for long periods of time—sometimes several years—but these affiliations sometimes changed abruptly. (For instance, J-10 might be seen with its calf J-18 for three years, and then when J-18 took up with J-17, J-10 would only be seen in the company of J-12.) These pods are year-round residents, and since the study was begun in 1976, hundreds of sightings have been documented, tens of thousands of photographs taken and correlated, and miles of tape have been recorded.

Bigg's continuing research (mostly in the waters of Vancouver Island) is continuing to produce surprising results. As the resident and transient pods were identified, certain characteristics of their behavior be-

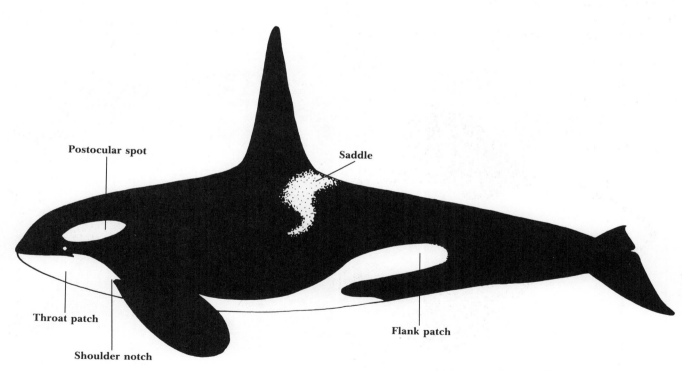

Identification of the various areas of white and gray on the black coloration of the killer whale. In this illustration of an adult male, the dorsal fin is particularly tall and vertical. (After Evans and Yablakov [1980])

DOLPHINS AND PORPOISES 171

came apparent. There were conspicuous differences: the residents had regular routes, while the travels of the transients seemed to be more random; residents also had shorter dive times on average, and the reproduction rate of the resident pods was almost twice that of the transients. Perhaps the most surprising observation that came from Bigg's comparison of the residents and the transients was that they actually looked different: females in the resident pods had sharply hooked dorsal fins, while in transient females the fins were more erect and "pointy." Bigg has speculated that the resident pods "spin off" the transients, somehow rejecting certain whales from the tight family groups. The life expectancy of the whales in a transient pod appears to be shorter than that of the resident whales, and there is no record of transients becoming reintegrated into a resident pod. Bigg has speculated that the transient pods, which are often quite small, sometimes consisting of five animals or less, are somehow "doomed," and will not perpetuate their line.

Since the behavior of residents differs so much from that of transients, it seems likely that a whale captured for exhibition would, by definition, have its behavior altered by removal from its family pod, especially if the pod was a resident one. It is traumatic enough for a wild killer whale to be put into a tank, but the stress may be increased substantially if a member of a "family" is suddenly isolated, or even thrown in with what amounts to "strangers." Of course, the capture and incarceration of any wild animal is likely to be traumatic, but with killer whales it has been shown that the family (or pod) structure affects the behavior of the individual. It is therefore possible to speculate that all captive killer whales are behaving uncharacteristically, since in their normal circumstances, they live in a permanent, integrated family unit.

Except where whales have been "cropped" (captured for display), there has been no noticeable decline in the sizes of the resident pods of the Vancouver Island area, indicating a long-term stability of the population. It would have to be stable, since the reproduc-

Male (top) and female killer whales, showing the difference in size of mature adults and the exaggerated, high dorsal fin of the male.

tion rate of the killer whale is the lowest known for any cetacean. Bigg estimates that the species may have a birth rate of only 9.5 percent per year, but since the observed death rate is also very low, the populations tend to remain at more or less fixed numbers. Because killer whales have no natural enemies, it might be assumed that they would reproduce themselves without restraint; but as the predators at the top of the food pyramid, they must depend on much larger numbers of smaller animals to provide them with their nutritional needs, and the supreme predators are never numerous.*

There are instances where killer whales come together to form much larger groups, but the reasons for these congregations are unknown. (Budylenko [1980] wrote, "One would think that killer whales, as typical predators, should not form large aggregations.") In virtually every study of killer whales, however, there are reports of huge schools. In their 1976 report, Bigg and colleagues noted separate incidents where 500, 225, 200, and 130 animals were seen together. Balcomb (1978) reports a number of instances in which J-, K-, and L-Pods were seen together, which would produce a total of some 70 whales. The Antarctic region, while still little studied, seems to be a

*In a book called *Why Big Fierce Animals Are Rare,* the zoologist Paul Colinvaux wrote,

For flesh eaters, the largest possible supply of food calories they can obtain is a fraction of the bodies of their plant-eating prey, and they must use this fraction both to make bodies and as a fuel supply. Moreover their bodies must be the big active bodies that let them hunt for a living. If one is higher still on the food chain, an eater of flesh-eater's flesh, one has yet a smaller fraction to support even bigger and fiercer bodies. Which is why large fierce animals are so astonishingly (or pleasingly) rare.

particularly rich area for killer whale research: Awbrey and colleagues (1980) reported observing pods of over 100 animals in the Ross Sea area, and on one occasion they saw "thousands of killer whales" off the Pennell Bank, also in the Ross Sea. There has been no satisfactory explanation for the massing of the killer whales, but Braham and colleagues (1981) wrote of an extraordinary gathering of some 2,500 whales in Alaskan waters, that "they may represent a multi-pod gathering grouped together for feeding or reproductive activities."

The killer whale is almost certainly "the most widely distributed marine mammal in the world" (Nishiwaki 1967), and we have discussed its well-documented appearance in the waters of Puget Sound (where, according to Rice [1968], "the killer whale population is denser than anywhere else in the world"), in the Antarctic, the islands of the Southern Ocean, Argentina, Iceland, and the eastern tropical Pacific. In addition to these areas, the killer whale is also relatively abundant off the coasts of Japan, eastern Canada, and Norway, where it has been the object of various small-whale fisheries throughout the years. One would expect to find killer whales in these areas, but they also turn up in some unexpected locations, including the warmer waters of Hawaii (Tomich 1969), the Bahamas (Backus 1961), the Caribbean (Caldwell et al. 1971), and in the western tropical Pacific, north of New Guinea (Miyazaki and Wada 1978). The two attacks on sailing ships, the *Lucette* and *Guia III,* took place in temperate waters. A thorough search of the historical records would be likely to produce sighting and stranding records of killer whales in al-

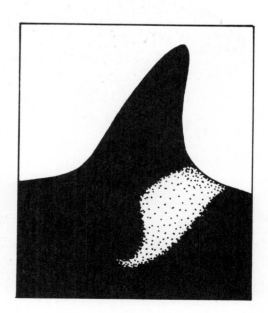

The dorsal fins of two female killer whales. According to Bigg (1980), the curved fin on the left is characteristic of resident pods, while the more erect, "pointy" fin is found in transients.

most every marine location. There is even a record of a killer whale in New Jersey (Ulmer 1941).

But killer whales do not restrict their travels to oceans: they have also been reported from various rivers, and Tomilin (1957) lists the Loire, the Seine, the Elbe, the Rhine, and the Thames as locations in which "killers used to be caught." There are numerous records of killers stranding on the British coasts, especially the west coast of Scotland, the Shetland and Orkney Islands, and Gavin Maxwell (1952) reported small packs of killers in the Hebrides, "perhaps a dozen times in the season." Killers are also known from the Mediterranean, and have been recorded from Monaco, Sicily, Malta, Corsica, Sardinia (Tomilin 1957). Duguy and Robineau (1973) indicate that the species is also known from the English Channel, and the Atlantic and Mediterranean coasts of France. On one well-documented occasion, a young killer whale swam 110 miles up the Columbia River, where it fed on carp that congregated around a packing plant until it was harpooned by local "sportsmen" (Shepherd 1932).

The world population of killer whales is unknown; only in certain areas have censuses been taken. (In the Vancouver Island–Puget Sound region, practically every individual has been identified and counted.) While studying the numbers of dolphins involved in the tuna fishery in the eastern tropical Pacific, scientists also counted the killer whales, and they were surprised to find many more killers than they had expected so far from shore. Often the tuna seiners work thousands of miles from the nearest land, and from aerial surveys, Leatherwood and colleagues (1980) reported, "Killer whales appear more abundant in the zone than heretofore thought and occur in a wider variety of depth and oceanographic zones." The possibility that the killer whales were attracted to the fishery was discounted by the investigators, who said that there were actually very few sightings from the tuna boats, and while other species, such as the pygmy killer whale and the false killer whale, often fed on porpoises "spilling" out of the nets, the orcas did not. Leatherwood and colleagues estimated a total killer whale population for the area studied (34°N to

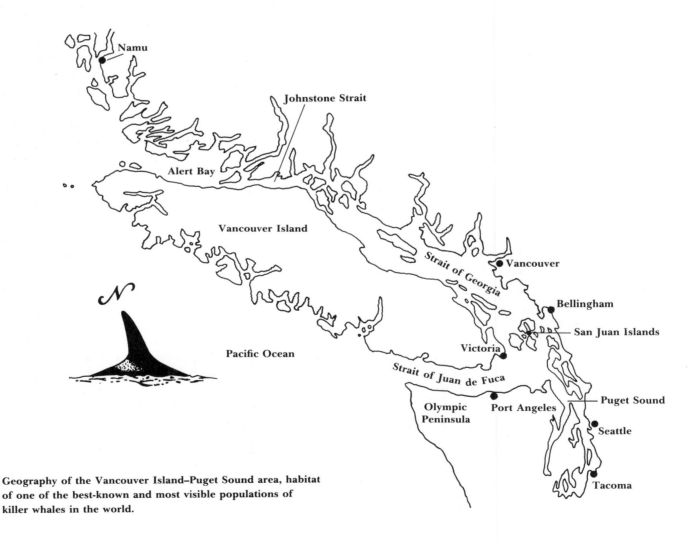

Geography of the Vancouver Island–Puget Sound area, habitat of one of the best-known and most visible populations of killer whales in the world.

15°S) of somewhere between 3,600 and 12,000 animals, and further suggested that the "conventional wisdom" about killer whales being found primarily in cold-water coastal areas may not be true. Only when comprehensive surveys can be conducted in open ocean areas can the number of orcas be estimated. That most killer whales have been spotted in coastal areas may be as much a function of the observer's location (people are more likely to be near land than in the middle of the Pacific Ocean) as it is of the whales' distribution patterns.

One area in which killer whales are particularly abundant is the Antarctic. In the 1979–80 whaling season, Soviet catcher boats killed 906 of them there; Awbrey reported "thousands" seen at once; and numerous population estimates have now been made. Best (1980) analyzed reports from minke whale cruises in Antarctic areas III and IV and obtained estimates of some 23,938 ($\pm$ 8,095) killer whales for these two areas. (At the 1980 Orca Symposium, Marilyn Dahlheim reported that Best had estimated that the total killer whale population for the Antarctic might be as high as 60,000, but more conservative estimates are probably more realistic.)

Killer whales are migratory in some portions of their range, and nonmigratory in others. In the eastern North Pacific around Washington and British Columbia, the whales are permanent residents—even the transient pods seem to cruise the inland waterways, although not in such predictable patterns—and are visible all year round. (Balcomb [1977] reported a great increase in sightings in Puget Sound in August, but he commented, "Basically, this tells us that the weather and visibility are good in August, and more potential observers are present.") In other areas, particularly the Antarctic, their movements are seasonal, and are probably related to the movements of prey species. According to a study conducted by Soviet scientists,* the killer whales begin to arrive in the Antarctic in November and remain through April: "By May they were registered only twice . . ." (Mikhalev et al. 1980). From April to November, therefore, the killers can be found farther north, and the data given in this paper corroborate this. When the killer whales are not in the Antarctic, they are in the coastal waters of southern South America, South Africa, Australia, New Zealand, and the various island groups in the Southern Ocean. Studies conducted in the Crozet and

Prince Edward groups in the southern Indian Ocean have confirmed this migratory inclination of Southern Hemisphere killer whales. Condy and colleagues (1978) reported that the seasonal occurrence of killer whales at Marion Island (in the Prince Edwards) was most numerous from October to December, which also coincides with the haul-out of the elephant seals, but also the seasonality of the king, rockhopper and macaroni penguins. It would appear that killer whales move even farther north during the months of June, July, and August, the height of the austral winter.

The months from November to March incorporate the Antarctic summer, and it is during this season that the krill population blossoms. This signals the arrival of the baleen whales to the Antarctic for their feeding season—and also the appearance of the whaling fleets. When the killer whales are in the Antarctic, they seem to feed primarily on minke whales and various species of seals (Mikhalev et al. 1980), but other food items are also listed, including fin whales, sei whales, and even sperm whales. From whales brought aboard Soviet factory ships, Shevchenko (1975) recorded killer whale bites on 53.4 percent of the fin whales examined, 29.4 percent of the sei whales, 6.4 percent of the minkes—perhaps they did not escape so often—and most remarkably, 65.3 percent of the sperm whales. (Perhaps sperm whales can avoid the predations of killer whales, but if these figures are correct, they would indicate a significant number of killer whale attacks on sperm whales, even if the attacks prove to be unsuccessful.) Budylenko (1980) concludes that "there exists a close agreement between the distribution of killer whales and little picked whales [minkes], in the Antarctic Zone, where the latter constitute 85% of the killer whale's diet."*

The teeth of the killer whale are well suited for its carnivorous habits; Nishiwaki (1972) says "they use their teeth to bite, tear off and chew certain food items." In fact, there is no evidence of killer whales actually chewing their food; all the teeth are large, sharp, conical, and interlocking in massive jaws. They are oval in crosssection, unlike the round teeth of the false killer whale, the one animal that might be confused with a killer whale. (The false killer reaches a maximum length of only about 18 feet; it has narrow, pointed pectoral fins, whereas those of the killer whale are broad and rounded; and it is an all-black animal.) When the whale does not take huge bites out of its prey, as with the bigger whales, elephant seals, and other large animals, it very often swallows them whole.

*In this study the Soviet cetologists plead for continued whaling on this species; otherwise, all the information we can obtain will have to come from captive specimens: "Our idea is there is no possibility to collect a large volume of material, which could serve as a base for a representative characteristic relating [to] this species of *Cetacea*, when it is not whaled at all or is taken in a very small number." Perhaps it was this recommendation that encouraged the Soviet whalers to take 906 killer whales during the 1979–80 season.

*The author suggests in this report that killer whales be used to locate "commercial objects, such as cetaceans, pinnipeds, cephalopods and fish aggregations," because of the "positive results obtained in taming and training." In other words, trained killer whales ought to be used to find the whales, seals, and other objects of the various fisheries.

This is probably the case with prey species such as fish, squid, birds, and juvenile seals and sea lions. In 1957, Tomilin described the dental equipment thus: "The form of the killer whale's teeth, compressed anteriorly, should be considered as an adaptation to feeding on large prey, which not only has to be snatched and held with considerable effort, but sometimes also torn into pieces for convenient swallowing." There are 10 to 13 pairs in both jaws, for an average total of 46 to 50 teeth. Often the teeth are worn, sometimes along the vertical surfaces, where the wear might be caused by violent feeding action, such as grasping or twisting a large body to tear large portions of flesh from the prey (Caldwell and Brown 1964), or sometimes the teeth are simply worn down with age.

Although Scheffer and Slipp (1948) recount a fisherman's description of "fighting," there are actually few other records of intraspecific conflict. There are, however, numerous illustrations (Scheffer 1969; Martinez and Klinghammer 1978; Lockyer 1979) of killers with scratches—usually on the back—that could only have come from other killer whales. It may be that some of the "play" activity sometimes becomes a little too energetic.

The killer whale is infamous for its predacious habits, and, as the world's largest predator of warm-blooded prey, it has acquired a fearsome reputation. (The sperm whale, which can grow to twice the size of the killer, is in fact the largest carnivore ever to have lived on earth, but here a distinction is drawn between

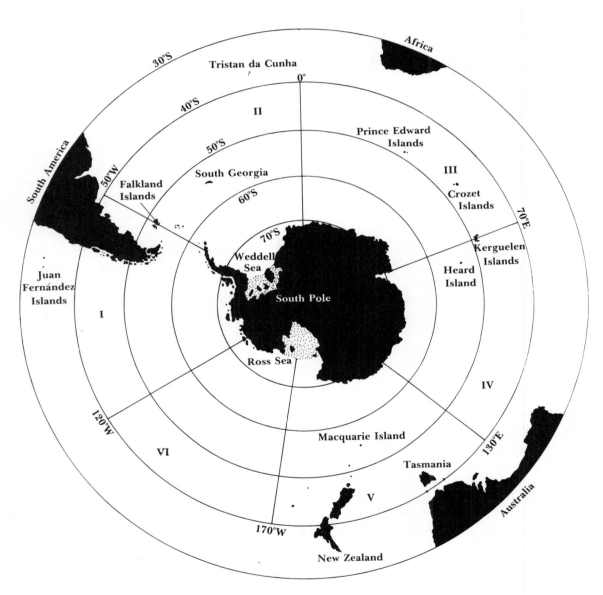

The Antarctic continent and its surrounding features. The roman numerals I–VI refer to the IWC statistical whaling areas, defined on their northern boundaries by 40°S. The island groups are those referred to in the text.

those animals that prey on invertebrates, such as squid, and those that prey upon mammals, such as whales, porpoises, and seals.) There are numerous accounts of killers attacking minke whales and holding the victim underwater, probably to drown, while they fed on it (Hancock 1965), but there are also records of minke whales unconcernedly feeding when killers were feeding on seals in their vicinity. Killer whales have been observed many times in some proximity to potential prey species, and the latter seem to be unconcerned. Mikhalev and colleagues wrote that killer whales were most often observed (in the Southern Hemisphere) in the same area as minkes and sperm whales, but they were also spotted among fin whales and sei whales. In Puget Sound there are numerous records of killer whales feeding on fish alongside Dall porpoises, harbor porpoises, and Steller sea lions (Jacobsen 1980).

When attacked by killers, gray whales are said to turn on their backs, paralyzed with fear, "and lie motionless at the surface of the water" while the killers tear them apart (Andrews 1914). Of course there are instances where the attack is not successful (e.g., Morejohn 1968), and Rice and Wolman (1971) found healed scars ("obviously the tooth marks of killer whales") on 18 percent of the gray whales they examined at California whaling stations. In one instance, a pack of 5 or 6 killers dragged a juvenile gray whale underwater, killed it, and fed on it while an adult—presumably its mother—swam back and forth in the kelp.

Killers are known to attack the larger rorquals, although there are still some cetologists who doubt it. Matthews (1978) wrote, "Dramatic illustrations of killers attacking rorquals, such as that painted by Millais, are products of imagination rather than observation."* Villiers (1925) reported an attack by five killers on a full-grown blue whale in the Antarctic: "Two of the pugnacious killers attached themselves, one on either side, to the great mammal's lower jaw, and appeared to be bearing down upon it with all the strength of their furiously struggling bodies, while two other of the assailants kept making short furious rushes at the great whale, and seemed to hurl themselves up and down on his exposed back, their writhing little bodies sounding on his body with great thwacks." In this instance, the blue whale was killed, and the killers fed on the tongue: "They had attacked the giant for nothing more than the delicacy of his tongue."

In 1977, an indisputable observation occurred in

which a pack of killers were seen and photographed in a five-hour attack on a blue whale off Baja California. From the *National Geographic* article describing the attack:

The predators exhibited marked divisions of labor. Some flanked the blue on either side, as if herding it. Two others went ahead and two stayed behind to foil any escape attempts. One group seemed intent on keeping the blue underwater to hinder its breathing. Another phalanx swam beneath its belly to make sure it didn't dive out of reach. The big whale's dorsal fin had been chewed off and its tail flukes shredded, impairing its movement. The dominant bulls led forays to pull off huge chunks of flesh. [Tarpy 1979]

The attack was not completed; the killers eventually left the great blue whale, which probably swam off to die. Perhaps they had fed sufficiently, and there was no need to pursue the attack any further.

In southeast Alaska in the spring of 1981, evidence that killer whales attack humpbacks was found by Charles Jurasz, an observer of cetaceans in the Glacier Bay area. An adult female humpback was found dead on the beach, and five days later (and two days after a pack of killer whales was observed in the area) a 29-foot juvenile male humpback washed ashore in the same location. In his reconstruction of the events, Jurasz suggested that the female had stranded, and the calf, in calling for its mother, had attracted the hunting killer whales. The calf was badly bitten, and examination of the wounds showed that they had been inflicted by killer whales (Jurasz, personal communication).

The predilection of killer whales to hunt and dispatch the larger whales was at least once put to practical use by whalers: In Twofold Bay, Australia, three generations of the Davidson family used killer whales "almost as drovers would use sheep dogs" (Mead

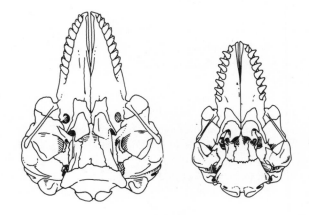

Ventral views of skulls of killer whale (*Orcinus orca*, left) and false killer whale (*Pseudorca crassidens*, right). (After Hall and Kelson [1959])

*Although L. H. Matthews is a respected cetologist, this reference is cause for suspicion. The painting by Millais that he refers to shows killer whales attacking a right whale, not a rorqual. It appears in Millais's *Mammals of Great Britain and Ireland* (1906).

1961).* As humpback whales (called "humpers") and right whales (called "black whales") came close to the whaling station at Eden, the killer whale pack, consisting of at least six identifiable whales (Tom, Hooky, Cooper, Stranger, Humpy and the Kinscher) and perhaps twenty others, would herd the whale into the bay while attacking it; then the various Davidsons and their crews would take to their boats, row out to the melee, and lance the struggling whale. "The tongue was the only part the killers would eat, and it was their reward for the help they gave." The dominant male, named Tom or Old Tom, easily recognizable by his forward-leaning, conspicuously notched dorsal fin, washed ashore dead on September 17, 1930. According to the story, this particular whale had been helping the whalers of Twofold Bay for over sixty years. (George Davidson, the last of the whalers, died in 1945 at the age of eighty-six. As a young boy he had been whaling with his father, and Tom had been present as early as 1866.)

The story is repeated in many accounts (e.g., Dakin 1938; Gaskin 1972, etc.), and it is usually considered to be true, although there is the possibility that no single whale lived that long, and that the story includes more than one individual named Tom or Old Tom. (Bigg [1980] estimated that male killer whales live for about twenty-eight years, but in 1981 he raised this estimate to 48 years.) In *Whalemen Adventurers,* Dakin's 1938 book on Australia's whaling history, the story of the Twofold Bay killer whales is investigated, and its veracity commented upon:

I am convinced (and I really am a most unbelieving person where stories of fish and sea-serpents are concerned) that the main outline given here is a correct statement of facts. Even if you discard part of it and suggest that the Killer Whales did not appreciate that any cooperation with man was taking place—even then the observation of the Killers at close quarters is unique.

Dakin, who was a professor of zoology at the University of Sydney, examined the skeleton of the killer whale in the museum at Eden, and wrote:

. . . no zoologist seeing the skull of "Old Tom" will have any doubts about his age. A great piece has been knocked out of one side of his jaw and he must have lost one or two teeth at the time of this accident, but the most striking is that all the teeth are worn down to rounded bosses, especially the front ones. From the fact that the toothed cetaceans do not use teeth for grinding, but only for capturing food or

fighting, the worn knobs of ivory tell their own story. I unhesitatingly accept the evidence of "Old Tom's" age being eighty years or more.

Killer whales will even "attack" dead whales lashed alongside whaling ships. The killers, "although they were frequently lanced and cut with boat spades . . . took the dead animals from their captors and hauled them under water, out of sight" (Scammon 1874). In the Southern Ocean, where much offshore whaling was conducted, it was considered unwise to leave rorquals "in flag"—tied to floats and set adrift until they could be hauled aboard the factory ships— for more than 24 hours, because the carcasses would be stripped by the killers after that time (Gaskin 1972). Jonsgard (1968b) described two instances of killer whales "attacking" bottlenose whales that had been harpooned by whalers off Spitsbergen, where they bit the flippers and flukes of the bottlenoses. (The Norwegian name for the killer whale is *spekhugger,* or "fat chopper.")

The list of known prey species for the killer whale is extensive, ranging from the great whales through all sorts of fishes, squid, porpoises, seals and sea lions, various birds, turtles, sting rays, and sharks. In other words, the killer whale feeds on anything it can catch —and it can catch almost anything that swims. Attacks on sperm whales are apparently restricted to females accompanied by nursing calves (Mikhalev et al. 1980). Bullen in *Cruise of the Cachalot* (1899) describes an attack by killers on a bowhead: "The first inkling I got of what was going on was the leaping of a killer high into the air by the side of the whale, and descending upon the victim's broad, smooth back with a resounding crash. . . ." He also includes a fanciful tale of an attack by two killers and a swordfish on a bull sperm whale: the sperm whale, "an avalanche of living, furious flesh," eats the swordfish, and after smashing one of the killers with its tail "like a shrimp under one's heel" chases the other with "enormous leaps half out of the sea every time." Bullen's colorful yarns are often wild fabrications, and his book, occasionally quoted to provide documentation for some of the more bizarre tales of whale behavior, is more a product of his vivid imagination than a description of actual events.

Estimates of the killer's speed in the water are as high as 34 mph (Scheffer 1976), which makes it one of the fastest animals in the sea. It has to be fast to catch the swift dolphins, seals, and fishes upon which it feeds. D. F. Eschricht, a nineteenth-century Danish zoologist, is credited with the account of the killer whale that choked on a seal: when it was examined, it was found to have the remains of thirteen porpoises and fourteen seals in its stomach. A careful reading of

*Tom Mead, an Australian journalist, wrote a comprehensive account of these events. His book *Killers of Eden*, from which much of this material is taken, was published in 1961, although the events took place from about 1860 to 1930.

the original account, however, reveals that these animals had been consumed over an unknown period of time ("most of them half decomposed, and only to be recognized by the fragments of skeletons"), and not eaten in a single frenzy. In a review of E. J. Slijper's 1958 book *Walvissen* (Whales), which includes an illustration of a killer whale and silhouettes of thirteen porpoises and fourteen seals, J. N. Tønnesen (1962) wrote, "I am not a biologist, but simple logic indicates that this is not possible. The total volume of the 27 animals would surely be as great as the volume of the whole killer whale."

The killer whale is an opportunistic feeder, and since its range is so great, its menu varies according to location. Awbrey and colleagues (1980) reported that killers in McMurdo Sound were feeding on "Antarctic cod (*Dissostichus mawsoni*) and also attacked a minke whale." In the high northern latitudes, killers eat harp seals, belugas, harbor porpoises, and various other cetaceans. In British Columbia waters, "salmon is the predominant, perhaps the sole food caught by *Orcinus orca* during the summer months" (Spong et al. 1972). During their annual summer observations of killer whales in B.C. waters, Spong and his coworkers frequently observed the killer whales ignoring cod, sei whales, harbor porpoises, and Dall porpoises, indicating a high selectivity in feeding.

There seems to be a difference of opinion as to whether killer whales feed on walruses. Scammon describes in detail how the "rapacious Orca" comes up beneath a female walrus and "with a spiteful thud throws the young one from the dam's back and into the water, when it is seized, and, with one crush, devoured by its adversary." Tomilin (1957) also includes the walrus in the list of food items of the killer whale, but Edward Griffin, the first man to swim with a captive killer whale, wrote, "Only the tusked walrus holds the orca at bay" (1966). It is likely that killers will take a young walrus if they can get at it without having to breach the ivory defenses of the massive adults.

Killer whales have been observed "herding" a school of dolphins before members of the pack darted in and fed on the massed animals (Brown and Norris 1956). While fishing in New Zealand waters, Frank Robson (1976) saw an organized attack on dolphins, which he described thus:

The Killers must have heard their chatter and closed in silently, intent on the kill. They had formed a circle round the dolphins and then they moved steadily in, closing the circle, driving the hapless dolphins before them into a crowded ring. And, as they closed, they kept up their terrible bleeping. . . . When the Killer circle had decreased to about fifty metres across, with the dolphins swimming round almost nose to tail, three or four of the hunters entered the

enclosure and selected as many victims as they needed to satisfy their hunger. These they maimed, biting some across the tail so they could not swim away.*

Norwegian fishermen (as reported in Christensen 1981) report similar behavior for killers that are feeding on herring:

Sometimes the school is seen to form a semi-circle when moving ahead. If a school of herring is found in the open sea, the pod concentrates the herring by swimming in circles around the school. When a compact school has been formed, some of the whales dive under the herring and eat, while the rest of the pod holds the school tightly together. Fishermen have reported that the herring may be so tightly packed that they can be picked directly out of the sea by hand.

In some areas, killers feed on fishes of all sorts, up to and including sharks. In *The Shark* (1970), Cousteau relates a story—told to him by Theodore Walker—of a killer whale that dived below a 9- or 10-foot shark, and a few moments later "the whale shot up just beneath the shark and leaped clear of the water holding the shark crosswise in his mouth." Similar behavior has been reported by Norris and Prescott (1961), where a 600-pound sea lion bull was the victim. Rice (1968) lists California sea lions, elephant seals, Dall porpoises, harbor porpoises, minke whales, and various fishes and sharks among the prey species of the killer whales examined in the eastern North Pacific. Caldwell and Caldwell (1969) added the leatherback sea turtle to the list of killer whale prey species, and Castello in 1977 found an eagle ray in the stomach of a specimen stranded in Brazil. In a study of killer whales in Japanese waters, Nishiwaki and Handa (1958) reported that the prey species, in order of occurrence, were fish, squid, and octopus, sharks, dolphins and whales, seals, miscellaneous.

There have been numerous observations of killer whales chasing birds of various species (Scheffer and Slipp 1948; etc.) and one account of the whales actually feeding on ducks: "A whale would spot a duck and start after it, the duck taking flight when it saw the large dorsal fin approaching. The ducks were unable

---

*Again, it is L. H. Matthews (1978) who would deny the killer whale its *modus operandi:* "Schools of killers are sometimes referred to as packs, thereby suggesting that the individuals in a school co-operate in pursuing their prey, and that the actions are the result of intelligence and foresight of the consequences. . . . It is quite unnecessary to invoke any concept of 'group feeding.' " In his review of the book in which this statement appeared, R. L. Eaton (1979b) wrote: "We are perplexed that a 'cetologist' could make such a statement! We can forgive Matthews for being ignorant of sociobiology which would describe the killer whale's behavior as highly social or co-operative. We cannot forgive blindness or ignorance of abundant literature: *clearly killer whales are highly co-operative* including their predatory behavior."

to gain altitude quickly enough, and were snapped up while they were flying with their wings pattering on the water as they tried to escape" (Odlum 1948).

Although penguins are usually listed among the prey of Southern Hemisphere killer whales (Norman and Fraser 1938; Kellogg 1940; Gaskin 1972; etc.), there are very few actual observations of the whales feeding on penguins. In a 1980 study of killer whales in the South Atlantic, Budylenko lists the following "food organisms" found in the stomachs of killer whales in temperate and Antarctic waters: "minke whales, dolphins, pinnipeds, fish, squid." The area covered by the study includes the range of numerous penguin species, but penguins are not included in the stomach contents of the whales examined. In another Soviet study, Mikhalev and colleagues (1980) list "penguins, pinnipeds, different species of dolphins and whales" as the food of the killer whales in the Southern Hemisphere, but in the section of the paper devoted to the analysis of the stomach contents of the 138 whales examined, there is no mention of penguins.

In the Crozet Islands of the southern Indian Ocean, Voisin (1972) saw killer whales unsuccessfully chasing royal penguins, and he "even saw penguins letting themselves be swept along in the wake of a killer whale." He wrote that the penguins "appeared to be too swift and too good at maneuvering to be caught by the whales other than haphazardly, after a great number of attempts."* When recorded killer whale "vocalizations" were played to jackass penguins in Table Bay, near Cape Town, "the birds formed a tight group and rapidly 'porpoised' away from the sound source," which the authors (Frost et al. 1975) interpreted as "an antipredator response." It appears that some penguins, such as the small and swift macaroni, rockhopper and royal varieties, are too agile—and perhaps too small—to be of major importance as a prey species. The larger species, such as the king penguin, much less agile and weighing as much as 46 pounds, are probably eaten regularly, and apparently swallowed whole (Condy et al. 1978).

Southern elephant seals are common in many islands of the Southern Ocean, such as the Macquarie, Heard, Falkland, Kerguelen, and South Georgia groups. There is also a large population in the waters of Península Valdés, Argentina. Killer whales are known visitors to these areas, and they frequently prey upon the elephant seals. Voisin (1972, 1976) described the hunting behavior of the killer whales as they "patrolled" the beaches and coves of the Crozets, and Condy and colleagues (1978) have shown a direct correlation between the arrival of the killer whales in the Prince Edward Islands and the seasonal activities of the elephant seals:

During October most of the elephant seal females arrive, give birth, wean their pups, and begin to depart. Some of these pups, henceforth referred to as yearlings when older than one month, begin to feed themselves during late October, staying close inshore. Killer whales reach a peak in numbers during this month, and it is undoubtedly due to the large number of elephant seals moving around the coast. By November most of the female elephant seals have departed, and there is an 18% decrease in the number of Killer whales. In December the adult females return to haul out for the annual moult. By this time the yearlings are feeding themselves (i.e. they are leaving the beaches) and there is an increase in the number of Killer whales as the number of elephant seals increases.

The killer whales seem to prey mainly on the juvenile elephant seals, but there are also indications that they do not hesitate to attack adults. There is at least one report (Condy et al. 1978) of killer whales consuming an adult female, and Voisin (1972) reported numerous adults with "large wounds" that probably were the result of killer whale attacks.

Another mammalian prey species in the Southern Hemisphere is the southern sea lion. Observers on the Patagonian coast filmed killer whales as they approached a herd of swimming sea lions, picking off stragglers that could not make it to shore in time. In water almost too shallow for them to swim, the killers tossed sea lion pups into the air with their flukes before devouring them, in what Wilson (1975) called "savage play."

Norris and Prescott (1961) reported a comparable incident in the North Pacific, where a pack of killer whales chased a school of California sea lions, coming under them at speed and knocking them out of the water before feeding on them. (The same authors recount the story of a 30-foot bull killer whale that came all the way out of the water to try to get a dog that was barking at it from a rock ledge. The dog wisely backed away, and, after much squirming and thrashing, the whale returned to the water.)

In the process of finding and herding their food, killer whales use echolocating clicks, as well as other physical and sound mechanisms. A pod of four killers feeding off St. John's, Newfoundland, were recorded and their behavior described by Steiner and colleagues (1979): They circled unseen quarry—although fishermen reported herring schools in the

---

*If this is the correct analysis of the interaction of killer whales and penguins, it is indeed unusual, since the whales are known to feed on leopard seals, animals which in turn eat penguins. According to King (1964) leopard seals feed mainly on penguins and fish, but they may even attack other pinnipeds. Siniff and Bengston (1977) wrote that many of the scars on crabeater seals that had earlier been attributed to killer whales were probably the work of leopard seals.

area, and "many gulls were working the circled area simultaneously"—with much "vigorous splashing, lunging and fluking, as a corralling behavior." Clicks, pulsed sounds, and tonal vocalizations were recorded. "The pulsed sounds," wrote the authors, "are consistent with those 'screams' reported by Schevill and Watkins (1966). . . . However, in addition to the standard 'screams' reported previously, we recorded a greater variety of pulsed sounds. Killer whales are able to vary their combinations of fundamental tones and pulsing rates to an extent not previously reported." The "strident scream" reported by Schevill and Watkins may be used to herd or frighten prey species, since there are a number of records of the sounds being played to known prey animals with predictable results. When the phonations were played to gray whales (Cummings and Thompson 1971), or belugas (Fish and Vania 1971), or even jackass penguins (Frost et al. 1975), the animals immediately turned and swam away from the sound. (The experiment with belugas was initiated in an attempt to keep the white whales from ascending certain rivers in Alaska where they were decimating the salmon population.) Robson's 1976 description of killer whales circling and attacking a school of dolphins includes "a sound from the sea [that] made my blood run cold. It was an incessant bleep-bleep-bleep, a terrifying sound." The dolphins were "hemmed in ever closer by a terrifying wall of sound." Right whales in Patagonia, also thought to be the sometime victims of killers, ignored the sounds when they were broadcast, and when Spong and colleagues (1970) played back killer whale sounds to the whales that had made the sounds, there were "no identifiable overt behavioral or vocal responses." In an attempt to resolve the problem of various dolphin species decimating the fish population of Iki Island, Japan—which resulted in the mass slaughter of the dolphins by Japanese fishermen—the fishing industry experimented with the broadcast of underwater sounds, including killer whale phonations, in an attempt to keep the dolphins away. Other sounds, such as ultrasonic wave transmissions, noises made by striking steel pipes, and an "inverted use of the ultrasonic wave emitted by the dolphins," were employed to "confuse the echo-location system of the dolphin" (Ichihara 1980). At first the sounds drove the dolphins off, but eventually they became accustomed to them—and probably realized that the hydrophones themselves were harmless—and they continued to prey upon the fish that the fishermen considered theirs.

From recordings made of thirteen captive killer whales at five West Coast oceanariums, Dahlheim (1981) identified twenty-one different sound categories, including a whistle, which was not previously included in the animal's sound repertoire. Also recorded were upscreams, downscreams, creaks, clicks, whines, tweets, and twelve other sounds, including a simultaneous whistle and click. In each oceanarium, the whales made individually recognizable sounds, leading Dahlheim to suggest that "acoustical mechanisms may figure significantly in the reproduction or social isolation among individuals and/or pods of wild killer whales."

Recording wild killer whales in the waters of British Columbia, Ford (1980) identified "echolocation-type clicks, pure-tone whistles and pulsed calls." Repeated recordings indicated that separate pods made stereotyped calls and maintained the integrity of the sounds within the pod over long periods of time. It is believed that since visibility is so limited in the killer whale's environment, sound plays a dominant role in the coordination of movement and enables individuals to identify each other and communicate over distance and ambient noise. Ford wrote: "Pods which frequently travel together may share the same stereotyped calls, while others which rarely, if ever, come into contact produce entirely different repertoires. It is possible that group-specific vocalizations are important in maintaining the cohesion and identity of killer whale social units."

A harpooned killer whale was heard to emit "shrill whistles so intense that they could be heard 100 meters away" (Newman and McGeer 1966), and a "tremendous roar" was attributed to the killers that appeared to be threatening Scott's expedition (Huxley 1978). As with almost all killer whale actions, the record is strongly affected by the predispositions of the observers. When killers were thought to be marine malevolence incarnate, intent upon dumping men into icy waters so they could gobble them up, the noises they made were "tremendous roars," but when they are performing in captivity or being observed from a kayak by moonlight, they make clever, friendly noises, consisting of clicks, whistles, and whines.

J. C. Lilly (1961) quotes a peculiar story to demonstrate the intelligence of killer whales and the fact that "the dolphin has a primitive language with predictable descriptive values." He tells of "several thousand killer whales" that came into an area of the Antarctic where a fishing fleet was operating. The killers were eating the fish that the fishermen were trying to catch and, to discourage this behavior, the fishermen called in a whaling catcher boat, or *shytter*, to shoot a harpoon at one of the whales. "Within half an hour the killer whales had completely disappeared from the vicinity of the *shytter* boats over fifty or more square miles and from then on, not a whale came within range of the harpoon gun. However, the fishing boats that were not next to the *shytter* boats were still plagued by the whales."* Lilly even goes so far as to re-create an imaginary conversation between the killer whales, which he "translates" as follows: "There is a thing sticking out on the front of some of those boats that can shoot a sharp thing that can go into our bodies and explode. There is a long line attached to it by which they can pull us in." Now killer whales certainly communicate with one another, as do most cetaceans (and also wolves, hyenas, lions, and any other animals that hunt in groups), but to postulate a warning like this is ludicrous, and only serves to trivialize and discredit the communications capabilities of killer whales. In Lilly's book, the story is attributed only to "a visiting scientist," and Wood (1973) points out that "fishing fleets do not operate in the Antarctic." It is difficult enough to learn anything about cetaceans, but the problem is compounded when one has to struggle through such unscientific hyperbole and anthropomorphism.

Observers of killer whales often comment on their organized swimming. Scammon saw them swimming "two, three, six, or even eight abreast—and, with the long pointed dorsal fins above their arched backs, together with their varied marks and colors, they present a pleasing and somewhat military aspect." "When following the prey," wrote Budylenko (1980), "the predators keep a bow-shaped line in an attempt to turn it from the side. In the first place, the prey is attacked by large and strong killer whale males. Afterwards, when the prey grows weak, the attacks are resumed by females and the young of both sexes." Off the Crozets, Voisin (1976) observed "synchronous sounding," where a school "departed from the surface of the water one after the other. They did not dive abruptly, but progressively, not raising their flukes above the water; their dorsal fins could be seen disappearing slowly into the water, sometimes in a sinuous trajectory."

When not hunting or traveling, killer whales have been seen playing—or at least performing activities that look remarkably like play. Voisin (1972) observed them swimming to and fro at random in all directions, sounding with their flukes raised high in the air, swimming belly up, and surfacing with large bundles of seaweed in their mouths. In Puget Sound the whales have been seen dragging pieces of kelp on their fins or flukes, and juveniles have engaged in what would appear to be play with Dall porpoises and harbor por-

*Lilly footnotes this story with a reference to R. B. Robertson's *Of Whales and Men*, but the only reference in Robertson that might apply is the word *shytter*, which Robertson spells *skytter* (p. 36). Surely one does not need to cite a book on Antarctic whaling to explain a single word, so the inference is that the *story* came from Robertson—which it did not. This is an example of what Tavolga and Tavolga, in a 1962 review of Lilly's book, called "an example of how not to do scientific research."

poises, swimming with them or half-heartedly chasing them. (That this is play rather than unsuccessful hunting can be deduced from the porpoises' willingness to remain in the area with the killer whales.) Probably the most spectacular manifestation of play in the killer whales is the leaping or breaching activity. The killer whale's natural tendency to leap from the water is the behavior that is so successfully demonstrated in captivity; if it were not a normal behavior, it would be very hard to teach an animal to do it. Juveniles are the most enthusiastic leapers, although adults jump as well. Osborne and colleagues (1980) report young killer whales leaping, jumping, and splashing for as much as seven hours at a time. In compiling an ethogram (a catalog of standard behavior patterns), Martinez and Klinghammer (1978) observed both captive and wild killer whales, and among the more than fifty actions noted are fin slapping, fluke slapping, rolling, headstanding, tongue-rubbing, chasing, and spy-hopping. Although the "meaning" of many of these actions is unknown, some of them may be communication-oriented, while others may be further demonstrations of playfulness. One type of behavior in which the function is fairly obvious is the "spy-hop," where the animal sticks its head out of the water so that its eyes are above the surface. In order to perceive activities above the water, the animal has to have its eyes in the air. An unusual demonstration of synchronized spy-hopping was recorded by MacAskie (1966) at Hanson Island, British Columbia: when five killer whales were startled by the simultaneous starting of three boat motors, all of them "popped up vertically and hung apparently motionless for 4 seconds. They seemed to be searching for an escape route, and found one."

Although it is not commonly observed, killer whales are also known to ride the bow wave of moving vessels. In Alaskan waters Dahlheim (1980b) observed a group of five killers "riding the shoulder pressure wave of the fishing vessel *Western Viking*," and noted that the large male "assumed a position nearest the bow and the water's surface. . . . Such positioning in other bow-riding cetaceans has often been interpreted as evidence of a dominance hierarchy within a group, since this position offers maximum assistance in the area of highest shoulder wave energy. . . ." In the waters of Prince William Sound, Alaska, Hall (1981) recorded two killer whales that "left the main group, approached the tagging vessel and rode the bow and stern wakes for a few moments before rejoining the herd. . . . The whales were generally quite curious and frequently approached the boat and swam around and under it, apparently examining the vessel visually."

There are at least two records of killer whales ramming sailing vessels and sinking them. In 1972 a Scotsman named Dougal Robertson was sailing his forty-three-foot schooner from the Galápagos to the Marquesas, when two days and some two hundred miles out, the boat was struck by something in the water:

"Killer whales," said Douglas. "All sizes, about twenty of them. Sandy saw one with a big V on its head. I think three of them hit us at once. . . ."

Three killer whales; I remembered the ones in captivity in the Miami Seaquarium weighed three tons and that they swam at about thirty knots into an attack; no wonder the holes in *Lucette!* The others had probably eaten the injured one with the V in its head, which must have split its skull when it hit *Lucette's* three-ton lead keel. [Robertson 1973]

There has always been some doubt about the identity of the whales that stove in Robertson's boat; they were seen only by two of the children, who may not have been that familiar with cetaceans. (But then the question must be asked, if they were not killer whales, what were they?)

In 1976, off the coast of Brazil, an Italian trans-oceanic "sailing boat" named *Guia III* was "attacked and sunk by a killer whale." Before anyone had seen the cetaceans "a dull stroke was heard, and suddenly the boat began to take on water. A leak 30–40 cm large, was located close to the bow, under the waterline, and in the port planking, built with stripes crossed and glued together to the total thickness of 20 mm" (Di Sciara 1978). After the attack, four or five "big Delphinidae appeared on the surface, easily recognizable as killer whales: very high, triangular shaped dorsal fin; coloration: dorsally black, ventrally white, clearly delimited, and two oval shaped patches behind the eyes; size: about 5–6 meters." The boat sank within fifteen minutes, and in the process of transferring from the sinking vessel to the lifeboats, the six crew members were in the water, "swimming a few meters from the whales without eliciting any observable reaction."

Whatever the whales' intentions—it is difficult to imagine animals as acoustically sensitive as killer whales accidentally ramming a boat—they were obviously not trying to dump the people in the water in order to eat them. In the case of Robertson's *Lucette,* the whales swam off immediately, but with the *Guia III* they stayed around. ("In no longer than fifteen minutes the boat sank and disappeared together with the cetaceans who caused its wreck.") It is difficult to draw any conclusions from these peculiar incidents, but we can take some small solace from the realization that killer whales have shown no inclination to attack people in the water.

In the wild, contact between man and killer whale has been limited to a few celebrated incidents, none of which resulted in any harm to the man. In 1911, H. L.

Ponting, the photographer on Scott's expedition to the South Pole, was standing on an ice floe, observing some six or seven killer whales. They began to hit the ice with their heads: "One could hear the 'booming' noise as the whales rose under the ice and struck it with their backs" (Scott 1912), but Ponting leaped to safety unharmed. More recently, Cousteau's divers have photographed wild killer whales in the Strait of Juan de Fuca, and other divers (Spong 1974; Hoyt 1975; etc.) have entered the water with free-swimming killer whales and emerged unharmed, but properly respectful. Daugherty (1972) lists a number of instances in which swimmers in California waters found themselves in the company of killer whales:

Three men had dived from a boat [near Anacapa Island in 1960] and were below the surface when a group of nine or more killers approached. One submerged where the bubbles were coming up from the divers. A diver surfaced, saw the whales, and dived again to warn his friends. All three men surfaced and got aboard, with the nearest killer 25 feet away. In another case, two divers near Pt. Hueneme were in the water when a killer came near; they swam as quickly as possible to their boat. The killer followed, raised up and looked them over, and swam away. One of the same men, on another occasion, had just climbed into his boat when a whale that he had not seen emerged in pursuit of a sea lion, grabbed it and carried it away. On still another occasion, at Pismo Beach, divers were followed through the surf by one or more curious killers. In 1962, at a competitive skindiving meet at Leo Carrillo State Park Beach, a school of killers worked upcoast just outside the kelp, while one large male traveled slowly through the kelp checking each skindiver in turn, finally disappearing to the northward.

Like almost all other cetaceans, killer whales strand occasionally. There are numerous records of single strandings; Fraser (1974) includes 39 individuals beached on the shores of the British Isles from 1913 to 1966. In Goodall's 1978 synopsis of stranded cetaceans on a single beach in Tierra del Fuego, she counted 23 stranded killers, including "series of 15 nearly complete orca skeletons spread out over an area of 8 km . . . almost surely representing a mass stranding." Another mass stranding of 17 animals occurred in Paraparaumu, New Zealand, in 1955. The stranding of killer whales makes extremely questionable one of the hypotheses advanced for the phenomenon in other cetaceans: the killer whales were not fleeing from predators, for there is no animal in the sea that is known to attack them. In this regard, Spong (1974) wrote, "One speculation I am particularly fond of is the thought that *Orcinus orca* is probably a creature which has little or no experiential reason to know fear; it may literally be fearless." Tomilin (1957) described attempts at tagging killer whales, where tags fired from rifles did not seem to disturb the whales, and they did not even react "to wounds inflicted in the course of marking." In 1979, Lockyer described a similar situation, where a large male, shot with a tag from a .410 shotgun, "remained unperturbed and continued his close scrutiny of us alongside the vessel, as if nothing had hit him at all."

In 1955, some 60 killer whales (along with 120 minkes and a southern bottlenose whale) were restricted to pools in the Antarctic ice that closed from "several kilometers" to "two holes in the ice each five meters long." (R. J. F. Taylor recorded this extraordinary occurrence, and the quotes in this discussion are from his 1957 account.) The ice had begun to close in April, and from then until August, the killer whales "were never seen to molest nor attack any animal in the pool, in spite of the frequent opportunity to do so." They breathed normally, and also with the head out of the water in the vertical position, where "there was a strong impression that the whales were watching the human spectators and using both eyes together." The minke whales decreased in numbers, the bottlenose was shot by Argentine soldiers, and in August, the killers abruptly disappeared. Taylor concluded, "It is impossible that they stayed alive in the neighborhood and were not recorded, and a plausible explanation of their disappearance is that they swam to the sea under 65 kilometers of ice."

For the most part, killer whales are not known to be deep divers; their normal activities take place mostly at or near the surface. (In their review of the behavior of this species, Martinez and Klinghammer [1970] wrote, "This larger amount of surface activity seems more true of the killer whale than of some other Cetacea.") There are, however, records of killer whales making deep dives, and Scheffer (1970) reports one individual, "carrying a harpoon, line and floats, [that] remained under water for 21 minutes." (The normal dive time for a killer whale is about 3 to 5 minutes.) The most extraordinary dive ever recorded for a killer whale is Heezen and Johnson's 1969 mention of a killer whale drowned in a submarine telegraph cable at 3,378 feet. (All other whales trapped and drowned in these cables have been sperm whales, which are known from other sources to descend to great depths. It is more than likely that this is a case of mistaken identity, but it is hard to imagine anyone confusing a killer whale with a sperm whale, even from fragmentary or skeletal remains.) That killer whales do not dive to great depths was suggested by Jonsgard (1968b) as the reason that some species—particularly bottlenose whales—escape their attacks. He wrote, "A plausible explanation for their succeeding in escaping from killer whales is that they have dived so deep that the killer whales have not been able to follow them."

A U.S. Navy program, known as Deep Ops, was begun in 1968 to train cetaceans to assist in rescue and salvage operations. Two killer whales, named Ishmael and Ahab, were captured in Puget Sound and eventually flown to Hawaii, where the training was to be conducted. (This was the series of experiments in which Morgan the pilot whale dived to a depth of 2,000 feet. Wood [1973] reports that the killer whales took almost a month before they would pass through a 10-foot-wide gate, while it took only an hour to train the pilot whales to do so.) The killers were being trained to dive to depth, and then to attach a clamp to an item on the bottom. Ahab's maximum depth of dive was 850 feet (259 meters), with a down time of 7 minutes and 40 seconds. For reasons not clearly understood by the experimenters, Ishmael decided not to participate in the training any longer, and he "slapped the water with his flukes and flippers in apparent anger or frustration," then swam away, never to be seen again. Ahab seemed to have the same inclinations, but the naval vessel followed him over 24 hours and 50 miles (he had an attached radio transmitter) and recovered him. F. G. Wood, who participated in the experiments, wrote, "After this incident diving sessions with Ahab were terminated."

Killer whales are protective of their young and members of their pod, but not to the extent shown in a recent Hollywood movie.* Female killers have been observed "standing by" when a juvenile has been killed, and refusing to leave the area. In Puget Sound a female had been lassoed for capture when a large male appeared. Both animals charged the boat at high speed, hitting it with their bodies "by veering sharply off at the last minute." They did this three times, and the crew, fearing for their own safety, had to "dispatch the attacking animals" (Caldwell and Caldwell 1966). In an instance in British Columbia, where a juvenile killer whale was injured by the propeller of a ferry, there were reports of presumably the same animal being suspended between two adults in the water, some fifteen days later (Dunn et al. 1974). One of the most dramatic examples of care-giving behavior in killer whales was recorded by Mikhalev and colleagues in 1980: A male was harpooned from a Soviet whaling vessel in the Southern Ocean, and as the whalers attempted to haul in the injured animal, "other individuals approached him and tried to push him to the surface. They were keeping motionless near this animal and touched him with their pectoral fins. The

*The film Orca, the Killer Whale was about a male killer who had to avenge the death of its mate, and for weeks he chased the people who had done it, smashing boats and houses in the process, and plucking unwary people from the decks of the boats that were pursuing it. In this silly movie—undoubtedly made to capitalize on the Jaws phenomenon—the killer whale was billed as "the only animal that kills for revenge," a most unlikely and implausible characterization.

animals rushed the line trying to bite it and pulled it from one side to another. A female remained near the male for almost 20 minutes, after the other animals had moved aside and were keeping at a safe distance." These instances of supportive behavior support the idea that killer whales that are closely involved in pod —and perhaps even family—groups.

Scheffer and Slipp (1948) have described some activities of male and female killer whales that appeared to be engaged in mating activities, and there is one photograph (in Nishiwaki and Handa 1958) of killer whales that are almost certainly in copulation. At Possession Island in the Crozet group, Voisin (1972) described what he believed was copulation activities:

A killer whale of moderate size, which had let itself sink belly up a couple of times among the *Macrocystis,* repeated its performance. An adult male came just behind this animal. It put itself exactly above the first whale's body hiding it completely except for the tail. Both animals remained in this position for a few seconds, then left one another and started their performance again at the same place a few minutes later. . . . Such behavior could last for hours.

The exact gestation time is unknown, but it is believed to be about 16 months, one of the longest for any cetacean. (At Marineland of the Pacific, four calves have been born to the resident pair of killer whales, Orky and Corky. Jacobsen (1980) observed and photographed the birth of a wild killer whale in the Johnstone Strait, British Columbia, in September 1980: "The calf was seen emerging from the vent flukes first as the female rolled onto her back. Within 20 minutes the calf was diving for up to 2 minutes and swimming freely with the pod. The mother, the adult bull, and another cow cared for the calf for the 2 1/2 hours after the birth that observations were maintained. The calf was recorded at close range vocalizing [a birdlike chirp] within 22 hours after birth." From some of the Orca Survey observations in Puget Sound, Haenel and colleagues noted that the newborn baby usually swims somewhat behind the dorsal fin of the mother, and that newborn calves often pop out of the water when they breathe. New mothers and their calves tend to group together, at least until the calves are weaned, which appears to take a minimum of two years, but in some instances the mother-calf association lasts considerably longer. In their first two years, calves form independent subgroups, whose main activities would seem to be chasing each other, jumping, and even harassing adults, including the large males (Haenel et al. 1980).

It is not surprising that the killer whale has been an object of man's long and bloody predation on whales. There were some cultures, however, that venerated rather than hunted it. Some of the North-

west Coast Indians, such as the Tlingit, Kwakiutl, and Haida, incorporated killer whale images into their totemic art, and stylized representations of this cetacean appear on masks, floats, dishes, helmets, blankets, and even totem poles and house fronts. Boas (1927) gives the following characteristics of the killer whale symbol as it appears in these various forms: "Large, long head; elongated large nostrils; round eye; large mouth set with teeth; blow-hole; and large dorsal fin." In discussing the use of the killer whale in the art of the Tlingit, Schildkraut (1979) wrote: "Most outstanding, perhaps, was the killerwhale's reputation for awesome ferocity, which invoked both fear and respect in the Indians. . . . Despite the fierce nature of the killerwhale, the Tlingit believed that they would never harm humans, and would in fact aid them with gifts of strength and health, and ocean food, of which the killerwhale was the guardian, and for which the Indians depended for their subsistence. . . . All of these native beliefs made the hunting of the killerwhales taboo." Daughterty (1972) employs a Canaliño Indian carving of a killer whale as the cover illustration for her *Marine Mammals of California,* and Ivashin and Votgorov (1980) wrote that the natives of the Chukotka coast (on the Bering Sea) "considered the killer whale a sacred animal . . . and it is for this reason that it has not been harvested." No such reservations affected the commercial whalers, and killer whales have been taken constantly.

For the most part, the exploitation of killer whales has been a small-scale operation, probably because the animal was not particularly abundant, and also because of its size, compared to the larger, more productive species. Dahlheim (1980) has calculated that the average yield of oil per killer whale was 4.88 barrels, or 830 kilograms, compared to an average of 27.4 barrels per sperm whale, or 106.7 barrels for a blue whale. (It would therefore require 21.9 killer whales to equal the oil production of one blue whale.)*

In the North Atlantic, the Norwegians have been hunting killer whales since the 1920s, but accurate records have been kept only since 1938 (Jonsgard and Lyshoel 1970). In addition, the International Whaling Statistics, maintained at Sandefjord, Norway, have recorded the annual catch of all whales by the whaling nations, a record that includes killer whales, pilot whales, bottlenose whales, and other "small cetaceans." The Norwegians hunted in their own coastal waters (Jonsgard and Long 1959), around the Barents Sea and Spitsbergen, Bear Island, Iceland, Greenland, and in the Antarctic. In all these areas, according to the International Whaling Statistics for 1954 to 1978,

*A barrel, as used for a measurement of whale oil, contained approximately 35 gallons. That worked out to 170.8 gallons of oil for a killer whale, 3,734.5 gallons for a blue whale.

they took 1,755 killer whales, an average of 29.3 per year. In a recent discussion, Christensen (1981) described the techniques used by the Norwegians, and also gave some insight into the behavior of hunted killer whales:

Whaling for killer whales is much more laborious and difficult than whaling for other small whales. Because of the way killers organize themselves when they are frightened, 5–6 whaling vessels usually have to cooperate during the hunt. When a scattered pod of killer whales is frightened they always gather before they run away. This seems to be organized by the old males. Females with calves run first, and then the rest of the whales side by side. During the flight the whales dive and surface synchronously. If the whalers succeed in splitting a pod or killing the big male, the organization often collapses. Small calves follow their mothers closely and appear to ride on the wave from the mother, but they have to blow more often.

The Japanese small-whale fishery killed 1,178 from 1954 to 1977, averaging 51.2 per year. According to a 1958 report on the use of the North Pacific killer whales, "The viscera and old meat are used for fertilizer or bait after boiled, cutted, chopped and dried" (Nishiwaki and Handa 1958).

Other whaling nations—including the United States from 1963 to 1970—took killer whales in limited numbers, but the Soviets seem to be the whalers with the most interest in the species. Tomilin (1957) has described the uses to which the killer whale ought to be put:

The Killer yields oil (the jaw oil being a good lubricant for precision instruments) and meat for animal consumption. The flesh, bones, and viscera of the Killer can be processed into meal (Killer whales' meat is unfit for human consumption, but the inhabitants of the Commander Islands eat the blubber). The skin of the Killer has a very thick dermis, in which the bundles of collagenic fibers are directed at different angles, and form a strong network. It can be used for manufacturing shoe soles.

But it is not only for the "products" that the killer whale ought to be harvested, according to some Soviet scientists; Tomilin also wrote that there ought to be a more active fishery for the species. "Killer whales should be hunted to protect marine mammals, the fur seal in particular. It is necessary to organize large scale Killer whale hunting in both the north of Europe and the Far East, using special low-tonnage fast vessels armed with small caliber harpoon guns. Males of this species show a great attachment to females, a condition that should facilitate extermination or, at least, aid in drastic reduction of the Killer whale's population" (Tomilin 1957).

From 1948 until 1979, the Russian whalers, working the areas of the Kamchatka Peninsula, the Kurile Islands and the Antarctic, took a total of 1,039 killer whales, or some 24.2 per year. In the 1979–80 Antarctic whaling season, however, for reasons never explained, the Soviets took 906 killer whales, almost as many as they had taken in all the preceeding 31 years.*

Prior to 1964, the killer whale was regarded as a vicious predator "of deliberate cunning and . . . singular intelligence" (Scoresby 1820). In *Moby-Dick,* Melville called it "very savage—a sort of Feegee fish," and Scammon (1874) wrote that "they seem always intent upon seeking something to destroy and devour." "Whalers detest them," wrote Bennett in 1932, "and often carry a rifle expressly for the Killer's benefit." In short, the animal was considered the terror of the seas, voracious and cruel in the extreme; a creature whose character was exemplified by its habits of eating the tongues of living whales or devouring large numbers of seal pups. In 1955, the government of Iceland asked for help in protecting their fishing industry from the predations of killer whales, and the U.S. Navy, in a program known as VP-18, "destroyed hundreds of killer whales with machine guns, rockets, and depth charges" (Mitchell 1975). In 1961 the first killer whale was captured alive and brought to Marineland of the Pacific. It lived for only two days, but it signaled the beginning of the end of the obsessive fear and hatred of *Orcinus orca* by *Homo sapiens.*

An adult female was "collected" in Puget Sound in 1962, but it died during the capture process. Then, in 1964, a small killer whale was captured in Puget Sound (and named Moby Doll, even though it was a male). For the first 54 days of its incarceration it ate nothing, finally beginning to feed by the beginning of the third month. It had been harpooned during its capture, and it succumbed to an infection approximately three months after it was caught (Newman and McGeer 1966).

Near the British Columbia village of Namu in 1965, an adult male orca was accidentally trapped in a salmon net. Edward Griffin, the owner of the Seattle Public Aquarium, raised $8000 and bought the whale from the fishermen who had it trapped. He towed it from Namu to Seattle in a makeshift floating cage, and from his very first days on exhibit, Namu began systematically to destroy the myths that had surrounded

*At the 1980 IWC meeting, the Soviets claimed that they did not know that the *Schedule* (the IWC document that gives the quotas for the following year) applied to killer whales, and that their word *kasatka* does not refer to a whale. In response to this flagrant infraction, the IWC amended the language of the *Schedule* for 1981, so that it now reads: "This moratorium [on the taking or killing of whales by factory ships] applies to sperm whales, killer whales, and baleen whales, excluding minke whales" (IWC 1980).

his species for so many years. The whale proved to be remarkably receptive to training and human contact; assertive to be sure, but cooperative and friendly as well. Griffin scratched the whale's back, hand-fed it salmon (200–400 pounds per day), swam with it, and even rode its broad back while hanging on to the tall dorsal fin. When asked "Aren't you risking death every time you swim with that whale?" Griffin replied: "In a way—yes. But from the very start I was convinced that neither Namu nor any other orca associates man with his feeding pattern. I also knew that killer whales in the wild have few if any enemies and should feel no fear. Hence, I reasoned, orcas don't have to use their teeth defensively. So I counted on my whale's regarding me with curiosity, but not with hunger or fear" (Griffin 1966). Namu lived for about a year in Seattle, and was drowned when he got tangled in his net enclosure.

There are a number of killer whales in captivity today: in a 1977 census of the marine mammals in captivity in North America, Cornell and Asper listed 17 of the species. They are so popular that when one dies and is replaced by another, the same name is used. Thus, Shamu at Sea World in San Diego has actually been several different animals. They have been trained to jump out of the water like dolphins one-tenth their size; they have their teeth brushed; they retrieve thrown objects; and they behave generally like overgrown dolphins, which is, taxonomically, exactly what they are. They eat fish in captivity, and while they are often housed with other small cetaceans, particularly the Pacific white-sided dolphin, they have shown no inclination to attack or even threaten the smaller animals. Summarizing the behavior of killer whales in captivity, Defran and Pryor (1980) wrote, "They play, invent games, interact with non-cetacean species, solicit stroking, and enjoy ball-play and other games with humans." Tom Otten, a West Coast killer whale trainer, warned that the animals are absolutely fearless and have phenomenal strength and excellent memories. At the 1980 Orca Symposium, he commented that "all training is done according to the will of the killer whale; you have the distinct feeling that the whale is in charge, and not the trainer."

It is always difficult to analyze intelligence in animals other than humans—and there are those who contend that it is difficult in humans as well—but whatever criterion is chosen, killer whales always rank extremely high among cetaceans. Gihr and Pilleri (1979) computed the body length–body weight and body weight–brain weight ratios, and plotted the degree of cephalization of various cetaceans. Among those that ranked highest were the bottlenose dolphin, Risso's dolphin, and the killer whale. The brain of the killer whale is one of the largest known for any animal: Ridgway (1980) weighed one from an 18.9-foot female at 11.6 pounds (6,215 grams). (The brain of a full-grown bull sperm whale, the largest brain ever to exist on earth, can weigh over 20 pounds.) Like the sperm whale, however, the killer whale is so large that the brain size–body size ratio is likely to be misleading, and in fact, Wood and Evans, in a 1980 discussion of the encephalization quotient (EQ) of various cetaceans, wrote:

The EQ of *Orcinus* is almost certainly too low. . . . The killer whale has probably the greatest geographic range of any odontocete (from the Arctic to the Antarctic), is found from shallow, restricted waters to the open sea, has a widely varied diet, and adapts very well to conditions of captivity. On the other hand, *Orcinus* preys on large fishes and also on other marine mammals, including whales, which are active noise sources. Locating food would appear to be less of a problem for killer whales than for most other odontocetes. . . . However, we suspect that if an accurate EQ could be computed for *Orcinus* it would be well up on the scale, possibly in the range of *Tursiops*. *

Given the number of killer whales in captivity, and the number of trainer-hours spent with them, it is surprising that there have been so few injuries—intentional or accidental—of the people who regularly cavort with these two- or three-ton carnivores. There have been some, of course, none of them particularly serious, but the apologists attribute these to carelessness on the part of the trainer, or an "off day" on the part of the whale. In one instance (at an unnamed institution), "the whale refused to bring the trainer to the landing stage upon a whistle signal, and when the trainer finally made a jump for it, pinned him against the wall, underwater; he was reportedly unconscious when pulled out" (Daugherty 1972). In another instance—this one at Marineland of the Pacific—there seems to have been a case of mistaken identity. The whale was used to being ridden by a diver in a black wet suit, but for publicity photographs, a bikini-clad diver was introduced into the tank. The whale grabbed the woman by the leg and dragged her around the tank. Given the strength of the killer whale's jaws, it is obvious that the animal was acting in a less than aggressive manner, although the best we can do is guess at its motivation. "It required a number of stitches to close the wounds in her leg," wrote Daugherty, "but

*There are even those who would raise the intelligence level of some cetaceans beyond that of man. Bunnell (1974) wrote: "Dolphins have a higher neocortical-limbic ratio than even healthy, intelligent humans, and captive dolphins and orcas have often shown humor, empathy, and self-control that few of us could match under comparable circumstances. . . . As regards our brain and our capacities as individual, conscious beings, we may actually be inferior to other kinds of large-brained mammals."

the animal could easily have killed the person if it had wished to do so."

Some observations of captive killer whales are useful in our continuing search for information on the life and habits of this animal. It is easier, for example, to record the sounds of killer whales in tanks than it is in the wild, and we can also observe with greater clarity the specific behavior patterns of the whales, even though it may be difficult to project these observations to the "natural" behavior of the whale. In 1977, the first killer whale was born, tail first, in captivity, at Marineland of the Pacific. The parents, Orky and Corky, had both been in captivity for about nine years, so it was obvious that the calf was conceived in the oceanarium. It was a male, about 8 feet long, and it weighed about 350 pounds. It never nursed; it lost weight, and after 15 days it died. The postmortem showed "no primary reason for the non-nursing behavior," and the attending veterinarians suggested that the difficult birth—it had taken over an hour and forty minutes—might have caused the baby to suffer from lack of oxygen to the brain (Otten 1977). Another baby was born, head first, to Orky and Corky in 1978, but it appeared to be unable to nurse, even though Corky was lactating heavily, and it died of an internal infection within a week. In April 1980, Corky again delivered a calf, tail first, but this one was stillborn (Sweeney 1980). On June 18, 1982, a female calf, the fourth calf for Orky and Corky, was born at Palos Verdes, and it was first observed with its flukes protruding.* Another baby orca, this one named Miracle, was found badly injured (she had been shot) in Menzies Bay, B.C. The fishermen who discovered the little whale thought she would die, but she was saved by the heroic combined efforts of cetologists, veterinarians, and Good Samaritans. After being carried by boat, truck, and helicopter—at one point she was in a hotel swimming pool—Miracle finally arrived at Sealand, Victoria, where she delighted crowds until 1982 (Jeune 1979). In January of that year, she was released from her pen by a self-styled "environmentalist" who thought she would be better off in the wild. She was trapped and drowned between her pen and a holding tank.

Because of the immense popularity of Namu and the public's fascination with killer whales, a fishery was started up in 1965 to provide other aquariums and oceanariums with specimens, unquestionably the most spectacular animals in captivity. From 1965 to 1973, some 300 killer whales were caught in the waters of California, Washington, and British Columbia, and of these, 237 were released (Asper and Cornell 1977). The great discrepancy between the number captured and the number retained is a function of the capture technique: nets were set up that encircled entire pods, and only the "salable" individuals were kept, the others being let go (Bigg and Wolman 1975). (Prior to the passage of the Marine Mammal Protection Act in the United States in 1972, and similar legislation in Canada in 1975, anyone who wanted to could go into the whale-collecting business; it now requires a federal permit to capture any species of cetacean.) Bigg and Wolman (1975) have estimated that from 1965 to 1973, the total revenue to the killer whale netters was about $1,000,000 for whales sold to aquariums and oceanariums. They wrote that "the sale prices for individual whales are a closely kept secret," but in the following year, Bigg (with MacAskie and Ellis) listed the following prices: 1966, $8,000 per whale; 1970, $20,000 per whale; and 1974, "possibly" $70,000.

With the record of captive births at zero, and only an occasional collection of an injured animal being successful, how do oceanariums replace their killer whales? It seems they are coming from Iceland. Canadian and Icelandic fishermen collect the whales, and then buyers are sought out. As far as can be determined from this fishery—the details are shrouded in secrecy—there are no controls over the capture, handling or sale of the Iceland killer whales. Most of those captured are juveniles, since they are presumably easier to train—and probably cheaper to feed as well. Frizell and colleagues (1980) have written, "In 1976, 1977, and 1978, several killer whales were caught, and in each year, several died." When the captive whales were seen to be badly stressed and, in some cases, severely frostbitten, they were released (at night) back to the sea, probably to their deaths. The whales collected in Iceland are for sale to the highest bidders, and although no one would encourage such odious capture techniques and conditions of captivity, it is often necessary for responsible institutions to purchase the Icelandic animals—at preposterous prices—rather than permit them to freeze to death or starve. At the Orca Symposium in Seattle in October 1980, the rumored price for one of these whales was $150,000, and by January 1981, it had escalated to an incredible $500,000.

What is it that can inspire an aquarium to spend half a million dollars for an animal to exhibit? Of course, the first element in such a transaction must be the inflation of greed: as long as there is someone willing to pay this amount for a captured whale, there will be someone else willing to provide the goods. And

---

*I saw the calf a week after it was born, and it seemed to be doing well. It was eight feet long, weighed 400 pounds, and was grayish in color as compared to the glossy black of its parents. It seemed unable to locate Corky's nipples, so the trainers had to feed it through a tube inserted in its mouth. Four times a day trainers entered the tank, gently grabbed the calf, and fed it a rich mixture of whipping cream, casein, safflower oil, and various vitamins. When its parents started butting the calf, she was moved to another tank. There she developed colic, and on August 3, she died.

there must also be people willing to pay money to see these animals perform, to justify the expense in the first place. There is also no question that the killer whale itself is responsible for its phenomenal popularity. Before Namu's capture, most oceanariums exhibited bottlenose dolphins, and perhaps pilot whales, along with various ichthyological exhibits. They were low-key attractions, and probably not geared to make a lot of money. But suddenly, here on exhibit was the most terrifying animal in the world, and the crowds beat a path to the turnstiles behind which Namu, Shamu, Hugo, Skana, Hyak, Orky, Corky, and all the other killer whales performed. When it was demonstrated that this beautiful animal—the largest predator of warm-blooded animals that has ever lived—could be trained to perform, it represented perhaps the epitome of man's dominance of the natural world. It proved once and for all that *we* are in charge.

This is not all of it, of course. Killer whales are totally fascinating animals, and just to be able to approach one of these fabulous creatures is a moving and emotional experience. Balcomb (1978) wrote of the killer whales of Puget Sound:

They do not seem to be violently aggressive toward each other, though they receive and inflict superficial injuries in play and sparring with one another. They are very social, and they cooperate within and between pods when feeding. Sexual activity seems to increase and peak in the month of September, and at this time of year adult males seem to be arrogant and disinclined to yield right of way to other whales and small boats. Adults and especially mothers are very protective of young whales. They are always on the move, averaging three to five knots swimming speed. They are often quite playful, with one another, with flotsam and kelp, or individually sportive, leaping into the air. They travel, feed, and play at night as they do in the day. They are very adaptable animals.

This description is a far cry from Hamilton's 1835 "warlike Grampus," or the "Feegee fish" of Melville.

The killer whale is not an unreconstructed murderer; neither is it a jolly circus clown, to be made to jump through hoops for our entertainment. The real orca lies somewhere between these extremes; or maybe we will find that it is beyond the scope of our understanding. If there is any argument against the killing of cetaceans, its basis may be found in the enigma of the killer whale—as mysterious, social, intelligent, powerful, and misunderstood an animal as can be found on this planet. If we can understand the killer whale—or even learn a little more about it—we might solve some tiny part of the mystery of our existence. But if we continue to misunderstand the killer whale, we will be demonstrating our fundamental inability to coexist with any of what Henry Beston referred to as the "other nations."

IRRAWADDY RIVER DOLPHIN

Orcaella brevirostris Gray 1866

This little dolphin is grayish blue to black above, and lighter below. It is essentially beakless, although various descriptions assign to it some small protuberance in the region of the mouth. For instance, Gibson-Hall (1950) says it has a "shelf-like beak," and Nishiwaki (1972) describes it as having "a lip-like swelling along the mouth." True (1889), on the other hand, brusquely writes "head globose; beak wanting." It is known to reach a maximum length of 7 feet (2.1 meters) and a weight of perhaps 220 pounds (484 kilograms). Adults have a constriction in the region of the neck, and only the first and second vertebrae of the neck are fused, which gives it great mobility in this region. The flippers are relatively large and rounded, and the dorsal fin is quite small: Banks (1931) described a specimen with a dorsal fin that was "only one inch or more high." This little fin is located well back of the midpoint of the back, and there are well-developed caudal keels on the tail stock. The species has more teeth in the upper jaw than in the lower: 15 to 17 pairs in the upper and 12 to 14 pairs in the lower. The teeth are sharply conical in young animals, but they become worn and flattened with age. The blowhole is asymmetrically positioned, more to the left side than the right.

Almost unique among the delphinids, this species has steadfastly resisted the multitude of name changes so frequently bestowed upon its relatives. It was named *Orcaella brevirostris* by Richard Owen in 1866, and with a few minor transgressions it has retained that name to this day. (When John Anderson, the superintendent of the Indian Museum in Calcutta from 1865 to 1886, wrote his exhaustive monograph on the animal [and also on the Ganges River dolphin], he referred to it as *Orcella*—and also described what he believed to be a second species, *Orcella fluminalis*. This can be translated as "little orca with a short beak," but there is very little about its habits or appearance that would warrant comparison with the killer whale. Anderson wrote that it is "not related to the orcas because the dorsal fin is low and placed behind the middle of the body.")

In 1938, Norman and Fraser wrote, "The genus has never been found away from this south-east corner of Asia," and the species was believed to be restricted to the coastal, estuarine, and riverine waters of Southeast Asia. Its common name is derived from one area where it was known to occur, the Irrawaddy River in Burma. It has been seen as far as 900 miles up this river (Mörzer Bruyns 1971). The species has been reported from the Bay of Bengal, Calcutta, Singapore, New Guinea, and northern Australia. Johnson (1964) discovered two skulls on the Arnhem Peninsula of Australia's Northern Territory, which "extended the range over 1600 miles and added a new genus and species to the list of Australian mammals." He wrote that the natives there are familiar with this animal, and use it for food. In 1966, Mörzer Bruyns said he had "never seen them at sea," which he defined as being more than one mile from the coast. Nevertheless, this animal is not strictly considered a freshwater dolphin, since it inhabits the mouths of rivers as well as tidal streams and estuaries, and is apparently at home in fresh as well as brackish and salt water. It is known to populate the rivers of Papua New Guinea, as well as the Mekong and the Ganges. In 1971 three animals stranded on the shore at Thale Sap, on a riverbank inland of the Gulf of Siam. They were alive when found, and, although they were placed in a pond, all three died within two days (Pilleri and Gihr 1973). In Borneo, the species is known as *lumbalumba*.

In muddy estuaries and farther up rivers, this little dolphin can be seen in small groups of 3 to 6 animals, slowly rising to the surface to breathe with "the short blowing sound which ends with the more feeble one of inspiration, and all night through this sound may be heard" (Anderson 1878). John Anderson, during his tenure as superintendent of the Indian Museum, was also the medical officer of two British expeditions to Western Yunnan (what is now Burma), where he "carried out fundamental researches of rare profoundness on the dolphins of the Ganges and the Irrawaddy Rivers"* (Pilleri 1970). His monographs on the species are models of anatomical examination, and he also observed the various species in the wild, adding materially to our still-limited knowledge of their natural history and behavior. He wrote, "The act of breathing is rapid, so much so that it requires a very expert marksman to take aim and fire before the animal disappears." Anderson also recorded the peculiarities of behavior of these animals in the wild:

They swim with a rolling motion near the surface, with their heads half out of the water, and every now and then fully exposed, when they ejected great volumes of water out of their mouths, generally straight before them, but sometimes nearly vertically. The sight of this curious habit at once recalled to me an incident on my voyage up the river. . . . On one occasion I noticed an individual standing upright in the water, so much so that one-half of its pectoral fins was exposed, producing the appearance against the background that the animal was standing on its flippers. It suddenly disappeared, and again, a little in advance of its former position, it bobbed up in the same attitude, and this it frequently repeated.

He also observed that they accompany river steamers, "careering in front and alongside of them, as is the custom of dolphins at sea," but this observation does not seem to have been substantiated in the later—but admittedly sparse—accounts. In his meticulous examination of a fetus, Anderson described the bristles on the upper lip: "The young have a distinct moustache occurring about one-half inch above the upper lip, and consisting of five brownish bristles; the first bristle being placed about one inch behind the tip of the snout, the line of bristles occupying an area of three-quarters of an inch." This full-term fetus was measured at 33.75 inches, or about two fifths the size of the mother.

Anderson actually described two species of *Orcella*: *O. brevirostris* from the estuaries and river mouths and *O. fluminalis* from the rivers themselves. (*Fluminalis* comes from the Latin for "stream.") He further differentiated them on differences in the size of the dorsal

*His work on the Ganges River dolphin was so complete that it was not until 1968 that a full-scale expedition was mounted to collect live specimens. The leader of that expedition, Earl Herald (1969), wrote, "His studies were so comprehensive that they may have served to stifle interest that zoologists of the region might otherwise have had in this interesting creature."

fin and the shape of the flippers, and noted that *fluminalis* had numerous streaks. In his *Review of the Delphindae*, True (1889) recognized the two species as distinct, but later authors believed that they were probably no more than subspecies, and Rice (1977) does not even mention *fluminalis*.

In the past, the species was valued by local fishermen because they believed it drove fish into their nets. (In 1878 Anderson wrote that "each fishing village has its particular guardian dolphin.") Indians were reported to use the blubber oil as an external remedy for rheumatism (Kellogg 1940). The Irrawaddy River dolphin is still poorly known, but some specimens have been successfully maintained in captivity at Green Island Marineland in Queensland (Mitchell 1975b), and also in Jakarta, Indonesia. At the Jaya Ancol Oceanarium, the Irrawaddy River dolphins were trained to perform an underwater ballet show, and in July 1979, the first specimen was born in captivity. A 65-centimeter (25-inch) female calf was produced by a female that had been in captivity since 1974 and a male that was taken in 1976. The first mating was observed in May 1978, so a gestation period of about a year has been suggested (Hendrokusomo 1979). At the same aquarium in February 1981, another calf was born to a different male and female (Hendrokusomo, personal communication).

HARBOR PORPOISE

Phocoena phocoena Linnaeus 1758

Although it has been reported to reach a maximum length of 6 feet (1.8 meters) and a weight of 150 pounds (68 kilograms), most specimens are considerably smaller, and do not often exceed 4 feet 9 inches (1.5 meters), or a weight of 130 pounds (60 kilograms). The harbor porpoise, therefore, is probably the smallest of all oceanic cetaceans. It is a common inshore inhabitant of the coastal waters of the temperate Northern Hemisphere, and can be easily recognized by its small size, its beakless profile, and its low, triangular dorsal fin. In color, it is a dark brownish gray to black above and lighter below, with a clearly defined eye-to-flipper stripe. In his description of the "bay porpoise" (which he called *Phocoena vomerina* but which is the same species that we now recognize as *P. phocoena*), Scammon (1874) wrote that "occasionally . . . both males and females are found with the larger portion, or the whole, of their dorsal and caudal fins white." Mörzer Bruyns (1971) suggests that "bigger and lighter animals are older." Recent studies have not borne out these observations, and it now appears that the dark dorsal coloration is constant throughout life, although there are recorded instances of lighter-colored animals.

Some specimens have tubercles on the leading edge of the dorsal fin, which led Gray (1865) to suggest that there might be a new species so characterized (*Phocoena tubercilifera*), but since some individuals in a given population have these tubercles and some do not, the distinction was rejected.*

There are about 25 pairs of small, spade-shaped teeth (Tomilin calls them "chisel-shaped") in each jaw. (These teeth characterize all the species of the genus *Phocoenidae*, and therefore, every cetacean with spade- or chisel-shaped teeth is a porpoise. If the animal does not have teeth with this shape, however, it is not automatically classified as a dolphin. There are animals with sharply pointed teeth that are also colloquially called porpoises.) One of the salient characteristics of this and other members of the genus is the

*Some authors, such as Tomilin (1957), Hershkovitz (1966), and Gaskin and colleagues (1974), discuss the existence of a Black Sea subspecies, *Phocoena phocoena relicta*. Since the differences between this subspecies and *P. phocoena* are to be found in cranial measurements, the two are not differentiated here.

loud puff made when the animal exhales at the surface. This noisy exhalation is believed to be responsible for the animal's common name—it is derived from *Porcus piscis,* "pig fish"—and among its other English names is "herring hog." The name "sea pig" is also applied in various European languages; for example, it is known as *marsouin* in French, *marsvin* in Danish, *Meerschwein* in German, and *puerco del mar* in Spanish. Beddard (1900) records a number of archaic spellings for its name, including "porpisce," "porpice," "porpesse," and "porpus." He also tells us that the porpoise was considered a delicacy in the days of Henry VIII, and "the sauce recommended for this 'fish' was made of crumbs of fine bread, vinegar and sugar. Considered to be a fish, it was allowed to be eaten on fast days." The generic name *Phocoena* is pronounced "fö-seen´-a," and according to Schevill and colleagues (1969), *Phocoena* is the correct spelling, even though variations such as *Phocaena* appear regularly in the literature.

As one might guess from the name harbor porpoise, this animal is known primarily from inshore and coastal waters, and even from rivers, sometimes traveling miles upstream. Tomilin (1957) lists records from the following European rivers: Thames, Seine, Rhine, Elbe, Garonne, Charente, Don, and Danube. According to Scheffer and Slipp (1948), "they are known to ascend the Columbia River for as far as the water is brackish," and Scammon also mentions his observations of this species in the Columbia. This species is circumpolar in its distribution in the ice-free inshore waters of the Northern Hemisphere.* In the eastern North Atlantic, it is by far the most common small cetacean. It is found in profusion in the coastal waters of Iceland, Norway, and Greenland, and in the Baltic, Azov, and Mediterranean Seas. In the western North Atlantic, it has been recorded as far north as Baffin Island, but "at the northern limit of its distribu-

tion the species appears to avoid truly polar seas" (Gaskin et al. 1974). It is commonly seen in Trinity Bay, Newfoundland, and the Bay of Fundy, and throughout the coastal waters of New England. On this coast it has been reported from New Jersey (Ulmer 1960), and the southernmost record seems to be Virginia (Reiger 1975). In the North Pacific the species is found in Japanese waters—where it is known as *nezumi-iruka,* or "rat dolphin"—but Nishiwaki (1967) considers the species "more scarce than on the American side." North of Japan it can be found in the waters of Kamchatka, the Sea of Okhotsk, the Bering Sea, and then down the west coast of North America from Alaska, Canada, and Washington, south to the San Pedro Channel off Los Angeles. Norris and Prescott (1961) wrote that "the species is uncommon south of Monterey Bay, California."

In much of its range, it is the commonest of all small cetaceans. For example, in the state of Washington, Scheffer and Slipp (1948) reported that it is "seen more than any other cetacean in the state," and Harmer (1927) called it the "smallest and commonest dolphin found in British seas." It ranks first among cetaceans stranded on the British coasts from 1913 to 1977, with a total of 779 individual strandings (Sheldrick 1979), but on the east coast of the United States it ranks second, behind the bottlenose dolphin (Mead 1979). There are no better explanations for the strandings of this species than there are for any other cetaceans; the large numbers would appear to be a function of the profusion of harbor porpoises in the waters adjacent to where they strand, and not a predisposition on the part of the species to ground itself.

Harbor porpoises are usually seen in small groups, from singles and pairs to six or ten animals, but there are reports of larger aggregations, especially when the animals are actively feeding. (Kellogg [1940] reports "schools numbering from a few to 50 or even 100," but there are not many accounts that support these numbers.) This porpoise feeds primarily on small, smooth, nonspiny fish (such as cod, whiting, and herring) within its extensive coastal and riverine range. Tomilin (1957) describes the species as "benthoichthyophagous," which means feeding on bottom-dwelling fishes, and there are records of harbor porpoises being trapped and drowned in nets set on the bottom in 40 to 44 fathoms off the Olympic Peninsula coast of the state of Washington (Scheffer and Slipp 1948). Groups of porpoises have been observed "herding" schools of herring, surrounding them until they ball up tightly, then dashing through the schools, snatching at the fish. Although they are active swimmers, these porpoises rarely jump clear of the water, and they do not ride the bow waves of passing boats, inclining instead to avoid all vessels. There are some

---

* During a whale marking expedition in the Southern Hemisphere, a group of cetologists observed "Porpoises (*Phocoena* sp.) on five occasions during the expedition to Chile in 1964. The sightings ranged from 50 to 85 nautical miles from the nearest land, which is unusual for *Phocoena* which is regarded as a coastal form" (Clarke et al. 1978). The animals were described as "small, stout porpoises ... between 0.9 m (3 ft) and 1.5 m (5 ft) long, mostly about 1.2 m (4 ft). The shapes of the head and dorsal fin were typical of the common porpoise, *Phocoena phocoena.* The animals were lead brown above and white beneath. The white of the ventral surface extended to the flanks, where it merged with the dorsal lead-brown in an area of dirty white. The flukes were darkly pigmented." This would be a fairly accurate description of the harbor porpoise, but the harbor porpoise is not known to occur in the Southern Hemisphere. Of the southern species of the genus *Phocoena,* the spectacled porpoise is strongly marked in black and white, and Burmeister's porpoise is all brown with a very distinctive upcurved dorsal fin. (The animals in Chilean waters most closely resembled the description given by Norris and McFarland in 1958 of the vaquita, but this animal is believed to exist only in the Gulf of California.) It is possible that another species of small porpoise exists in the little-traveled waters of southern South America.

A PORTFOLIO

OF PAINTINGS

OF DOLPHINS

Even though all cetaceans come to the surface to breathe, one tends to think of dolphins as creatures of air and water. Many of the dolphins in the following portfolio are shown partially or even completely out of the water. In these paintings I wanted to convey the exuberance of the dolphins as they demonstrate their mastery of the two elements of the interface. Since gigantic size is not one of the salient characteristics of dolphins, I have indicated the average length for the species shown, and not the maximum.

1

1   Common dolphin (*Delphinus delphis*)
    Average length: 7 feet (2.1 meters)

2   Amazon River dolphin (*Inia geoffrensis*)
    Average length: 8 feet (2.4 meters)

3   Bottlenose dolphin (*Tursiops truncatus*)
    Average length: 10 feet (3 meters)

4   Spinner dolphin (*Stenella longirostris*)
    Average length: 6 feet (1.8 meters)

5   Atlantic white-sided dolphin (*Lagenorhynchus acutus*)
    Average length: 8 feet (2.4 meters)

6   Hourglass dolphin (*Lagenorhynchus cruciger*)
    Average length: 5.5 feet (1.6 meters)

7   False killer whale (*Pseudorca crassidens*)
    and dolphin fish (*Coryphaena* sp.)
    Average length: 18 feet (5.4 meters)
    and 3 1/2 feet (1 meter), respectively

8   Killer whale (*Orcinus orca*)
    Average length, male: 27 feet (8 meters);
    female: 24 feet (7 meters)

9   Dusky dolphin (*Lagenorhynchus obscurus*)
    Average length: 6 feet (1.8 meters)

2   5

3   6

4   7

8

9

RICHARD ELLIS

reports, however, of more energetic swimming behavior; for example, Gaskin's (1977) remark that "the harbor porpoise is such an unobtrusive animal at sea unless actively pursuing fast-swimming prey such as mackerel, when individuals may jump vertically clear of the surface during fast swimming," or Scheffer and Slipp's observation that in "rough weather when foraging for active prey or when dodging boats, the surface action of the porpoises changed markedly. They speed up quickly, rise higher in the water when rolling, plunge with a splash, and breathe quickly and violently." When not feeding or dodging boats, the harbor porpoise surfaces, exhales loudly, and rolls smoothly, with little or no splash. Calves are more awkward, and their early breathing attempts resemble jumping rather than the smooth, easy roll of the adults. According to Amundin and Amundin (1973–74), who watched a small group of porpoises off the Danish Island of Æbelö, they show a "striking ability to disappear":

Although the surface of the water was absolutely calm and the animals were sighted in the middle of the observed area, they were sometimes seen only a few times as they surfaced to blow and then not again for hours. To be hidden by land, they would have had to swim without breathing for about 1500 m, which seems unlikely as they were not hunted.

They are not deep divers as a rule, and their average dive time was reported to be about four minutes, with a number of short, shallow breaths between each foraging dive. Prescott and Fiorelli (1980) wrote that they "moved in a relatively straight line, surfacing as often as 8 times in one minute." Harbor porpoises have also been observed "resting" on the surface for as much as 90 seconds (Gaskin et al. 1974), but this behavior has also been associated with nursing, since the cow lies still at the surface, turned on her side, while the calf suckles (Norman and Fraser 1938).

Females are thought to reach sexual maturity at about 3 to 4 years, and after an 11-month gestation period, they give birth to a calf that is about half their size. The calves average between 800 and 900 millimeters (31 and 35 inches), while the adult females are not much more than 1.5 meters (5 feet) in length. The calves appear to form a close bond with the mother and nurse for about 8 months. This is one of the few cetacean species in which pair bonds have been observed: a male and female will often remain together, suggesting the possibility of monogamy. There are a number of recorded instances of one animal "standing by" an injured or trapped animal, presumably its mate. Tomilin (1957) cites one observation when "an adult porpoise was caught . . . on hook-and-line gear designed for white sturgeon, [and] another animal, of the same size, remained at the side of the former till the arrival of the fishermen." (The same author also reports a rare observation of twins in cetaceans, where, "In September 1928, fishermen from Kerch caught a Harbor porpoise trailed by two calves attached to two umbilical cords.") While trying to capture a calf in Nova Scotia waters, Gaskin and colleagues (1974) observed: "The mother repeatedly swam across the bow of the boat, apparently attempting to divert attention from the calf. Later the same animal succeeded in joining with the calf and led it into a series of quite long dives, up to 3 minutes at a time, eventually resulting in the boat losing contact with them completely."

One newborn specimen of the harbor porpoise has been observed in captivity: In the Brighton (England) Aquarium in 1914, a calf was born to a female that had been captured some five days earlier. The calf was born tail first, and seemed to be doing well, but after ten days the mother died, and the calf shortly thereafter (James 1914). This is generally considered a difficult species to capture, since it avoids boats and does not ride bow waves. (The current method of catching small cetaceans at sea is to net or otherwise snare them as they come to or ride with the capture vessel, and those species that avoid boats are understandably hard to take alive and unharmed.) The harbor porpoise is also difficult to maintain in captivity, since it is likely to go into "terminal nervous shock" when taken, much like the Dall porpoise (Ridgway 1966). Both species seem to have a particularly high metabolic rate, which may account for this hyperactivity during capture, but unlike the Dall porpoise, the harbor variety is not known for its speed and power. Sergeant (1969) has estimated that this species eats approximately 10 percent of its body weight daily, almost twice the requirement of a captive bottlenose dolphin.

There are records of this species adjusting to captivity after stranding, a very unusual occurrence. According to Mead (1979), there is a low incidence—3 percent—of live strandings for this species, which suggests that "these are generally more capable of avoiding the beach when alive, even though they may be terminally ill or injured." In 1976, a young female stranded on the beach at Niantic, Connecticut, and was subsequently brought to the Mystic Marinelife Aquarium, some 35 minutes from the site of the stranding. The animal lived in captivity for nearly two years, and then died of a combination of causes, among them a fungus infection (esophageal candidiasis), bacterial bronchopneumonia, and trematodiasis (Spotte et al. 1978). Two years in captivity is about the average for this species; Prescott and Fiorelli (1980) wrote that "their health record in captivity is relatively poor . . . and few animals have survived for more than two years." Dudok van Heel (1962) wrote that the species is highly susceptible to shock, and frequently dies within minutes of being removed from the water.

Because of the availability of study specimens and the manageable size of these specimens—as contrasted with some of the other whales and dolphins—the harbor porpoise has been the subject of many anatomical studies which are considered applicable to the general subject of cetacean anatomy, and much of what we know about the functional morphology of cetaceans has come from dissections and examinations of this species. (It might therefore be said that this species has been more useful dead than alive, whereas the bottlenose dolphin, subject of many studies of captive animals, has led to the revelation of many of the behavioral characters of the odontocetes.) In 1680, Edward Tyson of London dissected a "porpess," and wrote:

. . . if we view a *Porpess* on the outside, there is nothing more than a fish; if we look within, there is nothing less. It cannot abide upon the Land so much as the *Phoca*, yet is often drowned in its own Element, and hath a constant need of the reciprocal motion of Air in Respiration. It is viviparous, does give suck, and hath all its Organs so contrived according to the standard of them in Land-Quadrupeds; that one would almost think of it to be such, but that it lives in the Sea and hath but two fore fins. The Contrivance and Structure of several of its parts are most curious and admirable; much illustrating divers late Inventions of some, and affording good hints for making others. And certainly by carefully perusing these Books of Nature, we shall not squander away our time in trifles, but may expect to meet with what will both please and ravish the Phancy, inform the Judgement and enrich the mind with the knowledge of God in his works, and of our selves.

Since Tyson's seventeenth-century discourse, specimens have been examined regularly. According to the extensive listing given by Gaskin and colleagues (1974), the harbor porpoise has been studied for its skin, oil composition, skeletal system, teeth, musculature, circulatory system, brain, larynx, lungs, liver, and urogenital system.* Although Gaskin and colleagues wrote, "No detailed study of the mammary glands appears to have been made," Arvy (1973) published an account of the mammaries of cetaceans which depended heavily on harbor porpoise examinations. In Slijper's 1966 discussion of the reproductive system in cetacea, he utilizes many examples and illustrations of harbor porpoise anatomy.

The phonations of harbor porpoises have been

recorded in captivity and in the wild, and the sounds heard were "low-frequency, narrow band clicks, produced singly or in bursts of up to 1000 per second" (Schevill et al. 1969). Busnel and Dziedzic (1966) also identified various click sequences from porpoises in captivity in Denmark, including identifiable sounds made during feeding ("the animal begins echo-ranging at 1 m from the fish"); a "dominance signal" (a large female seemed to inhibit a smaller male from feeding); courtship activity; and the reactions of animals newly introduced into the tank. In a discussion of the training and taming of this species, Andersen (1976) wrote that "harbor porpoises are compulsive echolocators in unknown surroundings."

In recent years, the harbor porpoise has been successfully maintained in captivity, and despite its poor health record, it can be taught to perform simple tricks such as jumping through a hoop, pressing a lever to receive a fish, towing a boat, retrieving objects, and throwing a ball (Andersen 1976). The beach-stranded female that was successfully exhibited at the Mystic (Connecticut) Aquarium was found to be "highly trainable," and her "repertoire of conditioned behaviors included vocalizing, retrieving objects, tail-walking, 'kissing' the trainer's cheek, breaching, porpoising, spinning in a circle with the head out of the water, presenting appendages to the trainer, slapping a rubber ball with the flukes, 'bowing' (leaping out of the water in a porpoising position) and performing a 2-m target jump vertically out of the water." (Spotte et al. 1978). This animal also showed an inclination to swallow foreign objects such as bolts and coins that she found in her tank. In their analysis of the cephalization ratios of small cetaceans, Gihr and Pilleri (1979) discovered that the harbor porpoise could be ranked among those odontocetes with the highest level of brain weight–body weight ratio, along with the bottlenose dolphin, Risso's dolphin, and the killer whale.

Like almost all other small cetaceans, harbor porpoises are subject to the attacks of sharks, killer whales, and men. Arnold (1972) describes the predations of a great white shark on the harbor porpoise, and there is one documented record of a porpoise found in the stomach of a Greenland shark. The white shark, of course, is one of the sea's paramount predators, so it is not surprising that the fish feeds on little harbor porpoises, but the Greenland shark is a slow-moving creature that could probably not catch a healthy harbor porpoise. An examination of the account (Williamson 1963) bears this out, for he wrote that the porpoise was only 31 inches (79 centimeters) long, and was "evidently stillborn," so the shark probably scavenged it from the bottom. In Eschricht's celebrated 1862 description of the killer whale that was

*Most of these are separate studies, but the listing of each one with its author(s) and date would be too cumbersome for this general account. Many of them, however, are listed in the bibliography for this species.

found with twenty-seven animals in its stomach, thirteen of these were harbor porpoises, and the other fourteen were seals. (Although it is now obvious that the killer whale could not have consumed all these animals at once, the account still supports the predatory habits of killer whales on harbor porpoises.)

In one instance, a porpoise died in the process of trying to turn the tables on a shark. A young female harbor porpoise had been found dead and was brought in for examination to the California Academy of Sciences in San Francisco. Upon examination, it was discovered that the 40-inch (106-centimeter) porpoise had tried to swallow a 22-inch (71-centimeter) smoothhound shark and had suffocated in the process. "Apparently," wrote Orr in 1937, "this young marine mammal had misjudged the size of its prey." Hult and colleagues (1980) found a dead harbor porpoise on the beach near Ozette, Washington, with a 44.5-centimeter (17 1/2-inch) herring "firmly lodged in her esophagus."

Because of its abundance and its inshore habitat, the harbor porpoise has been hunted throughout its range for centuries. In his 1834 *Natural History of the Order Cetacea*, W. H. Dewhurst wrote:

The Dutch, Danes, and most of the marine people of the North, pursue this animal into remote and inhospitable regions, to obtain its fat. The Laplanders and natives of Greenland, whose taste is not the most remarkably delicate, feed on all parts of it, the flesh of which they boil or roast, having first left it to putrefy in order that it may become more tender.

More recently, there have been directed fisheries in Canada, England, Scandinavia, Greenland (where Kapel [1975] estimated that 1,000 per year were still being killed for food), Iceland, and Japan. North American Indians on both coasts hunted them for food, and occasionally, in Newfoundland, Nova Scotia, or Quebec, the practice still continues. Prescott and colleagues (1981) report that the Passamaquoddy Indians of the Bay of Fundy regions of Maine and New Brunswick still hunt harbor porpoises from canoes, but "tribal sources maintain that four or five hunters are involved in a direct take today and that only one individual does so on a regular basis."

The most extensive fishery of all was conducted by the Soviets and the Turks in the Black Sea and the Sea of Azov. According to a recent summary (Smith 1976), the Soviet fishery is now shut down, although fishing continues in Turkey. Records of this enterprise have been maintained since about 1870, but it was only well into the twentieth century that the figures began to climb to astronomical heights. Tomilin (1957) describes the fishery, where "the porpoises,

which stay in small scattered groups, are driven together into a large herd. . . . Then the teams surround the herd and drive it into two purse seines. One such haul yields up to 2,000–2,500 porpoises." In 1927 the catch was 9,300, but by 1938 it had reached the astonishing number of 135,000 per year. (The figures quoted by Smith are for three different species: the harbor porpoise, common dolphin, and bottlenose dolphin, but no individual species totals are given.) Not surprisingly, the catch figures declined after that year, and by 1962 the Soviets had restricted their fishery to the summer months. In 1973 the Turks killed 129,600 porpoises and dolphins in the Black Sea. The most recent estimates of the original small-cetacean population for the Black and Azov Seas is 1.5 to 2 million animals, and "it is apparent that a fishery directed on these animals has reduced their abundance to marginal levels" (Smith 1976). Mitchell (1975a) quotes totals of 800 to 1,400 per year taken in the waters of Greenland, and in Iceland "this is the most common cetacean, and a good many are captured in nets or shot for the sake of the blubber, the meat and the intestines, which are used as bait for fish. . . ."

The species seems to be declining in European waters: "The migrations of the Baltic population have ceased almost entirely during the last decade. This is probably due, mostly, to the considerable decline in this population. In the Danish waters there is also an obvious decrease in population, and this is partly attributable to man-made disturbances like pollution, and the sport-fishermen's use of thin nylon nets which cannot be detected by the porpoise's sonar location apparatus" (Amundin and Amundin 1973–74). For a 1977 study of the small cetaceans off France, Duguy wrote, "This porpoise was formerly very common near the coasts; it is at present one of the least frequent species. On the Mediterranean coast there has not been a single report since the end of the nineteenth century. Along the Atlantic coast, according to sightings at sea and strandings, it is becoming increasingly rare; only one stranding is known since 1971."

Records have been kept of all cetacean strandings in the British Isles since 1913, and periodic summarizes are issued by the British Museum (Natural History). By examining the record over time, it is possible to identify trends in the stranding frequencies. Sheldrick (1979) reported that although harbor porpoises account for over 35 percent of the total strandings, there has been a tendency for the total number of stranded porpoises to decline, particularly on the south and east coasts. In the western North Atlantic, "some human activities may result in the degradation or destruction of harbor porpoise habitat" (Prescott and Fiorelli 1980). Because the inshore-offshore mi-

gration habits of this species are essentially unknown, we are able to consider only those effects on the inshore population that can be monitored. If the species breeds in the offshore portion of its range, we cannot even begin to determine the effects of oil spills, noise, ship traffic, or pollution, since virtually no studies are conducted away from coastal areas.

According to Prescott and Fiorelli, the Council of Europe has declared the harbor porpoise "endangered by pollution." Studies by Gaskin and colleagues (1976) have indicated a high level of DDT residues in the tissues of harbor porpoises in the Bay of Fundy, and although it may be considered a "periodic fluctuation" (IWC 1977), there is no question that the stocks of almost all harbor porpoise populations are in decline. In the conclusion of their 1980 study of the species in U.S. northwest Atlantic waters, Prescott and Fiorelli list the possible threats to the population:

In addition to incidental take, *P. phocoena* is subjected to subsistence take by native Americans. . . . Human-related environmental factors such as boat traffic, noise, and the pollution associated with coastal zone development, pesticide runoff, oil and gas exploration and development, and dumping and dredging, have an unknown impact on the species. The concentration of environmental contaminants, including heavy metals and organochlorines, is extremely high in this coastal species.

They recommend that research is needed in the following areas: "Population status, habitat use and human interactions, which includes incidental and subsistence takes, and human-related threats."

They concluded with the suggestion that "assessment and monitoring of harbor porpoise populations might yield an indirect indication of the health and stability of the ecosystems," a statement in modern jargon that merely parallels Tyson's 1680 observation that the study of these "Books of Nature" will "enrich the mind with the knowledge of God in his works, and of our selves."

VAQUITA

Phocoena sinus Norris and McFarland 1958

In 1950 a skull was found on a beach in the Gulf of California, the body of water that separates Baja California from the mainland of Mexico. Norris and McFarland (1958) wrote that it "could not be referred to as *P. phocoena*," because of numerous osteological differences, so they reported it as a new species. The cranial distinctions between this species and the harbor porpoise are too technical to be recorded here, but they are consistent and significant enough to separate the two species. The specific name *sinus* is Latin for "bay" or "gulf," and refers to the body of water in which the animal is found. In the fishery for *totoaba* (a species of drum) in the Gulf, the little porpoises have been caught incidentally in the nets for years, but Mexican *totoaba* and shark fishermen do not normally concern themselves with the taxonomic variations of the Phocoenoidae. It is known only from the upper reaches of the Gulf of California.

From the little information that is available, this species is believed to be somewhat smaller than the harbor porpoise, which makes this one of the smallest cetaceans. Mature individuals have been measured at 4.9 feet (1.5 meters), and it is thought that they do not get much larger. It is similar in coloration to the harbor porpoise, with a dark dorsal surface and white underside, and it also has an eye-to-flipper stripe. Where the harbor porpoise is reported to be lead-black or gray, however, the vaquita (Spanish for "small cow") is brownish. Prior to Norris and McFarland's description of this new species, any phocoenid in the gulf was thought to be a harbor porpoise, but now that this endemic species has been described, it is thought to be the only member of the genus in the gulf. Daugherty (1972) reports that since the original three skulls were collected at San Felipe, "four more skulls have been collected, plus three skeletons, making a total of perhaps 26 specimens through 1971."

It travels in small groups, sometimes only in pairs, and feeds on grunts, croakers, and species of squid that are common to the gulf (Fitch and Brownell 1968). When surfacing to breathe, it exhales with the loud puff that is characteristic of the genus. Norris and Prescott (1961) record various descriptions of the vaquita by fishermen and other observers, including I. McT. Cowan, who "observed what was probably this species in the harbor at Topolobampo, Sinaloa, Mexico." Cowan wrote: "On several occasions during the second week of March of 1959 they were within six or eight feet of my outboard motor boat, and on two occasions I was right over them and looking down their backs. They did not strike me as particularly small; I would say five to six feet long. They were dull lead grey in color with a slight brownish cast. No white showed from above. There was no discernible beak. The water in which they swam was very shallow."

Because of the extremely limited distribution of this species and its susceptibility to incidental catches, even a small number killed annually may have a detrimental effect on the total population. According to Mitchell (1975a), they are taken in the "net fishery for sharks and seabass," but a study of the shark fishery (Harris 1972) indicates that the fishermen of the area are converting from nets to the more efficient method of harpooning the sharks, and this may prove even more threatening to the porpoises. (According to Brownell [1976a] the Mexican government has closed down the *totoaba* fishery—as of 1975—and this may be of some benefit to the vaquita.) Brownell listed the following as research requirements necessary to learn enough about the species to ensure its continued survival: (1) examination of carcasses . . . to determine basic life parameters; (2) review of gill-net fisheries history to determine how long the species has been taken incidentally; (3) evaluation of the probable impact of future incidental takes of the vaquita by fishing operations in the upper gulf; (4) acquisition of more information on the total range of the species; (5) eval-

uation of the condition of the habitat due to the diversion of the Colorado River water for agricultural purposes and insecticide contamination into the river; and (6) evaluation of the probability of harassment from increasing tourist boat traffic in the upper gulf.

In the Report of the Sub-committee on Small Cetaceans (IWC 1977), it was reported that "a joint US–Mexican scientific meeting in February 1976 recommended that additional research be undertaken to determine its current status," and in the 1978 IWC Report of the Scientific Committee, the vaquita was one of three small cetacean species (the other two are the Indus River dolphin and the Chinese river dolphin) that are "in danger of biological extinction."

Officially discovered in 1958, this little porpoise may become extinct before anyone gets a really good look at a living specimen, and the bones collected on the beaches of the Gulf of California may be our only record of its existence.

SPECTACLED PORPOISE

Phocoena dioptrica Lahille 1912

This distinctive little black-and-white porpoise has been called "one of the rarest and most poorly known delphinids in the world" (Brownell 1974). It is black above and white below and sharply demarcated, but beyond this, descriptions vary, especially with regard to the flippers and flukes. In some illustrations the dorsal surface of the flipper is white (e.g., Lahille 1912; Bruch 1916), but in a 1968 description of an animal that had originally been collected in 1922, Sir Frances Fraser, of the British Museum of Natural History, quotes the collector: "Flipper about the same colour as back, on its upper surface." Since the back in this paper is described as "dark blue black," there can be no doubt that the flippers in this specimen were not white. (In the original drawing, also reproduced by Fraser, it is shown as dark.) Regarding the flukes, the same confusion exists. Norman and Fraser (1938) illustrate this species with flukes that are white on the upper surface. Brownell (1975) writes simply, "the dorsal surface of the flukes is black." Several descriptions contain the phrase, "the dorsal keel of the tailstock is white" (Brownell 1974a; Baker 1977). This is not very clear either, for it seems to suggest that there is a white line on an otherwise black tail stock. From the published illustrations, it appears that the flukes are black on the upper surface and white on the lower, with a gray border visible on the lower surface. The black coloration of the dorsal field does not extend to the tail stock, which is white. This variation in color, according to Hamilton (1941), is probably due to age, where the animal's light areas increase as it matures. That all this discussion can take place over the color of the flukes, flippers, and tail stock only points up the paucity of field observations of this species, since most of the specimens under discussion are badly preserved museum specimens or descriptions of animals that have been illustrated and then lost.

A characteristic that seems to be unique to this species is the pronounced dimorphism evident between male and female. In Bruch's 1916 illustration of the two sexes, the greatly exaggerated dorsal fin of the male can be clearly seen. Of all the other delphinids, only the killer whale manifests such a difference in the dorsal fin. Males are also thought to be somewhat larger than females (as is the case with most odon-

tocetes), but not enough of a sample has been collected to know if this is true. The known specimens seem to average about 6 1/2 feet (1.7 meters) in length. A fetus examined by Lahille was 19 inches (484 centimeters) in length, and was considered close to term, which would suggest the approximate size at birth.

The name *dioptrica* comes from the Greek, and refers to the "spectacle" effect of the white eye ring. ("Dioptric" means of or pertaining to a *diopter,* which was an optical instrument used for measuring the refraction of light.) In his original description, Lahille (1912) named the species "Focena de anteojos ó *Phocoena dioptrica,*" because of the resemblance of the eye rings to spectacles. (*Anteojos* is "eyeglasses" in Spanish.) As might be expected with this species, some of the illustrations show a white eye ring, and others do not. In the only head-on photograph (Lahille 1912), the animal—a female—is seen to have curiously pigmented black lips, and a faint dark line that runs up from the middle of the upper lip over the rostrum. The teeth are spade-shaped, as in all members of the genus, and there are 19 to 21 pairs in the upper and lower jaws.

This animal is rarely seen in its native habitat, and to further confuse matters, there are two other small black-and-white dolphins that inhabit the same Southern Ocean waters. One is the southern right whale dolphin, which has the same striking black-and-white coloration, but the right whale dolphin is a swift, slen-

Sexual dimorphism in the spectacled porpoise, *Phocoena dioptrica.* The male (top) has a greatly exaggerated, triangular dorsal fin. Male after Bruch (1916); female after Lahille (1912).

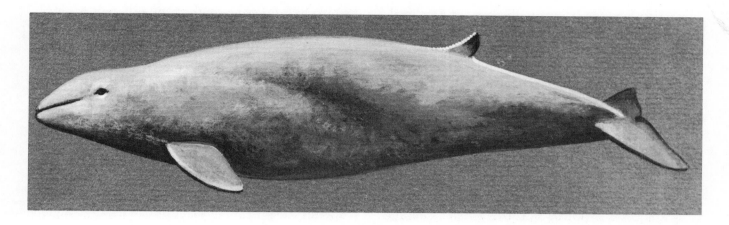

der creature with no dorsal fin. There is also Commerson's dolphin, which is a deep-bodied animal with a black head and tail, white in between, and a black, rounded dorsal fin.

When Brownell (1974a) wrote that this was one of the rarest of the dolphins, there were only nine specimens, and they had all been found on the shores of South America and the offshore islands, the Falklands, and South Georgia. Then a tenth, identified by a skull, was found in 1975 at Enderby Island, one of the Aucklands south of New Zealand, and "represented the first discovery of this species in the Pacific Ocean" (Baker 1977). The discovery of this skill suggested to Baker "the distinct possibility that *P. dioptrica* has a circumpolar distribution in subantarctic latitudes." To his summary of the literature on this species, Brownell (1976b) added: "Priority should be given to coastal surveys, initially in the areas around Tierra del Fuego, Falkland Islands, and South Georgia Island to look for additional stranded specimens of *P. dioptrica*. At a later date the southern coast of Argentina should also be searched. A coastal survey would probably be more productive than at sea surveys."

On the beaches of Bahía San Sebastián in Tierra del Fuego, Natalie Goodall made what must be considered a "productive" coastal survey: She discovered some 87 specimens of spectacled porpoises. Many of these were incomplete skeletons or just skulls, but from the remains strewn on a single beach, the spectacled porpoise became "the small cetacean most common in the waters off northeastern Tierra del Fuego," instead of one of the "rarest and most poorly known delphinoids in the world." In 1979, Goodall and Cameron published a report concerning four more specimens—again only skeletons—this time from the Chilean side of Tierra del Fuego, but still not so far west as to be considered part of the cetacean fauna of the Pacific Ocean.* In fact, both bays where the specimens

were found are on the northern end of the same island, Isla Grande, which is divided by a line that separates the Chilean and Argentine sectors.

Now that the "coastal surveys" recommended by Brownell have been implemented, what is needed is some at-sea observations, to fill in the gaps about how the animals live and what they look like in life. We know something now about where they die, but very little about how and where they live.

BURMEISTER'S PORPOISE

Phocoena spinipinnis Burmeister 1865

The name *spinipinnis* can be translated as "spiny fin" and refers to the unique dorsal fin of this species: on the sharply concave forward edge, there is a series of spiny denticles, which also account for the species name in Spanish, *marsopa espinosa*, or "spiny porpoise." The dorsal fin also has a convex rear margin, giving it a configuration that is peculiar to this species and can be seen in no other cetacean. Otherwise, this species is relatively nondescript. It is brown (*marrón* in Spanish) in color, with a less rounded head and somewhat larger and more pointed flippers than the other members of the genus. A photograph of a dead animal (Mitchell 1975a) shows a light area extending from the tip of the lower jaw to the area of the flippers. Hermann Burmeister (1807–92), who first described the porpoise that still bears his name, was the director of the Natural History Museum in Buenos Aires when the specimen was brought in; it had been taken in the harbor of that city.

The teeth, which number 14 to 19 pairs in each jaw, are spade-shaped as in the other phocoenids.

---

*There is a controversy concerning a species known as *Phocoena obtusata*, described by Philippi in 1893 from Talcahuano Bay on the

coast of Chile. Some authors (Allen 1925; Clarke et. al. 1978) consider this specimen as representing a western South American population of the spectacled porpoise, but others, such as Brownell (1974a) and Goodall and Cameron (1979), believe that the specimen was not a phocoenid at all, but rather an example of *Cephalorhynchus*.

Some discrepancies exist as to the size of this animal, but the differences are minimal, and from the literature we can assume that this species, like its relatives, does not much exceed 6 feet (1.83 meters) in length. According to Brownell and Praderi (1976), four specimens caught in the shark nets off Punta del Diablo, Uruguay, ranged in length from 1.79 to 1.83 meters.

Burmeister's porpoise is found in discrete populations in the coastal waters of the east and west coasts of South America, but it apparently occurs much farther north on the west coast. It has been recorded from Bahía de Paita, Peru, in the Pacific, but only as far north as the province of Rocha, Uruguay, on the Atlantic coast. Allen (1925) speculated that there was a single population, confined to the shallow waters from La Plata round the Horn "to the Chilean and Peruvian coasts, following the Humboldt Current to Peru." But Brownell and Praderi (1976) wrote, "We believe that the Atlantic and Pacific *Phocoena spinipinnis* are isolated populations. The connection between these two populations as illustrated by Pilleri and Gihr (1972) is unjustified, as no specimens or valid records

are known from the southern tip of South America." These "specimens or valid records" were revealed in 1978, when Goodall published her discovery of no fewer than eight specimens from the waters and beaches of Tierra del Fuego, "the southernmost known and the first from the Cape Horn area." Some of the specimens had been caught by fishermen in the Beagle Channel; some were caught in crab nets; and others were found as skeletal material from various beaches. It is now apparent that the species does "occur continuously around southern South America from Uruguay to Peru" (Goodall 1978). Because the species seems to prefer shallow coastal waters, and the continental shelf is wider on the Atlantic than on the Pacific, Brownell and Praderi wrote that "the population should be larger there. However, based on our survey of museum specimens and catch records, the Pacific population is by far the larger of the two."

Until recently, hardly anything was known about the behavior of this species in the wild; in 1975, Aguayo reported eight animals swimming together off the coast of Chile, and he described them as "com-

Recorded occurrence of *Phocoena spinipinnis* off South American coasts:

1. Buenos Aires, Argentina
2. Valparaíso, Chile
3. Talcahuano, Chile
4. Paita Harbor, Peru
5. Valdivia, Chile
6. Península Valdés, Argentina
7. Punta del Diablo, Uruguay
8. Tierra del Fuego, Argentina
9. Chimbote, Peru

pletely dark, and with knobs on the anterior border of the dorsal fin." During the course of their research on small cetaceans (dusky and bottlenose dolphins) in Golfo San José, Argentina, Bernd and Melany Würsig observed Burmeister's porpoise on numerous occasions, and were able to add substantially to our still-limited knowledge. They reported (in Würsig et al. 1977) that the animals were usually seen in small groups that ranged from two to eight. The porpoises were difficult to observe, even when the waters of the gulf were calm, because of their typically phocoenid behavior of rolling gently to the surface, exposing only the blowhole and the dorsal fin. Sometimes when the porpoises surfaced to breathe, they exposed the left flank so that the dorsal fin was tilted at an angle of 20° to 30° from the vertical. In one instance a group of them submerged for 30 seconds, and then emerged *todos* ("all together"), after a lapse of 8 to 12 seconds, some (30 to 50 meters) from where they had gone down. Previous reports had given the color of this species as "dark" or "completely black" (Norman and Fraser 1938), but from observations of the living animals. Würsig and colleagues were able to describe the porpoises as *marrón bastante claro*, or "rather light brown." In almost two years of observations (July 1974 to March 1976), the authors never heard the characteristically loud exhalation of the phocoenids, and they only saw one *spinipinnis* jump.

This was once thought to be an extremely rare species—in 1925 Allen wrote that "all four specimens have been collected in harbors"—but it has recently been referred to as "the most abundant small cetacean in southern South American waters" (Brownell and Praderi 1976). A "personal communication" from K. S. Norris is cited in various publications (Aguayo 1975; Mitchell 1975a; Brownell and Praderi 1975) as the source of the information that "250,000 pounds of meat from this species are marketed annually in Peru," but later interpretations of this figure (e.g., Brownell and Praderi 1976) have suggested that the figure refers to 250,000 pounds of *porpoise*, not por-

poise *meat*. They then write, "The correct figure is 'close to 2000/year,' " but again it is not clear whether it is porpoises or meat that is being discussed. Whatever the figure, it appears that this species is heavily exploited for human consumption on the Peruvian and Chilean coasts. Aguayo (1975) records the species as "common in the northern part of Chile (Iquique–Antofagasta)," and Grimwood (1969) indicated that it appears frequently in the fish markets at San Andrés, Peru.

Yet another "little-known" species has been discovered to be the object of human exploitation, and although science is just beginning to gather information on the distribution and behavior of Burmeister's porpoise, it appears that the small-boat fishermen of Peru and Chile have known about them for years.

FINLESS PORPOISE

Neophocaena phocaenoides Cuvier 1829

This is an unmistakable small porpoise, with a rounded forehead and no dorsal fin. In place of the fin, there is a subtle ridge that begins midway down the back and continues posteriorly to the origin of the flukes. Surrounding this ridge are a series of protrusions or tubercles, similar to those found on the dorsal fin of Burmeister's porpoise, and occasionally on the fin of the harbor porpoise. The teeth are spade-shaped like those of the Phocoenidae, but they are less numerous than those of the true porpoises. (The scientific name of this species can be roughly translated as "new porpoise like Phocoena.") There are 15 to 19 pairs of teeth in each jaw, but the figure varies considerably from individual to individual, and therefore cannot be diagnostic. These are small animals, probably not reaching a length of 6 feet (1.83 meters); Pilleri and Gihr (1972) listed six mature specimens from the Indus delta region that ranged in length from 98 to 155 centimeters (38 1/4 to 60 1/2 inches), and reached a maximum weight of 38 kilograms (83.6

pounds). The flippers are proportionally larger than those of any of the Phocoenoidae.

The animal used to be known as the black finless porpoise, and in virtually all early references where the color was given, it was black. In 1976, Pilleri and colleagues published the article "The Black Finless Porpoise . . . Is Not Black," in which they described the living animal as "pale grey with a bluish tinge on the back and sides." There are also white areas on the chin and throat, as shown in the color photographs that accompany the article. Tomilin (1957) gives the coloration as "body dusky, lead-black above, much lighter below. Throat and lips pale yellow-gray. A diffuse gray spot of variable size between the flippers and the region of the anal and urogenital openings. . . . Flippers and flukes dusky above, lighter below, sometimes with light and gray patches of variable size." Despite this description, however, Tomilin refers to the animal as the "finless black porpoise."*

The absence of a dorsal fin makes this species easy to identify, especially since it is restricted to the coastal and estuarine waters of eastern Asia and Japan. Because the finless porpoise occurs in many discrete areas, there are those who would identify some of the localized populations as subspecies, or even as full species. From an examination of the specimens caught in Pakistan, Pilleri and Gihr (1972) have suggested a new species, *Neomeris* (=*Neophocaena*) *asiaeorientalis*. As Fraser (1966) writes, there seem to be enough cranial differences to warrant a separation of the Chinese and Indian varieties, and Pilleri and Gihr (1975) suggest that the Japanese population, which they call *Neophocaena sunameri* (*sunameri* is the Japanese name for this

animal), should also be recognized as a separate species. In 1977, Rice wrote: "Specimens from China and Japan differ from Indian Ocean specimens, and are best regarded as a subspecies, *N.p. asiaeorientalis . . .* rather than a full species as originally described. Their published data are inadequate to reveal whether the Japanese and Chinese populations are sufficiently separable to warrant recognition of *sunameri* even as a subspecies."

In a 1980 discussion, however, Pilleri and Chen Peixun held that *N. phocaenoides* and *N. asiaeorientalis* should be regarded as distinct species, and wrote "that there is no difficulty in separating the two taxa at species level." They maintained that the 1975 identification of the Chinese variety as *N. asiaeorientalis* (by Pilleri and Gihr) "in recent cetological literature either has been passed over in silence or contested." In the 1980 paper, Pilleri and Chen Peixun pointed out that Chinese authors "regard the Changjiang finless porpoise as a separate taxon* and have always discussed it separately from *N. phocaenoides.*" According to this study, the species from South and Southwest Asia (*N. phocaenoides*) "is light grey in colour, but this changes rapidly to dark grey or black after death." The Chinese version (*N. asiaeorientalis*) is darker in life, and does not have the whitish areas around the snout of its Southwest Asian counterpart. The head differs in shape in the two species, with *phocaenoides* having a more prominent melon and a less projecting lower lip. The most significant feature, however, is the denticulated region on the back of *phocaenoides*, which feature is almost totally lacking in *asiaeorientalis*, sometimes represented by only a single row of tubercles running down the dorsal ridge. In a paper devoted specifically to comparative eye size, Chen, Shao, and Pilleri (1980) also indicate that the eyes of the Southwest Asian forms are considerably larger than those

*The eye color of this species was another aspect of its appearance that continued to cause confusion. Kellogg (1940) described the species as "pink-eyed," and the illustration, presumably prepared under his direction (Pl. XXII), shows this characteristic. Mörzer Bruyns (1971) lists Kellogg as a bibliographic source, and repeats this peculiarity with an additional geographic reference: "they are reported to have pink eyes in North East Asia." Other references do not mention the eye color, and Nishiwaki (1972) writes, "the eyes are small and very indistinct."

*A taxon (plural *taxa*) is a definite unit in classification; a unit in the science of taxonomy. The word comes from the Greek *taxis*, meaning "arrangement."

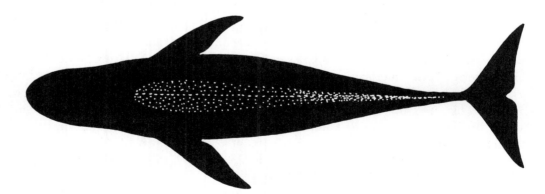

Dorsal view of *Neophocaena phocaenoides,* **showing pattern of tubercular elevations.**

of the Chinese finless porpoise, and attribute this degeneration to the reduced visibility of the Yangtze habitat.

The finless porpoise is not an open-ocean animal, and it is found only in the warmer inshore waters of river mouths, rivers, and littoral areas. It has been recorded from Pakistan, India, through the Indo-Malayan archipelago and the Arabian Sea, to China (including Hong Kong), Korea, and Japan. The species has been recorded from Tung Ting Lake in eastern China, hundreds of miles from the sea (Allen 1938), and numerous references to its appearance in the Yangtze River, now known as the Changjiang. There is a possibility that the range may extend as far south as New Zealand (Baker 1972), but according to the description ("swimming with a group of dusky dolphins . . . entirely black and without a dorsal fin"), it might have been some other species. (The finless porpoise is not black, and such a slow-swimming animal would have a difficult time keeping up with the swift, energetic dusky dolphins.) One of the two type specimens described by Cuvier was supposed to have come from the Cape of Good Hope (the other came from the Malabar coast of India), but recent authors, e.g., Fraser (1966), Mitchell (1975b), Rice (1977), have expressed doubts about this locality. (Rice quotes a personal communication from Peter Best to the effect that "there are no indisputable South African records.") On the other hand, Gibson-Hall, in a 1950 survey of the cetaceans of Sarawak (Borneo), states that he has seen the finless porpoise only off South Africa.

During a 1973 expedition to Southwest and monsoon Asia (the Persian Gulf, Indus delta, Malabar, Andaman Sea, and the Gulf of Siam), Pilleri and Gihr (1973) frequently observed this species, but they wrote, "It is very shy and since it has no dorsal fin it is more difficult to detect." In the Persian Gulf they sighted two finless porpoises swimming side by side: "Emerged suddenly almost without disturbing the surface of the water. During the short blowing period, the concave curve of the head observed dorsally, behind the blowhole, was clearly visible. This is much less evident in dead animals." This depression in the "neck" region has rarely been described before, and points up the importance of field observations of living animals as contrasted with the examination of stranded specimens or museum preparations in describing their actual appearance. The investigators encountered only single animals or pairs—"larger communities or schools are not formed"—and on one occasion they saw a pair of these normally shy animals approach a shrimp-fishing boat, "attracted nearer by the tantalizing bait."

Kasuya and Kurehara (1979) conducted an extensive survey of the finless porpoises in the Inland Sea of Japan, and they wrote, "The Inland Sea is a well known, and possibly the largest habitat of the finless porpoise in Japan. The species is legally protected since 1930 as a natural monument." (This was done, according to the authors, because feeding finless porpoises can serve as an indicator of the presence of certain species of fishes that fishermen were seeking.) In the study period, which began in April 1976 and ended in October 1978, some 1,194 finless porpoises were observed, and a maximum population for the Inland Sea was estimated at close to 5,000 animals.

In the past, this species was commercially fished in Japan, India, and China, but it is now unmolested throughout most of its range, except for some local net fisheries, such as that recorded by Dawson (1960), where 17 were landed in a seine at Malpe on the South Kanara coast of India. In 1923, Allen described the Chinese method of fishing for this species:

. . . the Chinese capture them by hanging a number of iron hooks from a stout cord, as sort of a barrage across part of the stream. If a porpoise strikes against a hook so that the point penetrates its skin, its subsequent struggles only serve to entangle it more firmly among the other hooks and cords, until it is drowned or captured.

During their 1979 expedition to China, Pilleri and colleagues had numerous opportunities to observe the finless porpoise in the lakes and rivers where they were seeking the Chinese river dolphin. The river dolphin and the finless porpoise were seen together on occasion, but the usual sighting consisted of small schools of each species, the finless porpoise occurring in pairs or groups of no more than five or six animals. The average dive time for the finless porpoise is about 17 seconds, with the longest recorded dive being 65 seconds. Like the river dolphin, this species changes direction and dives beneath a boat in order to escape, which may result in propeller injuries. This species seems to be less threatened by the boat traffic on the river than the river dolphin (Zhou et al. 1979). It feeds on squid, shrimp, and small fishes.

These recent observations of the finless porpoise in the wild have provided more information on its behavior and appearance, some of which is quite interesting. For example, the tubercles on its back have always puzzled cetologists. In 1938, Norman and Fraser wrote that they are "believed to be the last remnant of a scaly armor covering the whole of the body in the ancestors of these animals." Now a more practical explanation for this peculiarity has been identified: From on-site observations in China, Pilleri and Chen (1979) were able to corroborate what "Chinese fishermen and fishery scientists have long known," that finless porpoises carry their claves on their backs.*

We observed several instances of this interesting behavioural pattern during our co-investigation trip in May 1979. . . . Mothers with calves are extremely shy of boats, and maintain a much larger flight distance than when they are unaccompanied by young. It was interesting to watch the calf riding on its mother's back and being carried to safety through the Yangtze waves. The balance is perfect and when followed the mother can achieve a considerable speed, diving and coming up to blow still with the baby on her back.

The baby rides on the area of the tubercles, and the authors wrote, "On the basis of our ethological observations in the middle Changjiang it looked as if the rough, wart-covered area on the skin of the back could be a perfect structure to prevent the calf from slipping off." It is interesting to note that Kasuya and Kurehara (1979), in their lengthy discussion of the finless porpoise population in the Inland Sea of Japan, never noticed—or at least never mentioned—this unusual behavior. Their only reference to the behavior of mother and calf is as follows: "If an adult was accompanied by a calf, they were considered as a mother and calf. These individuals were always swimming in parallel, and usually stayed within the distance of 1 m, which is much closer than the ordinary two adults do."

This species has been maintained in captivity on numerous occasions, particularly in Japan, and on

*In this discussion, Pilleri and Chen point out that the Changjiang finless porpoise . . . have on the dorsal ridge of the back only a string of very tiny denticles, "while the specimens from the Indus have a much wider tubercle-covered area." They suggest that "this difference is remarkable and confirms the separation of the two taxa."

April 17, 1976, a baby finless porpoise was born to a female that had been in captivity for three years at the Toba Aquarium, Mie, Japan. Although the baby lived only seventeen days, its birth was an important one, since it was the first time that the parturition of this species had ever been observed. The baby was about 1 meter (3.28 feet) long and weighed 7 kilograms (15 pounds). There were ten male and three other female finless porpoises in the tank, but the baby died in just over two weeks (Anonymous 1976). From their observations of this species in the Inland Sea, Kasuya and Kurehara (1979) have estimated an 11-month gestation period, with newborn calves ranging in size from 60 to 100 centimeters (23 to 39 inches).

DALL PORPOISE

Phocoenoides dalli True 1885

Probably the fastest of all small cetaceans, the Dall porpoise is easily recognized by its prominent white "sidewalls" and its white-tipped dorsal fin and flukes. The name means "like *Phocoena.*" The animal is deep-bodied, muscular, and robust, with a relatively small head, prognathous profile, and pronounced dorsal keels on the caudal peduncle. In 1911, Andrews wrote of this configuration: "the caudal peduncle presents an extraordinary shape which is approximated by no other members of the delphinidae. This form is so remarkable that the question has been raised as to whether or not it might be a malformation due to injury." There are other cetaceans with pronounced caudal keels (e.g., the Atlantic white-sided dolphin), but they usually consist of muscle or connective tissue. Tomilin (1957) has written that in the Dall porpoise

The Chinese finless porpoise carrying its calf on its back. (After Pilleri and Chen [1979])

"the caudal peduncle has strongly developed dorsal (supported by the tall spinous processes of the caudal vertebrae) and ventral ridges. The ventral ridge is slightly smaller than the dorsal." In mature adults, these keels can also serve to distinguish males from females: The dorsal keel is much more pronounced in adult males, and there is also a secondary "central" keel, located on the ventral portion of the tail stock, and somewhat forward of the corresponding dorsal keel (Consiglieri, personal communication).

The Dall is a relatively small animal, reaching a maximum length of about 7 feet (2.13 meters) and a weight of perhaps 350 pounds (157 kilograms). As with all species of porpoises, its teeth are small and spade-shaped, and it has 23 to 27 pairs in each jaw. There are very few observations of eye color in cetaceans, but Cowan (1944) observed that in this species "the iris is black or dark blue, the pupil deep, iridescent blue-green."

The type specimen, now in the U.S. National Museum, was collected in the Aleutian Islands by the American naturalist W. H. Dall (1845–1927), and was named for him.* (The Dall sheep, *Ovis dalli*, and the Alaska blackfish, *Dallia pectoralis*, also share this distinction.)

Dall porpoises are typically seen in groups of two to ten animals, although they sometimes aggregate in larger numbers. Scheffer (1950) recounted a story of an enormous assemblage of porpoises—calculated to be in excess of 5,000—but the species could not be verified. Another account, quoted by the same author, mentions "several thousand" animals that were definitely identified as Dall porpoises. According to a National Marine Mammals Laboratory (NMML) report in 1981, "the largest group of *Phocoenoides* on record was

*This species is variously referred to as "the Dall porpoise" or "Dall's porpoise," both names appearing with equal frequency. Rice (1977) employs "Dall porpoise" and also gives the spelling of the trivial name as *dallii*. The name is often encountered, however, without the second "i."

sighted spring 1980, from a U.S. fisheries research vessel. An estimated 3,000 ($\pm$ 1,000) animals were observed moving northward through Stephens Passage in southeastern Alaska."

A type of schooling behavior was reported in the waters off Los Angeles by Norris and Prescott (1961), and since it appears to be unique in the cetacean literature, it is here reproduced in full:

On October 17, 1955, five adults were noted swimming single file, very evenly spaced about 100 feet apart, heading easterly down the San Pedro Channel. The animals could be heard venting a distinct whistle each time they blew, which sounded like high-pressure air escaping through a small opening. The spacing of the school members did not seem particularly noteworthy in view of the small size of the school. However, on December 15, 1956, the peculiar behavior was noted again on a much more striking scale. A single-file school was encountered in the San Pedro Channel, 5.5 miles south of the San Pedro Lighthouse. This school consisted of an estimated one hundred animals, all adults. All were spaced about 100 feet apart, head to tail, proceeding southeastward. The spacing was remarkably constant and the line quite straight. The boat zigzagged through the 2-mile long file, but the animals never allowed it to come closer than about 200 feet before breaking rank and fleeing. Four miles farther out in the channel another file was met, going approximately the same direction as the first. This school consisted of about twenty animals, again spaced about 100 feet apart. Still another file was met 2.5 miles farther south. This one was also composed of about twenty adults, again spaced about 100 feet apart, and again proceeding southeasterly. All the files were moving slowly, barely breaking the surface. All the animals were adults with white-tipped dorsal fins. No explanation can be offered for this peculiar schooling habit. It has been noted occasionally since, but the schools have not been as large.

These animals are rapid swimmers, and have been reported to be able to reach speeds of 30 knots (NMFS 1981). Although they are known bow-wave riders (Yocum [1946] recorded twelve animals "leap-ing and diving in front of the bow"), they are more likely to cross erratically in front of a moving vessel, and they can easily overtake boats moving at 12 to 15 knots. They do not jump often, but when swimming at speed they raise their heads out of the water to breathe, creating a "rooster tail" or "splash cone" of spray, which is characteristic and unique. Another typical behavior, known as the "slow roll," often follows the more energetic exercises. In discussing the swimming behavior of this species seen at sea, Morejohn (1979) wrote: "Often animals would appear close by seemingly from nowhere, race to our bow, criss-cross ahead with great swiftness, and then move off, perhaps occasionally splashing, then assume a slow, high, arched surfacing." Commenting on this behavior, Brown and Norris (1956) wrote that the animal "looks something like a large black and white square rolling over."

Early descriptions referred to the Dall porpoise merely as black and white, but intensified study of the species has shown that the coloration—like much about this animal—is not so simple. Younger animals, according to Morejohn (1979), are slate-gray or brownish, and "subadults" have slate-gray or brownish-gray heads, and "often these same colors were distributed along the flippers, caudal peduncle, and flukes." In his observations of the Dall porpoise population of Prince William Sound, Alaska, Hall (1981) noted that the newborn animals "frequently had light gray pigmentation on the dorsal surface of the head, and were thus distinct from adults in coloration as well as size. As the young porpoises grow the gray pigmentation fades to a 'skullcap' surrounding the blowhole. . . . Previous references to this color pattern phenomenon in young Dall porpoise has not been mentioned in the literature." The white tips of the dorsal and caudal fins (called "frosting" by Morejohn) is also a variable, and there have been animals reported with all-black or all-white dorsal fins, as well as many in-between variations. In addition to the sexual dimorphism manifest in the shape of the caudal keels, Dall porpoises also show a difference in coloration of males and females. On the belly, where the black area enters the white ventral field from the tail region, males show a single black protrusion, while on females the nipple slits are also accentuated, imparting to this area a trident-shaped appearance. "This distinction is probably related to sex recognition," wrote Morejohn and colleagues in 1973, "but its possible role in aiding nursing young to locate the mammae should not be overlooked." The same authors described a "banded" fetus from a normally pigmented female: it was white forward of the dorsal fin, while the flippers and posterior portion were black. Albino Dall porpoises are sometimes encountered, and Hall (1981) reported seeing these "uniquely marked" animals in Prince William Sound, southeast Alaska, in groups of normally colored porpoises.

The teeth of Dall porpoises are most unusual. They are tiny—Morejohn calls them "the smallest known teeth among the delphinids"—and they are separated by horny protuberances (also referred to as "gum teeth" or "palatal rugosities"), which often extend beyond the teeth themselves, and are believed to function as gripping organs. Miller, who described this phenomenon in 1929, saw it as a transitional stage in evolution between the toothed whales and the baleen whales, and assumed that the teeth of the Dall porpoise were on the way to becoming functionless. He wrote that the "gingival and dental structures of *Phocoenoides* represent anatomical structures closely parallel to those through which the corresponding parts of the toothed ancestors of the Mysteciti must have passed." In addition, this species has a "dental pad" at the tip of the upper jaw, which "appears to be a specialization of this species adapting it to better grasp and swallow cephalopods" (Morejohn 1979).

The Dall porpoise feeds on a variety of organisms, including squid and fish such as saury, herring,

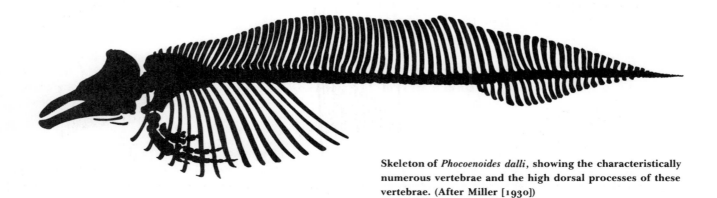

Skeleton of *Phocoenoides dalli*, showing the characteristically numerous vertebrae and the high dorsal processes of these vertebrae. (After Miller [1930])

capelin, jack mackerel and hake. Tomilin (1957) referred to various studies of the habits of this species (Cowan 1944; Scheffer 1953) and disputed those who felt it was primarily a fish eater: "We can hardly agree with this opinion [that Dall porpoises feed mostly on herring]: although Dall porpoises do consume gregarious fishes (capelin, herring and sardine), these are only marginal items in their diet, since the dentition of the Dall porpoise is rudimentary. In all probability, the main food of this species is cephalopod mollusks." In 1966, Ridgway wrote that it "appears to be a deep diver," and in a 1979 study, Treacy and Crawford confirmed this assumption: their preliminary findings indicate that many of the fish species consumed by Dall porpoises are bathypelagic; they are usually found between 3,000 and 10,000 feet below the surface, although some of them are known to approach the surface at night. (As we shall see, the predeliction of the prey species of Dall porpoises to approach the surface nocturnally might be an important factor in the death of thousands of porpoises.) Among the fish species found by Treacy and Crawford were lantern fishes and deepsea smelt, and in subsequent examinations of the stomach contents of Dall porpoises taken in the northwest Pacific, Boucher and colleagues (1980) discovered that the predominant food species was a lantern fish, which made up an average of 80 percent of the diet of the porpoises examined. In some areas, Dall porpoises eat mostly squid, while in other areas they consume deep-sea fishes. (Kellogg [1940] wrote that "its food consists almost entirely of squids, but occasionally small fish, such as the saddled blenny are eaten. The presence of this fish in the stomach contents suggests that this porpoise, when feeding, may nose around submerged rocks along the shore.") Hall (1981) observed that this species was "rarely seen in water less than 10 fathoms deep," and the NMML 1981 study stated that "Dall's porpoise are found over

the continental shelf adjacent to the slope and over deep oceanic waters (2500+ meters)."

The Dall porpoise is found only in the North Pacific, and is believed to be migratory in the western portion of its range—the waters of Japan—but perhaps not in the eastern North Pacific. There appear to be some inshore-offshore movements, but to date, these have not been resolved into a seasonal migratory pattern. Hall (1981) reported a population of "about 6,700 animals" in Prince William Sound, Alaska, in September 1977, and suggested that Dall porpoises (as well as other cetaceans), "habitually inhabit Prince William Sound during the summer season." In the eastern North Pacific, the species is found as far south as Ballenas Bay, Baja California, and northward to Alaska and the Pribilofs. Its range extends across the Bering Strait past Kamchatka and into Japanese waters as far south as Honshu.

Because of its offshore habitat and its poor record in captivity, little is known about the natural history of this species. Kasuya (1978) calculated the gestation period at 346 days (11.4 months) and the length of a newborn calf at about 39 inches (100 centimeters). The first recordings of the sounds of this species were made by Ridgway (1966), who reported that "the considerable acoustic activity . . . consisted entirely of repeated bursts of clicks similar in many ways to those produced . . . by *Phocoena phocoena.*" Subsequent studies in British Columbia have shown that "these animals produce high frequency (120–160 kHz), narrow-band, constant frequency echolocation pulses. This is the first report of such signals from any cetacean" (NMFS 1981). So far, there have been no whistles recorded from this species.

Attempts were made to keep Dall porpoises in captivity at Point Mugu, California, but the results were poor. Most of the animals died shortly after capture, and only one, a male named Marty, lived for

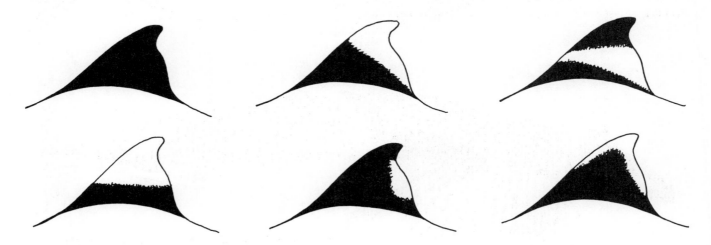

Variations in the coloration of the dorsal fins of Dall porpoises from California waters. (After Brownell [1966])

more than a few weeks. He was kept for over a year, and was observed to eat 28 to 30 pounds of fish per day, "twice the amount that a bottlenose of the same weight would eat" (Wood 1973). It is assumed that this substantial food requirement is related to the high metabolic rate of this unusually active animal. (Deborah Duffield, Marty's trainer at Point Mugu, said [quoted in Wood 1973] that she found it very difficult to get Marty to slow down.) All attempts discussed by Norris and Prescott (1961) to capture Dall porpoises resulted in the rapid death of the animal. They wrote: "Unlike most captive cetaceans with which we have worked, this individual battered us and the skiff with frenzied beatings of its tail. The same behavior has been exhibited by every Dall porpoise that has been captured. After taking two shallow breaths, the animal died, exhaling about half a pint of clear fluid from its blowhole." Another incident was described by the same authors, where "a mighty struggle ensued. After seven or eight minutes the animal arched its back, with head up in rigor, emitted a squeal, regurgitated about a bucketful of squid, and died." The same authors also commented on its "remarkable ability to disappear," sometimes remaining below for five minutes when pursued. Walker (1975) called the Dall porpoise "the most difficult to maintain of all the animals involved in the [Southern California] fishery" and attributed this to "the extreme power of the animal relative to its size." When the porpoises were finally captured, they would often dash wildly around the tank, crashing headlong into the walls or trying to dive through the bottom. Of the four specimens brought to the Navy Marine Bioscience Facility at Point Mugu, three died within a month, and the fourth (Marty) lived for over a year and a half. He was reported to be responsive but "nervous" to training, and he was taught to come to the trainer on signal, to wear a harness, and to allow himself to be hand-fed and handled (Ridgway 1966). In his examinations of the porpoises that died at Point Mugu, Ridgway wrote, "Dissections revealed the Dall porpoise to have a very large heart, very thin blubber and a small brain as compared to *Lagenorhynchus obliquidens* and *Tursiops truncatus.*" Green (1972) observed that "in the smaller, more active species, the relative heart size is much greater. The largest heart-to-body-weight ratio is reported for the Dall porpoise (*Phocoenoides dalli*), where the heart weight averages 1.3 per cent of the body weight." "The Dall porpoise," wrote Caldwell and Caldwell in 1972, "probably the most beautiful and active of all the well-known marine mammals, almost always dies very quickly in captivity."

In 1911, when R. C. Andrews erected the genus *Phocoenoides*, he differentiated it from *Phocoena* on the basis of its small teeth, pigmentation pattern, and the number of vertebrae. (Other species of porpoises have 60+ vertebrae, while *Phocoenoides* has over 90.) The taxonomy of this animal has always been troublesome, and it seems to have become even more complicated with the passage of time. (In 1938, Norman and Fraser referred to the species as *Phocoena dalli* and said that "it is known from the coast of Alaska, and it is very

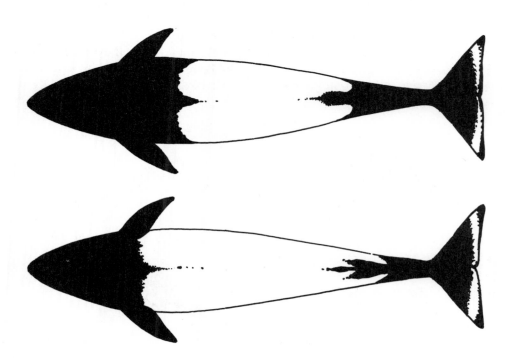

Comparison of ventral coloration of *Phocoenoides dalli* (top) and *Phocoenoides truei.*

rare.") Now that *Phocoenoides* is accepted as a valid species, it would seem that there should be no further taxonomic difficulties, but the presence of different-looking animals from different parts of the range has created a taxonomic tangle that has only recently become unsnarled.

When Andrews wrote of a new porpoise from Japan in 1911, he described an animal (and concurrently erected the genus *Phocoenoides*) that was different from *Phocoena dalli*, and he called it *Phocoenoides truei*. He separated the two on the basis of the obviously different white areas, the exaggerated caudal keels, and the different ventral markings. In the years that followed, there developed one of the most convoluted controversies in the already complicated taxonomy of the Delphinidae. It would further complicate matters to review the controversy here, but from year to year, from country to country, and from scientist to scientist, the synonomy of the species has been energetically debated. The particulars include pigmentation, range, integrated populations, and intermediate forms, and those involved in the controversy seem to have used the same material to support opposite sides of the argument. Simply stated, the discussions involve what may or may not be two species: *P. dalli*, with a white flank patch that begins approximately below the dorsal fin; and *P. truei*, whose white patch is much larger, and begins just behind the flippers. One would assume that the discovery of a *truei*-type fetus in the uterus of a *dalli*-type female would settle the argument in favor of conspecificity, but this apparently conclusive evidence notwithstanding, the argument continues. Nishiwaki (1972) distinguishes the two on the basis of "proportional skull measurements, dental formulae, vertebral formulae [but then he gives the same vertebral formula for both], distribution and adult size; these differences seem adequate to justify the establishment of a separate subspecies." Mitchell (1975b) wrote, "*P. truei* is probably a form of *P. dalli*, although further study is necessary." Fortunately, this "further study" has taken place. In 1978, Kasuya's study of *Phocoenoides* in Japanese waters was published, and in 1979, Morejohn's extensive survey on Dall porpoises in California waters was released. Most cetologists now agree that the *truei* form is restricted to the waters of northern Japan and the Kurile Islands, while the *dalli-type* is found from Japan north to the Bering Sea and into California waters. In a discussion of the color variations, Houck (1976) wrote, "The many examples of color intermediates plus the presence of a *truei*-type fetus from a *dalli*-type female indicate a considerable exchange of genetic material; therefore, the distinction of these two forms is below the species level." It can therefore be said that "True's porpoise"

is a color phase localized in Japanese waters (Rice 1977).

In the past, a Japanese drift gill-net fishery in the eastern North Pacific killed some 10,000 Dall porpoises annually (Ohsumi 1975). According to Ohsumi, "most cetaceans are lost at sea when they are caught by the salmon fisheries." There is also a directed market fishery for this species off the coast of Japan, and while the numbers do not approximate those killed "incidentally" to the salmon fishery, they are not insignificant. From January to April of 1972, 3,989 animals were caught off the Sanriku coast of Japan (Kasuya 1976). While one laments the slaughter of porpoises—especially those killed incidentally and then dumped overboard—from the viewpoint of science, this is one way to obtain a wide enough data base for population studies. (Kasuya was able to make a detailed study of *Phocoenoides* in Japan, but Morejohn wrote, "In the final analysis, nomenclatorial and systematic decisions will have to be made based on a larger series of specimens of both forms. . . .") There are, however, some aspects of the *truei-dalli* problem that have not been resolved by more intensive study, since the fishery has disclosed two more color variations: one that has the basic pattern of *truei*, but with spots on the white area, and an all-black variety. The black *Phocoenoides* could be just an anomalous melanistic specimen, were it not for the observation that it was seen swimming with another all-black animal, and in addition, it was found to be carrying an all-black fetus (Nishiwaki 1966). The spotted specimens do seem to be merely color variations, since individuals from any location will show a greater or lesser degree of spotting on the white area. The black Dall porpoises, however, seem to be a legitimate color variation, and they show up regularly along the Sanriku coast of Japan and elsewhere in the Northwest Pacific. Most publications nowadays recognize three types of *Phocoenoides*: the *truei*-type, with a very large white flank patch; the *dalli*-type, with a smaller patch; and the black type, with no patch at all. Morejohn (1979) describes several specimens that were grayish brown, but these are considered aberrant pigmentation patterns—like albinos—and not consistent color forms.

Besides man, the only predator that presents a threat to the swift Dall porpoise is the killer whale. In his examination of killer whale stomachs in the North Pacific, Rice (1978) found two instances of recognizable remains of Dall porpoises, and Morejohn (1979) includes photographs of what he calls "one that got away," where an animal (that did not get away from the scientists) was collected with "long raking tooth marks diagonally along both sides of the body. . . ." Morejohn has written that they "apparently swim too rapidly for sharks to attack them," and Matkin (1981) records the curious phenomenon of Dall porpoises swimming in the company of a school of killer whales. (It would appear that killer whales, like many other predators, send some sort of signal to prey species when they are actively hunting, and when they are not, the prey species appear to be unconcerned. The question, of course, is how quickly the predator can change its mind.)

In 1978, Leatherwood and Reeves wrote: "Of all the species [of porpoises and dolphins of the North Pacific], the Dall's porpoise may present the most serious conservation problem." Wilke and colleagues (1953) described the Japanese methods of hunting this species with harpoon and shotgun, but Kasuya (1978) reports that "in the recent years, the fishery at most of the places ceased the operation except for the

Sanriku coast." He records an annual catch of some 6,000 animals from the coastal population, which Nishiwaki (1972) has estimated at between 30,000 and 50,000 animals. Since this is also the stock that was involved in the western salmon fishery, "annual incidental catches in excess of 10,000 must have a major effect on this population" (Mitchell 1975a).

On the high seas of the North Pacific, quite a different situation now exists. As a signatory (with the United States and Canada) to the International Convention for the High Seas Fishery of the North Pacific (INPFC), Japan has been conducting a gill-net fishery for salmon since 1953. Some of this fishery occurred in Japanese as well as U.S. waters, but until the passage of the Marine Mammal Protection Act of 1972, the cetaceans and other marine mammals affected by it were not considered a problem. With the passage of

(A) *dalli* type

(B) *truei* type

(C) all-black form

Three color phases of *Phocoenoides*. The *dalli* type (A) shows the exaggerated dorsal and ventral keels of an adult male; the *truei* type (B) is an adult female, in which the keels are much less pronounced.

the MMPA, however, any marine mammals involved incidentally in fisheries within the U.S. Fisheries Conservation Zone (USFCZ) were subject to the controls of the act. (Mizue and Yoshida [1965] had estimated that some 10,000 Dall porpoises were killed annually in the pelagic salmon fishery in the northwest North Pacific, but the National Marine Mammal Laboratory staff wrote in 1981, "Since reporting of the take was on a volunteer basis . . . the authors estimated an equal amount might have been unreported by the catcher-boats, resulting in an estimate of up to 20,000 porpoise.") In 1977, an agreement was reached between Japan and the United States whereby Japanese salmon fishermen were granted an exemption from the MMPA, and they were permitted to fish within the zone. Although the USFCZ is well outside the 200-mile limit—its boundaries reach almost to Kamchatka—it was agreed to in principle by the signatories. According to a 1981 National Marine Fisheries Service report, "The chief motivation behind the Convention was the desire of the United States and Canada to minimize the interception of North American origin salmon by Japan in the North Pacific and Bering Sea. This Convention initiated the 'abstention principle' under which Japan agreed to abstain from fishing for salmon east of longitude 175°W in the Northeast Pacific and Bering Sea.") In return for the exemption, the Japanese agreed to implement an extensive research program to study the cetaceans involved in the fishery, and to attempt to determine how to reduce the incidental catch of Dall porpoises. (In 1975, Ohsumi had written: "Although many porpoises are incidentally caught by salmon gillnet fisheries annually, there is no evidence to show a decline in their population density. This means that the population size of cetaceans, mainly of Dall's porpoises, is remarkably large, and that the effect of incidental catches of cetaceans is negligible.")

In the Japanese salmon fishery each of the four "mother ships" has six scout boats and 37 catcher-boats, for a total of 172 boats. Each boat sets a total of 330 tans daily (a tan is a gill net of some 50 meters in length). The nets are made of 121- and 130-millimeter stretch mesh monofilament and extend from the surface to depths of 6 to 8 meters (20 to 26 feet). The nets are set at dusk and retrieved at dawn after a "soak time" of about ten hours. The total length of the nets set per night by the entire fleet is 2,838 kilometers (1,759 miles), and for the entire fishing season, which lasts from the beginning of June to the end of July, the total length of nets set is approximately three million tans, or 136,000 km (84,320 miles). This fishery has produced some 15,000 metric tons of salmon per year for 1978, 1979, and 1980, and

some 70 percent of this fishing takes place within the USFCZ. According to a U.S. environmental impact statement (NMFS 1981), "The total mothership fleet catch was valued at $73.9 million in 1978 or 15% of the value of Japan's entire salmon catch in that year. This represents about 0.75% of the value of Japan's total fisheries catch."

As part of the research program, the Japanese reported an incidental catch of Dall porpoises as follows: 449 in 1978, 682 in 1979, and 999 in 1980. U.S. scientists examined the Japanese data—and also served as observers aboard some of the Japanese fishing boats—and concluded that the 1980 catch was not 999 porpoises, but closer to 9,000 (NMML 1981).* The treaty came up for renegotiation in June 1981, and the alternatives were: (1) to grant Japan another incidental take permit; (2) to extend the current permit extension legislatively; and (3) to allow the treaty to expire, which would effectively end Japanese salmon fishing in the USFCZ. Alternative (3) would also end the International North Pacific Fisheries Convention, since the Japanese would terminate this agreement if they could no longer fish in our waters. "Beyond the impacts of the catch of salmon of North American origin which would result from the termination of the INPFC, impacts on the Dall porpoise would result from termination of research with the Japanese and the expected increase in incidental take outside U.S. jurisdiction" (NMFS 1981).

Although three years have passed since the initiation of the Japanese–U.S. research effort, such basic questions as the size of the Dall porpoise population in the North Pacific are still unresolved. Estimates range from 580,000 to 2.3 million, and with such a spread, it is almost impossible to determine what would be an "acceptable" number of porpoises that could be killed without harming the total population or its reproductive capacity. It is now believed that the earlier population estimates were too high, and the lower numbers—somewhere in the area of a half-million animals—are closer to the actual abundance (NMML 1981).

Still, the most important questions about this fishery have not been answered: Why do the porpoises become entangled in the nets, and how could this entanglement be reduced? Dall porpoises do not feed on salmon, so they are not hunting the fish that are trapped in the nets. It has been suggested that the type of netting used may not be "acoustically reflective" enough for the echolocating abilities of this particular

*All catch figures for porpoises in these studies are projections, based either on the number of animals taken aboard a "dedicated vessel" (i.e., with scientists aboard) or on the number extrapolated from occasional examinations of actual catcher boat operations.

species,* and they may simply blunder into the nets, oblivious to their presence. In the NMML report for 1981, the following statement appears: "For an animal to echolocate successfully, a perceivable amount of the pulse energy must be reflected by the target back to the porpoise ('target strength'). Because of the small diameter of the monofilament driftnet line, the target strength of the salmon gillnets may be very low, and consequently, the nets may be undetectable by the porpoise." In studies conducted of the feeding habits of the Dall porpoise (Treacy and Crawford 1979; Boucher et al. 1980), it was noted that the porpoises fed on deep-sea fish species that approached the surface at night. This means that the fish species—and therefore the Dall porpoises—are precisely in the area where the Japanese salmon fishermen are setting their nightly 1,759 miles of drift nets. Even in a great expanse of ocean like the North Pacific, when feeding porpoises find themselves in the same area as thousands of miles of nets probably undetectable to them, the porpoise mortality is going to be substantial.

Until we know what causes the porpoises to become entangled, we cannot prevent it from happening, short of closing down the Japanese salmon fishery. If the United States takes no action and simply lets the treaty expire, there is the distinct possibility that the Japanese will fish outside the USFCZ, and:

*Other marine mammals ensnared in these nets—but not in nearly comparable numbers—are the northern fur seal, the harbor porpoise, Pacific white-sided dolphin, killer whale, and Steller's sea lion. An estimated half-million seabirds (murres, shearwaters, puffins, fulmars, albatrosses, and petrels) are also entangled in the nets and drowned annually (King et al. 1975).

We would lose the ability to monitor incidental take in this fishery and influence efforts to reduce and eliminate it. Since we would no longer be able to obtain data on the extent of the problem, we would lose platforms of observation of the biology and ecology of this species, directed research on the incidental take of Dall porpoise by the National Marine Fisheries Service would probably cease.

It is possible that the total level of incidental take throughout the fishery would increase above the estimated 8,970 in 1980. Alternatively, total incidental take may decrease by closing the fishery to possible calving grounds of the Dall porpoise within the U.S. FCZ, areas of high density of pregnant females. [NMFS 1981]

In April 1981, a U.S. administrative law judge heard the arguments of both sides: the National Marine Fisheries Service, U.S. Marine Mammal Commission, and the Environmental Defense Fund on one side, and the Japanese Salmon Fisheries Cooperative Association on the other. Judge F. W. Vanderheyden ruled in favor of a three-year extension of the treaty permitting the Japanese to fish for salmon in the U.S. Fisheries Conservation Zone, with an incidental take of up to 5,500 Dall porpoises and 23 killer whales per year. The decision was obviously intended to reduce and control the porpoise mortality in the fishery, and a kill of 5,500 is better (for the porpoises) than a kill of 9,000. However, as long as people continue to think of these graceful little animals as pawns on the international fishing community's chessboard, it is the porpoises that will be expended in the interests of big business.

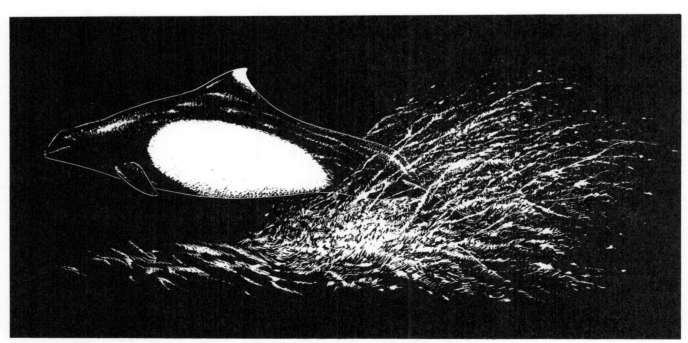

Dall porpoise (*Phocoenoides dallii*) **at speed, showing the characteristic "rooster tail" of spray.**

AFTERWORD

Now the various species of whales need some sort of popular comprehensive classification, if only an easy outline one for the present, hereafter to be filled in all its departments by subsequent laborers. As no better man advances to take this matter in hand, I hereupon offer my own poor endeavors. I promise nothing complete; because any human thing supposed to be complete, must, for that very reason infallibly be faulty. I shall not pretend to a minute anatomical description of various species—or in this place at least—to much of any description. My object here is simply to project the draught of a systemization of cetology. I am the architect, not the builder.

Finally: It was stated at the outset, that this system would not be here, and at once, perfected. You cannot but plainly see that I have kept my word. But now I leave my Cetological System standing thus unfinished, even as the great Cathedral of Cologne was left, with the crane still standing upon the top of the uncompleted tower. For small erections may be finished by their first architects; grand ones, true ones, ever leave the copestone to posterity. God keep me from ever completing anything. This whole book is but a draught— nay, but the draught of a draught. Oh Time, Strength, Cash, and Patience!

HERMAN MELVILLE
Moby-Dick

REFERENCES

Throughout the book the reader will encounter parenthetical references to authors—for example, (Alpers 1960). Even though this is intended to be a popular—that is, nontechnical—book, I have chosen to follow the style of scientific journals by incorporating the references into the text. In each case the date refers to the publication of the article or book and not to the date of the event discussed.

Each chapter in this volume is devoted to a single species of animal, and each list of references represents a working bibliography for that particular or related species. Many works are referred to frequently; these entries appear only in the bibliography and are not duplicated here in the individual lists of references.

INTRODUCTION

ALPERS, A. 1960. *Dolphins: The Myth and the Mammal.* Houghton Mifflin.

ANTRIM, J. E., and L. H. CORNELL. 1981. *Globicephala-Tursiops* hybrid. (Abstract) *Fourth Biennial Conf. Marine Mammals.* San Francisco.

ARISTOTLE. *Historia Animalium,* Book IX. 48, 631b. *The Works of Aristotle.* D'A. W. Thompson, trans. Oxford: Clarendon Press, 1910.

ASHLEY, C. W. 1942. *The Yankee Whaler.* Halcyon House.

BALCOMB, K. C., J. R. BORAN, R. W. OSBORNE, and N. J. HAENEL. 1980. Observations of killer whales (*Orcinus orca*) in greater Puget Sound, State of Washington. *Marine Mammal Commission Report.* MMC-78/13.

BATESON, G. 1974. Observations of a cetacean community. In J. McIntyre, ed., *Mind in the Waters,* pp. 146–64. Scribner's/ Sierra Club.

BEALE, T. 1839. *The Natural History of the Sperm Whale.* Voorst.

BEL'KOVICH, V. M., and A. V. YABLOKOV. 1963. The whale—an ultrasonic projector. *Yuchnyi Teknik* 3: 76–77.

BENNETT, F. D. 1840. *Narrative of a Whaling Voyage Around the Globe from the Year 1833 to 1836.* Richard Bentley.

BERZIN, A. A. 1972. *The Sperm Whale.* Israel Program for Scientific Translation, Jerusalem.

BIGG, M. A. 1981. An assessment of killer whale (*Orcinus orca*) stocks off Vancouver Island, British Columbia. *Sci. Com. Rep. Int. Whal. Commn.* SC/JN81/KW4.

BOWERS, C. A., and R. S. HENDERSON. 1972. Project Deep Ops: Deep object recovery with pilot and killer whales. *Naval Undersea Center TP 306.*

BROWNELL, R. L. 1964. Observations of odontocetes in central Californian waters. *Norsk Hvalfangst-tidende.* 55(3): 60–66.

BUNNELL, S. 1974. The evolution of cetacean intelligence. In J. McIntyre, ed., *Mind in the Waters,* pp. 52–59. Scribner's/ Sierra Club.

BUSNEL, R.-G., and J. F. FISH, eds. 1980. *Animal Sonar Systems.* Plenum.

CALDWELL, M. C., and D. K. CALDWELL. 1966. Epimeletic (caregiving) behavior in cetacea. In K. S. Norris, ed., *Whales, Dolphins and Porpoises,* pp. 755–89. University of California Press.

COCKRUM, E. L. 1962. *Introduction to Mammalogy.* Ronald Press.

COUSTEAU, J.-Y., and P. DIOLE. 1975. *Dolphins.* Doubleday.

DEFRAN, R. H., and K. PRYOR. 1980. The behavior and training of cetaceans in captivity. In L. M. Herman, ed., *Cetacean Behavior: Mechanisms and Functions,* pp. 319–62. John Wiley.

DEVINE, E., and M. CLARK. 1967. *The Dolphin Smile.* Macmillan.

EISLEY, L. 1978. *The Star Thrower.* Times Books.

ELLIS, R. 1980. *The Book of Whales.* Alfred A. Knopf.

EVANS, W. E. 1974. Radio-telemetric studies of two species of small odontocete cetaceans. In W. E. Schevill, ed., *The Whale Problem,* pp. 385–94. Harvard University Press.

FICHTELIUS, K.-E., and S. SJÖLANDER. 1972. *Smarter Than Man? Intelligence in Whales, Dolphins and Humans.* Ballantine Books.

FITCH, J. E., and R. L. BROWNELL. 1968. Fish otoliths in cetacean stomachs and their importance in interpreting feeding habits. *Jour. Fish. Res. Bd. Canada* 25(12): 2561–74.

FRASER, F. C. 1940. Three anomalous dolphins from Blacksod Bay, Ireland. *Proc. Royal Irish Acad.* 45(B): 413–55.

GIHR, M., and G. PILLERI. 1979. Interspecific body length–body weight ratio and body weight–brain weight ratio in cetacea. *Invest. on Cetacea* 10: 245–53.

GILBERT, P. W., B. IRVINE, and F. H. MARTINI. 1971. Shark-porpoise behavioral interactions. *American Zoologist* 11: 80.

GREEN, R. F., S. H. RIDGWAY, and W. E. EVANS. 1979. Functional and descriptive anatomy of the bottlenosed dolphin nasolaryngeal system with special reference to the musculature associated with sound production. In R.-G. Busnel and J. G. Fish, eds., *Animal Sonar Systems,* pp. 199–238. Plenum.

HEEZEN, B. C. 1957. Whales entangled in deep-sea cables. *Norsk Hvalfangst-tidende* 46(12): 665–81.

HEIMLICH, S. L., J. R. BORAN, K. C. BALCOMB, N. J., HAENEL, and R. W. OSBORNE. 1980. Surfacing associations of *Orcinus orca.* (Abstract) *Orca Symposium 1980.* Seattle.

HERMAN, L. M. 1980. Cognitive characteristics of dolphins. In L. M. Herman, ed., *Behavior of Cetaceans: Mechanisms and Functions,* pp. 363–429. John Wiley.

———, and W. N. TAVOLGA. 1980. The communication systems of cetaceans. In L. M. Herman, ed., *Cetacean Behavior: Mechanisms and Functions,* pp. 149–209. John Wiley.

HERTEL, H. 1969. Hydrodynamics of swimming and wave-riding dolphins. In H. T. Andersen, ed., *The Biology of Marine Mammals,* pp. 31–63. Academic Press.

HOESE, H. D. 1971. Dolphin feeding out of water in a salt marsh. *Jour. Mammal.* 52(1): 222–23.

HOLLIEN, H., P. HOLLIEN, D. K. CALDWELL, and M. C. CALDWELL. 1976. Sound production in the Atlantic bottlenosed dolphin (*Tursiops truncatus*). *Cetology* 26.

INTERNATIONAL WHALING COMMISSION. 1977. List of smaller cetaceans recognized. *Appendix 1*, 27: 30–31.

JACOBS, M. 1974. The whale brain: Input and behavior. In J. McIntyre, ed., *Mind in the Waters*, pp. 78–83. Scribner's/ Sierra Club.

JERISON, H. J. 1978. Brain and intelligence in whales. In S. Frost, ed., *Whales and Whaling*. Vol. II, pp. 161–97. Australian Government Publishing Service.

———. 1980. The nature of intelligence. Paper presented at the IWC Conference on Cetacean Behavior, Intelligence, and the Ethics of Killing Cetaceans, Washington, D.C., April 28–May 1, 1980. 12 pp. mimeo.

LAYNE, J. N., and D. K. CALDWELL. 1964. Behavior of the Amazon dolphin (*Inia geoffrensis*) in captivity. *Zoologica* 44(2): 81–108.

LEATHERWOOD, J. S., W. F. PERRIN, R. L. GARVIE, and J. C. LA GRANGE. 1973. Observations of sharks attacking porpoises (*Stenella* spp. and *Delphinus* cf. *D. delphis*). *Southwest Fisheries Center (NMFS)*. NUC TN 908.

LILLY, J. C. 1961. *Man and Dolphin*. Doubleday.

———. 1978. *Communication Between Man and Dolphin*. Crown.

MCBRIDE, A. F. 1940. Meet Mr. Porpoise. *Nat. Hist.* 45: 16–29.

———, and D. O. HEBB. 1948. Behavior of the captive bottle-nose dolphin, *Tursiops truncatus*. *Jour. Comp. and Physiol. Psych.* 41: 111–23.

MCCORMICK, J. G., E. G. WEVER, S. H. RIDGWAY, and J. PALIN. 1979. Sound reception in the porpoise as it is related to echolocation. In R.-G. Busnel and J. G. Fish, eds., *Animal Sonar Systems*. pp. 449–67. Plenum.

MITCHELL, E. D. 1975. Review of biology and fisheries for small cetaceans. *Jour. Fish. Res. Bd. Canada* 32(7): 889–983.

MIYAZAKI, N. 1980. Catch records of cetaceans off the coast of the Kii Peninsula. *Mem. Nat. Sci. Mus.* 13: 69–82.

MORGANE, P. 1974. The whale brain: The anatomical basis of intelligence. In J. McIntyre, ed., *Mind in the Waters*, pp. 84–93. Scribner's/Sierra Club.

———. 1978. Whale brains and their meaning for intelligence. In S. Frost, ed., *Whales and Whaling*. Vol. II, pp. 199–217. Australian Government Publishing Service.

NEMOTO, T., and K. NASU. 1963. Stones and other aliens in the stomachs of sperm whales in the Bering Sea. *Sci. Rep. Whales Res. Inst.* 17: 83–91.

NISHIWAKI, M., and K. NORRIS. 1966. A new genus *Peponocephala*. *Sci. Rep. Whales Res. Inst.* 20: 95–100.

NORRIS, K. S. 1964. Some problems of echolocation in cetaceans. In W. N. Tavolga, ed., *Marine Bio-Acoustics*, pp. 317–36. Pergamon Press.

———. 1969. The echolocation of marine mammals. In H. T. Andersen, ed., *The Biology of Marine Mammals*, pp. 425–75. Academic Press.

———. 1974. *The Porpoise Watcher*. W. W. Norton.

———. 1979. Peripheral sound processing in odontocetes. In R.-G. Busnel and J. G. Fish, eds., *Animal Sonar Systems*, pp. 495–509. Plenum.

———, and T. P. DOHL. 1980a. Behavior of Hawaiian spinner dolphin, *Stenella longirostris*. *Fish. Bull.* 77(4): 821–49.

———. 1980b. The structure and function of cetacean schools. In L. M. Herman, ed., *Cetacean Behavior: Mechanisms and Functions*, pp. 211–61. John Wiley.

NORRIS, K. S., and G. W. HARVEY. 1972. A theory for the function of the spermaceti organ of the sperm whale (*Physeter catodon*). In S. R. Galler, K. Schmidt-Koenig, G. J. Jacobs, and R. E. Belleville, eds., *Animal Orientation and Navigation*, pp. 397–417. NASA.

NORRIS, K. S., and B. MØHL, 1981. Do odontocetes debilitate their prey acoustically? (Abstract) *Fourth Biennial Conf. Biol. Marine Mammals*. San Francisco.

NORRIS, K. S., and J. H. PRESCOTT. 1961. Observations on Pacific cetaceans of Californian and Mexican waters. *Univ. Calif. Publ. Zool.* 63(4): 291–402.

NORRIS, K. S., K. J. DORMER, J. PEGG, and G. J. LIESE. 1971. The mechanism of sound production and air recycling in porpoises: A preliminary report. *Proc. Eighth Ann. Conf. Biol. Sonar and Diving Mammals*, pp. 113–29. Stanford Res. Inst.

PAYNE, R. 1974. A playground for whales—but for how long? *Animal Kingdom* 77(2): 7–12.

POPPER, A. N. 1979. Behavioral measures of odontocete hearing. In R.-G. Busnel and J. G. Fish, eds., *Animal Sonar Systems*, pp. 469–81. Plenum.

PRESCOTT, J. H. 1981. Clever Hans: Training the trainers, or the potential for misinterpreting the results of dolphin research. In T. A. Sebeok and R. Rosenthal, eds., *The Clever Hans Phenomenon: Communication with Horses, Whales, Apes, and People*, pp. 130–36. Ann. N.Y. Acad. Sci. 364.

PRYOR, K. W. 1973. Behavior and learning in porpoises and whales. *Naturwissenschaften* 60: 412–20.

PRYOR, K. 1975. *Lads Before the Wind*. Harper & Row.

———. 1981. Why porpoise trainers are not dolphin lovers: Real and false communication in the operant setting. In T. A. Sebeok and R. Rosenthal, eds., *The Clever Hans Phenomenon: Communication with Horses, Whales, Apes, and People*, pp. 137–43. Ann. N.Y. Acad. Sci. 364.

———, and K. S. NORRIS. 1978. The tuna/porpoise problem: Behavioral aspects. *Oceanus* 21(2): 31–37.

REED, D. C. 1981. *Notes from an Underwater Zoo*. Dial Press.

RICE, D. W. 1977. *A List of the Marine Mammals of the World*. NOAA Technical Report NMFS SSRF-711.

RIDGWAY, S. H. 1966. Studies on diving depth and duration in *Tursiops truncatus. Proc. Third Ann. Conf. Biol. Sonar and Diving Mammals*, pp. 151–58. Stanford Res. Inst.

——, and K. BENIRSCHKE (eds.). 1977. *Breeding Dolphins: Present Status, Suggestions for the Future.* Marine Mammal Commission Report No. MMC-76/07.

ROBSON, F. 1976. *Thinking Dolphins, Talking Whales.* A. H. & A. W. Reed.

SAAYMAN, G. S., D. BOWER, and C. K. TAYLER. 1972. Social organization of inshore dolphins (*Tursiops aduncus* and *Sousa*) in the Indian Ocean. *Koedoe* 15: 1–24.

SCAMMON, C. M. 1874. *The Marine Mammals of the Northwestern Coast of North America; Together with an Account of the American Whale-Fishery.* Carmany, San Francisco, and Putnam's, N. Y.

SCHEVILL, W. E. 1964. Underwater sounds of cetaceans. In W. N. Tavolga, ed., *Marine Bio-Acoustics*, pp. 307–16. Pergamon Press.

——, and B. LAWRENCE. 1956. Food-finding by a captive porpoise, *Tursiops truncatus. Breviora* 53: 1–15.

SCORESBY, W. 1820. *An Account of the Arctic Regions with History and a Description of the Northern Whale Fishery.* Archibald Constable, Edinburgh. (1969 ed., David & Charles.)

STUNTZ, W. E. 1980. Variation in age structure of the incidental kill of spotted dolphins, *Stenella attenuata*, in the U.S. tropical purse-seine fishery. *Southwest Fisheries Center (NMFS) Admin. Rep.* LJ-80-06.

TAVOLGA, M. C. 1966. Behavior of the bottlenose dolphin (*Tursiops truncatus*): Social interactions of a captive colony. In K. S. Norris, ed., *Whales, Dolphins and Porpoises*, pp. 718–30. Univ. of California Press.

——, and F. S. ESSEPIAN. 1957. The behavior of the bottlenosed dolphin (*Tursiops truncatus*): Mating, pregnancy, parturition, and mother-infant behavior. *Zoologica* 42: 11–31.

TAVOLGA, W. N., ed. 1964. *Marine Bio-Acoustics.* Pergamon Press.

——. 1967. *Marine Bio-Acoustics. Vol. II.* Pergamon Press.

WELLS, R. S., A. B. IRVINE, and M. D. SCOTT. 1980. The social ecology of inshore odontocetes. In L. M. Herman, ed., *Cetacean Behavior: Mechanisms and Functions*, pp. 263–17. John Wiley.

WOOD, F. G. 1953. Underwater sound production and concurrent behavior of captive porpoises, *Tursiops truncatus* and *Stenella plagiodon. Bull. Mar. Sci. Gulf and Caribbean* 3: 120–33.

——. 1977. Birth of porpoises at Marineland, Florida, 1939 to 1969, and comments on problems involved in captive breeding of small cetacea. In S. H. Ridgway and K. Benirschke, eds., *Breeding Dolphins: Present Status and Suggestions for the Future*, pp. 47–60. Marine Mammal Commission Report No. MMC-76/07.

——, and W. E. EVANS. 1980. Adaptiveness and ecology of echolocation in toothed whales. In R.-G. Busnel and J. F. Fish, eds., *Animal Sonar Systems*, pp. 381–425. Plenum.

WOOD, F. G., D. K. CALDWELL, and M. C. CALDWELL. 1970. Behavioral interactions between porpoises and sharks. *Invest. on Cetacea* 2: 264–77.

WÜRSIG, B., and M. WÜRSIG. 1979. Behavior and ecology of the bottlenose dolphin, *Tursiops truncatus*, in the South Atlantic. *Fish. Bull.* 77(2): 399–412.

——. 1980. Behavior and ecology of the dusky dolphin, *Lagenorhynchus obscurus*, in the South Atlantic. *Fish. Bull.* 77(4): 871–90.

WÜRSIG, M., B. WÜRSIG, and J. F. MERMOZ. 1977. Desplaziamentos, comportamiento general y un varamiento de la marsopa espinosa, *Phocoena spinipinnis*, en el Golfo San Jose (Chubut, Argentina). *Physis* 36(92): 71–79.

BOUTU (AMAZON DOLPHIN)

ALLEN, R., and W. T. NEILL. 1957. White whales of the Amazon. *Nat. Hist.* 66(6): 324–29.

BUSNEL, R.-G. 1973. Symbiotic relationship between man and dolphins. *Trans. N.Y. Acad. Sci.* Ser. 2, 35(2): 112–31.

CALDWELL, M. C., and D. K. CALDWELL. 1969a. The ugly dolphin. *Sea Frontiers* 15(5): 308–14.

——. 1969b. More about . . . the ugly dolphin. *Sea Frontiers* 15(6): 349–55.

DEFRAN, R. F., and K. W. PRYOR. 1980. The behavior and training of cetaceans in captivity. In L. H. Herman, ed., *Cetacean Behavior: Mechanisms and Functions*, pp. 319–62. John Wiley.

GIHR, M., and G. PILLERI. 1979. Interspecific body length–body weight ratio and body weight–brain weight ratio in Cetacea. *Invest. on Cetacea* 10: 245–53.

HERALD, E. S. 1967. Boutu and tookashee—Amazon dolphins. *Pacific Discovery* 20(1): 2–9.

——. 1969. Aquatic mammals at Steinhart Aquarium. *Pacific Discovery* 22(6): 26–30.

HUFFMAN, W. E. 1970. Notes on the first captive conception and live birth of an Amazon dolphin in North America. *Underwater Naturalist* 6(3): 9–11.

LAMB, F. B. 1954. The fisherman's porpoise. *Natural History* 63(5): 231–32.

LAYNE, J. N. 1958. Observations on the freshwater porpoises in the upper Amazon. *Jour. Mammal.* 39(1): 1–22.

——, and D. K. CALDWELL. 1964. Behavior of the Amazon dolphin (*Inia geoffrensis*) in captivity. *Zoologica* 44(2): 81–108.

NORRIS, K. S., G. W. HARVEY, L. A. BURZELL, and T. D. KRISHNA KARTHA. 1972. Sound production in the freshwater porpoises *Sotalia* cf. *fluviatilis* Gervais and Deville, and *Inia geoffrensis* Blainville, in the Rio Negro, Brazil. *Invest. on Cetacea* 4: 251–62.

PILLERI, G. 1969. On the behaviour of the Amazon dolphin, *Inia geoffrensis* in Beni (Bolivia). *Rev. Suisse Zool.* 76(4):57–91.

————. 1979. Observations on the ecology of *Inia geoffrensis* from the Río Apure, Venezuela. *Invest. on Cetacea* 10: 137–42.

————, and M. GIHR. 1976. The manus of the Amazon dolphin, *Inia geoffrensis* (de Blainville, 1817), and remarks concerning so-called "polydactyly." *Invest. on Cetacea* 7: 129–37.

————. 1977. Observations on the Bolivian (*Inia boliviensis* d'Orbigny, 1834) and the Amazon bufeo (*Inia geoffrensis* de Blainville, 1817) with description of a new subspecies (*Inia geoffrensis humboldtiana*). *Invest. on Cetacea* 8: 11–76.

————. 1980. Additional considerations on the taxonomy of the genus *Inia*. *Invest. on Cetacea* 11: 15–24.

————, and C. KRAUS. 1980. Play behaviour in the Indus and Orinoco dolphin (*Platanista indi* and *Inia geoffrensis*). *Invest. on Cetacea* 11: 57–108.

PILLERI, G., K. ZBINDEN, and C. KRAUS. 1979. The sonar field of *Inia geoffrensis*. *Invest. on Cetacea* 10: 157–76.

SANDERSON, I. T. 1956. *Follow the Whale*. Little, Brown.

WATERMAN, S. 1967. Dolphin collecting the Amazon. *Expl. Jour.* 45(4): 270–77.

WOOD, F. G., and W. E. EVANS. 1980. Adaptiveness and ecology of echolocation in toothed whales. In R.-G. Busnel and J. F. Fish eds., *Animal Sonar Systems*, pp. 381–425. Plenum.

FRANCISCANA (LA PLATA DOLPHIN)

BROWNELL, R. L. 1975. Progress report on the biology of the franciscana dolphin, *Pontoporia blainvillei*, in Uruguayan waters. *Jour. Fish. Res. Bd. Canada* 32(7): 1073–78.

————, and R. PRADERI. 1976. Present research and conservation problems with the franciscana, *Pontoporia blainvillei* in Uruguayan waters. *FAO, Bergen, Norway.* ACMRR/MM/SC/23.

GIHR, M., G. PILLERI, and K. ZHOU. 1979. Cephalization of the Chinese River Dolophin *Lipotes vexillifer* (Platanistidea, Lipotidae). *Invest. of Cetacea* 10: 217–74.

KASUYA, T., and R. L. BROWNELL. 1979. Age determination, reproduction, and growth of the franciscana dolphin *Pontoporia blainvillei*. *Sci. Rep. Whales Res. Inst.* 31: 45–67.

PILLERI, G. 1971a. On the La Plata dolphin, *Pontoporia blainvillei* off the Uraguayan coast. *Invest. on Cetacea* 3(1): 59–68.

————. 1971b. Epimeletic (nurturant) behavior by the La Plata dolphin *Pontoporia blainvillei*. *Invest. on Cetacea* 3(1): 74–76.

————, and M. GIHR. 1971. Brain–body weight ratio in *Pontoporia blainvillei*. *Invest. on Cetacea* 3(1): 69–73.

VAN ERP, I. 1969. In quest of the La Plata dolphin. *Pacific Discovery* 22(2): 18–24.

CHINESE RIVER DOLPHIN (BAIJI)

ALLEN, G. M. 1938. *The Mammals of China and Mongolia*. Natural History of Central Asia, 11(1). Chapter 9: "Cetacea." American Museum of Natural History.

BROWNELL, R. L. 1976. Conservation of the white-flag dolphin, *Lipotes vexillifer*. Scientific Consultation on Marine Mammals. ACMRR/MM/SC/24.

————, and E. S. HERALD. 1972. *Lipotes vexillifer*. Mammalian Species No. 10. American Society of Mammalogists.

CHEN PEIXUN. 1981. *Lipotes* research in the People's Republic of China. *Rep. Int. Whal. Comm.* 31: 475–78.

————, LIU PEILIN, LIU RENJUN, LIN KEJIE, and G. PILLERI. 1979. Distribution, ecology, behaviour and conservation of the dolphins of the middle reaches of Changjiang (Yangtze) River (Wuhan-Yueyang). *Invest. on Cetacea* 10: 87–103.

GIHR, M., and G. PILLERI. 1979. Interspecific body length–body weight ratio and body weight–brain weight ratio in Cetacea. *Invest. on Cetacea* 10: 245–53.

————, and K. ZHOU. 1979. Cephalization in the Chinese river dolphin *Lipotes vexillifer* (Platanistoidea, Lipotidae). *Invest. on Cetacea* 10: 257–74.

HINTON, M. A. C. 1936. Some interesting points in the anatomy of the freshwater dolphin *Lipotes* and its allies. *Proc. Linn. Soc. London* 148(3): 183–85.

————, and W. P. PYCRAFT. 1922. Preliminary note on the affinities of the genus *Lipotes*. *Ann. Mag. Nat. Hist.* 9(10): 232–234.

HOY, C. M. 1923. The "white-flag" dolphin of the Tung Ting Lake. *China Jour. Sci. and Arts* 1: 154–57.

MILLER, G. S. 1918. A new river dolphin from China. *Smithsonian Miscell. Coll.* 68: 1–12.

PILLERI, G. 1979. The Chinese river dolphin (*Lipotes vexillifer*) in poetry, literature and legend. *Invest. on Cetacea* 10: 335–49.

————, and M. GIHR. 1976. The current status of research on the Chinese river dolphin (*Lipotes vexillifer* Miller 1918). *Invest. on Cetacea* 7: 149–60.

POPE, C. H. 1932. Collecting in northern and central China. In R. C. Andrews, *The Conquest of Central Asia*. p. 475 ("A rare river dolphin.") Natural History of Central Asia, Vol. I. American Museum of Natural History.

RED DATA BOOK. 1976. *Lipotes vexillifer*. Mammalia 11.92.3.1. IUCN.

VAN BREE, P. J. H., and P. E. PURVES. 1975. On the dimensions of three skulls of the species of dolphin *Lipotes vexillifer* Miller, 1918 (Cetacea, Platanistoidea, Iniidae). *Beaufortia* 25(308): 1–5.

YEH, S. and G. PILLERI. 1980. The acoustic properties of the melon of the Chinese river dolphin—Biological transmission aperture, and considerations of the sonar field of *Lipotes vexillifer*. *Invest. on Cetacea* 11: 189–201.

ZHOU, K., G. PILLERI, and LI YUEMIN. 1979. Observations on the "Baiji" (*Lipotes vexillifer*) and the finless porpoise (*Neophocaena asiaeorientalis*) in the Changjing (Yangtze) River between Nanjing and Taiyandzhou, with remarks on some physiological adaptations of the Baiji to its environment. *Invest. on Cetacea* 10: 109–20.

GANGES RIVER DOLPHIN AND INDUS RIVER DOLPHIN

AMINUL HAQUE, A. K. M. 1976. Comments on the abundance of the Ganges susu, *Platanista gangetica,* and the effects of the Farakka barrage on its population. *Scientific Consultation on Marine Mammals* ACMRR/MM/SC/132

————, M. NISHIWAKI, T. KASUYA, and T. TOBAYAMA. 1977. Observations on the behavior and other biological aspects of the Ganges susu, *Platanista gangetica. Sci. Rep. Whales Res. Inst.* 29: 87–94.

ANDERSEN, S., and G. PILLERI. 1970. Audible sound production in captive *Platanista gangetica. Invest. on Cetacea* 2: 83–86.

ANDERSON, J. 1878. *Anatomical and zoological researches comprising an account of the zoological results of the two expeditions to Western Yunnan in 1868 and 1875; and a monograph of the two cetacean genera,* Platanista *and* Orcella. London.

ARVY, L., and G. PILLERI. 1970. The tongue of *Platanista gangetica* and remarks on the cetacean tongue. *Invest. on Cetacea* 2: 75–77.

BEDDARD, F. 1900. *A Book of Whales.* John Murray.

BLYTH, E. 1859. On the great rorqual of the Indian Ocean, with notices of other cetals, and of the sirenia or marine pachyderms. *J. Asiat. Soc. Bengal* 28: 481–98.

CORNELL, L. H., and E. D. ASPER. 1977. A census of captive marine mammals in North America. *International Zoo Yearbook* 18: 220–24.

DRAL, A. D. G. 1975. The "atrophic" eye of *Platanista gangetica. Aquatic Mammals* 3(1): 1–4.

GIHR, M., C. KRAUS, and G. PILLERI. 1972. Meteorological influences on the daily feeding rate of the Indus dolphin, *Platanista indi,* in captivity. *Invest. on Cetacea* 4: 33–43.

HARRISON, R. J. 1972. Reproduction and reproductive organs in *Platanista indi* and *Platanista gangetica. Invest. on Cetacea* 4: 71–82.

HERALD, E. S. 1969. Field and aquarium study of the blind river dolphin *(Platanista gangetica). Naval Undersea Research and Development Center Technical Paper.* 153.

————, R. L. BROWNELL, F. L. FRYE, E. J. MORRIS, W. E. EVANS, and A. B. SCOTT. 1969. Blind river dolphin: First side-swimming cetacean. *Science* 166: 1408–10.

JONES, S. 1976a. The present status of the Gangetic susu, *Platanista gangetica* (Roxburgh). *FAO Bergen, Norway.* ACMRR/MM/SC/15.

————. 1976b. A suggestion for the introduction of the Indus susu and the Gangetic susu into new sectors and river systems in the Indian subcontinent and the establishment of sanctuaries for them. *FAO, Bergen, Norway.* ACMRR/MM/EC/16.

KASUYA, T. 1972. Some information on the growth of the Ganges River dolphin with a comment on the Indus Dolphin. *Sci. Rep. Whales Res. Inst.* 24: 87–108.

————, and A. K. M. AMINUL HAQUE. 1972. Some information on distribution and seasonal movement of the Ganges dolphin. *Sci. Rep. Whales Res. Inst.* 24: 109–15.

————. 1976. Comments on the abundance and distribution of the Ganges susu, *Platanista gangetica,* and the effects of the Farakka barrage on its population. *FAO, Bergen, Norway.* ACMRR/MM/SC/132.

KASUYA, T., and M. NISHIWAKI. 1975. Recent status of the population of Indus dolphin. *Sci. Rep. Whales Res. Inst.* 27: 81–94.

KRAUS, C., and M. GIHR. 1972. On the research history and iconographic representation of the Indian river dolphin *Platanista gangetica* Roxburgh 1801. *Invest. on Cetacea* 4: 13–22.

MITCHELL, E. D. 1975. *Porpoise, Dolphin and Small Whale Fisheries of the World: Status and Problems.* IUCN Monograph No. 3. Morges, Switzerland.

NISHIWAKI, M. 1972. General biology. In S. H. Ridgway, ed., *Mammals of the Sea: Biology and Medicine.* Thomas. 3–204.

NORMAN, J. R., and F. C. FRASER. 1938. *Giant Fishes, Whales and Dolphins.* W. W. Norton.

NORRIS, K. S. 1964. Some problems of echolocation in cetaceans. In W. N. Tavolga, ed., *Marine Bio-Acoustics.* Pergamon Press. 317–36.

OWEN, R. 1866. On some Indian cetacea collected by Walter Elliot, Esq. *Trans. Zool. Soc. London* 6: 17–47.

PILLERI, G. 1970a. Observations on the behaviour of *Platanista gangetica* in the Indus and Brahmaputra River. *Invest. on Cetacea* 2: 27–60.

————. 1970b. The capture and transport to Switzerland of two live *Platanista gangetica* from the Indus River. *Invest. on Cetacea* 2: 61–68.

————. 1971. Observation on the copulatory behaviour of the Gangetic dolphin, *Platanista gangetica. Invest. on Cetacea* 3(1): 31–33.

————. 1972a. Field observations carried out on the Indus dolphin *Platanista indi* in the winter of 1972. *Invest. on Cetacea* 4: 23–29.

————. 1972b. Transport of a live *Platanista indi* from the Indus to Berne. *Invest. on Cetacea* 4: 30–31.

————. 1975. *Die Gehlimnisse de blinden Delphine.* Hallwag Verlag, Bern und Stuttgart.

————. 1978. William Roxburgh (1751–1815), Heinrich Julius Lebeck (?–1801) and the discovery of the Ganges Dolphin (*Platanista gangetica* Roxburgh 1801). *Invest. on Cetacea* 9: 11–21.

————. 1979. Sonar field patterns in cetaceans, feeding behavior and the functional significance of the pterygoschisis. *Invest. on Cetacea* 10: 147–55.

————, and M. GIHR. 1970. Brain-body weight ratio of *Platanista gangetica. Invest. on Cetacea* 2: 79–82.

————. 1971. Differences observed in the skulls of *Platanista gangetica* (Roxburgh 1801) and *indi* (Blyth 1859). *Invest. on Cetacea* 3(1): 13–21.

————. 1976. The function-and osteology of the manus of *Platanista gangetica* and *Platanista indi*. *Invest. on Cetacea* 4: 109–18.

————. 1977. Neotype for *Platanista indi* Blyth, 1859. *Invest. on Cetacea* 8: 77–81.

PILLERI, G., and N. U. BHATTI. 1978. Status of the Indus dolphin population (*Platanista indi* Blyth, 1859) between Guddu Bridge and Hyderabad in 1978. *Invest. on Cetacea.* 9: 25–38.

————. 1980. Status of the Indus dolphin population (*Platanista indi* Blyth, 1859) between Sukkur and Taunsa Barrages. *Invest. on Cetacea* 11: 205–14.

PILLERI, G., and O. PILLERI. 1979. Precarious situation of the dolphin population (*Platanista indi* Blyth 1859) in the Punjab, Upstream of the Taunsa Barrage, Indus River. *Invest. on Cetacea* 10: 121–27.

PILLERI, G., and K. ZBINDEN. 1973. Size and ecology of the dolphin population (*Platanista indi*) between the Sukkur and Guddu barrages, Indus River. *Invest. on Cetacea* 5: 59–70.

PILLERI, G., M. GIHR, and C. KRAUS. 1970. Feeding behavior of the Gangetic dolphin, *Platanista gangetica,* in captivity. *Invest. on Cetacea* 2: 69–73.

————. 1971. Further observations on the behaviour of *Platanista indi* in captivity. *Invest. on Cetacea* 3(1): 34–42.

————. 1980. Play behaviour in the Indus and Orinoco dolphins (*Platanista indi* and *Inia geoffrensis*). *Invest. on Cetacea* 11: 57–108 + 15 pls.

PILLERI, G., C. KRAUS, and M. GIHR. 1971. Physical analysis of the sounds emitted by *Platanista indi*. *Invest. on Cetacea* 3(1): 22–30.

PILLERI, G., M. GIHR, P. E. PURVES, K. ZBINDEN, and C. KRAUS. 1976. On the behavior, bioacoustics and functional morphology of the Indus River dolphin (*Platanista indi,* Blyth, 1859). *Invest. on Cetacea* 6: 14–69.

PILLERI, G., K. ZBINDEN, M. GIHR, and C. KRAUS. 1976. Sonar clicks, directionality of emission field and echolocating behaviour of the Indus dolphin (*Platanista indi* Blyth, 1859). *Invest. on Cetacea* 7: 13–44.

PURVES, P. E., and G. PILLERI. 1973. Observations on the ear, nose, throat and eye of *Platanista indi*. *Invest. on Cetacea* 5: 13–58.

RED DATA BOOK. 1976. *Platanista indi*. Mammalia. 11.92.1.1. IUCN.

RICE, D. W. 1967. Cetaceans. In S. Anderson and J. K. Jones, eds. *Recent Mammals of the World: A Synopsis of Families*. Ronald Press, 291–324.

————. 1977. *A List of the Marine Mammals of the World*. NOAA Technical Report NMFS SSRF—711: 1–15.

————, and V. B. SCHEFFER. 1968. *A List of the Marine Mammals of the World*. U.S. Fish and Wildlife Service. Special Scientific Report No. 579.

ROXBURGH, W. 1801. An account of a new species of *Delphinus,* an inhabitant of the Ganges. *Asiatick Researches* 7: 170–174.

TAYLOR, G. T. 1965. Water, history and the Indus plain. *Natural History* 74(5): 40–49.

ZBINDEN, K., C. KRAUS, and G. PILLERI. 1978. Auditory response of *Platanisita indi* (Blyth 1859). *Invest. on Cetacea* 9: 41–64.

ROUGH-TOOTHED DOLPHIN

BALCOMB, K. C. 1980. WA rough-toothed dolphin stranding. *Cetus.* 2(5): 8.

CALDWELL, D. K., M. C. CALDWELL, W. F. RATHJEN, and J. R. SULLIVAN. 1971. Cetaceans from the Lesser Antillean island of St. Vincent. *Fish. Bull.* 69(2): 303–12.

DEFRAN, R. F., and K. W. PRYOR. 1980. The behavior and training of cetaceans in captivity. In L. H. Herman, ed., *Cetacean Behavior: Mechanisms and Functions*, pp. 319–62. John Wiley.

DOHL, T. P., K. S. NORRIS, and I. KANG. 1974. A porpoise hybrid: *Tursiops × Steno. Jour. Mammal* 55(1): 217–21.

DUGUY, R., and D. ROBINEAU. 1973. Cétacés et phoques des côtes de France. *Ann. Soc. Sci. Nat. de la Charente-Maritime* (Supplement, juin 1973): 93 pp.

ELLERMAN, J. R., and T. C. S. MORRISON-SCOTT. 1951. Checklist of palearctic and Indian mammals 1758 to 1946. *Bull. Brit. Mus. (Nat. Hist.)* 810 pp.

FRASER, F. C. 1966. Comments on Delphinoidea. In K. S. Norris, ed., *Whales, Dolphins and Porpoises*, pp. 7–31. University of California Press.

HALL, E. R., and K. R. KELSON. 1959. *The Mammals of North America*. Ronald Press.

HAMILTON, R. 1835. Mammalia. Whales & c. In W. Jardine, ed., *The Naturalist's Library*, Vol. 26. London.

HIROSAKI, Y., M. HONDA, and T. KINUTA. 1981. On the three hybrids between *Tursiops truncatus* and *Grampus griseus. Jour. Japanese Assoc. Zool. Gar. and Aquariums.*

JONES, E. C. 1971. *Isistius brasiliensis,* a squaloid shark, the probable cause of crater wounds on fishes and cetaceans. *Fish. Bull.* 69(4): 791–98.

KELLOGG, R. 1940. Whales, giants of the sea. *National Geographic* 77(1): 35–90.

KOOYMAN, G. L., and H. T. ANDERSEN. 1969. Deep diving. In H. T. Andersen, ed., *The Biology of Marine Mammals*, pp. 65–94. Academic Press.

LAYNE, J. N. 1965. Observations of marine mammals in Florida waters. *Bull. Florida State Mus., Biol. Sci.* 9(4): 131–81.

LEATHERWOOD, S., W. E. EVANS, and D. W. RICE. 1972. *The Whales, Dolphins and Porpoises of the Eastern North Pacific: A guide to their identification in the water.* Naval Undersea Center, San Diego. NUC TP 282.

MILLER, G. S. and R. KELLOGG. 1955. List of North American recent mammals. *Bull. U.S. Nat. Mus.* 205: 1–954.

MITCHELL, E. D. 1975a. Report of the meeting on smaller cetaceans, Montreal, April 1–11, 1974. Subcommittee on Small Cetaceans, Scientific Committee, International Whaling Commission. *Jour. Fish Res. Bd. Canada* 32(7): 889–983.

———. 1975b. *Porpoise, Dolphin and Small Whale Fisheries of the World: Status and Problems.* IUCN Monograph No. 3. Morges, Switzerland.

NISHIWAKI, M. 1967. Distribution and migration of marine mammals in the North Pacific area. *Bull. Ocean Res. Inst. Univ. Tokyo* 1: 64 pp.

NORRIS, K. S. 1965. Trained porpoise released in the open sea. *Science* 147(3661): 1048–50.

———. 1969. The echolocation of marine mammals. In H. T. Andersen, ed., *The Biology of Marine Mammals*, pp. 391–423. Academic Press.

———. 1974. *The Porpoise Watcher.* W. W. Norton.

———, and W. E. EVANS. 1967. Directionality of echolocation clicks in the rough-toothed porpoise (*Steno bredanensis* (Lesson). In W. N. Tavolga, ed., *Marine Bio-Acoustics.* Vol. 2, pp. 305–16. Pergamon Press.

NORRIS, K. S., and K. W. PRYOR. 1970. A tagging method for small cetaceans. *Jour. Mammal.* 51(3): 609–10.

NORRIS, K. S., H. BALDWIN, and D. J. SAMPSON. 1965. Open ocean diving test with a trained porpoise (*Steno bredanensis*). *Deep-Sea Res.* 12: 505–09.

ORR, R. T. 1951. Cetacean records from the Pacific coast of North America. *Wassman Jour. Biol.* 9(2): 147–48.

———. 1965. The rough-toothed dolphin in the Galápagos archipelago. *Jour. Mammal.* 46(1): 101.

PERRIN, W. F. 1975. Distribution and differentiation of populations of dolphins of the genus *Stenella* in the eastern tropical Pacific. *Jour. Fish. Res. Bd. Canada* 32(7): 1059–67.

POPPER, A. N. 1980. Sound emission and detection by dolphins. In L. H. Herman, ed., *Cetacean Behavior: Mechanisms and Functions*, pp. 1–51. John Wiley.

PRYOR, K. W. 1969. Behavior modification: The porpoise caper. *Psychology Today* 3(7): 46–49.

———. 1973. Behavior and learning in porpoises and whales. *Naturwissenschaften* 60: 412–20.

———. 1975. *Lads Before the Wind: Adventures in Porpoise Training.* Harper & Row.

———, R. HAAG, and J. O'REILLY. 1969. The creative porpoise: Training for novel behavior. *Jour. Exp. Anal. Behav.* 12: 653–61.

RICHARDSON, J. I. 1973. A confirmed occurrence of the rough-toothed dolphin (*Steno bredanensis*) on the Atlantic coast of the United States. *Jour. Mammal.* 54(1): 275.

TOMICH, P. Q. 1969. *Mammals in Hawaii.* Bishop Museum Press.

TRUE, F. W. 1889. A review of the family Delphinidae. *Bull. U.S. Nat. Mus.* 36: 1–188.

WOOD, F. G. 1979. The cetacean stranding phenomenon: An hypothesis. In J. B. Geraci and D. J. St. Aubin, eds., *Biology of Marine Mammals: Insights through Strandings*, pp. 129–88. U.S. Marine Mammal Commission Report PB 293 890.

INDO-PACIFIC HUMPBACK DOLPHIN, ATLANTIC HUMPBACK DOLPHIN, AND TUCUXI

ALLEN, R., and W. T. NEILL. 1957. White Whales of the Amazon. *Natural History* 66(6): 324–29.

AL-ROBAAE, K. H. 1970. First record of the speckled dolphin *Sotalia lentiginosa* Gray, 1866, in the Arabian Gulf. *Saugetierk. Mttlg.* 18: 227–28.

ANDERSON, J. 1878. *Anatomical and Zoological Researches comprising an Account of the Zoological Results of the two Expeditions to Western Yunnan in 1868 and 1875, and a Monograph of the two Cetacean genera* Platanista *and* Orcaella. Vol. I Text, Vol. II, Plates. London.

BANKS, E. 1931. A popular account of the mammals of Borneo. *Jour. Malayan Branch Royal Asiat. Soc.* 9(2): 1–139.

BÖSSENECKER, P. J. 1978. The capture and care of *Sotalia guianensis. Aquatic Mammals* 6(1): 13–17.

BUSNEL, R.-G. 1973. Symbiotic relationship between man and dolphins. *Trans. N.Y. Acad. Sci.* Ser. II, 35(2): 112–31.

CADENAT, J. 1947. Observations on the Cetacea of Senegal. *Notes Africaines, Dakar.* 34: 20–23.

———. 1949. Notes sur les cétacés observés sur les côtes du Sénégal de 1941 à 1948. *Bull. Inst. Fran. Afrique Noir* 11(1–2): 1–15.

———. 1956. Sur un Delphinidé encore mal connu de la côte occidentale d'Afrique *Sotalia teuszii* Kükenthal 1892. *Bull. Inst. Fran. Afrique Noir* 18(2): 555–66.

———. 1957. Observation de Cétacés, Siréniens, Cheloniens et Sauriens en 1955–56. *Bull. Inst. Fran. Afrique Noir*, Ser. A, 19(4).

———, and F. PARAISO. 1957. Nouvelle observation de *Sotalia* (Cétacé, Delphinidae) sur les côtes du Sénégal. *Bull. Inst. Fran. Afrique Noir* 19(1): 324–32.

CARVALHO, C. T. de. 1963. Sobre um boto comun no litoral do Brasil (Cetacea, Delphinidae). *Revista Brasileira de Biologia* 23(3): 263–76.

FLOWER, W. H. 1870. Description of the skeleton of the Chinese white dolphin (*Delphinus sinensis* Osbeck). *Trans. Zool. Soc. London* 7: 151–60.

FRASER, F. C. 1949. A specimen of *Sotalia teuszii* Kükenthal from the coast of Senegal. *Jour. Mammal* 30(3): 274–76.

———. 1966. Comments on Delphinoidea. In K. S. Norris, ed., *Whales, Dolphins and Porpoises*. University of California Press, 7–31.

———. 1973. Record of a dolphin (*Sousa teuszii*) from the coast of Mauritania. *Trans. N.Y. Acad. Sci.* Ser. II, 35(2): 132–35.

GIBSON HILL, C. A. 1949. The whales, porpoises and dolphins known in Malayan waters. *Malayan Nat. Jour.* 4: 44–61.

———. 1951. The whales, porpoises and dolphins known in Sarawak waters. *Sarawak Mus. Jour.* 5: 288–96.

HARRISON, T. 1960. South China Seas Dolphins. *Malayan Nature Jour.* 14(1): 87–89.

HERALD, E. S. 1967. Boutu and tookashee—Amazon dolphins. *Pacific Discovery* 20(1): 2–9.

HERMAN, L. M., and W. N. TAVOLGA. 1980. The communication systems of cetaceans. In L. M. Herman, ed., *Cetacean Behavior: Mechanisms and Functions*, pp. 149–209. John Wiley.

INTERNATIONAL WHALING COMMISSION. 1977. List of small cetaceans recognized. *Appendix* 1, 27: 30–31.

KÜKENTHAL, W. 1892. Sotalia teuszii n. sp., ein pflanzenfressender (?) Delphin aus Kamerun. *Zoologische Jahrbücher* 6: 442–46.

LAMB, B. F. 1954. The fishermen's porpoise. *Natural History* 63(5): 231–34.

LAYNE, J. N. 1958. Observations on the fresh water dolphins in the upper Amazon. *Jour. Mammal.* 39(1): 1–22.

LYDEKKER, R. 1901. Notice of an apparently new estuarine dolphin from Borneo. *Proc. Zool. Soc. London* 88–91.

———. 1903. Notes on the Trivandrum cetaceans. *Jour. Bombay Nat. Hist. Soc.* 15: 40–41.

———. 1904. On two dolphins from Madras. *Jour. Bombay Nat. Hist. Soc.* 15: 408–14.

———. 1908. On an Indian dolphin and porpoise. *Proc. Zool. Soc. London* 802–08.

MÖRZER BRUYNS, W. F. J. 1960. The ridge-backed dolphin of the Indian Ocean. *Malay Nat. Jour.* 14: 159–65.

NORRIS, K. S., G. W. HARVEY, L. A. BURZELL, and T. D. KRISHNA KARTHA. 1972. Sound production in the Freshwater Porpoises *Sotalia* cf. *fluviatilis* Gervais, and Deville, and *Inia geoffrensis* Blainville, in the Río Negro, Brazil. *Invest. on Cetacea* 4: 251–59 + plates.

OWEN, R. 1866. On some Indian cetacea collected by Walter Elliot, Esq. *Trans. Zool. Soc. London* 6: 17–47.

PILLERI, G., and M. GIHR. 1972. Contribution to the knowledge of the cetaceans of Pakistan with particular reference to the genera *Neomeris*, *Sousa*, *Delphinus* and *Tursiops* and a description of a new Chinese porpoise (*Neomeris asiaeorientalis*). *Invest. on Cetacea* 4: 107–62.

———. 1973. Contribution to the knowledge of the cetaceans of southwest and monsoon Asia (Persian Gulf, Indus Delta, Malabar, Andaman Sea and Gulf of Siam). *Invest. on Cetacea* 5: 95–149.

PILLERI, G., and O. PILLERI. 1979. Observations on the dolphins in the Indus Delta (*Sousa plumbea* and *Neophocanea phocaenoides*) in winter 1978–1979. *Invest. on Cetacea* 10: 129–35 + plates.

ROBERTS, T. J. 1977. Cetacean records for Pakistan. *Invest. on Cetacea* 8: 95–99.

ROSS, G. J. B., P. B. BEST, and B. G. DONNELLY. 1975. New records of the pygmy right whale (*Caperea marginata*) from South Africa, with comments on distribution, migration, appearance, and behavior. *Jour. Fish. Res. Bd. Canada* 32(7): 1005–17.

SAAYMAN, G. S., and C. K. TAYLER. 1973. Social organisation of inshore dolphins (*Tursiops aduncus* and *Sousa*) in the Indian Ocean. *Jour. Mammal.* 54(4): 993–96.

———. 1979. The socioecology of humpback dolphins (*Sousa* spp.). In H. E. Winn and B. L. Olla, eds., *Behavior of Marine Animals, Volume 3: Cetaceans*, pp. 165–226. Plenum.

SAAYMAN, G. S., D. BOWER, and C. K. TAYLER. 1972. Observations on inshore and pelagic dolphins on the south-eastern Cape coast of South Africa. *Koedoe* 15: 1–24.

TIETZ, R. M. 1963. A record of the speckled dolphin from the south-east coast of South Africa. *Ann. Cape Prov. Mus.* 3: 68–74.

VAN BREE, P. J. H., and R. DUGUY. 1965. Sur un crâne de *Sotalia tëuszii* Kükenthal 1892 (Cetacea, Delphinidae). *Z. Saugetierkunde.* 30: 311–14.

WALKER, E. 1964. *Mammals of the World*. Johns Hopkins University Press.

WATERMAN, S. A. 1967. Dolphin collecting in the Amazon. *Expl. Jour.* 45(4): 270–77.

ZBINDEN, K., G. PILLERI, C. KRAUS, and O. BERNATH. 1977. Observations on the behaviour and the underwater sounds of the plumbeous dolphin (*Sousa plumbea* G. Cuvier 1829) in the Indus delta region. *Invest. on Cetacea* 8: 259–86.

BOTTLENOSE DOLPHIN

ADLER, H. E., and L. L. ADLER. 1978. What can dolphins (*Tursiops truncatus*) learn by observation? *Cetology* 30: 10 pp.

ALLEN, G. M. 1939. *Bats*. Harvard University Press.

ALPERS, ANTONY. 1960. *Dolphins: The Myth and the Mammal*. Houghton Mifflin.

ANDREWS, R. C. 1911. Description of an apparently new porpoise of the genus *Tursiops*, with remarks upon a skull of *Tursiops gillii* Dall. *Bull. Amer. Mus. Nat. Hist.* 30(9): 233–37.

———. 1916. *Whale Hunting with Gun and Camera*. D. Appleton.

ANONYMOUS. 1978. "Japanese Slaughter 1,000 Dolphins." *New York Times,* February 25, 1978.

AU, W. W. L. 1979. Echolocation signals of the Atlantic bottlenose dolphin (*Tursiops truncatus*) in open waters. In R.-G. Busnel and J. G. Fish, eds., *Animal Sonar Systems,* pp. 251–82. Plenum.

————, R. W. FLOYD, and J. E. HAUN. 1978. Propagation of Atlantic bottlenose dolphin echolocation signals. *Jour. Acoust. Soc. Amer.* 64(2): 411–22.

————, R. W. FLOYD, R. H. PENNER, and A. E. MURCHISON. 1974. Measurement of echolocation signals in the Atlantic bottlenose dolphin, *Tursiops truncatus* Montagu, in open waters. *Jour. Acoust. Soc. Amer.* 56(4): 1280–90.

BEL'KOVICH, V. M. 1978. Behavior and bioacoustics of dolphins. Academy of Sciences of USSR. P. P. Shizhov Inst. of Oceanography. Moscow. *In press.*

————, and A. V. YABLOKOV. 1963. The whale—an ultrasonic projector. *Yuchni Tekhnik* 3: 76–77.

BERZIN, A. A. 1972. *The Sperm Whale,* pp. 1–393. Israel Program for Scientific Translations. Jerusalem.

BROWN, D. H., and K. S. NORRIS. 1956. Observations of captive and wild cetaceans. *Jour. Mammal.* 37(3): 311–26.

BROWN, D. H., D. K. CALDWELL, and M. K. CALDWELL. 1966. Observations on the behavior of wild and captive false killer whales, with notes on associated behavior of other genera of captive delphinids. *Los. Ang. Cty. Mus. Contrib. Sci.* 95: 1–32.

BROWN, R. 1979. *The Lure of the Dolphin.* Avon Books.

BUNNELL, S. 1974. The evolution of cetacean intelligence. In J. McIntyre, ed., *Mind in the Waters,* pp. 52–59. Scribner's/ Sierra Club.

BUSNEL, R.-G. 1973. Symbiotic relationship between man and dolphins. *Trans. N.Y. Acad. Sci.* Series II, 35(2): 112–31.

————, and J. G. FISH, eds. 1979. *Animal Sonar Systems.* Plenum.

CALDWELL, D. K. 1955. Evidence of home range of an Atlantic bottlenose dolphin, *Jour. Mammal.* 36(2): 304–05.

————, and M. C. CALDWELL. 1968. The dolphin observed. *Natural History* 77(8): 58–63.

————. 1972a. Senses and communication. In S. H. Ridgway, ed., *Mammals of the Sea: Biology and Medicine,* pp. 466–98. Charles C. Thomas.

————. 1972b. *The World of the Bottlenosed Dolphin.* Lippincott.

————. 1972c. Dolphins communicate—but they do not talk. *Naval Research Reviews* 25(6–7): 23–27.

CALDWELL, M. C., and D. K. CALDWELL. 1966. Epimeletic (caregiving) behavior in cetacea. In K. S. Norris, ed., *Whales, Dolphins and Porpoises,* pp. 755–89. University of California Press.

————. 1970. Etiology of the chirp sounds emitted by the Atlantic bottlenosed dolphin: A controversial issue. *Underwater Naturalist* 6(3): 6–8.

————. 1972. Vocal mimicry in the whistle mode by an Atlantic bottlenosed dolphin. *Cetology* 9: 8 pp.

————. 1978. *Sound Communication by the Bottlenosed Dolphin.* (Phonograph record.) NR9686. Biological Systems.

————. 1979a. Communication in Atlantic bottlenosed dolphins. *Sea Frontiers* 25(3): 130–39.

————. 1979b. The whistle of the Atlantic bottlenosed dolphin (*Tursiops truncatus*)—Ontogeny. In H. E. Winn and B. L. Olla, eds., *Behavior of Marine Animals. Vol 3: Cetaceans,* pp. 369–401. Plenum.

CALDWELL, M. C., and H. M. FIELDS. 1959. Surf-riding by Atlantic bottle-nosed dolphins. *Jour. Mammal.* 40(3): 454–55.

CALDWELL, M. C., N. R. HALL, and D. K. CALDWELL. 1971. Ability of an Atlantic bottlenosed dolphin to discriminate between, and respond differentially to, whistles of eight conspecifics. *Proc. Eighth Ann. Conf. Biol. Sonar and Diving Mammals,* pp. 57–65. Stanford Research Institute.

CALDWELL, M. C., R. M. HAUGEN, and D. K. CALDWELL. 1962. High-energy sound associated with fright in the dolphin. *Science* 138(3543): 907–08.

CLARK, A. H. 1887. The blackfish and porpoise fisheries. In G. B. Goode et al., eds., *The Fisheries and Fishery Industries of the United States.* Part 16, Sect. 5, Vol. 2, pp. 297–310. Washington, D.C.

CORNELL, L. H., and E. D. ASPER. 1977. A census of captive marine mammals in North America. *Intl. Zoo Yearbook* 18: 220–24.

COUSTEAU, J.-Y. 1953. *The Silent World.* Harper & Row.

DALL, W. H. 1873. Descriptions of three new species of cetacea, from the coast of California. *Proc. Calif. Acad. Sci.* 5(1): 12–14.

DAWSON, W. W. 1980. The cetacean eye. In L. M. Herman, ed., *Cetacean Behavior: Mechanisms and Functions,* pp. 53–100. John Wiley.

DEFRAN, R. H., and K. PRYOR. 1980. The behavior and training of cetaceans in captivity. In L. M. Herman, ed., *Cetacean Behavior: Mechanisms and Processes,* pp. 319–62. John Wiley.

DEVINE, E., and M. CLARK. 1967. *The Dolphin Smile.* Macmillan.

DIERCKS, K. J., R. T. TROCHTA, C. F. GREENLAW, and W. E. EVANS. 1971. Recording and analysis of dolphin echolocation signals. *Jour. Acoust. Soc. Amer.* 49(6): 1729–32.

DOBBS, H. E. 1977. *Follow a Wild Dolphin.* Souvenir Press.

————. 1978. Donald the wild dolphin. *Wildlife* 22(5): 210–15.

DOHL, T. P., K. S. NORRIS, and I. KANG. 1974. A porpoise hybrid: *Tursiops* × *Steno. Jour. Mammal.* 55: 217–21.

DREHER, J. J., and W. E. EVANS. 1964. Cetacean communication. In W. N. Tavolga, ed., *Marine Bio-Acoustics*. Vol. 1: 373–93. Pergamon Press.

DUDOK VAN HEEL, W. H. 1966. Navigation in cetacea. In K. S. Norris, ed., *Whales, Dolphins and Porpoises*, pp. 597–602. University of California Press.

ESSAPIAN, F. S. 1953. The birth and growth of a porpoise. *Natural History* 62(9): 392–99.

————. 1955. Speed-induced skin folds in the bottle-nosed porpoise, *Tursiops truncatus*. *Breviora*. 43: 1–4.

————. 1962. An albino bottlenose dolphin (*Tursiops truncatus*) captured in the United States. *Norsk Hvalfangst-tidende*. 51: 341–44.

————. 1963. Observations on abnormalities of parturition in captive bottlenose dolphin *Tursiops truncatus*, and concurrent behavior of other porpoises. *Jour. Mammal.* 44(3): 404–14.

EVANS, W. E. 1967. Vocalization among marine mammals. In W. N. Tavolga, ed. *Marine Bio-Acoustics*. Vol. 2, 159–86. Pergamon Press.

————. 1973. Echolocation by marine delphinids and one species of fresh-water dolphin. *Jour. Acoust. Soc. Amer.* 54: 191.

————. 1980. Dolphins and their mysterious sixth sense. *Oceanus* 23(3): 69–75.

————, and J. BASTIAN. 1969. Marine mammal communication: Social and ecological factors. In H. T. Andersen, ed., *The Biology of Marine Mammals*, pp. 425–75. Academic Press.

EVANS, W. E., and J. J. DREHER. 1962. Observations on scouting behavior and associated sound production by the Pacific bottlenosed porpoise (*Tursiops gilli*). *Bull. So. Calif. Acad. Sci.* 61(4): 217–26.

EVANS, W. E., and B. A. POWELL. 1967. Discrimination of different metallic plates by an echolocating porpoise. In R.-G. Busnel, ed., *Animal Sonar Systems: Biology and Bionics*, pp. 363–83. Laboratoire de Physiologie Acoustique. Jouy-en-Josas, France.

EVANS, W. E., and J. H. PRESCOTT. 1962. Observations of the sound production capabilities of the bottlenose porpoise: A study of whistles and clicks. *Zoologica* 49(3): 121–28.

EVANS, W. E., W. W. SUTHERLAND, and R. G. BEIL. 1964. The directional characteristics of delphinid sounds. In W. N. Tavolga, ed. *Marine Bio-Acoustics*. Vol. 1, pp. 353–72. Pergamon Press.

FABRICIUS, O. 1780. *Fauna Groenlandica*. Hafniae et Lipsiae: Impensis Ioanis Gottlob Rothe.

FEJER, A. A., and R. H. BACKUS. 1960. Porpoises and the bow-riding of ships under way. *Nature* 188(4752): 700–03.

FLOWER, W. H. 1883. On the characters and divisions of the family Delphinidae. *Proc. Zool. Soc. London* 32: 466–513.

FRASER, F. C. 1934. Report on cetacea stranded on the British coasts from 1927 to 1932. *Bull. Brit. Mus. (Nat. Hist.)* 11: 1–41.

————. 1940. Three anomalous dolphins from Blacksod Bay, Ireland. *Proc. Royal Irish Acad.* 45(B): 413–55.

————. 1946. Report on cetacea stranded on the British Coasts from 1933 to 1937. *Bull. Brit. Mus. (Nat. Hist.)* 12: 1–55.

————. 1947. Sound emitted by dolphins. *Nature* 160: 759.

————. 1953. Report on cetacea stranded on the British Coasts from 1938 to 1947. *Bull. Brit. Mus. (Nat. Hist.)* 13: 1–48.

————. 1974. Report on cetacea stranded on the British Coasts from 1948 to 1966. *Bull. Brit. Mus. (Nat. Hist.)* 14: 1–65.

GILBERT, P. W., B. IRVINE, and F. H. MARTINI. 1971. Shark-porpoise behavioral interactions. *American Zoologist* 11: 80.

GOODE, G. B. 1884. The whales and porpoises. In G. B. Goode et al., eds., *The Fisheries and Fishery Industries of the United States*. Part IA, Sect. 1, pp. 7–32. Washington.

GRAY, J. 1936. Studies in animal locomotion, VI: The propulsive powers of the dolphin, *Jour. Exp. Biol.* 13: 192–99.

GREEN, R. F., S. H. RIDGWAY, and W. E. EVANS. 1979. Functional and descriptive anatomy of the bottlenosed dolphin nasolaryngeal system with special reference to the musculature associated with sound production. In R.-G. Busnel and J. G. Fish, eds., *Animal Sonar Systems*, pp. 199–238. Plenum.

GRIFFIN, D. R. 1958. *Listening in the Dark*. Yale University Press.

————. 1959. *Echoes of Bats and Men*. Anchor Books.

————. 1979. Early history of research on echolocation. In R.-G. Busnel and J. F. Fish, eds., *Animal Sonar Systems*, pp. 1–8. Plenum.

GRUBER, J. A. 1979. Aspects of the population biology of *Tursiops truncatus* with respect to the dolphin-shrimpboat association. (Abstract) *Third Bien. Conf. Biol. Marine Mammals*. Seattle.

GUNTER, G. 1942. Contributions to the natural history of the bottlenose dolphin *Tursiops truncatus* (Montague) on the Texas coast, with particular reference to food habits. *Jour. Mammal.* 23:267–76.

————. 1943. Swimming speed of *Tursiops*. *Jour. Mammal.* 24: 521.

HALL, H. 1981. Bloodbath at Iki. *Skin Diver* 30(3): 16–19.

HAMMER, C., and W. W. L. AU. 1978. Target recognition via echolocation by an Atlantic bottlenose porpoise (*Tursiops truncatus*). *Jour. Acoust. Soc. Amer.* 64: Suppl. 1: 587.

HARMER, S. F. 1927. Report on cetacea stranded on the British Coasts from 1913 to 1926. *Bull. Brit. Mus. (Nat. Hist.)* 10: 1–91.

HAYES, W. D. 1959. Wave-riding dolphins. *Science* 130: 1657–58.

HERMAN, L. M., ed. 1980. *Cetacean Behavior: Mechanisms and Functions.* John Wiley.

————. 1980. Cognitive characteristics of dolphins. In L. M. Herman, ed., *Cetacean Behavior: Mechanisms and Functions,* pp. 363–429. John Wiley.

————, and W. R. ARBEIT. 1973. Stimulus control and auditory discrimination learning sets in the bottlenose dolphin. *Jour. Exp. Anal. Behav.* 19: 379–94.

HERMAN, L. M., and W. N. TAVOLGA. 1980. The communication systems of cetaceans. In L. M. Herman, ed., *Cetacean Behavior: Mechanisms and Functions,* pp. 149–209. John Wiley.

HERTEL. H. 1969. Hydrodynamics of swimming and wave-riding dolphins. In H. T. Andersen, ed., *The Biology of Marine Mammals,* pp. 65–94. Academic Press.

HICKMAN, D. L., and E. M. GRIGSBY. 1978. Comparison of signature whistles in *Tursiops truncatus. Cetology* 31: 10 pp.

HIROSAKI, Y., M. HONDA, and T. KINUTA. 1981. On the three hybrids between *Tursiops truncatus* and *Grampus griseus. Jour. Jap. Assoc. Zool. Gardens and Aquariums.*

HOCKETT, C. F. 1978. In search of Jove's brow. *American Speech.* 53(4): 243–313.

HOESE, H. D. 1971. Dolphin feeding out of water in a salt marsh. *Jour. Mammal.* 52(1): 222–23.

HOLLIEN, H., P. HOLLIEN, D. K. CALDWELL, and M. C. CALDWELL. 1976. Sound production in the Atlantic bottlenosed dolphin (*Tursiops truncatus*). *Cetology* 26: 8 pp.

HOWELL, A. B. 1930. *Aquatic Mammals.* Charles C Thomas.

HUBBS, C. L. 1953. Dolphin protecting dead young. *Jour. Mammal.* 34: 498.

IRVINE, B. 1972. Behavioral changes in dolphins in a strange environment. *Q. Jour. Fla. Acad. Sci.* 34: 206–12.

————, R. S. WELLS, and P. GILBERT. 1973. Conditioning an Atlantic bottlenose dolphin *Tursiops truncatus* to repel various species of sharks. *Jour. Mammal.* 54(2): 503–05.

JACOBS, M. 1974. The whale brain: input and behavior. In J. McIntyre, ed., *Mind in the Waters,* pp. 78–83. Scribner's/Sierra Club.

JOHNSON, C. S. 1967. Sound detection thresholds in marine mammals. In W. N. Tavolga, ed., *Marine Bio-Acoustics* Vol. 2, pp. 247–60. Pergamon Press.

————. 1968. Masked tonal thresholds in the bottlenosed porpoise. *Jour. Acoust. Soc. Amer.* 44(4): 965–67.

JONES, H. 1980. Why the dolphins died. *International Wildlife* 10(5): 4–11.

KELLOGG, W. N. 1958. Echo ranging in the porpoise. *Science* 128: 982–88.

————. 1959. Auditory perception of submerged objects by porpoises. *Jour. Acoust. Soc. Amer.* 31: 1–6.

————. 1961. *Porpoises and Sonar.* University of Chicago Press.

————, and R. KOHLER. 1952. Responses of the porpoise to ultrasonic frequencies. *Science* 116: 250–52.

KELLOGG, W. N., and C. E. RICE. 1966. Visual discrimination and problem solving in a bottlenose dolphin. In K. S. Norris, ed., *Whales, Dolphins and Porpoises,* pp. 731–54. University of California Press.

KENYON, K. W. 1952. A bottlenose dolphin from the California coast. *Jour. Mammal.* 33(3): 385–87.

KOOYMAN, G. L. and H. T. ANDERSEN. 1969. Deep diving. In H. T. Andersen, ed., *The Biology of Marine Mammals,* pp. 65–94. Academic Press.

LANE, F. W. 1943. Speed of dolphins. *Jour. Mammal.* 24(2): 292–93.

LANG, T. G., and K. S. NORRIS. 1966. Swimming speed of a Pacific bottlenose porpoise. *Science* 151(3710): 588–90.

LANG, T. G., and K. PRYOR. 1966. Hydrodynamic performance of porpoises (*Stenella attenuata*). *Science* 152: 531–33.

LAWRENCE, B., and W. E. SCHEVILL. 1954. *Tursiops* as an experimental subject. *Jour. Mammal.* 35: 225–32.

————. 1956. The functional anatomy of the delphinid nose. *Bull. Mus. Comp. Zool. (Harvard)* 114(4): 103–51. Figs. 1–30.

LAWRENCE, C., K. EMERICK, and R. EATON. 1979. Beaky: wild but friendly dolphin. *Orca* 1(1): 20–27.

LILLY, J. C. 1961. *Man and Dolphin.* Doubleday.

————. 1966. Sonic-ultrasonic emissions of the bottlenose dolphin. In K. S. Norris, ed., *Whales, Dolphins and Porpoises,* pp. 503–09. University of California Press.

————. 1967. *The Mind of the Dolphin.* Doubleday.

————. 1974. A feeling of weirdness. In J. McIntyre, ed., *Mind in the Waters,* pp. 71–77. Scribner's/Sierra Club.

————. 1978. *Communication Between Man and Dolphin.* Crown.

————, and A. M. MILLER. 1961. Sounds emitted by the bottlenose dolphin. *Science* 133: 1689–93.

LINEHAN, E. J. 1979. The trouble with dolphins. *National Geographic* 155(4): 506–41.

LJUNGBLAD, D. K., S. LEATHERWOOD, R. A. JOHNSON, E. D. MITCHELL, and F. T. AWBREY. 1977. Echolocation signals of wild Pacific bottlenosed dolphins (*Tursiops* sp.). (Abstract) *Second Conf. Biol. Marine Mammals.* San Diego.

LOCKYER, C. 1978. The history and behavior of a solitary wild, but sociable, bottlenose dolphin (*Tursiops truncatus*) on the west coast of England and Wales. *Jour. Nat. Hist.* In press.

LUBOW, A. 1977. Riot in fish tank II. *New Times.* October 14: 36–53.

MADSEN, C. J., and L. M. HERMAN. 1980. Social and ecological correlates of cetacean vision and visual appearance. In L. M. Herman, ed., *Cetacean Behavior: Mechanisms and Functions*, pp. 101–47. John Wiley.

MAYER, W. V. 1950. *Tursiops gillii*, the bottlenosed dolphin, a new record from the Gulf of California, with remarks on *Tursiops nuuanu*. *Amer. Midl. Nat.* 43(1): 183–85.

MCBRIDE, A. F. 1940. Meet Mr. Porpoise. *Natural History* 45: 16–29.

———. 1956. Evidence for echolocation by cetaceans. *Deep Sea Res.* 3: 153–54.

———, and D. O. HEBB. 1948. Behavior of a captive bottlenose dolphin, *Tursiops truncatus*. *Jour. Comp. Physiol. Psychol.* 41(2): 111–23.

MCBRIDE, A. F., and H. KRITZLER. 1951. Observations on pregnancy, parturition, and post-natal behavior in the bottlenose dolphin. *Jour. Mammal.* 32: 251–56.

MEAD, J. G. 1975. Preliminary report on the former net fishery for *Tursiops truncatus* in the western North Atlantic. *Jour. Fish. Res. Bd. Canada* 32(7): 1155–62.

———. 1979. An analysis of cetacean strandings along the eastern coast of the United States. In J. B. Geraci and D. J. St. Aubin, eds., *Biology of Marine Mammals: Insights through Strandings*, pp. 54–68. U.S. Marine Mammal Commission Report PB-293 890.

MERLE, R. 1969. *The Day of the Dolphin*. Simon & Schuster.

MITCHELL, E. D. 1975. *Porpoise, Dolphin and Small Whale Fisheries of the World: Status and Problems*. IUCN Monograph No. 3, Morges, Switzerland.

MOORE, J. C. 1955. Bottlenose dolphins support remains of young. *Jour. Mammal.* 36(3): 466–67.

MOORE, P. W. B. 1979. Cetacean obstacle avoidance. In R.-G. Busnel and J. G. Fish, eds., *Animal Sonar Systems*, pp. 97–108. Plenum.

MORGANE, P. 1974. The whale brain: The anatomical basis of intelligence. In J. McIntyre, ed., *Mind in the Waters*, pp. 84–93. Scribner's/Sierra Club.

MURCHISON, A. E. 1979. Detection range and range resolution of echolocating bottlenose porpoise. In R.-G. Busnel and J. G. Fish, eds., *Animal Sonar Systems*, pp. 43–70. Plenum.

MYERS, W. A., and N. A. OVERSTROM. 1978. The role of daily observation in the husbandry of captive dolphins (*Tursiops truncatus*). *Cetology* 29: 7 pp.

NACHTIGALL, P. E. 1979. Odontocete echolocation performance on object size, shape and material. In R.-G. Busnel and J. G. Fish, eds., *Animal Sonar Systems*, pp. 71–95. Plenum.

NORRIS, K. S. 1964. Some problems of echolocation in cetaceans. In W. N. Tavolga, ed., *Marine Bio-Acoustics*. Vol. 1, pp. 317–36. Pergamon Press.

———. 1965. Trained porpoise released in the open sea. *Science.* 147(3661): 1048–50.

———. 1969. The echolocation of marine mammals. In H. T. Andersen, ed., *The Biology of Marine Mammals*, pp. 425–475. Academic Press.

———. 1974. *The Porpoise Watcher*. W. W. Norton.

———. 1979. Peripheral sound processing in odontocetes. In R.-G. Busnel and J. G. Fish, eds., *Animal Sonar Systems*, pp. 495–509. Plenum.

———, and T. P. DOHL. 1980. The structure and function of cetacean schools. In L. M. Herman, ed., *Cetacean Behavior: Mechanisms and Functions*, pp. 211–61. John Wiley.

NORRIS, K. S., and J. H. PRESCOTT. 1961. Observations on Pacific Cetaceans of Californian and Mexican Waters. *Univ. Calif. Publs. Zool.* 63(4): 291–402.

NORRIS, K. S., W. E. EVANS, and R. N. TURNER. 1967. Echolocation in an Atlantic bottlenose porpoise during discrimination. In R.-G. Busnel, ed., *Animal Sonar Systems: Biology and Bionics*, pp. 409–37. Laboratoire de Physiologie Acoustique. Jouy-en-Josas, France.

NORRIS, K. S., J. H. PRESCOTT, P. V. ASA-DORIAN, and P. PERKINS. 1961. An experimental demonstration of echolocation behavior in the porpoise *Tursiops truncatus* (Montagu). *Biol. Bull.* 120(2): 163–76.

ODELL, D. K. 1975. Status and aspects of the life history of the bottlenose dolphin, *Tursiops truncatus*, in Florida. *Jour. Fish. Res. Bd. Canada.* 32(7): 1055–58.

PARFIT, M. 1980. Are dolphins trying to say something, or is it all much ado about nothing? *Smithsonian* 11(7): 72–81.

PARRY, D. A. 1949. The swimming of whales and a discussion of Gray's paradox. *Jour. Exper. Biol.* 26: 24–34.

PEPPER, R. L., F. A. BEACH, and P. E. NACHTIGALL. 1972. In-air visual acuity of the bottlenose dolphin. *Proc. Ninth Ann. Conf. Biol. Sonar and Diving Mammals*, pp. 83–88. Stanford Research Institute.

PILLERI, G., and M. GIHR. 1972a. Contribution to the knowledge of the cetaceans of Pakistan with particular reference to the genera *Neomeris*, *Sousa*, *Delphinus* and *Tursiops* and a description of a new Chinese porpoise (*Neomeris asiaeorientalis*). *Invest. on Cetacea* 4: 107–62.

———. 1972b. On the record and taxonomy of *Tursiops gephyreus* Lahille, 1908, off Playa Coronilla, Uruguay. *Invest. on Cetacea* 4: 173–81.

POPPER, A. N. 1979. Behavioral measures of odontocete hearing. In R.-G. Busnel and J. G. Fish, eds., *Animal Sonar Systems*, pp. 469–81. Plenum.

PRYOR, K. 1973. Behavior and learning in porpoises and whales. *Naturwissenschaften* 60: 412–20.

———. 1975. *Lads Before the Wind*. Harper & Row.

———, and I. KANG. 1980. Social behavior and school structure in pelagic porpoises (*Stenella attenuata* and *S. longirostris*) during purse seining for tuna. *Southwest Fisheries Center Administrative Report LJ-80-11C*. NMFS.

REYSENBACH DE HAAN, F. W. 1966. Listening underwater: Thoughts on cetacean hearing. In K. S. Norris, ed., *Whales, Dolphins and Porpoises*, pp. 583–95. University of California Press.

RIDGWAY, S. H. 1966. Studies on diving depth and duration in *Tursiops truncatus*. *Proc. Third Ann. Conf. Biol. Sonar and Diving Mammals*, pp. 151–58. Stanford Research Institute.

——. 1980. Anatomical and physiological measures that might relate to cetacean intelligence. IWC Conference on Cetacean Behavior, Intelligence, and the Ethics of Killing Cetaceans. Washington, D.C. 2 pp. (Mimeo.)

——, and K. BENIRSCHKE, eds. 1977. *Breeding Dolphins: Present Status, Suggestions for the Future.* U.S. Marine Mammal Commission Report No. MMC-76/07.

RIDGWAY, S. H., B. L. SCRONCE, and J. KANWISHER. 1969. Respiration and deep diving in the bottlenose porpoise. *Science* 166: 1651–54.

ROSS, G. J. B. 1977. The taxonomy of bottlenosed dolphins *Tursiops* species in South African waters, with notes on their biology. *Ann. Cape Prov. Mus. (Nat. Hist.)* 11(9): 136–94.

SAAYMAN, G. S., and TAYLER, C. K. 1973. Social organization of inshore dolphins (*Tursiops aduncus* and *Sousa*) in the Indian Ocean. *Jour. Mammal.* 54(4): 993–96.

——, D. BOWER, and C. K. TAYLER. 1972. Observations on inshore and pelagic dolphins on the south-eastern Cape coast of South Africa. *Koedoe* 15: 1–24.

SAAYMAN, G. S., C. K. TAYLER, and D. BOWER. 1973. Diurnal activity cycles in captive and free-ranging Indian Ocean bottlenose dolphins (*Tursiops aduncus* Ehrenburg). *Behaviour* 44: 212–33.

SANDERSON, I. 1956. *Follow the Whale.* Little Brown and Company.

SCHEVILL, W. E. 1964. Underwater sounds of cetaceans. In W. N. Tavolga, ed., *Marine Bio-Acoustics*, Vol. 1, pp. 307–16. Pergamon Press.

——, and B. LAWRENCE. 1956. Food-finding by a captive porpoise (*Tursiops truncatus*). *Breviora* 53: 1–15.

SCHOLANDER, P. F. 1959. Wave-riding of dolphins: How do they do it? *Science* 129: 1085–87.

SERGEANT, D. E., D. K. CALDWELL, and M. K. CALDWELL. 1973. Age, growth, and maturity of bottlenosed dolphin (*Tursiops truncatus*) from northeast Florida. *Jour. Fish. Res. Bd. Canada.* 30: 1009–11.

SHANE, S. H. 1980. Occurrence, movements and distribution of bottlenose dolphin *Tursiops truncatus*, in southern Texas. *Fish. Bull.* 78(3): 593–601.

SHAPUNOV, V. M. 1973. Food requirements and energy balance in the Black Sea bottlenose dolphin (*Tursiops truncatus ponticus* Barabasch). In K. K. Chapskii and V. E. Sokolov, eds., *Morphology and Ecology of Marine Mammals: Seals, Dolphins, Porpoises*, pp. 207–12. John Wiley.

SHELDRICK, M. C. 1979. Cetacean strandings along the coasts of the British Isles 1913–1977. In J. B. Geraci and D. J. St. Aubin, eds., *Biology of Marine Mammals: Insights through Strandings*, pp. 35–53. U.S. Marine Mammal Commission Report PB-293 890.

SHUREPOVA, G. A. 1973. Aggressive behavior of captive *Tursiops truncatus* Barabasch. In K. K. Chapskii and V. E. Sokolov, eds. *Morphology and Ecology of Marine Mammals: Seals, Dolphins, Porpoises*, pp. 150–53. John Wiley.

SIEBENALER, J. B., and D. K. CALDWELL. 1956. Cooperation among adult dolphins. *Jour. Mammal.* 37: 126–28.

STENUIT, R. 1968. *The Dolphin, Cousin to Man.* Sterling.

TAVOLGA, M. C. 1966. Behavior of the bottlenose dolphin (*Tursiops truncatus*): Social interactions of a captive colony. In K. S. Norris, ed., *Whales, Dolphins and Porpoises*, pp. 718–30. University of California Press.

——, and F. S. ESSAPIAN. 1957. The behavior of the bottlenosed dolphin (*Tursiops truncatus*): Mating, pregnancy, parturition, and mother-infant behavior. *Zoologica* 42: 11–31.

TAVOLGA, M. C., and W. N. TAVOLGA. 1962. Man and dolphin. *Natural History* 71(1): 5–7 (book review).

TAVOLGA, W. N., ed. 1964. *Marine Bio-Acoustics* Vol. 1. Pergamon Press.

——, ed. 1967. *Marine Bio-Acoustics* Vol. 2. Pergamon Press.

TAYLER, C. K., and G. S. SAAYMAN. 1972. The social organisation and behaviour of dolphins (*Tursiops aduncus*) and baboons (*Papio ursinus*): Some comparisons and assessments. *Ann. Cape Prov. Mus. (Nat. Hist)* 9(2): 11–49.

——. 1973. Imitative behaviour by Indian Ocean bottlenose dolphins (*Tursiops aduncus*) in captivity. *Behaviour* 44: 286–97.

TOMICH, P. Q. 1969. *Mammals in Hawaii: A Synopsis and Notational Bibliography.* Bishop Museum Press.

TOWNSEND, C. H. 1914. The porpoise in captivity. *Zoologica* 1(16).

TRUE, F. W. 1884. Porpoise fishing at Cape May, New Jersey. *U.S. Fish. Comm. Bull.* 4: 431–32.

——. 1885. The porpoise fishery of Hatteras, N. C. *U.S. Fish Comm. Bull.* 5: 3–6.

——. 1889. A review of the family delphinidae. *Bull. U.S. Nat. Mus.* 36: 1–191.

——. 1890. Observations on the life history of the bottlenose porpoise. *Proc. U.S. Nat. Mus.* 13: 197–203.

——. 1914. On *Tursiops catalania* and other existing species of bottlenose porpoises of that genus. *Ann. Durban Mus.* 1: 10–24.

TURNER, R. N. 1964. Methodological problems in the study of cetacean behavior. In W. N. Tavolga, ed., *Marine Bio-Acoustics.* Vol. 1., pp. 343–52. Pergamon Press.

VAN GELDER, R. G. 1960. Results of the Puritan–American Museum expedition to western Mexico. 10. Marine Mammals from the coasts of Baja California and the Tres Marias Islands. *Amer. Mus. Novitates.* 1992: 1–27.

VORONIN, L. G., Y. D. STARODUBSTEV, and L. B. KOZAROVITSKII. 1973. Dynamics of behavior training in a Black Sea bottlenose dolphin. In K. K. Chapskii and V. E. Sokolov, eds., *Morphology and Ecology of Marine Mammals: Seals, Dolphins, Porpoises,* pp. 128–42. John Wiley.

WATKINS, W. A. 1980. Click sounds from animals at sea. In R. G. Busnel and J. F. Fish, eds., *Animal Sonar Systems,* pp. 291–97. Plenum.

WEBB, N. G. 1978a. Boat towing by a bottlenose dolphin. *Carnivore* 1(1): 122–30.

———. 1978b. Women and children abducted by a wild but sociable adult male bottlenose dolphin (*Tursiops truncatus*). *Carnivore* 1(2): 89–94.

WELLS, R. S., A. B. IRVINE, and M. D. SCOTT. 1980. The social ecology of inshore odontocetes. In L. M. Herman, ed., *Cetacean Behavior: Mechanisms and Functions,* pp. 263–317. John Wiley.

WILSON, E. O. 1975. *Sociobiology: The New Synthesis.* Harvard University Press.

WOOD, F. G. 1953. Underwater sound production and concurrent behavior of captive porpoises, *Tursiops truncatus* and *Stenella plagiodon. Bull. Mar. Sci. Gulf and Caribbean* 3: 120–33.

———. 1973. *Marine Mammals and Man.* Luce.

———. 1977. Births of dolphins at Marineland of Florida, 1939–1969, and comments on problems involved in captive breeding of small cetacea. In S. H. Ridgway and K. Benirschke, eds., *Breeding Dolphins: Present Status, Suggestions for the Future,* pp. 47–60. U.S. Marine Mammal Commission Report No. MMC-76/07.

———. 1979. The cetacean stranding phenomenon: An hypothesis. In J. B. Geraci and D. J. St. Aubin, eds., *Biology of Marine Mammals: Insights Through Strandings,* pp. 129–88. U.S. Marine Mammal Commission Report PB-293 890.

———, and W. E. EVANS. 1980. Adaptiveness and ecology of echolocation in toothed whales. In R. -G. Busnel and J. F. Fish, eds., *Animal Sonar Systems,* pp. 381–425. Plenum.

WOOD, F. G., D. K. CALDWELL, and M. C. CALDWELL. 1970. Behavioural interactions between porpoises and sharks. *Invest. on Cetacea* 2: 264–77.

WOODCOCK, A. H. 1948. The swimming of dolphins. *Nature* 161(4094): 602.

WÜRSIG, B. 1978. Occurrence and group organization of Atlantic bottlenose porpoises (*Tursiops truncatus*) in an Argentine bay. *Biol. Bull.* 154: 348–59.

———, and M. WÜRSIG. 1977. The photographic determination of group size, composition, and stability of coastal porpoises (*Tursiops truncatus*). *Science* 198: 755–56.

———. 1979. Behavior and ecology of the bottlenose dolphin *Tursiops truncatus,* in the South Atlantic. *Fish. Bull.* 77(2): 399–412.

YABLOKOV, A. V., V. M. BEL'KOVICH, and V. I. BORISOV. 1972. *Whales and Dolphins. (Kity i Del'finy.)* Israel Program for Scientific Translations. Jerusalem.

SPINNER DOLPHIN, CLYMENE DOLPHIN, SPOTTED DOLPHIN, ATLANTIC SPOTTED DOLPHIN, AND STRIPED DOLPHIN

ALLEN, G. M. 1925. The bridled dolphin (*Prodelphinus froenatus*) on the Florida coast. *Jour. Mammal.* 6: 59.

ALLEN, R. L., and M. D. GOLDSMITH. 1980. Dolphin mortality in the eastern tropical Pacific incidental to purse seining for yellowfin tunas, 1979. *Sci. Com. Rep. Intl. Whal. Commn.* SC/32/SM6.

AU, D., and D. WEIHS. 1980. At high speeds dolphins save energy by leaping. *Nature* 284(5756): 548–50.

BAKER, A. N. 1972. *New Zealand Whales and Dolphins.* Victoria University of Wellington. 49 pp.

———, and A. B. STEPHENSON. 1972. The occurrence of the dolphin genus *Stenella* in New Zealand Waters. *Rec. Dominion Mus.* 8(6): 107–14.

BENIRSCHKE, K., M. L. JOHNSON, and R. J. BENIRSCHKE. 1980. Is ovulation in dolphins, *Stenella longirostris* and *Stenella attenuata* always copulation-induced? *Fish. Bull.* 78(2): 507–28.

BEST, P. B. 1969. A dolphin (*Stenella attenuata*) from Durban, South Africa. *Ann. S. African Mus.* 52(5): 121–35.

BUSNEL, R. -G., G. PILLERI, and F. C. FRASER. 1968. Notes concernant le dauphin *Stenella styx* Gray 1846. *Mammalia* 32(2): 192–203.

CADENAT, J. and M. DOUTRE. 1958. Notes sur les Delphinides ouest-africains. I. Un *Prodelphinus?* indeterminé des côtes du Sénégal. *Bull. de l'Inst. Français d'Afrique Noir.* Serie A, 204(4): 1483–85.

CAHN, R. 1980. The porpoises resurface. *Audubon* 82(1): 5–8.

CALDWELL, D. K. 1955. Notes on the spotted dolphin, *Stenella plagiodon,* and the first record of the common dolphin, *Delphinus delphis,* in the Gulf of Mexico. *Jour. Mammal.* 36(3): 467–70.

———, 1960. Notes on the spotted dolphin in the Gulf of Mexico. *Jour. Mammal.* 41(1): 134–36.

———, and M. C. CALDWELL. 1966. Observations on the distribution, coloration, behavior and audible sound production of the spotted dolphin, *Stenella plagiodon* (Cope). *L.A. County Mus. Contrib. Sci.* 104: 1–28.

———. 1969. Gray's dolphin, *Stenella styx,* in the Gulf of Mexico. *Jour. Mammal.* 50(3): 612–14.

———. 1971. Underwater pulsed sounds produced by captive spotted dolphins, *Stenella plagiodon. Cetology* 1: 7 pp.

————. 1975. Pygmy killer whales and short-snouted spinner dolphins in Florida. *Cetology* 18: 1–5.

————, W. F. RATHJEN, and J. R. SULLIVAN. 1971. Cetaceans from the Lesser Antillean island of St. Vincent. *Fish. Bull.* 69(2): 303–12.

CASINOS, A., and J. -R. VERICAD. 1976. The cetaceans of the Spanish coasts: A survey. *Mammalia* 40(2): 267–90.

COE, J., and G. SOUSA. 1972. Removing porpoise from a tuna purse seine. *Mar. Fish. Rev.* 34(11–12): 15–19.

COE, J. M., and W. E. STUNTZ. 1980. Passive behavior by the spotted dolphin, *Stenella attenuata*, in tuna purse seine nets. *Fish. Bull.* 78(2): 535–37.

COMMITTEE FOR HUMANE LEGISLATION, INC. V. ELLIOT L. RICHARDSON *et al.* (C. A. No. 74-1465) and FUND FOR ANIMALS, *et al.* V. ELLIOT L. RICHARDSON *et al.*, 414 F. Supp. 296 (D.D.C. 1976); (C. A. No. 75-0277).

DAWBIN, W. H. 1966. Porpoises and porpoise hunting in Malaita. *Aust. Nat. Hist.* 15(7): 207–11.

DEFRAN, R. A., and K. W. PRYOR. 1980. The behavior and training of cetaceans in captivity. In L. M. Herman, ed., *Cetacean Behavior: Mechanisms and Functions*, pp. 319–362. John Wiley.

DUGUY, R. 1977. Notes on the small cetaceans off the coasts of France. *Rep. Int. Whal. Commn.* 27: 500–01.

ERDHEIM, E. 1979. The immediate goal test of the Marine Mammal Protection Act and the tuna/porpoise controversy. *Environmental Law* 9(2): 283–309.

ERDMAN, D. S., J. HARMS, and M. M. FLORES. Cetacean records from the northeastern Caribbean region. *Cetology* 17: 14 pp.

FOX, W. W. 1978. Tuna/dolphin program: Five years of progress. *Oceans* 11(3): 57–59.

FRASER, F. C. 1946. Report on cetacea stranded on the British coasts from 1933 to 1937. *Bull. Brit. Mus. (Nat. Hist.)* 12: 1–55.

————. 1950. Description of a dolphin *Stenella frontalis* (Cuvier) from the coast of French Equatorial Africa. *Atlantide-Report No. 1. Scientific Results of the Danish Expedition to the coasts of Tropical West Africa, 1945–1946.* 61–84.

————. 1966. Comments on Delphinoidea. In K. S. Norris, ed., *Whales, Dolphins and Porpoises*, pp. 7–31. University of California Press.

————. 1977. Royal fishes: the importance of the dolphin. In R. J. Harrison, ed., *Functional Anatomy of Marine Mammals.* Vol 3., pp. 1–44. Academic Press.

————, and B. A. NOBLE. 1970. Variation of pigmentation pattern in Meyen's dolphin, *Stenella coeruleoalba* (Meyen). *Invest. on Cetacea* 2: 147–63.

GIHR, M., and G. PILLERI. 1969. On the anatomy and biometry of *Stenella styx* and *Delphinus delphis*, (Cetacea, Delphinidae) of the western Mediterranean. *Invest. on Cetacea* 1: 15–65.

GRAY, J. E. 1850. Catalog of the specimens of mammalia in the collection of the British Museum. Pt. 1. *Cetacea.* Trustees, Brit. Mus., 153 pp.

GRAY, W. B. 1964. *Friendly Porpoises.* A. S. Barnes.

GUNTER, G. 1941. A record of the long-snouted dolphin, *Stenella plagiodon* (Cope), from the Texas coast. *Jour. Mammal.* 22(4): 447–48.

HALL, E. K., and K. R. KELSON. 1959. *The Mammals of North America.* Ronald Press.

HENDERSON, J. R., W. F. PERRIN, and R. B. MILLER. 1980. Rate of gross annual production in dolphin populations (*Stenella* spp. and *Delphinus delphis*) in the eastern tropical Pacific, 1973–1978. *Southwest Fisheries Center (NMFS) Admin. Rep.* LJ-80-02. 51 pp.

HERSHKOVITZ, P. 1966. Catalog of Living Whales. *U.S Nat. Mus. Bull.* 246.

HESTER, F. J., J. R. HUNTER, and R. R. WHITNEY. 1963. Jumping and spinning behavior in the spinner porpoise. *Jour. Mammal.* 44(4): 586–88.

HUBBS, C. L., W. F. PERRIN, and K. C. BALCOMB. 1973. *Stenella coeruleoalba* in the eastern and central tropical Pacific. *Jour. Mammal.* 54(2): 549–52.

JORDAN, A. M. 1974. Porpoises and purse seines. *Oceans* 7(3): 6–7.

KASUYA, T. 1971. Consideration of distribution and migration of toothed whales off the Pacific coast of Japan based upon aerial sighting record. *Sci. Rep. Whales Res. Inst.* 37–59. Pl. I–IV.

————. 1972. Growth and reproduction of *Stenella caeruleoalba* based on the age determination by means of dentinal growth layers. *Sci. Rep. Whales Res. Inst.* 24: 57–79.

————. 1976. Reconsiderations of life history parameters of the spotted and striped dolphins based on cemental layers. *Sci. Rep. Whales Res. Inst.* 28: 73–106.

————, and N. MIYAZAKI. 1975. The stock of *Stenella coeruleoalba* off the Pacific coast of Japan. *Advisory Committee on Marine Resources Research, FAO, Bergen, Norway.* ACMRR/MM/EC/25.

————, and W. H. DAWBIN. 1974. Growth and reproduction of *Stenella attenuata* in the Pacific coast of Japan. *Sci. Rep. Whales Res. Inst.* 26: 157–226.

KAMIYA, T., and N. MIYAZAKI. 1974. A malformed embryo of *Stenella coeruleoalba. Sci. Rep. Whales Res. Inst.* 26: 259–63.

KAWAMURA, A., and K. KASHITA. 1971. A rare double monster of dolphin, *Stenella caeruleoalba. Sci. Rep. Whales Res. Inst.* 23: 139–40.

KELLOGG, R., and V. B. SCHEFFER. 1947. Occurrence of *Stenella euphrosyne* off the Oregon coast. *Murrelet* 28(1): 9–10.

KENYON, K. W., and V. B. SCHEFFER. 1949. A long-snouted dolphin from the Washington coast. *Jour. Mammal.* 30(3): 267–68.

LANG, T. G., and K. S. NORRIS. 1966. Swimming speed of a Pacific bottlenose porpoise. *Science* 151(3710): 588–90.

LANG, T. G., and K. W. PRYOR. 1966. Hydrodynamic performance of porpoises (*Stenella attenuata*). *Science* 152: 531–33.

LAYNE, J. N. 1965. Observations on marine mammals in Florida waters. *Bull. Fla. State Mus.* 9(4): 131–81.

LEATHERWOOD, J. S., W. F. PERRIN, R. L. GARVIE, and J. C. LA GRANGE. 1973. Observations of sharks attacking porpoises. *Naval Undersea Center.* TN-908. 7 pp.

LEATHERWOOD, S., and D. K. LJUNGBLAD. 1979. Nighttime swimming and diving behavior of a radio-tagged spotted dolphin, *Stenella attenuata. Cetology* 34. 6 pp.

LEATHERWOOD, S., and R. R. REEVES. 1978. Porpoises and Dolphins. In D. Haley, ed., *Marine Mammals of Eastern North Pacific and Arctic Waters*, pp. 96–111. Pacific Search Press.

LINEHAN, T. 1979. The trouble with dolphins. *National Geographic* 155(4): 506–41.

MEAD, J. G. 1979. An analysis of cetacean strandings along the eastern coast of the United States. In J. B. Geraci and D. J. St. Aubin, eds., *Biology of Marine Mammals: Insights through Strandings*, pp. 54–68. U. S. Marine Mammal Commission Report PB-293 890.

————, D. K. ODELL, R. S. WELLS, and M. D. SCOTT. 1980. Observations on a mass stranding of spinner dolphin, *Stenella longirostris.* from the west coast of Florida. *Fish. Bull.* 78(2): 353–60.

MINASIAN, S. M. 1977. Dolphins and/or tuna. *Oceans* 10(6): 60–63.

MITCHELL, E. D., ed. 1975. Review of biology and fisheries for smaller cetaceans. *Jour. Fish. Res. Bd. Canada.* 32(7).

MIYAZAKI, N. 1976. School Structure of *Stenella coeruleoalba. Advisory Committee on Marine Resources Research*, FAO, Bergen, Norway. ACMRR/MM/SC/73.

————. 1977. Growth and reproduction of *Stenella coeruleoalba* off the Pacific coast of Japan. *Sci. Rep. Whales Res. Inst.* 29: 21–48.

————. 1980. Catch records of cetaceans off the coast of the Kii Peninsula. *Mem. Nat. Sci. Mus. Tokyo* 13: 69–82.

————, and M. NISHIWAKI. 1978. School structure of the striped dolphin off the Pacific coast of Japan. *Sci. Rep. Whales Res. Inst.* 30: 65–115.

MIYAZAKI, N., and S. WADA. 1978. Observation of cetacea during whale marking cruise in the western tropical Pacific, 1976. *Sci. Rep. Whales Res. Inst.* 30: 179–95.

MIYAZAKI, N., T. KASUYA, and M. NISHIWAKI. 1973. Food of *Stenella coeruleoalba. Sci. Rep. Whales Res. Inst.* 25: 265–75.

————. 1974. Distribution and migration of two species of *Stenella* in the Pacific coast of Japan. *Sci. Rep. Whales Res. Inst.* 26: 227–43.

MORRIS, R. A. and L. S. MOWBRAY. 1964. An unusual barnacle attachment on the teeth of the Hawaiian spinning dolphin. *Norsk Hvalfangst-tidende* 51(1): 15–16.

MURPHY, G. 1979. Discover the dolphins: Intelligent mammals of the sea. *Skin Diver* 28(8): 56–59.

NICOL, C. W. 1979. *Taiji—Winds of Change.* Japan Whaling Association.

NISHIWAKI, M. 1953. Hermaphroditism in a dolphin (*Prodelphinus caeruleo-albus*). *Sci. Rep. Whales Res. Inst.* 8: 215–18.

————. 1966. A discussion of rarities among the smaller cetaceans caught in Japanese waters. In K. S. Norris, ed., *Whales, Dolphins and Porpoises*, pp. 192–204. Univ. of California Press.

————. 1967. Distribution and migration of marine mammals in the North Pacific area. *Bull. Ocean Res. Inst., Univ. of Tokyo* I.

————. 1975. Ecological aspects of smaller cetaceans, with emphasis on the striped dolphin *Stenella coeruleoalba. Jour. Fish. Res. Bd. Canada* 32(7): 1069–72.

————. 1975. On the catch of the striped dolphin (*Stenella coeruleo-alba*) in Japan. *Advisory Committee on Marine Resources Research, FAO. Bergen, Norway.* ACMRR/MM/EC/30.

————, and T. YAGI. 1953. On the age and the growth of teeth in a dolphin (*Prodelphinus caeruleo-albus*). *Sci. Rep. Whales Res. Inst.* 8: 133–46.

NISHIWAKI, M., M. NAKAJIMA, and T. KAMIYA. 1965. A rare species of dolphin (*Stenella attenuata*) from Arari, Japan. *Sci. Rep. Whales Res. Inst.* 19: 53–64.

NORRIS, K. S. 1974. *The Porpoise Watcher.* W. W. Norton.

————. 1977. Tuna sandwiches cost at least 78,000 porpoise lives a year, but there is hope. *Smithsonian* 7(11): 44–53.

————, and T. P. DOHL. 1980. Behavior of the Hawaiian spinner dolphin, *Stenella longirostris. Fish. Bull.* 77(4): 821–49.

NORRIS, K. S., and J. H. PRESCOTT. 1961. Observations on Pacific Cetaceans of Californian and Mexican waters. *Univ. Calif. Publ. Zool.* 63(4): 291–402.

NORRIS, K. S., W. E. STUNTZ, and W. ROGERS. 1978. The behavior of porpoises and tuna in the eastern tropical Pacific yellowfin tuna fishery—preliminary studies. *U.S. Marine Mammal Commission Contract MM6ACO22.* Washington, D.C. 86 pp.

ODELL, D. K. and C. CHAPMAN. 1976. A striped dolphin, *Stenella coeruleoalba*, from Florida. *Cetology* 20: 6 pp.

O'FELDMAN, R. 1980. Dancing dolphins. *Oceans* 13(1): 12.

OHSUMI, S. 1965. A dolphin (*Stenella caeruleoalba*) with protruded rudimentary hind limbs. *Sci. Rep. Whales Res. Inst.* 19: 135–36.

————. 1972. Catch of marine mammals, mainly of small cetaceans, by local fisheries along the coast of Japan. *Bull. Far Seas Res. Lab.* 7: 137–66.

ORR, R. T. 1972. *Marine Mammals of California.* Univ. of California Press.

PERRIN, W. F. 1968. The porpoise and the tuna. *Sea Frontiers* 14(3): 166–74.

———. 1969a. Using porpoise to catch tuna. *World Fishing* 18(6): 42–45.

———. 1969b. The barnacle *Conchoderma auritum* on a porpoise (*Stenella graffmani*). *Jour. Mammal.* 50(1): 149–50.

———. 1969c. The problem of porpoise mortality in the U.S. tropical tuna fishery. *Proc. Sixth Ann. Conf. Biol. Sonar and Diving Mammals.* Stanford Research Institute. Menlo Park, California. 45–48.

———. 1969d. Color pattern of the Eastern Pacific Spotted Porpoise *Stenella graffmani* Lönnborg (Cetacea, Delphinidae). *Zoologica* 54(4): 135–42.

———. 1972. Color patterns of spinner porpoises (*Stenella* cf. *S. longirostris*) of the Eastern Pacific and Hawaii, with comments on delphinid pigmentation. *Fish. Bull.* 70(3): 983–1003.

———. 1973. Annotated bibliography of the genus *Stenella* (Cetacea, Delphinidae). *Marine Mammal Investigations,* NMFS. La Jolla, California.

———. 1975a. Distribution and differentiation of populations of dolphins of the genus *Stenella* in the eastern tropical Pacific. *Jour. Fish. Res. Bd. Canada* 32(7): 1059–67.

———. 1975b. *Variation of Spotted and Spinner Porpoise (Genus Stenella) in the Eastern Tropical Pacific and Hawaii.* University of California Press.

———, and J. R. HUNTER. 1972. Escape behavior of the Hawaiian spinner porpoise (*Stenella* cf. *S. longirostris*). *Fish. Bull.* 70(1): 49–60.

PERRIN, W. F., and J. E. POWERS. 1980. Role of a nematode in natural mortality of spotted dolphins. *Jour. Wildl. Manage.* 44(4): 960–63.

PERRIN, W. F., J. M. COE, and J. R. ZWEIFEL. 1976. Growth and reproduction of the spotted porpoise, *Stenella attenuata,* in the offshore eastern tropical Pacific. *Fish. Bull.* 74(2): 229–69.

PERRIN, W. F., E. D. MITCHELL, and P. J. H. VAN BREE. 1978. Historical zoogeography of tropical pelagic dolphins. (Abstract) *Congressus Theriologicus Internationalis.* Brno, Czechoslovakia.

PERRIN, W. F., P. A. SLOAN, and J. P. HENDERSON. 1979. Taxonomic status of the south-western stocks of spinner dolphin *Stenella longirostris* and spotted dolphin *S. attenuata. Rep. Int. Whal. Comm.* 29: 175–84.

PERRIN, W. F., T. D. SMITH, and G. T. SAKAGAWA. 1975. Status of populations of spotted dolphin, *Stenella attenuata,* and spinner dolphin, *Stenella longirostris,* in the eastern tropical Pacific. *FAO. Bergen, Norway.* ACMRR/MM/EC/27.

PERRIN, W. F., E. D. MITCHELL, P. J. H. VAN BREE, and D. K. CALDWELL. 1977. Spinner Dolphins, *Stenella* spp., in the Atlantic. (Abstract) *Second Conf. Biol. Marine Mammals.* San Diego.

PERRIN, W. F., R. R. WARNER, C. H. FISCUS, and D. B. HOLTS. 1973. Stomach contents of porpoise *Stenella* spp. and yellowfin tuna, *Thunnus albacares,* in mixed-species aggregations. *Fish. Bull.* 71(4): 1077–92.

PERRIN, W. F., E. D. MITCHELL, J. G. MEAD, D. K. CALDWELL, and P. J. H. VAN BREE. 1981. *Stenella clymene,* a rediscovered tropical dolphin of the Atlantic. *Jour. Mammal.* 62(3): 583–98.

PERRYMAN, W. L. and T. C. FOSTER. 1980. Preliminary report on predation by small whales, mainly the false killer whale, *Pseudorca crassidens,* on dolphins (*Stenella* spp. and *Delphinus delphis*) in the eastern tropical Pacific. *Southwest Fisheries Center (NMFS) Admin. Rep.* LJ-80-05.

PRYOR, K. W. 1973. Behavior and learning in porpoises and whales. *Naturwissenschaften* 60: 412–20.

———. 1975. *Lads Before the Wind: Adventures of a Porpoise Trainer.* Harper & Row.

———, and I. KANG. 1980. Social behavior and school structure in pelagic porpoises (*Stenella attenuata* and *S. longirostris*) during purse seining for tuna. *Southwest Fisheries Center (NMFS) Administrative Report* LJ-80-11C. 86 pp. + tables.

PRYOR, K., and K. S. NORRIS. 1978. The tuna/porpoise problem: behavioral aspects. *Oceanus* 21(2): 31–37.

SAAYMAN. G. S., and C. K. TAYLER. 1973. Social organization of inshore dolphins (*Tursiops aduncus* and *Sousa*) in the Indian Ocean. *Jour. Mammal.* 54(4): 993–96.

SAMPSON, W. F. 1970. *Stenella coeruleoalba* in the northern Pacific Ocean. *Jour. Mammal.* 51(4): 809.

SCHEFFER, V. B. 1960. A dolphin *Stenella* from Washington state. *Murrelet* 41(2): 23.

SCHEVILL, W. E., and W. A. WATKINS. 1962. Whale and porpoise voices. (Phonograph record + notes.) Woods Hole Oceanographic Institution. pp. 1–24.

SCHMIDLY, D. F., and S. H. SHANE. 1978. A biological assessment of the cetacean fauna of the Texas coast. *U. S. Marine Mammal Commission* PB 281763. 38 pp.

SCHMIDLY. D. J., M. H. BELEAU, and H. HILDEBRAN. 1972. First record of Cuvier's dolphin from the Gulf of Mexico with comments on the taxonomic status of *Stenella frontalis. Jour. Mammal.* 53(3): 625–28.

SHANE, S. H. 1977. The population biology of the Atlantic bottlenose dolphin, *Tursiops truncatus,* in the Aransas Pass area of Texas. M.S. Thesis, Texas A & M University, College Station, 237 pp.

SHEFFE, R. 1980. The dolphin project. *Sport Diver* 4(5): 60–67.

SHELDRICK, M. C. 1979. Cetacean strandings along the coasts of the British Isles 1913–1977. In J. B. Geraci and D. J. St.

Aubin, eds., *Biology of Marine Mammals: Insights through Strandings*, pp. 35–53. U.S. Marine Mammal Commission Report PB-293 890.

SMITH, T., ed. 1979. Report of the status of porpoise stocks workshop (August 27–31, 1979, La Jolla, California). *NMFS Southwest Fisheries Center Administrative Report LJ-79-41.* 62 pp. + plates, tables, appendices.

STUNTZ, W. E. 1980a. Preliminary investigations of the possible relationship between passive behavior by spotted dolphins, *Stenella attenuata*, and capture stress. *U. S. Marine Mammal Commission Report.* MMC-77-25.

———. 1980b. Variation in age structure of the incidental kill of spotted dolphins, *Stenella attenuata*, in the U.S. tropical purse-seine fishery. *Southwest Fisheries Center (NMFS), Admin. Rep.* LJ-80-06. 29 pp.

———, and T. B. SHAY. 1979. Report on capture stress workshop. *Southwest Fisheries Center (NMFS) Admin. Rep.* LJ-79-28.

SUTHERLAND, D. L., and L. L. MAY. 1977. Spotted dolphins, *Stenella plagiodon* (Cope): underwater observations using an unmanned submersible. *Cetology* 27: 9 pp.

TARUSKI, A. G., and H. E. WINN. 1976. Winter sightings of odontocetes in the West Indies. *Cetology,* 22: 12 pp.

TOBAYAMA, T., S. UCHIDA, and M. NISHIWAKI. 1970. Twin fetuses from a blue white dolphin. *Sci. Rep. Whales Res. Inst.* 22: 159–62.

TOMICH, P. Q. 1969. *Mammals in Hawaii: A Synopsis and Notational Bibliography.* Bishop Museum Press.

TRUE, F. W. 1889. Contributions to the natural history of the cetaceans, a review of the family Delphinidae. *Bull. U.S. Nat. Mus.* 36: 1–191.

ULMER, F. A. 1980. New Jersey's dolphins and porpoises. *N.J. Audubon Soc. Occasional Paper No. 137:* 11 pp.

VAN BREE, P. J. H. 1971. On skulls of *Stenella longirostris* (Gray, 1828) from the eastern Atlantic (Notes on Cetacea, Delphinoidea IV). *Beaufortia.* 19(251): 99–106.

VAN HALEWIJN, R., and P. J. H. VAN BREE. 1972. On the occurrence of the common dolphin, *Delphinus delphis,* and the spinner dolphin, *Stenella longirostris,* off the coast of Venezuela. *Invest. on Cetacea* 4: 187–88.

WHITTOW, G. C. 1977. The Hawaiian spinner. *Sea Frontiers* 25(3): 304–07.

WOOD, F. G. 1953. Underwater sound production and concurrent behavior of captive porpoises, *Tursiops truncatus* and *Stenella plagiodon. Bull. Mar. Sci. Gulf and Caribbean* 3: 120–33.

———. 1973. *Marine Mammals and Man.* Luce.

———. 1979. The cetacean stranding phenomenon: An hypothesis. In J. B. Geraci and D. J. St. Aubin, eds., *Biology of Marine Mammals: Insights through Strandings*, pp. 129–88. U.S. Marine Mammal Commission Report PB-293 890.

WÜRSIG, B., and M. WÜRSIG. 1980. Behavior and ecology of the dusky dolphin, *Lagenorhynchus obscurus*, in the South Atlantic. *Fish. Bull.* 77(4): 871–90.

COMMON DOLPHIN

ALPERS, A. 1960. *Dolphins: The Myth and the Mammal.* Houghton Mifflin.

BANKS, R. C., and R. L. BROWNELL. 1969. Taxonomy of the common dolphins of the eastern Pacific Ocean. *Jour. Mammal.* 50(2): 262–71.

BERKES, F. 1977. Turkish dolphin fisheries. *Oryx* 14(2): 163–67.

BROWN, D. H., and K. S. NORRIS. 1956. Observations of captive and wild cetaceans. *Jour. Mammal.* 37(3): 311–26.

BROWNELL, R. L. 1964. Observations of odontocetes in central Californian waters. *Norsk Hvalfangst-tidende* 53(3): 60–66.

BUSNEL, R. -G., and A. DZIEDZIC. 1966. Acoustic signals of the pilot whale *Globicephala melaena* and of the porpoises *Delphinus delphis* and *Phocoena phocoena*. In K. S. Norris, ed., *Whales, Dolphins and Porpoises*, pp. 607–46. University of California Press.

CALDWELL, M. C., and D. K. CALDWELL. 1966. Epimeletic (caregiving) behavior in cetacea. In K. S. Norris, ed., *Whales, Dolphins and Porpoises*, pp. 755–89. University of California Press.

CASINOS, A., and J. -R. VERICAD. 1976. The cetaceans of the Spanish coasts: A survey. *Mammalia* 40(2): 267–90.

CLARKE, R. 1980. Whales and dolphins of the Azores and their exploitation. *Int. Whal. Comm. Sci. Rep.* SC/32/01.

CORNELL, L. H., and E. D. ASPER. 1977. A census of captive marine mammals in North America. *Intl. Zoo Yearbook* 18: 220–24.

COUSTEAU. J. -Y., and P. DIOLÉ. 1975. *Dolphins.* Doubleday.

DALL, W. H. 1873. Descriptions of three new species of cetacea, from the coast of California. *Proc. Calif. Acad. Sci.* 5(1): 12–14.

———. 1874. Catalogue of the cetacea of the North Pacific. In C. M. Scammon, *The Marine Mammals of the Northwestern Coast of North America*, pp. 281–307. Carmany.

DAUGHERTY, A. 1972. *Marine Mammals of California.* Dept. of Fish and Game. Sacramento.

DEFRAN, R. F., and K. W. PRYOR. 1980. The behavior and training of cetaceans in captivity. In L. H. Herman, ed., *Cetacean Behavior: Mechanisms and Functions*, pp. 319–62. John Wiley.

DEVINE, E. and M. CLARK. 1967. *The Dolphin Smile: Twenty-nine Centuries of Dolphin Lore.* Macmillan.

DEWHURST, H. W. 1834. *The Natural History of the Order Cetacea and the Oceanic Inhabitants of the Arctic Regions.* London.

DIETZ, R. 1962. The sea's deep scattering layers. In *Oceanography.* Readings from *Scientific America.* W. H. Freeman.

DREHER, J. J., and W. E. EVANS. 1964. Cetacean communication. In W. N. Tavolga, ed., *Marine Bio-Acoustics.* Vol. 1, pp. 373–93. Pergamon Press.

EDWARDS, R. L., and R. LIVINGSTONE. 1960. Observations on the behavior of the porpoise *Delphinus delphis*. *Science.* 132 (3418): 35–36.

ESSAPIAN, F. S. 1962. Courtship in captive saddleback porpoises, *Delphinus delphis* L. 1758. *Zeitschrift fur Säugetierkunde* 27(4): 211–217.

EVANS, W. E. 1971. Orientation behavior of delphinids: Radio telemetric studies. *Ann. N.Y. Acad. Sci.* 188: 142–60.

———. 1974. Radio-telemetric studies of two small species of odontocete cetaceans. In W. E. Schevill, ed., *The Whale Problem*, pp. 385–94. Harvard University Press.

———. 1975. The biology of the common dolphin, *Delphinus delphis* Linnaeus. Ph. D. thesis. University of California.

———. 1976. Distribution and differentiation of stocks of *Delphinus delphis* Linnaeus in the northeastern Pacific. *FAO, Bergen, Norway.* SC/18.

———, W. W. SUTHERLAND, and R. G. BIEL. 1964. The directional characteristics of delphinid sounds. In W. N. Tavolga, ed., *Marine Bio-Acoustics*, pp. 353–70. Pergamon Press.

FITCH, J. E., and R. L. BROWNELL. 1968. Fish otoliths in cetacean stomachs and their importance in interpreting feeding habits. *Jour. Fish. Res. Bd. Canada.* 25(12): 2561–64.

FRASER, F. C. 1946. Report on cetacea stranded on the British coasts from 1933 to 1937. *Bull. Brit. Mus. (Nat. Hist.)* 12: 56 pp.

———. 1953. Report on cetacea stranded on the British coasts from 1938 to 1947. *Bull. Brit. Mus. (Nat. Hist)* 13: 48 pp.

———. 1977. Royal fishes: The importance of the dolphin. In R. J. Harrison, ed., *Functional Anatomy of Marine Mammals.* Vol. 3, pp. 1–44. Academic Press.

GASKIN, D. E. 1972. *Whales, Dolphins and Seals, with special reference to the New Zealand region.* Heinemann Educational Books.

GIHR, M., and G. PILLERI. 1969. On the anatomy and biometry of *Stenella styx* Gray and *Delphinus delphis* L. (Cetacea, Delphinidae) of the western Mediterranean. *Invest. on Cetacea* 1: 15–65.

GOODALL, N. R. P. 1977. Preliminary report on the small cetaceans stranded on the coasts of Tierra del Fuego. *Rep. Int. Whal. Commn.* 27: 505.

———. 1978. Report on the small cetaceans stranded on the coasts of Tierra del Fuego. *Sci. Rep. Whales Res. Inst.* 30: 197–230.

GUIGUET, C. J. 1954. A record of Baird's dolphin (*Delphinus bairdii* Dall) in British Columbia. *Can. Field Nat.* 68(3): 136.

GUNTER, G. 1942, Contributions to the natural history of the bottlenosed dolphin, *Tursiops truncatus* (Montagu), on the Texas coast, with particular reference to food habits. *Jour. Mammal.* 23: 267–76.

GWINN, S., and W. F. PERRIN. 1975. Distribution of melanin in the color pattern of *Delphinus delphis* (Cetacea; Delphinidae). *Fish. Bull.* 73(2): 439–44.

HARMER, S. F. 1927. Report on cetacea stranded on the British coasts from 1913 to 1926. *Bull. Brit. Mus. (Nat. Hist.)* 10: 91 pp.

HOUSBY, T. 1971. *The Hand of God: Whaling in the Azores.* Abelard-Schuman.

INTERNATIONAL WHALING COMMISSION. 1979. Report of the sub-committee on small cetaceans. *Rep. Intl. Whal. Commn.* (Annex H) 29: 87–89.

KASUYA, T. 1971. Consideration of distribution and migration of toothed whales off the Pacific coast of Japan based on aerial sighting records. *Sci. Rep. Whales Res. Inst.* 23: 37–66.

LEATHERWOOD, S., and R. R. REEVES. 1978. Porpoises and dolphins. In D. Haley, ed., *Marine Mammals of Eastern North Pacific and Arctic Waters*, pp. 96–111. Pacific Search Press.

LEATHERWOOD, J. S., W. F. PERRIN, R. L. GARVIE, and J. C. LA GRANGE. 1973. Observations of sharks attacking porpoises (*Stenella* spp. and *Delphinus* cf *Delphis*). *Naval Undersea Center* TN 908. 7 pp.

MARCUZZI, G., and G. PILLERI. 1971. On the zoogeography of cetacea. *Invest. on Cetacea* 3(1): 101–71.

MEAD, J. G. 1979. An analysis of cetacean strandings along the eastern coast of the United States. In J. R. Geraci and D. J. St. Aubin, eds., *Biology of Marine Mammals: Insights through Strandings*, pp. 54–68. U.S. Marine Mammal Commission Report PB 293 890.

MILLER, G. S. 1936. The status of *Delphinus bairdii* Dall. *Proc. Biol. Soc. Wash.* 49: 145–46.

MITCHELL, E. D. 1970. Pigmentation pattern evolution in delphinid cetaceans: an essay in adaptive coloration. *Canadian Journal of Zoology* 48(4): 717–40.

———. 1975a. Review of biology and fisheries for smaller cetaceans. *Jour. Fish. Res. Bd. Canada* 32(7): 889–983.

———. 1975b. *Porpoise, Dolphin and Small Whale Fisheries of the World: Status and Problems.* IUCN Monograph No. 3. Morges, Switzerland.

MIYAZAKI, N., and S. WADA. 1978. Observation of cetacea during whale marking cruise in the western tropical Pacific, 1976. *Sci. Rep. Whales Res. Inst.* 30: 179–95.

NISHIWAKI, M. 1967. Distribution and migration of marine mammals in the North Pacific area. *Bull. Ocean Res. Inst. Univ. Tokyo* 1: 1–64.

———. 1972. General biology. In S. H. Ridgway, ed., *Mammals of the Sea: Biology and Medicine*, pp. 3–202. Charles C. Thomas.

NORRIS, K. S., and J. H. PRESCOTT. 1961. Observations on Pacific cetaceans from Californian and Mexican waters. *Univ. Calif. Publ. Zool.* 63(4): 291–402.

NORRIS, K. S., and T. P. DOHL. 1980. The structure and function of cetacean schools. In L. H. Herman, ed., *Cetacean Behavior: Mechanisms and Functions*, pp. 211–61. John Wiley.

NORRIS, K. S., W. E. EVANS, and G. C. RAY. 1974. New tagging and tracking methods for the study of marine mammal biology and migration. In W. E. Schevill, ed., *The Whale Problem*, pp. 395–408. Harvard University Press.

PERRIN, W. F. 1972. Color patterns of spinner porpoises (*Stenella* cf. *S. longirostris*) of the eastern Pacific and Hawaii, with comments on delphinid pigmentation. *Fish. Bull.* 70(3): 983–1003.

————. 1975. Distribution and differentiation of populations of dolphins of the genus *Stenella* in the eastern tropical Pacific. *Jour. Fish. Res. Bd. Canada* 32(7): 1059–67.

PILLERI, G., and M. GIHR. 1972. Contribution to the knowledge of cetaceans of Pakistan with particular reference to the genera *Neomeris, Sousa, Delphinus* and *Tursiops* and description of a new Chinese porpoise (*Neomeris asiaeorientalis*). *Invest. on Cetacea* 4: 107–62.

PILLERI, G., and J. KNUCKEY. 1969. Behavior patterns of some delphinidae observed in the western Mediterranean. *Zeitschrift für Tierpsychologie* 26(1): 48–72.

ROBSON, F. 1976. *Thinking Dolphins, Talking Whales.* A. H. & A. W. Reed.

SANDERSON, I. T. 1956. *Follow the Whale.* Little, Brown.

SCHEFFER, V. B., and J. W. SLIPP. 1948. The whales and dolphins of Washington State with a key to the cetaceans of the west coast of North America. *Amer. Midl. Nat.* 39(2): 257–337.

SCHEVILL, W. E., and W. A. WATKINS. 1966. Sound structure and directionality in *Orcinus*. (Killer whale). *Zoologica* 51(2): 71–76.

SERGEANT. D. E. 1958. Dolphins in Newfoundland waters. *Canadian Field Nat.* 72: 156–59.

SHELDRICK, M. C. 1979. Cetacean strandings along the coasts of the British Isles 1913–1977. In J. R. Geraci and D. J. St. Aubin, eds., *Biology of Marine Mammals: Insights through Strandings*, pp. 35–53. U.S. Marine Mammal Commission Report PB-293 890.

SMITH, T. 1976. Current understanding of the status of the porpoise populations of the Black Sea. *FAO Scientific Consulation on Marine Mammals.* ACMRR/MM/SC/40.

STONER, D. 1938. New York State records for the common dolphin, *Delphinus delphis*. *N.Y.S. Mus. Circ.* 21: 1–16.

TOMICH, P. Q. 1969. *Mammals in Hawaii.* Bishop Museum Press.

TOMILIN, A. G. 1957. *Mammals of the USSR and Adjacent Countries. Vol. 9: Cetacea.* Izdatel'stvo Akademi Nauk SSR, Moscow. (Israel Program for Scientific Translations, Jerusalem, 1967.)

TRUE, F. W. 1889. A review of the family delphinidae. *Bull. U.S. Nat. Mus.* 36: 1–191.

ULMER, F. A. 1980. New Jersey's dolphins and porpoises. *New Jersey Audubon Society Occasional Papers* 137: 1–11.

VAN BREE, P. J. H. 1971. *Delphinus tropicalis*, a new name for *Delphinus longirostris* Cuvier. *Mammalia* 35: 345–46.

————, and M. D. GALLAGHER. 1978. On the taxonomic status of *Delphinus tropicalis* van Bree, 1971. (Notes on Cetacea, Delphinoidea IX.) *Beaufortia* 28(342): 1–8.

VAN BREE, P. J. H., and P. E. PURVES. 1972. Remarks on the validity of *Delphinus bairdii* (Cetacea, Delphinidae). *Jour. Mammal.* 53(2): 373–74.

WALKER, W. A. 1975. Review of the live-capture fishery for smaller cetaceans taken in Southern California waters for public display, 1966–1973. *Jour. Fish. Res. Bd. Canada.* 32(7): 1197–1211.

WILSON, E. O. 1975. *Sociobiology: The New Synthesis.* Harvard University Press.

WOOD, F. G. 1979. The cetacean stranding phenomenon: An hypothesis. In J. B. Geraci and D. J. St. Aubin, eds., *Biology of Marine Mammals: Insights through Strandings*, pp. 129–88. U.S. Marine Mammal Commission Report PB-293 890.

————, D. K. CALDWELL, and M. C. CALDWELL. 1970. Behavioral interactions between porpoises and sharks. *Invest. on Cetacea* 2: 264–77.

YABLOKOV, A. V., V. M. BEL'KOVICH, and V. I. BORISOV. 1972. *Whales and Dolphins (Kity i Del'finy).* (Israel Program for Scientific Translations, Jerusalem, 1974.)

FRASER'S DOLPHIN

BERZIN, A. A. 1978. Whale distribution in tropical eastern Pacific waters. *Rep. Int. Whal. Commn.* 28: 173–77.

CALDWELL, D. K., M. C. CALDWELL, and R. V. WALKER. 1976. First records for Fraser's dolphin (*Lagenodelphis hosei*) in the Atlantic and the melon-headed whale (*Peponocephala electra*) in the western Atlantic. *Cetology* 25: 4 pp.

DREHER, J. 1966. Cetacean communication: small group experiment. In K. S. Norris, ed., *Whales, Dolphins and Porpoises*, pp. 529–43. Univ. of California Press.

FRASER, F. C. 1956. A new Sarawak dolphin. *Sarawak Mus. Jour.* 7: 478–503.

HARRISON, T. 1957. Colour of the new Sarawak dolphin. *Sarawak Mus. Jour.* 8(10): 265.

LEATHERWOOD, S., D. K. CALDWELL, and H. E. WINN. 1976. *Whales, Dolphins and Porpoises of the Western North Atlantic: A Guide to Their Identification.* NOAA Technical Report NMFS CIRC-396.

MITCHELL, E. D. 1970. Pigmentation pattern evolution in delphinid cetaceans: an essay in adaptive coloration. *Canadian Jour. Zool.* 48(4): 717–40.

————, ed. 1975. Review of biology and fisheries for smaller cetaceans. *Jour. Fish. Res. Bd. Canada.* 32(7): 875–1239.

MIYAZAKI, N., and S. WADA. 1978a. Fraser's dolphin. *Lagenodelphis hosei* in the western North Pacific. *Sci. Rep. Whales Res. Inst.* 30: 231–44.

————, and S. WADA. 1978b. Observation of cetacea during whale marking cruise in the western tropical Pacific, 1976. *Sci. Rep. Whales Res. Inst.* 30: 179–95.

PERRIN, W. F. 1975. Distribution and differentiation of populations of dolphins of the genus *Stenella* in the eastern tropical Pacific. *Jour. Fish. Res. Bd. Canada.* 32(7): 1059–67.

————, P. B. BEST, W. H. DAWBIN, K. C. BALCOMB, R. GAMBELL, and G. J. B. ROSS. 1973. Rediscovery of Fraser's dolphin *Lagenodelphis hosei. Nature* 241(5388): 345–50.

TOBAYAMA, T., M. NISHIWAKI, and H. C. YANG. 1973. Records of the Fraser's Sarawak dolphin in the western North Pacific. *Sci. Rep. Whales Res. Inst.* 25: 251–363.

WHITE-BEAKED DOLPHIN, ATLANTIC WHITE-SIDED DOLPHIN, PACIFIC WHITE-SIDED DOLPHIN, DUSKY DOLPHIN, PEALE'S DOLPHIN, HOURGLASS DOLPHIN

AGUAYO, A. 1975. Progress report on small cetacean research in Chile. *Jour. Fish. Res. Bd. Canada* 32(7): 1123–43.

AMUNDIN, B., and M. AMUNDIN. 1975. Sightings of whitenose dolphins (*Lagenorhynchus albirostris*) in Danish waters. *Z. Saeugetierkd.* 40(1): 58–59.

ANDERSEN, S. H., and A. REBSDORFF. 1976. Polychlorinated hydrocarbons and heavy metals in harbor porpoise (*Phocoena phocoena*), and whitebeaked dolphin (*Lagenorhynchus albirostris*), from Danish waters. *Aquat. Mammals* 4(1): 14–20.

ASH, C. 1962. *Whaler's Eye*. Macmillan.

BAKER, A. N. 1972. New Zealand whales and dolphins. *Tuatara* 20(1): 49 pp.

BARTLETT, D., and J. BARTLETT. 1976. A wild shore where two worlds meet. *National Geographic* 149(3): 298–321.

BIERMAN, W. H., and E. J. SLIJPER. 1947. Remarks upon the species of the genus *Lagenorhynchus*. I. *Proc. K. Ned. Akad. Wet.* 50(10): 1353–64.

————. 1948. Remarks upon the species of the genus *Lagenorhynchus*. II. *Proc. K. Ned. Akad. Wet.* 51(1): 127–33.

BROWN, D. H., and K. S. NORRIS. 1956. Observations of captive and wild cetaceans. *Jour. Mammal.* 37(3): 311–26.

BROWNELL, R. L. 1964. Observations of odontocetes in Central Californian waters. *Norsk Hvalfangst-tidende* 55(3): 60–66.

————. 1965a. An anomalous color pattern in a Pacific striped dolphin. *Bull. So. Calif. Acad. Sci.* 64(4): 242–43.

————. 1965b. A record of the dusky dolphin, *Lagenorhynchus obscurus*, from New Zealand. *Norsk Hvalfangst-tidende* 54: 169–71.

————. 1974. Small odontocetes of the Antarctic. In V. C. Bushnell, ed. *Antarctic Mammals*. Antarctic Map Folio Series. American Geographical Society. Folio 18: 14–18.

CALDWELL, M. C., and D. K. CALDWELL. 1964. Experimental studies on factors involved in care-giving behavior in three species of the cetacean family Delphinidae. *Bull. So. Cal. Acad. Sci.* 63(1): 1–20.

————. 1966. Epimeletic (care-giving) behavior in cetacea. In K. S. Norris, ed., *Whales, Dolphins and Porpoises*, pp. 755–89. Univ. of California Press.

————. 1971. Statistical evidence for individual signature whistles in Pacific whitesided dolphins, *Lagenorhynchus obliquidens. Cetology* 3: 9 pp.

CAMPBELL, J. M. 1894. White-beaked dolphin in Kilbrannan Sound, Arran. *Zoologist* (3), 18: 424–26.

CASINOS, A., and J. -R. VERICAD. 1976. The cetaceans of the Spanish coasts: a survey. *Mammalia* 40(2): 267–90.

CASSIN, J. 1858. *Mammalogy and Ornithology. U.S. Exploring Expedition, 1838–1842*. Lippincott.

COFFEY, D. J. 1977. *Dolphins, Whales and Porpoises: An Encyclopedia of Sea Mammals*. Macmillan and George Rainbird.

CORNELL, L. H., and E. D. ASPER. 1977. A census of captive marine mammals in North America. *Intl. Zoo Yearbook* 18: 220–24.

COWAN, D. F., W. A. WALKER, and R. L. BROWNELL. 1981. Pathology of dolphins singly stranded on the coast of Southern California. (Abstract) *Fourth Biennial Conf. Biol. Marine Mammals*. San Francisco.

DAWBIN, W. H., B. A. NOBLE, and F. C. FRASER. 1970. Observations on the electra dolphin, *Peponocephala electra. Bull. Brit. Mus. (Nat. Hist.) Zool.* 20(6): 175–201.

DATHE, H. 1972. The occurrence of dolphins in the Mediterranean. *Zool. Gart.* 42(3–4): 204. (In German.)

DEARBORN, J. H. 1968. An unusual leap by a Pacific whitesided dolphin (*Lagenorhynchus obliquidens*). *Jour. Mammal.* 49: 328–29.

DE SMET, W. M. A. 1972. Concerning two white-beaked dolphins (*Lagenorhynchus albirostris*) of the Belgian coast. *Bull. Inst. R. Sci. Nat. Belg. Biol.* 48(10): 1–17.

————. 1974. Inventory of cetacea of the Flemish coast and the River Schelde, Belgium. *Bull. Inst. R. Sci. Nat. Belg. Biol.* 50(1): 1–156.

DUGUY, R. 1978. Un dauphin rare trouvé sur les côtes du Finistère: *Lagenorhynchus acutus* (Gray 1828). *Penn ar Bed.* 94: 365–66.

ELLIS, R. 1981. Diving with dolphins. *Oceans* 14(2): 38–40.

EVANS, W. E. 1973. Echolocation by marine delphinids and one species of freshwater dolphin. *Jour. Acoust. Soc. Amer.* 54(1): 191–99.

FRASER, F. C. 1934. Report on cetacea stranded on the British Coasts from 1927 to 1932. *Bull. Brit. Mus. (Nat. Hist.)* 11: 41 pp.

————. 1964. Whales and whaling. In Priestly, Adie, and Robin, eds., *A Review of British Scientific Achievement in Antarctica.* Butterworths, pp. 191–205.

————. 1966. Comments on Delphinoidea. In K. S. Norris, ed., *Whales, Dolphins and Porpoises*, pp. 7–31. University of California Press.

————. 1974. Report on cetacea stranded on the British coasts from 1948 to 1966. *Bull. Brit. Mus. (Nat. Hist.)* 14: 65 pp.

GALLARDO, A. 1912. El delfin *Lagenorhynchus fitzroyi* (Waterhouse) Flower capturado in Mar del Plata. *An. Mus. Nac. de Buenas Aires* 23: 391–97.

GASKIN, D. E. 1972. *Whales, Dolphins and Seals, with special reference to the New Zealand region.* Heinemann Educational Books

GOODALL, R. N. P. 1978. Report on the small cetaceans stranded on the coasts of Tierra del Fuego. *Sci. Rep. Whales Res. Inst.* 30: 197–230.

GRESSON, R. A. R. 1968. White-sided dolphins, *Lagenorhynchus acutus* (Gray) stranded at Ventry Harbor, Co. Kerry. *Irish Nat. Jour.* 16(1): 19–20.

————. 1969a. White-sided dolphins, *Lagenorhynchus acutus*, stranded at Brandon Bay, Co. Kerry. *Irish Nat. Jour.* 16(5): 140.

————. 1969b. White-sided dolphins, *Lagenorhynchus acutus*, stranded at Cloghane, Co. Kerry. *Irish Nat. Jour.* 16(8): 228.

HALL, J. D. 1970. Conditioning Pacific white-striped dolphins, *Lagenorhynchus obliquidens*, for open ocean release. *Naval Undersea Center.* TP 200.

HARMER, S. F. 1927. Report on cetacea stranded on the British coasts from 1913 to 1926. *Bull. Brit. Mus. (Nat. Hist.)* 10: 91 pp.

HERALD, E. S. 1969. Aquatic mammals at Steinhart Aquarium. *Pacific Discovery* 22(6): 26–30.

HERSHKOVITZ, P. 1966. *Catalog of Living Whales.* U.S. National Museum. Bull. 246.

HUBBS, C. L. 1953. Dolphin protecting dead young. *Jour. Mammal.* 34: 498.

HUSSON, A. M., and P. J. H. VAN BREE. 1972. Strandings of cetacea on the Dutch coast in 1970 and 1971. *Lutra* 14(1–3): 1–4. (In Dutch; English summary.)

————. 1976. On strandings of cetaceans on the Dutch coast. *Lutra* 18(2): 25–32. (In Dutch; English summary.)

JONSGARD, A. 1962. On the species of dolphins found on the coast of northern Norway and in adjacent waters. *Norsk Hvalfangst-tidende* 51(1): 1–13.

————, and E. J. LONG. 1959. Norway's small whales. *Sea Frontiers* 5(3): 168–74.

JONSGARD, A., and O. NORDLI. 1952. Concerning a catch of white-sided dolphins (*Lagenorhynchus acutus*) on the west coast of Norway, Winter, 1952. *Norsk Hvalfangst-tidende* 41(5): 229–32.

KASUYA, T., and N. MIYAZAKI. 1976. An observation of epimeletic behavior of *Lagenorhynchus obliquidens*. *Sci. Rep. Whales Res. Inst.* 28: 141–43.

KATONA, S. K., D. RICHARDSON, and R. HAZARD. 1975. *Field Guide to the Whales and Seals of the Gulf of Maine.* Maine Coast Printers.

KATONA, S. K., S. A. TESTAVERDE, and B. BARR. 1978. Observations on a white-sided dolphin, *Lagenorhynchus acutus*, probably killed in gill nets in the Gulf of Maine. *Fish Bull.* 76: 475–76.

KELLOGG, R. 1941. On the identity of the porpoise *Sagmatias amblodon. Zool. Ser. Field. Mus. Nat. Hist.* 27: 293–311.

KELLY, H. R. 1959. A two-body problem in echelon-formation swimming of porpoise. *U.S. Naval Ordnance Test Station, China Lake, California. Weapons Development Department, Aeromechanics Division.* Technical Note 40606–1: 1–7. (Mimeographed.)

LANG, T. G. 1966. Hydrodynamic analysis of cetacean performance. In K. S. Norris, ed., *Whales, Dolphins and Porpoises.* University of California Press pp. 410–32.

————, and D. A. DAYBELL. 1963. Porpoise performance tests in a seawater tank. *Naval Ordnance Test Station.* TP 3063.

LEATHERWOOD, S., R. REEVES, A. BOWLES, and B. STEWART. 1981. Distribution and relative abundance of the Pacific white-sided dolphin, *Lagenorhynchus obliquidens*, in the northeastern Pacific. (Abstract) *Fourth Biennial Conf. Biol. Marine Mammals.* San Francisco.

MATTHEWS, L. H. 1948. The swimming of dolphins. *Nature* 161(4097): 731.

MAXWELL, G. 1952. *Harpoon Venture.* Viking Press.

MERCER, M. C. 1973. Observations on distribution and intraspecific variation in pigmentation patterns of odontocete cetaceans in the western North Atlantic. *Jour. Fish. Res. Bd. Canada* 30: 1111–30.

MITCHELL, E. D. 1970. Pigmentation pattern evolution in delphinid cetaceans: An essay in adaptive coloration. *Canadian Jornal of Zoology* 48(4): 717–40.

————, ed. 1975a. Review of Biology and Fisheries for Smaller Cetaceans. *Journal of the Fisheries Research Board of Canada* 32(7): 875–1240.

————. 1975b. *Porpoise, Dolphin, and Small Whale Fisheries of the World: Status and Problems.* IUCN Monograph No. 3, Morges, Switzerland.

NICHOLS, J. T. 1908. Notes on two porpoises captured on a voyage into the Pacific Ocean. *Bull. Amer. Mus. Nat. Hist.* 24: 217–19.

NISHIWAKI, M. 1967. Distribution and Migration of Marine Mammals in the North Pacific Area. *Bull. Oceans Res. Inst. Univ. of Tokyo.*

NORMAN, J. R., and FRASER, F. C. 1938. *Giant Fishes, Whales and Dolphins.* W. W. Norton.

NORRIS, K. S., and J. H. PRESCOTT. 1961. Observations of Pacific cetaceans of Californian and Mexican waters. *Univ. Calif. Publ. Zool.* 63(4): 291–402.

PAYNE, R. 1974. A playground for whales. *Animal Kingdom* 77(2): 7–12.

PIKE, G. C. 1960. Pacific striped dolphin, *Lagenorhynchus obliquidens,* off the coast of British Columbia. *Jour. Fish. Res. Bd. Canada* 17(1): 123–24.

QUOY, J. R. C., and J. P. GAIMARD. 1824. Zoologie. Vol. I, L. C. D. Freycinet. *Voyage Autour du Monde, Exécuté sur les Corvettes de L.M. l'Uranie et la Physicienne, Pendant les Années 1817–1820.* Paris. 76–89.

RIDGWAY, S. H., and R. F. GREEN. 1967. Evidence for a sexual rhythm in male porpoises, *Lagenorhynchus obliquidens* and *Delphinus delphis bairdii. Norsk Hvalfangst-tidende* 56(1): 1–8.

ROBSON, F. 1976. *Thinking Dolphins, Talking Whales.* A. H. & A. W. Reed.

SANDERSON, I. 1956. *Follow the Whale.* Little Brown and Company.

SAPIN-JALOUSTRE, J. 1953. L'identification des cétacés antartiques à la mer. *Mammalia* 17: 221–59.

SCAMMON, C. M. 1874. *The Marine Mammals of the North-Western Coast of North America, Together with an Account of the American Whale-Fishery.* Carmany; Putnam's.

SCHEFFER, V. B. 1950. The striped dolphin *Lagenorhynchus obliquidens,* on the coast of North America. *Amer. Midl. Nat.* 44: 750–58.

———, and J. W. SLIPP. 1948. The whales and dolphins of Washington State with a key to the cetaceans of the West Coast of North America. *Amer. Midl. Nat.* 39(2): 257–337.

SCHEVILL, W. E. 1956. *Lagenorhynchus acutus* off Cape Cod. *Jour. Mammal.* 37(1): 128–29.

———, and W. A. WATKINS. 1971. Pulsed sounds of the porpoise *Lagenorhynchus australis. Breviora (Mus. Comp. Zool.)* 366, 10 pp.

SERGEANT, D. E. 1958. Dolphins in Newfoundland waters. *Norsk Hvalfangst-tidende* 48: 562–68.

———. 1979. Ecological aspects of cetacean strandings. In J. R. Geraci and D. J. St. Aubin, eds., *Biology of Marine Mammals: Insights Through Strandings,* pp. 94–113. U.S. Marine Mammal Commission Report MMC-77/13.

———, and H. D. FISHER. 1957. The smaller cetacea of eastern Canadian waters. *Jour. Fish. Res. Bd. Canada* 14(1): 83–115.

SERGEANT, D. E., D. J. ST. AUBIN, and J. R. GERACI. 1980. Life history and Northwest Atlantic status of the Atlantic whitesided dolphin, *Lagenorhynchus acutus. Cetology* 37: 1–12.

SPONG, P., and D. WHITE. Visual acuity and discrimination learning in the dolphin (*Lagenorhynchus obliquidens*). *Exp. Neurol.* 31(3): 431–36.

TESTAVERDE, S. A., and J. G. MEAD. 1980. Southern distribution of the Atlantic whitesided dolphin, *Lagenorhynchus acutus,* in the western North Atlantic. *Fish Bull.* 78(1): 167–69.

TOWNSEND, C. H. 1914. The porpoise in captivity. *Zoologica* 1(16): 289–99.

VAN BREE, P. J. H. 1977. On former and recent mass strandings of cetaceans on the coast of the Netherlands. *Z. Saeugetierkd.* 42(2): 101–07.

———. 1970. On the white nosed dolphin, *Lagenorhynchus albirostris* from the German coast of the North Sea. *Natur Mus.* 100(6): 264–68.

———, and A. M. HUSSON. 1974. Cetaceans washed ashore on the coast of the Netherlands in 1972 and 1973. *Lutra* 16(1): 1–10. (In Dutch; English summary.)

WAHL, T. R. 1977. Sight records of some marine mammals offshore from Westport, Washington. *Murrelet* 58(1): 21–23.

WALKER, W. A. 1975. Review of the live-capture fishery for smaller cetaceans taken in southern California waters for public display, 1966–73. *Jour. Fish. Res. Bd. Canada* 32(7): 1197–1211.

WALLER, G. H., and N. J. C. TYLER. 1979. Observations on *Lagenorhynchus acutus* stranded on the Yorkshire coast. *Naturalist* (Yorkshire) 104(949): 61–64.

WEBB. B. F. 1973a. Cetaceans sighted off the west coast of the South Island, New Zealand, Summer 1970. *N.Z. Jour. Mar. Freshwater Res.* 7(1–2): 179–82.

———. 1973b. Dolphin sightings, Tasman Bay to Cook Strait, New Zealand. *N.Z. Jour. Mar. Freshwater Res.* 7(4): 399–405.

WILKE, F., T. TANIWAKI, and N. KURODA. 1953. *Phocoenoides* and *Lagenorhynchus* in Japan with notes on hunting. *Jour. Mammal.* 34: 488–97.

WILSON, E. A. 1967. *Diary of the Discovery Expedition to the Antarctic Regions 1901–1904.* Humanities Press.

WOOD, F. G. 1973. *Marine Mammals and Man.* Luce.

———. 1979. The cetacean stranding phenomenon: An hypothesis. In J. R. Geraci and D. J. St. Aubin, eds., *Biology of Marine Mammals: Insights Through Strandings,* pp. 129–88. U.S. Marine Mammal Commission Report MMC-77/13.

———, and W. E. EVANS. 1980. Adaptiveness and ecology of echolocation in toothed whales. In R.-G. Busnel and J. F. Fish, eds., *Animal Sonar Systems,* pp. 381–425. Plenum.

WÜRSIG, B. 1976. Radio tracking of dusky porpoises (*Lagenorhynchus obscurus*) in the South Atlantic, a preliminary analysis. *Scientific Consultation on Marine Mammals, Bergen, Norway.* ACMRR/MM/SC/83. 20 pp.

———. 1979. Dolphins. *Scientific American* 240(3): 136–48.

————, and M. WÜRSIG. 1978. Day and night of the dolphin. *Natural History* 88(3): 60–67.

————. 1980. Behavior and ecology of the dusky dolphin, *Lagenorhynchus obscurus*, in the South Atlantic. *Fish. Bull.* 77(4): 871–90.

COMMERSON'S DOLPHIN, BLACK DOLPHIN, HEAVISIDE'S DOLPHIN, AND HECTOR'S DOLPHIN

ABEL, R. S., A. G. DOBBINS, and T. BROWN. 1971. *Cephalorhynchus hectori* subsp. *bicolor*. Sightings, capture, captivity. *Invest. on Cetacea* 3: 171–79.

AGUAYO, L. A. 1975. Progress report on small cetaceans research in Chile. *Jour. Fish. Res. Bd. Canada* 32(7): 1123–43.

ANGOT, M. 1954. Observations sur les mammifères marins de l'archipel de Kerguelen, avec un étude détaillée de l'éléphant de mer *Mirounga leonina* (L.). *Mammalia* 18: 1–111.

BAKER, A. N. 1972. New Zealand whales and dolphins. *Tuatara* 20(1): 49 pp.

————. 1978. The status of Hector's dolphin, *Cephalorhynchus hectori* (Van Beneden), in New Zealand waters. *Rep. Int. Whal. Commn.* 28: 331–34.

BEDDARD, F. 1900. *A Book of Whales*. John Murray.

BROWNELL, R. L. 1974. Small odontocetes of the Antarctic. In V. C. Bushnell, ed., *Antarctic Mammals*. Vol. 18, pp. 13–19. Antarctic Map Folio Series, American Geographical Society.

CABRERA, A. 1961. Catalogo de los mamiferos de America del Sur. II. Cetacea. *Rev. Mus. Arg. Cien. Nat.* 4(2): 603–25.

CLARKE, R., A. L. AGUAYO, and S. G. DEL CAMPO. 1978. Whale observation and whale marking off the coast of Chile in 1964. *Sci. Rep. Whales Res. Inst.* 30: 117–77.

FISCHER, G. M. 1957. Clave de determinación para las especies de mamiferos silvestres de Chile. *Invest. Zool. Chilenas* 4: 89–126.

FLOWER, W. H. 1883. On the characters and divisions of the family Delphinidae. *Proc. Zool. Soc. London* 32: 466–513.

FRASER, F. C. 1966. Comments on delphinoidea. In K. S. Norris, ed., *Whales, Dolphins and Porpoises*, pp. 7–31. Univ. of California Press.

GASKIN, D. E. 1972. *Whales, Dolphins and Seals, with Special Reference to the New Zealand Region*. Heinemann Educational Books.

GEWALT, W. 1979. The first Commerson's dolphin (*Cephalorhynchus commersonii*)—capture and first experiences. *Aquat. Mamm.* 7(2): 37–40.

GILMORE, R. M. 1961. Whales without flukes or flippers. *Jour. Mammal.* 42(3): 419–20.

GOODALL, R. N. P. 1978. Report on the small cetaceans stranded on the coasts of Tierra del Fuego. *Sci. Rep. Whales Res. Inst.* 28: 197–230.

————. 1979. *Tierra del Fuego*. Ediciones Shanamaiim, Buenos Aires.

————, and I. S. CAMERON. 1979. On the external characters of *Cephalorhynchus commersonii*. (Abstract) *Third Biennial Conf. Biol. Marine Mammals.* Seattle.

————. 1980. Exploitation of small cetaceans off southern South America. *Rep. Int. Whal. Commn.* 30: 445–50.

GRAY, J. E. 1849. Descriptions of three new species of Delphinidae. *Proc. Zool. Soc. London* 17: 1–3.

GRZIMEK, B., ed. 1975. *Grzimek's Animal Life Encyclopedia*. Vol. 11: *Mammals II*, p. 517.

HARMER, S. F. 1922. On Commerson's dolphin and other species of *Cephalorhynchus*. *Proc. Zool. Soc. London* 43: 627–38.

HARRISON, T. 1960. South China Seas Dolphins. *Malayan Nature Journal* 14(1): 87–89.

HECTOR, J. 1872. On the New Zealand bottlenose (*Lagenorhynchus clanculus* Gray). *Ann. Mag. Nat. Hist.* 4(9): 436–38.

————. 1873. On the whales and dolphins of the New Zealand seas. *Trans. Proc. N.Z. Inst.* 5: 154–70.

————. 1885. Notes on the dolphins of the New Zealand seas. *Trans. Proc. N.Z. Inst.* 17: 207–11.

KEZER, L. E. 1979. Commerson's dolphin. *Seaword* (Mystic Marinelife Aquarium, Mystic, Conn.) 5(3): 1–2.

MARCUZZI, G., and PILLERI, G. 1971. On the Zoogeography of Cetacea. *Investigations on Cetacea* 3:101–70.

MERMOZ, J. F. 1980. A brief report on the behavior of Commerson's dolphin, *Cephalorhynchus commersonii*, in Patagonian waters. *Sci. Rep. Whales Res. Inst.* 32: 149–54.

MITCHELL, E. D. 1970. Pigmentation pattern evolution in delphinid cetaceans: an essay in adaptive coloration. *Canadian Journal of Zoology* 48(4).

MÖRZER BRUYNS, W. F. J., and BAKER, A. N. 1973. Notes on Hector's Dolphin, *Cephalorhynchus hectori* (Van Beneden) from New Zealand. *Rec. Dominion Mus. Wellington* 8(9): 125–37.

OLIVER, W. R. B. 1922a. A review of the cetacea of the New Zealand seas. I. *Proc. Zool. Soc. London* 1922: 557–85.

————. 1922b. The whales and dolphins of New Zealand. *N.Z. Jour. Sci. Tech.* 5(3): 129–41.

————. 1946. A pied variety of the coastal porpoise. *Rec. Dom. Mus. Zool.* 1(1): 1–4.

OLROG, C. C. 1950. Notas sobre mamiferos y aves del archipelago de Cabo de Hornos. *Acta. Zool. Lilloana* 9: 505–32.

PEREZ CANTO, C. 1896. Description de deux nouveau cétacés de la côte du Chili. *Act. Soc. Sci. Chili* 5: 227–29.

PHILIPPI, R. A. 1893. Los delfines de la punta austral de la America del Sur. *An. Mus. Nac. Chile* I (Zoolojia). 1–18 + 5 plates.

————. 1896. Los cráneos de los delfines chilenos. *An. Mus. Nac. Chile* I (Zoolojia): 1–18 + 6 plates.

ROBSON, F. 1976. *Thinking Dolphins, Talking Whales.* Charles E. Tuttle.

SPOTTE, S., C. W. RADCLIFFE, and J. L. DUNNE. 1979. Notes on Commerson's dolphin (*Cephalorhynchus commersonii*) in captivity. *Cetology* 35: 9 pp.

STEPHEN, D. 1973. *Dolphins, Seals and other Sea Mammals.* Putnam's.

TRUE, F. W. 1903. On the species of South American Delphinidae described by Dr. R. A. Philippi in 1893 and 1896. *Proc. Biol. Soc. Wash.* 16: 133–43.

VAN BENEDEN, P. J. 1881. Notice sur un nouveau dauphin de la Nouvelle-Zélande. *Bull. Acad. Roy. Sci. Belgique.* Ser. 3. 1: 877–87.

VAN BREE, P. J. H. 1972. On the validity of the subspecies *Cephalorhynchus hectori bicolor* Oliver, 1946. *Invest. on Cetacea.* 4: 182–86.

WATKINS, W. A., and W. E. SCHEVILL. 1980. Characteristic features of the underwater sounds of *Cephalorhynchus commersonii. Jour. Mammal.* 61(4): 738–39.

———, and P. B. BEST. 1977. Underwater sounds of *Cephalorhynchus heavisidii* (Mammalia: Cetacea). *Jour. Mammal.* 58(3): 316–20.

YANEZ, A. P. 1948. Vertebrados marinos chilenos, I. Mamiferos. *Rev. Biol. Mar.* 1(2): 103–23.

NORTHERN RIGHT WHALE DOLPHIN AND SOUTHERN RIGHT WHALE DOLPHIN

AGUAYO, A. 1975. Progress report on small cetaceans research in Chile. *Jour. Fish Res. Bd. Canada* 32(7): 1123–43.

BAKER, A. N. 1972. New Zealand whales and dolphins. *Tuatara* 20(1): 1–49.

BROWNELL, R. L. 1964. Observations of odontocetes in central Californian waters. *Norsk Hvalfangst-tidende* 55(3): 60–66.

———. 1974. Small odeontocetes of the Antarctic. In V. C. Bushnell, ed., *Antarctic Mammals.* Vol. 18, pp. 13–19. Antarctic Folio Series. American Geographical Society.

CHAPMAN, W. M. 1940. A right whale dolphin collected in Washington. *Murrelet* 21(1): 10.

DAUGHERTY, A. 1972. *Marine Mammals of California.* California Department of Fish and Game, Sacramento. 91 pp.

FISH, J. F., and C. W. TURL. 1977. Acoustic source levels of four species of small toothed whales. *Naval Undersea Center Technical Publication* 547. 13 pp.

FITCH, J. E., and R. L. BROWNELL. 1968. Fish otoliths in cetacean stomachs and their importance in interpreting feeding habits. *Jour. Fish. Res. Bd. Canada* 25(12): 561–74.

FRASER, F. C. 1955. The southern right whale dolphin, *Lissodelphis peroni* (Lacepede). *Bull. Brit. Mus. Nat. Hist. (Zool.)* 2(11): 339–46.

GASKIN, D. E. 1972. *Whales, Dolphins and Seals, with special reference to the New Zealand region.* Heinemann Educational Books.

GOODALL, R. N. P. 1978. Report on the small cetaceans stranded on the coasts of Tierra del Fuego. *Sci. Rep. Whales Res. Inst.* 28: 197–230.

GUIGUET, C. J., and W. J. SCHICK. 1970. First record of a right whale dolphin from British Columbia. *Syesis* 3: 188.

KASUYA, T. 1971. Consideration of distribution and migration of toothed whales off the Pacific coast of Japan based on aerial sighting record. *Sci. Rep. Whales Res. Inst.* 23: 37–60.

LEATHERWOOD, S. 1974. A note on gray whale interactions with other marine mammals. *Mar. Fish. Rev.* 36(4): 50–51.

———, and R. R. REEVES. 1978. Porpoises and dolphins. In D. Haley, ed., *Marine Mammals of Eastern North Pacific and Arctic Waters*, pp. 96–111. Pacific Search Press.

LEATHERWOOD, S., and W. A. WALKER. 1979. The northern right whale dolphin *Lissodelphis borealis* Peale in the eastern north Pacific. In H. E. Winn and B. L. Olla, eds., *Behavior of Marine Animals.* Vol. 3: *Cetaceans*, pp. 85–141. Plenum.

LILLIE, D. G. 1915. British Antarctic (*Terra Nova*) Expedition 1910. *Nat. Hist. Repts. (Brit. Mus.) Zool.* 1: 85–124.

MITCHELL, E. D. 1975. *Porpoise, Dolphin and Small Whale Fisheries of the World: Status and Problems.* IUCN Monograph. 3: 129 pp.

NISHIWAKI, M. 1967. Distribution and migration of marine mammals in the North Pacific area. *Bull. Ocean Res. Inst.* 1: 1–64.

NORRIS, K. W., and T. P. DOHL. 1980. The structure and functions of cetacean schools. In L. M. Herman, ed., *Cetacean Behavior: Mechanisms and Functions*, pp. 211–61. John Wiley.

NORRIS, K. W., and J. H. PRESCOTT. 1961. Observations of Pacific cetaceans in Californian and Mexican waters. *Univ. Calif. Publ. Zool.* 63(4): 291–402.

OHSUMI, S. 1972. Catch of marine mammals, mainly of small cetaceans, by local fisheries along the coast of Japan. *Bull. Far Seas Res. Lab.* 7: 137–66.

PEALE, T. R. 1848. *U.S. Exploring Expedition 1838, 1839, 1840, 1841, 1842 under the Command of Charles Wilkes, U.S.N. Vol. 8, Mammalogy and Ornithology.* Asherman.

SCHEFFER, V. B., and J. W. SLIPP. 1948. The whales and dolphins of Washington State with a key to the cetaceans of the west coast of North America. *Amer. Midl. Nat.* 39(2): 257–37.

TOBAYAMA, T. S., S. UCHIDA, and M. NISHIWAKI. 1969. A white-bellied right whale dolphin caught in the waters off Ibaragi, Japan. *Jour. Mammal. Soc. Japan* 4(4): 112–20.

WALKER, W. A. 1975. Review of live-capture fishery for smaller cetaceans taken in Southern California waters for public display, 1966–73. *Jour. Fish. Res. Bd. Canada* 32(7): 1197–1221.

WICK, W. Q. 1969. Right whale dolphin from Cape Kiwanda, Tillamook County, Oregon. *Murrelet.* 50(1): 9.

WILKE, F., T. TANIWAKI, and N. KURODA. 1953. *Phocoenoides* and *Lagenorhynchus* in Japan with notes on hunting. *Jour. Mammal.* 34: 488–97.

WILSON, E. A. 1972. *Diary of the Terra Nova Expedition to the Antarctic 1910–1912.* Humanities Press.

RISSO'S DOLPHIN

ALPERS, A. 1960. *Dolphins: The Myth and the Mammal.* Houghton Mifflin.

BAKER, A. N. 1974. Risso's dolphin in New Zealand waters and the identity of "Pelorus Jack." *Rec. Dom. Mus. Wellington* 8(16): 267–76.

BLYTH, E. 1859. On the great rorqual of the Indian Ocean, with notices of other cetals, and of the sirenia or marine pachyderms. *Jour. Asiatic Society Bengal* 28(5): 481–98.

CALDWELL, D. K., M. C. CALDWELL, and J. F. MILLER. 1969. Three brief narrow-band sound emissions by a captive male Risso's dolphin, *Grampus griseus. Bull. S. Calif. Acad. Sci.* 68(4): 252–56.

CALDWELL, M. C., and D. K. CALDWELL. 1972. Behavior of marine mammals. In S. H. Ridgway, ed. *Mammals of the Sea: Biology and Medicine,* pp. 419–65. Charles C Thomas.

CLARKE, M. R. 1966. A review of the systematics and ecology of oceanic squids. *Advances in Marine Biology* 4: 91–300.

CLARKE, R., A. AGUAYO, and S. B. DEL CAMPO. 1978. Whale observation and whale marking off the coast of Chile in 1964. *Sci. Rep. Whales Res. Inst.* 30: 117–77, Pls. I–IV.

CRESS, C. 1955. Pelorus Jack, a dolphin diplomat. *Audubon* 57(3): 108–11.

CUVIER, G. 1812. Rapport fait à la classe des sciences mathématiques et physiques sur divers cétacés pris sur les côtes de France, principalement sur ceux qui sont échoués près de Paimpol, le 7 Janvier 1812. *Ann. Mus. Hist. Nat.* 19: 1–16.

——. 1817. *Le Règne Animal.* Tome IV. Paris.

DAWBIN, W. H. 1966. Porpoises and porpoise hunting in Malaita. *Aust. Nat. Hist.* 15(7): 207–11.

DAUGHERTY, A. 1972. *Marine Mammals of California.* State of California Dept. of Fish and Game. Sacramento. 1–91.

EVANS, W. E. 1967. Vocalization among marine mammals. In W. N. Tavolga, ed., *Marine Bio-Acoustics,* pp. 159–86. Pergamon Press.

FLOWER, W. H. 1872. On Risso's dolphin, *Grampus griseus. Trans. Zool. Soc. London* 8: 1–21 + 2 pl.

FRASER, F. C. 1934. Report on cetacea stranded on the British Coasts from 1927 to 1932. *Bull. Brit. Mus. (Nat. Hist.)* 11: 1–41.

——. 1940. Three anomalous dolphins from Blacksod Bay, Ireland. *Proc. Royal Irish Acad.* 45(B): 413–55.

——. 1946. Report on cetacea stranded on the British Coasts from 1933 to 1937. *Bull. Brit. Mus. (Nat. Hist.)* 12: 1–56.

——. 1953. Report on cetacea stranded on the British Coasts from 1938 to 1947. *Bull. Brit. Mus. (Nat. Hist.)* 13: 1–48.

——. 1974. Report on cetacea stranded on the British Coasts from 1948 to 1966. *Bull. Brit. Mus. (Nat. Hist.)* 14: 1–65.

GASKIN, D. E. 1972. *Whales, Dolphins and Seals, with Special Reference to the New Zealand Region.* Heinemann Educational Books.

GIHR, M., and G. PILLERI. 1979. Interspecific body length–body weight and body weight–brain weight ratio in cetacea. *Invest. on Cetacea* 10: 245–53.

GUIGUET, C. J., and G. C. PIKE. 1965. First record of the gray grampus or Risso Dolphin, *Grampus griseus* (Cuvier) from British Columbia. *Murrelet* 46(1): 16.

HAMILTON, R. 1835. *Mammalia. Whales &c.* In W. Jardine, ed., *The Naturalist's Library.* Vol. 26, pp. 233–34.

HARMER. S. F. 1927. Report on cetacea stranded on the British Coasts from 1913 to 1926. *Bull. Brit. Mus. (Nat. Hist.)* 10: 1–91.

——. 1930. Pelorus Jack. *Proc. Linn. Soc. London* 141: 48–50.

IREDALE, T., and E. L. TROUGHTON. 1933. The correct generic names for the grampus or killer whale, and the so-called grampus or Risso's dolphin. *Rec. Aust. Mus.* 19: 28–36.

KELLOGG, R. 1940. Whales, giants of the sea. *National Geographic* 77(1): 35–90.

LEATHERWOOD, S., and R. R. REEVES. 1978. Porpoises and dolphins. In D. Haley, ed., *Marine Mammals of Eastern North Pacific and Arctic Waters,* pp. 97–111. Pacific Search Press.

LEATHERWOOD, S., C. L. HUBBS, and M. FISHER. 1979. First records of Risso's dolphin (*Grampus griseus*) from the Gulf of California with detailed notes on a mass stranding. *Trans. San Diego Soc. Nat. Hist.* 19(3): 45–52.

LEATHERWOOD, S., W. F. PERRIN, V. L. KIRBY, C. L. HUBBS, and M. DALHEIM. 1980. Distribution and movements of Risso's dolphin, *Grampus griseus,* in the eastern North Pacific. *Fish. Bull.* 77(4): 951–63.

MAXWELL, G. 1952. *Harpoon Venture.* Viking Press.

MCCANN, C. 1974. Body scarring on cetacea—odontocetes. *Sci. Rep. Whales Res. Inst.* 26: 145–55.

MITCHELL, E. D. 1975. *Porpoise, Dolphin and Small Whale Fisheries of the World.* IUCN Monograph No. 3. pp. 1–125.

MURIE, J. 1871. On Risso's grampus, *G. rissoanus* (Desm.) *Jour. Anat. Physiol.* 5: 118–38.

NISHIWAKI, M. 1963. Taxonomical consideration on genera of *Delphinidae. Sci. Rep. Whales Res. Inst.* 17: 93–103.

NORMAN, J. R., and F. C. FRASER. 1937. *Giant Fishes, Whales and Dolphins.* W. W. Norton.

ORR, R. T. 1966. Risso's dolphin on the Pacific coast of North America. *Jour. Mammal.* 47(2): 341–43.

PAUL, J. R. 1968. Risso's dolphin, *Grampus griseus,* in the Gulf of Mexico. *Jour. Mammal.* 49(4): 746–48.

PILLERI, G., and M. GIHR. 1969. On the anatomy and behaviour of Risso's Dolphin (*Grampus griseus* G. Cuvier). *Invest. on Cetacea* 1: 74–93.

RISSO, A. 1826. *Histoire naturelle des principales productions de l'Europe meridionale et particulièrement de celles des environs de Nice et des Alpes Maritimes.* Paris.

SCAMMON, C. M. 1874. *The Marine Mammals of the Northwestern Coast of North America; Together with an Account of the American Whale-Fishery.* Carmany; Putnam's.

SERGEANT, D. E. 1978. Ecological isolation in some cetacea. *Novoe v Izuchenii Kitoobraznykh i Lastonogykh.* Academy of Sciences of the USSR. pp. 20–33.

SCHEVILLE, W. E. 1954. Sight records of the gray grampus, *Grampus griseus* (Cuvier). *Jour. Mammal.* 35(1): 123–24.

SHEFFER, V. B. 1976. *A Natural History of Marine Mammals.* Scribner's.

WATKINS, W. A. 1980. Click sounds from animals at sea. In R.-G. Busnel and J. F. Fish, eds., *Animal Sonar Systems.* Plenum.

MELON-HEADED WHALE

BRYDEN, M. M., W. H. DAWBIN, G. E. HEINSOHN, and D. H. BROWN. 1977. Melon-headed whale, *Peponocephala electra,* on the east coast of Australia. *Jour. Mammal.* 58(2): 180–87.

CALDWELL, D. K., M. C. CALDWELL, and R. V. WALKER. 1976. First records for Fraser's dolphin (*Lagenodelphis hosei*) in the Atlantic, and the melon-headed whale (*Peponocephala electra*) in the western Atlantic. *Cetology* 25: 1–4.

DAWBIN, W. H., B. A. NOBLE, and F. C. FRASER. 1970. Observations on the Electra Dolphin, *Peponocephala electra.* *Bull. Brit. Mus. (Nat. Hist.) Zoology* 20(6): 173–201.

GOODWIN, G. G. 1945. Record of a porpoise new to the Atlantic. *Jour. Mammal.* 26: 195.

NAKAJIMA, M., and M. NISHIWAKI. 1965. The first occurrence of a porpoise (*Electra electra*) in Japan. *Sci. Rep. Whales Res. Inst.* 19: 91–104.

NISHIWAKI, M., and K. NORRIS. 1966. A new genus *Peponocephala.* *Sci. Rep. Whales Res. Inst.* 20: 95–100.

PEALE, T. R. 1848. *Mammalia and Ornithology.* United States Exploring Expedition. Vol. VIII. Philadelphia.

PERRIN, W. F. 1976. First record of the melon-headed whale, *Peponocephala electra,* in the eastern Pacific, with a summary of world distribution. *Fish. Bull.* 74(2): 457–58.

PILLERI, G., and M. GIHR. 1972. Contribution to the knowledge of cetaceans of Pakistan with particular reference to the genera *Neomeris, Sousa, Delphinus* and *Tursiops* and a description of a new Chinese porpoise (*Neomeris asiaeorientalis*). *Invest. on Cetacea* 4: 107–162.

——. 1973. Contribution to the knowledge of the cetaceans of southwest and monsoon Asia (Persian Gulf, Indus Delta, Malabar, Anadaman Sea and Gulf of Siam). *Invest. on Cetacea* 5: 95–149.

TOMICH, P. Q. 1969. *Mammals in Hawaii: A Synopsis and Notational Bibliography.* Bishop Museum Press.

VAN BREE, P. J. H., and J. CADENAT. 1968. On a skull of *Peponocephala electra* (Gray, 1846) (Cetacea, Globicephalinae) from Senegal. *Beaufortia* 14: 193–202.

PYGMY KILLER WHALE

BASS, J. 1969. A rare whale stranded in Zululand. *Bull. S. Afr. Assoc. Mar. Biol. Res.* 7: 36.

BEST, P. 1970. Records of pygmy killer whale from South Africa. *Ann. South African Museum* 57(1): 1–14.

CADENAT, J. 1958. Notes sur les delphinides ouest-africaines. II. Un spécimen du genre *Feresa* capturé sur les côtes du Sénégal. *Bull. Inst. Français d'Afrique Noire.* Ser. A, 20: 1486–91.

CALDWELL, D. K., and M. C. CALDWELL. 1971. The pygmy killer whale, *Feresa attenuata,* in the western Atlantic, with a summary of world records. *Jour. Mammal.* 52(1): 206–09.

——. 1975a. Pygmy killer whales and short-snouted spinner dolphins in Florida. *Cetology* 18: 1–4.

——. 1975b. Dolphin and small whale fisheries of the Caribbean and the West Indies: Occurrence, history, and catch statistics—with special reference to the Lesser Antillean island of St. Vincent. *Jour. Fish. Res. Bd. Canada* 32(7): 1105–10.

DEFRAN, R. H., and K. PRYOR. 1980. The behavior and training of cetaceans in captivity. In L. M. Herman, ed., *Cetacean Behavior: Mechanisms and Functions,* pp. 319–62. John Wiley.

FRASER, F. C. 1960. A specimen of the genus *Feresa* from Senegal. *Bull. Inst. Français d'Afrique Noir.* Ser. A, 22: 699–707.

GRAY, J. E. 1871. Supplement to the catalog of whales and seals in the British Museum.

——. 1875. *Feresa attenuata. J. Mus. Godeffroy,* Hamburg. Vol. 8: 184 + 6 pl.

JAMES, P., F. W. JUDD, and J. C. MOORE. 1970. First western Atlantic occurrence of the pigmy killer whale. *Fieldiana Zool.* 58(1): 1–3.

JONES, J. K., and R. L. PACKARD. 1956. *Feresa intermedia* (Gray) preoccupied. *Proc. Biol. Soc. Washington* 69: 167.

NISHIWAKI, M. 1966. A discussion of rarities among the smaller cetaceans caught in Japanese waters. In K. S. Norris, ed., *Whales, Dolphins and Porpoises,* pp. 192–204. Univ. of California Press.

————, 1967. Distribution and migration of marine mammals in the North Pacific area. *Bull. Ocean Res. Inst. Univ. Tokyo* 1: 1–64.

————, T. KASUYA, T. TOBAYAMA, T. KAMIYA and M. NAKAJIMA. 1965. *Feresa attenuata* were caught and kept at Ito aquarium in 1963. *Sci. Rep. Whales Res. Inst.* 19: 65–90.

PERRIN, W. F., and C. L. HUBBS. 1969. Observations on the young pygmy killer whale from the eastern tropical Pacific. *Trans. San Diego Soc. Nat. Hist.* 15(18): 297–308.

PERRYMAN, W. L., and T. C. FOSTER. 1980. Preliminary report on predation by small whales, mainly the false killer whale, *Pseudorca crassidens*, on dolphins (*Stenella* spp. and *Delphinus delphis*) in the eastern tropical Pacific. *Southwest Fisheries Center (NMFS) Admin. Rep.* LJ-80-05.

PRYOR, K. 1975. *Lads Before the Wind: Adventures in Porpoise Training.* Harper & Row.

PRYOR, T. , K. PRYOR, and K. W. NORRIS. 1965. Observations on a pygmy killer whale (*Feresa attenuata* Gray) from Hawaii. *Jour. Mammal.* 46(3): 450–61.

TOMICH, P. Q. 1969. *Mammals in Hawaii: A Synopsis and Notational Bibliography.* Bishop Museum Press.

YAMADA, M. 1954. An account of a rare porpoise *Feresa* from Japan. *Sci. Rep. Whales Res. Inst.* 9: 59–88.

FALSE KILLER WHALE

ANONYMOUS. 1978. Japanese slaughter 1,000 dolphins. *New York Times*, Feb. 25, 1978.

BRIMLEY, H. H. 1937. The false killer whale on the North Carolina coast. *Jour. Mammal.* 18: 71–73.

BROWN, D. H., D. K. CALDWELL, and M. C. CALDWELL. 1966. Observations on the behavior of wild and captive false killer whales, with notes on associated behavior of other genera of captive delphinids. *Los Angeles County Museum Contributions in Science.* 95: 1–32.

BULLIS, H. R., and J. C. MOORE. 1956. Two occurrences of false killer whales and a summary of American records. *Am. Mus. Novitates.* 1756: 1–5.

CABRERA, A. 1946. Las falsas orcas de Mar del Plata. *Cienc. Investig.* 2(12): 505–09.

CAILLET-BOIS, T. 1948. Las pseudorcas de Mar del Plata. *Rev. Geogr. Americana* 28(172): 5–10.

CALDWELL, D. K., and M. C. CALDWELL. 1975. Dolphin and small whale fisheries of the Caribbean and West Indies: occurrence, history, and catch statistics—with special reference to the Lesser Antillean island of St. Vincent. *Jour. Fish. Res. Bd. Canada* 32(7): 1105–10.

————, and C. M. WALKER. 1970. Mass and individual strandings of false killer whales, *Pseudorca crassidens*, in Florida. *Jour. Mammal.* 51(3): 634–636.

————, W. F. RATHJEN, and J. R. SULLIVAN 1971. Cetaceans from the Lesser Antillean island of St. Vincent. *Fish. Bull.* 69(2): 303–11.

CASINOS, A., and J. R. VERICAD. 1976. The cetaceans of Spanish coasts: a survey. *Mammalia* 40(2): 267–89.

CASTELLO, H. P., and N. M. GIANUCA. 1976. Echouage de faux-orques, *Pseudorca crassidens* (Owen 1846), sur les côtes de l'Etat de Rio Grande do Sul, Brasil. *Mammalia* 40: 683–84.

DEFRAN, R. H., and K. PRYOR. 1980. The behavior and training of cetaceans in captivity. In L. M. Herman, ed., *Cetacean Behavior: Mechanisms and Functions*, pp. 319–62. John Wiley.

DERANIYAGALA, P. E. P. 1945. Some odontoceti from Ceylon. *Spolia Zeylanica* 24: 116–20.

DUDOK VAN HEEL, W. 1962. Sound and cetacea. *Neth. Jour. Sea Res.* 1(4): 407–508.

ELLIS, R. 1981. A visitor from inner space. *Animal Kingdom* 84(4): 5–11.

FERGUSON, H. S. 1903. On two cetaceans from Travancore. *Jour. Bombay Nat. Hist. Soc.* 15: 38–40.

FLOWER, W. H. 1865. Note on *Pseudorca meridonalis*. *Proc. Zool. Soc. London* 1865: 470.

FRASER, F. C. 1936. Recent strandings of the false killer whale, *Pseudorca crassidens*, with special reference to those found at Donna Nook, Lincolnshire. *Scot. Nat.* 217: 105–14.

————. 1946. Report on cetacea stranded on the British coasts from 1933 to 1937. *Bull. Br. Mus. (Nat. Hist.).* 12: 56 pp.

————. 1977. Royal fishes: the importance of the dolphin. In R. J. Harrison, ed., *Functional Anatomy of Marine Mammals.* Vol. 3, pp. 1–44. Academic Press.

GARROOD, J. R. 1924. Two skeletons of the cetacean *Pseudorca crassidens* from Thorney Fen. *Proc. Zool. Soc. London.* 177–193.

HARMER, S. F. 1931. The false killer dolphin. *Nature* 127: 60.

HECTOR, J. 1873. On the whales and dolphins of the New Zealand seas. *Trans. Proc. N.Z. Inst.* 5: 154–70.

HINTON, M. A. C. 1928. Stranded whales at Donoch Firth. *Nat. Hist.* 1: 131.

JONES, H. 1980. Report from Iki Island: Why the dolphins died. *International Wildlife* 10(5): 4–11.

LANGGUTH, A. 1977. Notas sobre la falsa orca *Pseudorca crassidens* (Owen) en el Atlantico sudoccidental. *Rev. Mus. Arg. Cien. Nat.* 12(6): 59–68.

LEATHERWOOD, S., W. F. PERRIN, and M. E. DALHEIM. 1980. Distribution and relative abundance of killer whales, *Orcinus orca*, in the warm temperate and tropical eastern Pacific (34° N to 15°S latitude). (Abstract) *Orca Symposium 1980.* Seattle.

LYDEKKER, R. 1903. Notes on the Trivandrum cetaceans. *Jour. Bombay Nat. Hist. Soc.* 15: 40–41.

MARELLI, C. A. 1953. Documentos iconograficos sobre cetaceos de las costas Argentinas. Falsa orca, Delphin blanco, Delphin de Berard, Tursión. *An. Mus. Nahuel Huapi, Buenos Aires* 3: 133–43.

MATHESON, C., and L. F. COWLEY. 1934. *Pseudorca crassidens* (Owen) on the Glamorgan coast. *Nature* 133: 870.

MEAD, J. G. 1979. An analysis of cetacean strandings along the eastern coast of the United States. In J.B. Geraci and D.J. St. Aubin, eds., *Biology of Marine Mammals: Insights through Strandings*, pp. 54–68. U.S. Marine Mammal Commission Report MMC-77/13.

MILLER. G. S. 1920. American records of whales of the genus Pseudorca. *Proc. U.S. Nat. Mus.* 57: 205–07.

MITCHELL, E. D. 1965. Evidence for the mass strandings of the false killer whale *(Pseudorca crassidens)* in the eastern North Pacific. *Norsk Hvalfangst-tidende* 54(8): 172–77.

MIYAZAKI, N. 1980. Catch records of cetaceans off the coast of the Kii Peninsula. *Mem. Nat. Sci. Mus. Tokyo* 13: 69–82.

————, and S. WADA. 1978. Observation of cetacea during whale marking cruise in the western tropical Pacific, 1976. *Sci. Rep. Whales Res. Inst.* 30: 179–95.

MIZUE, K., and K. YOSHIDA. 1961. Studies on the little toothed whales in the West Sea area of Kyushu—VII. About *Pseudorca crassidens* caught at Arikawa in Goto Is. Nagasaki Pref. *Bull. Fac. Fish. Nagasaki Univ.* 11: 39–48.

MIZUE, K., A. TAKEMURA, and K. NAKASAI. 1970. Studies on the little toothed whales in the West Sea area of Kyushu—XVI. Underwater sound of the false killer whale. *Bull. Fac. Fish. Nagasaki Univ.* 28: 19–29.

MOORE, J. C. 1953. Distribution of marine mammals to Florida waters. *Am. Midl. Nat.* 49: 117–58.

MÖRZER BRUYNS, W. F. J. 1969. Sight records and notes on the false killer whale *Pseudorca crassidens* (Owen 1846). *Saugetierk. Mttlg.* 17: 351–56.

NORRIS, K. S., and J. H. PRESCOTT. 1961. Observations on Pacific cetaceans of Californian and Mexican waters. *Univ. Calif. Publ. Zool.* 63(4): 291–402.

ODELL, D. K., E. D. ASPER, J. BAUCOM, and L. H. CORNELL. 1979. A summary of information derived from the recurrent mass stranding of a herd of false killer whales, *Pseudorca crassidens* (Cetacea: Delphinidae). In J. B. Geraci and D. J. St. Aubin, eds., *Biology of Marine Mammals: Insights through Strandings*, pp. 207–22. U.S. Marine Mammal Commission Report MMC-77/13.

OHSUMI, S. 1972. Catch of marine mammals, mainly of small cetaceans, by local fisheries along the coast of Japan. *Bull. Far Seas Res. Lab.* 7: 137–63.

OLIVER, W. R. B. 1922. A review of the cetacea of the New Zealand seas. *Proc. Zool. Soc. London* 557–85.

OWEN, R. 1846. *A History of British Fossil Mammals and Birds.* London.

PEACOCK, A. D., L. COMRIE, and F. GREENSHIELDS. 1936. The false killers stranded in the Tay Estuary. *Scot. Nat.* 1936: 93–104.

PEARSON, J. 1931. A note on the false killer whale, *Pseudorca crassidens. Spolia Zeylanica* 16: 199–203.

PERRYMAN, W. L., and T. C. FOSTER. 1980. Preliminary report on predation by small whales, mainly the false killer whale, *Pseudorca crassidens,* on dolphins *(Stenella* spp. and *Delphinus delphis)* in the eastern tropical Pacific. *Southwest Fisheries Center (NMFS) Admin. Rep.* LJ-80-05.

PILLERI, G. 1967. Behavior of *Pseudorca crassidens* (Owen) off the Spanish Mediterranean coast. *Rev. Suisse Zool.* 74: 679–83.

————, and M. GIHR. 1976. Record of *Pseudorca crassidens* off Karachi. *Invest. on Cetacea* 7: 205–07.

PORTER, J. W. 1977. *Pseudorca* Strandings: Eyewitness account of a beaching on Dry Tortugas. *Oceans* 10(4): 8–15.

PRESCOTT, J. H. 1981. Clever Hans: Training the trainers, or the potential for misinterpreting the results of dolphin research. In T. A. Sebeok and R. Rosenthal, eds., *The Clever Hans Phenomenon: Communication with Horses, Whales, Apes, and People. Ann. N.Y. Acad. Sci.* 364: 130–36.

PRYOR, K. 1973. Behavior and learning in porpoises and whales. *Naturwissenschaften* 60: 412–20.

————, 1981. Why porpoise trainers are not dolphin lovers: Real and false communication in the operant setting. In T. A. Sebeok and R. Rosenthal, eds., *The Clever Hans Phenomenon: Communication with Horses, Whales, Apes, and People. Ann. N.Y. Acad. Sci.* 364: 137–43.

PURVES, P. E., and G. PILLERI. 1978. The functional anatomy and general biology of *Pseudorca crassidens* (Owen) with a review of the hydrodynamics and acoustics in cetacea. *Invest. on Cetacea* 9: 68–227.

REINHARDT, J. 1866. *Pseudorca crassidens,* a cetacean hitherto unknown in the Danish fauna. *Proc. Ray Soc. London* 189–218.

SCHEFFER, V. B. 1978. False killer whale. In D. Haley, ed., *Marine Mammals of Eastern North Pacific and Arctic Waters,* pp. 128–31. Pacific Search Press.

————, and J. W. SLIPP. 1948. The whales and dolphins of Washington State with a key to the cetaceans of the West Coast of North America. *Amer. Midl. Nat.* 39(2): 257–337.

SCOTT, E. O. G. 1942. Records of Tasmanian cetacea. No. 1. Notes on various strandings at and near Stanley, north western Tasmania. *Rec. Queen Victoria Mus.* 1(1): 27–49.

————, and R. H. GREEN. 1975. Recent whale strandings in Northern Tasmania. *Proc. Roy. Soc. Tasmania* 109: 91–96.

SCOTT, H. H., and C. E. LORD. 1920. Studies of Tasmanian cetacea. Part 1. *(Orca gladiator, Pseudorca crassidens, Globicephalus melas). Pap. Proc. Roy. Soc. Tasmania* (1919): 1–17 + pls. I–IX.

SHELDRICK, M. C. 1979. Cetacean strandings along the coasts of the British Isles 1913–1977. In J. B. Geraci and D. J. St. Aubin, eds., *Biology of Marine Mammals: Insights through Strandings*, pp. 35–53. U.S. Marine Mammal Commission Report. MMC-77/13.

SILAS, E. G., and C. K. PILLAY. 1962. The stranding of two false killer whales *(Pseudorca crassidens* [Owen]) at Pozhikara, north of Cape Comorin. *Jour. Mar. Biol. Assoc. India* 2: 268–71.

SLIJPER, E. 1939. *Pseudorca crassidens* (Owen) ein Beiträg zur verleichenden Anatomie der Cetaceen. *Zool. Meded.* 21: 241–366.

SMITHERS, R. H. N. 1938. Notes on a stranding of a school of *Pseudorca crassidens* at the Berg River mouth, December 27, 1936. *Trans. R. Soc. S. Africa.* 25: 403–11.

STAGER, K. E., and W. REEDER. 1951. Occurrence of the false killer whale *Pseudorca* on the California coast. *Bull. S. Calif. Acad. Sci.* 50: 14–20.

TOMICH, P. Q. 1969. *Mammals in Hawaii: A Synopsis and Notational Bibliography.* Bishop Museum Press.

WASSIF, K. 1956. *Pseudorca crassidens* Owen from the Mediterranean shores of Egypt. *Jour. Mammal.* 37(3): 456.

WOOD, F. G. 1979. The cetacean stranding phenomenon: An hypothesis. In J. B. Geraci and D. J. St. Aubin, eds., *Biology of Marine Mammals: Insights through Strandings,* pp. 129–88. U.S. Marine Mammal Commission Report MMC-77/13.

LONG-FINNED PILOT WHALE AND SHORT-FINNED PILOT WHALE

ANDREWS, R. C. 1914. American Museum whale collection. *Amer. Mus. Jour.* 14(8): 275–94.

————, 1916. *Whale Hunting with Gun and Camera.* D. Appleton.

BANFIELD, A. W. F. 1977. *The Mammals of Canada.* University of Toronto Press.

BOWERS, C. A., and R. S. HENDERSON. 1972, Project Deep Ops: Deep object recovery with pilot and killer whales. *Naval Ordnance Systems Command.* NUC TP 306. 91 pp.

BROWN, D. H. 1960. Behavior of a captive Pacific pilot whale. *Jour. Mammal.* 41: 342–49.

————. 1962. Further observations on the pilot whale in captivity. *Zoologica* 47(1): 59–64.

————, and K. S. NORRIS. 1956. Observations of captive and wild cetaceans. *Jour. Mammal.* 37(3): 313–26.

BROWN, S. G. 1961. Observations on pilot whales in the North Atlantic. *Norsk Hvalfangst-tidende* 50(6): 225–54.

BROWNELL, R. L. 1964. Observations of odontocetes in central Californian waters. *Norsk Hvalfangst-tidende* 55(3): 60–66.

————. 1974. Small odontocetes of the Antarctic. In V. C. Bushnell, ed., *Antarctic Mammals,* folio 18, pp. 13–19. Antarctic Map Folio Series, American Geographical Society.

BUDKER, P. 1968. Stranding of pilot whales (*Globicephala melaena* [Traill]) on the coast of Normandy, France. *Norsk Hvalfangst-tidende* 57(1): 17–19.

BUSNEL, R.-G., and A. DZIEDZIC. 1966. Acoustic signals of the pilot whale *Globicephala melaena* and of the porpoises *Delphinus delphis* and *Phocoena phocoena.* In K. S. Norris, ed., *Whales, Dolphins and Porpoises,* pp. 607–46. University of California Press.

CALDWELL, D. K., and M. C. CALDWELL. 1975. Dolphin and small whale fisheries of the Caribbean and the West Indies: occurrence, history, and catch statistics—with special reference to the Lesser Antillean island of St. Vincent. *Jour. Fish. Res. Bd. Canada* 32(7): 1105–10.

CALDWELL, D. K., and D. S. ERDMAN. 1963. The pilot whale in the West Indies. *Jour. Mammal.* 44: 113–15.

CALDWELL, D. K., W. F. RATHJEN, and M. C. CALDWELL. 1970. Pilot whales mass stranded at Nevis, West Indies. *Quart. Jour. Florida Acad. Sci.* 33(4): 241–43.

CALDWELL, D. K., M. C. CALDWELL, W. F. RATHJEN, and J. R. SULLIVAN. 1971. Cetaceans from the Lesser Antillean Island of St. Vincent. *Fish. Bull.* 69(2): 303–12.

CALDWELL, M. C., and D. K. CALDWELL. 1966. Epimeletic (caregiving) behavior in cetacea. In K. S. Norris, ed., *Whales, Dolphins and Porpoises,* pp. 755–89. University of California Press.

CALDWELL, M. C., D. H. BROWN, and D. K. CALDWELL. 1963. Intergeneric behavior by a captive Pacific pilot whale. *L.A. County Mus. Contrib. Sci.* 70: 1–12.

CASINOS, A., and J. R. VERICAD. 1976. The cetaceans of the Spanish coasts: A survey. *Mammalia* 40: 267–89.

CHACE, L. 1954. Blackfish bonanza. *Natural History* 63: 38–40.

CLARK, A. H. 1887. The blackfish and porpoise fisheries. In G. B. Goode et al., eds., *The Fisheries and Fishery Industries of the United States.* Part 16, Sect. 5, Vol. 2. pp. 297–310. Washington, D.C.

CLARKE, R., A. AGUAYO, and S. G. DEL CAMPO. 1978. Whale observation and whale marking off the coast of Chile in 1964. *Sci. Rep. Whales Res. Inst.* 30: 117–77.

CORNELL, L. H., and E. D. ASPER. 1977. A census of captive marine mammals in North America. *Intl. Zoo Yearbook* 18: 220–24.

DAMMERMAN, K. W. 1926. On *Globicephala* and some Delphinidae from the Indo-Australian archipelago. *Treubia* 5(+): 340–52.

DAVIES, J. L. 1960. The southern form of the pilot whale. *Jour. Mammal.* 41: 27–34.

DEFRAN, R. H., and K. PRYOR. 1980. The behavior and training of cetaceans in captivity. In L. M. Herman, ed., *Cetacean Behavior: Mechanisms and Processes,* pp. 319–62. John Wiley.

DUDOK VAN HEEL, W. H. 1966. Navigation in cetacea. In K. S. Norris, ed., *Whales, Dolphins and Porpoises,* pp. 597–606. University of California Press.

DUGUY, R. 1968. Note sur *Globicephala macrorhyncha* Gray 1846; un cétacé nouveau pour les côtes de France. *Mammalia* 32(1): 113–17.

————, and D. ROBINEAU. 1973. Cétacés et phoques des côtes de France. *Annales de la Société des Sciences, Naturelles de la Charente-Maritime.* 93 pp.

ERDMAN, D. S. 1970. Marine mammals from Puerto Rico to Antigua. *Jour. Mammal.* 51(3): 636–38.

————, J. HARMS, and M. M. FLORES. 1973. Cetacean records from the northeastern Caribbean region. *Cetology* 17: 1–14.

EVANS, P. 1977. Herded by whales. *Cruising World Magazine*, January 1977. Newport, Rhode Island.

EVANS, W. E. 1967. Vocalization among marine mammals. In W. N. Tavolga, ed., *Marine Bio-Acoustics*, Vol. II, pp. 159–86. Pergamon Press.

————. 1974. Radio-telemetric studies of two species of small odontocete cetaceans. In W. E. Schevill, ed., *The Whale Problem*, pp. 385–94. Harvard University Press.

————, W. W. SUTHERLAND, and R. G. BEIL. 1964. The directional characteristics of delphinid sounds. In W. N. Tavolga, ed., *Marine Bio-Acoustics*, pp. 353–72. Pergamon Press.

FEHRING, W. K., and R. S. WELLS. 1976. A series of strandings by a single herd of pilot whales on the west coast of Florida. *Jour. Mammal.* 57(1): 191–94.

FISCUS, C. H., and K. NIGGOL. 1965. Observations of cetaceans of California, Oregon and Washington. *U.S. Fish and Wildlife Service Special Report 498*.

FRASER, F. C. 1934. Report on cetacea stranded on the British Coasts from 1927 to 1932. *Bull. Brit. Mus. (Nat. Hist.)* 11: 1–41.

————. 1946. Report on cetacea stranded on the British Coasts from 1933 to 1937. *Bull. Brit. Mus. (Nat. Hist.)* 12: 1–55.

————. 1950. Two skulls of *Globicephala macrorhyncha* (Gray) from Dakar. *Atlantide Rep.* 1: 49–60.

————. 1953. Report on cetacea stranded on the British Coasts from 1938 to 1947. *Bull Brit. Mus. (Nat. Hist.)* 13: 1–48.

————. 1974. Report on cetacea stranded on the British Coasts from 1948 to 1966. *Bull. Brit. Mus. (Nat. Hist.)* 14: 1–65.

GASKIN, D. E., G. J. D. SMITH, P. W. ARNOLD, M. V. LOUISY, R. FRANK, M. HOLDRINET, and J. W. MCWADE. 1974. Mercury, DDT, dieldrin, and PCB in two species of Odontoceti (Cetacea) from St. Lucia, Lesser Antilles. *Jour. Fish. Res. Bd. Canada* 31: 1235–39.

GERACI, J. R. 1978. The enigma of marine mammal strandings. *Oceanus* 21(2): 38–47.

————, and D. J. ST. AUBIN. 1967. Mass stranding of the long-finned pilot whale, *Globicephala melaena*, on Sable Island, Nova Scotia. *Jour. Fish. Res. Bd. Canada* 24(11): 2196–99.

GRESSON, R. A. R. 1966. Pilot whales, *Globicephala melaena* (Traill) stranded at Cloghane, Co. Kerry. *Irish. Nat. Jour.* 15: 163–66.

GUNTER, G. 1946. Records of the blackfish or pilot whale from the Texas coast. *Jour. Mammal.* 27(4): 374–77.

HAIN, J. H. W., and S. LEATHERWOOD. 1982. Two sightings of white pilot whales, *Globicephala melaena*, and summarized records of anomalously white cetaceans. *Jour. Mammal.* 63(2): 338–43.

HARMER, S. F. 1927. Report on cetacea stranded on the British Coasts from 1913 to 1926. *Bull. Brit. Mus. (Nat. Hist.)* 10: 1–91.

JONES, S. 1976. The short-finned pilot whale, *Globicephala macrorhyncha* Gray, of the Indian Ocean. *Scientific Consultation on Marine Mammals, Bergen, Norway.* ACMRR/MM/SC/31. 1–35.

JONSGARD, A., and E. J. LONG. 1959. Norway's small whales. *Sea Frontiers* 5(9): 168–74.

KASUYA, T. 1971. Consideration of distribution and migration of toothed whales off the Pacific coast of Japan based on aerial sighting record. *Sci. Rep. Whales Res. Inst.* 23: 37–60.

————. 1975. Past occurrence of *Globicephala melaena* in the western North Pacific. *Sci. Rep. Whales Res. Inst.* 27: 95–110.

KOOYMAN, G. L., and H. T. ANDERSEN. 1969. Deep diving. In H. T. Andersen, ed., *The Biology of Marine Mammals*. Academic Press. pp. 65–94.

KRAUS, C., and M. GHIR. 1971. On the presence of *Tursiops truncatus* in schools of *Globicephala melaena* off the Faeroe Islands. *Invest. on Cetacea* 3(1): 180–82.

KRITZLER, H. 1952. Observations on the pilot whale in captivity. *Jour. Mammal.* 33: 321–34.

LEATHERWOOD, J. S., and M. E. DALHEIM. 1978. Worldwide distribution of pilot whales and killer whales. *Naval Oceans Systems Center Technical Note 443*.

MATTHEWSON, S. J. 1935. Blackfish in the Gulf of St. Lawrence. *Jour. Mammal.* 16: 234.

MERCER, M. C. 1967. Wintering of pilot whales, *Globicephala melaena*, in Newfoundland inshore waters. *Jour. Fish. Res. Bd. Canada* 24(11): 2481–84.

————. 1975. Modified Leslie–DeLury population models of the long-finned pilot whale (*Globicephala melaena*) and the annual production of the short-finned squid (*Illex illecebrocus*) based on their interaction at Newfoundland. *Jour. Fish. Res. Bd. Canada* 32(7): 1145–54.

MITCHELL, E. D. 1970. Pigmentation pattern evolution in delphinid cetaceans: an essay in adaptive coloration. *Canadian Jour. Zool.* 48(4): 717–40.

————. 1975a. Review of Biology and Fisheries for Smaller Cetaceans. *Jour. Fish. Res. Bd. Canada* 32(7).

————. 1975b. *Porpoise, Dolphin and Small Whale Fisheries of the World: Status and Problems.* IUCN Monograph No. 3, Morges, Switzerland.

MIYAZAKI, N., and S. WADA. 1978. Observation of cetacea during whale marking cruise in the western tropical Pacific, 1976. *Sci. Rep. Whales Res. Inst.* 30: 179–95.

NISHIWAKI, M. 1967. Distribution and migration of marine mammals in the North Pacific area. *Bull. Ocean. Res. Inst. Univ. Tokyo* I.

——. 1972. General biology. In S. H. Ridgway, ed., *Mammals of the Sea: Biology and Medicine*, pp. 3–204. Charles C. Thomas.

NORMAN, J. R., and F. C. FRASER. 1938. *Giant Fishes, Whales and Dolphins*. W. W. Norton & Co.

NORRIS, K. S. 1974. *The Porpoise Watcher*. W. W. Norton.

——, and J. H. PRESCOTT. 1961. Observations on Pacific cetaceans of Californian and Mexican waters. *Univ. Calif. Publ. Zool.* 63(4): 291–402.

NORRIS, K. S., H. A. BALDWIN, and D. J. SAMSON, 1965. Open ocean diving test with a trained porpoise. *Deep-Sea Research* 12: 505–09.

O'RIORDAN, C. E. 1975. Pilot whales, *Globicephala melaena*, driven ashore in Ireland, 1800–1973. *Jour. Fish. Res. Bd. Canada* 32(7): 1101–03.

PARADISO, J. L. 1958. The common blackfish in Virginia coastal waters. *Jour. Mammal.* 39: 440.

PIKE, G. C., and I. B. MACASKIE. 1969. Marine mammals of British Columbia. *Bull. Fish. Res. Bd. Canada* 171: 1–54.

PINERO, M. E., and H. P. CASTELLO. 1975. Sobre "ballenas piloto" *Globicephala melaena edwardi* (Cetacea, Delphinidae), variadas en la Isla Trinidad, Provincia de Buenos Aires. *Rev. Mus. Arg. Cien. Nat.* 12(2): 13–24.

RAY, C. 1961. A question in whale behavior. *Natural History* 70: 46–53.

RAYNER, G. W. 1939. *Globicephala leucosagamorpha*, a new species of the genus *Globicephala. Ann. Mag. Natl. Hist.* Ser. II, 4: 543–44.

REILLY, S. B. 1978. Pilot whale. In D. Haley, ed., *Marine Mammals of Eastern North Pacific and Arctic Waters*. Pacific Search Press. pp. 112–119.

SCHEFFER, V. B., and SLIPP, J. W. 1948. The whales and dolphins of Washington State with a key to the cetaceans of the West Coast of North America. *Amer. Midl. Nat.* 39(2): 257–357.

SCHEVILL, W. E. 1964. Underwater sounds of cetaceans. In W. N. Tavolga, ed., *Marine Bio-Acoustics*, pp. 307–16. Pergamon Press.

SCORESBY, W. 1820. *An Account of the Arctic Regions and of the Whale-Fishery*. Archibald Constable, London. (Reprint, 1969, David & Charles, Devon, England.)

SERGEANT, D. E. 1962a. The biology of the pilot or pothead whale *Globicephala melaena* (Traill) in Newfoundland waters. *Fish. Res. Bd. Canada. Bull.* No. 132.

——. 1962b. On the external characteristics of the blackfish or pilot whales (genus *Globicephala*). *Jour. Mammal.* 43(3): 395–413.

——. 1979. Ecological aspects of cetacean strandings. U. S. Marine Mammal Commission Report MMC-77/13.

——, A. W. MANSFIELD, and B. BECK. 1970. Inshore records of Cetacea for eastern Canada, 1949–68. *Jour. Fish. Res. Bd. Canada* 27: 1903–15.

STARRETT, A., and P. STARRETT. 1955. Observations on a young blackfish, *Globicephala. Jour. Mammal.* 36(3): 424–29.

STEVEN, D. 1950. Notes on a school of pilot whales stranded in East Lothian. *Scot. Nat.* 62(1): 153–56.

TARUSKI, A. G. 1979. The whistle repertoire of the North Atlantic pilot whale (*Globicephala melaena*) and its relationship to behavior and environment. In H. E. Winn and B. L. Olla, eds., *Behavior of Marine Animals, Vol. 3: Cetaceans.* pp. 345–68. Plenum Press.

——, and H. E. WINN. 1976. Winter sightings of odontocetes in the West Indies. *Cetology.* 22: 1–12.

TOMICH, P. Q. 1969. *Mammals in Hawaii: A Synopsis and Notational Bibliography*. Bishop Museum Press.

TOMILIN, A. G. 1957. *Mammals of the U.S.S.R. and Adjacent Countries.* Vol. 9: *Cetacea*. Izdatel'stvo Akademi Nauk SSR, Moscow. (Israel Program for Scientific Translations, Jerusalem, 1967.)

ULMER, F. A. 1961. New Jersey's whales and dolphins. N.J. Audubon Society. 16(3): 80–93.

VAN BREE, P. J. H. 1971. On *Globicephala sieboldii* Gray, 1846, and other species of pilot whales. *Beaufortia* 19(247): 79–87.

——. 1975. On two skeletons of pilot whales, *Globicephala melaena* (Traill 1809), from the mass stranding on the Island of Tholen, the Netherlands, on April 9, 1825. *Lutra* 17: 6–8.

——, P. B. BEST, and G. J. B. ROSS. 1976. Occurrence of the two species of pilot whales (Genus *Globicephala*) on the coast of South Africa. *Scientific Consultation on Marine Mammals, Bergen, Norway.* ACMRR/MM/SC/128. 1–12.

WATKINS, W. A. 1980. Click sounds from animals at sea. In R.-G. Busnel and J. F. Fish, eds., *Animal Sonar Systems.* pp. 291–97. Plenum.

WILLIAMSON, K. 1949. Notes on the caaing whale. *Scot. Nat.* 61(1): 68–72.

WOOD, F. G. 1973. *Marine Mammals and Man.* Luce.

——. 1979. The cetacean stranding phenomenon: An hypothesis. In J. B. Geraci and D. J. St. Aubin, eds., *Biology of Marine Mammals: Insights through Strandings*, pp. 129–88. U.S. Marine Mammal Commission Report PB 293 890.

KILLER WHALE

ANDREWS, B., and T. DESMOND. 1981. Killer whale births. *Whalewatcher* 15(1): 8–9.

ANDREWS. R. C. 1914. American Museum whale collection. *Amer. Mus. Jour.* 14(8): 275–294.

ASPER, E. D., and L. H. CORNELL. 1977. Live capture statistics for the killer whale (*Orcinus orca*) 1961–1976 in California,

Washington, and British Columbia. *Aquatic Mammals* 5(1): 21–26.

AWBREY, F. T., W. S. DREISCHMAN, and W. E. EVANS. 1980. Ross Sea killer whales. (Abstract) *Orca Symposium 1980.* Seattle.

BACKUS, R. H. 1961. Stranded killer whale in the Bahamas. *Jour. Mammal.* 42: 418–19.

BAKER, A. N. 1972. New Zealand Whales and Dolphins. *Tuatara* 20(1). Victoria University of Wellington.

BALCOMB, K. C. 1978. Orca survey—1977. *A report to the Marine Mammal Division, U.S. National Marine Fisheries Service.* 10 pp.

————, J. R. BORAN, and S. L. HEIMLICH. 1981. Killer whales in greater Puget Sound: A population ideally suited for statistical modeling. *Int. Whal. Commn. Sci. Com. Rep.* SC/JN81/KW9.

————, J. R. BORAN, R. W. OSBORNE, and N. J. HAENEL. 1980. Observations of killer whales (*Orcinus orca*) in greater Puget Sound, State of Washington. U.S. Marine Mammal Commission Report MMC-78/13. 42 pp.

BALDRIDGE, A. 1972. Killer Whales attack and eat a gray whale. *Jour. Mammal.* 53(4): 898–900.

BANFIELD, A. W. F. 1977. *The Mammals of Canada.* University of Toronto Press.

BENNETT, A. G. 1932. *Whaling in the Antarctic.* Henry Holt.

BEST, P. B. 1980. Notes on abundance of killer whales in Antarctic areas III and IV. *Int. Whal. Commn. Sci. Com. Rep.* SC/32/SM 10.

BEST, R., and C. ANGUS. 1970. White killer whale captured. *Vancouver Public Aquarium Newsletter* 14(2): 6–7.

BIGG, M. A. 1980. The life cycle of killer whale pods in British Columbia. (Abstract) *Orca Symposium 1980.* Seattle.

————. 1981. An assesment of killer whale (*Orcinus orca*) stocks off Vancouver Island, British Columbia. *Int. Whal. Commn. Sci. Com. Rep.* SC/JN81/KW4.

————, and A. A. WOLMAN. 1975. Live capture killer whale (*Orcinus orca*) fishery, British Columbia and Washington, 1962–73. *Jour. Fish. Res. Bd. Canada* 32(7): 1213–21.

BIGG, M. A., I. B. MAC ASKIE, and G. ELLIS. 1976. Abundance and movements of killer whales off eastern and southern Vancouver Island with comments on management. *Prelim. unpub. rep., Arctic Biol. Sta., Ste. Anne de Bellevue, Quebec.* 21 pp.

BOAS, F. 1927. *Primitive Art.* (Dover edition, 1955.)

BOWERS, C. A., and R. S. HENDERSON. 1972. Project Deep Ops: Deep object recovery with pilot and killer whales. *NUC, San Diego. NUC TP306.* 86 pp.

BRAHAM, H. W., M. E. DALHEIM, and L. D. CONSIGLIERI. 1981. Killer whales in Alaska from at-sea sightings documented in the U.S. platforms of opportunity program. *Int. Whal. Commn. Sci. Com. Rep.* SC/JN81/KW2.

BROWN, D. H., and K. S. NORRIS. 1956. Observations on captive and wild cetaceans. *Jour. Mammal.* 37(3): 311–26.

BROWNELL, R. L. 1974. Small odontocetes of the Antarctic. In V. C. Bushnell, ed., *Antarctic Mammals.* Antarctic Map Folio Series. American Geographical Society. Folio 18: 13–19.

BUDYLENKO, G. A. 1980. Distribution and some aspects of biology of killer whales in the South Atlantic. *Int. Whal. Commn. Sci. Com. Rep.* SC/32/SM 3.

BULLEN, F. 1899. *The Cruise of the Cachalot.* D. Appleton.

BUNNELL, S. 1974. The evolution of cetacean intelligence. In J. McIntyre, ed., *Mind in the Waters.* pp. 52–59. Scribner's.

BURRAGE, B. R. 1964. An observation regarding gray whales and killer whales. *Trans. Kansas Acad. Sci.* 67: 550–51.

CALDWELL, D. K., and D. H. BROWN. 1964. Tooth wear as a correlate of described feeding behavior by the killer whale, with notes on a captive specimen. *Bull. S. Calif. Acad. Sci.* 63: 128–40.

CALDWELL, D. K., and M. C. CALDWELL. 1969. Addition of the leatherback sea turtle to the known prey of the killer whale, *Orcinus orca. Jour. Mammal.* 50(4): 636.

————, W. F. RATHJEN, and J. R. SULLIVAN 1971. Cetaceans from the Lesser Antillean island of St. Vincent. *Fish. Bull.* 69(2): 303–12.

CALDWELL, M. C., and D. K. CALDWELL. 1966. Epimiletic (caregiving) behavior in cetacea. In K. S. Norris, ed., *Whales, Dolphins and Porpoises,* pp. 755–89. University of California Press.

CARL, G. C. 1946. A school of killer whales stranded at Estevan Point, Vancouver Island. *Prov. Mus. Nat. Hist. Anthrop. Rep.* (Victoria, B.C.) 1945: 21–28.

————. 1960. Albinistic killer whales in British Columbia. *Prov. Mus. Nat. Hist. Anthrop. Rep.* (Victoria, B.C.) 1959: 1–8.

CASTELLO, H. P. 1977. Food of a killer whale: Eagle sting-ray, *Mylobatis* found in the stomach of a stranded *Orcinus orca. Sci. Rep. Whales Res. Inst.* 29: 107–11.

————, A. P. TOMO, and J. S. PANIZZA. 1974. First Antarctic record of a killer whale stranding. *Sci. Rep. Whales Res. Inst.* 26: 255–58.

CHANDLER, R., C. GOEBEL, and K. BALCOMB. 1977. Who is that killer whale? A new key to whale watching. *Whalewatcher* 11(3): 10–11.

CHRISTENSEN, I. 1980. Miscellaneous data on killer whales caught in Norwegian coastal waters 1978–79. *Int. Whal. Commn. Sci. Com. Rep.* SC/32/SM 14.

————. 1981. Killer whales in Norwegian coastal waters. *Int. Whal. Commn. Sci. Com. Rep.* SC/33/KW1.

————, A. JONSGARD, and C. J. RØRVIK. 1981. Catch statistics for minke whales (*Balaenoptera acutorostrata*) and killer whales (*Orcinus orca*) caught off Norway in 1980. *Int. Whal. Commn. Sci. Com. Rep.* SC/33/06.

COLINVAUX, P. 1978. *Why Big Fierce Animals Are Rare.* Princeton University Press.

CONDY, P. R., R. J. VAN AARDE, and M. N. BESTER. 1978. The seasonal occurrence and behaviour of killer whales *Orcinus orca,* at Marion Island. *Jour. Zoology* 184(4): 449–64.

CORNELL, L. H., and E. D. ASPER. 1977. A census of captive marine mammals in North America. *Intl. Zoo Yearbook* 18: 220–24.

COUSTEAU, J.-Y, and P. COUSTEAU. 1970. *The Shark: Splendid Savage of the Sea.* Doubleday.

COUSTEAU, J.-Y., and P. DIOLÉ. 1972. *The Whale: Mighty Monarch of the Sea.* Doubleday.

CUMMINGS, W. C., and P. O. THOMPSON. 1971. Gray whales avoid the underwater sounds of killer whales. *Fish. Bull.* 69(3): 525–30.

CUMMINGS, W. C., J. F. FISH, and P. O. THOMPSON. 1972. Sound production and other behavior of southern right whales *Eubalaena glacialis. Trans. San Diego Soc. Nat. Hist.* 17(1): 1–14.

DAKIN, W. J. 1938. *Whaleman Adventurers.* Angus and Robertson.

DAHLHEIM, M. E. 1980a. A review of the biology and exploitation of the killer whale, *Orcinus orca,* with comments on recent sightings from Antarctica. *Int. Whal. Commn. Sci. Com. Rep.* SC/32/SM 9.

———. 1980b. Killer whales observed bowriding. *Murrelet* 61(2): 78.

———. 1981. Signature information in killer whale calls. *Whalewatcher* 15(1): 12–13, 19.

———, S. LEATHERWOOD, and W. F. PERRIN. 1981. Distribution of killer whales in the warm temperate and tropical eastern Pacific. *Int. Whal. Commn. Sci. Com. Rep.* SC/JW81/KW3.

DAUGHERTY, A. E. 1972. *Marine Mammals of California.* California Dept. of Fish and Game, Sacramento.

DEARDEN, J. C. 1958. A stranding of killer whales in Newfoundland. *Canadian Field. Nat.* 72: 166–67.

DEFRAN, R. F., and K. W. PRYOR. 1980. The behavior and training of cetaceans in captivity. In L. H. Herman, ed., *Cetacean Behavior: Mechanisms and Functions,* pp. 319–62. John Wiley.

DI SCIARA, G. N. 1978. A killer whale (*Orcinus orca* L.) attacks and sinks a sailing boat. *Natura* (Milano) 68(3–4): 218–20.

DUFFIELD, D., and L. CORNELL. 1979. Observations on population structure and dynamics in *Orcinus orca.* (Abstract) *Third Bien. Conf. Biol. Marine Mammals.* Seattle.

DUGUY, R., and D. ROBINEAU. 1973. Cétacés et phoques des côtes de France. *Annales de la Société des Sciences Naturelles de la Charente-Maritime.* 93 pp.

DUNN, D., S. HEWLETT, and K. MICHAELIS. 1974. The killer whale. *Vancouver Public Aquarium Newsletter* 18(5): 1–10.

EATON, R. L. 1979a. Selfishness, philosophy, and why ORCA. *Orca* 1(1): 3.

———. 1979b. Meditations on cetology and the cost of professionalism. (Review of *The Natural History of the Whale,* by L. H. Matthews.) *Carnivore* 2(3): 25–27.

ELLIS, R. 1982. The biggest, brightest dolphin. *Geo* 4(1): 34–45.

ESCHRICHT, D. F. 1862. On the species of orca inhabiting the northern seas: recent memoirs on the cetacea. *Proc. Roy. Danish Soc.* 151–88.

EVANS, W., and A. V. YABLOKOV. 1978. The peculiarities of the intraspecific variations of the killer whale colouration. *Izdatel'stvo Nauka,* 102–15.

———. 1980. Geographic variation in the pigmentation pattern of killer whales (*Orcinus orca*). (Abstract) *Orca Symposium 1980.* Seattle.

FISH, J. F., and J. S. VANIA. 1971. Killer whale (*Orcinus orca*) sounds repel white whales (*Delphinapterus leucas*). *Fish. Bull.* 69(3): 531–36.

FORD, J. K. B. 1980. Dialects in British Columbia killer whales. (Abstract) *Orca Symposium 1980.* Seattle.

———, and H. D. FISHER. 1981. Killer whale (*Orcinus orca*) dialects as an indicator of stocks in British Columbia. *Int. Whal. Commn. Sci. Com. Rep.* SC/JN81/KW8.

FRASER, F. C. 1934. Report on cetacea stranded on the British Coasts from 1927 to 1932. *Bull Brit. Mus. (Nat. Hist.)* 11: 1–41.

———. 1974. Report on cetacea stranded on the British coasts from 1948 to 1966. *Bull Brit. Mus. (Nat. Hist.)* 14: 1–65.

FRIZELL, J., C. PLOWDEN, and A. THORNTON. 1980. *Outlaw Whalers 1980.* Greenpeace, San Francisco.

FROST, P. G. H., P. D. SHAUGHNESSY, A. SEMMELINK, M. SKETCH, and W. R. SIEGFRIED. 1975. The response of jackass penguins to killer whale vocalisations. *S. Afr. Jour. Sci.* 71(5): 157–58.

GASKIN, D. E. 1972. *Whales, Dolphins and Seals, with Special Reference to the New Zealand Region.* Heinemann Educational Books.

GIHR, M., and G. PILLERI. 1979. Interspecific body length–body weight ratio and body weight–brain weight ratio in cetacea. *Invest. on Cetacea* 10: 245–53.

GOLDSBERRY, D. G., E. D. ASPER, and L. H. CORNELL. 1978. A live capture technique for the killer whale *Orcinus orca. Aquatic Mammals* 6(3): 91–96.

GOODALL, R. N. P. 1978. Report on the small cetaceans stranded on the coasts of Tierra del Fuego. *Sci. Rep. Whales Res. Inst.* 30: 197–230.

GRIFFIN, E. I. 1966. Making friends with a killer whale. *National Geographic* 129(3): 418–46.

HAENEL, N. J., K. C. BALCOMB, J. R. BORAN, S. L. HEIMLICH, and R. W. OSBORNE. 1980. Observations of nurturant behavior of

Puget Sound killer whales. (Abstract) *Orca Symposium 1980.* Seattle.

HALL, J. D. 1981. *Aspects of the Natural History of Cetaceans of Prince William Sound, Alaska.* Ph.D. dissertation, University of California, Santa Cruz.

————, and C. S. JOHNSON. 1972. Auditory thresholds of a killer whale *Orcinus orca* Linnaeus. *Jour. Acoust. Soc. Amer.* 51(2): 515–17.

HAMILTON, R. 1835. *Mammalia. Whales &c.* In W. Jardine, ed., The Naturalist's Library. Vol. 26, pp. 228–32.

HANCOCK, D. 1965. Killer whales kill and eat a minke whale. *Jour. Mammal.* 46: 341–42.

HARMER, S. F. 1927. Report on cetacea stranded on the British coasts from 1913 to 1926. *Bull. Brit. Mus. (Nat. Hist).* 10: 1–91.

HAWLEY, F. 1961. *Whales and Whaling in Japan.* Kyoto.

HEEZEN, B. C., and G. L. JOHNSON. 1969. Alaskan submarine cables: A struggle with a harsh environment. *Arctic* 22(4): 413–24.

HEIMLICH, S. L., J. R. BORAN, K. C. BALCOMB, N. J. HAENEL, and R. W. OSBORNE. 1980. Surfacing associations of *Orcinus orca.* (Abstract) *Orca Symposium 1980.* Seattle.

HOEY, A., and K. R. THORNTON. 1971. Techniques of management of killer whales in capture in a cold water environment. In *Proc. 8th Ann. Conf. Biol. Sonar and Diving Mammals.* Stanford Research Inst. 13–22.

HOYT, E. 1975. Singing with killer whales. *Pacific Discovery* 28(5): 28–32.

————. 1981. *A Whale Called Killer.* E. P. Dutton.

HUXLEY, E. 1978. *Scott of the Antarctic.* Atheneum.

ICHIHARA, T. 1980. The researches conducted on the dolphins around Iki and results of using devices. Unpub. rep. presented at the *IWC Conference on Cetacean Behaviour and Intelligence and the Ethics of Killing Cetaceans.* April 1980. 3 pp.

INTERNATIONAL WHALING COMMISSION. 1980. *Schedule.* (As amended by the commission at the 31st annual meeting, London, July 1979 and replacing that dated April 1979.) Cambridge, England.

INTERNATIONAL WHALING STATISTICS. 1930–1978. The Committee for Whaling Statistics, Sandefjord, Norway. Nos. 1–82 *(et seq.).*

IVASHIN, M. V., and L. M. VOTGOROV. 1980. Killer whales, *Orcinus orca,* inhabiting inshore waters of the Chukotka coast. *Int. Whal. Commn. Sci. Com. Rep.* SC/32/SM 2.

————. 1981. Occurrences of baleen and killer whales in the waters off the Chukotka Peninsula. *Int. Whal. Commn. Sci. Com. Rep.* SC/33/08.

JACOBSEN, J. 1980. Behavior of the killer whales (*Orcinus orca*) in the Johnstone Strait, British Columbia. (Abstract) *Orca Symposium 1980.* Seattle.

————. 1980. The birth of a wild killer whale (*Orcinus orca*). (Abstract) *Orca Symposium 1980.* Seattle.

JEHL, J. R., W. E. EVANS, F. T. AWBREY, and W. S. DRIESCHMAN. 1980. Distribution and geographic variation in the killer whale (*Orcinus orca*) populations of the Antarctic and adjacent waters. *Antarctic Jour.* 15(5): 161–63.

————. 1981. Distribution and geographic variation in the killer whale (*Orcinus orca*) populations of the Antarctic and adjacent waters. *Int. Whal. Commn. Sci. Com. Rep.* SC/JN81/KW5.

JEUNE, P. 1979. *The Whale Who Wouldn't Die: The True Story of "Miracle."* Follett.

JONSGARD, A. 1968a. A note on the attacking behavior of the killer whale (*Orcinus orca*). *Norsk Hvalfangst-tidende* 57(4): 84–85.

————. 1968b. Another note on the attacking behavior of the killer whale (*Orcinus orca*). *Norsk Hvalfangst-tidende* 57(6): 175–76.

————, and E. J. LONG. 1959. Norway's small whales. *Sea Frontiers* 5(3): 168–74.

JONSGARD, A., and P. B. LYSHOEL. 1970. A contribution to the biology of the killer whale, *Orcinus orca. Norw. Jour. Zool.* 18(1): 41–48.

JONSGARD, A., and P. ÖYNES. 1952. Om bottlenosen (*Hyperoodon rostratus*) og spekhoggeren (*Orcinus orca*). *Fauna* (Oslo). 1: 1–17.

KELLOGG, R. 1940. Whales, giants of the sea. *National Geographic* 77(1): 35–90.

KING, J. E. 1964. *Seals of the World.* British Museum (Natural History).

LEATHERWOOD, J. S., and M. E. DALHEIM. 1978. Worldwide distribution of pilot whales and killer whales. *Naval Oceans Systems Center.* TN 443. 39 pp.

LEATHERWOOD, S., W. F. PERRIN, and M. DALHEIM. 1980. Distribution and relative abundance of killer whales, *Orcinus orca,* in the warm temperate and tropical eastern Pacific (34° N to 15° S latitude). (Abstract) *Orca Symposium 1980.* Seattle.

LILLY, J. C. 1961. *Man and Dolphin.* Doubleday.

LIOUVILLE, J. 1913. *Cétacés de l'Antarctique (Baleinoptères, Ziphiides, Delphinides). Deuxième Expédition Antarctique Française, 1908–1910.* Masson.

LOCKYER, C. 1979. Response of orcas to tagging. *Carnivore* 2(3): 19–21.

MAC ASKIE, I. B. 1966. Unusual example of group behavior by killer whales (*Orcinus rectipinna*). *Murrelet* 47(2): 38.

MARTINEZ, D. R., and E. KLINGHAMMER. 1970. The behavior of the whale *Orcinus orca:* a review of the literature. *Zeitschrift fur Tierpsychologie* 27: 828–39.

————. 1978. A partial ethogram of the killer whale (*Orcinus orca* L.) *Carnivore* 1(3): 13–27.

MATKIN, C. 1981. Orca: Killer whale. *Whalewatcher* 15(1): 3–4.

MATTHEWS, A. 1978. Air transportation by helicopter of juvenile *Orcinus orca*. Aquatic Mammals. 6(3): 97–98.

MATTHEWS, L. H. 1978. *The Natural History of the Whale.* Columbia University Press.

MAXWELL, G. 1952. *Harpoon Venture.* Viking Press.

MEAD, T. 1961. *Killers of Eden.* Angus and Robertson.

MELVILLE, H. 1851. *Moby-Dick, or The Whale.* 1930 edition. Random House.

MIKHALEV, Y. A., M. V. IVASHIN, V. P. SAVUSIN, and F. E. ZELE-NAYA. 1980. Materials on the distribution of the killer whales (*Orcinus orca*) in the Southern Hemisphere. *Int. Whal. Commn. Sci. Com. Rep.* SC/32/SM 12.

MITCHELL, E. D. 1970. Pigmentation pattern evolution in delphinid cetaceans: an essay in adaptive coloration. *Canadian Jour. Zool.* 48(4): 717–40.

———. 1975. *Porpoise, Dolphin and Small Whale Fisheries of the World: Status and Problems.* IUCN Monograph No. 3, Morges, Switzerland.

MIYAZAKI, N., and S. WADA. 1978. Observation of cetacea during whale marking cruise in the western tropical Pacific, 1976. *Sci. Rep. Whales Res. Inst.* 30: 179–95.

MOREJOHN, J. V. 1968. A killer whale–gray whale encounter. *Jour. Mammal.* 49(2): 327–28.

NEWMAN, M. A., and P. L. MC GEER. 1966. The capture and care of a killer whale *Orcinus orca* in British Columbia. *Zoologica* 51: 59–70 + 8 pl.

NISHIWAKI, M. 1967. Distribution and Migration of Marine Mammals in the North Pacific Area. *Bull. Ocean Res. Inst. Univ. Tokyo.*

———, and C. HANDA. 1958. Killer whales caught in the coastal waters off Japan for recent 10 years. *Sci. Rep. Whales Res. Inst.* 13: 85–96.

NORMAN, J. R. and F. C. FRASER. 1938. *Giant Fishes, Whales and Dolphins.* W. W. Norton.

NORRIS, K. S., and J. H. PRESCOTT. 1961. Observations on Pacific cetaceans of Californian and Mexican waters. *Univ. Calif. Publ. Zool.* 63(4): 291–402.

ODLUM, G. C. 1948. An instance of killer whales feeding on ducks. *Canadian Field Nat.* 62: 42.

OHSUMI, S. 1981. Distribution and abundance of killer whales in the Southern Hemisphere. *Int. Whal. Commn. Sci. Com. Rep.* SC/JN81/KW10.

OSBORNE, R. W., K. C. BALCOMB, J. R. BORAN, N. HAENEL, and S. L. HEIMLICH. 1980. A behavior budget of Puget Sound Killer Whales. (Abstract) *Orca Symposium 1980.* Seattle.

OTTEN, T. 1977. First killer whale (*Orcinus orca*) ever born in captivity. *Whalewatcher* 11(3): 13–14.

———. 1980. Considerations for training mature killer whales. (Abstract) *Orca Symposium 1980.* Seattle.

RICE, D. W. 1968. Stomach contents and feeding behavior of killer whales in the eastern North Pacific. *Norsk Hvalfangst-tidende* 57(2): 35–38.

———, and A. A. WOLMAN. 1971. *The Life History and Ecology of the Gray Whale,* (Eschrichtius robustus). *Am. Soc. Mammal. Spec. Publ. No. 3.*

RIDGWAY, S. H. 1980. Brain size and surface area in neonatal and adult killer whales. (Abstract) *Orca Symposium 1980.* Seattle.

ROBERTSON, D. 1973. *Survive the Savage Sea.* Praeger.

ROBERTSON, R. B. 1954. *Of Whales and Men.* Alfred A. Knopf.

ROBSON, F. 1976. *Thinking Dolphins, Talking Whales.* A. H. & A. W. Reed.

SALDEN, D. R. 1979. Supplementary observations concerning an ethogram of the killer whale. *Carnivore* 2(3): 17–18.

SALISBURY, D. F. 1978. A whale called killer. *National Wildlife* 16(2): 4–9.

SANDERSON, I. T. 1956. *Follow the Whale.* Little, Brown.

SAPIN-JALOUSTRE, J. 1953. L'identification des cétacés antarctiques à la mer. *Mammalia* 17: 221–59.

SCAMMON, C. M. 1874. *The Marine Mammals of the Northwestern Coast of North America; Together with an Account of the Whale-Fishery.* Carmany; and Putnam's.

SCHEFFER, V. B. 1969. Marks on the skin of a killer whale. *Jour. Mammal.* 50(1): 151.

———. 1970. The cliché of the killer. *Natural History* 79(8): 28–29, 76–78.

———. 1971. Killer Whales: Fat Choppers. In A. Seed, ed., *Toothed Whales in Eastern Pacific and Arctic Waters.* Pacific Search Books.

———. 1976. *A Natural History of Marine Mammals.* Scribner's.

———. 1978. Killer whale. In D. Haley, ed., *Marine Mammals of Eastern North Pacific and Arctic Waters.* Pacific Search Press. 120–127.

———, and J. W. SLIPP. 1948. The whales and dolphins of Washington State with a key to the cetaceans of the west coast of North America. *Amer. Midl. Nat.* 39(2): 257–337.

SCHEVILL, W. E., and W. A. WATKINS. 1966. Sound structure and directionality in Orcinus (killer whale). *Zoologica* 51(2): 71–76.

SCHILDKRAUT, L. 1979. The killer whale in the art and myth of the Tlingit Indians. *Carnivore* 2(3): 4–9.

SCORESBY, W. 1820. *An Account of the Arctic Regions with History and a Description of the Northern Whale-Fishery.* Archibald Constable, Edinburgh. (1969 edition.) David & Charles.

SCOTT, R. F. 1912. *Scott's Last Expedition.* (1964 edition.) The Folio Society, London.

SHEPHERD, G. S. 1932. Killer whale in slough at Portland, Oregon. *Jour. Mammal.* 13(2): 171–72.

SHEVCHENKO, V. I. 1975. The nature of interrelations between killer whales and other cetaceans. *Sea Mammals Part 2, Rep. to the 6th AU Union Meeting. Ed. Naukova Dunika, Kiev.* 173–78 (In Russian.)

SINIFF, D. B., and J. L. BENGSTON. 1977. Observations and hypotheses concerning the interactions among crabeater seals, leopard seals and killer whales. *Jour. Mammal.* 58(3): 414–16.

SPONG, P. 1974. The whale show. In J. McIntyre, ed., *Mind in the Waters.* Scribner's/Sierra Club. pp. 170–85.

————, and D. WHITE. 1970. Sensory guidance of behavior in the killer whale (*Orcinus orca*). In *Proc. 7th Ann. Conf. Biol. Sonar and Diving Mammals*, pp. 175–83. Stanford Research Inst.

SPONG, P., J. BRADFORD, and D. WHITE. 1970. Field studies of the behavior of the killer whale *Orcinus orca*. In *Proc. 7th Ann. Conf. Biol. Sonar and Diving Mammals*, pp. 169–74. Stanford Research Inst.

SPONG, P., H. MICHAELS and L. SPONG. 1972. Field studies in the behavior of the killer whale (*Orcinus orca*). II. *Proc. 9th Ann. Conf. Biol. Sonar and Diving Mammals*, pp. 181–85. Stanford Research Inst.

SPONG, P., L. SPONG, and Y. SPONG. 1972. Field studies of the behavior of the killer whale (*Orcinus orca*). III. *Proc. 9th Ann. Conf. Biol. Sonar and Diving Mammals*, pp. 187–92. Stanford Research Inst.

STEINER, W. W., J. H. HAIN, H. E. WINN, and P. J. PERKINS. 1979. Vocalizations and feeding behavior of the killer whale (*Orcinus orca*). *Jour. Mammal.* 60(4): 823–27.

STEPHENS. W. M. 1963. The killer. *Sea Frontiers* 9(5): 262–73.

SWEENEY, J. C. 1980. Observations on the breeding, pregnancy and problems with the neonate in *Orcinus orca*. (Abstract) *Orca Symposium 1980.* Seattle.

TALBOT, B. 1981. Diving with orcas. *Whalewatcher* 15(1): 16.

TARPY, C. 1979. Killer whale attack! *National Geographic* 155(4): 542–45.

TAYLOR, R. J. F. 1957. An unusual record of three species of whale being restricted to pools in Antarctic sea-ice. *Proc. Zool. Soc. London.* 129: 325–31.

THOMAS, J. A., F. T. AWBREY, S. LEATHERWOOD, W. E. EVANS, and J. R. JEHL. 1981. Ross Sea killer whale (*Orcinus orca*) distribution, behavior, color pattern, and vocalizations. *Int. Whal. Commn. Sci. Com. Rep.* SC/JN81/KW6.

THORNTON, K. R., and A. HOEY. 1979. Management of inflammatory skin granuloma in an albino *Orcinus orca*. *Proc. 8th Ann. Conf. Biol. Sonar and Diving Mammals.* Stanford Research Inst. pp. 25–33.

TOMICH, P. Q. 1969. *Mammals in Hawaii.* Bishop Museum Press.

TOMILIN, A. G. 1957. *Mammals of the U.S.S.R. and Adjacent Countries. Vol. IX: Cetacea.* Izdatel'stvo Akademi Nauk SSR, Moscow. (Israel Program for Scientific Translations, Jerusalem, 1967).

TØNNESEN, J. N. 1962. Et storverk om hval. *Norsk Hvalfangsttidende* 51(12): 473–80.

ULMER, F. A. 1941. Notes on a killer whale (*Grampus orca*) from the coast of New Jersey. *Notulae Naturae* 83: 1–5.

VILLIERS, A. J. 1925. *Whaling in the Frozen South.* Bobbs-Merrill.

VOISIN, J.-F. 1972. Notes on the behaviour of the killer whale, *Orcinus orca* (L.). *Norw. Jour. Zool.* 20: 93–96.

————. 1976. On the behaviour of the killer whale, *Orcinus orca* L. *Nor. Jour. Zool.* 24(1): 69–71.

WILSON, J. 1975. Killers in the surf. *Audubon* 77(5): 2–5.

WOOD, F. G. 1973. *Marine Mammals and Man.* Luce.

————, and W. E. EVANS. 1980. Adaptiveness and ecology of echolocation in toothed whales. In R.-G. Busnel and J.F. Fish, eds, *Animal Sonar Systems*, pp. 381–425. Plenum.

YABLOKOV, A. V. 1974. *Whales and Dolphins.* Joint Publications Research Service; Arlington, Virginia. JPRS-62150-2 1–452.

————, and W. E. EVANS. 1981. Geographic variation in the color pattern of killer whales (*Orcinus orca*). *Int. Whal. Commn. Sci. Com. Rep.* SC/JN81/KW11.

IRRAWADDY RIVER DOLPHIN

ANDERSON, J. 1878. *Anatomical and Zoological Researches Comprising an Account of the Zoological Results of the Two Expeditions to Western Yunnan in 1868 and 1875, and a Monograph on the Two Cetacean Genera Platanista and Orcella.* Vol I, text; Vol. II, plates. London.

BANKS, E. 1931. A popular account of the mammals of Borneo. *Jour. Malayan Branch Roy. Asiat. Soc.* 9(2): 1–139.

GIBSON-HALL, C. A. 1950. The whales, dolphins and porpoises known in Sarawak waters. *Sarawak Mus. Jour.* 5(2): 288–96.

GRAY, J. E. 1866. *Catalogue of Seals and Whales in the British Museum.* British Museum, London.

HENDROKUSOMO, S. 1979. Freshwater dolphin baby (*Orcaella* sp) born in Jaya Ancol Oceanarium. (Jakarta, Indonesia.) Mimeo letter + photo. July 16, 1979.

HERALD, E. S. 1969. Field and aquarium study of the blind river dolphin (*Platanista gangetica*). *Naval Undersea Research and Development Center.* NUC-TP 153.

JOHNSON, D. H. 1964. Mammals of the Arnhem Land Expedition. In R. L. Specht, ed., *Records of the American-Australian Scientific Expedition to Arnhem Land* (Zoology) 4: 427–515.

KELLOGG, R. 1940. Whales, giants of the sea. *National Geographic* 77(1): 35–90.

MITCHELL, E. D. 1975a. *Porpoise, Dolphin and Small Whale Fisheries of the World: Status and Problems.* IUCN Monograph No. 3, Morges, Switzerland.

———. 1975b. Review of smaller cetacea, identity and status of species and stocks. *Jour. Fish. Res. Bd. Canada* 32(7): 889–983.

MÖRZER BRUYNS, W. F. J. 1966. Some notes on the Irrawaddy dolphin, *Orcaella brevirostris* (Owen, 1866). *Zeit. für Saugetierk.* 31(5): 367–70.

———. 1971. *Field Guide of Whales and Dolphins.* Amsterdam.

OWEN, R. 1866. On some Indian cetacea collected by Walter Elliot, Esq. *Trans. Zool. Soc. London* 6: 17–47.

PILLERI, G. 1970. Forward. *Invest. on Cetacea* 2: 9–10.

———, and M. GIHR, 1973. Contribution to the knowledge of the cetacea of southwest and monsoon Asia (Persian Gulf, Indus Delta, Malabar, Andaman Sea and the Gulf of Siam). *Invest. on Cetacea* 5: 95–149.

RICE, D. W. 1977. *A List of the Marine Mammals of the World.* NOAA Technical Report NMFS SSRF-711.

TRUE, F. W. 1889. A review of the family Delphinidae. *Bull. U.S. Nat. Mus.* 36: 1–191.

HARBOR PORPOISE, VAQUITA, SPECTACLED PORPOISE, AND BURMEISTER'S PORPOISE

AGUAYO, L. A. 1975. Progress report on small cetaceans research in Chile. *Jour. Fish. Res. Bd. Canada* 32(7): 1123–43.

ALLEN, G. M. 1925. Burmeister's porpoise (*Phocoena spinipinnis*). *Bull. Museum of Comparative Zoology* 67(5): 251–61.

AMUNDIN, M., and B. AMUNDIN. 1973–74. On the behavior and study of the harbor porpoise (*Phocoena phocoena*), in the wild. *Invest. on Cetacea.* 5: 317–28.

ANDERSEN, S. 1969. Epimeletic behavior in captive harbor porpoise *Phocoena phocoena. Invest on Cetacea* 1: 203–05.

———. 1970a. Auditory sensitivity of the harbour porpoise, *Phocoena phocoena. Invest. on Cetacea* 2: 255–59.

———. 1970b. Directional hearing in the harbour porpoise *Phocoena phocoena. Invest on Cetacea* 2: 260–63.

———. 1975. Change of migratory behavior in the harbor porpoise, *Phocoena phocoena,* illustrated by catch statistics from 1834–1944. Marine Mammals Symposium. ACMRR/MM/EC/32. 1–3.

———. 1976. The taming and training of the harbor porpoise *Phocoena phocoena. Cetology* 24: 1–9.

ARNOLD, P. W. 1972. Predation on harbor porpoise *Phocoena phocoena* by a white shark *Carcharodon carcharias. Jour. Fish. Res. Canada* 29(8): 1213–14.

ARVY, L. 1973. Mammary glands, milk, and lactation in cetaceans. *Invest. on Cetacea* 5: 157–202.

BAKER, A. N. 1977. Spectacled porpoise, *Phocoena dioptrica,* new to the subantarctic Pacific Ocean. *N. Z. Jour. Mar. and Freshw. Res.* 11(2): 401–06.

BEDDARD, F. 1900. *A Book of Whales.* John Murray.

BROWN, D. H., and K. S. NORRIS. 1956. Observations of captive and wild cetaceans. *Jour. Mammal.* 37(3): 311–26.

BROWN, S. G. 1975. Relation between stranding mortality and population abundance of smaller cetacea in the northeast Atlantic Ocean. *J. Fish. Res. Bd. Canada* 32(7): 1095–99.

BROWNELL, R. L. 1974a. *Phocoena dioptrica.* Mammalian Species. *Amer. Soc. Mamm.* No. 66.

———. 1974b. Small odontocetes of the Antarctic. In V.C. Bushnell, ed., *Antarctic Mammals.* Folio 18 pp. 13–19. Antarctic Map Folio Series, American Geographical Society.

———. 1976a. Status of the cochito, *Phocoena sinus.* in the Gulf of California. *FAO Scientific Consultation on Marine Mammals.* ACMMR/MM/SC/63.

———. 1976b. Status of the spectacled porpoise, *Phocoena dioptrica,* in the western South Atlantic. *FAO Scientific Consultation on Marine Mammals.* ACMMR/MM/SC/19.

———, and R. PRADERI. 1976. Status of the Burmeister's porpoise, *Phocoena spinipinnis,* in South American waters. *FAO Scientific Consultation on Marine Mammals.* ACMMR/MM/SC/20.

BRUCH, C. 1916. El macho de *Phocaena dioptrica* Lah. *Physis* 2(12): 461–62.

BURMEISTER, H. 1865. Description of a new species of porpoise in the Museum of Buenos Aires, *Phocoena spinipinnis* sp. nov. *Proc. Zool. Soc. London.* 1865: 228–31.

BUSNEL, R.-G., and A. DZIEDZIC. 1966. Acoustic signals of the pilot whale *Globicephala melaena* and of the porpoises *Delphinus delphis* and *Phocoena phocoena.* In K. S. Norris, ed., *Whales, Dolphins and Porpoises,* pp. 607–46. University of Calif. Press.

CLARKE, R., A. AGUAYO, and S. B. DEL CAMPO. 1978. Whale observation and whale marking off the coast of Chile in 1964. *Sci. Rep. Whales Res. Inst.* 30: 117–77.

DAUGHTERTY, A. 1972. *Marine Mammals of California.* State of California Dept. of Fish and Game. Sacramento. 91 pp.

DEWHURST, H. W. 1834. *The Natural History of the Order Cetacea, and the Oceanic Inhabitants of the Arctic Regions.* London.

DUDOK VAN HEEL, W. H. 1959. Audio-direction finding in the porpoise (*Phocoena phocoena*). *Nature* 183: 1063.

———. 1962. Catching *Phocoena phocoena* for scientific purposes. *Bull. Inst. Oceanogr. Monaco.* Spec. No. 1A: 23–27.

DUGUY, R. 1977. Notes on the small cetaceans off the coasts of France. *Rep. Int. Whal. Commn.* 27: 500–01.

EASTON, D. F., M. KLINOWSKA, and M. C. SHELDRICK. 1981. A preliminary analysis of the British stranding records of the harbor porpoise (*Phocoena phocoena*). *Sci. Com. Rep. Int. Whal. Commn.* SC/33/SM4

ESCHRICHT, D. F. 1862. On the species of Orca inhabiting the northern seas. Recent Memoirs of the Cetacea. *Proc. Roy. Danish Soc.* 151–88.

FISHER, H. D., and R. J. HARRISON. 1970. Reproduction in the common porpoise (*Phocoena phocoena*) of the North Atlantic. *Jour. Zool.* 161: 471–86 +2 pls.

FRASER, F. C. 1934. Report on cetacea stranded on the British Coasts from 1927 to 1932. *Bull. Brit. Mus. (Nat. Hist.)* 11: 1–41.

———. 1946. Report on cetacea stranded on the British Coasts from 1933 to 1937. *Bull. Brit. Mus. (Nat. Hist.)* 12: 1–56.

———. 1953. Report on cetacea stranded on the British Coasts from 1938 to 1947. *Bull. Brit. Mus. (Nat. Hist.)* 13: 1–48.

———. 1966. Comments on Delphinoidiea. In K. S. Norris, ed., *Whales, Dolphins, and Porpoises*, pp. 7–31. Univ. of California Press.

———. 1968. Notes on a specimen of *Phocoena dioptrica* from South Georgia. *Brit. Antarctic Surv. Bull.* 16: 51–56.

———. 1974. Report on cetacea stranded on the British Coasts from 1948 to 1966. *Bull. Brit. Mus. (Nat. Hist.).* 14: 1–65.

GALLARDO, A. 1917. Sobre el tipo de la *Phocaena spinipinnis* Burmeister. *Physis, Rev. Soc. Argentina Cien. Nat.* 3: 83–84.

GASKIN, D. E. 1977. Harbour porpoise *Phocoena phocoena* (L.) in the western approaches to the Bay of Fundy. *Rep. Int. Whal. Commn.* 27: 487–492.

———, P. W. ARNOLD, and B. A. BLAIR. 1974. *Phocoena phocoena*. Mammalian species. *Am. Soc. Mammal.* no. 42.

GASKIN, D. E., M. HOLDRINET, and R. FRANK. 1971. Organochlorine pesticide residues in harbour porpoises from the Bay of Fundy region. *Nature* (London) 233: 499–500.

———. 1976. DDT residues in blubber of harbour porpoise, *Phocoena phocoena* (L.) from eastern Canadian waters during the five-year period 1969–1973. *Scientific Consultation on Marine Mammals, Bergen, Norway.* ACMRR/MM/SC/96. 1–11.

GASKIN, D. E., K. ISHIDA, and R. FRANK. 1972. Mercury in harbor porpoises (*Phocoena phocoena*) from the Bay of Fundy region. *Jour. Fish. Res. Bd. Canada.* 29: 1644–46.

GOODALL, R. N. P. 1977. Preliminary report on the small cetaceans stranded on the coasts of Tierra del Fuego. *Rep. Intl. Whal. Commn.* 27: 505.

———. 1978. Report on the small cetaceans stranded on the coasts of Tierra del Fuego. *Sci. Rep. Whales Res. Inst.* 30: 197–230.

———, and I. S. CAMERON. 1979. *Phocoena dioptrica*, una nueva especie para aguas Chilenas. *Rev. Mus. Arg. Cien. Nat.* 12(11): 143–52.

GRAY, J. E. 1865. Notice of a new species of porpoise (*Phocoena tuberculifera*) inhabiting the mouth of the Thames. *Proc. Zool. Soc. London.* 318–21.

GRIMWOOD, I. R. 1969. Notes on the distribution and status of some Peruvian mammals 1968. *Spec. Publ. N.Y. Zool. Soc.* 21. 86 pp.

HALL, E. R., and J. W. BEE. 1954. Occurrence of the harbor porpoise at Point Barrow, Alaska. *Jour. Mammal.* 35: 122–23.

HAMILTON, J. E. 1941. A rare porpoise of the South Atlantic, *Phocoena dioptrica* (Lahille 1912) *Disc. Rep.* 21: 229–34.

HARMER, S. F. 1927. Report on cetacea stranded on the British Coasts from 1913 to 1926. *Bull. Brit. Mus. (Nat. Hist.)* 10: 1–91.

HARRIS, D. 1972. Vagabundos del mar: Shark fishermen of the Sea of Cortez. *Oceans* 5(1): 60–72.

HULT, R. W., S. E. DUPEY, and R. W. BADLEY. 1980. Mortalities associated with prey ingestions by small cetaceans. *Cetology* 38: 1–2.

INTERNATIONAL WHALING COMMISSION. 1977. Report of the sub-committee on small cetaceans—London 7–9 June 1976. Annex L. SC/28/Rep. 3. *Rep. Intl. Whal. Commn.* 27: 474–84.

———. 1978. Report of the scientific committee. *Rep. Intl. Whal. Commn.* 28: 38–74.

JAMES, H. L. 1914. Birth of a porpoise at the Brighton Aquarium. *Proc. Zool. Soc. London.* 1061–62.

KAPEL, F. O. 1975. Preliminary notes on the occurrence and exploitation of smaller cetacea in Greenland. *J. Fish. Res. Bd. Canada.* 32(7): 1079–82.

———. 1977. Catch of belugas, narwhals and harbor porpoises in Greenland, 1954–75, by year, month and region. *Rep. Intl. Whal. Commn.* 27: 507–20.

KELLOGG, R. 1940. Whales, giants of the sea. *National Geographic* 77(1): 35–90.

LAHILLE, F. 1912. Nota preliminar sobre una nueva especie de marsopa del Río de la Plata. *An. Mus. Hist. Nat. Buenos Aires* 23: 269–78.

LAURIN, J. 1976. Preliminary study of the distribution, hunting and incidental catch of harbour porpoise, *Phocoena phocoena* L. in the gulf and estuary of the St. Lawrence. *Scientific Consultation on Marine Mammals, Bergen, Norway.* ACMRR/MM/SC/93. 1–14.

LEAR, W. H., and O. CHRISTIANSEN. 1975. By-catches of harbour porpoise (*Phocoena phocoena*) in salmon driftnets at West Greenland in 1972. *Jour. Fish. Res. Bd. Canada* 32(7): 1223–28.

LEIGHTON, A. H. 1937. The twilight of the Indian porpoise hunters. *Natural History* 40(1): 410–16, 458.

MARCUZZI, G., and G. PILLERI. 1971. On the zoogeography of cetaceans. *Invest. on Cetacea* 3(1): 101–70.

MEAD, J. G. 1979. An analysis of cetacean strandings along the eastern coast of the United States. In J. B. Geraci and D. J. St. Aubin, eds., *Biology of Marine Mammals: Insights Through Strandings*, pp. 54–68. National Technical Information Service. PB-293 890.

MERCER, M. C. 1973. Observations on distribution and intraspecific variation in pigmentation patterns of odontocete cetacea in the Western North Atlantic. *Jour. Fish. Res. Bd. Canada.* 30(8): 1111–30 +4 pls.

MITCHELL, E. D. 1975a. *Porpoise, Dolphin and Small Whale Fisheries of the World: Status and Problems.* IUCN Monograph No. 3. Morges, Switzerland. 129 pp.

———. 1975b. Review of Biology and Fisheries for Smaller Cetaceans. *Jour. Fish. Res. Bd. Canada.* 32(7): 889–983.

MØHL-HANSEN, U. 1954. Investigations on reproduction and growth of the porpoise (*Phocoena phocoena* L.) from the Baltic. *Vidensk. Medd. fra Danish Naturh. Foren.* 116: 369–98.

MORIS, F. 1969. Etude anatomique de la région céphalique du marsouin *Phocaena phocaena* L. (Cétacé Odontocète). *Mammalia.* 33: 666–726.

MÖRZER BRUYNS, W. F. J. 1971. *Field Guide of Whales and Dolphins.* Amsterdam.

NEAVE, D. J., and B. S. WRIGHT. 1968. Seasonal migrations of the harbor porpoise (*Phocoena phocoena*) and other cetacea in the Bay of Fundy. *Jour. Mammal.* 49(2): 259–64.

———. 1969. Observations of *Phocoena phocoena* in the Bay of Fundy. *Jour. Mammal.* 50(3): 653–54.

NIELSEN, H. G. 1972. Age determination of the harbour porpoise *Phocoena phocoena* (L.) (Cetacea). *Vidensk. Medd. fra Dansk Naturh. Foren.* 135: 61–84.

NOBLE, B. A., and F. C. FRASER. 1971. Description of a skeleton and supplementary notes on the skull of a rare porpoise *Phocoena sinus* Norris & McFarland 1958. *Jour. Nat. Hist.* 5: 447–64.

NORMAN, J. R., and FRASER, F. C. 1938. *Giant Fishes, Whales and Dolphins.* W. W. Norton.

NORRIS, K. S., and MC FARLAND, W. N. 1958. A new porpoise of the genus *Phocoena* from the Gulf of California. *Jour. Mammal.* 39: 22–39.

NORRIS, K. S., and J. H. PRESCOTT. 1961. Observations on Pacific cetaceans of Californian and Mexican waters. *Univ. Calif. Publ. Zool.* 63(4): 291–402.

OHSUMI, S. 1975. Incidental catch of cetaceans with salmon gill net. *Jour. Fish Res. Bd. Canada* 32(7): 1229–35.

ORR, R. T. 1937. A porpoise chokes on a shark. *Jour. Mammal.* 18: 370.

———. 1969. An additional record of *Phocoena sinus. Jour. Mammal.* 50(2): 384.

PARKER, G. H. 1932. The respiratory rate of the common porpoise. *Jour. Mammal.* 13: 68–69.

PEREZ CANTO, C. 1896. Descriptions de deux nouveaux cétacés de la côte du Chili. *Act. Soc. Sci. Chili.* 5: 227–29

PHILIPPI, R. A. 1893. Los delfines de la Punta Austral de la América del Sur. *Anales Mus. Nac. Chile* 1 (Zool.) 6:1–16.

PILLERI, G., and M. GIHR. 1972. Burmeister's porpoise, *Phocoena spinipinnis* Burmeister 1865, off the Punta del Diablo, Uruguay. *Invest. on Cetacea* 4: 163–72.

———. 1974. Second record of Burmeister's porpoise (*Phocoena spinipinnis*) of Los Cerros, Uruguay. *Invest. on Cetacea* 5: 150–53.

PRADERI, R. 1971. Contribución al conocimiento del género *Phocoena.* (Cetacea, Phocoenidae.) *Rev. Mus. Arg. Cienc. Nat., Zool.* 7(2): 251–66.

———, and E. PALERM. 1971. Hallazgo de *Phocoena dioptrica* Lahille (Cetacea, Phocoenoidae) en la costa Uruguaya. *Bol. Soc. Zool. Uruguay* 1: 19–21.

PRESCOTT, J. H., and P. M. FIORELLI. 1980. Review of the harbor porpoise (*Phocoena phocoena*) in the U.S. northwest Atlantic. U.S. Marine Mammal Commission Report. MMC-78/08.

PRESCOTT, J. H., S. D. KRAUS, P. FIORELLI, D. E. GASKIN, G. J. D. SMITH, and M. BRANDER. 1981. Harbor porpoise (*Phocoena phocoena*): Distribution, abundance, survey methodology and preliminary notes on habitat use and threats. *NOAA NMFS Contract NA-80-FA-D-00009.*

RAE, B. B. 1965. The food of the common porpoise (*Phocoena phocoena*). *Proc. Zool. Soc. London* 146: 114–22.

REIGER, G. 1975. Dolphin sacred, porpoise profane. *Audubon* 77(1): 3–29.

ROEST, A. I., W. THURMOND, and D. H. MONTGOMERY. 1959. Notes on a female harbor porpoise. *Jour. Mammal.* 40(3): 452–53.

SCAMMON, C. M. 1874. *The Marine Mammals of the Northwestern Coast of North America, together with an account of the American Whale-Fishery.* Carmany and Putnam's.

SCHEFFER, V. B., and J. W. SLIPP. 1948. The whales and dolphins of Washington state, with a key to the cetaceans of the west coast of North America. *Amer. Midl. Nat.* 39(2): 257–337.

SCHEVILL, W. E. 1968. Sight records of *Phocoena phocoena* and cetaceans in general. *Jour. Mammal.* 49(4): 794–96.

———, W. A. WATKINS, and C. RAY. 1969. Click structure in the porpoise, *Phocoena phocoena. Jour. Mammal.* 50(4): 721–28.

SERGEANT, D. E. 1969. Feeding rates of Cetacea. *Fisk. Dir. Skr. Ser. Havunders.* 15: 246–48.

———, and H. D. FISHER. 1957. The smaller cetacea of eastern Canadian waters. *Jour. Fish. Res. Bd. Canada* 14(1): 83–115.

SHELDRICK, M. C. 1979. Cetacean strandings along the coasts of the British Isles 1913–1977. In J. B. Geraci and D. J. St. Aubin, eds., *Biology of Marine Mammals: Insights Through Strandings,* pp. 35–53. National Technical Information Service. PB-293 890.

SLIJPER, E. J. 1966. Functional morphology of the reproductive system in cetacea. In K. S. Norris, ed., *Whales, Dolphins, and Porpoises,* pp. 277–319. Univ. of California Press.

SMITH, T. 1976. Current understanding of the status of the porpoise populations in the Black Sea. *FAO Scientific Consultation on Marine Mammals.* ACMRR/MM/SC/40. 1–11.

SOKOLOV, V. E., M. M. KALASHNIKOVA, and V. A. RODIONOV. 1973. Micro- and ultrastructure of the skin in the harbor porpoise (*Phocaena phocaena relicta* Abel.) In K. K. Chapskii and V. E. Sokolov, eds., *Morphology and Ecology of Marine Animals; Seals Dolphins, Porpoises,* pp. 82–101. John Wiley.

SPOTTE, S., J. L. DUNN, L. E. KEZER, and F. M. HEARD. 1978. Notes on the care of a beach-stranded harbor porpoise (*Phocoena phocoena*). *Cetology* 32: 1–6.

TESTAVERDE, S. A. 1978. Possible capture of a harbour porpoise, *Phocoena phocoena,* on a tuna longline. *Aquat. Mammals.* 6(3): 90.

TOMILIN, A. G. 1957. *Mammals of the U.S.S.R. and Adjacent Countries.* Vol. 9: Cetacea. Izdatel'stvo Akademi Nauk SSR, Moscow. (Israel Program for Scientific Translations, Jerusalem, 1967).

TRUE, F. W. 1903. On species of South American delphinidae described by Dr. R. A. Philippi in 1893 and 1896. *Proc. Biol. Soc. Wash.* 16: 133–44.

TYSON, E. 1680. *Phocaena, or the Anatomy of a Porpess, dissected at Gresham College: With a Præliminary Discourse concerning Anatomy, and a Natural History of Animals.* London. (Reprinted 1980, Brain Anatomy Institute, Bern, Switzerland.)

ULMER, F. A. 1960. New Jersey's whales and dolphins. *New Jersey Nature News* 16(3): 80–93.

———. 1980. New Jersey's dolphins and porpoises. *New Jersey Audubon Society Occasional Paper No. 137.* 11 pp.

VAN UTRECHT, W. L. 1959. Wounds and scars in the skin of the common porpoise *Phocoena phocoena. Mammalia* 23: 100–22.

WATKINS, W. A. 1980. Click sounds from animals at sea. In R.-G. Busnel and J. F. Fish, eds., *Animal Sonar Systems,* pp. 291–97. Plenum.

WILLIAMSON, G. R. 1963. Common porpoise from stomach of Greenland shark. *Jour. Fish. Res. Bd. Canada* 20(4): 1085–86.

WISLOCKI, G. B. 1933. On the placentation of the harbor porpoise (*Phocoena phocoena* Linnaeus). *Biol. Bull.* 65: 80–98.

———. 1942. The lungs of cetacea, with special reference to the harbor porpoise (*Phocoena phocoena* Linnaeus). *Anat. Rec.* 84: 117–23.

WOOD, F. G. 1979. The cetacean stranding phenomenon: an hypothesis. In J. B. Geraci and D. J. St. Aubin, eds., *Biology of Marine Mammals: Insights Through Strandings,* pp. 129–88. National Technical Information Service. PB-293 890.

———, and W. E. EVANS. 1980. Adaptiveness and ecology of echolocation in toothed whales. In R.-G. Busnel and J. F. Fish, eds., *Animal Sonar Systems,* pp. 381–425. Plenum.

WÜRSIG, M., B. WÜRSIG, and J. F. MERMOZ. 1977. Desplazamientos, comportamiento general y un varamiento de la mariposa espinosa, *Phocoena spinipinnis,* en el Golfo San José (Chubut, Argentina). *Physis* 36(92): 71–79.

FINLESS PORPOISE

ALLEN, G. M. 1923. *Meomeris,* the black finless porpoise. *Bull. Mus. Comp. Zool.* 65(7): 233–57. (Note: For taxonomic and typographical reasons far too complex to review here, the spelling "*Meomeris,*" although obviously incorrect, was used in the title of this paper.)

———. 1938. *The Mammals of China and Mongolia.* Cetaceans. pp. 494–513. American Museum of Natural History.

ANONYMOUS. 1976. The birth of a finless porpoise, *Neophocaena phocaenoides. Toba Aquarium Newsletter.* 18.

BAKER, A. N. 1972. *New Zealand Whales and Dolphins.* Tuatara, Vol. 20(1). Victoria University of Wellington.

CHEN PEIXUN, SHAO ZUOHUA, and G. PILLERI. 1980. Regression of the optic system in the Changjiang (Yangtze) finless porpoise (*Neophocaena asiaeorientalis*) as a result of lack of light. *Invest. on Cetacea* 11: 115–20.

DAWSON, E. 1960. On a large catch of the finless black porpoise *Neomeris phocaenoides* (Cuvier). *Jour. Mar. Biol. Assoc. India.* 1: 259–60.

FRASER, F. C. 1966. Comments on Delphinoidea. In K. S. Norris, ed., *Whales, Dolphins and Porpoises,* pp. 7–31. University of California Press.

GIBSON-HALL, C. A. 1950. The whales, porpoises and dolphins known in Sarawak waters. *Sarawak Mus. Jour.* 5(2): 288–96.

HOWELL, A. B. 1927. Contribution to the anatomy of the Chinese finless porpoise *Neomeris phocaenoides. Proc. U.S. Natl. Mus.* 70(13): 1–43.

———. 1930. *Aquatic Mammals.* Charles C. Thomas.

KASUYA, T., and K. KUREHARA. 1979. The population of finless porpoise in the Inland Sea of Japan. *Sci. Rep. Whales Res. Inst.* 31: 1–44.

KELLOGG, R. 1940. Whales, giants of the sea. *National Geographic* 77(1): 35–90.

LYDEKKER, R. 1908. On an Indian dolphin and porpoise. *Proc. Zool. Soc. London* 802–08.

MITCHELL, E. D. 1975a. Review of biology and fisheries for smaller cetaceans. *Jour. Fish. Res. Bd. Canada* 32(7): 889–983.

———. 1975b. *Porpoise, Dolphin and Small Whale Fisheries of the World: Status and Problems.* IUCN Monograph No. 3. Morges, Switzerland.

MÖRZER BRUYNS, W. F. J. 1971. *Field Guide of Whales and Dolphins.* Amsterdam.

NISHIWAKI, M. 1972. General biology. In S.H. Ridgway, ed., *Mammals of the Sea, Biology and Medicine,* pp. 3–204. Charles C. Thomas.

————, and K. KUREHARA. 1975. Strange organ in the anal region of the finless porpoise. *Sci. Rep. Whales Res. Inst.* 27: 139–40.

NORMAN, J. R. and F. C. FRASER. 1938. *Giant Fishes, Whales and Dolphins.* W. W. Norton & Co.

PILLERI, G., and CHEN PEIXUN. 1979. How the finless porpoise (*Neophocaena asiaeorientalis*) carries its calves on its back, and the function of the denticulate area of skin, as observed in the Changjiang River, China. *Invest. on Cetacea* 10: 105–08.

————. 1980. *Neophocaena phocaenoides* and *Neophocaena asiaeorientalis:* Taxonomical differences. *Invest. on Cetacea* 11: 25–32 +4 pls.

PILLERI, G., and M. GIHR. 1972. Contributions to the knowledge of the cetaceans of Pakistan with a particular reference to *Neomeris*, and a description of a new Chinese porpoise, *Neomeris asiaeorientalis*. *Invest. on Cetacea* 4: 107–62.

————. 1973. Contribution to the knowledge of the cetacea of southwest and monsoon Asia (Persian Gulf, Indus Delta, Malabar, Andaman Sea and the Gulf of Siam). *Invest. on Cetacea* 5: 95–149.

————. 1975. On the taxonomy and ecology of the finless black porpoise, *Neophocaena*. (Cetacea, Delphinidae). *Mammalia* 39: 657–73.

PILLERI, G., K. ZBINDEN, and M. GIHR. 1976. The "black finless porpoise" (*Neophocaena phocaenoides* Cuvier 1829) is not black. *Invest. on Cetacea* 7: 161–64.

RICE, D. W. 1977. *A List of the Marine Mammals of the World.* NOAA Technical Report NMFS SSRF-711.

TOMILIN, A. G. 1957. *Mammals of the U.S.S.R. and Adjacent Countries. Vol. IX: Cetacea.* Izdatel'stvo Akademi Nauk SSR, Moscow. (Israel Program for Scientific Translations, Jerusalem, 1967).

VAN BREE, P. J. H. 1973. *Neophocaena phocaenoides asiaeorientalis* (Pilleri and Gihr, 1973), a synonym of the preoccupied name *Delphinus melas* Schlegel, 1841. *Beaufortia* 21: 17–24.

ZHOU KAIYA, G. PILLERI, and YUEMEN LI. 1979. Observations on the baiji (*Lipotes vexillifer*) and the finless porpoise (*Neophocaena asiaeorientalis*) in the Changjiang (Yangtze) River between Nanjing and Taiyangzhou, with remarks on some physiological adaptations of the baiji to its environment. *Invest. on Cetacea* 10: 109–20.

DALL PORPOISE

ANDREWS. R. C. 1911. A new porpoise from Japan. *Bull. Amer. Mus. Nat. Hist.* II(4): 31–51.

BENSON, S. B. 1946. Further notes on the Dall porpoise. *Jour. Mammal.* 27(4): 368–74.

————, and T. C. GROODY. 1942. Notes on the Dall porpoise (*Phocoenoides dalli*). *Jour. Mammal.* 37(3): 311–23.

BOUCHER, G. C., L. D. CONSIGLIERI, and L. L. JONES. 1980. Report on the distribution and the preliminary analyses of the abundance of Dall's porpoise. Document submitted to the meeting of the Scientific Subcommittee on Marine Mammals, International North Pacific Fisheries Commission, Tokyo, Japan. Feb. 25–29, 1980. 27 pp.

BOUCHER, G. C., T. W. CRAWFORD, L. L. JONES, and T. C. NEWBY. 1980. Preliminary results of studies of the Dall's porpoise, *Phocoenoides dalli* True, incidentally taken in Japanese salmon gillnets, 1978–1979. *Int. Whal. Commn. Sci. Com. Rep.* SC/32/SM 8.

BROWNELL, R. L. 1964. Observations of odontocetes in central California waters. *Norsk Hvalfangst-tidende* 53(3): 60–66.

BUTTERWORTH, B. B. 1957. *Phocoenoides dalli* washed ashore in California. *Jour. Mammal.* 38(1): 126.

CALDWELL, M. C., and D. K. CALDWELL. 1972. Behavior of marine mammals. In S. H. Ridgway, ed., *Mammals of the Sea: Biology and Medicine*, pp. 419–65. Charles C. Thomas.

COWAN, I. M. 1944. The Dall porpoise (*Phocoenoides dalli* True) of the northern Pacific Ocean. *Jour. Mammal.* 25(3): 295–306.

FITCH, J. E., and R. L. BROWNELL. 1968. Fish otoliths in cetacean stomachs and their importance in interpreting feeding habits. *Jour. Fish Res. Bd. Canada* 25(12): 2561–64.

GREEN, R. F. 1972. Observations on the anatomy of some cetaceans and pinnipeds. In S. H. Ridgway, ed., *Mammals of the Sea: Biology and Medicine*, pp. 247–97. Charles C. Thomas.

HALL, J. D. 1981. Aspects of the natural history of cetaceans of Prince William Sound, Alaska. Ph.D. Dissertation, University of California, Santa Cruz.

HOUCK, W. J. 1976. The taxonomic status of the porpoise genus *Phocoenoides*. *FAO Scientific Consultation on Marine Mammals*. ACMMR/MM/SC/114.

KASUYA, T. 1976. Preliminary report of the biology, catch and population of *Phocoenoides* in the western North Pacific. *FAO Scientific Consultation on Marine Mammals*. ACMRR/MM/SC/21.

————. 1978. The life history of Dall's porpoise with special reference to the stock off the Pacific coast of Japan. *Sci. Rep. Whales Res. Inst.* 30: 1–63.

KING, W. B., R. G. BROWN, and G. SANGER. 1975. Mortality to marine birds through commercial fisheries. NMFS Report. Northwest and Alaska Fisheries Center. Seattle. 14 pp.

LEATHERWOOD, S., and R. R. REEVES. 1978. Porpoises and dolphins. In D. Haley, ed., *Marine Mammals of Eastern North Pacific and Arctic Waters*, pp. 96–111. Pacific Search Press.

LUSTIG, B. L. 1948. Sight records of Dall porpoises off the Channel Islands, California. *Jour. Mammal.* 29(2): 183.

MATKIN, C. 1981. Orca: killer whale. *Whalewatcher* 15(1): 3–4.

MILLER, G. S. 1929. The gums of the porpoise *Phocoenoides dalli* (True) *Proc. U.S. Natl. Mus.* 2771(79): 1–4.

————. 1930. A note on the skeletons of two Alaskan porpoises. *Smithsonian Misc. Coll.* 82(13): 1–2.

MIZUE, L., and K. YOSHIDA. 1965. On the porpoises caught by the salmon fishing gill-net in Bering Sea and the north Pacific Ocean. *Bull. Fac. Fish. Nagasaki Univ.* 19: 1–36.

MOREJOHN, G. V. 1979. The natural history of Dall's porpoise in the North Pacific ocean. In H. E. Winn and B. L. Olla, eds., *Behavior of Marine Animals,* Vol. 3: *Cetaceans,* pp. 45–83. Plenum.

——, V. LOEB, and D. M. BALTZ. 1973. Coloration and sexual dimorphism in the Dall porpoise. *Jour. Mammal.* 54(4): 977–82.

NMFS (NATIONAL MARINE FISHERIES SERVICE). 1981. Draft environmental impact statement on the incidental take of Dall porpoise in the Japanese salmon fishery. *U.S. Department of Commerce, National Oceanic and Atmospheric Administration.* 36 pp. (Mimeo.)

NMML (NATIONAL MARINE MAMMAL LABORATORY). 1981. Report on studies of the incidental take of marine mammals particularly Dall's porpoise, *Phocoenoides dalli,* in the Japanese salmon fishery. *Northwest and Alaska Fisheries Center, National Marine Fisheries Service, NOAA.* 70 pp. (Mimeo.)

NICHOLS, J. T. 1950. Additional data on the occurrence of Dall's porpoise. *Jour. Mammal.* 31(1): 99.

NISHIWAKI, M. 1966. A discussion of rarities among the smaller cetaceans caught in Japanese waters. In K. S. Norris, ed., *Whales, Porpoises and Dolphins,* pp. 192–204. University of California Press.

——. 1967. Distribution and migration of marine mammals in the North Pacific area. *Bull. Ocean Res. Inst. Univ. Tokyo* 1: 1–64.

OHSUMI, S. 1975. Incidental catch of cetaceans with salmon gill net. *Jour. Fish. Res. Bd. Canada.* 32(7): 1229–35.

RICE, D. W. 1968. Stomach contents and feeding behavior of killer whales in the eastern North Pacific. *Norsk Hvalfangst-tidende* 57(2): 35–38.

——. 1977. *A List of the Marine Mammals of the World.* NOAA Technical Report NMFS SSRF-711.

RIDGWAY, S. H. 1966. Dall porpoise, *Phocoenoides dalli* (True): observations in captivity and at sea. *Norsk Hvalfangst-tidende* 55(5): 97–110.

SCHEFFER, V. B. 1949. The Dall porpoise (*Phocoenoides dalli*) in Alaska. *Jour. Mammal.* 30(2): 116–21.

——. 1950. Porpoises assembling in the North Pacific Ocean. *Murrelet* 31(1): 16.

——. 1953. Measurements and stomach contents of eleven delphinids from the northeast Pacific. *Murrelet* 34: 27–30.

TREACY, S. D., and T. W. CRAWFORD. 1979. Preliminary report on the food habits of the Dall porpoise (*Phocoenoides dallii*) caught incidentally by the Japanese high seas salmon drift-net fishery. (Abstract) *Third Biennial Conf. Biol. Marine Mammals.* Seattle.

TRUE, F. W. 1885. On a new species of porpoise, *Phocoena dalli,* from Alaska. *Proc. U.S. Natl. Mus.* 8: 95–98.

WALKER, W. A. 1975. Review of the live-capture fishery for smaller cetaceans taken in southern California waters for public display. *Jour. Fish. Res. Bd. Canada* 32(7): 1197–1211.

WILKE, F., and A. J. NICHOLSON. 1958. Food of porpoises in the waters off Japan. *Jour. Mammal.* 39(3): 441–43.

WILKE, F., T. TANIWAKI, and N. KURODA. 1953. *Phocoenoides* and *Lagenorhynchus* in Japan with notes on hunting. *Jour. Mammal.* 34(4): 488–97.

WOOD, F. G. 1973. *Marine Mammals and Man.* Luce.

YOCUM, C. F. 1946. Notes on the Dall porpoise off California. *Jour. Mammal.* 24(4): 364–68.

BIBLIOGRAPHY

Because there have been very few books written exclusively about the smaller cetaceans, many of the listings in this bibliography deal with cetology and cetaceans inclusively. The most pronounced difference between this bibliography and the one included in *The Book of Whales* is the absence of books about whaling. In any study of the great whales, much of our knowledge has come from those who were actively involved in killing them, or alternatively, from those who chronicled and documented the whaling industry. Since the study of dolphins and porpoises cannot be defined as an "industry"—certainly not one where profit-making was its primarily motivation—we lack the eloquence of the whalers. We have no Scoresbys, no Scammons, no Melvilles. Specific studies are more often devoted to classification, training, acoustics, intelligence, or the benign interactions of cetaceans and people. Except in those instances where I wished to make a particular reference to one of the works listed below, they will not be found in the species bibliographies. This was done for the obvious reason of not having to list "Kellogg 1940," or "Nishiwaki 1972" a great number of times. Only books and popular magazine articles are listed here; the reader is referred to the references for monographs or scientific papers dealing with one species or a particular aspect of cetacean behavior.

ALPERS, A. 1960. *Dolphins: The Myth and the Mammal.* Houghton Mifflin.

ANDERSEN, H. T., ed. 1969. *The Biology of Marine Mammals.* Academic Press.

BEDDARD, F. 1900. *A Book of Whales.* John Murray.

BUSNEL, R.-G., and J. F. FISH, eds. 1980. *Animal Sonar Systems.* Plenum.

CALDWELL, D. K., and M. C. CALDWELL. 1972. *The World of the Bottlenosed Dolphin.* J. B. Lippincott.

COFFEY, D. J. 1977. *Dolphins, Whales and Porpoises: An Encyclopedia of Sea Mammals.* Macmillan.

DAUGHERTY, A. 1972. *Marine Mammals of California.* State of California Department of Fish and Game.

GASKIN, D. E. 1972. *Whales, Dolphins and Seals, with Special Reference to the New Zealand Region.* Heinemann Educational Books.

HALEY, D., ed. 1978. *Marine Mammals of Eastern North Pacific and Arctic Waters.* Pacific Search Press.

HERMAN, L. M., ed. 1980. *Cetacean Behavior: Mechanisms and Functions.* John Wiley.

HERSHKOVITZ, P. 1966. *Catalog of Living Whales.* U.S. National Museum, Bulletin 246.

HOYT, E. 1981. *The Whale Called Killer.* E. P. Dutton.

KATONA, S. 1975. *A Field Guide to the Whales and Seals of the Gulf of Maine.* Maine Coast Printers.

KELLOGG, R. 1940. Whales, giants of the sea. *National Geographic* 77(1): 35–90.

KELLOGG, W. N. 1961. *Porpoises and Sonar.* Univ. of Chicago Press.

LEATHERWOOD, S., D. K. CALDWELL, and H. WINN. 1976. *Whales, Dolphins and Porpoises of the Western North Atlantic: A Guide to Their Identification.* NOAA Technical Report NMFS CIRC-396.

LEATHERWOOD, S., W. E. EVANS, and D. W. RICE. 1972. *The Whales, Dolphins, and Porpoises of the Eastern North Pacific: A Guide to their Identification in the Water.* Naval Undersea Center, San Diego.

LINEHAN, E. J. 1979. The trouble with dolphins. *National Geographic* 155(4): 506–41.

MCINTYRE, J. 1974. *Mind in the Waters.* Scribner's/Sierra Club.

MITCHELL, E. D. 1975a. *Porpoise, Dolphin, and Small Whale Fisheries of the World: Status and Problems.* IUCN Monograph No. 3, Morges, Switzerland.

———, ed. 1975b. Review of Biology and Fisheries for Smaller Cetaceans. *Journal of the Fisheries Research Board of Canada* 32(7).

MÖRZER BRUYNS, W. F. J. 1971. *Field Guide of Whales and Dolphins.* Amsterdam.

NISHIWAKI, M. 1972. General biology. In S. H. Ridgway, ed., *Mammals of the Sea: Biology and Medicine,* pp. 3–204. Charles C Thomas.

NORMAN, J. R., and F. C. FRASER. 1938. *Giant Fishes, Whales and Dolphins.* W. W. Norton.

NORRIS, K. S., ed. 1966. *Whales, Dolphins and Porpoises.* University of California Press.

———. 1974. *The Porpoise Watcher.* W. W. Norton.

PRYOR, K. W. 1975. *Lads Before the Wind: Adventures in Porpoise Training.* Harper & Row.

RIDGWAY, S. H., ed. 1972. *Mammals of the Sea: Biology and Medicine.* Charles C. Thomas.

RICE, D. W. 1977. *A List of the Marine Mammals of the World.* NOAA Technical Report NMFS SSRF-711.

———, and V. B. SCHEFFER. 1968. *A List of the Marine Mammals of the World.* U.S. Fish and Wildlife Service. Special Scientific Report No. 579.

SCHEFFER, V. B., and D. W. RICE. 1963. *A List of the Marine Mammals of the World.* U.S. Fish and Wildlife Service, Special Scientific Report No. 431.

SLIJPER, E. J. 1962. *Whales: The Biology of Cetaceans.* Trans. A. J. Pomerans. Basic Books.

———. 1977. *Whales and Dolphins.* University of Michigan Press.

TOMILIN, A. G. 1957. *Mammals of the U.S.S.R. and Adjacent Countries.* Vol. 9. *Cetacea.* Izdatel'stvo Akademi Nauk SSR, Moscow. (Israel Program for Scientific Translations, Jerusalem 1967.)

TRUE, F. W. 1889. Contributions to the natural history of the cetaceans, a review of the family Delphinidae. *Bull. U.S. Nat. Mus.* 36: 1–191.

WOOD, F. G. 1973. *Marine Mammals and Man.* Luce.

INDEX

melon oil, 15
    of long-finned pilot whale, 160
    of short-finned pilot whale, 167
Melville, Herman, 9, 20 n., 66, 106,
    138, 162–63, 186, 213
memory, 19
Mercer, M. C., 140, 162
Merle, Robert, 71
Mermoz, J. F., 127, 128
Meyen, 99 and n.
Meyen's dolphin, see striped dolphin
Miami Seaquarium, 95
Mikhalev, Y. A., 170 n., 175, 177, 178,
    180, 184
military uses of dolphins, 72
Miller, G. S., 29, 42, 206 (and
    illus.)
mimicry, see imitative behavior
minke whales, 175, 177
Mitchell, E. D., 3, 25, 42, 48, 50, 67,
    85, 86, 88 n., 89 n., 103–05, 110,
    112–15, 117, 124, 127, 130 and
    n., 131, 150, 156, 158, 160, 162,
    166–69, 186, 191, 195, 197, 199,
    201, 203, 209, 210
Miyazaki, N., 10, 89, 90, 97, 99, 100
    and n., 101, 103, 112, 113, 152,
    153, 166, 173
Mizue, L., 211
Mohl, 17, 18
Moore, J. C., 152
Moore, P. W. B., 63
Morejohn, J. V., 177, 206, 209
Morgane, P., 21
Morrison-Scott, T. C. S., 42
Mörzer-Bruyns, W. F. J., 38, 43, 48 n.,
    51, 129, 132, 133, 144, 145, 152,
    190, 191
mother-calf relationship
    bottlenose dolphin, 63
    common dolphin, 110
    dusky dolphin, 123
    finless porpoise, 204 (and illus.)
    harbor porpoise, 193
    killer whale, 171, 185
    short-finned pilot whale, 165–66
    striped dolphins, 99
    see also nursing behavior
mullet, 55, 61
Murchison, A. E., 72
Murie, J., 140, 141 (illus.)
Murphy, G., 96
Murphy, Robert Cushman, 145
mythology, 5–6, 185
    see also folklore; literature, dolphins
        in

Nachtigall, P. E., 72
Nakajima, M., 145, 146

nasal sacs, sound production and,
    14–15
Nasu, K., 17
National Marine Fisheries Service, 79,
    88, 128, 211, 212
National Marine Mammals Laboratory
    (NMML), 205, 207, 211
Navy, U. S., 184, 186
Neill, W. T., 25, 26
Nemoto, T., 17
newborn, see birth
Newman, M. A., 181, 186
New York Aquarium, 10, 67
Niagara Falls Aquarium (New York,
    26, 57
Nicol, C. W., 100
Nichols, J. T., 59 n., 125
Nishiwaki, M., 4, 26, 30 n., 40, 41, 43,
    51, 54–56, 75 n., 79, 89, 98–100,
    99 n., 100 n., 103, 104, 118, 121,
    129, 133 n., 134–36, 139, 145–47,
    150, 152, 161, 163 and n., 173,
    175, 179, 185, 186, 189, 192,
    209
Noble, B. A., 98
nomenclature, 3–5
    see also taxonomy of under individual
        species
Nordli, O., 117
Norman, J. R., 23, 26, 29, 33, 40, 48
    n., 49, 50, 56, 98, 121, 127, 129,
    131, 132, 137, 140, 150, 162, 164
    n., 190, 193, 198, 201, 203, 208
Norris, K. S., 3, 4, 8, 10, 12–18, 22,
    25, 35–36, 36 n., 42–46, 42 n., 43
    n., 45 n., 55, 57, 60, 61, 63, 65,
    69 and n., 70, 72, 73 and n., 76
    n., 79, 82–84, 90–93, 91 n., 99,
    106–09, 117 n., 117–19, 120 n.,
    134, 135, 145, 146, 150, 153, 156,
    160, 163–66, 164 n., 179, 180,
    192 and n., 196, 197, 201, 205,
    206, 208
northern right whale dolphin
    (Lissodelphis borealis), 133–36,
    134–36 (illus.)
    anomalously colored, 136 (and illus.)
    in captivity, 135
    feeding, 135–36
    population of, 134
    sightings of, 134
    swimming habits of, 134–35
Northwest Coast Indians, 185
Norway, killer whale fishery in, 185,
    186
nursing behavior
    of bottlenose dolphin, 62–63
    of striped dolphins, 99, 100
nurturant behavior, 7

Odell, D. K., 155, 156
Odlum, G. C., 180
odontocetes, 4
    cranial asymmetry in, 17
    echolocation capabilities of, 14
Ohsumi, S., 89, 99, 100 and n., 101,
    134, 136, 153, 167, 209, 211
oil
    porpoise-jaw, 67
    see also melon oil
Oliver, W. R. B., 131–33
Omura, Hideo, 143
operant conditioning, 19
Optimum Sustainable Population
    (OSP), 94 and n.
orca, see killer whale
Orca, the Killer Whale (film), 184 n.
Orca Survey, 171 n.
Orr, R. T., 42, 99, 139 n., 140, 195
Osbeck, Peter, 48
Osborne, R. W., 182
Otten, Tom, 187, 188
Owen, Sir Richard, 149, 190
Owen, Sir Robert, 39, 50

Pacific spotted dolphin, see spotted
    dolphin
Pacific striped dolphin, see Pacific
    white-sided dolphin
Pacific white-sided dolphin
    (Lagenorhynchus obliquidens), 12,
    107, 117–20, 118 (illus.)
    care-giving behavior of, 119
    dusky dolphin compared to, 121,
        122 (and illus.)
    echelon swimming, 119, 120 (illus.)
    habitats and range of, 118
    hunting for, 120
    leaping behavior of, 117, 118
    strandings of, 119
    swimming habits, 117–19
    training of, 118, 120
    visual acuity of, 120
    whales and, 119, 120
    whistling, 120
Paraiso, F., 54
parasites, 93
passive sonar, of common dolphin,
    108
Payne, R., 13, 121
Peale, Titian Ramsay, 124, 134–36,
    145, 146
Peale's dolphin (Lagenorhynchus
    australis), 123–25, 124 (illus.), 126
    (illus.)
Pearson, J., 154
Pelorus Jack, 143–44
penguins, as killer whales' prey, 180
Pepper, R. L., 68

266

Peron, François, 137
Perrin, W. F., 8, 79, 80 and n., 84–89,
    88 n., 93, 94, 97–98, 103, 105,
    110–13, 145, 147
Perryman, W. L., 93, 148, 150, 152
Philippi, R. A., 129, 199 n.
Phocoenida, see porpoises
piebald dolphin, see Commerson's
    dolphin
Pilleri, G., 8, 21, 23–28, 30–32, 32 n.,
    34–41, 48 n., 50–53, 55, 59, 103,
    104, 106, 108–10, 130, 131, 142,
    150, 152, 153, 155 n., 190, 194,
    200–04, 204 n.
Pilleri, O., 41, 52
pilot whales (genus Globicephala), 4, 8,
    10, 151 (illus.)
    Atlantic white-sided dolphin and,
        116
    depth of dives of, 12
    taxonomy of, 157–58, 163–64
    white, 157
    see also long-finned pilot whale;
        short-finned pilot whale
Platanistidae (platanistids), 4–5, 8
play behavior
    of Amazon River dolphin, 40
    of Atlantic spotted dolphin, 95,
        97
    of bottlenose dolphin, 65–67
    of boutu, 26–27
    defined, 40 n.
    of dusky dolphin, 121, 122
    of Indus River dolphin, 40
    of killer whale, 182, 187, 189
    of Pacific white-sided dolphin, 117
    of Risso's dolphin, 141
    of short-finned pilot whale, 164
Pliny, 66, 102
plumbeous dolphins (Sousa plumbea),
    49 (illus.), 50–52
pods
    of killer whales, 170–71, 173, 181
    see also schools
Ponting, H. L., 170, 183
Pope, C. H., 29
Popper, A. N., 16, 46
porpoise-jaw oil, 67
porpoises (Phocoenidae), 8
    classification of, 3–5
    defined, 164 n.
porpoising behavior, 59
Porter, J. W., 153, 154 and n., 156
Powell, B. A., 72
Powers, J. E., 93
Praderi, R., 27, 28, 200
Prescott, J. H., 3, 12, 14, 19, 60, 61,
    63, 65, 69, 99, 106–08, 117 n.,
    119, 120 n., 134, 135, 150, 152,

153, 156, 163–66, 179, 180,
    192–97, 205, 208
Pryor, K. 10, 19, 26, 43–47, 46 n., 61,
    65, 75 n., 76, 79, 82, 84, 89–91,
    109, 120, 147–49, 152, 153, 164,
    187
purse-seine fishery, see tuna fishery
Purves, P. E., 35, 104, 150, 153, 155 n.
pygmy killer whale (Feresa attenuata), 4,
    92, 146–49, 146 (illus.), 147
    (illus.), 151 (illus.)
    aggressive behavior of, 148
    dolphins as prey of, 148
    range of, 148–49
pygmy right whale, 53

Quoy, J. R. C., 126

radiotelemetric studies of common
    dolphins, 107
Rayner, G. W., 156 n.
red-bellied dolphin, 103
Reed, D. C., 18
Reeves, R. R., 97, 107, 133, 135, 140,
    210
Reiger, G., 192
Reinhardt, J., 149
remora, 95
respiration, see breathing
resting behavior
    of harbor porpoise, 193
    of short-finned pilot whale, 166
    of spinner dolphin, 82, 84
    see also sleeping
Rice, D. W., 3, 4, 30 n., 38, 39, 45,
    48, 50, 56 n., 59, 89, 98, 104,
    157, 165 n., 173, 177, 179, 191,
    202, 203, 205 n., 209
Richey, Charles, 79–80
Ridgway, S. H., 11, 12, 66, 74, 77,
    187, 193, 207, 208
right whale dolphin, 118
    see also northern right whale dolphin;
        southern right whale dolphin
right whales, 13, 181
    dusky dolphin and, 121
Risso, Giovanni Antonio, 139
Risso's dolphin (Grampus griseus), 4,
    119, 138–44, 138 (illus.)
    in captivity, 142, 143
    hybrid, 62, 143
    juvenile, 141 (and illus.)
    length of, 140
    names of, 139–40
    play behavior, 141
    schools of, 140, 141
    skull of, 140 (illus.)
    speed of, 141
    strandings of, 142, 143

swimming habits of, 141
    ventral view of, 139 (illus.)
Robertson, Dougal, 182–83
Robertson, R. B., 182 n.
Robineau, D., 174
Robson, F., 8, 97 n., 105, 106 and n.,
    108–10, 109 n., 123, 179, 181
Rogers, W., 90
rorquals, as killer whales' prey, 177,
    178
Ross, G. J. B., 53, 59, 63, 64
rough-toothed dolphin (Steno
    bredanensis), 13 (illus.), 41–47, 42
    (illus.)
    bottlenose dolphin crossbred with,
        62
    coloration of, 42, 43
    distribution of, 42, 43
    diving capabilities of, 44, 45
    echolocation, 45–46
    emotional responses of, 45
    feeding, 44
    jaw of, 43 (and illus.)
    physical appearance of, 42, 43
    skull of, 44 (illus.)
    strandings of, 43, 44
    swimming habits of, 42–43
    teeth of, 42, 43
    training of, 46–47
Roxburgh, William, 32 and n., 39

Saayman, G. S., 7, 16, 48, 51–53,
    58–61, 65, 75, 77, 91 n.
salmon, as killer whales' prey, 179
salmon fishery, Dall porpoise and,
    210–12
Samson, Dottie, 44 n.
Sanderson, Ivan, 24 n., 29–30, 66, 101
    n., 114, 169
San Diego Zoo, 62 n.
Sarawak dolphin, see Fraser's dolphin
Scammon, Charles Melville, 9, 59, 103,
    117, 134, 138, 166, 167, 169, 170,
    178, 179, 186, 191
Scheffer, V. B., 39, 48, 56 n., 135, 144,
    150, 152, 153 n., 169, 176, 178–
    80, 184, 185, 192, 193, 205, 207
Schevill, W. E., 14, 16 n., 46, 66, 69,
    72, 73, 97, 106, 115, 117, 124,
    128, 130, 138, 140, 157, 165, 181,
    192, 194
Schildkraut, L., 185
Schmidly, D. F., 82, 86, 96
schools (herds or aggregations), 8, 9,
    84
    of Atlantic spotted dolphin, 95
    of Atlantic white-sided dolphin, 114,
        116
    of bottlenose dolphin, 60

clymene dolphin and, 85, 86 (and illus.)

dorsal fins of, 80, 81 (illus.)

feeding, 82

habitats of, 81, 86–87

physical appearance of, 79

population estimates of, 80

resting behavior, 82, 84

skull of, 85

sound production of, 15

spinning behavior of, 82–83, 83 (illus.)

strandings of, 82

taxonomy of, 80–81, 81 (illus.)

teeth of, 81

tuna fishery and, 78–80, 84–85

ventral keel of, 80–81, 81 (illus.)

spinning behavior

of clymene dolphin, 86

of dusky dolphin, 122

of false killer whale, 153

of hourglass dolphin, 126

of spinner dolphin, 82–83, 83 (illus.)

of white-beaked dolphins, 114

Spong, P., 120, 167, 179, 181, 183

Spotte, S., 193, 194

spotted dolphin (*Stenella attenuata*), 10, 87–94, 87 (illus.), 142

in captivity, 91

habitats of, 89, 90

kill quotas for, 93–94

natural causes of death in, 93

nets, behavior in, 90–93

optimum sustainable population (OSP) of, 94

physical appearance of, 89

population estimates, 94

schools of, 9

senior male squads of, 91, 92 (illus.)

social behavior and school structure of, 90–92

speed of, 65, 90

spinner dolphins and, 84

stages in maturation of, 89

taxonomy of, 87–89

teeth, 89

tuna fishery and, 85, 87–88, 90–94

see also Atlantic spotted dolphin

spy-hopping, killer whales, 182

squid, 17 (and illus.)

as long-finned pilot whale food, 158–59

as Risso's dolphin prey, 140

standing by, 7

harbor porpoise, 193

killer whale, 184

Starrett, A., 159

Starrett, P., 159

Status of Porpoise Stocks Workshop (La Jolla), 93, 94

Steiner, W. W., 180–81

Stenuit, Robert, 72

Stephen, D., 127

Stephenson, A. B., 97

Stoner, D., 103

strandings, 9

of Atlantic spotted dolphin, 96

of Atlantic white-sided dolphin, 116, 117

of bottlenose dolphin, 64–65

of common dolphins, 103

of dusky dolphin, 123

of false killer whale, 153–56

of harbor porpoise, 192, 193

of killer whale, 183

of long-finned pilot whale, 160–61

of northern right whale dolphin, 135

of Pacific white-sided dolphin, 119

of Peale's dolphin, 124

of Risso's dolphin, 142, 143

of rough-toothed dolphin, 43, 44

of short-finned pilot whale, 166

of spinner dolphins, 82

of striped dolphins, 99

of white-beaked dolphins, 114, 117

streaker dolphin, *see* striped dolphin

striped dolphin (*Stenella coeruleoalba*), 10 (and illus.), 97–101, 97 (illus.)

feeding, 99

Fraser's dolphin differentiated from, 112–13

habitats of, 97, 98

names of, 98–99

physical appearance of, 99, 100

population of, 101

strandings of, 99

variations in the eye-to-flipper stripe, 98 (and illus.)

Stuntz, W. E., 9, 90

suckling, *see* nursing behavior

supporting behavior, 7

surfing, bottlenose dolphins, 65

susu, *see* Ganges River dolphin

Sutherland, D. L., 96

Sweeney, J. C., 188

swimming habits

of Atlantic spotted dolphin, 95

of bottlenose dolphin, 59, 65, 67

of boutu, 23, 24, 26

of Burmeister's porpoise, 201

of Commerson's dolphin, 127, 128

of common dolphin, 106, 108

of Dall porpoise, 205–06

of dusky dolphin, 122, 123

echelon, 45, 119, 120 (illus.)

of false killer whale, 152

of finless porpoise, 203

of Ganges River dolphin, 34, 36–38, 38 (illus.)

of harbor porpoise, 192–93

of Heaviside's dolphin, 131

of humpback dolphins, 52

of Indus River dolphin, 40

of Irrawaddy dolphin, 190

of killer whale, 182, 186

of long-finned pilot whale, 160

of melon-headed whale, 145

of northern right whale dolphin, 134–35

of Pacific white-sided dolphin, 117–19

of Risso's dolphin, 141

of rough-toothed dolphin, 42–43

of short-finned pilot whale, 164

of spotted dolphins, 90

of tucuxi, 56

of white-beaked dolphins, 114

see also bow-wave riding; deep diving; leaping behavior; speed; spinning behavior

Swinhoe, Robert, 48, 49

symbiotic relationship between man and dolphins

Atlantic humpback dolphin, 55, 61

boutu, 26, 55 n.

tail grabber, 96

Tarpy, C., 177

Taruski, A. G., 161

Tavolga, M. C., 8, 11, 61, 63, 72, 77–78, 182 n.

Tavolga, W. N., 14, 72, 182 n.

taxonomy, *see* classification of cetaceans

Tayler, C. K., 48, 51–53, 59–61, 65, 75, 77, 91 n.

Taylor, G. T., 40

Taylor, R. J. F., 170, 184

teeth, 17

of Atlantic humpback dolphin, 54

of Atlantic spotted dolphin, 95

of bottlenose dolphin, 58, 60

of boutu, 23–25

of Burmeister's porpoise, 199

of clymene dolphin, 86

of Commerson's dolphin, 127

of common dolphin, 105

of Dall porpoise, 8, 206

of dusky dolphin, 121

of finless porpoise, 201

of Franciscana, 27, 28

of Fraser's dolphin, 113

of Ganges River dolphin, 34

of harbor porpoise, 191

of Irrawaddy dolphin, 190

of killer whale, 175, 176

of long-finned pilot whale, 159